THE BIBLE

in Greek Christian Antiquity

THE BIBLE
THROUGH THE AGES

Volume 1

SERIES DIRECTORS

Charles Kannengiesser & Pamela Bright

The University of Notre Dame Press
gratefully acknowledges the generous support of
THE ESTATE OF NANCY R. DREUX
in the publication of this Great Work in Translation.

THE BIBLE

in Greek Christian Antiquity

EDITED AND
TRANSLATED BY

Paul M. Blowers

Based on BIBLE DE TOUS LES TEMPS, volume 1,
Le monde grec ancien et la Bible, edited by C. Mondésert

UNIVERSITY OF NOTRE DAME PRESS / NOTRE DAME, INDIANA

Copyright © 1997 by
University of Notre Dame Press
Notre Dame, Indiana 46556

All Rights Reserved

Book design by
Designer's Ink

Set in text type—10 on 13 Palatino

Manufactured in the United States of America by
Rand McNally Book Services Group

Binding by
Nicholstone Companies

Library of Congress Cataloging-in-Publication Data

The Bible in Greek Christian Antiquity

Edited by
Paul M. Blowers

P. cm.

Based on: Le monde grec ancien et la Bible, c1984.
Includes bibliographical references and index.
ISBN 0-268-00701-2 (alk. paper).
ISBN 0-268-00702-0 (pbk. : alk. paper)
1. Bible—Criticism, interpretation, etc.—
History—Early church, ca. 30-600.
2. Fathers of the church, Greek,
I. Blowers, Paul M., 1955-
BS500.B542 1997
220′.09′015—dc21
CIP 97-13525

Contents

Preface

The present volume represents a translation, revision, adaptation, and expansion of *Le monde grec ancien et la Bible*, volume 1 in the series "Bible de tous les temps" published by Beauchesne of Paris beginning in 1984. Credit here must certainly be given to Charles Kannengiesser, Huisking Professor Emeritus of Theology in the University of Notre Dame, who directed the original French series and who, together with Pamela Bright, currently Professor in the Department of Theological Studies at Concordia University in Montreal, pioneered the plan for an English edition of this series. I am grateful for the opportunity to have worked with them, and with several others, including James Langford of the University of Notre Dame Press, in the conception of an English edition and adaptation of this series.

What follows in the present volume is not a simple reproduction of the original French edition in English. All but four of the original French essays do appear in translation in this English edition, but they have, in some cases, been revised slightly to reflect more recent developments in early Christian studies, and have been adapted so as to include English translations of primary or secondary works that are quoted or referred to in the essays. Where the authors have quoted ancient writings, I have made use of available English translations. Where such translations have not already been available, I have checked the original source, and provided my own English translation, respecting as far as possible the spirit of the French translation. In some of the essays, there have been significant additions to, or revisions in, the notes. In the essays by Pierre de Bourguet and Pierre Maraval, I have added notes where there were none in the original French so as to aid the reader in locating supporting primary documents and relevant secondary literature.

As I already mentioned, four of the original essays from *Le monde grec ancien et la Bible,* a few of which were considered too specialized for a broad audience of readers, were not selected for translation here. The four essays (Roger Arnaldez on Philo's biblical interpretation; Nicole Thierry on the illustrated Bible in Cappadocia; Paul Gallay on Gregory Nazianzen's use of the Bible; and Gilles Dorival on the catena commentaries in the early Church) are superb studies and certainly to be recommended for further reading. Yet it is my pleasure to introduce in the present volume four new essays by American scholars—Ronald Heine, Frederick Norris, Douglas Burton-Christie, and myself—which I hope will provide some additional perspective on the profound influence of the Bible in various aspects of the life, thought, and culture of the early Greek Church. I am especially grateful to my colleague Fred Norris, who has furnished an essay on Gregory Nazianzen's use of Scripture which is intended to be not a "replacement" of Paul Gallay's original study but a fresh perspective from a scholar who has lately produced a commentary on Gregory's *Theological Orations.* A lacuna in *Le monde grec ancien et la Bible* was the absence of an essay on the achievement of Origen and its ongoing significance in the Greek Church. Hopes for a single volume on Origen in the series "Bible de tous les temps" did not materialize, but that gap may well have been filled elsewhere more recently by the publication of the collected papers of the Sixth International Colloquium on Origen of Alexandria (Chantilly, France, September 1993), which was specifically devoted to the theme of "Origen and the Bible" (*Origeniana Sexta,* ed. A. le Boulluec and G. Dorival, Leuven, 1995). Publication of our volume, however, was unthinkable without at least one essay dedicated to the greatest biblical scholar of the early Church. Ronald Heine has therefore provided a thoughtful introductory essay on Origen the exegete. The essays by Douglas Burton-Christie and myself address one very important context of biblical interpretation which also did not receive concentrated attention in the original French edition, namely, the biblical culture of early Christian monasticism.

As for the actual work of rendering the French, I am grateful for assistance from Constance McLeese of the University of Montreal, who provided a preliminary translation of some of the essays, and to Charles Kannengiesser, who kindly supplied me with a translation and slight revision of his contribution on the Bible in the Arian controversy. Many of the essays from *Le monde grec ancien et la Bible* I translated myself; and the final translation of all the essays from the French edition is my own, for which reason I must humbly assume responsibility for any errors that may have been missed in the final stages of editing.

My final thanks go to Jeff Gainey and Jeannette Morgenroth of the University of Notre Dame Press, for services rendered in preparing the manuscript for production, and to John Mark Wade, Assistant Librarian at Emmanuel School of Religion, who has been of immeasurable help to me in the "technical support" and computer services which today are truly indispensible to the production of books.

The Bible in Greek Christian Antiquity comes as something of an international labor, with French, Swiss, Australian, and now Canadian and American collaboration. My hope is that the present volume will do justice to the original labors of Claude Mondésert, who edited *Le monde grec ancien et la Bible,* and to the esteemed circle of scholars—including Marcel Simon, Marcel Borret, and Pierre du Bourguet, honored here posthumously—who have contributed immensely to the study of the Bible's influence in the early Christian world from out of their varied perspectives and areas of expertise.

PAUL M. BLOWERS
Emmanuel School of Religion
October 1996

Abbreviations

CCSG   Corpus christianorum, series graeca
CCSL   Corpus christianorum, series latina
CSEL   Corpus scriptorum ecclesiasticorum latinorum
ANF   A Select Library of the Ante-Nicene Fathers
NPNF   A Select Library of the Nicene and Post-Nicene Fathers
PG   Patrologia Graeca
PL   Patrologia latina
PO   Patrologia orientalis
SC   Sources chrétiennes

Introduction

PAUL BLOWERS

Early Christians heard, read, sang, prayed, produced, interpreted, memorized, preached, debated, defended, and developed canons of Holy Scripture. But only in rare instances did they reflect historically on precisely how the Hebrew Scriptures had come together and been handed down to them or on the process by which new Christian Scriptures had come into being for the edification of the Church. And in these cases such reflection was usually occasioned by the need to address particular crises of Christian identity. The classic example is the response to the anti-Judaic theology and biblical canon of the Marcionite movement in the second century, which prompted a number of Christian writers to try to confirm the historical and theological connections between the Old and New Testaments and to look more keenly toward the ultimate finalization of an orthodox Christian Bible. For the most part, however, early Christians simply presupposed that "Scripture" was foundational to their identity, that it contained the very oracles of God, that its language was the sacred language of salvation rendered all the more hallowed—as Origen and other Greek patristic exegetes professed—because the Very Logos who was in Jesus of Nazareth was also "incarnate" in the Bible, accommodating himself to humanity through the flesh of *text,* even through the Bible's fine details and diverse modes of expression.

Accordingly, the world of early Christian biblical usage and interpretation appears to be a far distant world from that of contemporary biblical-critical science. Typically, modern biblical scholarship has referred to this period (usually without disguising the pejorative connotations) as the "pre-critical" age in the evolution of biblical interpretation. And yet early Christians perceived little need for distanced reflection on sacred texts that were already the lifeblood of their communities, texts that were thoroughly woven into their preaching, instruction, liturgical celebrations, spirituality, and pastoral and ethical commitments. The "sacramental" nature of Scripture—the quickening, judging, saving Word—needed no verification or vindication beyond the Church itself. Scripture (text) and Church (interpreting community) were assumed to constitute one living tradition handed down from prophets and apostles, a tradition tested and verified through the churches' continued performance and enactment of the Word. The hermeneutical circle thus established, however, is a circle that biblical-critical science in the twentieth century has largely sought to break down. Biblical texts and canons have come to be viewed—through the lenses of form criticism, tradition criticism, theories of redaction, and the analytical history of religions—principally in terms of their historically- and culturally-conditioned nature. Roughly the last 75 years in biblical-critical studies have seen a fairly systematic emphasis on the formation history of the Bible, on the ways that communities of faith—often constrained by their own needs for normative self-definition—produced, shaped, and reshaped traditions of Holy Scripture over time. Generally speaking, there has not been a converse emphasis on the ways in which received traditions or canons of Holy Scripture have produced, shaped, and reshaped ecclesial communities.

More recently, however, shifts within the disciplines of theological and biblical hermeneutics have served to open up new ways of understanding, appreciating, and even reclaiming certain aspects of the biblical vision of the early Christians. Of particular note are the broadening in philosophical approaches to categories like "text" and "interpretation," the rediscovery of the central role of narrative within the Bible and the life of the Church, and the emergence of more carefully nuanced understandings of the dynamic relation between sacred texts and interpreting communities. One can detect a certain shift of interest, in some circles at least, away from the antecedent formation history of the Bible toward a new concentration on the *datum,* the given or received state of texts, and the ways in which those texts have been (and are) appropriated in various ways, and at various levels, in the life of religious communities. From this kind of perspective, the Bible comes to light not merely as the harvest of ancient communities of faith, but truly as having a life of its own, shaping religious communities linguistically, symbolically, and theologically, and continuing to impact whole cultures of interpretation.

It is now possible, therefore, to argue that the *history of interpretation*—or what we might call more broadly the "reception history" of the Bible, as contrasted with its formation history—is an adjunct task of critical study of the Bible, and not just a fully separate theological discipline; for indeed, that history of interpretation begins not only with, but *within*, the sacred texts themselves. Christian communities, from the primitive Christian period onward, can be viewed within their own contexts as "reader-respondent" communities aware of their own historical distance from the ancient witnesses but striving to make sense of the texts in their own times and circumstances and in response to the constantly new challenges to Christian identity in the world. Such a perspective frustrates the hope of locating an absolutely "original" meaning of the biblical writings, especially since the various traditions of interpretation have always made divergent claims about what that original meaning is, but it properly recognizes the "world" created between sacred texts and interpreting communities, the continuum of interpretation which naturally and necessarily obtains between the two. To use an idiom from contemporary theological hermeneutics, the authority and integrity of the Bible, as comprising the "classic repertoire" for Christian faith and practice, is born out only through ongoing "performance" and "re-performance." The Bible's "claim" upon the Church is realized only as the Bible is appropriated and interpreted within the many and varied dimensions of the Church's life: in theology and doctrine, preaching and catechesis, liturgy and sacrament, ministry and ethics.

In the field of early Christian studies itself, there has been a pronounced revival in recent years in the investigation of the reception and use of Scripture in early Christian communities and in the canons and methods of patristic biblical interpretation. Older studies are reappearing and newer studies being published all the time.[1] In some cases, newer approaches from "postmodern" literary criticism, linguistic theory, or philosophical hermeneutics are being directly applied to the study of early Christian interpretation.[2] Given these kinds of interests, the essays which follow in the present volume should be a welcome contribution, for they deliver a panoramic view of diverse aspects of the appropriation of the Bible in the early Greek Church. Not all these studies fall strictly within the category of the history of biblical interpretation, if we take that to

3

mean, narrowly speaking, the "traditioning" or evolution of the exegesis of specific texts. But virtually all the essays, at one level or another, address the early Christian *interpretation* of the Bible, provided we honor two caveats: (1) that "interpretation," in a fittingly broad sense, is something done not only by trained exegetes in the technical study of texts or by bishops locked in doctrinal controversies, but also, for example, by pilgrims locating holy places with Bibles in hand, by monks fighting demons in the desert with the weapon of memorized Scripture, or by Christian communities gathered for the hearing of Scripture in the liturgy; and (2) the *media* of interpretation are broader than commentaries or homilies, inclusive also of such things as the visual arts or stone epigraphs on Christian buildings.

The essays in Part I afford insights into precisely how the Bible functioned as a foundation of Christianity. Invariably that "foundational" role has to be qualified and nuanced. Contemporary critical scholarship has rightly discouraged attempts to locate one "Bible," or more specifically one "Christian canon" as utterly and completely original or foundational to Christianity, since the Hebrew Bible (Masoretic Text), the Septuagint, the Syriac, and the Old Latin and Vulgate recensions all ultimately played a formative role in the early Church. Without doubt, however, the early Christians understood the Septuagint, a Greek "rereading" of the Hebrew Scriptures, to be the privileged Bible of the Church, a fact which Paul Lamarche brings out in his essay. Yet, as Lamarche further illustrates, the "Septuagint" really subsumed a living tradition of multiple Greek translations which vied, as it were, for inclusion in the Church's "Old Testament." The Christian Bible, from the beginning, was born of the dynamic relation between texts and interpreting communities and of the struggle for unity amid enduring diversity.[3]

Jacques Guillet's essay adds another important qualifier, indicating how the primary experience of Jesus Christ as the risen Lord, the tradition from Jesus and about Jesus (in word and in sacrament), was the true *foundation* of Christianity, insofar as it was the very basis for the Christian reinterpretation of the Hebrew Scriptures. That reinterpretation was a long and painstaking process beginning, of course, in the New Testament itself, but continuing well into the second and third centuries. It was a process critical to the Church's departure from (albeit amid a continuing dependence on) the mother faith of Judaism. Externally, it engaged Christian and Jewish communities in an ongoing contention over precisely what they had in common, a legacy of Holy Scripture. As Marcel

4

Simon points out in his essay, the battle lines were drawn not over the canonicity of biblical books, but over the integrity of the Greek translations, and more importantly over the proper hermeneutical key to reading the Bible: for Jews the living Torah and for Christians the centrality of Jesus the Christ as the agent of salvation prefigured in Law and in prophecy. Internally, as Willy Rordorf demonstrates, the process of the Christian reinterpretation of the Hebrew Scriptures (and indeed, the dogged refusal of the Church to repudiate that ancient biblical heritage) was integral to the shaping of Christian identity and to the conception of a full Christian Bible (Old and New Testaments), as attested in the preaching, catechesis, liturgy, and sacraments of early Christian communities. Indeed, Rordorf's study stands out in providing a comprehensive portrait of the formative role of Scripture and the accompanying christocentric Rule of Faith in most aspects of the Church's ecclesial life.

Part II of our volume turns to the work of some representative Greek patristic interpreters of the Bible. More than just the "methods" of patristic hermeneutics are highlighted here, for those methods were in fact tied up with larger theological presuppositions about the nature and scope of Scripture. Here the work of Irenaeus of Lyons is especially important, since the great second-century bishop, as Maurice Jourjon clarifies in his essay, pioneered an entire "program of biblical theology," an understanding of theology precisely as the science of Scripture. Irenaeus established the parameters of a "spiritual" interpretation of Scripture as rooted in the *historical* revelation of God in Jesus Christ, a revelation which is entrusted to the Church, and the prophetic fullness of which is realized in the Church. Irenaeus likewise originated a principle that was destined to become basic to early Christian exegesis as a whole: the conviction that the living Christ himself (together with his Spirit) discloses the meaning of the Bible in the Church.[4] For Clement of Alexandria in turn, as Eric Osborn ably demonstrates, Christ is the ever-present Pedagogue opening up the moral and spiritual ramifications of the Bible for those needing instruction. To use Clement's own analogy, the Logos-Christ is a bee gathering honey from the flowers in the meadow of prophets and apostles to produce pure knowledge and virtue in the souls of his audience. Clement thus appears as something of an early master of "interscriptural" exegesis, building a model of Christian ascetic life from the diverse biblical riches of law, prophets, and gospel.

It is Origen, however, who truly made a science of the moral and spiritual interpretation of the Bible on the basis of the conviction that the

Logos (and the Spirit) were "in" the text and "in" the interpretative encounter with the text. Numerous scholarly studies have been devoted to Origen's hermeneutics, but Ronald Heine's essay provides a valuable short tour through that rich legacy, one which views Origen not only as an exegete but as an instructor to readers of the Bible. Jean-Noël Guinot's excellent essay similarly takes us through the hermeneutical science of Theodoret of Cyrus, one of the later representatives of the Antiochene "school" which, while certainly independent of the Alexandrian tradition of Origen, shared many of the same general presuppositions about the nature of the biblical revelation (e.g., its fundamental inspiration, its internal integrity and *symphônia* as vindicated through exegesis, the importance of non-literal meanings, its christocentric focus, and so on). But the achievement of Theodoret and his tradition was noticeably different. With scientific and logical rigor, Theodoret highlighted the constraints imposed by texts from within (i.e., through an irreducible "literal" sense) and tried to set out a scheme that truly freed the texts to speak for themselves as the oracles of God.

Frederick Norris's essay on Gregory Nazianzen's use of the Bible in his *Theological Orations* provides a much needed balance both to the tendency in modern biblical scholarship to dismiss much patristic exegesis as undisciplined allegory lacking an "objective" or critical base and to the tendency, in patristic studies, to underestimate the subtle dynamics of language and context in the Fathers' interpretation of Scripture. It is easy to forget that the early churches did not operate with an absolutely original or stable biblical text: variants in Greek biblical translations were a fact of life. Moreover, "textuality," as we have come to discover, bespeaks not only the sacred text but the interpreting community which receives, reads, and in some sense "reconstructs" the text for itself within its own context; selective reading and (intertextual) reconfiguration of the sacred texts has always been a reality of Christian biblical interpretation. As Norris reveals, Gregory Nazianzen, in his careful management of biblical language and his firm adherence to the principle of a singular, overarching intentionality or *skopos* of the Bible that is necessary to guide and stabilize the interpretative task in an ecclesial setting, anticipates many of the concerns of Christian hermeneutics in postmodernity.

Part III of our volume provides some glimpses into the varied use of Scripture in particular theological and doctrinal controversies in the early Church. We need not look further than the New Testament to find diversity in the primitive Christian interpretation of Scripture. The reality of difference and of a more ominous heterodoxy became ever more pronounced in the second, third, and fourth centuries. It comes as something of a shock to students of early Christian history to discover that Marcion developed the first singularly Christian Bible or that Gnostics were among the earliest composers of commentaries on Scripture in this period. From Alain le Boulluec's careful analysis of the use of the Bible among the marginally orthodox, we can see how Marcionites and Gnostics created such a profound challenge to the Great Church precisely by their unique claims on Scripture. Marcion's radical program to disconnect Christianity from the sacred tradition of the Jews—resulting in his discarding of the Hebrew Scriptures and formation of a heavily edited New Testament—was motivated by a compelling affirmation of the utterly unprecedented genius and *novelty* of the gospel, the revelation, through Jesus Christ, of the once-hidden and merciful God (being the "divine" gospel which Paul upheld [Gal. 1:12] and opposed to law). Marcion not only developed a canon of Scripture, but a rule of faith (that is, a theological and hermeneutical criterion) to go with it. The Gnostic schools, by contrast, used much the same Scripture (including the Old Testament) as the Church, but were already pioneering methods of allegorical and intertextual exegesis so as to propound their own cosmological and soteriological ideas. Little wonder, then, that they were accused by patristic critics of pulling the biblical revelation apart and putting it back together again.

Charles Kannengiesser moves us beyond these early disputes to later developments in the fourth-century Church, and provides a sketch of the overarching patterns of biblical exegesis in the long and grueling Arian controversy. Here the task of reconstructing those patterns, particularly on the Arian side, is complicated by the fact that the evidence comes to us largely through the vehicle of polemical literature. Kannengiesser rightly seeks to penetrate beneath the foil which Arian exegesis became in the works of its ecclesiastical opponents, since Arius's basic intuition, the starting-point of his hermeneutical enterprise, was a strict monotheism grounded solidly in traditional Christian catechesis. But ultimately as important, and much more far-reaching in its ramifications, was the anti-Arian exegetical tradition which Arianism inadvertently helped to spawn, pioneered by Athanasius and the Cappadocian Fathers. Theological interpretation of Scripture, ecclesiastical politics, and ecclesial and pastoral concerns all intersected in the Arian controversy, but in the end, the heart of the controversy appears in much the same light as the Marcionite and Gnostic crises, namely, as a fierce dispute over the precise hermeneutical lens through which Scripture must be selected and interpreted.

My own essay in this section is intended to demonstrate how theology, interpretation of Scripture, and the ideals of ascetic praxis overlapped and intersected in some of the significant controversies over "spiritual doctrine" in early Eastern Christian monasticism. The monastic culture of biblical interpretation, as observed here and in Douglas Burton-Christie's essay later on, was one in which the *pragmatic* or performative character of biblical interpretation was clearly at the forefront. But the more deeply we analyze the monastic appropriation of the Bible, the more we discover how animated and constructively controversial it was, and the more we discover its theological complexity and its interconnection with theological and hermeneutical concerns of the larger Church in the fourth and fifth centuries.

The essays in Part IV give a sense of just how broad the contexts of biblical interpretation in the early Christian period really were. We dare not ignore, for example, the fact that there was, however restricted, a properly *pagan* context of interpretation, for there were certain educated pagans who had read at least parts of the Bible. As we see in Marcel Borret's essay on Celsus, the most sophisticated and effective pagan criticism of Christianity was precisely that which attacked the faith at its sources. Scripture, especially the Old Testament and the Gospels, found a cherished place in Celsus's invective against Christianity. Later on it would serve the same purpose in the more scholarly critique of the pagan philosopher Porphyry. Such criticism reflected the perceived novelty of Judaism and Christianity as religions of the Book in the highly pluralistic cultural setting of the Mediterranean world in late antiquity. But it also challenged the Church, in response, to recognize the necessarily "public" dimension of its biblical interpretation and to factor into its interpretation an "audience" larger than its own constituencies.

The two studies by Denis Feissel and Pierre du Bourguet display examples of the significant impact of the Bible on cultural expression within the Christian communities of the Mediterranean world and the Syrian frontier. Feissel has discerned certain basic patterns in the quotation of Scripture in Christian inscriptions on homes, churches, and tombs dating mainly from the fourth century on. Such inscriptions served a variety of purposes—apotropaic, benedictive, doxological, etc.—with the Psalms enjoying a privileged place. Only a cynical assessment would suggest that such inscriptions represented merely a Christian "domestication" of Scripture, for these quotations in stone were intended precisely to enshrine the transcendent power of the Bible and to celebrate its direct claims on all aspects of Christian life—*and* death. Bourguet's masterful survey of the earliest biblical scenes and themes depicted in Christian visual arts builds on his own extensive research in the field. His contribution to our volume as a collective whole is enormous. For the interpretation of the Bible in these iconographic media is no more frozen away in paint, wood, and stone, than the interpretation of the Bible in commentaries and homilies is frozen away in writing. Such artistic *re-presentation* of the Bible bespeaks, in some respects more profoundly than words, the living engagement between biblical text and interpreting communities in the early Christian age, and retains, for many Christians today, an evocative power that has not diminished with the centuries.

The essays in Part V concentrate on the Bible's integral role in the development of diverse forms and expressions of religious devotion in early Greek Christianity. The two studies by Irénée-Henri Dalmais and Charles Renoux highlight the formative role of biblical themes and biblical readings in the ancient liturgy. Dalmais effectively points out how, in its various Greco-Byzantine recensions, the anaphora, the eucharistic prayer which was a focal point of the liturgy, was consistently replete with biblical references and allusions and served as a crucial medium (over and beyond the creed) for celebrating, in the presence of the Christian community gathered for the Eucharist, the central biblical narrative of salvation history. It is difficult for modern Christians in the Western world to fathom the profound impact of *audibly read* Scripture in the early Christian period (let alone the common custom in this era of privately reading Scripture *aloud*). Carefully reconstructing the ancient lectionary of the Jerusalem church from available Armenian translations, Charles Renoux furthermore demonstrates how, in this important and influential liturgical tradition, the celebration of the Christian Year was itself framed and guided precisely by the disciplined liturgical reading of the Bible in the worshipping assembly (be it in the setting of a church or at the station of a holy site).

Bible reading fired the imaginations not only of whole churches in the liturgical context, but of individual Christians and groups of Christians in their respective spiritual vocations or pursuits. In his essay on the Bible's influence in early Christian martyrology, Victor Saxer details how biblical language, imagery, symbolism, ethical ideals, and eschatology permeated every aspect of the martyrs' "witness" and experience, as well as the testaments of their hagiographers. Pierre Maraval meanwhile shows how early Christian pilgrims to the Holy Land, whose travels began in earnest mainly in the fourth century, found inspiration precisely in the sacred topography mapped out for them in Holy Scripture, a topography which promised to bring them into closer identification with the Bible's own saints and martyrs.

Douglas Burton-Christie's fine essay brings into focus a world unto itself in the history of early Christian biblical interpretation and spirituality, a world also largely untouched by much of the antecedent scholarship on the Bible in the early Church. This is the oral/aural biblical culture of desert monasticism, where written Scriptures were largely absent and the practice of the Christian life turned on the power of memory, oral transmission of texts, and the inspired interpretations of charismatic elder monks. But as Burton-Christie demonstrates, it was precisely this austere culture that produced its own unique "desert hermeneutic" devoted to the practical embodiment of the Word and to the power of Holy Scripture to transform lives.

At last, it must be reiterated that this volume of collected essays in no way aspires to be a comprehensive portrait of the Bible's varied role and influences in the life of the early Greek Church. But the rich and diverse perspectives thus presented will hopefully furnish readers with an enlarged vision of that role. Meanwhile, much work still remains to be done in sorting out the many and precise ways in which biblical thought, symbolism, and language continued to be processed in the theological, ecclesial, and spiritual life of the early Christian communities.

NOTES

1. Currently in preparation, for example, is an English translation of H. de Lubac's groundbreaking study *Exégèse médiévale* (Paris, 1959-1964; new Eng. ed., Grand Rapids, forthcoming), as well as a multi-volumed patristic commentary on Scripture, *The Church's Bible*, ed. R. L. Wilken (Grand Rapids, forthcoming). Newer general studies of patristic exegesis have also begun to appear of late, such as B. de Margerie, *Introduction à l'histoire d'Exégèse*, vol. 1: *Les Pères grecs et orientaux* (Paris, 1980); J. Kugel and R. Greer, *Early Biblical Interpretation* (Philadelphia, 1986); William Horbury, "Old Testament Interpretation in the Writings of the Church Fathers," in *Mikra: Text, Translation, Reading and Interpretation of the Hebrew Bible in Ancient Judaism and Early Christianity*, ed. M. J. Mulder and H. Sysling, Compendia Rerum Iudaicarum ad Novum Testamentum, Section 2, Part 1 (Assen and Minneapolis, 1988), 727-787;

F. Young, *Virtuoso Theology: The Bible and Its Interpretation* (Cleveland, 1993); M. Simonetti, *Lettera e/o allegoria: un contributo alla storia dell'esegesi patristica* (Rome, 1985); idem, *The Interpretation of the Bible in the Early Church: An Introduction to Patristic Exegesis* (Edinburgh,1994); T. Finan and V. Twomey, eds., *Scriptural Interpretation in the Fathers: Letter and Spirit* (Blackrock, Co. Dublin, 1995); M. S. Burrows and P. Rorem, eds., *Biblical Hermeneutics in Historical Perspective* (Grand Rapids, 1991); T. F. Torrance, *Divine Meaning: Studies in Patristic Hermeneutics* (Edinburgh, 1995); and a soon-to-be-published *Handbook of Patristic Exegesis*, ed. C. Kannengiesser (Leiden, forthcoming). See also some useful anthologies of primary sources in early Christian biblical interpretation: K. Froelich, ed., *Biblical Interpretation in the Early Church*, Sources of Early Christian Thought (Philadelphia, 1984); J. Trigg, ed., *Biblical Interpretation*, Message of the Fathers of the Church, vol. 9 (Wilmington, Del., 1988); F. Sadowski, ed., *The Church Fathers on the Bible: Selected Readings* (New York, 1987). Works on the exegesis and use of Scripture in individual Greek patristic authors and traditions have also been abundant of late: e.g., K. J. Torjeson, *Hermeneutical Procedure and Theological Method in Origen's Exegesis* (New York, 1986); A. le Boulluec and G. Dorival, eds., *Origeniana Sexta: Origène et la Bible/Origen and the Bible. Actes du Colloquium Origenianum Sextum, Chantilly, 30 août - 3 septembre 1993* (Leuven, 1995); D. Dawson, *Allegorical Readers and Cultural Revision in Ancient Alexandria* (Berkeley, 1992); M. Canévet, *Grégoire de Nysse et l'herméneutique biblique: Étude des rapports entre le langage et la connaissance de Dieu* (Paris, 1983); P. Rorem, *Biblical and Liturgical Symbols within the Pseudo-Dionysian Synthesis* (Toronto, 1984); D. Zaharopoulos, *Theodore of Mopsuestia on the Bible: A Study of His Old Testament Exegesis* (New York, 1989); J.-N. Guinot, *L'exégèse de Théodoret de Cyr* (Paris, 1995); D. Burton-Christie, *The Word in the Desert: Scripture and the Quest for Holiness in Early Christian Monasticism* (New York, 1993); P. M. Blowers, *Exegesis and Spiritual Pedagogy in Maximus the Confessor* (Notre Dame, Ind., 1991).

2. See, e.g., P. Cox Miller, "Poetic Words, Abysmal Words: Reflections on Origen's Hermeneutics," in *Origen: His World and His Legacy*, ed. C. Kannengiesser and W. Petersen (Notre Dame, Ind., 1988), 165-178; A. Mosshammer, "Disclosing but Not Disclosed: Gregory of Nyssa as Deconstructionist," in *Studien zu Gregor von Nyssa und der christliche Spätantike*, ed. H. Dröbner and C. Klock (Leiden, 1990), 103-120.; F. W. Norris, "Blackmarks on the Communities' Manuscripts," *Journal of Early Christian Studies* 2 (1994): 443-466.

3. Still of tremendous value is the work of H. von Campenhausen, *The Formation of the Christian Bible*, trans. J. Baker (Philadelphia, 1972).

4. A fact which renders rather superfluous the search for "theories" of inspiration per se in early Christian hermeneutics.

PART I

The Bible as a Foundation
of Christianity

1

The Septuagint:
Bible of the Earliest Christians

PAUL LAMARCHE, S.J.

In what version was the Old Testament used and commented on by early Christians? Excluding the text used by the earliest Syriac Christian authors, it is the Septuagint, the Greek translation which, directly or indirectly, was fundamental for all writings of the early Christian centuries, and even after Jerome it is the text which the Greek Fathers, including the Antiochenes, customarily used.

This fact opens us to interesting and fruitful investigations in the Fathers' engagement with the Septuagint, but unfortunately we must also face multiple problems posed by a text that is in so many respects enigmatic. The label "Septuagint" attaches to such a multiplicity and variety of textual traditions that it leaves doubts about the unity of this translation: ancient manuscripts, diverse translations made of the Greek, and Greek quotations of the Old Testament proposed by the New Testament and the Fathers admit of so many variants that it may be justly asked whether we are dealing with texts originating from a common root or rather with mutually independent translations.

The problem is further complicated when we attempt to reconstruct the history of the Septuagint. Strictly speaking, it is the Pentateuch that should be called the Septuagint. The legend in the *Letter of Aristeas* indicates that the Pentateuch alone was the work of the 72 translators. Only over the course of subsequent centuries were the other books of the Bible translated into Greek, and in very different ways. The Septuagint collection is thus only a relative unity. So how can we explain both its diversity and its unity?

Starting with historical evidence and thereupon stressing those things which have favored certain hypotheses over others concerning the formation of this version, we will try to reconstruct how the Septuagint came together before turning to examine its characteristic literary and theological principles.

The History of the Septuagint: Origins and Formation

In investigating the origins and evolution of the Septuagint, we must distinguish between the Pentateuch and the rest of the Old Testament.

The Pentateuch

The Pentateuch was the first part of the Bible to be translated into Greek. Antiquity has afforded us a unique testimony to this translation in the *Letter of Aristeas*,[1] the precise value of which is debatable. Its author is presented as a Greek (§16) living in Alexandria in the period of Ptolemy II Philadelphus (king from 285 to 246 B.C.E.).[2] The *Letter* portrays Demetrius of Phalerum[3] as head of the royal library. By Aristeas's account, Demetrius counseled Philadelphus to have the Law of the Jews translated in order to expand the Library of Alexandria. A delegation dispatched to Jerusalem secured from the Jewish authorities not only an excellent Hebrew text, but also the services of 72 translators learned in Hebrew and Greek. Their work, carried out piously and methodically, was finished in 69 days. Authenticated by a heavenly sign, promulgated by the Jewish authorities of Alexandria, and acclaimed by the community, the translation appeared perfect: "Inasmuch as the translation has been well and piously made and is in every respect accurate, it is right that it should remain in its present form and that no revision of any sort take place."[4]

Date and Purpose of the Letter of Aristeas. Today it is universally admitted that the *Letter* was not written by the true Aristeas, and that its story was in large part legendary. Its date and purpose are more difficult to determine. Most modern scholars date the *Letter* to the second century B.C.E (some date it to the first century B.C.E.). P. E. Kahle dated it right around 100, while S. Jellicoe and A. Pelletier envisaged it rather from the first half or beginning of the second century B.C.E. The latter seems the more probable to us.[5] The letter appears to combine Jewish propaganda with an apology for the Greek translation itself, though the latter motif clearly dominates the text. As for the problem of why such an apology would be composed more than a century after the translation was completed, Kahle theorized that over the course of the third and second centuries B.C.E., the liturgical reading of the Pentateuch had engendered diverse Greek translations.[6] The process would have been similar to that which gave rise to diverse forms of the Aramaic targum. At the end of the second century, one of the translations had to be chosen in order to produce an official text. A Jewish author would have had this purpose in mind in creating the legend recounted in the *Letter of Aristeas* (ca. 100 B.C.E.). For Kahle this would explain the tremendous diversity of Greek texts of the Bible (quotations in Alexandrian authors; ancient papyri, etc.). As a consequence, the desire to establish the text of a primitive Septuagint on the basis of these diverse testimonies would be a vain enterprise, a search for a text that had never existed.

This is a brilliant hypothesis; nonetheless, critical studies of late do not favor it. Indeed, given the lack of decisive arguments, there is mounting evidence against Kahle's theory. For one thing, the Greek translation for which the *Letter of Aristeas* is an apology was a century old and not recently chosen from among the others. The end of the letter (especially § 310) could very well indicate the desire to defend a translation (already ancient) against recent criticisms and concurrent corrections. Detailed examination of the ancient papyri[7] and analysis of the Greek fragments of the Minor Prophets discovered in the Judean desert[8] demonstrate that these texts are not parallels to the Septuagint, but that they depend on it. It seems that Eupolemus (ca. 160 B.C.E.) knew and used the Septuagint.[9] In about the same period, Aristobulus alludes to the origin of the Septuagint, which he refers back to the preceding century.[10] Finally, allusions in the Prologue to Sirach (ca. 132 B.C.E.) are better understood by taking into account the classic hypothesis.

Reasons for the Translation. The *Letter of Aristeas* thus refers us to a Greek translation[11] made in the period either of Demetrius of Phalerum (under Ptolemy Soter, 323-285 B.C.E.) or of Ptolemy Philadelphus (285-246 B.C.E.). If on this point we can accept the information in the *Letter,* even if some of it is dubious,[12] is it not clear that the rest of the *Letter* is legendary? In particular, many modern authors do not take into account the motives that the *Letter* gives for the production of the Greek translation. In their view, it was a liturgical need that led the Jewish community in Alexandria to compose a translation of the Pentateuch. Enticing though this thesis is, it encounters several difficulties. Had the real reason been liturgical, it would not have been necessary to translate the whole Pentateuch. And indeed, not until the second century C.E. do we find the continuous reading of the Pentateuch in the synagogue. Moreover, it is not clear why the *Letter of Aristeas* would itself have remained silent about this liturgical motivation.

For a while, another hypothesis began to be put forth,[13] according to which the Alexandrian authorities were permitting diverse communities to live by their own laws, such that it was useful and necessary for the King and his entourage to know the Law of the Jewish community. Doubtless a political motive and the King's almighty will were necessary in order to convince reticent Jews and to render the translation open to the Greek intellectual spirit. But it is quite clear that this principal motive (at least if this hypothesis is accepted) does not exclude other important factors. The intellectual curiosity of the cultured people of Alexandria must have played a significant role.[14] The *Letter of Aristeas* undoubtedly had good reason for emphasizing this motivation for the translation. Certainly from the standpoint of the Jewish community there was an interest to make known the doctrine of the true God.[15] Finally, it seems likely that this translation also corresponded to the liturgical needs of the Jewish community of Alexandria—a motivation which may not have been determinative, but certainly could be added to the overall list of reasons for the Greek translation.

Hence, while understanding the *Letter of Aristeas* as a legend, we are still led to take it seriously since legend is more or less common for this literary genre. Significant segments of the *Letter* are "confirmed" by similar or slightly variable external witnesses: Aristobulus, Philo, the Babylonian Talmud (*Megillah* 9), Justin, Irenaeus, the *Exhortatio ad Graecos*, Clement of Alexandria, Anatolius of Laodicea, Cyril of Alexandria, Epiphanius, Justinian, the *Paschal Chronicon*, Nicetas of Remesiana, and Georgius Syncellus.[16]

We can reasonably conclude, then, that around 285 a Greek translation of the Pentateuch was produced. Far from being a mere slavish word-for-word copying of the Hebrew words into the Greek, this translation showed up remarkable characteristics and qualities. It was to engender a whole religious language, a language that was to make possible the completion of the translation itself and that would find its culmination in the New Testament and in the works of the Fathers.

18

Translation of the Other Books of the Bible

The "purists," chiefly Jerome,[17] reserved the title "Septuagint" only for the translation of the Pentateuch.[18] But it was by no mere accidental misnomer that the title was customarily used of the whole Greek Old Testament. Under the influence of the translation of the Pentateuch, the translation enterprise was extended progressively to the rest of the Hebrew Bible, so that beyond the diversity of genres and translations, the Septuagint was able to boast a minimal unity.

Normally the books of the Septuagint are classified by considering certain characteristics that indicate a more or less substantial literal fidelity to the Hebrew text. The Psalter, the Minor Prophets, and the ancient Septuagint version of Daniel are found in between the Pentateuch and the *Kaige* group. In these books, the Hebrew particle *gam* is practically never translated using the Greek *kaige*. But the rendering of *gam* with *kaige* is resumed again in Lamentations, the Song of Songs, Ruth, and the Theodotionic recension of Daniel. Literalism makes still further progress in translating, in certain cases, the Hebrew particle *'et*, signifying the accusative, with the Greek *syn*. This is the case in Ecclesiastes.

Yet this simplified scheme needs explaining and complementary evidence. These translation characteristics are typical and exemplify a group of procedures which progressively seek always to give a more faithful account of the Hebrew text.[19] A particular hermeneutics is expressed through this literal fidelity to the Hebrew; indeed this was a current Jewish trend represented especially by Aqiba and Aquila.[20] The originality and audacity of the translators of the Greek Pentateuch is better understood in relation to this exegetical school. It is no surprise to find in this connection an ongoing conflict between two tendencies: the one more liberal, at times approaching correction or adaptation; the other more faithful, to the point of clinging tightly to the letter of the text. The latter tendency, then, would unceasingly attempt to rectify what it considered to be excessive liberties in the initial Greek translations. Ordinarily Jewish authors, in using the Septuagint, corrected it in order to harmonize it with the Hebrew text.[21] Ancient papyri from the second century C.E., while dependent on the Septuagint, drew closer to the Hebrew text. We see here that an offensive strategy was developed: limited improvements were made on certain Septuagint texts, but the ancient translation persisted in a part of the manuscripts.[22] Some books (Lamentations, the Song of Songs, Ruth) were doubtless translated by taking into account principles which must have led to the exegesis of Aqiba and Aquila. In the end, a work of Aquila—the translation of Ecclesiastes—succeeded in making its way into the Septuagint.[23] Clearly the bitter struggle between liberal and conservative tendencies complicated the history of the Septuagint recension.

Scarcely had the Septuagint been put together than it was continuing to run into the same problems. It had to face the competition of translations made according to diverse principles: Theodotion, Aquila, Symmachus. It had to struggle against criticisms coming from within Judaism.[24] It was for the purpose of countering those attacks that Origen, without in the process abandoning the Septuagint as the primitive Church had received and transmitted it, agreed for polemical purposes to correct and complete it. A little more slowly, then, Jerome, perhaps not comprehending all that the Septuagint had of the original text, attempted to return strictly to the *hebraica veritas*.

Other Translations

It is impossible to present the Septuagint without saying something about the other Greek translations of the Hebrew Bible. Not only did Origen and numerous patristic writers know of them and use them, but at times there was tampering between the Septuagint and the other translations, such that the Daniel of Theodotion and the Qoheleth of Aquila managed to penetrate manuscripts of the Septuagint.

Theodotion. Based on evidence from Irenaeus, Epiphanius, and Jerome,[25] Theodotion is often presented as an Ephesian proselyte, an Ebionite, living somewhere around 180-190 C.E. In reality, nearly all this evidence is debatable.

We are on firmer ground if we start with the texts attributed to him. His simple and precise translation (fitting the *kaige* group) is characterized by a fairly sizeable number of transliterations. One of his books in particular that has been preserved is his translation of Daniel, which, according to Origen,[26] was used by Christians and found its way into the Septuagint to the point of replacing the ancient translation in the majority of manuscripts.

But Hebrews 11:23 and 1 Corinthians 15:54, which quote Isaiah according to Theodotion's text, and Clement of Rome (*1 Clem.* 34.6), who appears to have used Theodotion's version of Daniel, throw into question the date customarily attributed to this translator (i.e. 180-190 C.E.). Two hypotheses have been proposed in response. Some authors, like S. Jellicoe, distinguish two stages in this translation-recension: a first stage during the first century B.C.E. resulted in what could be called a proto-Theodotion; and a second stage, the work of Theodotion himself, who recovered and revised the translation of proto-Theodotion. A second hypothesis, that of D. Barthélemy,[27] chooses to locate Theodotion not at the end of the second century C.E., but somewhere in 30-50 C.E. Representative of the *kaige* group, he would thus precede Aquila. Several indications would tend to identify Theodotion with Jonathan ben 'Uzziel. As for clues to the identity of Theodotion originating from ancient authors (date, proselyte, Ebionite), they can be explained and corrected. It is more important to recover texts that can and must be attributed to Theodotion.[28] Moreover, we can confirm that his translation is in fact only a revision based on the Septuagint.

Aquila. A disciple of Rabbi Aqiba (at the end of the first century or beginning of the second century C.E.), Aquila produced his translation around 130. Undoubtedly making use of earlier recensions, especially those of the *kaige* group, which were already endeavoring to draw nearer to the Hebrew text, Aquila went a step further in order to copy the Greek off of the semitic original. Thus he usually translated the particle of the accusative *'et* with the Greek *syn*. Sometimes these barbarisms and the servility of this kind of translation is ridiculed. Actually the *syn* of Aquila is an archaism imitating Homeric usage and its employment is adverbial. Furthermore, this literal transference from Hebrew to Greek actually serves an exegetical approach made famous by Aqiba.[29] Some modern authors propose identifying Aquila with Onqelos, but such an equation is impossible. Besides (and this is perhaps more important), the particularities of Aquila's style have been specified such that we can very likely attribute to Aquila the translation of Ecclesiastes transmitted by Septuagint manuscripts.[30]

Symmachus. Little is known of Symmachus. Irenaeus says nothing of him, as if this translator was too recent or had yet to publish anything. Moreover, Palladius,[31] Eusebius,[32] and Epiphanius[33] are not very precise in the information they give. Considered an Ebionite by Eusebius, one wonders whether Symmachus had ever really been a Jewish Christian, since much evidence runs counter to such a thesis.[34] A Samaritan by birth, he converted to Judaism. His translation of Isaiah 7:14 (*neanis*), like those of Theodotion and Aquila, was able to provide a point of support for the Ebionites.[35] Moreover, according to Eusebius, Ebionism was not only the heresy of certain Christians, but was also the stance of certain Jews as well. Symmachus's translation, finished around 165 C.E. (or sometime around 200), is less literal than those of Theodotion and Aquila, but

21

in its elegance and accuracy it was destined to influence Jerome's Latin translation of the Old Testament.[36]

Quinta, Sexta, Septima. Besides these Greek versions, Origen had at times used other translations, one of which, it appears, was found in a jar (reminiscent of the Qumran discoveries) with some other volumes at Jericho at the beginning of the third century. In fact, little or nothing is known of the extent of these translations or of their author. Their very existence, at least that of the last (Septima), is sometimes doubted. Furthermore, it must be remembered that the various columns of the Hexapla were not always reserved for the same translation, and occasionally several recensions of the same translation could effectively leave the other versions unaccounted for, subsequently leading, no doubt, to confusions and errors.[37]

The Originality of the Septuagint

Through its long and winding history we already get a glimpse of the importance and complexity of the Septuagint. The originality of this text requires now a more detailed assessment.

Textual Criticism

For a long time ancient versions, and in particular the Septuagint, were used for improving the Masoretic text of the Hebrew Bible. So in embarking on a retroversion beginning with the Greek, it was sometimes possible to establish that a word had unfortunately disappeared from the Hebrew text, or indeed that the vocalization of a certain Hebrew word underlying the Greek was better than that of the Masoretic text. Hence, the aid provided to biblical scholars by the Septuagint until recent times was indeed not insignificant, but it was restricted.

The discoveries at Qumran have changed the landscape. Hebrew biblical texts found in the Qumran corpus often stand in the middle between the concise form of the Masoretic text and the Septuagint version, with its theological corrections and various complements. In short, it is believed today that visible changes in the Septuagint in relation to the Masoretic text do not all stem from the translators, but are more often derived from a subjacent Hebrew text. And so the text-critical problems posed by the Septuagint have once again been revived and amplified.

At the same time, through the Qumran discoveries, we have obtained a better grasp of the diversity of manuscript traditions of this period. Undoubtedly, according to different regions[38] and situations, there were slightly different texts. These living and dynamic traditions were destined to be dangerously dispersed after the destruction of Jerusalem in 70 C.E. At Jamnia (ca. 90 C.E.), the rabbis apparently decided to guard a single orientation of the biblical text (that which became the Masoretic text) and to destroy the others. Undoubtedly the choice was intelligently made; yet, there was no reason at all to remove all other forms of the Bible. The primitive Church certainly had understood that fact, in never accepting the decision of Jamnia and in adopting as its Bible a text enriched by complements present in the Septuagint.

The Septuagint as Biblical Text[39]

In the presence of a living text, there is no reason to be slaves to the primitive "original." Must we automatically prefer the Hebrew form of Sirach to its Greek form? Do we have to exclude the books of Chronicles on the pretext that they are a late rereading of the books of Samuel and Kings? But indeed, the Septuagint as a whole is a rereading of the Hebrew Bible, and it is in this Greek form that the primitive Church received the "Old Testament," beginning with the New Testament writers themselves. It should be no surprise, then, that patristic authors read and commented on the Septuagint, that they argued from it, that they supported themselves with it—including its alleged "mistranslations." And they did so without the least naiveté. On the contrary, they were conscious that revelation as a whole had followed a progression and that it had come to the Church in this renewed Greek form. This "rereading" was replete with philosophical and theological developments, which is precisely how we must understand the originality of the Septuagint.

The Originality of the Septuagint

Philosophical Originality. "With the Septuagint," writes A. Neher, "the Bible attains, for the first time in history, to the resolute standard of a philosophical value; it takes its place among the masterworks of philosophy. For, far from being literal, as are later Jewish or Christian versions which want to react to the philosophical baptism of the Bible, the Septuagint is consciously interpretative, and certain tendencies of this exegesis, among the most fundamental, are clearly philosophical."[40] Undoubtedly such assertions are open to refinement,[41] but to a great degree they are justified. Thus for the Septuagint, in Exodus 3:14 and elsewhere throughout, the God who reveals himself and his name is no longer hidden and disclosed through the Tetragrammaton (*YHWH*) in terms of mysterious signification; rather, he is the great Existent (*ho ôn*), the Lord.[42] It is not a matter of depersonalizing God, for the God of the Septuagint is indeed a personal being; yet there is a distinct effort to remove God from any local, exotic, particularized context, and to ascribe to him a universal dimension. Only then can a bridge between the Bible and Greek reflection on God be established.

On the other hand, through some variants, transpositions, and nuances, the Greek translation divulges another cultural and philosophical world, seen in the following two examples.

From Genesis 1:2, it is established that the material to be used in creating and modelling the world is no longer a chaos, as in the semitic outlook, but is rather something invisible and unorganized. We see into a Greek cosmogony that opens the way into the notion of an intelligible and invisible world,[43] or, to put it more simply, a cosmogony that is oriented toward a comprehension of the world in which the illumination and organization of the cosmos plays a capital role.

Elsewhere in the Septuagint, the richness of the Greek language made it possible for the translators at times to nuance the primitive narratives. Thus in the Masoretic text of Genesis 30 and 31, words from the Hebrew root 'BD are always used to designate the labor that Jacob furnished for fourteen years. But the Greek with great finesse employs two different themes: when Jacob speaks, he insinuates that his labor is that of a slave (*douleuein*); when Laban answers him, he indicates a labor (*ergazesthai*) without any pejorative connotation.[44] The spirit of the Greek has not only used shades of meaning here which characterize the labor and lend greater color and poignancy to the narrative, it introduces to the biblical world social and philosophical conceptions largely foreign to Jewish society. In ancient Israel, slavery, far from being generally institutionalized, was hardly practiced anywhere, and justly the Septuagint usually avoided attributing a slave's status to Israelites. Under the influence of Greek social concepts, then, the possibility became readily apparent of ascribing two different qualifications to one and the same "labor."

Theological Originality. Often certain theological developments are pointed out as proper to the Septuagint, such as the tendency to spiritualize language about God, an accentuated universalism, and more refinement in messianic expectation.

This tremendous tendency to spiritualize language about God, even if it is neither systematic nor exclusive to the Septuagint, habitually eliminates or tones down anthropomorphisms and material metaphors that the Hebrew text customarily uses in speaking of God. Yet since to-day there is no longer any danger of taking these images literally, it is regrettable to find the disappearance in the Greek of poetic analogies where God is likened to a mighty rock, a shield, or someone who is given to wrath or who repents. At the time that the Septuagint was composed, it was the tendency among Jews as much as Greeks to transpose these seemingly offensive images and to use a more intellectual and spiritual language for God. For example, at the beginning of Psalm 17 (18 in the Hebrew Bible) the Lord is a rock, a fortress, a mighty rock, a shield in the Masoretic text, whereas in the Greek he becomes a support, a refuge, a help, a protector.

Quite often, of course, the Fathers of the Church supported their theological arguments with finepoints from the Septuagint, a classic instance being the christological and mariological discussions of the importance of the Greek *parthenos*, "virgin," (substituting the Hebrew *almah*, which can designate simply "young woman") in Isaiah 7:14.[45] On the other hand, the idea of a *created* Wisdom was, with the Septuagint reading, retained for Proverbs 8:22 before Eusebius, Basil, and Jerome searched other translations for an interpretation more conducive to their christological position.

Most important, however, is the birth of a language, indeed of a whole cultural and religious world that was destined to be adopted and perpetuated in the New Testament, and still further commented on and developed in patristic authors. Undoubtedly there is no absolute beginning to this development: Greek and semitic sources (especially the Hebrew Bible) are both conspicuous enough. Nonetheless, through a multitude of small linguistic phenomena, a threshold was passed: something new appeared on the scene.

An example would be the first two Psalms. Amid all the small textual variations and linguistic transpositions certain expressions emerge. As nearly everywhere in the Bible, in Psalm 1:2 the Hebrew *torah* is translated *nomos* ("law") in the Septuagint. The significance is not immediately obvious and demands further reflection. We would rather expect to find *torah* translated with *didachê* ("teaching") or a similar term. Sometimes we find *torah* attaining a meaning quite close to the Greek *logos*, in clear contrast with *nomos*. Indeed, biblical usage causes the primary sense of *nomos* as "law" to break down; thus, even in Paul the term *nomos* defies a purely legislative meaning and can go beyond the Pentateuch and its teaching to refer to the Prophets.[46] Yet it would be unnecessary to jump to the conclusion that the translation of *torah* with *nomos* subverted or betrayed the Hebrew concept, opening the door to narrowly legalistic and reproachable attitudes. In fact the most elevated things are capable of the worst and best results alike. Before excesses and abuses were recognized, law was originally for ancient civilizations a marvelous discovery, guaranteeing harmony and peace in human relations. At the time of the Septuagint, though there was no attempt to account for the full richness of the Hebrew concept of *torah*, there had nonetheless been a desire to capture from it a vital element characterizing the covenant relation between God and his people. Yet while choosing to render *torah* with *nomos*, the Septuagint, in spite of itself, made the boundaries of this covenant impossible to define absolutely. And we see how this perspective was further reinforced in the New Testament by Paul.

In Psalm 1:2, not only is the proper name of the God of Israel not pronounced, but the sacred Tetragrammaton disappears altogether, being translated and completely replaced by the equivalent of *Adonai: Kyrios* or "Lord." As we have seen above, it would be unnecessary to conclude that there was a commensurate depersonalization of God. The *Kyrios* of the Septuagint retains all the characteristics of the personal God as they are found in the Hebrew Bible. Yet, besides its never being pronounced, he loses his proper name. What is doubtless abandoned is the local aspect and the archaizing of a God who had been tied exclusively to certain tribes before revealing his universality. The Lord of the Septuagint is personal, and he certainly remains the God of Moses and Abraham, but he is Lord of heaven and earth, the universal God for whom all peoples grope, especially the Greeks.

In Psalm 2 there appears one who is anointed through royal unction and enthroned to establish the reign of God. Because of this anointing, he is called *Christos*. The New Testament, basing itself in this translation and all that it represents, does not hesitate applying this title to Jesus. It may be that Aquila searched for another translation of this word in reaction to the linguistic and theological continuity thus established between the Old Testament and Jesus.

Let us return to Psalm 1, where the vocabulary concerning sinners and righteous begins to take shape. In Greek as well as in Hebrew there is a great richness of words to designate sin and the sinner. Certain equivalences regularly appear between the two languages: the Greek root *hamart-* corresponds to the Hebrew root *ḤṬ'*. A crucial agreement in thought obtains on both sides, the idea of the sinner falling short of the goal, and this idea in Psalm 1, as in Psalm 24:8 (LXX, = 25:8, Masoretic text) is reinforced by the image of a directional course. If the root HṬ' dominates the terminology for sin in the Hebrew Bible, the root *hamart-* is even more frequent in the Septuagint. Thus in a dramatic way a concept emerges that underscores the religious dimension of sin. Humanity on its own has deviated from the course that leads to God; it falls short of the goal. This notion would be indispensable to the reasonings of Paul in Romans, as well as to later developments in the Church's theological tradition. At the same time, however, the Septuagint lends a certain importance to words like *anomia* ("lawlessness"). This evolution does not necessarily represent a reinforced legalism but emphasizes the relation that exists between sin and rejection of the Law understood in its complete scope. Since the sinner does not know the Law and is not obedient to it, pagans are *ipso facto* sinners. There is perhaps also an opposition established between the *asebeis* ("ungodly," Ps. 1:1, 4) and "God-fearers" which tends still to reconcile the two categories of "pagans" and "sinners."

There is no reason to read into this language a narrow or sectarian element, but it is clear that this manner of speaking was to aid Christian writers in accentuating the limitations of the Law.

A certain counterpoised tendency toward universalism appears in the first two Psalms, and especially Psalm 2, where the violent threats against the nations (2:9b) are partially mitigated by the Septuagint. Thus in 2:9a, in place of "breaking" the nations with a rod of iron, the messianic king will "shepherd" them with it. Moreover, at two points where God's anger against the nations is expressed in Psalm 2, the term is not *orgê* (the "fury" that destroys the nations) but the milder *thymos*, designating in the Psalms that divine wrath which heals and saves (2:5, 12).[47] Finally, the word in Greek designating "the nations," *ethnê*, does not bear the pejorative connotation of the Hebrew *goïm*. Each of these slight mutations is not so significant individually, but their accumulation here and elsewhere leaves a lasting impression.

Twice we discover in this Psalm an interesting cognate: in 2:10 *paideuthête*, and in 2:12 *paideias*. These words can designate punishments and corrections as well as instruction and formation, all simultaneously applicable to a child being educated. As in 2:10, where the imperative, because of its referent, probably has a noble sense ("instruct yourselves!" or "let yourselves be instructed!"), it is possible that in 2:12 the sense of "instruction" must equally be preferred to that of "correction." Moreover, this typically Greek term *paideia* very nearly epitomizes the cultural humanism which was the very ideal of Greek education. In the Bible, the term can, as we see in Sirach (Prol. 3), where it stands in parallel with wisdom, designate the ultimate formation or education of Israel by God. In Psalm 2:12, even if we cannot separate the sense of "correction" in the term *paideia* without violating the context, it is still necessary, in view of the parallel with 2:10 and because of the general meaning of this word, not to neglect the sense of *paideia* as instruction or formation.

Also in Psalm 2:12 we encounter the idea of trust in God. The image suggested by the underlying Hebrew verb ("seeking refuge") disappears here for the sake of a more general notion, less poetic no doubt yet in the end more dynamic. Progressively in the Septuagint, and especially in the Psalms, this idea of confidence was to emerge in the notion of hope. This notion of hope would become the focal point of several other semitic verbs as well, certain of which would form a straight line between hope and firmness of faith, while the biblical "hope," through usage, would assume a vast messianic and eschatological content. Thus in our view there appears in the Septuagint a notion which transcended its Greek and semitic origins and which, in its New Testament development, would become a premier concept, one that the modern person, whether a Christian or not, can no longer do without.

By just these few examples taken from Psalms 1 and 2 we see how a multitude of small linguistic phenomena in the Greek text reread, transformed, adapted, and developed—but did not deform—the original Hebrew text. In the larger perspective of the development of "the Bible," this process of rereading and adaption, in all its originality and novelty, constitutes a crucial step that we have no right to neglect.

Conclusion

By way of conclusion it would perhaps be useful briefly to say a word on some relatively recent developments in Septuagint studies.

Earlier research on the *Letter of Aristeas* was rightly critical of this story, but in too negative a manner. We are well advised today to take this legend more seriously as a source. Thus P. E. Kahle's brilliant "Greek targum" theory about the origins of the Septuagint has been more and more discussed. Without doubt the Pentateuch was translated into Greek at Alexandria in the first half of the third century B.C.E. The liturgical motif at one time introduced as the rationale for this translation is less often invoked today; instead, appeal is made to juridical factors (e.g., the

Alexandrian Jewish community's indulging their authorities' desire to know the Law) and the curiosity of Alexandria's Jewish intellectuals.

A better knowledge of the characteristics of the *kaige* and *kaige-syn* groups in the Septuagint would doubtless facilitate a better understanding of the succession of recensions that attempted to bring the Greek translation judged too liberal closer to the Hebrew text. Owing to these characteristics, which were demonstrated largely by D. Barthélemy, we can certainly concur with his attribution of the Septuagint version of Qoheleth to Aquila.

The identification of Aquila with Onqelos, and of Theodotion with Jonathan ben 'Uzziel is gaining ground. Instead of dating Theo–dotion to around 180 C.E., we could envisage him in the years 30-50, or else it might be necessary to "divide him in two," distinguishing the pre-New Testament Theodotion and the Theodotian at the end of the second century.

Interest in the Septuagint today has taken on a whole new look. At one time Septuagint research was conducted primarily for purposes of resolving certain text-critical problems. Yet even in this context, the bearing of the Septuagint on text criticism is far more important than was once thought, and thanks to it we have greater insight into the diversity of manuscript traditions of the Hebrew text prior to Jamnia (at the end of the of the first century C.E.). But above all, we are beginning to move beyond the very obstacle that leads to a misunderstanding of the Septuagint, and we are less obsessed today with the authority of a text said to be "original" when confronted with a living text with a whole evolutionary history. To Christians, the Septuagint appears more and more as a rereading of the Old Testament, and of course it is precisely this Greek recension that was formative for primitive Christian understanding, and proclamation, of the biblical revelation. As one scholar has forcefully argued of late, when faced with the dilemma of "choosing" between the Hebrew Bible and the Septuagint as the "original" Bible of the Church, the choice has already been dictated by the New Testament writers themselves: it it the Septuagint.[48] Today we are obliged to uncover the originality of the Septuagint—its textual, philological, philosophical, and theological originality. Such research is of immediate interest in Old Testament studies, but it is no less important and decisive for a better comprehension of the literary, cultural, and religious sources of the New Testament and the Fathers.

NOTES

1. See the critical edition in Moses Hadas, ed. and trans., *Aristeas to Philocrates (Letter of Aristeas)*, Jewish Apocryphal Literature series (New York, 1973). A score of manuscripts (the more ancient of which date to the twelfth century), numerous Church Fathers, and Philo of Alexandria (*De vita Moysis* 2.37) all attest to the *Letter*. Eusebius of Caesarea (*Praeparatio evangelica* 8.1.7-8.5.9 and 8.9.38), and Josephus (*Antiquities* 12.12-118) also amply cite the *Letter of Aristeas*. Cf. also Justin, *Apologia* 1.31; Irenaeus, *Adversus haereses* 3.21.2 (*ap.* Eusebius, *Hist. eccl.* 5.8.11-15); *Exhortatio ad Graecos* (PG 6: 241-326); Clement of Alexandria, *Stromateis* 1.148; Tertullian, *Apologeticus* 18; Cyril of Jerusalem, *Catecheses* 4.34; Epiphanius, *De mensuris et ponderibus* 3; John Chrysostom, *Homiliae in Matthaeum* 5.2; Jerome, *Praef. in Pentateuchum* (PL 28: 150-152), etc.

2. We already know that after the death of Alexander (323 B.C.E.), his empire was quickly divided: Egypt went to Ptolemy, son of Lagos; the vast possessions from Asia to Syria went to Seleucus, and then to his son Antiochus I (281-261). Palestine, for a long time politically tied to Egypt, fell under the protection of the Seleucids after the battle of Panion (ca. 200). In Egypt, the first Ptolemy (surnamed Soter), after having reigned from 323 to 283, abdicated so that the throne could be assumed by his younger son, Ptolemy II, subsequently called Philadelphus (285-246). After this shining cultural period, Egypt came to experience gradually more severe hardships under the reigns of Ptolemy III Euergetes (246-222), Ptolemy IV Philopator (221-205), and Ptolemy V Epiphanes (204-180).

3. By ancient account (see, e.g., Diogenes Laertius 5.78), Demetrius had been the friend and counselor of Ptolemy Soter. When the latter had wanted to place his younger son on the throne (who was to become Ptolemy Philadelphus), Demetrius attempted to deter the king. Upon the death of Ptolemy Soter in 283, the new king had Demetrius put in prison, where he died. Ptolemy Philadelphus contributed greatly to the Library of Alexandria, but his father and Demetrius could claim to be its true founders (see E. A. Parsons, *The Alexandrian Library: Glory of the Hellenic World* [Amsterdam, London, and New York, 1952]).

4. *Letter of Aristeas* 310 (trans. Hadas, 221). For a fresh look at the *Letter's* significance, see M. Müller, *The First Bible of the Church: A Plea for the Septuagint* (Sheffield, 1996), 46-58.

5. It is interesting here to take into account the testimony of Aristobulus, cited by Clement of Alexandria (*Strom.* 1.22.150): "They were translated by others before Demetrius, yet before the rule of Alexander and the Persians..." Likewise see Eusebius of Caesarea, *Praeparatio evangelica* 13.12.2. Did Aristobulus, who wrote during the decade 160-150 B.C.E., depend on the *Letter of Aristeas* or was he rather representing a tradition earlier than the *Letter*? The latter hypothesis would valorize the *Letter of Aristeas*, but it is the first hypothesis that appears simpler and more probable.

6. See P. E. Kahle, *The Cairo Geniza*, 2nd ed. (Oxford, 1959).

7. Papyrus Rylands 458 (around 150 B.C.E.), Papyrus Fouad 266 (around 100 B.C.E.). According to the analyses of P. Walters (*The Text of the Septuagint* [London, 1973], 273ff), confirmed by D. Barthélemy (*Études d'histoire du texte de l'AT* [Fribourg, 1978], 322), these two texts are close to the Septuagint and dependent on it.
8. D. Barthélemy, *Les devanciers d'Aquila* (Leiden, 1963).
9. See Eusebius of Caesarea, *Praep. evang.* 9.30-34. Cf. perhaps 1 Macc. 8:17.
10. See note 5. For the date of Aristobulus, see N. Walter, *Der Thoraausleger Aristobulos* (Berlin, 1964).
11. Certain authors, like F. X. Wutz, have proposed the hypothesis of a transcription of the Hebrew text in Greek characters, a transcription which would have served as the basis of the translation of the LXX. This hypothesis has an air of probability, as is proven by the second column of Origen's Hexapla, and could explain certain "translations" which were in fact transcriptions. Yet on the whole this theory has not been retained and, at any rate, this problem appears marginal in relation to more pressing questions raised by the LXX.
12. Upon the accession of Ptolemy Philadelphus, Demetrius of Phalerum was in disfavor (see n. 3). To set the stage for these two personalities, it is as if the foundation of the French Academy were attributed to joint decisions of Richelieu and King Louis XIV. Personal glory takes precedence over chronology.
13. See L. Rost, "Vermutungen über den Anlass zur griechischen Übersetzung der Tora," in *Wort–Gebot– Glaube: Beiträge zur Theologie des Alten Testaments,* ed. H. J. Stoebe (Zürich, 1970); also D. Barthélemy, *Études d'histoire du texte d'AT,* 328ff.
14. Indeed, a great intellectual flowering marked this period in Alexandria: the Library saw the collection of great works from the world over, while the Museum assembled the city's great sages. Theophrastus (who died ca. 287) founded the discipline of natural history. During the third century B.C.E., Euclid wrote his *Elements,* while Eratosthenes invented the science of geography.
15. This desire and this spirit show through in certain comments of other Jewish authors of Alexandria. Several, like Aristobulus, refer, boastfully and certainly not without illusions, to Moses's influence on Plato and Greek thought.
16. These authors lend details to the legend in the *Letter of Aristeas,* or else modify some of the facts it gives (e.g., the 72, or 70 translators working separately from one another; the name of the king), as if they are using other traditions. Some of the authors have visited the sites; another notes a mysterious anthology of Ptolemaica. For more detail on these references, see the edition of A. Pelletier, *Lettre d'Aristée,* SC 89, Introduction, 78-97; on Anatolius, cf. Barthélemy, *Études d'histoire du texte de l'AT,* 326. On the Jewish defense of the *Letter of Aristeas* and the tradition of the translation of the LXX, and the Christian reception of that tradition, see also Müller, *The First Bible of the Church,* 58-97.

17. *Comm. in Mich.* 2.9 (PL 25: 1227).
18. According to the *Letter of Aristeas*, the translators numbered 72; but, based on Josephus, the number was frequently given as 70.
19. See a list of characteristics that one finds in the *kaige* group, and in the *kaige-syn* group, in D. Barthélemy, *Les devanciers de'Aquila*, 48-80, 81-88.
20. See ibid., 3-15. These two figures are from the end of the first century and beginning of the second century C.E.
21. E.g., see Aristobulus quoting Exod. 3:20 (*ap.* Eusebius, *Praep. evang.* 8.10). Again it is to be noted that the *Letter of Aristeas* had aspired to defend the Septuagint against attempts at correction and revision.
22. Such is the case with the section from 2 Kings 11:2 (or 4) to 3 Kings 2:11 (= 2 Sam. 11:2-1 Kings 2:11, Masoretic text), the ancient Septuagint being represented by the Antiochene manuscripts (constituting what we call the Lucianic recension).
23. On the attribution of the LXX version of Ecclesiastes to Aquila, see Barthélemy, *Les devanciers d'Aquila*, 21-30.
24. See *Massakhet Soferim* I.7-10, in particular: "It happened one time that five ancients wrote the Law in Greek for King Ptolemy. That was a bad day for Israel, as it was the day when Israel fashioned the calf, for the Law could not be translated according to all his demands" (text cited by A. Pelletier, *Lettre à Aristée*, 97). Elsewhere we find in Justin echoes of these discussions (*Dialogue with Trypho* 68, 71).
25. Irenaeus, *Adv. haer.* 3.21.1; Epiphanius, *De mensuris et ponderibus* (PG 43: 264); Jerome (PL 25: 1326; PL 23: 702; PL 28: 1142; CSEL 55: 389; PL 25: 493).
26. *Ep. ad Africanum* (PG 11: 49-52).
27. Barthélemy, *Les devanciers d'Aquila*, 144-157.
28. Barthélemy (*Les devanciers d'Aquila*), with the support of abundant evidence, suggests on the one hand that the text of Greek fragments of the Minor Prophets (from the Judean Desert) is to be identified with the text used by Justin and with the "Quinta" of the Hexapla. On the other hand, he argues, this text (one and the same as it appears in these three places) corresponds to the usual translations of Theodotion, whereas the text attributed to Theodotion in writings which are dependent on the Hexapla does not show up the characteristics of this translator: undoubtedly we are dealing with a false attribution (based perhaps on a staggering of the columns of the Hexapla).
29. See ibid., 3-15.
30. See ibid., 81-88, 15-30. For the identification with Onqelos, ibid., 152-154.
31. *Historia Lausiaca* 147.
32. *Hist. eccl.* 6.17.
33. *De mensuris et ponderibus* 16-17.
34. See Barthélemy's arguments in "Qui est Symmaque?," in *Études d'histoire du texte de l'AT*, 307-321.
35. Cf. Eusebius, *Hist Eccl.* 5.8.10, using Irenaeus, *Adv. haer.* 3.21.1.
36. Cf. Jerome (PL 23: 2012; 1048; 1059, etc.).

37. Thus the "Quinta" of the Minor Prophets could very well actually be the work of Theodotion.
38. See the research of F. M. Cross and his collaborators.
39. For more recent perspectives, see G. Dorival, M. Harl, and O. Munnich, *La Bible grecque des Septante: Du judaïsme hellénistique au christianisme ancien* (Paris, 1988); E. Tov, "The Septuagint," in *Mikra: Text, Translation, Reading and Interpretation of the Hebrew Bible in Ancient Judaism and Early Christianity*, ed. M. J. Mulder and H. Sysling, Compendia Rerum Iudaicarum ad Novum Testamentum, Section 2, Part 1 (Assen and Minneapolis, 1988), 161-188; idem, *Textual Criticism of the Hebrew Bible* (Assen and Minneapolis, 1992), 134-148.
40. A. Neher, "La philosophie hébraique et juive dans l'Antiquité," in *Histoire de la philosophie*, Encyclopédie de la Pléiade (Paris, 1966), 1: 69f.
41. M. Harl lends some important nuances to these assertions of Neher: "The recent pages of A. Neher devoted to the Septuagint..., quite suggestive (the Septuagint, on the linguistic level, had rendered the Bible more 'philosophical') merit a discussion.... At the very most it can be said that it is a first landmark in the 'philosophical' interpretation of the Bible" ("Y a-t-il une influence du 'grec biblique' sur la langue spirituelle des chrétiens?" in *La Bible et les Pères* [Paris, 1971], 244).
42. In point of fact the Tetragrammaton is still found in some manuscripts of the Septuagint. Undoubtedly it was the sacred name that was replaced with *Kyrios* only slowly and progressively.
43. Cf. Philo, *De opificio mundi* 29.
44. S. Daniel, *Recherches sur le vocabulaire du culte dans la Septante* (Paris, 1966), 56-57.
45. E.g., Origen, *Contra Celsum* 1.34.
46. Cf. Rom. 3:10-19 and 1 Cor. 14:21 where *nomos* refers to Isaiah and the Psalms. See also Ps. 77:1, LXX (=78:1, Masoretic Text).
47. See M. Flashar, *ZATW* 32 (1912): 261-265; also J. Gribomont and A. Thibaut, "Méthode et esprit des traducteurs du psautier grec," dans *Richesses et déficiences des psautiers latins* (Rome, 1959).
48. Müller, *The First Bible of the Church*, 23-24, 98-144. Müller writes: "Because the Old Testament is relativized in this way, first by being the earliest Bible of the Church and then the earliest part of the Christian canon, the question of what the Old Testament represents in a biblical theological context becomes more than just a question about the original text of the Hebrew Bible. *The question of the Old Testament text cannot be separated from the question of what the early church regarded as its Bible. It is unreasonable to say that the 'true' text actually differs from what the early church believed it to be.* A historical determination of what early Christians believed to be the biblical text cannot be replaced by the text-critical question of its original appearance, if this can be answered at all" (p. 23, emphasis added).

2

The Role of the Bible in the Birth of the Church

JACQUES GUILLET, S.J.

Strictly speaking, Scripture did not give rise to Israel or to the Church. The true starting-point in each case was an event, an experience lived by human beings in which God communicated and spoke to them. The faith of Abraham, the deliverance from Egypt, the covenant at Sinai, the assembly around Moses and his God—all these events are difficult to situate historically, let alone rank in order of importance, but it is certain that Israel was born of these experiences. The character and meaning ascribed to these events by Israel have for centuries, and even in the present day, provided the Jewish people with their sense of vocation and destiny.

Scripture nonetheless occupies a unique place in this history, again not in the actual birth of Israel but at every step, every stage of Israel's self-awareness. Each time that the people of Israel, whether in victory or defeat, in times of glory or disaster, lived through a decisive moment, a text was born which recorded the experience and gave it form: from the testing in the wilderness (Exod. 15:25) and the entry into Palestine (Josh. 24:25) emerged the law and customs; from the victory at Kishon, the Song of Deborah (Judges 5:1); from the story of David's ascendancy (1 Sam. 16-2 Sam. 5 [1 Kings 16-2 Kings 5, LXX) and that of his succession (2 Sam. 7-20 [2 Kings 7-20, LXX], 1 Kings 1-2 [3 Kings 1-2, LXX]), the deuteronomic reform under Josiah (Deut. 12:1-26:19); upon the return from Exile in Babylon, the law of the Temple (Leviticus). In the time of Christ's ministry, writing continued with the Jewish people and always in the name of the same faith; but these newer texts were no longer adjoined to the sacred canon as though God had finished modeling the physical character of his people and had only to send them their promised salvation.

It is hardly accidental that at the same time as the Jews were constituting their canon (the Greek Septuagint in Egypt, and Hebrew canon in Jamnia after 70 C.E.), Christian writings began to appear, those which would form the New Testament.

A Reading of the Scriptures

The New Testament writings were not born immediately with the Christian faith any more than the Hebrew Scriptures were born immediately with Israel's faith; they deliver an original experience after the fact. Moreover, they do not aspire to oppose the Christian experience to that of Israel, to erect in the face of the Hebrew Scriptures a new and concurrent corpus. Indeed, they do not themselves originate the expression "New Testament" in opposition to the Old, a title that would thrive later on. Even if they are all born of the conviction that with Jesus an event has occurred in the world which opens up an absolutely new reality, (Matt. 9:17, 26:28; John 13:34; 2 Cor. 5:17; Gal. 6:15; Eph. 2:15; Heb. 8:8, 9:15; 2 Peter 3:13; Rev. 3:12, 21:1) the writings of the New Testament did not appear right alongside those of Israel but in their wake and at their end. They are at bottom a reading of, and commentary on, the Jewish Scriptures.

This is verified in the most characteristic forms of primitive Christian literature. The oldest confessions of faith proclaim that Christ rose on the third day "in accordance with the Scriptures" (1 Cor. 15:4) and that after his last supper, he shared with them "my blood of the covenant" (Mark 14:24; cf. Exod. 24:8). Paul presents himself as the apostle who is "set apart for the gospel of God...promised beforehand through his prophets in the holy scriptures" (Rom. 1:1-2). It is from the Law conceived in all its vastness that Paul builds and formulates his most original theology, that of salvation by faith. The gospels, which are entirely focused upon the figure and acts of Jesus, constantly relate them to the Scriptures. The Kingdom of God which Jesus announces is the great hope of the Psalms and the prophets (Mark 1:15, Matt. 4:15-17, Luke 4:14-15). The deeds Jesus performs—his healings on the Sabbath (Mark 3:1-6), his contacts with lepers (Mark 1:41) and with sinful men and women (Mark 2:15; Luke 7:39), his liberties with regard to purity laws (Mark 7:1-23), his forgiveness of sins (Mark 2:5,10)—are all founded on Jesus's coherent and radical vision of the authority of the Law and of the will of God. When, beginning with Peter's confession at Caesarea Philippi, Jesus starts to speak with his disciples about the death which is his destiny, he always bases its necessity on Scripture (Mark 8:31, 9:31, 10:33). He never moves outside of Scripture. All that he does and is aims only at giving the Scriptures their true dimension—God's own dimension. If the Scriptures truly come from God, who is the common faith of both Jews and Christians, the latter had no sense of departing from the Scriptures when they saw them fulfilled in the person of the Son of God.

This explains why Christians, even when they most strongly opposed the Jews, never pretended to set their own writings in opposition to Jewish Scripture, but only their *reading* of the Scriptures in the light of Jesus Christ. In all cases this christocentric reading was of such magnitude, the person of Jesus exhibited such originality and richness, and the development of Christian communities revealed such a strong and new experience that little by little, without ever relinquishing a foundation in the Jewish Scriptures, a properly Christian literature was born. From this literature, inseparable from the Christian Church itself, the Church found its own sense of the authority of the Scriptures and the power of the Word of God. This genesis and growth of Christian Scripture merits further description and explanation.

The Word about Jesus, the Word of Jesus

The literary forms of the New Testament are diverse.[1] Some are absolutely unique, such as Paul's letters; other genres like apocalypses or hymns are found outside of the New Testament. Although it is interesting to identify the various forms, it is perhaps more important to note that even though the common denominator of all these writings is the person of Jesus, two distinct categories clearly stand out: one in which Jesus is the object of the literature, the other in which he is the active subject. The first series is quite varied. They announce Jesus (Paul in all his letters more or less directly; the majority of the sermons in Acts; the record of missionary activity in Acts; the whole of Revelation). They confess the mystery of Christ's person and work (1 Cor. 15:3-5; 1 Tim. 3:16, 6:15-16; 2 Tim. 2:8-13; 1 Peter 1:8-9, 2:22-25). They enlarge that confession into a hymn of adoration (Col. 1:13-20) or thanksgiving to God (Eph. 1:3-13). They develop the theme of thanksgiving, as Paul does in Romans and the Hebrew writer in his epistle, by reflecting on the work of Christ in the world and his role in God's creation, thereby constructing two grand models of Christian theology. These writings even share the news, the worries, the joys, and the reproaches which are all part of correspondence among friends. Such is the fabric of Paul's letters, and no communication better illustrates the extent to which the person of Christ and the power of his action are present in the heart of the apostle Paul and, even if they are less aware of it, in the lives of Christians and their communities in the background of the New Testament.

Finally this category of writing evokes the Lord in a more direct way than mere words. The action of baptism performed in his name (Acts 2:38, 8:16, 10:48, 19:5) signifies that, through the words of the apostles and the faith of those who listen to them, the personal power of Jesus such as the original followers of Jesus experienced is a present reality at work in the world and capable of transforming it. Reference to the Lord in the breaking of the bread is even more direct. Rather than the community doing it "in his name" it is performed "in remembrance" (*eis anamnêsin*) of him (Luke 22:19; 1 Cor. 11:24-25) like a gesture of Jesus himself giving his body and blood. This action is nevertheless carried out by his disciples: "Do this... "; and from this point of view, Jesus remains the object rather than the subject, for in doing it "you proclaim the Lord's death." (1 Cor. 11:26).

Despite its diversity of forms there is throughout this series of writings a certain homogeneity. Even without the assurance of pure textual interrelationships, a coherent logic obtains among their various formulations of faith in Christ; indeed, one often finds strong verbal connections and real textual dependencies. Conceived as an expression of what the nascent Church had to say of Christ, the christology of the New Testament, while assuredly posing numerous literary and historical problems, is an enterprise capable of being undertaken. While it contains gaps, the fundamental structure of New Testament christology is solid and its expression comprehensible. Even though Peter, Paul, and the author of Hebrews speak a different language from our own, translation is possible and interpretation justifiable.

The same cannot be said of the texts wherein Jesus is the subject, the character who speaks and acts: the four gospels. Here we are confronted with authors in a position to manipulate what Jesus says and does, and thus with the problem of the distance between Jesus and the evangelists. It is a distance in time, a distance between situations and especially between persons. Who or what makes Jesus speak?

The Tradition of Jesus

If the faith of the Church, even with its various authors and diverse forms, is relatively easy to grasp, the tradition of Jesus which gave birth to the gospels is quite another story. It is said that this tradition constitutes an isolated block in the New Testament, unconnected to the other writings.[2] In the letters of Peter, Paul, James, or John, references to the words of Jesus himself seem to be surprisingly rare. How can we explain the fact that the pastors who composed these letters, and who were so preoccupied with nurturing their communities in faith and fidelity to the Lord, make so few references to the teachings of Christ or his earthly existence? Why do they seem only to acknowledge Christ's death and resurrection? Does this mean that by their time the gospel tradition had not yet come together?

This is the conclusion that many exegetes frequently reach, and is the conviction notably of the *Formgeschichte* school. Without wishing to deny that many of the words and gospel stories originate with Jesus, they argue that these traditions, in order to be communicated and transmitted, must have taken a certain form. They must have been poured into models which rendered them suitable for use and repetition. Furthermore, these models, isolated sentences or groups of sentences, anecdotes couching a word, miracle stories, controversies, prayers, and so on, were products of the community, born of the community's needs and diverse activities. They were anonymous creations which truly took shape only when the community adopted them and held on to them. *Formgeschichte* does not pretend to substitute the creative power of the community for that of Jesus, but it does believe that the tradition of Jesus truly took shape only within communities of faith. It observes therefore that at this stage, the formulation of the words and actions of Jesus derived only from isolated units and that there was as yet no genuine gospel or continuous narrative. Such would be the work of so-called "redactors," who are effectively the authors of our gospels. Mark is doubtless the first to have created a continuous narrative from this traditional material. But between the time of the isolated units and the final composition ensued a period when units of the same type were assembled and grouped into series. Mark has brought together several series of different genres such as miracle stories (1:21-45; 4:35-5:43), controversy stories (2:1-3:6, 12:13-37), and parables (4:1-34). Consequently, between the actual deeds of Jesus and the final redaction of the gospels stretch not only a lapse of time, a good thirty years a least, but a considerable labor of elaboration, adaptation and regrouping.

To all of these factors, which are more or less traceable through the history of the communities and literary analysis, must be added the essential element internal to the tradition, namely, the initial experience of the Resurrection, and the shock that such an experience would have upon all antecedent perspectives and memories. Nothing was as it had been, and yet the Resurrection event caused the whole past to be rediscovered in a new light. John's gospel expresses well the nature and effect of this shock: "When therefore he was raised from the dead, his disciples remembered that he had said this." (John 2:22; cf. 13:7). John's gospel is also, however, precisely the one which best manifests the entire labor of reflection, the deepening and the transformation that Christian faith, in its very fidelity, exercised upon the first recollections of Jesus.

To be sure, the facts accounted for here can be given several interpretations. The experience of the Resurrection, for example, would obviously modify the perspective of Jesus's disciples upon the events they had experienced in his company. They could no longer see his acts as other than the Messiah's nor see in his person anyone but God's only Son. It is a genuinely radical shift.

Yet we must be careful not to distort this experience of the Resurrection. Far from making Jesus appear as a new person, on the contrary, it is the former man and master who has been resurrected. Not only is the Resurrected also the Crucified (Mark 16:6), he comes to prove to his companions that the Resurrection, while supplanting his death, and introducing him into the power and the glory of God, and seating him at the right hand of the Father, changes absolutely nothing in his relationship with them, his original physical appearance, or the secret of his person. The accounts of the post-Resurrection meal in particular, which are naive and posterior creations wherein the resurrected Jesus is easily seen, indeed casually observed, attest on the contrary to the fact that the witnesses of the Resurrection, whatever its impact on them, were incapable of describing their experience in other than familiar terms, terms identical to those used before and totally different from the terms that they themselves would have used to picture the Messiah who conquered death. They proclaim a Christ "exalted at the right hand of God...having received from the Father the promise of the Holy Spirit." (Acts 2:33). They prostrate themselves before the Lord to whom God has "bestowed...the name which is above every name" (Phil. 2:9), but at the same time they describe Jesus as he was before, sharing bread and eating fish (Luke 24:30, 43).

Much more than a transformation in their memory of Jesus, the Resurrection creates fidelity and continuity. The resurrected Jesus is the Jesus of Nazareth, the Jesus in Galilee, the Jesus who confronted the authorities in Jerusalem. Resurrection has not given this Jesus a new personality. His appearances, always extremely brief, change nothing in his former physical appearance. Consequently it is the Jesus prior to death to whom one must refer in order to know who is the Lord that has been raised in the glory of the Father. The more faithful the memory, the more accurate and profound will be the knowledge. Fallibilities and alterations are technically possible, but faith is not based on them.

The Jesus Tradition and Apostolic Preaching

Even so, the silence of the "Jesus tradition" during the years when the letters of the Apostles were appearing is not necessarily the sign of absence or proof that this tradition is a sheer creation of the Christian communities. Though he certainly had had no contact with the earthly Jesus, there are positive indications in the writings of Paul himself that he knew Christ's teachings, which he clearly distinguished from his own.[3] Writing to the Corinthians about problems erupting among them over marriage, he distinguishes what "I say to the unmarried and widows" (1 Cor. 7:8), what "not I but the Lord" decrees (1 Cor. 7:10), what "I say, I and not the Lord" (1 Cor. 7:12), what "I prescribe in all the churches" (1 Cor. 7:17), and the advice which is "my opinion" since "I have no command of the Lord" (1 Cor. 7:25). Yet the very point on which Paul refers to the Lord's commandment, the indissolubility of marriage, figures in the gospel tradition (Matt. 5:32, 19:9; Mark 10:9-12). In addition, without directly citing Matt. 10:10 ("the laborer deserves his food"), Paul refers to the word of Jesus when he writes: "The Lord commanded that those who proclaim the gospel should get their living by the gospel" (1 Cor. 9:14).

Such cases are rare, it is true, and their rarity can be surprising; but the fact that they exist at all suggests an explanation. Could it not be the presence and knowledge of this "Jesus tradition" in the Christian communities that explain the habitual silence in the apostolic letters? They respect the priority of this tradition. But that does not mean that they are condemned to silence. Those whom God has appointed "apostles and prophets" (1 Cor. 12: 28; Eph. 2:20, 3:5, 4:11) in the Church have the authority to speak in his name, to proclaim the gospel message, to recall authentic traditions and to safeguard the truth of the faith. They do not, however, confuse their authority with that of the Lord and the tradition issuing from him. Their silence concerning the Jesus tradition does not come from their ignorance but from their wariness and their refusal to appropriate an authority which is not theirs.

Not wishing to overestimate the force of a hypothesis which has limited support, although its implications are immense since it covers the entire gospel tradition, an important fact in its favor must be pointed out, namely, the allusion to and the importance of the tradition of the Lord's Supper in Paul (1 Cor. 11:23-26). Here is a tradition "received from the Lord" (*apo tou Kyriou*) and transmitted in the churches virtually hand to hand by those responsible for the communities. There is no reference to a written document or a letter. The authority, if one can call it that, is the transmission itself of a faithfulness which comes from the Lord. But the object of this transmission is rightly part of the gospel tradition, the story of the institution of the Eucharist at the Last Supper. It is striking that when Paul refers to this tradition, he insists upon its importance as being derived from this very event. In contrast he presents with the very same solemnity the tradition of the Resurrection, a tradition which evidently does not originate with the Lord himself (1 Cor. 15:3-5), in which case he refrains from adding the phrase "received from the Lord." Nonetheless, the common point with both traditions is that they have foundations antecedent to the communities which receive them.

It would be ill advised to extend to all of the Jesus tradition, to all the sayings of Jesus and gospel stories, the exceptional value Paul accords to the tradition of the Last Supper. For example, when Paul in his discussion of marriage and celibacy refers to the commands of the Lord, he is not concerned with reproducing them word for word in his letter (1 Cor. 7:10) but contents himself with allusions. In the case of the Last Supper, if Paul, like those before him who had received this tradition, feels compelled to state that he is repeating the words of Jesus, it is because at precisely that moment Jesus himself is there in person, gathering together his community, offering his body and his blood. The word, the action, and the gift are all present and express, amid the visible absence, the active and immediate presence of the Lord. But Jesus could only achieve this fullness at the end of his life in the hour when he gave his life for us and when God received his life in its glory in order to make it the life of the world. All prior moments in the Savior's life were incomplete: "I have earnestly desired to eat this Passover with you before I suffer." The preceding events of Jesus's life derive their full meaning from this supreme act. This is also why, like all the moments of a person's life, the words of Jesus and stories of him in the gospels took on their full meaning only when they had been reassembled from all the texts and clarified in the light of the Last Supper, the Passion and the Resurrection. Thus we

41

can understand how the Jesus tradition did not in its entirety take on the same gravity and rigor . At any rate, it remains true that never was a word of the Lord placed on the same level as a word of his disciples, for his word was a pillar of the Church. Yet we cannot avoid asking how these words of the Lord were transmitted before ending up in our gospels.

Oral Transmission Prior to Writing

If there is some hesitation in assuming that the Christian community gave birth to the diverse forms which constitute the gospel tradition, and if it is obviously impossible that the gospel writers themselves created these forms, there remains one other option: to admit that these forms truly, and more or less directly, descend from Jesus himself. This brings us back to saying these words of Jesus reach us not only in their conceptualizable substance but with all their own emphasis and style, a style capable of being maintained even in translations.

Were this solely a case of an unavoidable but unverifiable assumption, we would be forced to choose between resignation to ignorance and blind faith. Even though research in this area is hard to come by, primarily because exegetes educated in the critical reading of texts hesitate to trust oral transmissions, the rules of which are not well known, we are not totally without resources. Three scholars in particular stand out for their contributions in the field of oral transmission: Harald Riesenfeld and Birger Gerhardsson in Sweden and Marcel Jousse in France.[4] Their work and their conclusions coincide on many points although their methodologies vary considerably.

Riesenfeld and Gerhardsson, both exegetes by profession, have pursued their research in their homeland following the lines of the "Scandinavian school" of biblical-critical studies.[5] Comparing their own positions with their colleagues', submitting to criticism and criticizing their opposition, these scholars have remained exegetes. M. Jousse, on the other hand, has never been an exegete and always refused to become one.[6] True to his peasant background, to his mother who had never seen a written version of the gospels and who made rhymes of the gospel reading of the year, which she sang using melodies of unknown origin, he wrote: "In the end I know only my mother and Jesus and their lullabies."[7] In his passion for anthropological research and for the study of spontaneous gesture, its passage into language and from language into memory, Jousse never forsook his origins. The Bible was a privileged example of this world of oral performance, and the gospels its unique flowering. Jousse started with the

"rhythmic catechism of Rabbi Jeshua" and its four reproductions (as opposed to translations) in the four gospel targums. Jousse devoted his life to
this oral world and its riches and scarcely concealed his lack of interest in
scribal civilizations. Consequently exegetes have largely treated him with
disdain and have with few exceptions ignored his work.

If, however, we set the insights of M. Jousse into the larger context of the work of the Scandinavian school, we will feel better equipped
to explore the literary void which appears to characterize the Jesus tradition up until the redaction of the gospels. This is the time of witnesses
and servants of the Word who "delivered to us" (Luke 1:2) the material
from which Luke produced his work. It is the time when Christians were
congregating around the "apostles' teaching" (Acts 2:42). *Formgeschichte*
was not wrong to situate in this period the development of gospel forms
in Christian communities. But it confined itself within too narrow limits
by minimizing the importance of memory and oral transmission. Historians and exegetes today sense the necessity to focus on the history of
these traditions before they were gathered together in the gospels. It is a
complex endeavor, which presupposes all at once a deep knowledge of
the laws of oral communication, of the customs of Jewish tradition, and
of the tendencies, resources, and practices within Christian milieus.[8]

The Lord's Supper: Word and Body

Among these diverse practices, the best attested is the Lord's
Supper (1 Cor. 11:20), or in Luke's words "the breaking of bread" (Luke
24:35; Acts 2:42,46 and 20: 7-11). Whether in Jerusalem, Troas, or Corinth,
this was the essential act around which the community reunited; it was
the Lord's act. Christ's words were repeated (1 Cor. 11:27), his body received, and in his blood the participants communed (1 Cor. 10:16). Yet
this was not an isolated action; it was part of a whole. The episode in
Troas shows Paul, before and after the breaking of the bread, prolonging
a speech which is more than a simple farewell (Acts 20:7-11). The first
summary, wherein Luke describes the life of the Jerusalem community,
recounts four elements: "the apostles' teaching, fellowship, the breaking
of bread and prayers" (Acts 2:42). When mentioned with these other practices, "fellowship" is certainly something more than a warm atmosphere
among friends.[9] It designates the service of mutual help which the Christians inherited from the Jews, but to which they gave a new and original
form by situating it precisely in the context of the common meal.[10] As for
the "prayers," rather than using those which they uttered in the Temple

(Acts 2:46, 3:1), these earliest Christians expressed in unison their thanks-givings and their supplications (Acts 4:24, 6:4, 12:5). The "apostles' teach-ing" could evidently include admonitions and elaborations similar to those found in their letters. But more than likely that teaching was first and foremost the Word of God, the Word for which the apostles had primary responsibility, such that no one else could replace them (Acts 6:2,4). The Word of God was addressed to Christians by men who specialized in it, to instruct them and form them. It is hard to imagine anything fitting this bill better than the tradition of Christ. Accordingly it was at the moment of the Lord's Supper, at the very time it received the Body of the Lord, that the community also received his Word. Made present in his Church by the breaking of bread, Christ indwelled the Church by his word and his whole existence.[11]

How is this word living? R. Bultmann and E. Käsemann in par-ticular emphasize Christian prophets at this point. Speaking in the name of the Lord and invested with his authority, such prophets would have originated the gospel commandments, the words wherein Jesus defined the laws of Christian conduct.[12] This hypothesis, based invariably upon the theory that a break occurred between the historical Jesus and the birth of the gospels, hardly has any support in the texts of the New Testament. The role more accurately associated with prophets appears to be that of encouragement (*parakalein*), of making known the will of God in the present moment.[13] A tradition cannot be based upon these sorts of inter-ventions. The natural hypothesis for explaining the gospels remains the Jesus tradition, based upon the apostles and eyewitnesses. And if it is a living tradition, it is perhaps due in part to the prophets who recall it and bring it up to date,[14] but it is primarily alive because the word of Jesus, transmitted during the Lord's Supper, is inseparable from the resurrected body of the Lord.

It is possible that the gospels themselves contain traces of their original connection with the Lord's Supper. One example would be the story of two apostles' encounter with the resurrected Jesus on the road to Emmaus (Luke 24:13-35), which is immediately followed by the breaking of the bread and the instruction given by Jesus. A parallel example would be the episode with the Ethiopian eunuch on the road to Gaza, where Philip, having explained the Passion within the context of the Suffering Servant theme of Isaiah 52-53, baptizes the Ethiopian.[15] This structure connecting teaching and sacrament is perhaps Luke's own compositional model. Indeed it is found again in the episode at Pentecost where the proclamation of Jesus culminates in the baptism of three thousand and the description of the first community focusing on the breaking of bread (Acts 2:14-47). But it might also be the case that, in the gospel of Mark, the evangelist directs the movement which, beginning with Peter's confession at Caesarea and the first announcement of the Passion, conducts Jesus to that hour when, " in order that the Scriptures may be fulfilled" (Mark 14:49), he falls into the hands of "the one who betrays him" (Mark 14:42,44). We would thus have, in this advance toward the Passion, the first form of our gospels: a continuous story mixing teaching with narrative episodes, taking the form of a history of Jesus, and culminating with the Last Supper and the gift of the betrayed body.[16] It would be wrong to see in this composition the reproduction of a Christian assembly around the Lord's Supper, but we are not prevented from asking whether it naturally led to such a reproduction.

Tradition and Translation

We seem to have forgotten a most fundamental point. In discussing tradition and its faithfulness, we dare not leave out the factor of translation, particularly when we presume to be going back to Jesus himself and the memories of those who witnessed him. All of these witnesses spoke Aramaic, the language of Palestine at the time. The distance between the original Aramaic and the Greek of our gospels is as vast as that between a conversation in modern Arabic and a journal article written in French. Does not this basic fact destroy all possibility of ever reconstructing the words of Jesus?

This issue must be taken seriously and its dimensions precisely measured. Perhaps they do not have the range of the example mentioned above. Between Arabic and French there are no bridges, at least at the literary level. Many Arabic authors write in excellent French but they are not transposing originally Arabic works. At the time of the gospels the translation of biblical books into Greek had been a cultural and religious fact for two centuries. Greek-speaking Judaism flourished in Egypt and beyond, and was very much alive even in Palestine.[17] The Greek Bible, known as the Septuagint, became very quickly the Bible of the Christian communities of Palestine as well as Antioch and Corinth. Translating the Aramaic of Jesus and his disciples was not an unprecedented task.

Certainly the type of translation which took place should be noted. It was not a literal translation, such as is so often proclaimed to be normative. M. Jousse, who is passionately devoted to going back to Jesus's own

45

words themselves, insists constantly, and rightly so, on the difference between translation, as is typical of civilizations having written language, and the kind of "imitation" found in oral cultures. The Jewish world of Jesus's time thrived on these imitations or impressions. They were called targums and were the transposition of the Hebrew Bible into popular Aramaic.[18] The "Christian Targums," as Jousse calls the gospels, were created in this living milieu, and must be read from this perspective, without asking for a precision with which they were not concerned, rather paying attention to their own aims, rhythms, and accents.

Having noted these essential points and bearing them in mind, we must all the same turn to the evangelists, the gospel authors themselves, for they themselves indeed had their own aims, their own thoughts, public purview, theology and interpretative horizon. All of these factors, which are so profoundly personal, also pertain to our written gospels and to the revelation of Jesus Christ. This is why exegesis and the literary study of the texts remain an irreplaceable access route and have never ceased throughout the centuries to nourish Christian faith and thinking.

Even the gospel writers were translators, and not in the simple manner of the first Christian "targums" of which Jousse speaks. With time, distance, diverse experiences, emerging problems, complicating questions, new perspectives opening up, the tradition of Jesus still always dominates. With each evangelist, however, this tradition takes on a new appearance. These writers represent the end of an era, being the last to transmit the Jesus tradition, the last to have received this tradition from actual witnesses.

They are also the first in a long and glorious line, because translation, and foremost the translation of the gospels, has always been a preeminent labor in the Church. Through the centuries, implanting the Church among a new people or in a new culture almost always involved first translating the Gospel into in a new language. How many of the great apostles were also great translators! Not only was this a basic condition of apostleship, it was inherently demanded by the Gospel itself. Certainly it is not merely by chance or by accident that we possess no Aramaic gospel and that the gospels have existed from the very beginning only in translations. The reason for this is clear. A literal reproduction of the words of Jesus would have frozen them forever in his original language and milieu. All of the translations would have been inferior adaptations of the original text. On the contrary, in the Church, through the power of the Holy Spirit, all translations can carry the authentic Word of God since all can follow the example of the first translations, our four gospels.

Notes

1. On the characteristics of these forms, their role in the life of the Christian communities, and their place in the earliest Christian literature, see P. Grelot in A. George and P. Grelot, *Introduction à la Bible, Édition nouvelle, Nouveau Testament*, t. III, vol. 5: *L'achèvement des Écritures* (Paris, 1977), 48-87. See also C.F.D. Moule, *The Birth of the New Testament*, 3rd ed. (San Francisco, 1982); and more recently, D. Aune, *The New Testament in Its Literary Environment*, Library of Early Christianity 8 (Philadelphia, 1987).

2. See B. Gerhardsson, *The Origins of the Gospel Traditions* (Philadelphia, 1979), esp. 47-49, 67-77.

3. See ibid., 33-41. More recently, see L. T. Johnson, *The Real Jesus: The Misguided Quest for the Historical Jesus and the Truth of the Traditional Gospels* (San Francisco, 1996), 117-122.

4. More recently, see also the work of W. A. Graham, *Beyond the Written Word: Oral Aspects of Scripture in the History of Religion* (Cambridge, 1987), who has extended the analysis of the category of "sacred scripture" to include the process of oral traditioning before *and after*, or beyond, the state of written text.

5. H. Riesenfeld, *The Gospel Tradition and Its Beginnings: A Study in the Limits of 'Formgeschichte'* (London, 1957); B. Gerhardsson, *Memory and Manuscript: Oral Transmission and Written Tradition in Rabbinic Judaism and Early Christianity* (Uppsala, 1964).

6. M. Jousse's theories have been accumulated in the three volumes of his *L'anthropologie du geste* (Paris, 1974, 1975, 1978).

7. G. Baron, *Marcel Jousse: Introduction à sa vie et à son oeuvre* (Tournai, 1965).

8. P. Grelot, *L'achèvement des Écritures*, 15-18.

9. J. Dupont, "L'union entre les premiers chrétiens dans les Acts des Apôtres," *Nouvelle revue théologique* 91 (1969): 897-915.

10. C. Perrot, *Jésus et l'histoire*, Jésus et Jésus Christ 11 (Paris, 1979), 298-304.

11. Ibid., 304-309.

12. E. Käsemann, *Exegetische Versuche und Besinnungen* (Göttingen, 1970), vol. 2, 69-104.

13. E. Cothenet, "Prophétisme et Nouveau Testament," in the *Supplément* to the *Dictionnaire de la Bible*, vol. 8, col. 1265-1267, 1285-1286.

14. Perrot, *Jésus et l'histoire*, 299, 306-309.

15. J. Dupont, "Les pèlerins d'Emmaüs (Luc XXIV, 13-35)," in *Miscellanea Biblica Bonaventura Ubagh* (Monserrat, 1953), 349-374.

16. R. Pesch, *Das Markusevangelium*, pt. 2, Herders theologischer Kommentar zum Neuen Testament 2 (Freiburg-im-Breisgau, 1977), 1-27.

17. In particular, see the studies of S. Lieberman, *Hellenism in Jewish Palestine*, 2nd ed. (New York, 1962); idem, *Greek in Jewish Palestine*, 2nd ed.

(New York, 1965); also M. Hengel, *Judaism and Hellenism: Studies in Their Encounter in Palestine during the Early Hellenistic Period*, 2 vols. (Philadelphia, 1981).

18. M. Jousse, *L'anthropologie du geste*, vol. 3: *Le parlant, la parole et le souffle* (Paris, 1978), 168-197.

3

The Bible in the Earliest Controversies
between Jews and Christians

MARCEL SIMON

The Christian Church, whose first recruits were native Israelites, and which considered itself the true Israel and the heir to Israel's promises, spontaneously adopted the Jewish Bible as its sacred Scripture from the very beginning. Just as quickly it laid claim to exclusive ownership of that Bible, since the Church alone was capable of apprehending its true meaning. "Your Scriptures," said Justin Martyr to his imaginary Jewish interlocutor Rabbi Trypho, "are rather not yours, but ours, for we are left persuaded by them, while you read them without comprehending the spirit that is in them." (*Dialogue with Trypho the Jew* 29.2). Pseudo-Barnabas for his part adjures his readers not "to heap sin upon sin by repeating that the covenant is simultaneously both theirs and ours. It is in truth ours, but they lost forever the covenant formerly received by Moses" (*Epistle of Barnabas* 4.6-7). A foundation of Christian faith, what we call the "Old Testament" is at the same time the arsenal from which anti-Jewish polemical writings drew their weapons. For in order to have some effect on the Jews, any demonstration of Christian truth was obliged to support itself on biblical texts, the revealed character and infallible authority of which are recognized by Christians and Jews alike. From this angle the conflict between Jews and Christians appears to be a quarrel over one common heritage.

But in what precisely does that heritage consist? In other words, from which collection of biblical writings were the arguments fomenting this controversy drawn? Constitutionally the Old Testament canon was not yet fixed *ne varietur* when Christianity entered the scene. At least the tripartite division of Law, Prophets, and "Writings" (what we generally call the Hagiographa) was already universally received, in Palestine as well as in the Jewish communities of the Diaspora. The Greek prologue of Ecclesiasticus or Sirach (2nd century B.C.E.) already mentions it, referring to the "Writings" as "other ancestral books." Philo knew the tripartite division (*De vita contemplativa* 25). It appears for the first time in a Christian writer, in simplified form, in Luke's gospel where Jesus, giving the apostles his final instructions, declares that "everything written about me in the law of Moses and in the prophets and the psalms must be fulfilled" (Luke 24:44).

For a long time a certain vacillation persisted over the content of the third part of the Hebrew Bible. The canon ostensibly was finally closed only at the rabbinic synod of Jamnia (Jabneh) around 90 C.E. About the same time the Jewish historian Flavius Josephus expressed a view doubtless already quite common in Israel when he wrote that only twenty-two books were received, "which contain the annals of all times and obtain a just credence." Josephus enumerates them this way: "First the books of Moses, five in number, which comprehend the laws and the tradition (*paradôsin*) from the creation of humanity to Moses's own death. From the death of Moses to the time of Artaxerxes...the prophets who came after Moses have recounted the history of their time in thirteen books. The four remaining books contain hymns to God and moral precepts for humanity" (*Contra Apionem* 1.8.39-40). It should be remembered that when speaking of the biblical canon the term "Prophets" (*nebiim*) designates, in addition to the prophetic writings properly speaking (Isaiah, Jeremiah, etc.), narrative and historical works (Judges, Ruth, etc.).

The Palestinian canon recognized twenty-four, not twenty-two, books. Josephus perhaps retained the number twenty-two on the basis of the idea that the scriptural canon had to embrace as many writings as the letters of the Hebrew alphabet. But the number twenty-two is not peculiar to Josephus, since the Septuagint too recognizes a total of twenty-two—if no account is taken of the books which figure into the Septuagint list over and above those in the Hebrew Bible—from the fact that Ruth is attached to Judges and Lamentations to Jeremiah. Thus between the canon of Josephus, ostensibly tributary from the Septuagint, and the Palestinian canon, there is only a difference of numbering: the content of the Bible remains the same for both. The twelve minor prophets are always counted as a single book. The four "writings" acknowledged by Josephus are probably Psalms, Proverbs, Ecclesiastes, and the Song of Songs.

The number twenty-two is also that which various early Christian authors retained, such as Melito of Sardis (cited by Eusebius, *Hist. eccl.* 4.26.14), Origen (Eusebius, *Hist. eccl.* 6.25.2),[1] and even Jerome. It appears certain that these authors directly adopted the Jewish canon fixed at Jamnia, all the while keeping the number of books retained by the Septuagint and, we can now see, without modifying in any way the text of the inspired Bible.

By no means, then, did Jewish and Christian representatives confront each other on problems of the authenticity of given books of the Hebrew Bible. It is always fitting to add that a variable, but sufficiently high number of writings which the synagogal canon did not admit sometimes benefited, in certain environments (Jewish and Christian alike), from a veneration almost equal to that applied to canonical books. These would include, above all, the so-called Apocryphal or Deutero-canonical works, certain of which were welcomed into the Septuagint (1 and 2 Maccabees, Wisdom of Solomon, Sirach, etc.) and later on into the Catholic Bible such as was fixed by the Council of Trent, whereas the churches of the Protestant Reformation held fast to the more restricted canon of the Hebrew Bible, the only one which had official value in Judaism.

Abundant religious literature discovered in the Essene library at Qumran illustrates in a particularly striking way this tendency to expand the limits of inspiration so as to benefit works ultimately excluded from the canon but held in high esteem as surely on the shores of the Dead Sea as in the Diaspora, or at least in Alexandrian Judaism. Josephus gives testimony of this fact when, speaking of certain of these works without actually naming them, he writes: "From the time of Artaxerxes to our own day, all events have been recounted, but one does not accord these writings the same credence as to the preceding ones, because the prophets are no longer exactly succeeded" (*Contra Apionem* 1.8.41). In fact the difference has not always been very carefully observed in practice between writings considered truly inspired and those which, not having this character and consequently not the equivalent authority, nonetheless deserve to be read by the faithful with pious interest and, indeed, to be used in public worship.

On the Christian side, rigidity with regard to necessary fidelity to the strict Hebrew canon is asserted especially with authors who were themselves hebraizers or in contact with Palestinian Judaism. Melito, in the passage already cited, insists that he had gone "to the place where Scripture had been preached and fulfilled" and there had "acquired with exactitude the books of the Old Testament," of which he then gives a list. Apparently Melito searched for his information in close proximity to Jews. Origen, whose close contacts with rabbis are well known,[2] and who was initiated in the language of the Bible, also invoked for his own use "the Hebrew tradition" and, in the passage cited by Eusebius, juxtaposed to the Greek title of each book of the Bible its corresponding Hebrew title, more or less exactly transliterated. Jerome's example is even more interesting. His criterion for canonicity is of a linguistic order: any work not attested in Hebrew is to be ranked among the Apocryphal works.[3] Thus, precisely while refusing the Jews any right to reclaim the Bible, Christians rely absolutely on their authority when it is a question of defining the content of the canon—which is tantamount to recognizing their possession of these sacred writings, at least retrospectively. There is no contradiction here, for Israel, in the view of the Fathers, fell from its privileges only from the moment that it refused to recognize Jesus as the true Messiah, the point at which election was transferred to the ransomed Gentiles.

It remains true that, beyond the apostolic generation, the only Christians initiated in Hebrew were a handful of intellectuals in succession down through the centuries. As far as the vast majority of Greek-speaking Christians and the authority of the Church were concerned, the Septuagint version carried a halo of such prestige that its adoption by Christianity meant the automatic inclusion as well of its deutero-canonical writings. It does not appear, however, that Jews made this into an argument against their Christian adversaries, since there were those Jews who, in the Diaspora, had made these additions to a canon still incompletely defined and continued to consider them, if not inspired, at least edifying.

In fact, Christians and Jews attacked each other not on the content of the canon but rather on the authority of the Septuagint. Being the official Bible of Alexandrian Judaism and probably of the whole Greek-speaking Diaspora, the Septuagint was venerated as an inspired text enjoying the same claim as the original Hebrew. Philo, who used only the Septuagint, tells us that at Alexandria an annual thanksgiving feast celebrated "this ancient but ever young benefit of God" (*Vita Moysis* 2.7). From the moment the Church started appropriating and using the Septuagint to confute them, the Jews could be seen throwing it into question and turning more and more away from using it: "I put no confidence," writes Justin, "in your teachers who refuse to recognize as accurate the translation made by the seventy elders in the court of King Ptolemy of Egypt, and try instead to do their own translation" (*Dial.* 71.1; cf. 68.7;

72-74). The translations of Theodotion, Symmachus, and Aquila, worked out during the second century, responded to the need for refuting interpretations which the Church grounded in the Septuagint.

These translations, too, in their turn, were attacked by Christians. The *Dialogue of Timothy and Aquila* in particular, which can with certainty be dated around 200 C.E., and which gives the name of Aquila to its Jewish interlocutor probably intentionally, vigorously inveighs against Aquila's version, accusing him of having deliberately falsified and mutilated the sacred text.[4] In the rabbinic writings, Jewish distrust of the Septuagint grew into deliberate hostility. There we find that the day of translation was as painful for Israel as the day when the golden calf was fashioned, for the Torah had not been able to be translated adequately. Following the translation, in the form of chastisement, darkness covered the world for thirty days (*Tosephta, Tr. Sopherim* 1.7; *Meg. Taanit* 13). It appears that as early as the third century the Septuagint had been commonly supplanted in the synagogues by new translations the slavish literalism of which did violence to the genius of the Greek language. Aquila's translation in particular was received with great favor and was still in use in Diaspora communities by Justinian's time. It is in this epoch, it seems, that the liturgical use of the Greek was gradually lost.

The Jewish-Christian controversy over the Bible therefore does not rest on the canonicity of individual books; it is rather articulated around three essential points: (1) the text itself, its integrity, and the falsifications, additions, and abridgements of which it could be the object; (2) the proper method for reading it in order to recover its exact meaning; and (3), having traversed the problem of interpretative method, the application that one was or was not entitled to make of the text, in a prophetic or typological perspective, to the person and work of Christ and to the realities of the Church. All patristic biblical exegesis, and with it the Fathers' anti-Jewish polemic, is from the outset guided by this fundamental conviction that the Old Testament, in order to be clearly understood, does not suffice by itself and that it needs a kind of retrospective illumination. This conviction would ultimately find expression, once the Old Testament had been joined in a single canon with the fundamental writings of Christianity, in the famous adage: *Novum Testamentum in Vetere latet, Vetus Testamentum in Novo patet* ("The New Testament is hidden in the Old, the Old Testament is manifest in the New"). For want of having grasped this key to the Bible, "the Jews do not understand the Scriptures" (Justin, *Dial.* 9.1).

53

Concerning the first point of debate, the integrity of the biblical text itself, we find the Jewish and Christian communities in antiquity bandying about, for the sake of controversy, the accusation of having disfigured the Scriptures.[5] In order to be absolutely certain of how precisely the Bible had been libeled, Origen, the veritable founder of biblical text criticism, launched into a remarkable scientific enterprise. In the six parallel columns of his *Hexapla* (completed ca. 250 C.E.), he brought together the original scriptural text in Hebrew characters and the same text in Greek letters; moreover, alongside the Septuagint he set the three aforementioned Greek translations that were in the process of supplanting the Septuagint in synagogal usage. Origen takes note in the Septuagint of all the words or passages that are missing in the Hebrew. Conversely, he fills in the lacunas by taking his inspiration from other Greek versions, most often that of Theodotion, or else corrects passages that have been poorly translated. Such an effort betrayed Origen's idea, scarcely prevalent among Christians of the time, that the Septuagint in its initial form did not merit absolute confidence. In order to render the Church all the services expected of it, especially in allowing the Church to counter Jewish attacks by supporting itself with the word of the Eternal down to the very letter, the Septuagint needed to be rectified, even at its minute levels, through continuous reference to the Hebrew text.

Yet Christian authors before Origen, and most often those coming after him, clung to the traditional text of the Septuagint and favored it, if necessary, to the original Hebrew. "There is much of the Scriptures," Justin can thus affirm, that the Jews have entirely deleted from the translation made by the elders in the court of Ptolemy" (*Dial.* 71.2). Thereafter, at Trypho's request, he cites, as eliminated from the text by the Jews, a certain number of biblical passages, some of which are also mentioned by subsequent Christian authors, and which, while actually absent from our Septuagint, do not figure at all in the original Hebrew. Consequently we are fully justified in seeing here, not suppressions by Jews, but Christian interpolations. Undoubtedly we must see here commentators' glosses inadvertently integrated into the biblical verses to which they referred. This is the case, for example, with the words "from the tree" that Justin (*Dial.* 73.1), followed by numerous Greek and Latin authors, claims to have read in Psalm 96:10 [95:10, LXX] right after the phrase "The Lord has reigned." This expression, which the Fathers naturally applied to the crucified Christ, actually appears neither in the Septuagint nor, for more obvious reasons, in the original Hebrew.

manner as *paradôsis*, designates in Jewish usage itself the oral tradition finally fixed in written form in the Mishnah. From the Christian side the term was also applied at times to the second codification of the Covenant at Sinai following the episode of the golden calf and the destruction of the original tablets of the Law by Moses.[7] This second legislation, of a particularly ritual character, was considered, then, as punishment for Israel's apostasy, yet, despite this, its divine origin was not questioned. The originality of the *Dialogue of Timothy and Aquila*, in playing on the kinship of the two Greek terms, lies in considering this *deuterôsis* to be codified in the book of Deuteronomy and, moreover, favoring the more customary usage of the term *deuterôsis*, in seeing in Deuteronomy, with the same title as in the oral tradition of the rabbis and in the Mishnah, a purely human initiative, even if it is Moses who has received it.

However exceptional it is, the position of the *Dialogue of Timothy and Aquila* with regard to Deuteronomy leads us to concern ourselves with the problem of the exegetical method according to which the Bible had to be interpreted. For Jews there was hardly a problem. Whatever their nature, be they narrative, normative, or prophetic, the biblical texts were to be understood in their plain sense. When a passage created a difficulty by virtue of an obscure or defective text, one had to strive to restore its most natural meaning. In any case, everything recorded in Scripture had to be rendered to the letter.[8] A symbolic meaning could be added to the literal but not supplant it, save in a work like the Song of Songs which, by all appearances, showed all the characteristics of a quite profane love song that was surprising to find among the inspired books. The pious reader was therefore to acknowledge in the Song the allegorical exaltation of God's love for his chosen people or for the mystic soul.

Excluding this restricted and unique case, absolute priority would always be given to the literal sense of the scriptural text. Even an allegorist as enthusiastic as Philo never loses sight of this basic axiom. The symbolic meaning aims only to reinforce the literal sense. In the same way, it is because he refuses to read between the lines of Deuteronomy in order to discover a hidden significance, and because he furthermore judges this trifling ritual legislation to be unworthy of God, that the author of our *Dialogue* denies the book its place among the inspired writings and sees in it a purely human work. Yet there were comparable considerations which induce the heresiarch Marcion, a man hostile to all allegorical exegesis, to deny the authorship of the Old Testament to the benevolent God, revealed for the first time by Jesus, and to ascribe it instead to the

Demiurge, the God of wrath, Lord of Israel, subordinate of the good God, whose existence Marcion furthermore ignores, thereby usurping his place at the summit of the hierarchy of beings.

Marcion's position in early Christianity is equally exceptional. It is hardly peripheral in the Gnostic and gnosticizing spheres beyond the limits of the Great Church. It is worth noting, for this purpose, the equally original and quite ingenious perspective of Ptolemy's *Letter to Flora*. A Gnostic work of the second century C.E., this letter testifies to a quite interesting critical and exegetical sense that foreshadows modern biblical exegesis in some ways. The ancient Law, Ptolemy says, is composite. None of its elements come from the supreme God (a point of agreement with Marcion). The fundamental core of the Law is ascribable to a subaltern deity who does not, however, stand in opposition to the supreme God. Certain other legal prescriptions come from Moses, and they have a sort of custodial purpose, namely, to hinder the hard-hearted Jews from completing their sins by rejecting the law as a whole. Other clauses in the law derive from "the Ancients," that is, in all probability, the rabbinic schools.

From this interesting tripartition, which indicates a chronological succession and a descending order of value, derives the attitude to be adopted concerning the Law. Its two purely human elements—the Mosaic legislation and that of "the Ancients"—must be rejected. Yet even with the legislation of divine origin, there must be discrimination. The moral Law, deposited in the Decalogue, represents the immutable divine will which, even after Christ, retains all its value. Another part of the commandments dictated by God is destined, just like the Mosaic contribution (and here there are overlaps that are difficult to explain in detail), to thwart the bad instincts of the Jews, such as the law of retaliation; it is to be thrown out. Finally, every detail of the ritual Law must be interpreted allegorically and must find is spiritual fulfillment in Christ.

Repudiating the extremist views of Marcion as well as Ptolemy's nuanced exegesis, the Great Church made allegory its official method for interpreting the Hebrew Bible. The Church did not generally impugn the literal sense of the commandments and ritual injunctions in confronting the rabbis, but it did restrict its value solely to the pre-Christian Jewish past. The Law, being in Paul's own words "a pedagogue until the coming of Christ" (Gal. 3:24), no longer had any *raison d'être* after this crucial moment in human history. Faith was henceforth the only means of justification. Attaining therefore to spiritual maturity in Christ, human beings won to the Christian message no longer need any ancient pedagogue.

Pressing this idea of a spiritual sense of Scripture to its extreme, the *Epistle of Barnabas* goes so far as to reject the literal sense even for the historical past itself. The fatal error of the Jews was to get caught up in the literal sense by considering it lawful and necessary. In fact, however, the rites of the Old Covenant, even considered independently of the Christian rites, have never been of anything more than of symbolic value. They are the image of spiritual realities and nothing more. Some of the precepts which codify the rites are prefigurative, such as the scapegoat or circumcision (*Epistle of Barnabas* 7-9). Others are the image of a moral truth, such as the dietary laws: "It is not a commandment of God not to eat. But Moses spoke in the spirit; first of swine, in this sense: You shall not have relations with men who resemble swine, that is, who forget the Lord when they live in pleasures and remember him when they are in need, as does the swine who does not acknowledge his master when he is eating, but grunts when he is hungry" (*Epistle of Barnabas* 10.2-3).

Between the extreme views of Marcion, who rejects allegory and wants to acknowledge only the letter of scripture, and Pseudo-Barnabas, for whom Scripture never had any true meaning other than the spiritual one, the Church rested content with a via media which it justified chronologically. The establishment of the new economy totally modified all perspectives on salvation history; the ritual commandments of the ancient Law no longer had more than an archaeological interest for a Christian, as their true *raison d'être* was to elucidate what came after them.

Such is the fundamental difference between the Philonic and early Christian uses of allegory. In Philo, the temporal dimension is absent, so that allegorical interpretation can be spoken of "vertically": the literal sense contains moral or metaphysical truths, precepts of the Law or biblical-historical episodes and personages which convey heavenly and eternal realities. Christian allegory, on the contrary, without totally spurning this vertical aspect, adjoined another, more important "horizontal" dimension, as it were: precepts, institutions, figures and personages in the Old Testament signaled Christian realities. Allegory thus became for Christians essentially prefigurative, turning into typology. Already the Epistle to the Hebrews proclaimed: "The Law has but a shadow of things to come" (10:1). This perspective is fully exploited in turn through patristic exegesis: "Everything," comments John Chrysostom, "is a figure, everything a shadow, circumcision, sacrifices, sabbath..." (*In Ep. ad Hebr.* 7, *Hom.* 13).

The Old Testament thus comes to hold a double role as a forerunner of the New Covenant. It is such in a direct way, a way obvious to anyone who is not voluntarily blinded to it, through the prophecies; and it is such, equally indisputably, through the oblique significance of typology. In both cases, the Old Testament refers to Christ and Christianity.

On the prophetic level, the Christian apologists essentially strive to demonstrate that all scriptural texts capable of a messianic interpretation apply perfectly to the person of Jesus. Such is the case especially with texts like Isaiah 53 and Psalm 22 (21, LXX) which illustrate the sufferings of the Righteous One. Abundantly cited ever since Justin (*Dialogue with Trypho* 97, 106), they bear proof that the Passion of Christ conforms with the plan of God. The same holds true for the other biblical passages which, indicating a priest or an eschatological sovereign, such as Psalms 110 (109, LXX) and 72 (71, LXX), refer in the view of Christian exegetes not to the Passion but to Christ's glorious Parousia. Unfortunately we do not possess any rabbinic texts (even from within the majority of Christian anti-Jewish sources) which directly counter these interpretations: the rabbinic response, even if it is aimed at countering the Church's exegetical arguments in a way that is difficult to contest, is often only indirect and allusive; indeed, in most cases we know of the rabbinic response only as it is made known to us by the Christian authors themselves.

If Justin is to be believed, for example, the rabbis were contesting the very possibility of a messianic reading of the two Psalms that I just mentioned, understanding Psalm 110 (109, LXX) to refer to King Hezekiah (*Dial.* 33.1; 67.1; 68.7), and Psalm 72 (71, LXX) to refer to Solomon himself (*Dial.* 34; 64.5-6). No trace of these interpretations remains in rabbinic literature. *B. Sanhedrin* 94a says that Hezekiah had been chosen to be Messiah, but he was found unworthy of that election. An application of Psalm 72 (71, LXX) to Solomon is conceivable, strictly speaking, only if we accept its Davidic origin, as Justin's Jewish interlocutor Trypho does, whereas an equally ancient tradition, one that is moreover unstable, attributes its very composition to Solomon. Most likely the messianic interpretation of certain texts, accepted at first, was abandoned for a time in Israel precisely in order to respond to Christian utilization of those texts.[9] As for texts relating to the Suffering Servant figure, Jewish exegesis, rather than acknowledging here the figure of a suffering Messiah, who was only accepted slowly and with great difficulty in Judaism, envisioned instead the people of Israel.[10]

Christian apologists invoked typology as much as prophecy to support their christological positions. A quite exacting exegesis enabled Justin to find prefigurative images of the crucified Jesus in the bronze serpent and in Moses's act of praying with his arms extended during the battle with the Amalekites (Num. 21:8-9; Exod. 17:8ff; *Dial.* 90.3-4; 94.5; 111.1; 112.2). He found the symbol both of Jesus's cross and his baptism in the wood of Noah's ark sailing on the waters, which saved Noah (Gen. 6-7; *Dial.* 138.1-2), and in the wood which Elisha threw into the Jordan (4 Kings 6:6-7, LXX; *Dial.* 86). Justin goes so far as to interpret all miraculous sticks in the Bible along the same lines (*Dial.* 86).

The Jewish objections not only touched on Jesus's earthly career, however; they undoubtedly targeted even more the essential doctrinal affirmations of the Church's christology, in particular the preexistence and divinity of the Christ-Messiah. The essence of Christian counterargument was often aimed at refuting these kinds of objections. Trypho is explicit on this point: "If you mean to say that Christ is God, that he preexisted the ages, since he consented to become a man and to be born and since he was not from among men, that seems to me not only paradoxical but foolish" (*Dial.* 48.1; cf. Origen, *Contra Celsum* 1.49; 4.2). Without going as far as to profess Christ's absolute equality with the Father, as does later Nicene theology in speaking of the three Persons of the Trinity, Justin responds by affirming still the divine nature of Christ, who is *theos* but not *ho theos*, the article being used only with respect to the Father (*Dial.* 46.4, 10; 60.1-5).

A considerable place is given in these demonstrations to the idea of another God, present, according to Scripture, alongside the Father in the work of creation and in the administration of the world. Justin further tries to show how the biblical history is made fully effective through him (*Dial.* passim, esp. 55-63). Arguments are drawn in particular from the theophanies recorded in Scripture. Since the agent of these theophanies could not be "him who is invisible to men, who has never himself conversed with anyone, the one whom we acknowledge as Creator of all things and as Father" (Justin, *Dial.* 56.1; cf. *Dialogue of Simon and Theophilus* 6), it can be none other than Christ the Logos.

This principle is in turn applied to all passages that give account of a divine apparition, and especially to the most celebrated of these stories, Abraham's vision under the oak of Mamre (Gen. 18:1-15). Philo sees in these three heavenly visitors God the Father flanked by two hypostases, creative Power and royal Power (*De Abrahamo* 24). It is rather strange to see Justin in some way trying to outdo the Alexandrian thinker on the issue of divine transcendence. Philo allows for God himself, *the* God, to descend to earth, while Justin confines him to the heavens and reserves all direct contact with the world below for his proxy in power, the Logos-Christ, whom he therefore also calls an Angel. Indeed for Justin, it is in effect the Logos who appears, accompanied by two subordinate angels, whereas for Trypho it is three angels. This recalls the way, characteristic of his subordinationist christology, that Justin qualifies Christ here as "the Lord who serves him who is in heaven" (*Dial.* 56.22).

Numerous works in the *adversus Judaeos* tradition insist on the role of Christ in creation, for which two verses in particular provide scriptural warrant. Some writings consider the phase "in the beginning" in Genesis 1:1 not in its more natural sense but as applying to a primordial, personal being, the Logos himself. The *Dialogue of Timothy and Aquila* (ch. 78) understands it this way; and we know that the lost Dialogue of Jason and Papiscus reads in the Latin Bible not *in principio* but *in Filio fecit Deus caelum et terram* (*ap.* Jerome, *Quaest. Hebr. in Gen.* 1.1). More often, however, there is reference to Genesis 1:26, with its use of the plural in describing the creation of humanity ("Let *us* make humanity in *our* image"), or else to Genesis 3:22, where God declares that "Adam has become like one of us" (Justin, *Dial.* 62.2; *Dial. of Athanasius and Zacchaeus* 3; *Dial. of Simon and Theophilus* 8; John Chrysostom, *Hom. against the Judaizers* 7.3). Justin, who brings together both verses, concludes from them that God speaks to someone numerically distinct and of a *verbal* (*logikon*) nature.

The Jewish interlocutor of these controversial dialogues typically responds on this point that these scriptural texts refer to angels—a view attested now and then in rabbinic literature—or else, conforming with the positions of Alexandrian Judaism, that God has hypostatic Wisdom as his associate (Prov. 8:22ff; Wisdom of Sol., passim; Sirach 1.1-10; 24, etc.). Justin supports this view, but immediately specifies that this divine hypostasis, called Angel, God, Lord, and Word alike, is none other than Christ (*Dial.* 61.1). Trypho, like the rabbi of the *Dialogue of Athanasius and Zacchaeus* (ch. 22), cries blasphemy at this point: Wisdom, he says, cannot become incarnate in a human body.

Yet here is the stumbling-block: the presence in Judaism itself of belief in a preexistent agent of God. We see this in certain more or less marginal Jewish communities, for example those from which emerged the writings of the cycle of Enoch, which gave rise to the idea of the Son of Man, the figure sketched in Daniel 7:13-14, a preexistent being on whose person are concentrated some of the traditional attributes of the Messiah, indeed a figure who takes the place of the Messiah. This current of thought, however, does not seem to have flowed with the Alexandrian Jewish current which reserved a central place in its speculations for the hypostasized divine Wisdom. While the messianic Son of Man descends to and is active on the earth, Wisdom does not abandon its heavenly spheres or at least never takes human form. Of the currents of religious thought circulating at this time in the Jewish world, only Christianity seems to have brought together and combined in a single figure the grand attributes of the human Messiah, indeed the heavenly Son of Man, and transcendent divine Wisdom, which were both, in differing degrees, familiar to Jews. It was the idea of a divine Incarnation that remained utterly incapable of assimilation into Jewish thought.

Neither prophetic argument nor typology was sufficient, however, to uproot positions taken by Jewish apologists. It was not enough to prove the truth of Christ and the Church on the basis of Scripture. The Law (Torah) still had to be overturned, for Jews believed, virtually down to every line, that the Law in its totality enjoyed eternal value. Christian argumentation at this point made a distinction, unceasingly invoked, between the moral Law, which is once and for all valuable, and the ritual Law. The former was effective for Gentiles as well as Jews because, in its biblical expression, it was merely the transcription of a natural Law inscribed on all human hearts from the very beginning, before the Sinaitic codification: "God established among the whole human race what is eternally and absolutely righteous" (Justin, *Dial.* 93.1; cf. Irenaeus, *Against Heresies* 4.13.1).

Over against this universal moral Law stood the particular precepts of the ritual Law, binding on Jews alone. But while Jews saw here the evidence of a unique privilege, Christian authors endeavored to show that the ritual Law was little more than an infamous sign, "precepts of servitude" as Irenaeus called it (*Against Heresies* 4.16.5). Even the foundational rite of circumcision carried no saving value. All wise men before Abraham had been justified without it! As for the mass of properly Mosaic prescriptions, they were imposed on Israel "because of your iniquity and hardness of heart" (Justin, *Dial.* 18.2; Irenaeus, *Against Heresies* 4.15.2). Having been given directly as a consequence of the worship of the golden calf (Exod. 32), they are at once punitive and preventative. They punish the sin committed and hinder its repetition, and furthermore help the sinful people of Israel to keep ever spiritually present the remembrance of their God.

Destined for Jews only, these commandments are, moreover, transitory. The coming of Christ spells their end, for the New Covenant instates the rule of faith in place of the rule of law. In addition, circumstances themselves render them impracticable. Whoever has himself circumcised, Paul already declares, "is bound to keep the whole Law" (Gal. 5:3). Recalling this principle, Christian polemicists estimated that the Law could not become partially impracticable without all of its prescriptions being abrogated at one and the same time. Passover would have had to disappear simultaneously with the Temple, since its celebration was limited, like that of the sacrifices, exclusively to the place that God had chosen as his residence (Deut. 16:5-6; John Chrysostom, *Hom. against the Judaizers* 4.4). These things had all had to disappear together in virtue of the internal solidarity that connected all the elements of the Law, in particular all those rites whose performance was linked to the existence of the priesthood, which had itself vanished with the Temple. This circumstantial impossibility of observing the ritual Law demonstrated all the more the rejection of the fallen people of Israel, who had now been replaced with the Gentiles by divine election.

This election of the Gentiles is illustrated, from the Christian apologists' perspective, by a number of premonitory episodes from the Old Testament where the younger take precedence over the elder: the dual lineage of Abraham, through Ishmael, son of Hagar, and through Isaac, son of Sarah (Gen. 16 and 21); the two peoples issuing from Rebecca (Gen. 25:19-28); Esau's abandonment of his birthright (Gen. 25:29-34); the blessing of Jacob by Isaac (Gen. 27); and the story of Joseph (Gen. 37ff).

Better still than this typology, which could always be challenged, was the argument based on the episode of Melchizedek (Gen. 14:18-20), the uncircumcised priest, father of the Gentiles as well as of the Christian priesthood (cf. Heb. 7), who was called to the worship of the true God even before Abraham himself, who paid him the tithe and appeared before him like a mere layman (John Chrysostom, *Hom. against the Judaizers* 7.5). Above all, Christian apologists invoked all biblical texts that announced the arrival of a new community of the faithful, gathering the chosen from all the peoples of the universe in the spiritual worship of the one God. These texts were read not in terms of a grand addition of proselytes to the Jewish community, but rather of a usurping or substitution of the community (*Ep. of Barnabas* 13; Origen, *Contra Celsum* 2.78). At best Jews would be able, by converting, to be incorporated into this Church, which was being built up outside the Jewish people.

The Church's priesthood, according to the order of Melchizedek, supplanted that of Aaron. But before it was to reach definitive form, the gift of prophecy was transferred to Christianity: "From the fact that even now we Christians have among us the gifts of prophecy, you should understand that those gifts which your people once possessed have now been transferred over to us" (Justin, *Dial.* 82.1; cf. Irenaeus, *Against Heresies* 2.32.4; 5.6.1; Clement of Alexandria, *Strom.* 1.21.135-136; Eusebius, *Hist. eccl.* 4.18.8). From these accumulated arguments springs the conclusion, already formulated in advance by Justin: "We, whom the crucified Christ has led to God, are the true spiritual race of Israel, descendents of Judah, of Jacob, of Isaac, and of Abraham (who without being circumcised received from God testimony to his faith, and was blessed and called father of many nations)" (*Dial.* 11.5).

We cannot fail to pose the question: did this kind of argumentation represent actual controversies between Christians and Jews? Even when works present such debate in the form of a dialogue, it is not certain that this always transcribes actual rhetorical bouts. We could indisputably answer this question in the affirmative if we only had similar works from the Jewish side, providing clear verification. But such works are not available. In the present state of the evidence, Judaism in the early centuries C.E. knows no specific genre of anti-Christian literature. In addition, since we do not possess any Jewish text in Greek after the second century C.E., we must turn to the rabbinic literature to search for echoes of this polemic and for eventual proof that these anti-Jewish polemical treatises were nothing more than academic exercises or a form of apologetic for the Church's internal use. If such echoes could be found, we could also, a fortiori, in all likelihood confirm that, in the hellenized or latinized Jewish milieu, the controversy between Christianity and Judaism was being actively carried on. Already we have some indications that it was. The *Dialogue of Simon and Theophilus* opens with the phrase: *Fuit igitur altercatio legis,* which seems difficult to understand except with regard to a real-life dispute. Tertullian for his part informs us that his treatise *Adversus Judaeos* records the substance of a discussion carried on in a public place for an entire day. As well, the fact that the pagan philosopher Celsus, in his *The True Doctrine,* calls to the rescue a Jewish interlocutor leads us to think that he knew of actual cases of verbal debate between Jewish and Christian teachers.

As for the rabbinic writings, although they derive from a Jewish milieu that was more retired to itself than Greek-speaking Judaism, they furnish abundant texts which explicitly reflect an anti-Christian inspiration. Christians are never designated by name in this literature, but they are firmly lumped together under the rubric of *minim,* a term indicating all manner of deviations from synagogal orthodoxy. In fact all rabbinic literature, Talmud and Midrash, to the extent that it is concerned with vindicating the oneness of God, the immutability of the Law, and the perpetuity of Israel's election, conveys at least the echo of Christian attacks on these doctrines. Elsewhere I have attempted to provide proof of this.[11] If I may be permitted one example here to make my point, I would turn again to the verse already cited, Genesis 1:26, "Let us make humanity in our image," which is used so abundantly by Christian apologists. Here we are met with a classic problem of monotheistic interpretation.

Occasionally the *minim* have been identified as dissidents of a Gnostic type.[12] But such an interpretation does not resist testing. For the Gnostic systems invested themselves in a dualistic perspective in which one or more subordinate divinities, steeped in matter and responsible for the material creation (among whom the Gnostics gladly identify the God of the Bible), stand in opposition to the one supreme God who is pure spirit and alone worthy of the title of God. But our verse from Genesis alleges no such antagonism. "The other god" is not some adversary ignoring or deliberately rebelling against the supreme God; he is rather his collaborator and associate. Only two interpretations were therefore possible: the polemic concerns either Alexandrian-Jewish speculations on the Logos or Wisdom, or rather, as would seem all the more probable the further we move into the Christian era, the Christian doctrine of Christ the Logos.

The rabbis resolved this exegetical difficulty in different ways. Sometimes they neutralized the plural signification of God by referring to the next verse, where God is cited in the singular: "and God created humanity in his (sing.) image" (*J. Ber.* 9.1). Sometimes they mustered all biblical passages in which the oneness of God is firmly asserted, most importantly the text of the *Shema,* Deuteronomy 6:4: "Here O Israel, the Lord our God is one Lord" (*Sifre Deut.* 32-39; *B. Pesach.* 56a; *Midr. Deut. r.* on 6:4). At other times still they would explain the plural by saying that God addressed Adam before he was even created, and, through Adam, his whole human posterity (*J. Ber.* 9.1). Justin perhaps recollects this response when he writes: "You are perhaps about to say, by distorting the words that I just quoted, what your teachers tell you, either that God said to himself 'Let us make,' or else that he addressed the elements, that is, the earth and the other things of which we think that humanity was made" (*Dial.* 62.2).

We could add numerous other examples. We could give in two

parallel columns the essential anti-Jewish arguments of Christian authors and the responses set forth directly or indirectly in rabbinic literature. The comparison would doubtless be quite revealing. Due to the brevity of this essay, I must content myself merely with the following conclusions.

Christian anti-Jewish literature, which always based itself on the Bible, was, with few exceptions, no mere academic exercise disconnected from daily reality. More often than not this polemical literature registered arguments that Christians actually levelled against Jews, or, what amounted to practically the same thing, against Christian judaizers.[13] Judaism did not remain indifferent to the attacks of its Christian adversary and determined to neutralize them. Judaism did not, as has often been believed and asserted, simply stiffen, in the very wake of two Judean wars, into an isolated indifference. Jewish withdrawal took place slowly, under the pressure of Christian propaganda and later that of the post-Constantinian imperial authorities, rather than out of sheer wantonness or indifference. The polemic which Christian authors stubbornly kept up against this ancient religion testified to its persistent vitality.

NOTES

1. Origen is among those authors who related the number of inspired biblical books to the number of letters in the Hebrew alphabet. For further discussion see A. Loisy, *Histoire du canon de l'Ancien Testament* (Paris, 1890); and more recently H. von Campenhausen, *The Formation of the Christian Bible*, trans. J. A. Baker (London and Philadelphia, 1972); P. R. Ackroyd and C. F. Evans, eds., *The Cambridge History of the Bible*, vol. 1 (Cambridge, 1970), 113-159.

2. See N. de Lange, *Origen and the Jews* (Cambridge, 1976), 20-28; also P. M. Blowers, "Origen, the Rabbis, and the Bible: Toward a Picture of Judaism and Christianity in Third-Century Caesarea," in *Origen: His World and His Legacy* (Notre Dame, Ind., 1988), 96-116.

3. *Prologue* to the *Books of Kings,* called Prologue *galeatus;* cf. A. Loisy, *Histoire du canon de l'Ancien Testament,* 113ff.

4. Cf. A. Lukyn Williams, *Adversus Judaeos: A Bird's Eye View of Christian Apologiae until the Renaissance* (Cambridge, 1935), 71.

5. For a recent study of this question, see R. A. Kraft, "Christian Transmission of Greek Jewish Scriptures," in *Paganisme, judaïsme, christianisme (Mélanges Marcel Simon)* (Paris, 1978), 207-226.

6. Cf. Williams, *Adversus Judaeos,* 72, n. 1.

7. See M. Simon, *Verus Israel,* trans. H. McKeating (Oxford and New York, 1986), 88-91; also idem, "The Ancient Church and Rabbinic Tradition, " in *Holy Book and Holy Tradition,* ed. F. F. Bruce and E. G. Rupp (Manchester and Grand Rapids, 1968), 94-112.

8. On the principles of rabbinic exegesis, see J. Bonsirven, *Exégèse rabbinique et exégèse paulinienne* (Paris, 1939); D. Daube, "Rabbinic Methods of Interpretation and Hellenistic Rhetoric," *Hebrew Union College Annual* 22 (1949): 239-264; idem, "Alexandrian Methods of Interpretation and the Rabbis," in *Festschrift H. Lewald*, ed. M. Gerwig et al. (reprinted Vaduz, 1978), 27-44; R. Loewe, "The 'Plain' Meaning of Scripture in Early Jewish Exegesis," in *Papers of the Institute of Jewish Studies* (London, 1964); and more recently the useful introductions by R. Kasher, "The Interpretation of Scripture in Rabbinic Literature," in *Mikra: Text, Translation, Reading and Interpretation of the Hebrew Bible in Ancient Judaism and Early Christianity*, ed. M. J. Mulder and H. Sysling, Compendia Rerum Iudaicarum ad Novum Testamentum, Section 2, Part 1 (Assen and Minneapolis, 1988), 547-594; M. Fishbane, "Jewish Biblical Exegesis: Presuppositions and Principles," in *Scripture in the Jewish and Christian Traditions: Authority, Interpretation, Relevance*, ed. F. E. Greenspahn (Nashville, 1982), esp. 94-108; R. Brooks, *The Spirit of the Ten Commandments: Shattering the Myth of Rabbinic Legalism* (San Francisco, 1990). The fundamental principle, which has by no means always been respected in rabbinic exegesis, is the following: "Scripture must not part from its simple sense" (*B. Jebam.* 11b, 24a). In Jewish and Christian interpretation alike, however, the "plain sense" has often turned out to be quite ("spiritually") complex.

9. On Jewish messianic exegesis, see J. J. Brierre-Narbonne, *Les prophéties messianiques de l'Ancien Testament dans la littérature juive* (Paris, 1933); idem, *Exégèse rabbinique des prophéties messianiques*, 5 vols. (Paris, 1934-1938).

10. Cf. J. J. Brierre-Narbonne, *Le Messie souffrant dans la littérature rabbinique* (Paris, 1940).

11. Simon, *Verus Israel*, 186-196.

12. In particular, see M. Friedländer, *Der vorchristliche jüdische Gnostizismus* (Göttingen, 1898), who is followed by more recent researchers who extend the same Gnostic interpretation to all usages of the term *minim.*

13. The parameters and substance of the earliest controversies between Christians and Jews (and judaizers) has been taken up again more recently in the excellent study of S. G. Wilson, *Related Strangers: Jews and Christians 70-170 C.E.* (Minneapolis, 1995).

4

The Bible in the Teaching and the Liturgy of Early Christian Communities

WILLY RORDORF

Before launching headway into our discussion, four preliminary observations are in order:

1. Until the end of the second century, the "Bible" such as we know it today, consisting of "Old" and "New" Testaments, did not yet exist. The Bible of the early Christians was the Old Testament—and as a general rule the Old Testament in its Greek translation, the Septuagint—to which was added the written tradition about Jesus, as well as the epistles of the apostle Paul and other "apostolic men." But the whole was not in any actual form united and had not yet received "canonical" status. As we will see later on, teaching and the liturgy in early Christian communities were largely instrumental in determining which of these latter writings would be incorporated into the Bible in the form of a "New Testament."

2. The history of the formation of the New Testament canon is simultaneously the history of the progressive elimination of non-canonical or "apocryphal" writings. Our actual New Testament represents only a very limited selection among the mass of dominical Sayings, Gospels, Acts, Epistles, and Apocalypses which were circulating at the time of the primitive Church. The discovery of the Nag Hammadi corpus in Egypt brought to our attention a number of unedited texts along these lines. Interestingly in these writings, Old Testament and New Testament traditions alike are utilized, combated, or ignored. It is thus a matter of a literature that the orthodox tradition of the Church has not acknowledged as authentic.

3. But even within the orthodox tradition, there is a troubling phenomenon, namely, the quite liberal manner in which the Scriptures are quoted. We see this with the Old Testament, which has for so long been considered a sacred text. The freedom with which its texts were interpreted by Christians is not explained solely by the differences existing between the original Hebrew and its Greek translations, but must be traceable in part to Jewish traditions of paraphrasing the biblical text (*midrashim*). More disconcerting still is the variety of textual forms in which gospel accounts appear in early post-apostolic writers. There was thus a multiplicity of textual traditions and the received text must have been established only little by little.

4. The first commentaries on whole books of the Bible appear only beginning in the third century. Before that we find, on the one hand, isolated quotations of biblical verses, from the Old and New Testaments alike, and on the other hand, florilegia serving as *testimonia* or scriptural "proof-texts" for theological purposes. In this essay we will be touching on a need of Christian instruction which was inspired by a Jewish model. Scattered quotations of the Old and New Testaments in primitive Christian literature make it difficult for one doing research in the history of exegesis of particular verses of Scripture in the early period. For this reason we can only hail the publication of the multi-volumed *Biblia Patristica*, which is aspiring to provide as thorough information as possible in this regard.

Having mentioned these facts we can move on to our principal subject, the Bible's place in education and in the liturgy in early Christian communities. It would perhaps be better to speak first of the liturgy and then teaching, in order better to see at what point the liturgy was not only the framework but the vital source of instruction. Nevertheless, it is useful to draw attention first to certain theological principles connected with the exegesis of the Bible and their formal place in instruction, before investigating the impact of the Bible in the liturgical life of the early churches.

The Bible in Early Christian Teaching

Teaching assumed a number of different forms in the early Christian period. In the first place, we must mention the sermons of ministers in the context of weekly Christian assemblies, preaching being the most regular form of instruction. Unfortunately we have precious few remains of preaching activity from the first two centuries, since at the time there was no thought of putting sermons into writing and preserving them. Beyond the New Testament, the first Christian homily available to us is *2 Clement* (first half of the second century); from the second half of the second century, we have a *Homily on the Pascha* by the bishop Melito of Sardis in Asia Minor. Lately we have come to know one or the other model of Gnostic preaching. The examples of preaching in the Pseudo-Clementine literature and in the apocryphal Acts of the Apostles are literary fictions which inform us more of the theology of their respective authors than of the theology of those to whom these sermons are attributed.

In the second place, we must mention the epistolary literature, which is most strongly represented among our extant sources. As is the case with the New Testament epistles, we are dealing with works addressed to specific historical situations or else theological treatises disguised as letters. In the first category belong, for example, *1 Clement*, the letters of Ignatius of Antioch, Polycarp of Smyrna's *Letter(s) to the Philippians*, the correspondence of Dionysius of Corinth, as well as the letters of the church of Smyrna on the martyrdom of Polycarp and of the church of Lyons on the martyrs who died in the persecution of 177. In the second category we could include, for example, the *Epistle of Barnabas*, the *Epistle to Diognetus*, and several Gnostic letters discovered at Nag Hammadi.

Christian instruction was also delivered, though more rarely, in the form of theological works of an apologetic type, whether aimed at countering pagan or Jewish interlocutors (cf. Justin Martyr's *Dialogue with Trypho the Jew*) or at refuting a false doctrine being propagated within the Church (cf. the celebrated five books of Irenaeus of Lyons's *Adversus haereses*, or numerous treatises of Tertullian of Carthage, Hippolytus of Rome, et al.).

In this mass of literature reflecting Christian teaching, the Bible played a central role. It is impossible in what follows to assess every work in detail. We will limit ourselves to presenting some fundamental problems of biblical interpretation such as were posed within Christian communities in this early period.

The Place of the Old Testament in the Christian Church

In simple terms, three dispositions toward the Old Testament are distinguishable in the early Christian communities: a radical repudiation of it, as seen with Marcion and in heretical Gnosticism; a fundamentally positive attitude toward it in Jewish Christianity; and a rather nuanced position toward it in the Great Church, one which would prevail in the Church's later history.

Marcion and the heretical Gnosticism of the second century contested the very value of the Old Testament. Whereas Marcion, on the bases of his *Antitheses*, set in opposition the loving God of Jesus and the jealous, cruel, and ignorant deity of the Old Testament, and accordingly spurned the Old Testament as a whole (even those parts of it to which the New Testament alludes), the various Gnostic sects laid waste to the central message of the Old Testament through skillful exegesis. Gnostic exegetes are reputed especially for their exegesis of the opening chapters of Genesis: the good creation of the beneficent Creator becomes in their hands the rather controversial work of a Demiurge who is even more controversial; the insubordination of the first human being toward the Demiurge's commandment becomes for them the signal of the human's superior knowledge; the serpent of the temptation becomes the veritable benefactor of humanity, and so on. In short, the Genesis cosmogony is manipulated as an illustration of the Gnostic myth; and all Gnostic exegesis, including that of the New Testament (in particular Jesus's parables) follows the same tendency.

On the other hand, the Jewish Christian wing of the early Christian movement upheld as much as possible the Old Testament as a whole. Since we have little evidence overall, it is difficult to determine precisely the theology of Jewish Christianity in its beginnings, but the twenty *Homilies of Peter*, dating to around 200 and representing the earliest stratum of the so-called Pseudo-Clementine literature, reflect this theology faithfully enough. The true prophets, from Adam to Jesus and Peter, revealed the Law of God (roughly corresponding to the Mosaic Law); but the false prophets from Eve to the apostle Paul (!) tried to abolish it. The true Christian believer, however, would excel through his or her faith in the law, both the moral and ceremonial regulations (Jewish Christians had in fact continued observing circumcision, the Sabbath, the custom of saying prayers in the direction of Jerusalem, etc.). Jewish Christians nonetheless admitted that fallacious material had insinuated itself into the Mosaic Law (also under the influence of false prophecy), namely in the form of everything concerning the cult of blood sacrifices, the royal dynasty of David, and anthropomorphic conceptions of God. The true prophet Jesus came to purify the Law of these corrupt elements which had altered the will of the Lawgiver.

How did the Church find its way between the two extremes represented by Marcion and heretical Gnosticism on the one hand, and Jewish Christianity on the other? It is thrilling to observe how it searched out its own position toward the Old Testament throughout the course of the second century. For the sake of examples and in order to illustrate this evolution, let us speak briefly of the respective solutions of *1 Clement*, the *Epistle of Barnabas*, the *Preaching of Peter*, Justin Martyr's *Dialogue with Trypho the Jew*, and Melito of Sardis's *Homily on the Pascha*.

1 Clement (composed in Rome in 96 C.E.) largely employs the Old Testament as a collection of examples of Christian moral conduct. The Old Testament accordingly speaks in an immediate way to Christians: God's will for the Israelites is God's will for Christians as well. *1 Clement* thus teaches what is customarily called the moral sense of Scripture. It is an *ad hominem* application of the Old Testament such as has always been highly valued in Christian preaching even up to our own time, but which easily fails to notice the newness of the revelation in Christ. We get the impression that nothing has changed since Christ's coming except the fact that Christian preaching is now addressed to all human beings without distinction and that a part of the ritual Law of the Old Testament is no longer observed.

The *Epistle of Barnabas* (originating in Syria-Palestine during the second quarter of the second century) follows a different approach, laying claim to the totality of the Old Testament for Christian use and considering the Old Testament itself as a written testament of Christ. To do that it radically opposes literal interpretation of the Old Testament, which it identifies as the erroneous interpretation of the Jews. Spiritual exegesis is the only valuable interpretation for the Church. In effect the *Epistle of Barnabas* is responsible for introducing allegorical exegesis into Christianity, the quest for an alternative meaning to the literal sense.

The exegetical approaches represented by *1 Clement* and the *Epistle to Barnabas* are not wholly satisfactory. Both works commit the same error. Both identify the Old and New Testaments too closely, although doing so in contradictory ways. *1 Clement* interprets the Old Testament literally; it takes it as it is and thus risks a failure to appreciate the fullness of Christ. The *Epistle of Barnabas* interprets it in the light of the revelation of Christ, but risks failing to appreciate the historical truth of the Old Testament.

Consequently we come to the New Testament conviction that salvation history, to which the Old Testament testifies, is real or actual, but that it has found its culmination in the person and work of Jesus, and that it finds its actual continuation in the mission of the Church. The basic principle of this conception of the Old Testament is clearly expressed in the *Preaching of Peter*, a work from the beginning of the second century known to us from fragments in Clement of Alexandria's *Stromateis*, Book 6. The *Preaching* appears to have been the original apologetic work that influenced subsequent apologists like Aristides, Justin Martyr, and the author of the *Epistle to Diognetus*. Two principal passages are worth quoting here. Having spoken of the Greeks who worship God in a false manner, the text continues

> Do not worship him any longer as do the Jews, who in effect imagine that they alone know God, and yet do not know him, worshipping angels, archangels, the month, and the moon. If the moon does not appear, they neither celebrate the Sabbath that they say is the first thing to celebrate, nor the new moon, nor the Feast of the Unleavened (of Passover), nor the Feast of the Tabernacles, nor the Great Day of Atonement... So guard in piety and righteousness the tradition that we proclaim to you, rendering to God a new worship through Jesus Christ. For we find in Scripture the words, "Behold, I make a new covenant with you, not like that which I made with your fathers on Mount Horeb" (Jer. 31:31 [38:31, LXX]). He has given us a new covenant: the manner of worship of the Greeks and that of the Jews are ancient. As Christians we render to God a new and third kind of worship. (*Preaching of Peter, ap.* Clement of Alexandria, *Strom.* 6.5.41).

Recalling the scheme of Romans 1-2, the *Preaching of Peter* claims that pagans as well as Jews are culpable before God, and that they must convert to the New Covenant finalized by Christ and proclaimed by the apostles. As in the New Testament, the major argument for convincing the Jews is scriptural proof. They must be shown that the messianic prophecies are fulfilled in Jesus Christ:

> Having perused the books left to us by the prophets, in which Jesus Christ is signified sometimes in parables, sometimes in enigmas, sometimes in explicit and indisputable terms, we discover here his coming, his death, his cross and all the rest of the torments with which the Jews burdened him, his resurrection, and his ascension into heaven, before the foundation of [the New] Jerusalem. Likewise these books write about what he must suffer and about who must come after him. Having made this examination (of the scriptures) we have believed in God on account of what is written here of him... Indeed we came to know that God had truly ordained him, and we say nothing that is not supported by Scripture. (*Preaching of Peter, ap.* Clement of Alexandria, *Strom.* 6.15.128).

The Old Testament as a whole is therefore a prophetic testimony to Christ, and it is unnecessary to eliminate from it that which does not "stick" to the New Testament, either by deleting it or allegorizing it. There are, however, different levels of witness in the Old Testament, passages that more explicitly testify to Christ and those in which the testimony remains relatively obscure.

This is the basis on which the second-century Fathers desired to understand their exegetical task. We will observe here two examples, Justin Martyr and Melito of Sardis. Following the two great options of Old Testament exegesis, Justin will serve to illustrate Christian interpretation of the Old Testament Law, and Melito the christological exegesis of the Old Testament.

Justin Martyr develops his interpretation of the Old Testament Law in his *Dialogue with Trypho the Jew*. First he recounts the story of his own conversion, and then he engages Trypho in a discussion of the value of the Law. Trypho poses the fundamental question as follows:

> This is what surprises us most, that you who claim to be pious and believe yourselves to be different from the others do not segregate yourselves from them, nor do you practice the rite of circumcision. You place your hope in a crucified man, and still expect to receive favors from God when you disregard his commandments. (*Dial.* 10.3).[1]

Justin responds:

> Trypho, there will never be, nor has there ever been from eternity, any other God except Him who created and formed this universe. Furthermore, we do not claim that our God is different from yours, for He is the God who, with a strong hand and outstretched arm, led your forefathers out of the land of Egypt... But, our hope is not through Moses or through the Law, otherwise our customs would be the same as yours. Now, indeed, for I have read, Trypho, that there should be a definitive law and a covenant, more binding than all others, which now must be respected by all those who aspire to the heritage of God... An everlasting and final law, Christ himself, and a trustworthy covenant has been given to us, after which there shall be no law, or commandment, or precept. (*Dial.* 11:1-2).[2]

We see here already that Justin is fundamentally opposed to the Gnostics and to Marcion: the God of the Old Testament is the God of Christians; he who created heaven and earth, the God of the people of Israel, is at once the Father of Jesus Christ. But if so, why did God give an earlier body of law to the Israelites that would now be null and void since the coming of Christ? This change had to be explained as part of the

divine plan. The first human beings mentioned in the Bible, and the patriarchs themselves, did not have the Law of Moses. The only valid explanation was that human sin had necessitated God's intervention (cf.
Dial. 23.2).

Justin at this point opposes the perspective represented in the
Epistle of Barnabas: the first body of law was valid, had existed (for the
term of its purpose), and was perfectly understood by the Jews; but now,
in Christ, that law had passed away and been abolished, since now the
Spirit of Christ bestowed a means of practicing righteousness without
the exterior "enclosure" of the commandments. There was thus a progression in salvation history: the transition from the Old to the New Covenant was the sign of the pedagogy of God who, in his philanthropy, desired to draw humanity to himself through a long process of maturation.
Shortly after Justin, this conception of the history of salvation was developed into a grand fresco by Irenaeus of Lyons.

But was it the entire Old Testament law that was abolished and
ineffectual for Christians? Justin says no, for the law of love, which is the
law of Christ, is eternal and concerns all human beings alike.

> God shows every race of man that which is always and in all places
> just, and every type of man knows that adultery, fornication, murder,
> and so on are evil. Though they all commit such acts, they cannot es-
> cape the knowledge that they sin whenever they do so, except those
> who, possessed by an unclean spirit, and corrupted by bad education
> and evil habits and wicked laws, have lost (or rather have stifled and
> stamped out) their natural feelings of guilt... Hence, I am of the opinion
> that our Lord and Savior Jesus Christ very aptly explained that all jus-
> tice and piety are summed up in the these two commandments: "Thou
> shalt love the Lord thy God with thy whole heart, and with thy whole
> strength, and thy neighbor as thyself" (cf. Matt. 22:37-40).
>
> Therefore, since all justice is directed toward two ends, namely, God
> and man, whoever loves the Lord God with all his heart, says the Scrip-
> ture, and with all his strength, and his neighbor as himself, will surely
> be a just man. (*Dial.* 93).[3]

Justin thus follows here traces of the apostle Paul: there is a "natural" law, inscribed in the heart, or "conscience," of every human being, the
clarity of which can be obscured by sin, but the universal truth of which is
plainly revealed in the light of the Gospel. This conviction is but a corollary
of Justin's axiom of the *logoi spermatikoi* found in Jews and Gentiles alike,
which have their origin in the eternal Logos incarnate in Jesus of Nazareth.
Such a vision of things was quite compelling, and explains in large part the

missionary success of Christianity in the early centuries.

Melito of Sardis. Of the numerous works of this Christian author of the second half of the second century, only his *Homily on the Pascha* has survived in complete form; preached during the paschal feast, it is our primary source of information.[4] Here Melito again connects up the typological interpretation of the Old Testament with New Testament exegesis. Let us look at some characteristic passages:

> *For the model* (typos) *indeed existed,*
> *but then the reality* (alêtheia) *appeared.*
> *For instead of the lamb there was a Son,*
> *and instead of the sheep a Man,*
> *and in the Man Christ who has comprised all things.*
> *Hence the slaying of the sheep*
> *and the distribution of the blood*
> *and the scripture from the law have reached as far as Christ,*
> on whose account were all things *(Heb. 2:10) in the ancient law...*
>
> (HOM. ON THE PASCHA 4-6).[5]

Melito describes the prefiguration in terms of an image:

> *This is just what happens in the case of a preliminary structure:*
> *it does not arise as a finished work,*
> *but because of what is going to be visible through its image*
>   *acting as a model.*
> *For this reason a preliminary sketch is made of the future thing*
> *out of wax or of clay or of wood,*
> *in order that what will soon arise*
> *taller in height, and stronger in power,*
> *and beautiful in form,*
> *and rich in its construction,*
> *may be seen through a small and perishable sketch.*
> *But when that of which it is the model arises,*

that which once bore the image of the future thing
is itself destroyed as growing useless
having yielded to what is truly real the image of it;
and what once was precious becomes worthless
when what is truly precious has been revealed.

(HOM. ON THE PASCHA 36-37).[6]

Melito also gives the application of this principle:

For the very salvation and reality of the Lord were prefigured
in the people [of Israel],
and the decrees of the gospel were proclaimed in advance by
the law.
The people then was a model by way of preliminary sketch,
and the law was the writing of a parable;
the gospel is the recounting and fulfilment of the law,
and the church is the repository of the reality.

(HOM. ON THE PASCHA 39-40).[7]

The Passion of Christ was prefigured and announced:

But first the Lord made prior arrangements for his own sufferings
in patriarchs and in prophets and in the whole people [of Israel],
setting his seal to them through both law and prophets...
Therefore if you wish to see the mystery of the Lord,
look at Abel who is similarly murdered,
at Isaac who is similarly sold,
at Moses who is similarly exposed,
at David who is similarly persecuted,
at the prophets who similarly suffer for the sake of Christ.

(HOM. ON THE PASCHA 57, 59).[8]

This exegesis appears not as an artificial game, but flows from Melito's sense of the progress of salvation history itself.

The Canonical Value of the New Testament

Up to now, we have only spoken of the interpretation of the Old Testament in the Church. But beginning in the second century, the New Testament writings would also be quoted more and more and made the object of exegesis. We will first recall some of the established evidence concerning the history of the formation of the New Testament, and then observe what the Fathers of the second century considered to be the hermeneutical center of the New Testament.

The Formation of the New Testament. In the beginning, the Christian message was preached and transmitted in oral form. The Pauline scriptures were occasional or circumstantial writings, but they already referred to a pre-Pauline tradition (cf. the confession of faith in 1 Cor. 15:3ff; the hymn in Phil. 2:6-11). Elsewhere as well, Paul refers to certain sayings of Jesus (1 Cor. 7:10; 9:14; 11:23-26; 1 Thess. 4:15). In fact, collections of dominical sayings must have existed from very early on, as evidenced by the "Q" Source in the Synoptics, as well as the *Gospel of Thomas*. The redaction of the first Gospel (undoubtedly Mark's Gospel, though its priority has more recently been questioned) marked a turning-point: the desire now was to conserve the tradition intact, including all the tradition about Jesus; the other canonical Gospels wished, each in its own way, to complete this first attempt.

In the second century, we witness an impressive proliferation of apocryphal writings claiming apostolic origin (gospels, acts of apostles, letters, apocalypses). Gnostics, in particular, loved to refer to secret traditions, and their preferred apostle was Paul, which consequently led to Paul being quoted less and less by orthodox authors.

It was Marcion who first had the idea of forming a canon of authentic New Testament books (ca. 150 C.E.). It was indeed a matter of making a choice, and Marcion included only one Gospel, Luke's (due to its affinities with Paul, though even here Marcion had to eliminate any traces of Judaism[9]), which he placed at the front of his canon, followed then by ten Pauline epistles (Gal.; 1-2 Cor.; Rom.; 1-2 Thess.; Eph.; Col.; Phil.; Philemon; and the apocryphal *Letter to the Laodiceans*). The Great Church could only counter by expanding what it saw with Marcion as too limited a canon; to do this it collected the apostolic writings generally in use in the majority of local churches (in preaching, catechesis, worship: cf. Justin, *1 Apol.* 67). Based on the concurring testimonies of Irenaeus, Tertullian, and the canonical list discovered by Muratori, we know that this canon comprised the four Gospels, the Acts of the Apostles, 13 Pauline epistles (plus Hebrews, which was considered Pauline), 1 Peter, 1 and 2 John, Jude, and Revelation. The essential canon was thus constituted. The value of Hebrews and of Revelation still remained contested for two centuries.

Irenaeus of Lyons, in the five books of his "Refutation and Destruction of the False Gnosis" (*Against Heresies*, composed ca. 180) was systematically basing himself on this new canon of the Great Church: by quoting book after book in canonical order, he demonstrated that the Lord and his Apostles were in agreement in order to refute heretical teachings. In a celebrated passage, Irenaeus writes:

> Such, then, are the first principles of the Gospel: that there is one God, the Maker of this universe; He who was also announced by the prophets, and who by Moses set forth the dispensation of the law—[principles] which proclaim the Father of our Lord Jesus Christ and ignore any other God or Father except Him. So firm is the ground upon which these Gospels rest, that the very heretics themselves bear witness to them, and, starting from these [documents], each one of them endeavours to establish his own peculiar doctrine. For the Ebionites, who use Matthew's Gospel only, are confuted out of this very same, making false suppositions with regard to the Lord. But Marcion, mutilating that according to Luke, is proved to be a blasphemer of the only existing God, from those [passages] which he still retains. Those, again, who separate Jesus from Christ, alleging that Christ remained impassible, but that it was Jesus who suffered, preferring the Gospel of Mark, if they read it with a love of truth, may have their errors rectified. Those, moreover, who follow Valentinus, making copious use of that according to John, to illustrate their conjunctions, shall be proved to be totally in error by means of this very Gospel, as I have shown in the first book... It is not possible that the Gospels can be either more or fewer in number than they are. For, since there are four zones of the world in which we live, and four principal winds, while the Church is scattered throughout all the world, and the "pillar and ground" (1 Tim. 3:15) of the Church is the Gospel and the spirit of life; it is fitting that she should have four pillars, breathing out immortality on every side, and vivifying men afresh. From which fact, it is evident that the Word, the Artificer of all, He that sitteth upon the cherubim, and contains all things, He who was manifested to men, has given us the Gospel under four aspects, but bound together by one Spirit. (*Against Heresies* 3.11.7-8). [10]

What follows next is an interpretation of the four creatures of Ezekiel 1 and Revelation 4:7: John = lion; Luke = ox; Matthew = human being; Mark = eagle; later, the symbols of John and of Mark would be inverted.

The formation of the New Testament canon had a profound theological significance: the written Gospel was placed beside the Jewish Bible, thus demonstrating that there was a continuity between the first and second part of Scripture, but at the same time a real progress moving from the "Old" Testament to the "New" Testament, from the "Old" Covenant to the "New" Covenant.

The Hermeneutical Center of the New Testament. There remained a crucial problem: How must the New Testament itself be interpreted? The second part of the canon included 27 writings that were of a very different nature and content, and these writings did not themselves self-evidently provide the criterion of their interpretation. One could easily think that one already had the unity of the New Testament, but it was still necessary to explain that of which its unity consists.

The Church Fathers of the second century were very clear on this subject. Once again, Irenaeus is our principal witness (but Tertullian as well). He refers us to the Rule of Faith (or as he sometimes calls it, the "Canon of Truth") as the *hermeneutical center* of Scripture, and of the New Testament in particular. At bottom it is the Truth itself which is the rule of faith. That Truth was revealed on the one hand in the divine Scriptures, and in the Tradition of the apostolic faith on the other. What is this tradition? It is summed up in the fundamental articles of the baptismal confession of faith. Irenaeus has preserved several confessional formulas. We quote two of them here:

> To [this] course many nations of those barbarians who believe in Christ do assent, having salvation written in their hearts by the Spirit, without paper or ink, and, carefully preserving the ancient tradition, believing in one God, the Creator of heaven and earth, and all things therein, by means of Christ Jesus, the Son of God; who, because of His surpassing love towards His creation, condescended to be born of the virgin, He Himself uniting man through Himself to God, and having suffered under Pontius Pilate, and rising again, and having been received up in splendour, shall come in glory, the Saviour of those who are saved, and the Judge of those who are judged, and sending into eternal fire those who transform the truth, and despise His Father and His advent. (*Against Heresies* 3.4.2).[11]

> And this is the drawing up of our faith, the foundation of the building, and the consolidation of a way of life. God, the Father, uncreated, beyond grasp, invisible, one God the maker of all; this is the first and foremost article of our faith. But the second article is the Word of God,

the Son of God, Christ Jesus our Lord, who was shown forth by the prophets according to the design of their prophecy and according to the manner in which the Father disposed; and through Him were made all things whatsoever. He also, *in the end of times* (cf. Heb. 9:26), for the recapitulation of all things, is become a man among men, visible and tangible, in order to abolish death and bring to light life, and bring about the communion of God and man. And the third article is the Holy Spirit, through whom the prophets prophesied and the patriarchs were taught about God and the just were led in the path of justice, and who in the end of times has been poured forth in a new manner upon humanity over all the earth renewing man to God. Therefore the baptism of our rebirth comes through these articles, granting us rebirth unto God the Father, through His Son, by the Holy Spirit. (*Proof of the Apostolic Preaching* 6-7).[12]

The relationship between these confessional formulas and the Apostles' Creed is obvious. Hence, the confession of trinitarian faith which expresses in scriptural terms the faith of Christian communities becomes the hermeneutical key to the interpretation of the canon, and, conversely, the confession of faith refers to Scripture, which guarantees the authenticity of the confession's content. We find ourselves faced with a hermeneutical circle between the two traditions that the Church of the second century had given as the rule of truth: the canon of Scriptures and the confession of faith. From that time on, the Church's preaching would rest on these two pillars, which were both, meanwhile, products of the apostolic and ecclesiastical tradition.

The Bible in the Early Christian Liturgy

In the Church's instruction, theological problems were discussed, and often their discussion was provoked by the challenge of an aberrant concept; in the liturgy, we find ourselves on the level of the lived faith and, as it were, at the source from which springs the fresh and living water of worship, prayer, and hope.

In the section on teaching, we already had occasion to mention certain writings which allude to the liturgy (cf. Melito's *Homily On the Pascha*; Irenaeus's *Proof of the Apostolic Preaching*). Now we will approach the study of documents more directly related to the liturgy.

For example, we have two catechetical and liturgical sources of primary importance, dating from the period in which we are interested here: the *Didache*, written probably at the end of the first century in western Syria, and the *Apostolic Tradition* of Hippolytus, from the beginning of the third century. Several catechetical treatises of Tertullian supplement the information we have from these works. In addition, we cannot pass over in silence, in this context, prophetic and poetic works from the early Christian period: among prophetic writings, the apocalypses (e.g., several christianized Jewish apocalypses, as well as the *Apocalypse of Peter*, the *Sibylline Oracles*, and the *Shepherd of Hermas*); and among poetic works, hymnological fragments which are sometimes of tremendous value (e.g., the *Odes of Solomon*, some specimens from apocryphal and Gnostic literature, as well as some prayers written on papyri or in stone inscriptions).

We will first look at Christian initiation, then at some instances of the dominical cult in early Christianity, and finally at the annual Christian feasts. In each case we will concentrate on the Bible's formative role in the liturgical life of the Christian communities.

Christian Initiation

According to New Testament witnesses, baptism occurred quickly, without any preliminary conditions being imposed; faith in Jesus Christ was sufficient by itself in order to be baptized (cf. Acts 2:38-41; 8:36-38; 9:18; 10:47-48; 16:33; etc.). This practice was possible so long as Christian missionaries were addressing themselves to Jews and "God-fearers," since these converts had a sufficient religious and ethical base; however, when pagans began to be converted, they had to be taught the rudiments of Christian faith and ethics. The catechumenate therefore had to be devised as a means to prepare candidates for baptism. Beginning in the third century, the catechumenate was in place in all the churches, but its origins go back to the end of the first century.

Catechesis. Beginning in the fourth century, catechesis focused primarily on Christian doctrine and consisted in highly detailed commentary on the confession of faith. By contrast, its original focus was on ethics, the application of the faith in Christian living. This is confirmed by all the sources at our disposal: in part in the New Testament itself, then in the *Didache*, in the works of the Greek apologists, in the catechetical treatises of Tertullian, in the *Apostolic Tradition* of Hippolytus, and even in Clement of Alexandria, who teaches ethics before doctrine.

As for the content of this catechetical instruction, one passage from the *Didache* is especially revealing:

> Two ways there are, one of Life and one of Death, and there is a great difference between the Two Ways. Now, the Way of Life is this: "first, love the God who made you; secondly, your neighbor as yourself" (Matt. 22:37, 39; Deut. 6:5; Lev. 19:18): do not do to another "what

you do not wish to be done to yourself" (Matt. 7:12).... "Do not murder; do not commit adultery"; do not commit pederasty; do not fornicate; "do not steal"; do not deal in magic; do not practice sorcery; do not kill a fetus by abortion, or commit infanticide. "Do not covet your neighbor's goods." (Cf. Matt. 19:18; Ex. 20:13-15, 17; *Ep. of Barnabas* 19.4). "Do not perjure yourself; do not bear false witness" (Matt. 5:33; 15:19; 19:18); do not calumniate; do not bear malice. Do not be double-minded or double-tongued, for a double tongue is a "deadly snare" (Prov. 21:6). Your speech must not be false or meaningless, but made good by action. Do not be covetous, or rapacious, or hypocritical, or malicious, or arrogant. Do not have designs upon your neighbor. Hate no man; but correct some, pray for others, for still others sacrifice your life as proof of your love. My child, shun evil of any kind and everything resembling it.... On the contrary, be gentle, for "the gentle will inherit the land" (Ps. 37:11[36:11, LXX]; Matt. 5:4). Be long-suffering and merciful, and guileless, and quiet (cf. 1 Thess. 4:11), and good, and "with trembling treasure" forever "the instructions" you have received (Isa. 66:2). Do not carry your head high, or open your heart to presumption. Do not be on intimate terms with the mighty, but associate with holy and lowly folk. Accept as blessings the casualties that befall you, assured that nothing happens without God. (*Didache* 1.1-2; 2.2-3.10).[13]

In subsequent chapters, the author gives instruction on the Christian's demeanor toward his or her fellow believers, on almsgiving, on domestic duties, and of course on the "way of Death" that must be avoided since it leads to destruction.

This instruction is replete with biblical allusions; herein we find the double commandment of love (cf. Deut. 6:5; Lev. 19:18; Matt. 22:37-39), the Golden Rule (Matt. 7:12; cf. Tobit 4:15; also Acts 15:20, 28 in the Western text), several references to the Ten Commandments and to the Sermon on the Mount, and more. The theme of the "two ways" is itself biblical (cf. Deut. 31:15-20; Jer. 21:8; Matt. 7:13-14). In Second Temple Judaism (at Qumran, for example), the theme of the "two ways" served as a framework for ethical instruction.

Why was this ethics taught in connection with baptism? Attempts have been made to establish a relation between the baptismal rite of "renunciation" and this ethical teaching. At the time of baptism, a candidate had to renounce Satan and "all his works" (= the "way of Death") in order to cling to Christ and follow his teaching (= the "way of Life"). The first pagan testimony to Christian worship, Pliny the Younger's *Letter* 96 (*to the Emperor Trajan*), seems to confirm this hypothesis; he says, probably referring to candidates for baptism, that they were pledging "by oath, not to perpetrate any crime, but not to commit theft, or robbery, or adultery, not to break their word or to deny a deposit when it was required." In their oath, these baptismal candidates were therefore engaging in observing commandments recalling those in the Decalogue, and other testimonies confirm that the Decalogue, explained in the light of what Jesus said of it in his Sermon on the Mount, enjoyed an important role in ethical teaching in the earliest Christian communities.

Toward the end of the second century, ethical instruction was becoming even more systematic: apostasy, murder, and adultery were thereupon considered the three mortal sins (cf. 1 John 5:16ff). When individuals were registered for the catechumenate, they had to change professions if their work carried the risk of having occasion to commit one of these mortal sins (e.g., public offices, military service, arts and crafts, school teaching, circus games, etc.). In principle, a mortal sin (as its name indicates) could not be pardoned by the Church. Gradually, however, ecclesiastical discipline eased up and penitence became accessible for all sinners.

The Rite of Baptism. The commission to baptize is found in Matthew 28:19-20, and already in this text, the baptismal formula is trinitarian. The same trinitarian formula is found in the *Didache* 7.1; the invocation of the three names of God is accompanied by the triple immersion or aspersion of the candidate for baptism.

At the beginning of the third century, the *Apostolic Tradition* of Hippolytus preserves for us the liturgy of baptism. The following passage describes the confession of faith and triple immersion:

> A deacon will descend with him (the candidate for baptism) in this manner. When he who is being baptized descends into the water, he who is baptizing him will say, while laying his hand on him, "Do you believe in God the Father almighty?" And the one who is being baptized will say in turn, "I believe." And immediately (he who is baptizing), having his hand positioned on his head, will baptize him once. And then he will say, "Do you believe in Christ Jesus, Son of God, who was born by the Holy Spirit of the Virgin Mary, and was crucified under Pontius Pilate, died, and rose the third day living from the dead, and ascended into the heavens and was seated at the right hand of the Father; who will come to judge the living and the dead?" And when he says, "I believe," he will baptize him a second time. Again, he (who is baptizing) will say, "Do you believe in the Holy Spirit in the Holy Church?" He who is being baptized will say, "I believe," and so he will baptize him a third time. (*Apostolic Tradition* 21).

We have never sufficiently emphasized the importance of this rite for the evolution of all Christian doctrine. We have already said that the baptismal confession of faith in three articles, as we find it in the *Apostolic Tradition*, toward the end of the second century, played the role of a hermeneutical principle for the correct interpretation of the New Testament and of the entire Bible. The Church's whole trinitarian theology, moreover, would spring from this very source; we see it already in Justin Martyr, for example, and will see it especially in the fourth and fifth centuries when the first ecumenical councils develop Christian dogma as explanatory of the Church's baptismal confessions of faith.

The text of the *Apostolic Tradition* that we quoted mentions the laying on of hands at the time of baptism. According to this document, hands are also imposed on the newly baptized when they are anointed with oil. We do not know precisely at what time these supplementary rites originated; the *Didache*, for example, does not mention them, but it is clear that they were inspired by the Old Testament tradition.

Baptismal Typology. Baptismal typology would be richly embellished beginning in the fourth century.[14] But we find the roots of it in the New Testament (cf., for example, 1 Cor. 10:1ff; 1 Peter 3:19ff; Col. 2:11), and at the beginning of the third century, for example, in Tertullian's treatise *On Baptism*. Tertullian explains for us the rites of post-baptismal unction and the laying on of hands:

> After leaving the font, we receive an unction of blessed oil, conforming to the ancient discipline. According to this discipline, it was customary to be elevated to the priesthood by an unction of oil poured from a horn, in the manner that Aaron was anointed by Moses. And our name of "Christ" comes from that, the "chrism" which signifies unction and which also gives the Lord his name. For it is this unction transposed onto the spiritual level that the Lord, in the Spirit, received from God the Father, as it says in Acts, "they gathered together in this city against your holy Son whom you anointed" (Acts 4:27). For us too the unction runs over the body , but profits us spiritually, just as the rite of baptism is a corporeal action since we are immersed in water and yet its effect is spiritual since it delivers us from our sins. Next, hands are laid on us , while the Holy Spirit is invoked and invited through a benediction... This rite as well derives from the ancient sacrament in which Jacob blessed his grandsons, Ephraim and Manasseh, sons of Joseph; he positioned his hands on their heads cross-wise, indeed he placed them thus in the form of a cross with the idea that by forming on them the image of Christ, they would announce right then the benediction which would come to us through Christ. Then this very Holy Spirit leaves the Father and willingly descends on these cleansed and blessed bodies of ours. Being the very one who descended on the Lord in the form of a

dove, he reposes over the waters of baptism as though recognizing there his primeval throne. (*On Baptism* 7-8).

We must also note, however, the curious fact that the Pauline typology in Romans 6:1ff, depicting the baptized believer's participation in the death and resurrection of Christ, is absent in Christian literature in these earliest centuries.

Worship on the Lord's Day

The heart of the Christian liturgy throughout the ages was the dominical cult, the service of worship for the Lord's Day. The first detailed description of it comes in Justin Martyr:

> On the day which is called Sunday we have a common assembly of all who live in the cities or in the outlying districts, and the memoirs of the Apostles or the writings of the Prophets are read, as long as there is time. Then, when the reader has finished, the president of the assembly verbally admonishes and invites all to imitate such examples of virtue. Then we all stand up together and offer up our prayers, and, as we said before, after we finish our prayers, bread and wine and water are presented. He who presides likewise offers up prayers and thanksgivings, to the best of his ability, and the people express their approval by saying 'Amen.' The Eucharistic elements are distributed and consumed by those present, and to those who are absent they are sent through the deacons. The wealthy, if they wish, contribute whatever they desire, and the collection is placed in the custody of the president. [With it] he helps the orphans and widows, those who are needy because of sickness or some other reason, and the captives and strangers in our midst; in short, he takes care of all those in need. (*1 Apol.* 67).[15]

It is striking to be able to confirm at what point there is continuity in the different elements of the Church's dominical cult through the centuries. Let us follow these different components in sequence.

Biblical Readings and Preaching. In the text just quoted, Justin speaks of the reading of the "memoirs of the apostles" (gospel readings) and of the "writings of the prophets" (doubtless from the Old Testament). Following in this practice the model of synagogue worship (cf., for example, Luke 4:16ff), the early Christians read and explained the Old Testament accordingly. Yet we see here that the New Testament also constituted a part of this cultic reading. The written word of the apostles thus received consecration as inspired, divine Scripture. Already in the New Testament, we read that the letters of the apostle Paul were read in the context of worship (1 Thess. 5:22; Col. 4:16; cf. 1 Tim. 4:13), and a hundred years later, the tradition of reading the letters of sister-churches on the Lord's Day is still attested.[16] It is clear that this regular practice of reading the apostolic writings within the framework of worship greatly contributed to preparing the way for the formation of the New Testament canon.

We have already said that few sermons from this early period of the Church's history have been preserved, and we have had occasion to mention Melito's *Homily on the Pascha*. Another important text comes from the so-called *Second Epistle of Clement*:

> But in what way do we acknowledge him? By doing what he says and not disobeying his commandments, and by honoring him not only with our lips but "with all our heart and all our mind" (Deut. 6:5; Mark 12:30 and par.). For he also says in Isaiah, "This people honors me with their lips, but their heart is far from me" (Isa. 29:13; Matt. 15:8; Mark 7:6). Let us not merely call him Lord, for this will not save us. For he says, "Not every one that says to me, 'Lord, Lord,' will be saved, but he who does righteousness" (Matt. 7:21 and par.). So then, brethren, let us acknowledge him in deeds (by loving one another, by refraining from adultery and slander and jealousy, being instead self-controlled, merciful, kind. We ought also to share each other's lot and not be avaricious. In behavior of that kind and not its opposite we acknowledge him. Further, we must fear not men but God. That is why, assuming you do these things, the Lord said, "Even if you are with me, gathered to my bosom, but keep not my commandments, I shall cast you out and I shall say to you, 'Go from me, I do not know you nor whence you are, you workers of iniquity' (cf. Matt. 7:23)." (*2 Clement* 3.4-4.5).[17]

It should be noted that this homily quotes abundantly from the Old and New Testaments. But his last scriptural quotation (and it is not the only one in the homily) shows that the author referred also to apocryphal sources, for his text does not faithfully reproduce Matthew 7:23.

Prayer. I must limit myself here to the communal prayer of which Justin speaks. Such prayer was offered standing up, with the hands lifted in a praying position, turned toward the east. As for content, we unfortunately have few written vestiges of this communal prayer, since it was often the business of Christian prophets who prayed freely under the inspiration of the moment. But we find a quite beautiful example of an intercessory prayer in *1 Clement*:

> *[Through Jesus Christ the Creator has called us]...*
> *to hope in thy Name as the source of all creation.*
> *Thou hast opened the eyes of our hearts to recognize that*

thou alone art highest among the highest,

ever remaining holy among the holy (Isa. 57:15).

Thou dost humble the pride of the arrogant (Isa. 13:11),

overthrow the calculations of the nations (Ps. 33:10 [32:10, LXX]),

raise up the humble and

humble the proud (Job 5:11; Isa. 10:33; Ezek. 17:24; 21:31);

thou dost make rich and make poor (1 Sam. 2:7),

kill and make alive (Deut. 32:39);

thou alone art the benefactor of spirits and the God of all flesh
    (Num. 16:22; 27:16).

Thou seest into the depths (Dan. 3:55) and lookest upon men's
    deeds (cf. Esther 5:1a);

thou art the aid of those in peril, Savior of those in despair
    (Jud. 9:11),

the Creator of every spirit and the Watcher over it (cf. Amos 4:13;
    Job 10:12).

Thou dost multiply the nations upon the earth and

from them all thou hast chosen those who love thee

through Jesus Christ thy beloved Servant,

through whom thou dost discipline, sanctify, and honor us
    (cf. John 12:26; 17:17).

We beseech thee, Master, to be our helper and defender (Ps. 119:114
    [118:114, LXX]; Jud. 9:11).

Save those of us in affliction, have mercy on the humble,

raise up the fallen,

show thyself to those in need,

heal the sick,

turn back those of thy people who have gone astray (Ezek. 34:16).

Feed the hungry,

release our imprisoned ones,

revive the weak (Job 4:4),

encourage the fainthearted.

Let all the heathen know that thou art God alone (1 Kings 8:60
  [3 Kings 8:60, LXX]; 2 Kings 19:19 [4 Kings 19:19, LXX];
  Isa. 37:20; Ezek. 36:23; John 17:3), and that Jesus Christ is thy
  servant, and that we are thy people and the sheep of thy pasture
  (Ps. 79:13 [78:13, LXX]).

For thou through thy works didst reveal the everlasting
structure of the universe;
thou, Lord, didst create the world.
Thou art faithful in all generations (Deut. 7:9),
righteous in judgment,
marvelous in might and majesty,
wise in creating,
understanding in establishing what exists,
good toward what is visible, and
kind to those who put their trust in thee,
merciful and compassionate (Joel 4:13; Sir. 2:14).
Forgive us our lawlessness and unrighteousness,
our transgressions and faults.
Reckon not every sin of thy slaves and maidservants, but
cleanse us with the cleansing of thy truth (cf. Ps. 119:33 [118:33,
  LXX]), and guide our
steps (Ps. 40:1 [39:3, LXX], 119:133 [118:133, LXX]), that we may
  walk in holiness of
heart (1 Kings 9:4) and do what is good
and pleasing before thee (Deut. 6:18; 12:25, 28; 13:19; 21:9) and
  before our rulers.
Yea, Lord, let thy face shine upon us (Ps. 67:1 [66:2, LXX]) in peace
  for our good,
that we may be shielded by thy mighty hand and delivered
from every sin by thy uplifted arm (Deut. 4:34; 5:15, etc.);
and deliver us from those who hate us without a cause.

(1 CLEMENT 59.3-60.3).[18]

Biblical allusions abound in this text. Christian prayer is virtually impregnated with reminiscences drawn especially from the Old Testament.

Christian worship services were without doubt embellished with hymnological compositions. Already Pliny the Younger, in his *Letter to Trajan*, is aware that it was the custom of Christians in their morning worship "to recite by turns a form of words to Christ as a god." Unfortunately it is difficult to determine the precise content of this hymn.

In any case, hymns directed toward the glorification of the work of Christ had to have been composed from very early on in the Church's history. We need look no further than John's Revelation in the New Testament itself (cf. Rev. 4:8, 11; 5:9-10, 12, 13; 15:3-4; etc.), but we will further quote an extract from the *Odes of Solomon*, dating probably from the beginning of the second century and originating in eastern Syria:

> *Sheol saw me and was shattered,*
>
> *And Death ejected me and many with me.*
>
> *I have been vinegar and bitterness to it,*
>
> *And I went down with it as far as its depth.*
>
> *Then the feet and the head it released,*
>
> *Because it was not able to endure my face.*
>
> *And I made a congregation of living among his dead;*
>
> *And I spoke with them by living lips;*
>
> *In order that my word may not be unprofitable.*
>
> (ODES OF SOL. 42)[19]

At the beginning of the third century, Clement of Alexandria provides us as well with a hymn composed in honor of Christ:

> *Bridle, mastering unbroken foals,*
>
> *Wing of the never-wearied bird,*
>
> *Steady rudder of ships at sea,*
>
> *Shepherd of the King's own flock:*
>
> *Call your children together,*
>
> *Bid them, in their innocence, sing*
>
> *A song of holy praise,*
>
> *Hymns from the heart;*

91

Let them chant melodies from pure lips
To Christ, their leader and their guide.

You reign over the saints,
Conqueror of the world,
Word and Son of the Most High God, the heavenly Father,
Citadel of Wisdom,
Sure comforter of all who suffer,
Eternal Joy of the ages,
Jesus, you are the Savior of our mortal race.
Shepherd and laborer,
Rudder and bridle,
Wing, bearing aloft to the heavens a sanctified flock;
Fisher of those men and women
Who have not been swallowed up in an ocean of wickedness,
Unsullied fish drawn by the sweet bait of life out of the violent
tempest.
O Holy Shepherd of the lambs of the Word,
Be their guide, O King of innocent children,
Christ, they wind their way toward heaven,
Walking in your footsteps...[20]

Clearly in this hymn, biblical titles of Christ are found combined with titles drawn from Clement's Greek cultural background.

We would love to know the role that the Psalms of the Old Testament played in the worship of earliest Christian communities, but unfortunately the evidence is quite patchy. From the beginning, Christians undoubtedly continued this synagogal practice as well; the frequent use of the Psalms in patristic exegesis of the second century confirms this hypothesis.

Even our knowledge of the liturgical use of the Lord's Prayer in the second century is limited. The *Didache* categorically prescribes its use: "Pray in this manner three times a day" (8.3). This text appears to connect up with the Jewish tradition of prayer three times a day, the Lord's Prayer replacing, for Christians, the Jewish *Shema* and *Tefillah*. But can we positively affirm that the Lord's Prayer was regularly used in worship on the Lord's Day? Numerous allusions in the earliest commentaries on the Lord's Prayer, those of Tertullian and Origen, leave us supposing that it came to enjoy an established place in the Lord's Day liturgy in this period.

The Eucharist. Returning once again to Justin's description of worship on the Lord's Day in his *Apology* addressed to Antoninus Pius, we find a description of the Eucharist:

> Then bread and a chalice containing wine mixed with water are presented to the one presiding over the brethren. He takes them and offers praise and glory to the Father of all, through the name of the Son and of the Holy Spirit, and he recites lengthy prayers of thanksgiving to God in the name of those to whom He granted such favors. At the end of these prayers and thanksgivings, all present express their approval by saying "Amen." This Hebrew word, "Amen," means "So be it." And when he who presides has celebrated the Eucharist, they whom we call deacons permit each one present to partake of the Eucharistic bread, and wine and water; and they carry it also to the absentees.
>
> We call this food the Eucharist, of which only he can partake who has acknowledged the truth of our teachings, who has been cleansed by baptism for the remission of his sins and for his regeneration, and who regulates his life upon the principles laid down by Christ. Not as ordinary bread or as ordinary drink do we partake of them, but just as, through the word of God, our Savior Jesus Christ became Incarnate and took upon Himself flesh and blood for our salvation, so, we have been taught, the food which has been made the Eucharist by the prayer of His word, and which nourishes our flesh and blood by assimilation, is both the flesh and blood of that Jesus who was made flesh. The Apostles in their memoirs, which are called Gospels, have handed down what Jesus ordered them to do; that He took bread and, after giving thanks, said: "Do this in remembrance of Me; this is My body" (Matt. 26:26-28 and par.). In like manner, He took also the chalice, gave thanks, and said: "This is my My blood" (Matt. 26:26-27 and par.); and to them only did He give it. (*1 Apol.* 65-66).[21]

Clearly the Eucharist is the central part of Christian worship, being directly based on an institution of Christ and serving as the Testament of the Lord which the Church has re-actualized throughout its history. But we must try to observe to what extent early Christians understood this Eucharist, or "thanksgiving," of the Church, as standing within the tradition of Israel, the people of God. The first eucharistic prayers (anaphoras) provide us with ample evidence. We have a premier illustration of this process in the *Didache*:

Regarding the Eucharist. Give thanks as follows: First, concerning the cup: "We give Thee thanks, O Father, for the Holy Vine (cf. John 15:1) of David Thy servant, which Thou hast made known to us through Jesus, thy Servant (cf. Acts 3:13). To Thee be glory for evermore." Next, concerning the broken bread: "We give Thee thanks, Our Father, for the life and knowledge which Thou hast made known to us through Jesus, Thy Servant. To thee be the glory for evermore. As this broken bread was scattered over the hills and then, when gathered, became our mass, so may Thy Church be gathered from the ends of the earth into Thy Kingdom. For Thine is the glory and the power through Jesus Christ for evermore." Let no one eat and drink of the Eucharist but those baptized in the name of the Lord; to this, too, the saying of the Lord is applicable: "Do not give to dogs what is sacred" (Matt. 7:6).

After you have taken your fill of food, give thanks as follows: "We give thanks, O Holy Father, for Thy holy name which Thou hast enshrined in our hearts, and for the knowledge and faith and immortality which Thou hast made known to us through Jesus, Thy Servant. To Thee be the glory for evermore. Thou, Lord Almighty, 'hast created all things' (cf. Wisd. 1:14; Sir. 18:1; Rev. 4:11) for the sake of Thy name and hast given food and drink for men to enjoy, that they may give Thanks to Thee; but to us Thou hast vouchsafed spiritual food and drink and eternal life through [Jesus] Thy Servant. Above all, we give Thee thanks because Thou art mighty. To thee be the glory for evermore. Remember, O Lord, Thy Church: deliver her from all evil, perfect her in Thy love, and 'from the four winds assemble' her (cf. Matt. 24:31), the sanctified, in Thy kingdom which Thou hast prepared for her. For Thine is the power and the glory for evermore. May Grace come, and this world pass away! 'Hosanna to the God of David' (Matt. 21:9, 15; 22:42-45)! If anyone is holy, let him advance; if anyone is not, let him be converted. Maranatha! Amen." (*Didache* 9-10).[22]

It is a fact that these prayers very closely followed Jewish prayers pronounced at the table. The biblical reminiscences are clearly numerous. It might seem surprising that Jesus's words of institution for the Eucharist are not mentioned, but it would be a mistake to use this as an argument *e silentio* in order to claim that they were not pronounced. We need go no further than the text from Justin quoted above: in chapter 65 he does not mention this part of the liturgy, but then in chapter 66 clearly alludes to it.

We cannot help but be impressed by the emphatic eschatological character of the eucharistic prayers in the *Didache*. It is truly significant that the gathered Christian community experienced the living presence of its Lord and quite naturally and fervently anticipated the full achievement of communion with him.

We should also note that the Eucharist was for the first time called a "sacrifice" in the *Didache*:

> On the Lord's Day, assemble in common to break bread and offer thanks; but first confess your sins, so that your sacrifice may be pure. However, no one quarreling with his brother may join your meeting until they are reconciled; your sacrifice must not be defiled. For here we have the saying of the Lord: "In every place and time offer me a pure sacrifice; for I am a mighty King, says the Lord; and my name spreads terror among the nations (Mal. 1:11, 14). (*Didache* 14).[23]

At the beginning of the third century, an entire eucharistic liturgy is preserved for us in the *Apostolic Tradition* of Hippolytus. Since one of the new eucharistic prayers of the Roman Mass, after the liturgical reforms of Vatican II, is directly connected with this liturgy, we will quote the text here in full:

> Let the deacons present the offering to the bishop. When he lays his hands upon it, with all the presbyters, let him say the thanksgiving. "The Lord be with you." And the people shall say: "And with thy spirit." [And the bishop shall say:] "Lift up your hearts." [And the people shall say:] "We have them with the Lord." [And the bishop shall say:] "Let us give thanks unto the Lord." [And the people shall say:] "It is meet and right." Let him continue thus: "We give thanks to you, O God, through your beloved Servant Jesus Christ, whom in the last times you sent to us as a Savior and Redeemer, and Messenger of your will; who is your inseparable Word, through whom you made all things and in whom you were well pleased; whom you sent from heaven into the virgin's womb and who was conceived within her and was made flesh and demonstrated to be your Son being born of Holy Spirit and a virgin; who fulfilling your will and preparing for you a holy people stretched forth his hands for suffering that he might release from sufferings them who have believed in you; who when he was betrayed to voluntary suffering that he might abolish death and rend the bonds of the devil and tread down hell and enlighten the righteous and establish the covenant and demonstrate the resurrection: Taking he offered thanks to you and said, "Take eat; this is my body which is broken for you." Likewise also the cup, saying, "This is my blood which is shed for you. When you do this, make my memorial (*anamnêsis*)." Remembering therefore his death and resurrection we offer to you the bread and the cup giving thanks to you because you made us worthy to stand before you and minister to you. And we pray that you would send your Holy Spirit upon the offering of your holy church, that you would grant to all who partake of your holy [mysteries] to be united that they may be filled with the Holy Spirit for the confirmation of faith in truth. That we may praise and glorify you through your Servant Jesus Christ through whom glory and honor be to

you with the Holy Spirit in your holy church now and for ever world without end. Amen. (*Apostolic Tradition* 4).[24]

Since we are unable to give a detailed analysis of this text here, it will suffice to emphasize its "anamnetic" character. The text epitomizes the entire history of salvation from creation to the advent of Christ, then recalls the saving work of Christ and the institution of the Eucharist, and finally ends with the invocation (*epiclêsis*) of the Holy Spirit over the elements and over the community of the faithful. This liturgy recalls very nearly everything that we discussed, in the first section of this study, which was devoted to teaching, on the interpretation of the Old Testament in a christological and salvation-historical sense, and on the confession of faith as the hermeneutical center of the New Testament. We noted earlier our impression that teaching in the earliest Christian communities was nourished by the lived experience of the liturgy. *Lex orandi* is the very matrix of *lex credendi*! The eucharistic liturgy in the *Apostolic Tradition* was destined to serve as a model for later liturgies of the Mass in Western and Eastern churches alike.[25]

The Collection. The last element of early Christian worship on the Lord's Day mentioned by Justin is the collection:

> The wealthy, if they wish, contribute whatever they desire, and the collection is placed in the custody of the president. [With it] he helps the orphans and widows, those who are needy because of sickness or any other reason, and the captives and strangers in our midst; in short, he takes care of all those in need. (*1 Apol.* 67).[26]

Tertullian describes the practice in nearly identical terms in his *Apology*:

> Even if there is some kind of treasury, it is not accumulated from a high initiation fee as if religion were something bought and paid for. Each man deposits a small amount on a certain day of the month or whenever he wishes, and only on condition that he is willing and able to do so. No one is forced; each makes his contribution voluntarily. These are, so to speak, deposits of piety. The money therefrom is spent not for banquets or drinking parties or good-for-nothing eating houses, but for the support and burial of the poor, for children who are without their parents and means of subsistence, for aged men who are confined to the house; likewise, for shipwrecked sailors, and for any in the mines, on islands or in prisons. Provided only it be for the sake of fellowship with God, they become entitled to loving and protective care for their confession. (*Apol.* 39.5-6).[27]

We need not emphasize that the practice of the "diaconate" was already a well-established biblical tradition (cf., for example, Deut. 14:28-29; 15:1-11; 16:11-14; 24:14-22; 26:12-15). Liturgical and social life are intrinsically linked both in Judaism and in Christianity. The subject is treated well in a 1968 monograph of Fr. A. G. Hamman.[28] The agape meal, a meal offered to poor brothers and sisters, as well as gifts offered to the clergy (first-fruits, the tithe) were also set within the same framework.

Annual Feasts

In the early centuries of the Church's history, there were only two kinds of annual feasts, the Paschal feast and the annual commemorations of the martyrs. Here we want to examine both forms of annual feasts within our own perspective, hoping to be able to discern the Bible's impact on their origin and development.

The Paschal Feast. Jesus died and was resurrected during the Jewish Passover. In annually commemorating the events foundational to their faith, Christians began to remember as well the framework in which those events had unfolded. The earliest Christian communities first commemorated the death and resurrection of Christ precisely when Jews were celebrating their Passover, namely, in the fourteenth day of Nisan, the first month in the Jewish calendar, which fairly nearly corresponds to our month of March. This primitive Christian practice of celebrating Easter on the fourteenth of Nisan came to be known as the Quartodeciman ("from the fourteenth day") usage. Such was the ordinary practice in Palestine and Asia Minor up until the fourth century. At the end of the second century, Pope Victor attempted to impose on all churches the more recent Western practice of celebrating Easter on the Sunday following 14 Nisan, but was unsuccessful. Not until the Council of Nicea in 325 was the rule formulated for fixing the date of Easter which has remained in effect to this day, placing it on the first Sunday after the full moon which follows the vernal equinox.[29]

According to the Johannine chronology of the Passion, Jesus died precisely when the Paschal lambs were killed (John 19:14, 31ff). The apostle Paul himself compares Christ with the Paschal lamb: "Clean out the old yeast so that you may be a new batch, as you really are unleavened. For our Paschal lamb, Christ, has been sacrificed. Therefore, let us celebrate the festival, not with the old yeast, the yeast of malice and evil, but with the unleavened bread of sincerity and truth" (1 Cor. 5:7-8, NRSV). This is

97

essentially the perspective in which the death and resurrection of Jesus are celebrated during the Paschal feast. Let us quote once more from Melito of Sardis's *Homily on the Pascha*, which is itself based in the Quartodeciman tradition in Asia Minor:

> *For, himself led as a lamb*
> *and slain as a sheep,*
> *he ransomed us from the world's service*
> *as from the land of Egypt,*
> *and freed us from the devil's slavery*
> *as from the hand of Pharaoh;*
> *and he marked our souls with his own Spirit*
> *and the members of our body with his own blood.*
> *It is he that clouded death with shame*
> *and stood the devil in grief*
> *as Moses did Pharaoh.*
> *It is he that struck down crime*
> *and made injustice childless*
> *as Moses did Egypt.*
> *It is he that delivered us from slavery to liberty,*
> *from darkness to light,*
> *from death to life,*
> *from tyranny to eternal royalty...*
> *It is he that was enfleshed in a virgin,*
> *that was hanged on a tree,*
> *that was buried in the earth,*
> *that was raised from the dead,*
> *that was taken up to the heights of the heavens.*
> *He is the lamb being slain;*
> *he is the lamb that is speechless;*
> *he is the one born from Mary the lovely ewe-lamb;*
> *he is the one "taken from the flock" (cf. Ex. 12:5; 1 Sam. 17:34),*
> *and dragged "to slaughter" (cf. Isa. 53:7),*

and sacrificed "at evening" (cf. Ex. 12:6),

and buried "at night" (cf. Ex. 12:8, 10),

who on the tree was "not broken" (cf. Ex. 12:10),

in the earth was not dissolved,

arose from the dead,

and raised up man from the grave below.

(HOM. ON THE PASCHA 67-69, 70-71).[30]

Other fragments from Melito reveal the importance of the typology of Abraham's sacrifice (Gen. 22:1-19) in second-century Christian theology:

On behalf of Isaac the righteous one, a ram appeared for slaughter,

so that Isaac might be released from bonds.

That ram, slain, ransomed Isaac;

so also the Lord, slain, saved us,

and bound, released us,

and sacrificed, ransomed us.

And a little further on:

For the Lord was a lamb like the "ram"

which "Abraham saw caught in a Sabek-tree" (Gen. 22:13).

But the tree displayed the cross,

and that place, Jerusalem,

and the lamb, the Lord fettered for slaughter.

(MELITO, FRAGMENTS 10-11).[31]

Another inheritance from Judaism is likewise emphasized in the Christian Paschal feast: like the Jews awaiting the Messiah during Passover night, Christians await the return of their Lord.

The precise evolution of the Paschal feast is difficult to determine. According to Melito's *Homily on the Pascha* and other sources, it seems that the chapter in the Bible on the Exodus of the people of God had been read, then the preacher had given a christological interpretation of the events of the story, and that Christians had fasted while pondering the obdurate Jewish people; at dawn (precisely, then, at the beginning of the Jewish "abstention" from the unleavened bread!), Christians were, on the contrary, devoting themselves to the exultation of the resurrection by celebrating the Eucharist.

The Paschal rites basically did not change from the original practice of celebrating the Pascha during the night from Saturday to Sunday. Ultimately, the pre-Paschal fast was prolonged, as was the time of the Paschal celebration. The full term of the Paschal feast is the fifty-day period between Easter and Pentecost. The Paschal vigil became the preferred time for administering baptism in the Church.

The Annual Commemorations of the Martyrs. Very soon within the history of the early Church, Christians began associating the martyrs, those who had died for their love of Christ, with the glory of their resurrected Lord. Indeed, the martyrs came to be known as "witnesses" to the truth of the Christian hope in and through their suffering,. The story of their martyrdom was composed and subsequently read on the anniversary day of their death, the day of their triumph and birth into eternal life. We see this attested in the *Martyrdom of Polycarp*:

> Accordingly, we later took up his bones, more precious than costly stones and finer than gold, and deposited them in a suitable place. And there, in so far as it is possible, the Lord will grant that we come together with joy and gladness and celebrate the birthday of his martyrdom both in memory of those who have contended in former times and for the exercise and training of those who will do so in the future (*Martyrdom of Polycarp* 18.2-3).[32]

Biblical influence is immediately in evidence in the martyrological literature. The martyr is considered here to be an imitator of Christ who has the privilege to suffer like his Master. Once again the *Martyrdom of Polycarp* is exemplary in this regard, with its depiction of the bishop's execution:

> They did not nail him, but set about binding him. Now when he had put his hands behind him and had been bound, like a splendid ram from a great flock (ready) for sacrifice, prepared as a burnt offering (cf. Lev. 6:1-7; 16:5) acceptable unto God, he looked up to heaven and said: "Lord God Almighty (Rev. 4:8; 11:17; 15:3; 16:7; 21:22), Father of your beloved (Isa. 42:1; Matt. 12:18; cf. 3:17) and blessed Son, Jesus Christ through whom we have received knowledge of you, God of angels, and powers, and every created thing (cf. Ps. 59:5 [58:6, LXX]; Jud. 9:12, 14) and all the race of the just who dwell before you, I bless you because you have considered me worthy of this day and hour, to receive a portion among the number of the martyrs, in the cup (cf. John 18:11; Mark 10:38)

of your Christ unto the resurrection of eternal life (John 5:29) both of soul and body in the incorruption of the Holy Spirit, among whom I may be received today as a rich and acceptable sacrifice (cf. Phil. 4:18), just as you have prepared beforehand, and revealed beforehand, and fulfilled, O undeceiving and true God. For this reason and for all these things I praise you, I bless you, I glorify you, through the eternal and heavenly high priest Jesus Christ (cf. Heb. 5:10; 6:20; 7:26; 8:1; 9:11), your beloved Son (Isa. 42:1; Matt. 12:18), through whom to you with him and the Holy Spirit be glory now and forever. Amen. (*Martyrdom of Polycarp* 14.1-3).[33]

Concluding this general survey of the function of the Bible in the liturgy of the early Christian communities compels us to confirm that the Bible was omnipresent in the life of Christian believers. It accompanied them from the moment of their preparation for baptism; they encountered it every Sunday through preaching and the liturgy; and it was recalled for them at every annual feast. The Christian Bible, being ultimately composed of the Old and New Testaments, attested the permanent Covenant ratified by God with humanity in Jesus Christ. It was literally the source of faith, love, and hope for early Christians, and has remained so through the course of the Church's history.

Notes

1. Trans. T. B. Falls, *Writings of Justin Martyr*, Fathers of the Church, vol. 6 (Washington, 1965), 163.
2. Trans. Falls, 163-164.
3. Trans. Falls, 295-296.
4. See the critical edition of the full Greek text, with English trans. by S. G. Hall, *Melito of Sardis: On Pascha and Fragments*, Oxford Early Christian Texts (Oxford, 1979).
5. Trans. Hall, 5.
6. Trans. Hall, 19.
7. Trans. Hall, 21.
8. Trans. Hall, 31, 33.
9. See, in this volume, A. le Boulluec, "The Bible in Use among the Marginally Orthodox," 197-216.
10. Trans. A. Roberts and J. Donaldson, ANF 1 (reprint ed., Grand Rapids, 1975), 428.
11. Trans. Roberts and Donaldson, 417.
12. Trans. J. Smith, *St. Irenaeus: Proof of the Apostolic Preaching*, Ancient Christian Writers, vol. 16 (New York and Ramsey, N. J., 1952), 51.
13. Trans. J. A. Kleist, *The Didache* (et al.), Ancient Christian Writers, vol. 6 (Mahwah, N. J., 1948), 15-17.

14. See P. Lundberg, *La typologie baptismale dans l'ancienne Église* (Leipzig-Uppsala, 1942); also J. Daniélou, *The Bible and the Liturgy* (Notre Dame, Ind., 1956), 70-113.
15. Trans. Falls, 106-107.
16. Cf. the testimony of Dionysius of Corinth, *ap.* Eusebius of Caesarea's *Ecclesiastical History* 4.23.11.
17. Trans. H. H. Graham, *The Apostolic Fathers: A New Translation and Commentary* (New York, 1965), vol. 2, 115-116.
18. Trans. Graham, ibid., 93-95.
19. Trans. J. Charlesworth, *The Odes of Solomon: The Syriac Texts*, SBL Texts and Translations 13, Pseudepigrapha Series 7 (Missoula, Mont., 1977), 145.
20. *Paedagogus*, Bk. 3, appendix, trans. A. Cunningham, in *Prayer: Personal and Liturgical*, Message of the Fathers of the Church 16 (Wilmington, Del., 1985), 68-69.
21. Trans. Falls, 105-106.
22. Trans. Kleist, 20-21.
23. Trans. Kleist, 23-24. The quoted text from Mal. 1:11 and 14 would come to play a prominent role in Christian tradition.
24. Trans. E. Ferguson, in *Early Christians Speak: Faith and Life in the First Three Centuries*, revised ed. (Abilene, Texas, 1981), 94-95. This is essentially a revision of the translation by G. Dix, *The Apostolic Tradition of St. Hippolytus* (New York, 1937), 7-9.
25. We would add that the *Apostolic Tradition* mentions the eucharistic liturgy within the framework of episcopal ordination, which itself also took place on Sundays. We cannot comment further on this here, other than to say that this eucharistic prayer, which is so profoundly biblical, became a model for the new liturgy of episcopal ordination after Vatican II.
26. Trans. Falls, 107.
27. Trans. E. J. Daly, *Tertullian: Apologetical Works*, Fathers of the Church, vol. 10 (New York, 1950), 98.
28. See A. G. Hamman, *Vie liturgique et vie sociale* (Paris, 1968).
29. Unfortunately, calendar reforms have split this ecumenical unity in dating Easter. There have been ongoing consultations among the churches for determining a fixed date for the celebration of the Paschal feast.
30. Trans. Hall, 35-37, 37-39.
31. Trans. Hall, 77.
32. Trans. W. R. Schoedel, *The Apostolic Fathers: A New Translation and Commentary* (Camden, N. J., 1967), vol. 5, 75-76.
33. Trans. Schoedel, 69-71. (Schoedel, in the notes to his translation, provides an even more complete listing of the biblical references and allusions in this passage).

PART II

The Bible in Use among the
Greek Church Fathers

5

Irenaeus's Reading of the Bible

MAURICE JOURJON

Anyone who reads Irenaeus even occasionally or superficially cannot deny the importance of Holy Scripture for the great second-century bishop of Lyons. All the reader need do is glance over page after page of his massive treatise *Against Heresies* to discover that each of its five books contains passages on Scripture which are of tremendous importance, and which have for centuries animated the life of the churches and provided a foundation and exemplary models for exegesis, hermeneutics, and biblical theology.[1]

The first book of Irenaeus's treatise accordingly presents us with a program of biblical studies that could very well be entitled "On Theology as the Science of the Scriptures."[2] The second book gives us what was destined to become the great hermeneutical principle of Greek (Antiochene as well as Alexandrian) and Latin patristic interpretation.[3] The third book enlightens us on the Old Testament in the Septuagint version and on the New Testament with its fourfold Gospel.[4] Irenaeus's fourth book teaches us which reading of Scripture calls for the pedagogy of God,[5] while his fifth book places the Church's message in relation to Scripture and the Word of God, in a manner not unworthy of an ecumenical council of the twentieth century.[6]

If this outline is accurate, it can undoubtedly provide a helpful method for analyzing Irenaeus and his use of the Bible: first, because quite often it suffices simply to read Irenaeus in order to understand him, and one must surely benefit from reading his work in the critical edition available in the "Sources chrétiennes" collection[7]; second, because the modern commentator, desiring perhaps to set in order this collection of testimonies on Scripture in the *Against Heresies,* risks doing so in fidelity to theological conventions of which Irenaeus himself was unaware; and finally, because if these Irenaean sequences deserve to be read and reread in their own right, they lose nothing (far from it!) by remaining rooted within their native context.

A Program of Biblical Theology
(Against Heresies 1.10.3)[8]

Irenaeus estimates in this section of his great treatise that the study of Scripture, which reveals the plan of God, amply suffices for Christian research and renders completely useless the deceitful Gnostics' fatuous speculations about another God or another Christ. He paints a truly grandiose picture of the work that has to be done on the contents of the Bible. We discover again here the importance that Irenaeus frequently attaches to "bringing out more fully the meaning of what was spoken in parables," recalling in the same connection the "activity and plan of God on behalf of humankind." Significant Pauline and Johannine influences are represented, for example, when he speaks of the prerogative of intelligent Christians, in probing the mysteries of the faith,

> to search out why God "consigned all things to disobedience in order to have mercy on all" (Rom. 11:32); and to make known with thanksgiving why "the Word" of God "was made flesh" (John 1:14) and suffered his Passion.

Such a statement demonstrates quite well that Irenaeus did not simply select what he wanted in the Bible. In spite of the indisputable presence in his work of biblical florilegia,[9] and considering even his preference from his Christian childhood for the Beloved Disciple, author of the fourth Gospel under whom his fellow bishop Polycarp had allegedly studied, it is Scripture in its entirety—conserved without forgery, a complete account of the truth, admitting no addition or subtraction[10]—which for Irenaeus prompts the Apostle's cry of adoring admiration, "O the depth of the riches and wisdom and knowledge of God" (Rom. 11:33).

Scripture is Spiritual Throughout
(Against Heresies 2.28.3)[11]

Why this choice of the whole Bible as "spiritual"? Irenaeus, incidentally, recalls this choice in the second book of *Against Heresies*—and for once we have his Greek text! "These Scriptures which are spiritual throughout..."

They are completely spiritual in the sense certainly that they are authored by the Holy Spirit through human agents. The *Epideixis* (or *Proof of the Apostolic Preaching*) affirms that the Spirit is the one "through whom the prophets prophesied and the patriarchs were taught about God."[12] Likewise it is the Spirit, according to the same passage in the *Epideixis,* who guides the righteous and who, having now been poured forth in a new way on our humanity, renews humanity on the whole earth before God. Since the Author of the Scriptures is also the Creator of the new heart, it can be said that inspired Scripture becomes inspiring in the human heart. Composed by the Spirit, Scripture must be understood spiritually in order for the dead letter to be transcended. "Therefore if someone reads the Scriptures in this way, he will discover there a word about Christ and a foreshadowing of the new vocation."[13] And finally Scripture is spiritual in the sense that, through the Spirit, it extends beyond itself. Thus the faith of the Gentiles is "nobler because they followed the Word of God without the instruction of the Scriptures."[14] So too the barbarian peoples possess "the salvation written without pen or ink by the Spirit on their hearts."[15] We say: the Bible, Book par excellence, but Scripture is no more a book than the Decalogue is a stone. It is in the heart that God writes: the "Fathers were righteous who had the virtue of the Decalogue inscribed in their hearts and in their souls, seeing as they loved the God who created them and abstained from any injustice toward their neighbor; they did not need a Scripture to admonish them, since they possessed within themselves the righteousness of the law."[16]

Old and New Testament: Septuagint and Gospel (Against Heresies 3.1.1; 3.11.7-8; 3.21.1-3)[17]

Book 3 of Irenaeus's treatise *Against Heresies* is a basic testimony concerning Scripture that Christ has fulfilled (the Old Testament) and Scripture which emanates from him via the apostles (the New Testament). Yet in order to use the two terms that Irenaeus himself knows and appreciates, we should say that his testimony relates to the Septuagint annunciating Jesus the Messiah and to the four gospels, written text of the Good News of Jesus.

It is undeniable from the outset that for Irenaeus, the Scripture of the Church is the Old Testament in its Septuagint recension. The manner in which he takes up the legend of Aristeas plainly indicates that for him, as a catholic bishop, the Scriptures "by which God prepared and fashioned in advance our faith in his Son" were in the Septuagint version "truly divine" and "translated under divine inspiration." Between Justin before him and Origen after, Irenaeus is an irrefutable representative of the Great Church's belief in reading the messianic identity of Jesus, and particularly the prophecy of the Virgin Mother, into the text, which perfectly reflects the plan of God and which is "in accordance with the tradition of the apostles."

This Scripture, on which Jesus relied precisely in order to fulfill it, finds its flowering, as it were, in the Church, thanks to the apostles. Certainly it cannot be duplicated in a second edition, but, transfigured in Christ, it confers its title of inspired Scripture on the written register of the Good News of salvation: "First they [the apostles] preached this Gospel; then, by the will of God, they handed it down to us in the Scriptures to be the ground and pillar of our faith."

It would be useless here to dwell on Irenaeus's magisterial account of the formation of the four gospels beginning with the preaching of the one Gospel. Neither the weight nor the tumultuousness of history can ultimately contradict the basic affirmation that we have come to know the economy of our salvation through the very ones who handed down to us as Scripture the Gospel which at first they preached orally. When, during his discourse, Irenaeus confirms that the one Gospel of the Lord Jesus was recorded four times and by four different writers, he establishes—with arguments which captured the Christian audience of his own time, but were purposed for Christian conviction in all times—that this necessary plurality constituted a plenitude, rather than a dividing up, of the evangelical truth. "The Word, Artificer of the universe...gave us one Gospel in quadruple form...maintained by one Spirit."

The Mind of Holy Scripture
(Against Heresies 4.14.3)[18]

And yet the Gospel is by no means the ultimate fulfillment of an imperfect body of Scripture, for which reason the "Old" in Old Testament must be qualified so as not to mean "obsolete." God's pedagogy does not intend to lead us from the Old Testament to the New but, through the unity of the writings of the Old Covenant and the New, toward the definitive truth of heaven and the Kingdom. Thus no Scripture is to be rejected, but neither is any of it to be idolized any more. God leads us "through secondary things to the things of prime importance, that is, through figurative things to realities, through carnal things to spiritual, through earthly things to heavenly."

This spirit or mind of Scripture makes for quite a typological and anagogical project—Origen would certainly approve of it!—and indeed, the discourse that follows this notice of Irenaeus's essential hermeneutical intention is quite daring in this respect. Reading carefully through his discourse, Scripture is understood to be above all Word *and Spirit,* and, since it consists of prophecy, it is fulfilled in acts that the Church performs, for the Spirit inspires the Church to carry out its acts on the basis of the Word of the Lord. A classic example of this is the Eucharistic oblation, in which the prophecy of Malachi (1:10-11) is fulfilled,[19] in which also the Lord's order is carried out, and in which is impressed, at last, the distinctive mark of the freedom God expects of his children.[20] For that matter, Marcion's sorting out of choice works for his canon and Tatian's harmonization of the gospels are not merely rude manipulations of the sacred writings; each in its own way is an attempt aimed at the unity of God and his comprehensive plan, that of the Gospel in its fullness. On the contrary, if "someone reads the Scriptures in the way...that the Lord explained them to his disciples after his resurrection...he will be a perfect disciple 'like the master of the house who extracted from his treasure new things and old' (Matt. 13:52)."[21]

The Message of the Church, Scripture, Word of God (Against Heresies 5, Preface)[22]

But when the Christian, the true gnostic and by no means a fraud,[23] thus draws old things and new from his or her treasure,[24] through the work of the cross of Christ, what exactly is the Christian's deeper reference point? Scripture? The tradition of the apostles? The messsage of the Church in his or her own time? We know that Irenaeus did not oppose these authorities, but connected them all together without inhibiting the issue with the human emotion that we attach to it today, and without imposing a solemn dogmatism. It is this living link between Scripture, tradition, and proclamation that enables the Church's preaching to be conformed to Scripture in organic fidelity to the apostles, in a web not woven by human hands but by "the one steadfast and truthful Teacher, the Word of God."

In the preface to Book 5 of his treatise, Irenaeus repeats this point in a serene and assured manner. The prophets have announced the message. Christ brought it to perfection. The apostles transmitted it. The Church receives, protects, and communicates it. Once more, it is a matter of choosing the whole and, in order to receive the Son of God who sows himself throughout the Scriptures,[25] listening to the Church where the apostles speak. Only the plow of the cross can turn up the field of the Scriptures where the secret of the Kingdom lies (cf. Matt. 13:44).[26] Already innumerable hands have grasped in their turn this witness of wood, and the Church's attention has always been directed toward the front of the furrow.[27] But the one sure and truthful Teacher is not the one who has been appointed for the ministry of the word in the Church, nor even the sacred text which continues to endure in the Church, but the One who prevents that text from remaining a dead letter, "the Word of God, Jesus Christ our Lord, who, on account of his superabundant love, became what we are in order to make us what he is."

Such is Irenaeus's reading of the Bible, one sufficient for his understanding of the apostolic preaching as the projection of a scenario, in the history of salvation, of the fulfilment of Scripture considered as perfect prophecy of the incarnation of the Word. The apostles' preaching has no other support than the Scriptures which announce the New Covenant, and no other goal than to affirm that that Covenant has been accomplished in Jesus "in his blood," that it has been sealed in the baptismal faith and expeditiously set to Scripture in the writings of the New Testament.[28]

But if, by way of conclusion, we must present, as in a sort of thesis—but utilizing Irenaeus's own words—what the bishop of Lyons thinks of Scripture, we would say this: since all of Scripture is spiritual, it is necessary to take precise account of it in order to read it in the manner of Christ and to proclaim, teach, and transmit the faith[29] just as the apostles do so, namely, in conformity with the Scriptures.[30]

NOTES

1. On Irenaeus's use of the Bible, see also the earlier studies of A. Benoît, *Saint Irénée: introduction à l'étude de sa théologie* (Paris, 1960), 74-102 ("Irénée et l'Ancien Testament"), 103-147 ("Irénée et les écrits néo-testamentaires"); B. Sesboüé, "La preuve par les Écritures chez saint Irénée: a propos d'un texte difficile du Livre III de l'*Adversus Haereses*," *Nouvelle revue théologique* 103 (1981): 872-887; D. Farkasfalvy, "Theology of Scripture in St. Irenaeus," *Revue Bénédictine* 78 (1968): 319-333; J. Lawson, *The Biblical Theology of Irenaeus* (London, 1948).

2. *Adversus haereses* 1.10.3 (SC 264: 160-165).
3. Ibid., 2.28.3 (SC 294: 274-275).
4. Ibid., 3.1.1; 3.11.7-8 (SC 211: 20-25, 158-171, 398-409.
5. Ibid., 4.14.3 (SC 100: 546-547).
6. Ibid., 5, Pref. (SC 153: 10-15).
7. All references to Irenaeus in this essay are to the multi-volumed critical edition of *Adversus Haereses* in this series.
8. SC 264:160-165.
9. See A. Benoît, "Irenaeus *Adversus Haereses* 4, 17, 1-5 et les Testimonia," *Studia Patristica* 4 (Berlin, 1961), 20-27.
10. *Adv. haer.* 4.33.8 (SC 100: 820-821).
11. SC 294: 274-275.
12. *Epideixis* 6, trans. J. Smith, *St. Irenaeus: Proof of the Apostolic Preaching,* Ancient Christian Writers 16 (Ramsey, N.J., 1952), 51.
13. *Adv. haer.* 4.26.1 (SC 100: 712-713).
14. Ibid. 4.24.2 (SC 100: 704-705).
15. Ibid. 3.4.2 (SC 211: 46-47).
16. Ibid. 4.16.3 (SC 100: 564-567).
17. SC 211: 20-25; 158-171; 398-409.
18. SC 100: 546-547.
19. *Adv. haer.* 4.17.5 (SC 100: 592-593).
20. See also ibid. 4.13.2 (SC 100: 528-529); 4.13.4 (534-537); 4.16.5 (572-573); 4.18.2 (598-599).
21. Ibid. 4.26.1 (SC 100: 716-717).
22. SC 153: 10-15.
23. See in this sense *Adv. haer.* 4.33.1-10 (SC 100: 802-825).
24. Ibid. 4.26.1 (SC 100: 714-717).
25. Ibid. 4.10.1 (SC 100: 492-493).
26. See again ibid. 4.26.1 (SC 100: 714-717).
27. See, in this connection, M. Jourjon, "La tradition apostolique chez Irénée," *L'Anée canonique* 23 (1979): 193-202.
28. Yet no reference to Scriptures of the New Covenant appears here—nor was it necessary; such is the sense of Irenaeus's *Epideixis*. The terminology of a "New Testament" appears in earnest beginning with Clement of Alexandria. Cf. C. Mondésert, *Clément d'Alexandrie: Introduction à l'étude de sa pensée religieuse à partir de l'Écriture* (Paris, 1944), 65ff; H. von Campenhausen, *The Formation of the Christian Bible* (London and New York, 1972), 293ff.
29. *Adv. haer.* 1.10.2 (SC 264: 158-159).
30. Several passages from the *Adversus Haereses* are worth citing again in this connection: 2.28.3 (SC 294: 274-275); 4.33.8 (SC 100: 820-821); 4.26.1 (SC 100: 716-717); 4.33.8 (SC 100: 820-821).

6

The Bible and Christian Morality
in Clement of Alexandria

Clement of Alexandria's use of Scripture is remarkable for two reasons.[1]

The first is his use of the New Testament side by side with the Old. The New Testament consists in the writings of the new covenant which is the fulfillment of the old. In Clement there are 700 references to Matthew's Gospel, while John and Luke follow with 400 each. The letters of Paul, in particular 1 Corinthians (400) and Romans (300), are uniformly utilized. 3 John and Philemon are the only New Testament writings that Clement does not quote. This compares favorably with the Old Testament references: 240 for Isaiah, 320 for Proverbs, 300 for the Psalms, 260 for Genesis. Clement's Old Testament references total about 3200, his New Testament references about 5000.

The contrast with Justin, who antedates Clement by at least fifty years, is striking. Justin uses the Old Testament much more than the New, and his allusions to the latter are generally not explicit. We must remember that Justin's most extensive work was a dialogue with Jewish thought (the *Dialogue with Trypho the Jew*), in which case particular importance was obviously attached to the Old Testament. With Irenaeus, the balance already favors the New Testament, but the use of Scripture does not hold the predominant place in his writing that it does in Clement.

The other striking feature in Clement is precisely this dominant role of Scripture in his work.[2] In 992 pages of text and 32 pages of fragments, there are 8000 references or allusions to Scripture. The first impression we get is that Clement is more a compiler than a writer, but what renders this impression specious is the obvious coherence and delicacy with which he uses the quotations. They consequently express a theology of God as Word,[3] which requires theologians to think within Scripture's own purview and to utilize its own categories.

In the case of Clement's moral teaching, the reason for constant quotations of Scripture is clear. Having treated at length the various methods which "the Pedagogue" (Jesus Christ) uses to instruct us, Clement speaks of thousands of precepts that orient us to the good and turn us from evil, "for there is no reward for the impious, says the Lord" (Isa. 57:21; 48:22; *Paedagogus* 1.10.94). To fortify this fact, Clement further quotes three verses from Proverbs and six from Ezekiel. He insists on the various ways in which the precept is expressed and on the teaching method employed by the Word, and he never quotes a verse singly when it is possible to quote more of them. Yet because his theology develops on the basis of one or two central principles, there is a brevity and an order which counterbalances the mass of material that he accumulates.

What does Clement mean by the old and the new Covenant? In one passage, he seems to identify the covenants with the texts that substantiate them. It is faith in the Son of God that is "declared and affirmed by the old and the new Covenant" (*Stromateis* 4.21.134).[4] Clement prefers to explore the Scriptures rather than reduce them to a practical summary. While he still accords the Old Testament an important place, it cannot be said that he desires his readers to understand it foremost.[5] His premier axiom is the unity shared among the Law, the Prophets, and the new Covenant of the incarnate Lord (*Strom.* 6.15.125). For Clement, the true interpretation is none other than the tradition that has been orally transmitted beginning with the Apostles. The argument of the first chapter of his *Stromateis* ("Miscellanies") precludes the concept of a secret tradition that cannot be divulged. Certain things cannot be written down, but they are not hidden. Scripture and Tradition are not mutually exclusive.[6] Teaching has a central role in Christian development. It sows seed and nourishes souls. It provides a connecting link in Christian tradition; it is the messenger of God, and is a father to those whom it instructs.

The great Pedagogue of Clement, like a bee, gathers his honey from flowers in the meadow of Prophets and Apostles in order to produce pure knowledge in the souls of his hearers (*Strom.* 1.1.11). Clement follows the same method as his divine ideal. His use of Scripture shows little interest in the context out of which a verse is drawn; he occasionally quotes long passages and often groups his quotations under themes. His use of Scripture is distinctly theological, since he surmises that in Jesus

Christ all truth has at once been communicated. This one truth of Jesus Christ must be be discovered everywhere that it is hidden. Thousands of verses of Scripture, just like the quotations he draws from other sources, are uprooted from their old context so that they can be situated in the new context of Christ. Clement's theological method aims at recovering unity and truth in Christ by regathering the different elements of the truth: a concern for the unity of the whole body of truth presupposes the appreciation of its parts. Clement often assembles his quotations (as in *Strom.* 2.22) with an aesthetic sensibility that an attentive reader will pick up on. This sense of relations and connections comes from the fact that Clement lives within the Bible as did Origen and, much later, Luther.[7] If Clement is not an exegete in the technical sense,[8] "he was under the profound influence of Scripture and that influence on him is as indisputable as that of Plato."[9] We will verify it by examining texts that Clement uses in his moral teaching.

Philo of Alexandria presents a special case in the background of Clement's work and deserves mention here. His influence on Clement is not in question, but it is difficult to determine its precise nature. Philo had already effected a synthesis of Hellenistic culture and Scripture. Clement was therefore not the first to pursue this course. But a close analysis leads to the conclusion that "if in philosophy, properly speaking (psychology and moral teaching), Clement could have borrowed more from Philo and through Philo from others as well, it must be said that as far as the interpretation of Scripture is concerned, he basically owed him rather little."[10]

A Biblical Morality

Likeness to God

The veritable leitmotif of Clement's moral teaching is assimilation to God, the invitation to pursue God or to imitate Christ. He finds two principal foundations for this theme in Scripture. First, in Genesis, humanity is created in the image and likeness of God.[11] Clement selects this text to indicate that humanity does not yet possess pure likeness to God as the image requires. As well, Moses demands humanity to walk in the way of God and to obey his commandments. There is a beginning, the divine image (*eikôn*), and an end, perfect likeness (*homoiôsis*), and the path of progress in divine assimilation that connects the two.[12]

The eschatology of Paul explains the relation between the beginning and the end and constitutes the second major biblical foundation of

114

Clement's moral teaching. Humanity has a dual hope,[13] one part of which is present or current (Rom. 8:24) and the other part eschatological. Human beings now enjoy a real participation in the end, but their hope is not confused because the love of God has already been poured into their heart (Rom. 5:4-5). Those who have been liberated from sin and become slaves of God must bear fruit for sanctification, and their end or goal is eternal life (Rom. 6:22). Paul describes the course that leads to the end as the imitation of Christ; Plato called it assimilation to God.[14]

The *beginning* is the image of God (present) in all human beings, the proximity or closeness of God in virtue of his word, of which Isaiah speaks. That proximity is the source of good, the word by which human beings grow in righteousness.

The *movement* that leads from the beginning to the end is guided by Scripture, which speaks of the whole armor of God that humanity must utilize for ethical progress (Eph. 6:14ff; *Protrepticus* 11.116). Clement juxtaposes the unity of the end with the infinite variety of means. The Pedagogue is a Pastor who leads the sheep into one flock and who teaches that which relates to life in the good (John 10; Exod. 20; *Paed.* 1.7.53ff). The salvation of humanity is entirely the achievement of the Word of God, who is God himself. He created his people and protects them from foreign gods; he was with them in everything that they did (Deut. 32:10ff; *Paed.* 1.7.56). It is the Word who gave the Law through Moses, which was the grace of old (John 1:17; *Paed.* 1.7.60). The righteous person is described in great detail in the words of Ezekiel the prophet, who displayed the single way of life in obedience to God (Ezek. 18:4ff; *Paed.* 1.10.95). In a long list of Pauline exhortations, Clement begins with Ephesians 4 and shows how the forgiveness of God is the basis of mutual forgiveness among human beings (*Paed.* 3.12.94ff).

The end is none other than than the deification of humanity and adoption by the Most-High (Ps. 82:6 [81:6, LXX]; *Prot.* 12.123). The one God attracts to Himself those who are like him and introduces them into his Unity (John 17:21ff; Exod. 3:14). Christians are merciful because their Father in heaven is merciful (Luke 6:35; *Paed.* 1.8.72). Human beings can behold God face to face and fulfill their destiny. For this reason the Word struggled with Jacob and Jacob saw God face to face (Gen. 32:30; *Paed.* 1.7.57). Likeness to God is the only beauty that endures. This beauty is displayed in the way that the Lord abased himself and in his long-suffering and benevolent love (Phil. 2; 1 Cor. 13; *Paed.* 3.1.2ff). This divine beauty surpasses human beauty. It is the beauty of the humiliated condition of the uniquely Righteous One, as described by the prophet Isaiah (Isa. 53:2ff; *Paed.* 3.1.3).

Clement refers in particular to Genesis in his exposition of the image and likeness of God, and to Paul in his description of the moral-spiritual progress of humanity from beginning to end. John's Gospel and Hebrews, which speak of the final unity and promised rest, are used to support Clement's vision of the goal of Christian morality. Isaiah is important to him as well, since the prophet speaks of the ways of a God who is different from human beings and yet near to them. Indeed, Isaiah saw the strange beauty of God just as Ezekiel envisioned the way of life that depends on God.

Wisdom and Word

The way which leads from beginning to end is that of the Wisdom and the Word of God. He is the one who calls those who are heavy-laden to enter into his rest and to take his yoke upon their shoulders. Wisdom and Word are united in him (Matt. 9:28ff; *Prot.* 12.120). The different manners in which Wisdom has spoken come from the one Spirit of the Lord who fills the universe (Wisd. 1:7), and they find their fulfilment in the coming of Christ (Matt. 23:37; *Strom.* 1.5.29). The Wisdom and Word of God are close to all human beings (Rom. 2:14ff; *Strom.* 1.19.95), while heretics are attacked by the Word and Wisdom himself (Prov. 9:12, 17; *Strom.* 1.19.95ff).

Divine wisdom has practical consequences, since it springs from "the Ancient of Days" who controls the dispositions of humanity. The crown of old men is their past experience; yet the ancient wisdom of God is a new wisdom because God has nothing to do with falsehood and deceit (Sir. 25:6; Eph. 4:20ff; *Paed.* 3.3.17). Those who follow God's wisdom will always be few in number, since "you shall not go with a multitude" (Exod. 23:2; *Paed.* 3.4.27). The wise man gives no place to trickery and impurity, but instead searches for justice and the fear of the Lord (Sir. 11:29; 9:16; *Paed.* 3.4.29). Love of wisdom is practical and helps to produce other wise persons (Prov. 29:3; Matt. 5:15; *Strom.* 1.1.12). The way of wisdom is the way of life and turns from hatred and strife (Prov. 10:12, 17; *Strom.* 1.6.35). Like Plato in his own way, Paul calls for obedience to the Word who, all things considered, appears to be the superior Truth (*Strom.* 1.8.41-1.9.45). One follows the Word wherever he leads (Eccl. 1:16-18; *Strom.* 1.13.58).

The Word, Wisdom of God, is perfect and has accomplished everything that has gone before; he is more precious than any precious stone

(Eccl. 7:13; Prov. 8:9-11; *Strom.* 1.13.58). In its perfection this wisdom surpasses the ideas of the Jews as well as the Greeks and makes the wisdom of the world appear foolish (1 Cor. 1:19-20; *Strom.* 1.18.88); for the Word not only displays the Truth, he is the Truth (John 14:6; *Strom.* 5.3.16). He leads human beings to that wisdom which is perfect, mysterious, and hidden (1 Cor. 2:6ff; *Strom.* 5.4.25); for, just as he is the goal, he was also at the beginning with God, the wisdom in which God took delight (Prov. 8:30; *Strom.* 7.2.7).

Thus in his exposition of the Word and Wisdom of God, Clement refers in particular to the Wisdom literature and Matthew's Gospel for support, and, in order to repudiate false wisdom, he refers to Paul and his opposition between the wisdom of God and the wisdom of the world.

The Law

God's Law is universal. It is true that his people belong to heaven and receive their laws from the God who is the legislator of heaven (Exod. 20:13ff; Deut. 6:3; *Prot.* 10.108). Yet these words, laws of reason and words of holiness, are inscribed in the hearts of human beings (Luke 6:29; Matt. 5:28; *Prot.* 10.108ff). God has inscribed his Law in the hearts of human beings so that they can know him (Heb. 8:10-12; Jer. 31:33ff; *Prot.* 11.114). Scripture and the great tradition of the Greeks are in agreement: the commandments of God give light and illuminate humanity's way (Prov. 6:23; *Strom.* 1.29.181). The Greeks actually borrowed their morality from Moses and duplicated his exposition of virtue in their own writings.

The Gentiles were not excluded from the Law because by nature they followed its precepts, thanks to the natural law which was inscribed in their hearts (Rom. 2:14; *Strom.* 2.9.44). The laws are guided by reason. The Law of Moses shows this when, for example, it prohibits men from wearing women's clothes and encourages them toward masculine virtues (Deut. 22:5; *Strom.* 2.18.81).[15] The same Law emphasizes the need for practical concern for one's neighbor (Lev. 19:9-10; 23:22; Deut. 24:14-22; *Strom.* 2.18.85). Whatever is reasonable in the Law is developed in Christ in that love and solicitude expressed by the Golden Rule (Matt. 5:7; 6:14-15; 7:1-2, 12; *Strom.* 2.18.91).

So too there is change and newness in the Law. The Hebrews did not understand the Law when they made God into a Master and not a Father. It is the God of mercy who turned from his wrath (Ps. 77:38, LXX; *Paed.* 1.9.87). The Ten Commandments have a higher and larger meaning which, without destroying them, transcends their basic literal meaning

(Exod. 20; *Strom.* 6.16). It is also crucial to note that all the commandments are summarized by Christ in one commandment alone: "Love your neighbor as yourself" (Rom. 13:9; *Strom.* 7.16.105).

Thus on the theme of the Law Clement inevitably refers to the writings of Moses (the Pentateuch) and the Wisdom literature. Clement understands these texts within the framework of Jeremiah's prophecy of the internal law and its fulfilment according to the Epistle to the Hebrews. Once again Paul is an important source for Clement's moral teaching, in particular the apostle's conception of the law of nature and reason, and his recapitulation of all the commandments in one.

The Ascetic Virtues

Clement refers to Scripture to support his appeal for a life of ascetic simplicity, and he bases that appeal on two principles. First, there is a good superior to food, money, and pleasure for which human beings must eagerly search. Second, reason and sobriety (or moderation) are goods in themselves. Clement warns of the dangers of the rich man's delicacies and the coming destruction of gluttons (Prov. 23:3; 1 Cor. 6:13; *Paed.* 2.1.4). But love (*agapê*) is a heavenly food, a banquet of the Logos which will never end and endures forever. This is the beatitude of those who will eat their bread in the Kingdom of God (1 Cor. 13; Luke 14:15; *Paed.* 2.1.5).

Practical questions cannot be decided solely on precedents (that we see) in the life of Jesus. The anointing of Jesus's feet does not justify the use of perfumes. This action took place before the woman had received the Word; it was more a symbol than a teaching. The feet of Jesus in this instance symbolized the disciples, who went to the extremities of the earth in preaching the Gospel; they received the spiritual unction with the oil of divine mercy, which also symbolizes the Passion of the Lord and the treachery of Judas (Matt. 26:7; Luke 7:47; Ps. 19:4 [18:5, LXX]; *Paed.* 2.8.61ff).

It is necessary to refuse sleep because there is something better. The Word is light, and the one who has that light is not submerged in darkness and sleep, but remains awake, since the companions of the Word are the children of the day (Prov. 8:34; 1 Thess. 5:5-11; *Paed.* 2.9.80). The ascetic simplicity of those who are close to the Lord is exemplified by Elijah, to whom the angel brought a barley cake and a jar of water (3 Kings 19:4ff, LXX; *Paed.* 3.7.38). One's possessions can be a burden on the journey that leads to the Truth; the Lord himself forbade the carrying of a purse, bag, or sandals (Luke 10:4; *Paed.* 3.7.38). In the same vein, Rachel is an example of simplicity and of personal discipline in the way that she tended her father's sheep and concerned herself with practical and useful things, things which occupy women so well; concern for the poor and for wayfarers, as modeled by Sarah, elicited the same simplicity and the same interest (Gen. 29:9; Prov. 31:19-20; Gen. 18:6, *Paed.* 3.10.49). Clement found scores of verses of Scripture directing humanity toward a simpler life, far from the ways of luxury and excess (1 Peter 1:17; 4:3; *Paed.* 3.12.85).

The Christian's asceticism is not a negative virtue but rather a concern for a higher good. Those who are persecuted suffer in the cause of righteousness, and for that virtue they are declared blessed (Matt. 5:10; *Strom.* 4.6.25). The only genuine treasure is the righteousness which belongs to the Kingdom of heaven (Matt. 6:32-33; *Strom.* 4.6.34). For the sake of this higher good there can be no compromise between the way of the cross and the way of the flesh; the flesh desires things contrary to the spirit (Gal. 5:17; *Strom.* 7.12.79).

What is more, asceticism is a good in itself. Paul speaks of the utility of a small amount of wine (1 Tim. 1:25; *Paed.* 2.2.19) and Wisdom quite often decries the evils of too much of it (Sir. 31 and Prov. 23; *Paed.* 2.2). Money proves to be as well the source of all forms of evil and warnings against it are found throughout Scripture (Haggai 1:6; 1 Tim. 6:10; *Paed.* 2.3.39). Job and Jonah are both examples of patience and constancy who light the way for the Christian, one who is crucified to the world and to whom the world is crucified (Jonah 2; Gal. 6:14; *Strom.* 2.20.104). Constancy, which is a gift of God, is connected with his promise never to abandon or forsake those who pursue this way of life. His constant presence is the source of their endurance and their constancy (Heb. 13:5; *Strom.* 2.20.126). Those who can become as gods live like mere mortal human beings when they fail to overcome the ways of the flesh (Ps. 81 [80, LXX]; *Strom.* 2.20.125).

Clement therefore makes abundant use of Scripture in speaking of the ascetic virtues of endurance, simplicity, and self-control, and in showing that endurance, for the sake of a superior good and for the sake of self-control, possesses a value in and of itself. With these themes he refers in particular to Matthew's Gospel and to Paul, as well as to *exempla* from the Old Testament and exhortations from the Wisdom literature.

Purity

Purity begins as self-control and is governed by four principal factors. In the first place, purity is connected with likeness to God: the people of God must be holy because He is holy. The Apostles' feet were washed and they were sent into the world pure and clean, in order that their freshness could be spread everywhere (John 13:5; 2 Cor. 2:14-17; *Paed.* 2.8.63). From the beginning, purity has been required of human beings and angels. Those angels who abandon their divine beauty for earthly beauty fall from heaven; the inhabitants of Shechem were even massacred for their impurity (Gen. 6:1-4; Gen. 34; *Paed.* 3.2.14). The true Christian gnostic, however, follows his Lord in holiness and is pure in flesh and in heart. The world is crucified to him just as he is crucified to the world.

Purity is furthermore the fundamental issue in Clement's debate with heretics in the *Stromateis*. The temple of God must remain holy, as Paul says, and defilement has no place in it. The bride of Christ must be pure and free of any blemish in her flesh and in her spirit. It is Paul once again who asserts that it is impossible for those who are dead to sin to continue living in sin, while Peter beseeches those who are aliens and exiles to guard against the lusts of the flesh (Exod. 19:15; 2 Cor. 7:1; Rom. 6:2, 13; 1 Peter 2:11-12; *Strom.* 3.11.73). Peter incites his readers to purity and obedience in order that they may be holy as their God is holy (1 Peter 1:14-21; *Strom.* 3.18.110).

On the question of marriage, Clement gives the following exposition by way of summary: "In general, all the Apostle's letters teach responsible self-control. They embrace thousands of instructions about marriage, the production of children, and domestic life. Nowhere do they blackball marriage, provided that it is responsible. They preserve the connection between the Law and the gospel." Clement's own position on marriage and celibacy is born out when he further says here that the epistles "welcome the man who embarks responsibly on marriage with gratitude to God, and the man who takes celibacy as his life companion in accordance with the Lord's will, each, as he has been called, making his choice in maturity and firmness" (*Strom.* 3.12.86).[16]

What is more, because purity is a means to be like God, it is a matter of internal disposition rather than of external ritual observance. It must rule a person's language precisely because, as the Lord says, speech reveals the person within, the heart (Matt. 5:22; 15:18; *Paed.* 2.6.49). The language of the Christian is free of impurity (Eph. 4:29; 5:3ff; *Paed.* 2.6.50). It is wrong to be preoccupied with external propriety if the person within is impure. The Scribes and Pharisees whitewashed sepulchres. They washed the outside of the cup, but left the inside dirty. It is the impurity of the soul that must be cleansed, and the hands covered with the blood of the prophets that must be purified (Matt. 23:25ff; *Paed.* 3.9.47ff; Isa.

4:4). External beauty is very misleading: it does not lead to the love and beauty which are imperishable (Sir. 9:8; *Paed.* 3.11.83). For Clement, purity is above all a reasonable virtue, which prevents human beings from becoming like beasts and renders them capable of seeing God (Ps. 49:12, 20 [48:13, 21, LXX]; Sir. 33:6; *Paed.* 1.13.101ff). Many times Clement insists on the fact that only the pure of heart see God (Matt. 5:8; *Strom.* 2.10.50). The vision of God face to face is the vision of the Truth, and only a small number can attain to it, for only the pure of heart see God. The Savior came down in order to lead us to this purity and definitive vision (Matt. 5:8; *Strom.* 5.1.7).

Thus we see that when Clement addresses Christian purity, he finds emphatic support in a single verse of Matthew's Gospel and in the appeal to assimilation to God through holiness as taught in the Law. He also refers to Paul and to 1 Peter to support his treatment of this theme.

Faith

Faith is essential in Clement's view and he dedicates much of his time to defending it against pagan objections. Faith begins with trust in God, which is the foundation of life and its very perfection. It seeks the will of God and leads to eternal life (John 6:40; 3:36; *Paed.* 1.6.28ff). The believer confides in God when he or she sees God's concern for the birds of the sky and the lilies of the field. The believer rejects anxiety about food and clothing because he or she has the faith which is founded on God (Luke 12:22-24, 27-29; *Paed.* 2.10.102-103). Faith bespeaks stability, avoiding the capricious impulses of those who prefer agitation and trouble. Here Clement uses the symbolism of the story of Cain (Gen. 4:16) and refers to Proverbs as well (Prov. 11:14; *Strom.* 2.11.51). Abraham's faith, which reckoned him righteous in the eyes of God, is presented as paradigmatic (Rom. 4:3; *Strom.* 5.15). For Clement, faith is the means by which we receive the divine word, and is a reasonable and critical power. If human beings do not believe, they will not understand. The need for faith is a dominant theme in Books 2 and 5 of the *Stromateis*. Clement views faith here as the means by which we discover God's wisdom; the fear of God guards us against evil. Through faith we receive the perfect philosophy, the true wisdom, as well as a sure knowledge of existent beings and of the structure of the world (Prov. 3:5-7; 12:23; Isa. 7:9; *Strom.* 2.2.4-8). Faith is the evidence of things that we cannot see, and without it it is impossible to please God. Those who do not see, yet believe, find the blessing of God (Heb. 11:1-6; *Strom.* 2.2.8).

For Clement, this intellectual aspect of faith is never separated from the trust and surrender that are the foundation of life. Indeed, the writer of Hebrews, describing the heroic exemplars of faith from the ancient past, tells us that faith is the basis of knowledge (Heb. 11:3-25, 32ff; *Strom.* 2.4.13). Isaiah also speaks of the value of the faith which comes from hearing and from the preaching of the Apostles. Faith lays hold of the word of the Lord and unites the believing person to the Son of God (Isa. 53:1; Rom. 10:14-17; Isa. 52:7; *Strom.* 2.6.25ff). The virtue of intellectual courage is essential for Clement, just as it was for Plato (*Rep.* 503), for the author of Hebrews, and much later for Thomas Aquinas, who calls faith "the courage of the spirit." Faith is linked to the development of maturity. Only faith in Christ can provide understanding of the Law. The ancient Hebrews were told that unless they believed, they would not understand (Isaiah 7:9; *Strom.* 4.21.134). Whoever progresses in the way of faith penetrates the very presence of God. At this stage in the journey, the believer groans in expectation of his or her heavenly dwelling (2 Cor. 5:1-7; *Strom.* 4.26.166). The believer has a double faith since the righteousness of God is revealed "from faith to faith": salvation is the developing recovery of faith. By faith the Apostles moved mountains and trees. Faith has a cutting edge that penetrates into the human soul, like a grain of mustard seed planted in the soul and developing there (Rom. 1:11ff, 17; Matt. 17:20; Luke 17:5; *Strom.* 5.1.2ff).

Martyrdom

Clement sees in the crown of martyrdom the beatitude of those who are persecuted. Martyrdom is the fulfillment of the spiritual life (Matt. 5:10; *Strom.* 4.6.41; Matt. 10:39; *Strom.* 2.20.108). Paul himself suffered for Christ and in that experience saw a gift granted him in addition to the gift of faith (Phil. 1:29-30; 2:1ff, 17; *Strom.* 4.13.92). Paul speaks at length of the perseverance of the martyr, or witness, who confesses the name of Christ and blesses his persecutors. Clement likewise fills two entire pages with verses drawn from Paul on this theme (Rom. 10ff; *Strom.* 4.16.99ff).

The martyr suffers only for a time and his or her patience will be requited. Hebrews speaks of the salvation which comes from suffering (Heb. 10:32-39; 11:36-40; 12:1ff; *Strom.* 4.16.101ff). The great heroes of the faith were tested and found worthy of God (Wisd. 3:2-8; *Strom.* 4.16.103ff). Jesus frequently speaks of confessing his name in the face of human opposition, of confronting the courts in the power of the Spirit, of refusing to deny him, and of ultimately prevailing with him. In all of this, the martyr follows his or her Lord and drinks the cup that the Father has given (Luke 12:8-12; Matt. 10:32; Luke 22:31-34; *Strom.* 4.9.70-75).

For Paul, following Christ, to be martyred is to become a spectacle of death for the world and to be despised by the multitude (1 Cor. 4:9-13; *Strom.* 4.7.51).

Love

Paul sees in love (*agapê*) the supreme virtue (1 Cor. 13:4; *Paed.* 3.1.2). Its perfection, Peter says, covers a multitude of sins (1 Peter 4:8; *Paed.* 3.12.91). Love manifests the likeness of the children of God to their heavenly Father. They love their enemies and are quickly reconciled with their adversaries. Nothing can separate them from the love of God which is shown in Christ their Savior (Matt. 5:24, 44; Rom. 8:38ff; *Strom.* 4.14.95ff).

The love of God consists in keeping his commandments, not in some vague emotion (1 John 4:7; *Paed.* 3.11.82). The Lord himself summarized the commandments in the love of God and love of neighbor (Matt. 22:37-40; *Paed.* 3.12.88).

The ancient law preceded this charity and oriented humanity toward patience and generosity. It leads one to return the stray animal to its rightful owner, requiring that one assume care of it until the owner can again take possession of it. The law imposes respect for the rights of strangers, Egyptians, and prisoners, and demands one to give alms to the poor (Deut. 23:7; 20:10; *Strom.* 2.18.87-96). In all of this, the goodness and love of God are evident. On this specific theme of the sweetness of the law, Clement is especially indebted to Philo.

Jerusalem or Athens?

We must now assess the relative importance in Clement of biblical and non-biblical sources.[17] By their sheer mass, the biblical documents transmit a rich theological content. By contrast, non-biblical sources— particularly of a Hellenistic and philosophical origin—loom large in Clement's background and project a philosophical structure on his thought. As far as Clement's interests are concerned, there is no problem here of an inherent conflict of sources. Like Justin (2 *Apol.* 13.4), he estimates that "everything that has been rightly spoken to all humanity belongs to us, Christians," and that Christianity is the true philosophy. Other philosophies have simply extracted pieces of the total truth which is Christ, and claimed that their portion is the total truth (*Strom.* 1.13.57). For Clement it was already obvious that Greek thought and Hebrew thought were identical. The Greeks had stolen their ideas from the Hebrews, which meant that it was only normal for Christians to avail themselves of these ideas wherever they found them. Nothing that the Greek philosophers said was original; all of it had already been said by Moses and the prophets.

For Clement, terms and ideas had to be found, at least in fragmentary form, simultaneously in philosophy and in the Bible. Was their significance above all theological and "Christian," rather than philosophical or "Greek"? It is a perplexing question, but one which must be posed. What is Clement's theology and how does he connect his moral ideas to it? Is it inevitable that moral ideas are not easily integrated into a Christian theology, whatever that may be, while they are conspicuously integrated into the structure of a Hellenistic philosophy? For each group of ideas that we have examined, we can pose four questions: Are the two tendencies, theological and philosophical, equally present? Which is the dominant tendency? Is the non-Christian element being modified? How can Clement's synthesis of theology and philosophy be compared with that of his rivals, the Gnostic sects?

The theme of *assimilation to God* (*homoiôsis theô*) unquestionably owes its origin to Plato. Clement cites the celebrated passage in *Theaetetus* 176 B and acknowledges his debt. Yet at the same time he copiously quotes Scripture on the image and likeness of God, the call to follow and imitate Christ, the hope which has not deceived us, and the promised rest which we expect. Two tendencies are therefore operative. The Platonic tendency appears dominant, since the theme of dynamic assimilation to God cannot be drawn from Genesis 1:26-27. Thus Plato furnishes the framework into which Clement introduces his moral teaching. Yet it can still be argued that the Pauline notion of the dual hope is a central theme of Christian theology and that the theological aspect prevails in Clement. The balance seems therefore to lean toward Plato, but Paul is the object of a more frequent attention and the theme of the dual hope elicits their substantial unity in numerous quotations. We can thus answer our third question in short order: the non-Christian element in Clement is modified by his insistence on Christian hope and by many references drawn from Scripture, which are joined with the formula that Clement borrows from Plato concerning assimilation to God. For example, the story of the creation of humanity in Genesis gives a distinctly biblical significance to the Platonic motif. Quite to the contrary, the Gnostic teaching on the image and likeness had no connection with their genuine Old Testament meaning. Clement's use of the texts and terminology was quite different from the use made of them by heretics, since he took both the Old Testament and divine creation seriously.

Wisdom and *Word* clearly are biblical terms, yet they are connected with Scriptural texts that already betray a strong Hellenistic influence. The question thus posed—theological or philosophical, Christian or Greek?—is scarcely pertinent. Clement had no need to introduce here elements of Greek philosophy; they were already present in Scripture. The Wisdom of Solomon (from the Apocrypha) was included among the New Testament Scriptures in the Muratori canon.[18] We can therefore ask whether parts of Scripture which reflected Greek influence had less grounds than other parts for being accepted into Christian theology. The answer certainly has to be negative, provided that a critical reading keeps in mind the tensions existing among different parts of the Bible. Within the Gospels, particularly in Matthew and John, sapiential theology is an integral part of the Christian message. Once again, Clement differs from his Gnostic opponents because, while they accept wisdom and word, they alienate them from the world, failing to bear in mind that the Creator and the Redeemer are one, and so distorting this theology by removing it from its biblical foundations. Wisdom and Word do not imply a dualistic view of the world. But with Gnosticism, dualism estranges flesh and spirit; body and soul can find no meeting-point.

The theme of *the Law* in Clement has more foundation in Stoicism than in the theology of the Pentateuch. Yet the Wisdom literature in the Bible had already integrated the Hebrew concept of *Torah* with the notion of law (*nomos*) in Stoic philosophy. Already Philo had connected the Mosaic law to the natural law, and between the two conceptions (both of which are present), the Greek philosophical concept appears to predominate.[19] Yet Clement's dependence on Scripture leads him to describe the law in terms that are not easily harmonized with the static notion of law in Stoicism. The deeply personal content of the Law in the Bible modifies the meaning of law stemming from Hellenistic tradition.[20] The God who gives the Law in the Bible speaks to his people and his commandments constitute his will for the world, not some impersonal and universal structure. Clement's Gnostic opponents in Book 3 of the *Stromateis* believed, on the contrary, in an autonomous system of natural law (*Strom.* 3.2.6). There was an order of justice established in heaven and human beings had to conform to that order. In this happy universal system of justice, human beings had to live without private property and private marriages. Part of the Gnostic error was the unqualified acceptance of a theory of natural law, which was destined to be an influential force, but also a problem, throughout the history of Christianity.

The appeal for *self-control* was a common ascetic exigency in Hellenistic philosophies,[21] but the same demand for moderation and restraint is clear in the New Testament. Suffering with a view to a superior good and patience in hardship are inherent in the way of the Cross. If Clement is influenced by the philosophical motif of self-control, it is precisely because he wants to prove the superiority of Christianity on this point. Accordingly, the soul is superior to the body, but both belong among the intermediate realities between good and evil (*Strom.* 4.26.164).[22] Clement transforms the non-Christian tendencies of this theme: restraint is not a negative virtue nor a repudiation of the goodness of creation. In certain Gnostic and Marcionite sects, self-renunciation and ascetic behavior were signs of human preeminence over the world. The elitist element in the Stoic ascetic ideal was pressed far beyond the wiser limits of Stoicism.

As far as the theme of *purity* is concerned, Clement once again followed in the footsteps of Hellenistic philosophy. Philosophers in antiquity proved their greatness by their detachment from the world; the true wise man for them was one who was impassible (*apathês*), or free from passion.[23] Paralleling that, Clement unveils an entirely biblical idea of purity owing to four factors: the divine holiness ("Be holy because I am holy"); the purity of the Bride of Christ (whence arises Clement's views on marriage and celibacy); the superiority of internal dispositions to superficial holiness; and lastly the role of purity in knowledge, since it is the pure of heart who see God. The dangers in discussing this theme are clearly present to him; nevertheless, Clement does little more than present what in his own eyes is obvious. When we compare him to his Gnostic adversaries, we see how their exposition lacks any biblical basis. For Gnostics, purity depended on a predetermined disposition more than on discipline and obedience; marriage had no place, either because it was a useless constraint or because it was a compromise with wicked carnality and with a creator hostile to the one true God. Therefore Clement shows the Gnostics that their pretensions of moral greatness are not supported by a moral integrity. Only good trees can bear good fruit.[24] They must be bad trees because their fruit is bad. The evil of their life proves their lack of purity. Finally, the pure of heart who see God do not behold him by some mystical and particular privilege, but because this vision is the apogee of rational inquiry. This progress toward the dialectical summit is made possible by the Savior who descended to earth and led humanity toward purity and vision. On all these points, Clement adopts the Gnostic ideal of the final vision and transforms it through his theology of the Incarnation.

The theme of *faith* in Clement bears the mark of his biblical and philosophical background. Faith is the faith of Abraham, the confidence of believing in a God of love. It is the proof of things unseen, which presses humanity forward in a heroic confidence.[25] Yet because Clement must prove to critics that Christian faith is intellectually respectable, faith becomes for him more philosophical and rational than is the case in the New Testament. He demonstrates that faith is not servile, that it is not a denial of reason but that it is necessary for all human inquiry. The text of the New Testament aids him in emphasizing the perfection of faith and avoiding Gnosticism. For Clement, everything is present in the perfection of faith: it is like the perfection of the newborn infant. The philosophical and logical elements are refashioned thanks to Isaiah's union of faith and comprehension, and owing to the Wisdom literature and the Epistle to the Hebrews, where the activity of faith is at once intellectual and heroic. In the end, Clement's exposition has nothing in common with Gnostic thought, since for him faith is intellectual and essential. Gnostics, on the contrary, scorned faith and ignored reason: their teaching was a theosophy, not a philosophy or theology.

In Clement's discussion of *martyrdom,* biblical and non-biblical elements are simultaneously present. Paul has his theology of the Cross and the Epistle to the Hebrews shows us the paths of suffering. Jesus called his disciples to confess him before hostile judges, whereas for Plato philosophy was the apprenticeship of death, the struggle of the soul to separate itself from the body, which anticipates the definitive liberation brought by death.[26] In Clement there is a clear influence of the philosophical ideal. The martyr abandons his or her humanity in order to ascend to God; the soul separates itself from the body; yet any dualistic tendencies are buried by the mass of exhortations that Clement draws from Scripture, as we have noted. The body is not scorned and martyrdom in the flesh is shown to be the crown of all life and virtue, since at this stage the disciple more resembles the Lord. The contrast with Gnosticism is truly dramatic on this point, since there are no proofs of there having been any Gnostic martyrs. The fluidity of the Gnostics' beliefs and their slighting of actions that were manifestly earthly rendered the confession of Christ useless in the face of danger. For the Gnostic, the ritual act of loyalty to the emperor had no significance since it did not belong to the order of knowledge and spirit. What is more, Gnostics objected to Clement that martyrdom was proof that the God of Christians was not a God of love. How could he, in his love and supreme power, allow his faithful followers to be able to be put to death on account of their loyalty to him?

Clement's theme of *love* is not peculiar to Christianity, but it bears the mark of the Christian tradition. Love of neighbor and even of enemies was combined with the Golden Rule, which was recommended by many an ancient moral theory.[27] Clement's use of Paul is based on the central place that the apostle gives to love and to the perfection that this love requires, and Clement only desires a Christian love. Since love is of God, it is a matter of keeping his commandments and obeying his sovereign will. The tendencies of the pagan ideal of love are modified by the radical biblical requirement of the love of God and love of neighbor. When compared with the Gnostics on this point, Clement manifests a more realistic and practical orientation. He indicates that the ancient Law announces love and shows its sweetness and its benevolence. He clearly rejects the Gnostic opposition between Law and Gospel, between Old and New Testaments.

Conclusion

In his use of Scripture, Clement of Alexandria resorts especially to Matthew, Romans, 1 and 2 Corinthians, Proverbs, Psalms, and Genesis, but he quotes the rest of the Bible as well. The varied forms of the moral tradition found in the New Testament are all presented in his quotations: instructions, maxims, wisdom sayings, proverbs, prophetic oracles, as well as beatitudes, similitudes, parables, discussions or debates, and miracle stories.[28]

From the exegetical standpoint, Clement does not take context into account in any rigorous way, and often he more or less neglects the original sense of the scriptural phrase. This stems from his basic conviction that Scripture is one, like Truth, because there is only one living Word of God; thus, he intermingles verses so that the Word can be clearly understood. Clement gathers honey from the flowers of prophetic and apostolic meadows in order to communicate immortal knowledge to his audience—an analogy that effectively conveys the aesthetic sensibility and evangelical fervor of most of his writings. He reunites the dislocated members of the body of truth—an analogy which conveys his discovery of curious unities in Scripture and his enthusiasm for reconciling a multitude of texts.

Method is decisive when considering the manner in which Clement's morality is Christian. The parallels discovered with non-Christian sources prove that he addressed the world of his time, not that that world dominated him. He was a Greek moralist of the second century, just as many of his readers today are Western moralists of the twentieth century; we have entirely our own place marked in history. There is only one question: Did Clement integrate these non-biblical sources into a visible theological unity? It is clear that he presented a simple and predominant theology, the theology of the Logos, and that the bulk of his scriptural quotations reshaped non-Christian values into new forms. Disarray and distortion remained, but they were no different from the disarray already found in the moral teaching of the New Testament. The Bible is full of non-biblical elements and it requires a critical approach if it is to be understood.

Notes

1. For a general discussion of Clement's use of Scripture, see C. Mondésert, *Clement d'Alexandrie: Introduction à l'étude de sa pensée religieuse à partir de l'Ecriture* (Paris, 1944).
2. The similarity (on this point) with Philo has already been emphasized by Mondésert, *Clement d'Alexandrie*, 2; and E. Bréhier, *Les idées philosophiques et religieuses de Philon d'Alexandrie* (Paris, 1950), 317; and W. Völker, *Der wahre Gnostiker nach Clemens Alexandrinus* (Berlin, 1952), 508ff.
3. As Mondésert notes (*Clement d'Alexandrie*, 95), "L'Ecriture...c'est un intermediare qui le met en contact avec Dieu, avec surtout son Logos révélateur et sauveur."
4. Cf. H. von Campenhausen, *The Formation of the Christian Bible,* trans. J. Baker (Philadelphia, 1972), 266.
5. Ibid., 293.
6. E. Osborn, "Teaching and Writing in the First Chapter of the *Stromateis* of Clement of Alexandria," *Journal of Theological Studies* 10 (1959): 39ff.
7. H. Lietzmann, *The Founding of the Church Universal* (London, 1953), 316.
8. Mondésert, *Clément d'Alexandrie*, 263.
9. Ibid., 264.
10. Ibid., 183.
11. Cf. Philo, *De opificio mundi* 25, 65-88 and passim.
12. E. Osborn, *Ethical Patterns in Early Christian Thought* (Cambridge, 1976), 67; idem, *The Philosophy of Clement of Alexandria* (Cambridge, 1957), 84-94.
13. Ibid.
14. See Völker, *Der wahre Gnostiker,* 577-597.

15. Cf. Philo, *De virtutibus* 18-20 (*de fortitudine*). In all of his discussion of the Law, Clement's dependence on Philo is obvious.
16. Trans. J. Ferguson, *Clement of Alexandria: Stromateis, Books 1-3*, Fathers of the Church, vol. 85 (Washington, D.C., 1991), 310.
17. For a general introduction to this problem, see M. Spanneut, *Le stoïcisme des Pères de l'Église* (Paris, 1957), 54-77; J. Daniélou, *Gospel Message and Hellenistic Culture*, trans. J. Baker (Philadelphia, 1973); H. Chadwick, *Early Christian Thought and the Classical Tradition* (Oxford, 1966).
18. *et Sapientia ab amicis Salomonis in honorem ipsius scripta.*
19. See J. Daniélou, *Philon d'Alexandrie* (Paris, 1958), 128ff, on Philo's treatment of the Law. But see also Bréhier's conclusion in *Les idées*, 317: "Philo did not take Greek philosophy as his point of departure, but that Alexandrian theology which must have produced the Gnostic systems and the Hermetic literature."
20. Precisely as in Philo: "The God whom Philo worships is the God of Abraham, Isaac and Jacob, a personal God," notes H. Chadwick in *The Cambridge History of Later Greek and Early Medieval Philosophy*, ed. A. H. Armstrong (Cambridge, 1967), 140; cf. Daniélou, *Philon*, 148: "The language may be Platonic and anticipate Plotinus, but the reality is precisely that of the living God of the Bible."
21. Völker, *Der wahre Gnostiker*, 474-475, 532ff.
22. See Spanneut, *Le stoïcisme*, 245.
23. Ibid., 248.
24. *Strom.* 3.5.44. Cf. Osborn, *Ethical Patterns*, 46-49.
25. Clement believes that Paul was the author of the Epistle to the Hebrews, and so it is rather easy for him to connect the double hope to the promised rest.
26. *Phaedo* 65, 67.
27. See Cicero's remarks on benevolence (*De legibus* 1.33ff). I owe this part of the discussion to the comments of Fr. G. Strecker. Cf. his "Compliance—Love of One's Enemy—The Golden Rule," *Australian Biblical Review* 29 (1981): 38-46.
28. See G. Strecker, "Strukturen einer neutestamentlichen Ethik," *Zeitschrift für Theologie und Kirche* 75 (1978): 120ff.

7

Reading the Bible with Origen

RONALD HEINE

Whoever would understand Origen must take the Bible into serious account, for it stood at the center of his work, his thought, and his entire life. Eusebius relates that Origen had been trained in the Scriptures from his childhood, and that his father pressed him with daily memorization of the Scriptures. He adds that Origen was an eager student, going beyond what his father demanded and seeking the deeper meaning in Scripture even at that early age.[1] While Eusebius' stories about Origen's boyhood may be exaggerated, they cannot be completely false, for the ready knowledge of the Scriptures that Origen's adult work demonstrates could have been acquired only by long experience with them. One of the criticisms that Origen directed at the majority of Christians later in his life was that they lacked this long and diligent experience with the Scriptures.[2]

Much has been written about the influence of Greek philosophy on Origen's thought and methodology, and that influence is certainly present. Origen himself advises his student Gregory to study philosophy and the other disciplines of Greek education. Origen was always a critical reader, however, and this applied especially to his reading of Greek philosophy. The purpose of studying philosophy was to take *from it* those things which could serve the Christian faith as "assistants."[3] He illustrated this for Gregory with the story from Exodus in which the Israelites were instructed to "spoil the Egyptians" before leaving Egypt. The materials they obtained had, he said, been misused by the Egyptians, but were used for godly purposes by the Israelites in the construction of the tabernacle. Origen was aware that this placed one in proximity with the heathen, and that one had to exercise great critical acumen in accepting any doctrines of the philosophers.[4] He concludes the letter with an urgent exhortation that Gregory give his main attention to the reading of the Scriptures.[5] This was where the emphasis lay in Origen's own life. He always attempted, at least, to judge philosophy by Scripture, and to accept from the former only what he thought was in harmony with the latter.

This essay will address three questions to Origen as a reader of the Bible. First, what did he conceive the nature and purpose of the Bible to be? Second, how did he think one should read the Bible? And third, what kind of person did he think the interpreter of the Bible must be? In attempting to answer these questions we will occasionally notice the influence of Greek culture on Origen's thought. We will notice, however, that even when this influence is present, it is brought into contact with and under the judgment of Scripture, and is (usually) modified in the process.

The Nature and Purpose of the Bible

Origen had a very high view of the Bible. He considered Scripture to be divine and inspired. He begins his discussion of hermeneutics in his treatise *On First Principles* with an argument for the divine nature of the Bible based on Christ's fulfillment of prophecy. This shows, he argues, that Christ is divine and, at the same time, that the prophecies about him are divinely inspired.[6] In his many sermons and commentaries Origen makes it clear that he considered the Holy Spirit to be the author of the Biblical books. When the text of Genesis, for example, relates that Abraham was standing under a tree, we ought not think, he asserts, that the Holy Spirit was concerned to tell us simply where Abraham was standing.[7] Or, when Rebecca is said to come daily to the wells, he remarks that such details are significant, for the Holy Spirit is not just telling stories in the Scriptures.[8] Even such minor details as Abraham's position and Rebecca's daily duties have been placed in the Scriptures by the Holy Spirit. We will not understand the way Origen reads the Bible if we miss this basic point, that it is always the Holy Spirit who speaks in the text of the Bible.

Origen's understanding, however, of what it meant for the Holy Spirit to be the speaker in the Bible is far different from that of modern Protestant fundamentalism which might make a similar statement. Modern fundamentalism uses the doctrine of the inspiration of the Scriptures to guarantee the accuracy of the historical and scientific information in the Bible. For Origen, the inspiration of the Scriptures had nothing to do with the accuracy of their historical or scientific accounts. He did not think that everything in the Bible was historically accurate. He begins Book 10 of his *Commentary on John*, for example, by calling attention to the discrepancies between John and the Synoptic Gospels in both chronological and geographical references clustered around the story of Jesus cleansing the temple and the events both preceding and following the cleansing in John 2. He does not think these discrepancies can be reconciled at the historical level, and he thinks that such discrepancies between the four Gospels are numerous. He is concerned, however, to defend the truthfulness of these accounts. Truthfulness and historical accuracy are neither synonymous nor necessarily interdependent for Origen.

He assumes that the evangelists sometimes made "minor changes in what happened so far as history is concerned" in order to communicate the spiritual truth. "They have related," he asserts, "what happened in this place as though it happened in another, or what happened at this time as though at another time, and they have composed what is reported in this manner with a certain degree of distortion."[9] It was the intention of the evangelists "to speak the truth spiritually and historically at the same time where that was possible," but where the spiritual truth could be communicated only through the distortion of historical information they chose the spiritual truth at the expense of the historical.[10] In *On First Principles*,[11] Origen suggests that historical problems were sometimes slipped into the text of Scripture to alert the reader to the fact that one must not depend on the literal meaning, but must search out the spiritual meaning.

Origen also did not think that all the scientific information in the Bible was accurate. He was concerned especially with the accounts of creation in Genesis. He did not think it possible to believe that the first three days existed, along with an evening and a morning for each, without the prior existence of the sun, moon, and stars, nor that the first day even lacked a heaven.[12] He thought such statements must be figurative, indicating mysteries through semblance, but not through actual events.

Origen was careful to note, however, that his assertions about historical truthfulness did not mean that there was no accurate historical information in Scripture,[13] nor did he take refuge in his view of the spiritual meaning every time he encountered a historical problem in the text of Scripture. In his treatise *On Prayer*,[14] he notes the differences between the way the Lord's Prayer is recorded in Matthew and Luke, and the different settings for the prayer in each Gospel. He knows that many assume it to be the same prayer in both Gospels. He concludes that the two accounts describe two separate occasions on which Jesus gave instructions on prayer, with certain parts of the prayer being the same in each case. He offers a similar explanation for the differences in a saying of John the Baptist.[15]

Origen's chief concern was always with the spiritual teaching of the gospel, but he did not neglect the literal sense, and sometimes went to great pains to explain it. He recognized early in his career that the majority of believers held a very simple faith, and understood the Bible literally.[16] Although he often attacked the views held by these, whom he called "the simple," he never dismissed them from his concern.[17] His homilies may be seen as a kind of popularization of those points of his thought which he considered most relevant to "the simple" in his attempt to lead them to a higher level of understanding of the Christian faith.[18] In *Against Celsus*, the last book that Origen wrote, he takes note at various places of Celsus's derision of Christians as ignoble, uneducated, and ignorant, and responds that in contrast to the teachings of Celsus's philosophers, the revelation of God through Moses and Jesus reached not just the educated elite, but extended also to the common people, improving the life they lived and communicating concepts of God which they could understand.[19]

While Origen believed the words of the Bible to be inspired, it was the teachings communicated by these words that were divine for him.[20] He considered it to be the interpreter's task to translate the literal words of the gospel into the spiritual gospel.[21] In doing this the interpreter was seeking what the Spirit intended in the words of the Bible.

Origen understood the purpose of the Spirit to be twofold in Scripture. The first aim (*skopos*) of the Spirit was to reveal those doctrines necessary for the perfection of souls.[22] The doctrines concerning God and His Son and the nature and work of the Son in relation both to God and humanity were of first importance. After these came teachings concerning other spiritual beings, the world and its purpose, and the origin of evil.[23] At the same time, there was a second aim (*skopos*) of the Spirit in Scripture. Recognizing that the investigation of such doctrines is beyond the capabilities of many, the Spirit concealed these primary teachings in the secondary story of the visible creation and the Biblical account of human history.[24] It is this dual purpose of the Spirit that has produced the complex mixture of spiritual truth and historical narrative in the Bible.[25] The purpose of the various stories and laws in Scripture is to communicate those hidden doctrines which will lead advanced souls to perfection. The secondary narrative hull in which the kernel of primary spiritual teachings is enclosed has its own usefulness, however, in instructing the simple.[26] Each person, then, can be instructed from the Bible in accordance with his or her own capacity, and can experience improvement in both deeds and understanding from this instruction.[27]

The Way to Read the Bible

Origen's understanding of the way to read the Bible goes hand in hand with his understanding of the nature and purpose of the Bible. Just as the Bible consists of two levels of meaning, the deeper spiritual meaning and the surface level of the literal stories and laws, the advanced reader, or teacher,[28] such as Origen himself, interprets both levels, but is primarily concerned with the deeper meaning.

When Origen works at the literal level he draws on the techniques of the Greek *grammaticus* that had been employed over the past several centuries at Alexandria to establish and explain the classical Greek texts.[29] Among his efforts to illumine the literal text are discussions of textual variants,[30] the geography of Palestine,[31] the etymology of words,[32] the general context,[33] grammar,[34] logic,[35] and, when treating the Gospels, the parallel accounts.[36] Origen occasionally does not go beyond a technical discussion of the literal level of the text. The problems connected with the prophecy of Caiaphas, for example, are treated at the literal level alone,[37] as are the statements in John 1:1-5.[38] His usual concern, however, is to penetrate beneath the hull of the literal text to the spiritual truth contained within it.

To discover this spiritual meaning in the Biblical texts, Origen applied the allegorical method long used by philosophers to find symbolic meaning in the texts of Homer and the other poets. This allegorical method of reading texts is one of Origen's most significant borrowings from Greek philosophy. It also illustrates well how he accepted from philosophy only that which he thought to be harmonious with Scripture. He does not think he stands in the tradition of the philosophers, whether Greek or Jewish, when he practices allegory. He thinks he stands in the tradition of the apostle Paul.

He offers a programmatic statement about the use of allegory in the prologue of his fifth homily on Exodus. Paul, he says, taught the Church of the Gentiles how to interpret the books of law by providing some examples. He then narrates a literal reading of the story of the departure of the Israelites from Egypt, the crossing of the sea, and the early encampments, which he calls the Jewish understanding of the text. To

135

this literal reading he juxtaposes Paul's reading of these events in 1 Corinthians 10, where Paul says that the crossing of the sea was a baptism, the cloud was the Holy Spirit, and the rock which followed them was Christ. The principles seen in these examples, Origen argues, should be applied to other texts as well, for it is incumbent on the Christian to read the Bible as Paul did, and not as the Jews.[39]

There is a cluster of Pauline texts (Rom. 7:14; 1 Cor. 2:10-16; 9:9-10; 10:11; 2 Cor. 3:6; 3:15-16; and Gal. 4:24) to which Origen appeals whenever he finds it necessary to discuss or to defend the way in which he reads the Bible. His frequent citations of these texts demonstrate that he was convinced that he was following the Pauline model found in the Scriptures themselves when he looked for the deeper meaning.

Among these Pauline texts used by Origen, various statements found in 1 Corinthians 2:10-16 were especially important, and they take us to the heart of Origen's spiritual reading of the Bible. Paul's words, "Which things also we speak, not in words taught by human wisdom, but in words taught by the Spirit, comparing spiritual things with spiritual" (1 Cor. 2:13), provide Origen with one of his most used and most important techniques for discerning the spiritual meaning in a text. It is the principle which would later be called "interpreting Scripture by Scripture." The practice of comparing texts within the corpus of an author's own works to determine what was meant in a particular text was a common procedure among exegetes of all types in the ancient world. It was used by the Greek grammarians to interpret Homer, by philosophers to interpret Aristotle or Plato, and by Hellenistic Jews such as Philo, but also by the rabbis, to interpret the Old Testament.[40] In his commentary on Psalm 1, which was perhaps his earliest writing, Origen claims to have learned the principle from a Jewish teacher. The teacher compared Scripture to a house with many locked rooms. A key lies before each door, but it is not the key to that door. The difficulty in understanding the obscurities in the Scriptures is likened to the difficulty in discovering the right key for the right door. The proper procedure for unlocking the mysteries in a passage of Scripture is to search in other passages, since the Scriptures "hold the explanation scattered among themselves." Origen comments, "The apostle, I think, suggested such a way of coming to a knowledge of the divine words when he said, 'Which things also we speak, not in words taught by human wisdom, but in words taught by the Spirit, comparing spiritual things with spiritual.'"[41]

The significance Origen attached to 1 Corinthians 2:13 as an exegetical key is made quite explicit in the extant fragments of his comments on 1 Corinthians. He sees the comparison of Biblical texts with one another to be the way in which the Holy Spirit illuminates the meaning of those texts in the mind of the interpreter. He asks, "How is one 'taught by the Spirit'?," and answers, "By comparing one text with another."[42] This, of course, is directly related to his view of the nature of the Bible in that he understood it to be the Spirit who speaks in the texts. When, therefore, he arrives at a meaning for a text by comparing other Biblical texts containing similar terminology, it is the Spirit speaking in the auxiliary texts which teaches him the meaning of the text in question.

Origen makes a very self-conscious application of this principle in commenting on the meaning of the "hart" in Song of Songs 2:9. He first cites various references to the hart in other passages of the Old Testament, and then says that he has cited these passages "that 'we may not speak in the teaching of human wisdom, but in the teaching of the Spirit, comparing spiritual things with spiritual.'" Then he prays that God may reveal the secrets of his word, and that he will remove his understanding from "'the teaching of human wisdom'" and lift it up to the "teaching of the Spirit."[43]

Not only did Origen see this principle as the key for opening the meaning of the Biblical texts, he also saw it functioning as a control on the possible range of meanings of a text. Celsus had asserted that the words of the prophetic books were meaningless, and afforded the opportunity to any fool to give them any meaning he wished. Origen responded that the words of the prophets cannot be taken in any chance way one wishes, and bases his argument on 1 Corinthians 2:13. Only the person in Christ can interpret the obscure passages of the prophets "by 'comparing spiritual things with spiritual' and by explaining each phrase he found in the text from the common usage of that phrase elsewhere in scripture."[44]

One of the by-products of this comparison of texts containing the same key terminology was the creation of a core of Biblical symbolism. Origen inherited some of this symbolism from his predecessors, both Christians and Jews, and created some of it himself. This symbolism, once established, could then function without the continual repetition of the web of comparative texts from which it had been created. Particular persons, places, and events in the Bible came to symbolize key persons, places and events in the drama of salvation being played out below the surface level of the texts. The appearance of these indicators in a text immediately alerted the spiritual reader to this symbolic meaning.

How this process of the creation and use of a Biblical symbol worked can be illustrated in Origen's equation of Pharaoh with the devil, and consequently of Egypt with this (evil) world.[45] In *On First Principles*,[46] he brings together various passages from the Old Testament which he considers to speak of the devil. Pharaoh is not specifically mentioned here, but the Biblical image of the "dragon" occurs in some of the texts. This latter is a key image in Origen's concept of how the Bible speaks of the devil.[47] The association seems to have developed as follows. Origen begins by referring to the "serpent" who seduced Eve in Genesis 3. The apocryphal *Ascension of Moses* is then cited where the "serpent" is said to have been inspired by the *devil* in his seduction of Eve. Other images from the Old Testament related to the devil, which have no direct bearing on our point, follow. Then comes a citation of Isaiah 27:1, where "the dragon" is identified with "the crooked serpent," and this is followed by two allusions to Ezekiel, the latter of which is Ezekiel 27:3, which refers to "the great dragon sitting in the midst of the rivers." This verse, in the portion not expressly cited here by Origen, identifies this "great dragon" as Pharaoh. Ezekiel 27:3 was the key verse for Origen's subsequent symbolic reading of Pharaoh. He sometimes cites it explicitly to identify Pharaoh as symbolic of the devil,[48] but more often references to Pharaoh are simply taken to mean the devil with no supporting Biblical texts cited for the identification.[49] That "'king who knew not Joseph,'" and who subjected the Israelites to slavery in Egypt is "the devil."[50] Pharaoh, fearing the increasing number of the Israelites, says, "'The race of Israel is stronger than us.'" Origen comments, assuming the symbolic meaning of Pharaoh: "Would that he might also say this about us; that he might feel that we are stronger than himself!"[51] Pharaoh does not want us to leave his land, therefore he "appoints 'taskmasters' to teach us their skills, to make us contrivers of malice, to tutor us in evils." When the Lord Jesus comes, he sets other taskmasters over us who subdue those of Pharaoh, and "teach us the works of Israel. They teach us again to see God with the mind, to leave the works of Pharaoh, to depart from the land of Egypt, to cast aside Egyptian and barbarian customs."[52]

Origen summarizes his overall program for the symbolic reading of the Bible in the treatise *On First Principles*.[53] It is again texts of Paul that provide his justification. Paul spoke of "Israel after the flesh" (1 Cor. 10:18), which, Origen says, implies an "Israel after the spirit." Again Paul said, "It is not the children of the flesh that are children of God" (Rom. 9:8), and, "Not all who are of Israel are Israel" (Rom. 9:6). These and other Pauline texts, such as those which contrast the earthly and heavenly Jerusalem, and the inner and outer Jew, teach Origen to read the history of the Israelites as symbolic of the race of souls. But if this is true of the Israelites, it must be true also that the other peoples mentioned in the Bible, such as the Egyptians, Babylonians, Tyrians, etc., along with their rulers are spiritual as well. And, as there is a heavenly Jerusalem and Judaea, so there are adjacent spiritual places called Egypt, or Babylon, or Tyre. These latter regions are where souls are taken into captivity.[54] The Savior was sent to gather these "lost sheep of the house of Israel" (cf. Matt. 10:6; 15:24).[55] The Holy Spirit has buried these spiritual truths concerning the soul's salvation deeply in narratives "in which people are said to go down into Egypt or to be led captive to Babylon."[56]

Origen's allegorical reading of the Bible was a coherent and controlled reading. The principle of comparing Biblical texts, which he based on 1 Corinthians 2:13, was a primary factor in both the coherence and the controlled nature of his reading.

The Reader of the Bible

Origen's view of the reader of the Bible is correlate with both his view of the nature of the Bible, and his hermeneutical principle taken from 1 Corinthians 2:13. He recognized, of course, that anyone could read and understand the historical narrative contained in the Bible, and, as we noted above, such a reading was not without its usefulness. The goal of reading the Bible, however, is to "understand in a worthy manner the word which is stored up in the earthen treasures of paltry language."[57] This hidden treasure was not available to just any reader, but only to the spiritual person who could say with Paul, "'but we have the mind of Christ, that we may know the things which have been given to us by God.'"[58] The spiritual truth which has been buried in the Bible can be understood only by one in whom the same Spirit who was present and worked through the writers of the Bible dwells and works.[59] This Spirit works in the interpreter primarily in the process of "comparing spiritual things with spiritual" (1 Cor. 2:13).

Paul's statements in 1 Corinthians 2:10-16 were important to Origen's understanding of the reader of the Bible as well as to his understanding of the method of reading the Bible. We have already cited 1 Corinthians 2:16 and 12 above, and we shall return to those verses later, but we begin with his use of 1 Corinthians 2:10: "God has given us a revelation through his Spirit. For the Spirit searches all things, even the depths of God." In commenting on this verse, Origen stresses the necessity of the presence of the Holy Spirit in the person who would understand the deeper meaning in the Bible. "It is the 'Spirit'," he says, "which is able to search 'all things.' The soul of man cannot search all things, but the higher Spirit must come to be in us so that, when he who searches 'all things, even the depths of God' has come to be in us, and has been united with us, we, together with him, may search 'all things, even the depths of God.'"[60]

This dependence on the presence of the Spirit which Origen perceived in his understanding of the Bible is expressed in various ways. Sometimes he speaks of it as being filled with the same Spirit which filled the prophets, and consequently, in a sense, as being a prophet himself in his interpretation of the Bible.[61] Origen expresses this explicitly in an echo of Isaiah 22:22, when he says, "Not only must I have learned the things of the Spirit who moved Isaiah, but I must also have had the same Spirit which closed and sealed Isaiah's words. For unless the Spirit opens the words of the prophets, the things which have been closed cannot be opened."[62] He makes this statement in the context of his discussion of the principle of "comparing spiritual things with spiritual" (1 Cor. 2:13). He must have been thinking partially, at least, of the application of this comparative principle to Biblical texts when he speaks here of the Spirit opening "the words of the prophets." It is clear, however, that he thinks of 1 Corinthians 2:13 as providing a principle that can be used only by a person in whom the Spirit is present. Origen must have impressed these matters on his students by his own practice as well as by his lectures. In the *Panegyric* addressed to him, one of Origen's students, basing his remarks on Isaiah 22:22, says that the words of the prophets can be understood correctly only by those to whom the Spirit who spoke in the prophets has given the ability to understand. He then comments that Origen had himself received this divine gift.[63]

Origen refers specifically to the necessity of the Spirit's presence based on 1 Corinthians 2:10 in relation to all our knowledge of God[64] and for understanding such problems as the inequalities in the human condition exemplified in the Biblical story of Jacob and Esau[65] and those posed by the story of the hardening of Pharaoh's heart.[66] In his first homily on Exodus, however, Origen makes it clear that he did not think that insight into the deeper meaning of the Biblical text was given by the Spirit apart from the intense exegetical effort of the reader. He compares the inter-

140

preter of the Bible to a farmer who must diligently work the earth.[67] Origen also notes, since he is addressing a congregation, that the nature of the audience, which he compares to the fertility of the earth, is a further factor in the result of the interpreter's work. But he also asks his audience to pray for the leading of the Logos in his discourse.[68] It is the cooperative effort of the Spirit and the interpreter which yields the desired result.

Origen appeals even more frequently to 1 Corinthians 2:16 and 12 when he speaks of the reader of the Bible.[69] He usually combines the two verses in the form, "But we have the mind of Christ, that we may know the things which have been given to us by God." Clement of Alexandria had identified "the mind of Christ" in 1 Corinthians 2:16 with the Holy Spirit.[70] This identification may be the basis for Origen's combination of the two verses. He replaces the major clause of verse 12, "But we received the Spirit of God," with the clause, "But we have the mind of Christ" from 1 Corinthians 2:16. He never, however, makes such an explicit identification as Clement had done. Furthermore, although he certainly considered the presence of the Holy Spirit in the reader of the Bible to be a necessity, as we have just noted in our discussion of his use of 1 Corinthians 2:10, he seems, in fact, to use the phrase "mind of Christ" more in the sense of the "understanding of Christ" than in the specific sense of the Holy Spirit.

The following passages may serve to show how Origen understands the "mind of Christ" to be formed in a person and what he understands it to mean for the reader of the Bible. The first is his discussion of the "living water" that Jesus gives in contrast to the water from the well of Jacob in John 4. Origen identifies Jacob's well with the Scriptures, and he says that one must have come regularly and frequently to Jacob's well before one can receive the living water that Jesus gives. He means that one must have read the Bible diligently over a long period of time, and have had one's life shaped by its teachings. Most people, he says, are very deficient in this sustained drinking from Jacob's well and cannot, therefore, receive the "living water." The higher teachings of the "living water" are revealed only "to those who no longer have the heart of man, but who are able to say, 'But we have the mind of Christ, that we may know the things which have been given to us by God.'"[71] A part of the formation of the "mind of Christ" in a person was a broad knowledge of the whole of Scripture which could then be brought to bear on individual texts. This much might be taken to be little different from the hermeneutical circle in which one understands the whole in terms of the details and the details in terms of the whole. The issue, however, is more complex. Origen did not mean simply a broad knowledge of the literal details of the Biblical writings, as our next example makes clear.

In the ninth homily on Joshua Origen treats Joshua 8:34-5, where Joshua is said to have read all the words of the Law to the Israelites. Because Joshua's name in Greek is "Jesus," Origen passes easily from Joshua to "the Lord Jesus" and asserts that whenever the "veil of the letter" is removed and we begin to understand that "the Law is spiritual," and that when it speaks of "not muzzling an oxen" it is not concerned for oxen, and when it says that Abraham "had two sons," it is referring to two covenants and two peoples, then the Lord Jesus is reading the Law to us.

> In this way, we can understand the Law correctly, if Jesus reads it to us, so that, as he reads, we may receive his "mind" and understanding. Or is it not to be thought that he understood "mind" from this, who said, "But we have the mind of Christ, that we may know the things which have been given to us by God, which things also we speak"? And [did not] those [have the same understanding] who said, "Was not our heart burning within us when he opened the Scriptures to us in this way?" when he read everything to them, beginning from the Law of Moses up to the prophets, and revealed the things which had been written about himself?[72]

This passage makes clear that a part of the formation of the "mind of Christ" in a person depends on learning to recognize the spiritual meaning in the Scriptural texts. The spiritual reading of the Bible is, in effect, Origen thinks, a kind of *imitatio Christi* in relation to Christ's understanding of the Law.

In his discussion of drinking from "Jacob's well," Origen divides readers of the Bible into three categories. Some drink as Jacob and his sons. These are those who "are wise in the Scriptures," i.e. the spiritual readers. Others drink as Jacob's livestock. These are the "so-called 'sheep of Christ,'" or the simple. Still others drink as the Samaritan woman drank "before she believed in Jesus." These are the heretics who misunderstand the Scriptures.[73] It is the spiritual readers, who drink from the well of Scripture as Jacob and his sons, in whom the "mind of Christ" is formed. For these persons the Scriptures are no more than "introductions" to the higher spiritual truth which is "beyond that which is written" (1 Cor. 4:6), and which is associated with the "living water" that Jesus gives.[74] One goes up from the spiritual understanding of the Scriptures. This latter is made more explicit in a passage in his *Commentary on the Song of Songs*.

142

In commenting on Song of Songs 2:8 ("Behold, he comes leaping on the mountains, skipping on the hills") Origen makes applications to both the Church and the soul. In an application to the Church, he identifies the "mountains" and "hills" as the books of the Law and the prophets. When the "veil" is removed from the reading of these books, the Church finds "Christ springing forth from them."[75] He also notes in his exposition how the bridegroom is sometimes depicted as present with the bride and sometimes absent from her. Taking this in relation to the soul, he says that when she attempts unsuccessfully to understand some obscure matter, then "the Word of God is surely absent from her." When, however, what she is seeking "appears to her, who doubts but that the Word of God is present, illuminating her mind and offering to her the light of knowledge?" But then he withdraws again, and later returns "in every matter that is either opened or closed to our understanding." This alternation of the bridegroom's presence and absence, which is taken, with its echo of the "opened" and "closed" terminology of Isaiah 22:22 discussed above, to mean the understanding or lack of understanding of Scripture's obscurities, continues, Origen says, "until we become such people as He may condescend not only often to revisit, but to remain with."[76] It is important to note that the continual presence of the bridegroom to which Origen here alludes refers to the continual ability to understand the spiritual meaning in the Scriptures. Finally, he identifies those souls who have drunk the "living water" that Jesus gives with the "mountains and hills" of Song of Songs 2:8. These are souls "who are more able to receive the Word of God." The "Word of God bursts forth" in these souls "in frequent and abundant perceptions like ever-flowing streams." They have become "mountains and hills" as a result of their "life and knowledge and teaching."[77] This latter statement shows that the spiritual readers of whom Origen speaks are the exegetes, or teachers of the Church like himself.[78]

Origen treats the theme of the repeated presence and absence of the bridegroom with the bride in the Song of Songs again in his first homily on that book. He comments that no one can understand this who has not personally experienced it. Then he relates his own experience. "I have often perceived the Bridegroom drawing near me and being most intensely present with me; then suddenly He has withdrawn and I could not find Him, though I sought to do so." This he says, has been his repeated experience, and each time the bridegroom slips away the "search for Him begins anew."[79] It may be correct to speak of this as a mystical experience,[80] but if so, it is a mysticism that is directly related to Origen's reading of the Bible, for it was there that he looked for Christ. It is, in my view, Origen's description of his experience in reading the Bible. Sometimes Christ is clearly manifest to him in the passage he is reading, but as he proceeds, he loses Christ and must again struggle to find him in the text. Something very similar to this is expressed clearly near the end of his discussion of how to read the Bible in *On First Principles* when he asserts that no one can ever understand everything in the Scriptures. "For however far one may advance in the search and make progress through an increasingly earnest study, even when aided and enlightened in mind by God's grace, he will never be able to reach the final goal of his inquiries." Rather, as soon as the mind "has discovered a small fragment of what it is seeking, it again sees other things that must be sought for; and if in turn it comes to know these, it will again see arising out of them many more things that demand investigation." Consequently, he concludes with Paul's words from Philippians 3:14, that each person, in accordance with his own capacity should "ever 'reach out to the things which are before, forgetting those things which are behind,'" which means, he says, reaching out "both to better works and also to a clearer understanding and knowledge, through Jesus Christ our Saviour, to whom is the glory for ever."[81]

There is one other necessary factor in Origen's concept of the reader who would properly understand the Bible. He or she must be a person of prayer. Many of his homilies, and some of the books of his commentaries, either begin or end with a prayer, or the request for prayer, for divine help in understanding the Scriptures. He addresses the subject most clearly in the conclusion of his letter to his student Gregory. He urges Gregory, as we noted above, to give his priority to the reading of the Scriptures. In doing this, he says, Gregory should "knock" at Scripture's "closed" doors, and they will be opened. He should "seek" the hidden meaning in the Scriptures. But most important of all, he should pray, for "prayer," Origen says, "is most necessary for understanding the divine Scriptures." Consequently, "the Saviour not only said, 'Knock and it will be opened to you,' and, 'Seek and you will find,' but he also said, 'Ask and it will be given to you (Matt. 7:7).'"[82] Understanding the Bible for Origen, in the final analysis, was a gift of God's grace.

In conclusion, I return to the hermeneutical circle I referred to above, in which the whole is understood in terms of the details, and the details in terms of the whole. I noted there that Origen's view is more complex. One might say that Origen's hermeneutical circle is larger or that he thinks in terms of more than one circle. There is the narrower circle of the comparison of texts in which the literal terminology is used to bring together texts which share words or ideas. From these texts which have elements in common, the key to the spiritual meaning of a word or concept in the text in question is established, and this meaning then functions to provide the symbolic significance wherever else the term may occur. This circle involves the text in relation to itself. The next larger circle involves the reader and the text. Only the spiritual person can discern the hidden meaning of the text, but the hidden meaning of the text itself plays a major role in the formation of the spiritual person. Finally, there is the circle that involves the Holy Spirit, the text, and the reader. Both the text and the spiritual reader are formed ultimately by the Holy Spirit. The Spirit works independently in both the text (by inspiration) and the reader (through prayer). But the Spirit also works conjointly in them in the illumination of the reader through the comparison of texts. To separate things in this way misconstrues them slightly, for the circles all collapse in on one another in Origen's thought and work, and all, apart from the inspiration of the Scriptures by the Spirit, operate more or less simultaneously.

NOTES

1. Eusebius of Caesarea, *Hist. Eccl.* 6.2.7-9.
2. *Comm. in Joannem* 13.42.
3. *Ep. ad Gregorium* 1 (*ap. Origenis Philocalia* 13, ed. J. A. Robinson, Cambridge, 1893), 64.
4. Ibid. 2-3 (*Origenis Philocalia* 13, ed. Robinson), 65-66.
5. Ibid. 4 (*Origenis Philocalia* 13, ed. Robinson), 67.
6. *De principiis* 4.1.6.
7. *Homiliae in Genesim* 4.3.
8. Ibid. 10.2.
9. *Comm. in Joannem* 10.19-20.
10. Ibid.
11. *De princ.* 4.2.9.
12. Ibid. 4.3.1.
13. Ibid. 4.3.4.
14. *De oratione* 18.2-3.
15. *Comm. in Joannem* 6.170-172.
16. *De princ.* 4.2.6, 8.
17. *Comm. in Joannem* 1.43. This may have been a part of the legacy Origen inherited from the faith of his father. Eusebius notes that when the young

Origen would ask his father about the deeper meaning of Scripture, his father would advise him not to seek beyond the "manifest meaning" (*Hist. Eccl.* 6.2.10). This may suggest that Origen's father read the Bible as one of "the simple." The faith of his father appears to have had a profound influence on Origen, and his continual concern for, and dialogue with, "the simple" may be yet another part of that influence.

18. See E. de Faye, *Origène: sa vie, son oeuvre, sa pensée*, vol. 1 (Paris, 1923), 106-137.

19. *Contra Celsum* 7.41; cf. also 3.44, 59. See also H. Koch, *Pronoia und Paideusis* (Berlin and Leipzig, 1932), 56.

20. See K. J. Torjesen, "'Body,' 'Soul,' and 'Spirit' in Origen's Theology of Exegesis," *Anglican Theological Review* 67 (1985): 17-30, esp. 19.

21. *Comm. in Joannem* 1.45.

22. See M. Harl, "Le guetteur et la cible: les deux sens de *skopos* dans la langue religieuse des chrétiens," *Revue des études grecques* 74 (1961): 455-456. Harl suggests that *skopos* in Origen means God's plan to save humanity as revealed in the Scriptures, and the interpreter's task, then, is to discover, under the historical narrative, those saving indicators which correspond to God's essential plan.

23. *De princ.* 4.2.7.

24. Ibid. 4.2.8.

25. Ibid. 4.2.9.

26. Ibid.

27. Ibid. 4.3.14.

28. Torjesen ("'Body,' 'Soul,' and 'Spirit,'" 20) has correctly noted that Origen thinks of an exegete as someone who interprets Scripture for others, not for himself.

29. See de Faye, *Origène*, vol. 1, 75, 89-90; B. Neuschäfer, *Origenes als Philologe*, 2 vols. (Basel, 1987); R. M. Grant, *The Earliest Lives of Jesus* (New York, 1961); R. E. Heine, "Stoic Logic as Handmaid to Exegesis and Theology in Origen's Commentary on the Gospel of John," *Journal of Theological Studies* 44 (1993): 90-117.

30. *Comm. in Joannem* 6.204.

31. Ibid. 6.204-205.

32. Ibid. 6.206.

33. Ibid. 6.53.

34. Ibid. 2.13-15.

35. Ibid. 2.37-38.

36. Ibid. 10.3-14.

37. Ibid. 28.98-191.

38. Ibid. 1.90-92, 174.

39. *Hom. in Exodum* 5.1; cf. *Comm. in Joannem* 6.227.

40. See J. Lamberton, *Homer the Theologian* (Berkeley, 1986), 109; L. G. Westerink, "The Alexandrian Commentators and the Introductions to Their Commentaries," in *Aristotle Transformed: The Ancient Commenta-*

tors and Their Influence, ed. R. Sorabji (Ithaca, N.Y., 1990); P. Sellew, "Achilles or Christ? Porphyry and Didymus in Debate over Allegorical Interpretation," *Harvard Theological Review* 82 (1989): 83; N. R. M. de Lange, *Origen and the Jews* (Cambridge, 1976), 110-111.

41. *Selecta in Psalmos* (PG 12: 1080C).

42. Text in C. Jenkins, ed., "Origen on 1 Corinthians," *Journal of Theological Studies* (Old Series) 9 (1908): 240.

43. *Comm. in Canticum* 3.13.8.

44. *Contra Celsum* 7.11; trans. H. Chadwick, *Origen: Contra Celsum* (Cambridge, 1965), 404.

45. Pharaoh was not the only symbol of the devil in the Bible for Origen. The prince of Tyre was another, and nearly any ruler considered evil in the Old Testament.

46. *De princ.* 3.2.1

47. See especially *Comm. in Joannem* 1.95-98, and the importance of Job 40:19 there, and also ibid., 20.181-182; 32.233-234.

48. *Comm. in Joannem* 6.248-249; *Hom. in Ezech.* 13.1; *Contra Celsum* 4.50.

49. *Comm. in Cant.* 2.6.1-2; repeatedly in the *Hom. in Exod.* 1-6.

50. *Hom. in Exod.* 1.5.

51. Ibid.

52. Ibid.

53. *De princ.* 4.3.6-15.

54. *De princ.* 4.3.9.

55. Ibid. 4.3.10.

56. Ibid. 4.3.11.

57. *Comm. in Joannem* 1.24.

58. Ibid.; 1 Cor. 2:16, 12.

59. *De princ.* 4.2.7.

60. Jenkins, ed., "Origen on 1 Corinthians," 239.

61. *Hom. in Jeremiah* 19.14; *Hom. in Ezech.* 2.2. See also P. Cox, *Biography in Late Antiquity* (Berkeley, 1983), 94-95; H. Crouzel, *Origen*, trans. A. S. Worrall (Edinburgh, 1989), 74-75; G. Hällström, *Charismatic Succession: A Study on Origen's Concept of Prophecy* (Helsinki, 1985), 42ff.

62. Jenkins, ed., "Origen on 1 Corinthians," 240. Cf. *Hom. in Exod.* 4.5.

63. *In Origenem oratio panegyrica* (PG 10: 1093D-1096A). The panegyric has traditionally been attributed to Gregory Thaumaturgus.

64. *De princ.* 1.3.4; *Contra Celsum* 6.17.

65. *De princ.* 2.9.5.

66. *Hom. in Exod.* 4.2.

67. Origen also notes, since he is addressing a congregation, that the nature of the audience, which he compares to the fertility of the earth, is a further factor in the result of the interpreter's work.

68. *Hom. in Exod.* 1.1.

69. See L. Brésard, H. Crouzel, and M. Borret, eds., *Origène: Commentaire sur le cantique des cantiques*, SC 375 (Paris, 1991), 242-243, n. 1.

70. *Stromateis* 5.4.25.5. Clement discusses several of the same verses from 1 Cor. 2:10-16 which Origen uses in relation to understanding the mysteries of Scripture in the whole of *Strom.* 5.4. *Strom.* 5.4-12 is a discussion of the symbolic veiling of truth in general as seen in philosophers, poets, and Egyptian mysteries, as well as in the Bible.

71. *Comm. in Joannem* 13.23-42.

72. *Hom. in Jesu Nave* 9.8.

73. *Comm. in Joannem* 13.38-39.

74. Ibid. 13.30-37.

75. *Comm. in Cant.* 3.12.4; trans. R. P. Lawson, *Origen: The Song of Songs Commentary and Homilies,* Ancient Christian Writers, no. 26 (New York, 1957), 214.

76. *Comm. in Cant.* 3.11.18-19; trans. Lawson, 216.

77. Ibid., 3.12.12; trans. Lawson, 216.

78. See note 28 above.

79. *Hom. in Cant.* 1.7; trans. Lawson, 280.

80. See Lawson, ibid., 364, n. 66.

81. *De princ.* 4.3.14; trans. G. W. Butterworth, *Origen: On First Principles* (New York, 1966), 311-312.

82. *Ep. ad Gregorium* 4 (*Origenis Philocalia* 13, ed. Robinson), 67.

8

Gregory Nazianzen: Constructing and Constructed by Scripture

FREDERICK NORRIS

The corpus of Gregory the Theologian offers us a remarkable opportunity when raising the question of how early Christians interpreted the Bible. Church Fathers such as Origen and John Chrysostom, or Augustine and Jerome, created commentaries or preached a series of homilies on entire biblical books. At other times when there is nothing extant on a full scriptural book, we have from these four either partial treatments of originally large works or pieces designed to cover sections of the Bible, sometimes encompassing a few chapters as, for example, the Sermon on the Mount. In the twelfth century Elias of Crete spoke of a treatise by Nazianzen which he refers to as *The History of Ezekiel the Prophet*. It might have been a commentary on the biblical book or the scriptural cycles about that figure, but we do not have a copy.[1] The bulk of Gregory's works are not concerned with consecutive exegesis of a selected portion of Holy Writ. *Oration 37* deals with Matthew 19:1-12 and will be treated below. But Nazianzen's writings always represent the thought of a constructive theologian who teaches and preaches within a context shaped both by polemical adversaries and by confessional friends.

Thus when we investigate the Theologian's use of Holy Writ, we will have to approach it in specifically theological ways. We cannot pretend, as some do, that at its best commentary on biblical texts offers us some kind of distanced, controlled interpretation of scriptural verses. Those who study early Christian exegesis seldom if ever suggest that neither Augustine nor Origen was involved in or changed by the theological debates of his day when he meditated on the Bible. But too often there is a modern fantasy that the paradigm against which ancient insights, whether grammatical, historical or allegorical, must be judged is the "objective" historical, critical exegesis of the modern era.

Such pristine objectivity has never existed except as an ethereal goal. Twentieth-century exegesis with its psychological and political insights is surely a contemporary form of allegory, and no less useful because it is. Positivistic historical treatments of Scripture depend upon their own worldviews and assumptions. Both modern and early exegesis has arisen out of communities with deep theological or sometimes anti-theological views which inform what they "find" in the text.[2] Differences between ancient and modern efforts exist, but they shift in importance. Modern critical texts have the variants set off in footnotes. Alternatives are printed, but they appear to be "handled" or at least "handleable." Before the onslaught of printed books, however, texts had a fluidity which both influenced and was influenced by theological debate, a malleability that we frequently forget. They were usually read aloud with the clear expectation that they had been marred by scribal error as all texts were. Reading meant constructing a text somewhat different from the transcription in hand.

Textual variants within the Bible were and are at times significant. For example, in his discussion of both Jesus Christ and the Holy Spirit with Neo-Arian opponents, Nazianzen continually returns to baptism into the name of the Father, the Son, and the Holy Spirit as a basic insight. Christians would not have been baptized into the Son or into the Holy Spirit if the Son and the Spirit were not of the same nature as the Father. Believers share in the intended *theôsis*, "deification," only if each person of the Trinity in whose name they were baptized is divine and thus can offer them divine life. As we would expect, there are allusions to a series of texts, but surely one of the more prominent ones behind the Theologian's argument is Matthew 28:19-20, the command so to baptize. Threefold immersion into Father, Son, and Spirit, the practice of Gregory's Church, provided a liturgical setting for his arguments about Christology and Trinity, arguments which relied on the threefold character of that command in Matthew.[3]

A number of Christian theologians had referred to that "triune" text for baptism well before Gregory.[4] His colleagues Basil and Gregory of Nyssa found it normative.[5] But we also have the nagging testimony from Eusebius of Caesarea that there well may have been a textual tradition for Matthew 28:19-20 which did not have the threefold formula. That form of the text, unattested in extant manuscripts, seems to have spoken only of baptism in the name of Jesus. Such a reading is particularly important because it appears in the corpus of Eusebius of Caesarea,[6] one who had difficulty understanding and/or accepting the early Nicene refusal of Arian views as heretical. We do not hear much about a single immersion of Christians into the name of Jesus until Socrates and Sozomen speak of it in describing the views of later Arians. Both those historians insist that such a baptism was an innovation which marked some non-Nicene communities.[7] But the Biblical text and the Neo-Arian practice may represent a conservative tradition, one in place before the time of Arius, let alone Aetius and Eunomius. In itself such Arian views and acts were theologically astute and quite possibly related to a different text of Matthew's command about baptism as well as Pauline verses about baptism in Jesus' name.

This alternative textual tradition shows yet again that we cannot separate neatly the text an early theologian used from the theological traditions and the worshipping community within which that theologian lived. Arians may have handed on a biblical text and liturgical practice which probably both formed and was formed by their communities. It is certainly no accident that the basic biblical text of Gregory the Theologian and the rest of the Cappadocian circle appears to have been the common Byzantine one,[8] circulated by a Church that accepted the Cappadocians as theologically sound—with some serious questioning of views like Nyssa's universalism.[9] Here chicken/egg arguments are futile. Modern "objective" textual study can argue that the single immersion "in Jesus' name" variant is the earliest because it explains the existence of the threefold text as a corrective addition. The point is focused on the question of who would have shortened the text from the threefold to single form. The question has merit, but modern textual study also is not capable of drawing itself up into uninvolved positions which clearly show us how the texts developed. Textual studies themselves must come to terms with the more holistic interrelations of community, theology and text, their own and those of the texts they study.[10] We may not be able to settle the question whether the text "in the name of Jesus" referred to by Eusebius was the original. Perhaps Eusebius found a text of Matthew in the Caesarean library that agreed with Pauline and Luke/Acts models. Or he may have repeated a misremembered conflation based on those same models.[11]

A similar kind of communal need within a particular polemical context bears on the question of what canon Gregory employed. He evidently read the Septuagint for he quotes as Scripture passages from Tobit,

Judith, 1 & 2 Maccabees, Wisdom of Solomon, Ben Sirach and Baruch.[12] But the selections from those books, specifically in his *Theological Orations*, are to be understood in terms of their usefulness in his debates with later Arians and Pneumatomachians. They provide scriptural Trinitarian and Christological backing important to the propagation and defense of what he confesses as orthodox. The Wisdom of Solomon is among the most frequently used of the so-called apocryphal books. Wisdom 1:7, 7:21, 23, 27 and 8:1 help the Theologian establish from Scripture that God the Father and the Holy Spirit are not to be made subject to containment arguments. They fill the world but are not limited to it. Placed between references to Hebrews 1:3 and John 6:27, the phrase "image of goodness" from Wisdom 7:26 provides Gregory with a model of the Son that challenges the Arian interpretation of Jesus himself saying God alone is good. Jesus said that, but Holy Writ also says that he was the "image of goodness." Nazianzen refers to Baruch 3:36-38 precisely because he sees that section as a reference to the Son as God; it insists that *God* "was seen on earth and lived among men."

The Theologian's exegesis of Scripture, always set within homilies, poems or letters with specific theological purposes, forms a continuum with one end respecting the rather strong resistance to any interpretation that a text offers and the other end treating a text as something more akin to a springboard. Gregory adopts a fourfold calculus for dealing with biblical texts, one he found in Origen. "(1) Some things that do not occur in reality are mentioned in Holy Writ. (2) Some things that occur are not mentioned. (3) Some things that do not occur are not mentioned. (4) Some things that occur are mentioned."[13] The first principle is particularly helpful in theological debate because it contains the many anthropomorphic characteristics of God which in Gregory's view surely do not exist. At the same time Origen's principle of Scripture never saying things unworthy of God, things often seen as unworthy from rather sophisticated acceptance of philosophical principles, provides guidance for selecting from a series of options what a specific text means. The Theologian worries that a kind of literalism may support Jewish rejection of Jesus as the Messiah; a love of the letter may serve as a "cloak of irreligion" that blinds even Christians to the truth in Holy Writ about the Holy Spirit. Nazianzen accepts that the text written has an inner meaning which appears only when the Bible is read with great care.[14] He knows that the interpretation of texts, for example the parable of the laborers in the vineyard, could be quite dangerous. Holy Writ can cause injury when proper information is not in the reader's hands.[15] Gregory would be reticent to think of the Bible as a totally separate component in theology, but what it says is of utmost importance; no position should ever be taken without scriptural support. Yet the totality of revelation should be involved in the interpretation of each text. Holy Writ has its own *skopos*, its own intent. And that intent is made known to the Church in worship.

Although Nazianzen's interpretation is always deeply enmeshed in his community's theological concerns, R.P.C. Hanson has insisted correctly that much of the Theologian's exegesis is rather common-sensical and grammatical.[16] Gregory depends upon his circle of fellow theologians for concordant lists of where the words "holy" and "spirit" appear in Scripture.[17] They probably shared similar guides to various biblical themes. Within an oration on baptism, Nazianzen enumerates five kinds of baptism and assembles about a half dozen scriptural references for each, references he welds together to make his point.[18] The actual words from Holy Writ are important, but they can be arranged together in a harmonious whole which is led by his theological commitments as well as the actual words themselves.

Gregory the Theologian's education in philosophical rhetoric is evident in his grammatical exegesis. Certain understandings of language dominate all his exegetical work. As a master rhetorician, Nazianzen knows that language is often a puzzle. It rarely tells us anything definite.[19] It does represent certain "things" (*pragmata*); thus we can talk with each other and make some kind of sense.[20] Indeed language has a positive character which must be honored. Even in a discipline such as theology, a theologian cannot develop only an apophatic approach to the nature of God. Although we must concede the severe limitations of our meager minds, we also must attempt to say some things about deity that state rather than negate. We could truthfully answer that two times five is neither "two," nor "three," nor "four" on *ad infinitum*, skipping over "ten." But at some point it might be best just to say "ten." Deciding that a term like "unbegotten" is the most helpful designation for God both denies that sense of things and overlooks a group of positive words used for God in Scripture.[21]

Second, following Aristotle[22] and rejecting Plato,[23] Nazianzen views all language as conventional rather than natural. We decide how to use the words which we choose; there is no necessary connection between the name of something and its nature. Trying to work out the relationship of a "dog" and a "dogshark" on the assumption that both somehow share a "dog" essence or that one has that nature and the other is referred to as a "dog" only because of some similarity to that essence creates an unsolvable conundrum.[24] The Theologian criticizes his later Arian opponents for this category mistake about names[25] and is probably aware that both Clement and Origen had themselves fallen into what he considers to be a trap.[26]

Third, most language does not fit easily into propositions that can be formed into syllogisms. The Theologian builds his sense of argument on Aristotle's concept of an enthymeme. His main concern is not that a three-part classic syllogism of major premise, minor premise and conclusion could be shortened into a two-part enthymeme: "if . . ., then" or "because . . ., therefore." That contraction was designed to draw the audience into supplying the missing premise and thereby becoming actively involved in the debate. His approach, on the contrary, depends upon the Stagirite's observation that much human conversation deals with probability issues which are not suited to the formal demonstration of syllogisms. For Gregory, theology and biblical interpretation raise probability questions. They look to authority in maxims or topics and thus are seldom amenable to syllogistic tests of validity.[27]

All human language suffers these limitations. Therefore all theologians are at bottom philologists;[28] indeed the best theologian is a poet, someone who offers better images and provides vivid but fleeting glimpses into the deep mysteries.[29] Anyone interpreting the Bible does not come upon crystal clear statements, names for God's essence or God's actions which somehow magically reveal in their fullness those aspects of God. Only rarely do logical propositions appear in Scripture, ones that may be demonstrated through syllogisms. In theology the nature of language is only heightened, not changed. Plato was wrong to think that the nature of God is merely inexpressible;[30] it is instead incomprehensible.[31]

These general perspectives on language and theological language and thus on biblical texts are developed through a clear understanding of grammatical rules that gives the text a chance to resist certain interpretations while at the same time allowing theologians to read Scripture through the convictions of their communities. But before turning to those rules, it is important to insist, in ways the textbooks seldom tell us, that the Trinitarian controversy which so defined Gregory's life was itself a debate about the interpretation of Holy Writ, about the meaning of biblical texts within the context of worshipping communities.[32] The development by the Cappadocians of philosophically astute concepts and terminology like *homoousios, physis, ousia,* etc. was shorthand contextualization of a large amount of exegesis. The Theologian argued that his positions were the true ones because they made more sense of more Scripture than did the views of the later Arians. After citing or alluding to over 150 biblical texts set within an almost hymnic counterpoint which stresses both the humanity and the divinity of Jesus Christ, Nazianzen says: "If the first set of expressions starts you going astray, the second set takes your error away."[33] The great theological issues that the Cappadocians debated with their opponents can be followed rather closely by paying attention to how they interpreted Scripture and what principles they applied from within their community of faith.

For Gregory, the meaning of a word depended upon its use in a specific context. 1 Corinthians 15:25, Acts 3:21, and Psalm 110:1 (109:1, LXX) cause consternation and debate because they are read by later Arians as saying that the Son would reign "only until" the kingdom was restored to the Father. That reading supports their sense of the Son's subordination to the Father, his secondary status as a divine being. Yet Nazianzen responds with Luke 1:33 which states that the Son's royal rule will not end. The problem depends upon the meaning of the word "until." It can designate what happens up to a point and not deny anything about what occurs after that point. For example, in Matthew 28:20 Jesus says that he will be with his disciples "until" the end of the age. That cannot mean that he will not be with them after the age has ended. The 1 Corinthians, Acts, and Psalms passages do not establish that the Son is of a second rank, less than the Father. They only state that when all those inferior to him have submitted to his rule, he no longer needs to produce submission in them. Only in that sense will his rule end. Nazianzen's opponents have misunderstood these passage because they have denied the plain sense of Luke 1:33 and have supplied the wrong meaning for "until" by not comparing it with its use in other biblical verses.[34]

Determining the meaning of a word in Scripture can also be enhanced by knowing what options exist for the meaning of that word in everyday language as well as in the Bible. Gregory's Eunomian opponents insist that John 5:19 shows the secondary nature of the Son when it claims that he "can do nothing of himself, but what he sees the Father do." To understand what "can do nothing" means, the interpreter must ask what "cannot" means. Nazianzen offers five possibilities. First, the word may refer to an ability at a particular time in relation to a specific object. Young children are not accomplished athletes, but they may grow

155

to be such. A little puppy with closed eyes certainly cannot fight, but later he may both see and attack. Second, "cannot" might speak of something that is usually true but is not true from a particular perspective. When Scripture says "A city set on a hill cannot be hidden," it does not mean it could never be hidden. If one stands with a higher hill in the line of sight, the city cannot be seen. Third, "cannot" could mean something unthinkable, something not considered sensible. At the celebration of a wedding feast, the friends of the bridegroom "cannot" fast while everyone around them is celebrating. Fourth, "cannot" might designate a lack of will as when Jesus "could not" do miracles because of the people's lack of faith. Jesus did no mighty works in his home town, but that did not mean that he had no power to do them. Fifth, "cannot" could speak of things that are utterly impossible like God not existing or being evil, or something non-existent existing, or two plus two equaling ten, not four.

Because John 6:57, 16:15, and 17:10 make it clear that the Son has his being from God before the existence of time and without the involvement of some extraneous cause, John 5:19 must be read as using "cannot" in the fifth sense, that of something impossible. Surely Wisdom does not need to be taught. The Father does not model acts for the Son because the Son is ignorant and has to learn them. In context John 5:19 emphasizes that the Son has the same authority as the Father.[35]

Another rule assists the interpreter in understanding what a biblical passages means. Some later Arians take John 6:38 to mean that the Son has a divine will different from that of his Father. They see it as yet another indication that the two are separate and thus that the Son is indeed subordinate. The John passage says only that the Son did not come to do his own will but the will of the one who sent him. The rule which these Eunomians have broken is one which indicates that not every negative statement can be turned into a positive one. To say that the Son did not come to do his own will but that of the Father may not mean that he has his own separate divine will. In Psalm 59:3 (58:4, LXX) the phrase "not my transgression nor my sin" speaks of the Psalmist's enemies preparing to harm him. The point is that those fierce men plan to harm him in spite of his lack of transgression or sin. To turn the negative into a positive creates the opposite meaning from what the text says. The Psalmist is not at fault for his opponents' actions; his transgression and sin are not the cause. When Titus 3:5 insists God saved us "not for righteousness we have done," its sense is destroyed if the negative phrase is turned into a positive one. Then it would mean that God saved us because of "righteousness we have done." Understood in terms of this principle, John 5:19 means precisely that the divine Son does not have a divine will of his own; His divine will is one with that of the Father.[36]

A final grammatical principle offers guidance in interpreting Holy Writ. The tense of a verb, although represented by a specific form, may not designate the exact time when something occurred. Psalm 2:1 uses the past tense to ask "Why did the heathen rage?" But the context insists that the heathen have not yet raged. Psalm 66:6 (65:6, LXX) uses the future tense "They shall cross over the river on foot" when it clearly means that they had already made the crossing. The tense of a verb does not necessarily determine the time of the action that the verb designates. The context does that. Thus when Scripture speaks of the Son as the "only begotten of the Father," with the sense that the Father begat the Son or the Son was begotten by the Father, "time" cannot be brought in to prove that "begetting" had a beginning and an end. A wrong analogy of how humans are fathers and sons with beginning and ending upsets the meaning and makes too much of the tenses of verbs.[37]

These principles were important for Nazianzen's *Theological Orations*. But they are not always evident in his exegesis. Only one work in Gregory's corpus is focused primarily on a consecutive biblical passage. *Oration* 37 comments on Matthew 19:1-12.[38] This homily shows just how much Gregory interprets Scripture from within his theological confession rather than from within a tightly limited philological exegesis. Here Nazianzen uses the first five sections of the homily, not to set the stage from the biblical text, but to detail his community's confession of who Jesus Christ is.

> He moves from place to place, who is not contained in any place; the timeless, the bodiless, the uncircumscribed, the same who was and is; who was both above time and came under time, and was invisible and is seen. He was in the beginning and was with God, and was God. The word "was" occurs the third time to be confirmed by number. What he was he laid aside. What he was not he assumed; not that he became two but that he accepted being made one out of the two. For both are God, that which assumed, and that which was assumed; two natures united in one, not two sons—let us give no false account of the blending. . . If he had stayed in his eminence, if he had not condescended to weakness, if he had remained what he was, keeping himself unapproachable and incomprehensible, a few perhaps would have followed him—perhaps not even a few, possibly only Moses . . . But inasmuch as he strips himself for us, inasmuch as he comes down (and I speak of an emptying, as it were, a lowering and a diminution of his glory) he becomes by this comprehensible.[39]

With this confession expressed, the Theologian returns to the text and has rather grand things to say about marriage. Jesus noted that the Biblical legislation was hard on women. God is not like that. He made both men and women. Eve sinned but so did Adam.

> Christ saves both by his passion. Was he made flesh for the man? So he was also for the woman. Did he die for the man? The woman is also saved by his death. He is called of the seed of David; and so perhaps you think the man is honored, but he is born of a virgin, and this is on the woman's side. They two, he says, shall be one flesh; so let the one flesh have equal honor.[40]

Gregory thinks that the passage speaks against a second marriage, and without knowledge of modern serial polygamy, he says: "The first is lawful, the second is indulgent, the third is law-breaking, and anything beyond this is swinish."[41] He counsels patience and care for a spouse that errs and warns that it is unclear who is most endangered, the one cast out or the one casting out.

From there he almost leaves the actual wording of the passage to speak of honoring marriage but pursuing virginity. Yet for him in his context the two are inseparable. Virginity is the most honored, but if there were no marriage there would be none to choose virginity.

Nazianzen returns to the text by referring only to the cryptic twelfth verse about some being able to receive the saying. He then invokes his own context and warns that chastity of body is not all that is needed; chastity of mind must refuse the heretical. But haughtiness is out of place.

> For since there are some who are so proud of their virtue that they attribute all to themselves and nothing to Him that made them and gave them wisdom and supplied them with good, such are taught by this word that even to wish well needs help from God, or rather even to choose what is right is divine and a gift of the mercy of God. For it is necessary both that we bear the responsibility and that we be saved by God. . . but to God it belongs both to win the victory and to bring the small boat safe to port.[42]

Gregory insists that a strong mind, work, reasoning, philosophy, fasting, vigils and the like have merit. The soul is not punished for having lived badly in a previous life. Against such an absurd doctrine one might here add to the Matthean text, "to whom it has been given," the sense of those "'who are worthy,' who have not only received this character from the Father, but have given it to themselves."[43]

The deepest problem is not whoring after another human, but whoring after a false idea of God the Father, the Son and the Holy Spirit.

> Cut off the bodily passions; cut off also the spiritual [ones]. . . Cut away the Arian impiety; cut away Sabellius' false opinion. Neither join more than is right nor wrongly sever. Neither compress the three persons into one nor make three diversities of nature. "One" is praiseworthy if rightly understood, also "three" when rightly divided, when the division is of persons, not of Godhead.[44]

Little in this homily represents the careful grammatical exegesis that Nazianzen employs in his *Theological Orations* when he is skewering his opponents. There the rules appear both straightforward and persuasive. All of them certainly can be applied to the texts which Gregory needed to explain there. But here his exegesis of Matthew 19:1-12 and the context of the grammatical rules show that the confession of his community—Jesus is God, the Son incarnate—and its moral concerns—virginity as well as marriage and divorce—are the driving reasons for his application of such rules elsewhere.

Yet in fairness to Gregory, he rejects the claims that biblical words do not mean what they appear to say because they are actually homonyms, a principle which his later Arian opponents used to their advantage.[45] He also shows that his Eunomian antagonists twisted or avoided a number of passages of Scripture that, in his view, clearly indicate the divinity of Jesus Christ. One of the strengths of his theological hermeneutic is that he can treat many passages about Jesus Christ rather well by designating the subject either as the Son before time or before incarnation, the Son incarnate and the man Jesus. His confession empowers this threefold predication, but it also is able to deal with a larger collection of texts than even Athanasius treated in his *Discourses Against the Arians*,[46] and certainly more passages than we find in the truncated extant corpus of Eunomius and Aetius. When we concede that priority arguments for either Biblical texts or the interpreter's context are difficult to formulate, we must also notice that the Theologian has the upper hand in the ability to make rather consistent sense of large blocks of texts that deal with the Son and the Holy Spirit. He not only forms the biblical texts to his context but in many ways he is formed by them.

The stability of his exegesis is liturgical: a Christian consumes the Word sacramentally. Just as one eats the Eucharist, one devours scripture.

> Whatever then is meaty and nourishing in the Word, shall be eaten and consumed along with the inward and hidden [thoughts] of the mind, and shall be given up to spiritual digestion; so it is from head to foot,

that is, from the first contemplations of Godhead to the very last thoughts about the Incarnation.[47]

As a constructive theologian Gregory Nazianzen both deconstructs scriptural verses and is constructed by them. His use of scripture to build up the body of Christ always occurs within that community and in faithful response to what he considers to be its best confession.

NOTES

1. Elias of Crete, in J. Billius, ed., *Eliae Cretensis Metropolitani Commentarius in Gregorii Nazianzeni, Gregorii Nazianzenii Theologi, Opera*, Tomus Secundus (Coloniae, 1690), col. 230A.

2. See my "Black Marks on the Communities' Manuscripts" (North American Patristics Society presidential address), *Journal of Early Christian Studies* 2 (1994), 443-466.

3. *Or.* 31.28-39 (PG 36: 164C-168B).

4. Justin, *1 Apol.* 61; Irenaeus, *Adv. haer.* 3.17.1; Theodotus, in Clement of Alexandria, *Excerpta Theodotus* 76.3; Tertullian, *Bapt.* 13.3.

5. *Biblia Patristica* 5 (Paris, 1991), 284-285, lists nearly eighty texts in which either Basil or Gregory of Nyssa referred to Matthew 28:19.

6. H. Benedict Green, "Matthew 28:19, Eusebius, and the *Lex Orandi*," *The Making of Orthodoxy: Essays in Honour of Henry Chadwick*, ed. R. Williams (Cambridge, 1989), 124-141.

7. Socrates, *Hist. Eccl.* 5.24 (PG 67: 649A); Sozomen, *Hist. Eccl.* 6.26 (PG 67: 1361C). Also see T. Kopecek, *A History of Neo-Arianism*, (Cambridge, Mass., 1979), vol. 2, 397-400.

8. P. Gallay, *Grégoire de Nazianze, Discours 27-31 (Discours théologiques)*, SC 250 (Paris, 1978), 24, mentions an unpublished report by P. Sablier, "Le Nouveau Testament dans les "Discours théologiques" de Grégoire de Nazianze," Travail d'étude et de recherche pour la Maîtrise en Lettres Classiques, Université Paul Valéry, Montpellier III, Octobre, 1976, which says that the New Testament text used by Gregory is usually like the Byzantine text or D, manuscript Beza.

9. See my "Universal Salvation in Origen and Maximus," in *Universalism and the Doctrine of Hell: Papers presented at the Fourth Edinburgh Conference in Christian Dogmatics, 1991*, ed. N. M. de S. Cameron (Carlisle, U.K; Grand Rapids, Mich., 1992), 35-72.

10. B. Ehrman, *The Orthodox Corruption of Scripture: The Effect of Early Christological Controversies on the Text of the New Testament* (Oxford, 1993) has raised these kinds of questions quite provocatively. But his sense of modern critical textual study is not as open as is his sense that the Orthodox changed texts. He apparently believes that his understanding of textual variants is quite objective and available as a template for judging what early Christian interpreters did.

11. Until corrected by a student, for over a decade I told the story of the Syro-Phoenician (Canaanite) woman, who looked to him for the healing of her daughter (Mark 7:24-30; Matt. 15:21-28), using Jesus' statement about not finding such faith in Israel, which was actually his response to the centurion seeking help for his servant (Matt. 8:5-13; Luke 7:1-10). I have heard others make the same mistake. Any hermeneutic of suspicion so strong that it would never consider that Eusebius could have done something similar is too suspicious.

12. *Biblia Patristica* 5: 248-252.

13. *Or.* 31.22 (PG 36: 157A). Origen, *On First Principles* 4.2.9. See my *Faith Gives Fullness to Reasoning: The Five Theological Orations of Gregory Nazianzen,* Supplements to *Vigiliae Christianae* 13, intro. and comm. by F. Norris, trans. L.Wickham and F. Williams (Leiden, 1991), 204.

14. *Or.* 31.3 and 21 (PG 36: 136B and 156D).

15. *Or.* 40.20 (PG 36: 384D-385C).

16. R.P.C. Hanson, *The Search for the Christian Doctrine of God: The Arian Controversy 318-381* (Edinburgh, 1988), 846.

17. *Or.* 31.2 (PG 36: 133D-136A).

18. *Or.* 39.17 (PG 36: 329D-332B).

19. *Or.* 28.4 (PG 36: 28C-32A).

20. *Or.* 29.13 (PG 36: 92A). *Or.* 30.20 (PG 36: 129A-132A) *Or.* 31.7, 9, 20-21 (PG 36: 140C-141A, 141C-144A, 156A-157A).

21. *Or.* 28.9 (PG 36: 36C-37B); *Or.* 29.11 (PG 36: 88C).

22. Aristotle, *On Interpretation* 16A-B.

23. Plato, *Cratylus* 430A-431E.

24. *Or.* 29.14 (PG 36: 92B-93A).

25. *Or.* 28.9 (PG 36: 36C-37B); *Or.* 29.12 (PG 36: 88B-89C).

26. Clement of Alexandria, *Stromata* 1.143.6 (GCS 2: 89); Origen, *Contra Celsum* 1.24 (GCS 1: 74).

27. *Or.* 28.7 and 29 (PG 36: 33B-C, 68B-C); *Or.* 29.10-11 (PG 36: 85D-89A); *Or.* 31.7-8 (PG 36: 140C-141C).

28. *Or.* 30.16 (PG 36: 124C).

29. *Or.* 30.17 (PG 36: 125B-C); *Or.* 28.30 (PG 36: 69A).

30. Plato, *Timaeus* 28E.

31. *Or.* 28.4-5 (PG 36: 29C-32C).

32. See my "Wonder, Worship and Writ: Patristic Christology," *Ex Auditu* 7 (1991): 59-72.

33. *Or.* 29.17-20 (PG 36: 96B-101C)

34. *Or.* 30.4 (PG 36: 108A-B).

35. *Or.* 30.10-11 (PG 36, 113C-117B).

36. *Or.* 30.12 (PG 36: 117C-120B).

37. *Or.* 29.4 (PG 36: 80A-C). For a treatment of these grammatical rules in a different context see my "Theology as Grammar: Nazianzen and Wittgenstein," *Arianism After Arius: Essays on the Development of the Fourth Century Trinitarian Conflicts,* ed. M. Barnes and D. Williams (Edinburgh, 1993), 237-249.

38. P. Gallay looks at this text in his "La Bible dans l'oeuvre de Grégoire de Nazianze le Théologien," *Le monde grec ancien et la Bible*, Bible de tous les temps 1 (Paris, 1984), 330-333.
39. *Or.* 37.2-3 (PG 36: 283C-285C). All translations of *Or.* 37 are adapted from C. G. Browne and J. E. Swallow, NPNF 7 (reprint ed., Grand Rapids, Mich., 1952).
40. *Or.* 37.7 (PG 36: 289C-292A). See V. Harrison, "Male and Female in Cappadocian Theology," *Journal of Theological Studies*, n. s. 41 (1990): 441-471.
41. *Or.* 37.8 (PG 36: 292B).
42. *Or.* 37.13 (PG 36: 298C-300A).
43. *Or.* 37.15 (PG 36: 300D-301A).
44. *Or.* 37.22 (PG 36: 308A).
45. Eunomius, *Apology* 11, 16, 19 in *Eunomius: The Extant Works*, trans. and ed. R. Vaggione, Oxford Early Christian Texts (Oxford, 1987), 46-47, 52-55, 56-59.
46. Norris, "Wonder, Worship and Writ: Patristic Christology."
47. *Or.* 45.16 (PG 36: 645A).

9

Theodoret of Cyrus:
Bishop and Exegete[1]

JEAN-NOËL GUINOT

Following in the footsteps of his illustrious Alexandrian and Antiochene predecessors, Theodoret of Cyrus undertook in the fifth century to compose a series of commentaries on Scripture which actually cover almost the whole Bible. An enterprise of such magnitude was not new in itself, but it holds particular interest for us because Theodoret is one of the few Greek patristic exegetes the bulk of whose work is extant. Certainly this is true for Theodoret's Old Testament commentaries, all of which are available to us and which will serve as the primary foundation for this essay,[2] though we will also have occasion to mention his *Commentary on the Epistles of St. Paul,* the only testimony to his New Testament exegesis. It would take too long to examine here the reasons why the writings of authors long touted as masters of Christian exegesis were lost, while the commentaries of Theodoret, who considered himself to be merely a "gnat" among "bees,"[2] have survived the centuries. We can nonetheless be assured of two facts. On the one hand, the reasonably restricted scope of his commentaries, owing to an intentional conciseness which Theodoret proved time and time again,[4] was less discouraging to copyists than the long and prolix commentaries of the Alexandrians. On the other hand, the manner in which Theodoret's interpretation struck a balance between the extremes of Antiochene and Alexandrian exegesis was conducive early on to the reading of his commentaries. Indeed, the frequency with which Theodoret is quoted in the collections of exegetical *catenae* unquestionably testifies to the high estimation of his exegesis.[5]

An exegetical enterprise of this stature in the fifth century leaves us with two fundamentally important questions. Wherein lay Theodoret's originality, and what were his goals? Within the limits of this article we can only make passing reference to the first query, in order to confirm that Theodoret saw himself as the heir to an exegetical tradition that he revered. Far from concealing his borrowings from earlier authorities,[6] he had a tendency in our view rather to exaggerate their importance. At the same time, however, he wanted to bring his own personal contribution to what he saw, in a way, as a collective task.[7] We must not let ourselves be deceived by Theodoret's insistence on his debt to his predecessors, to the point of viewing him merely as a clever compiler. Not only did he never slavishly borrow from earlier sources, but a close study of his commentaries reveals that he often separated himself quite clearly from the very ones to whom we could presume he owed the greatest debt.[8] It will therefore be easier, no doubt, to answer our second query about the ultimate objective of Theodoret's exegetical enterprise. Beyond his avowed goals (the solicitation of friends, a pastor's sense of moral obligation, etc.), and beyond his overtly polemical stance against idols, Jews, and heretics, were there not perhaps other, more latent motives that led Theodoret to undertake such a long and patient labor of interpreting Scripture? An examination of his exegesis may provide at least some basic elements of an answer.

But before launching into a precise study of his exegesis, we should underscore some of Theodoret's fundamental hermeneutical principles. In the first place, like Origen[9] and many other patristic authors after him, Theodoret believed that Scripture was inspired in its entirety. Here we must refer again to the long preface to his *Commentary on the Song of Songs,* where Theodoret vigorously opposes those who contest the inspired character of the Song and at once slander the Holy Spirit.[10] While he deems it necessary, for example, to make a distinction between the three writings of Solomon (Proverbs, Ecclesiastes, and the Song of Songs), and even views them as three rungs on a spiritual ladder, he would not always agree to speaking of three degrees of inspiration.[11] It is indeed the same Spirit, under the same name, who inspires all three books. To support his point, Theodoret even goes so far as to claim that after the blasphemous destruction of part of the holy books during the reign of Manasseh and their complete disappearance in the burning of the Temple under Nebuchadnezzar, Ezra, inspired by the Spirit and without the help of copies that might have escaped the disaster, was able to restore the whole corpus of biblical writings.[12] How then could the Holy Spirit have "re-inspired" texts unworthy of him? The argument certainly appears weak, but it shows the extent to which Theodoret considered Scripture to be inspired. For the same reason, it would no longer be possible to establish a classification of prophetic books according to greater or lesser degrees of inspiration. Theodoret's asserts this unambiguously: "All the prophets are instruments of the divine Spirit," and to want to dispute the title of prophet for Daniel is undoubtedly a hidden way of "making war on God."[13]

From this unity of inspiration arises, in Theodoret's view, the perfect harmony of all Scripture, its *symphônia*. Consequently there are no contradictions within any given book or among diverse scriptural texts, notably among the various prophecies, and there is no disharmony between the Old and New Testaments. "The divine prophets and holy apostles were all deemed worthy of the same Spirit; thus, they do not contradict one another in what they say, for the Holy Spirit is a spirit of truth."[14]

This principle governs all of Theodoret's exegesis, and he is consistently concerned to show the internal coherence of the sacred text (quotations often serve this function) or to resolve ostensible contradictions in order to silence those who would use them to denigrate Scripture.[15]

Such a conception of the *symphônia* of Scripture at the same time demands a certain attitude on the part of the exegete toward the sacred text—an attitude at once of respect, humility, and sincere desire to discover the truth.[16] Though Scripture is inspired and internally coherent, we are not prohibited from investigating the reasons for its obscurity or its structure. Theodoret admits that Scripture is often obscure: first, without doubt, because it is divinely inspired, but also because its obscurity functions "pedagogically" to incite research into Scripture's "hidden treasure."[17] But there are other reasons as well for its obscurity, such as the very preservation of the text that evil spirits could have destroyed or falsified had the prophecies been too clearly composed.[18] More simply, obscurity was already characteristic of the prophetic style, and there was always the factor of greater or lesser competency in translating Scripture from the original Hebrew.[19] This obscurity is, moreover, the very *raison d'être* of Christian hermeneutics. The exegete's task is to lift "the veil which covers the oracles of the divine prophets" and even to enable the reader to discover the hidden sense of a text beyond its superficial simplicity and "the appearance of the letter."[20] On the other hand, without questioning the authenticity of the text or its authorial attribution, Theodoret exercises enough critical discernment to demonstrate that the order in which we read the Psalms, the prophecies of Isaiah, or the epistles of Paul do not always correspond to the order of their original composition.[21] He is even conscious of rearrangements that could have been effected in the sacred texts and sometimes of the reasons for the adoption of an order other than the original chronological one.[22] Respect for Scripture therefore did not induce Theodoret to abandon critical inquiry. This is even more obvious in his desire to base his exegesis on legitimate textual criticism.

Textual Criticism

Such a conviction might seem surprising for an exegete who considered even the Septuagint version divinely inspired.[23] What would be the need, under these circumstances, to control the text, or more importantly, to add to it? Once again it is a matter of an attitude of respect, and Theodoret's respect for the Septuagint version is immense, but he is not blind. As a serious exegete he is fully conscious of running up against a difficult language, the obscurity of which is further enhanced by the fact that the Septuagint is the translation of Hebrew originals. Every translation has its weaknesses and the admirable desire to remain faithful to the Hebrew, with the accompanying bias toward literalness, is not always conducive to clarity. Theodoret knows this,[24] and in order to see things more clearly he resorts to versions in which the Greek translation is more immediately intelligible. But the version of the Septuagint on which he bases his commentary is that used in the Church of Antioch, accordingly known as the "Antiochene text."[25] Whatever its degree of originality, this text is in any case not reducible to the fifth column of the Hexapla, since, in at least two of his commentaries (*In Psalmos* and *In Isaiam*), Theodoret openly compares these two texts and notes certain differences between them.[26] Thus, despite the periodic appearance of asterisks that we could believe indicated traces of Origen's work,[27] we must submit to the evidence: The text of the Septuagint that Theodoret regularly used is not that of Origen's *Hexapla*.

More consistently, Theodoret compares his text with the versions of Aquila, Symmachus, and Theodotion, whose principal merit, in his view, is clarity. This is especially true of Symmachus, for whose work Theodoret, like most exegetes of his age, shows a definite preference.[28] In the event that these versions present a variant capable of elucidating the text of the Septuagint, or better yet, if this variant can lead to an alternative interpretation, Theodoret includes it, at least partially,[29] accompanied with the specific translator's name. But in numerous other cases where these three versions agree at least on the basic sense of a scriptural passage, regardless of whether they support or contradict the Septuagint text, Theodoret refers more generally to them as "the three interpreters," "the other interpreters," or "the rest of the interpreters," and does not hesitate to articulate after the fact the particular readings of each.

What Theodoret looks for most often from these versions is a text which is clearer than that of the Septuagint, of which these translations offer in many cases a first interpretation. The synonyms, doublets, constructions that are clearer or have greater textual support[30] that these versions propose are able to render the biblical text more intelligible. In addition, a good many of the Hebrew terms which the Septuagint preserves, and which cause obscurity or ambiguity,[31] are translated by "the three interpreters;" or else, quite simply, their less literal versions make it much easier to grasp the exact sense of the scriptural text.[32] Occasionally it happens that Theodoret shows, without admitting it, a rather obvious preference for the reading of these interpreters, even basing his commentary on one of their readings to the detriment of the Septuagint text. At other times still, he hesitates to choose between the Septuagint text and their readings, thereupon indicating that the difference is only apparent, that the "the three interpreters" and the Septuagint are really saying the same thing.[33] In some instances Theodoret finds the difference irreducible and, recognizing that the alternative readings are each justified, retains both under the same heading.[34] As a general rule, however, he taxes his ingenuity to demonstrate[35] that the testimony of the three interpreters confirms the Septuagint text, and that there obtains between them, on the level of meaning at least, a *symphônia* which guarantees the authority of his interpretation.

Does this mean that for Theodoret these three versions enjoyed an authority comparable to that of the Septuagint? One could opt for such a conclusion, in view of the fact that Theodoret largely uses them to control his text, that he recognizes in them the merits of expressing "clearly" or "more clearly" what the Septuagint expresses obscurely, and, finally, that he sometimes notes their readings for their own value or else retains them concurrently with the Septuagint's. But such a deduction would ultimately be mistaken, for these alternative versions only have a relative authority and actually serve only as explanatory tools in the hands of the exegete. It is important to observe in this connection how Theodoret normally proceeds after having quoted the verse from the Septuagint. In some cases it is enough for him simply to note, most often with a *houtô*, that the version of the three interpreters (which he does not always quote) is identical to that of the Septuagint. Elsewhere, he introduces the interpreters' version, accompanied if need be by a brief commentary before returning to the initial text (henceforth rendered more intelligible), in order to demonstrate that the Septuagint reading is confirmed by other versions.[36] Aquila, Symmachus, and Theodotion nonetheless only have a referential value. Having their interpretation at his disposal, Theodoret ordinarily refuses to dodge the difficulty posed by his text,[37] which is to say it is extremely rare for their interpretation to cause him to impugn the Septuagint text.[38] The contrary is rather true to the extent that the three interpreters hardly enjoy, in his mind, the Septuagint's prestige.[39] Theodoret remains suspicious of these translators, accusing them in his *Commentary on Isaiah* of voluntarily altering Scripture in a sectarian spirit.[40] While it is true that what was at stake in the prophecy here (Isa. 7:14) could explain Theodoret's severity, it nonetheless remains true that the three interpreters hardly enjoyed more than an auxiliary role in his own interpretation.

Aside from these versions,[41] Theodoret often remarks, especially in his commentaries on Psalms and Isaiah, on readings posed by Greek manuscripts which he rather vaguely refers to as "some copies." He is not referring, properly speaking, to an original biblical version, or *ekdosis*, but rather, as indicated by the term *antigrapha*, to a collection of manuscripts which appear to form an homogeneous group. Along with precise variants, often limited to a single word but still occasionally interesting,[42] these "copies" present, in comparison with other versions, an expanded biblical text. Indeed, very rarely are they not as full as the Septuagint text.[43] Theodoret's respect for them seems real enough, but is perhaps restricted once again to benefiting his own text.[44] Nevertheless, the attention which Theodoret pays to these "copies" attests to his concern for textual criticism, and he thus seems to be aware of the relative uncertainty surrounding the manuscript tradition of the Bible.

Considering the Septuagint to be divinely inspired does not, therefore, exempt Theodoret from referring to other Greek versions of the Bible, any more than to the Hebrew text itself.[45] In addition to variations between his text and the original Hebrew that he targets for comment, Theodoret uses the Hebrew Bible, in particular, to verify the Septuagint text. Much like Origen in his *Hexapla*, he uses it to point out the presence or absence of one or more words in the Greek text.[46]

Finally, Theodoret avails himself of the resource of the Syriac version, the Peshitta.[47] He uses it more rarely than the other versions,[48] but its contribution is not negligible. In accordance with the Hebrew, which it often seems to reflect more faithfully than does the Septuagint, the Peshitta provides him with a number of variants that he retains. It also serves, jointly with the Hebrew, to show up additions in the Greek text. Perhaps more often, however, the Syriac text contributes to Theodoret's interpretation by offering translations of Hebrew terms that the Septuagint merely transcribes.

Thanks to his knowledge of Syriac, and perhaps Hebrew, Theodoret enjoyed a greater potential than other exegetes for controlling his biblical text. While he rather consistently tries to exercise such control, and knows how to profit from lessons learned notably from Aquila, Symmachus, and Theodotion, none of the versions that he consults really and truly, for Theodoret, prevails over the Septuagint text, his own text, the text that he intends to interpret such as it appears to him.[49]

The Three Levels of Interpretation

To guide his interpretation, Theodoret observes a rule, quite simple in appearance, which defines rather well a statement from the *Commentary on Isaiah*: "In considering the collection of the prophet's writings, some are clear and have a plain sense, while others are presented in a figurative way and demand a commentary."[50] From this rule naturally arises the explanation of the sacred text according to the literal sense and its interpretation according to the figurative sense. In practice, things are not so clearly distinguished and the frontiers between the literal sense and the figurative sense are sometimes dynamic or unfixed. But in particular there is a third mode of interpretation which allows one to penetrate beyond the literal surface of the text in order to arrive at its "mystical and hidden" meaning.[51] This is the typological interpretation which, according to Theodoret, can properly be said to form a third level of explanation.

Literal Interpretation

In a very great number of cases, this interpretation proceeds on the first level, according to the literal sense. Theodoret definitely bears, in this respect, the legacy of the great Antiochene exegetes, and, like them, shows little inclination toward an interpretation that neglects or denies the "reality" of the text. He was frankly suspicious of allegory and of the excesses to which it could lead[52] if the exegete was not careful precisely to base his interpretation on the first sense of the text. It was not necessary to consider the literal sense inferior or negligible, since quite often it is the only meaning of the text, and because it grants direct access to essential realities affecting theology, christology, and the whole history of salvation. Literal interpretation, therefore, did not lead to investing the text with a meaning that was not its own, but rather to determining clearly its true sense. Although not hidden beyond the words of the text, this true sense was often obscured by scriptural language and allusions. Properly speaking, it was more an explanation than an interpretation of the text. Here Theodoret had recourse to a number of helps, among the most significant being grammar, style, history, and geography, such that interpretation according to the literal sense—"the plain sense" (*procheiros*)—is commonly designated by expressions which conveyed this attention to the letter or historical reality of the text. Understood this way, literal explanation appears most often as an explanatory reading of the scriptural text, a paraphrase rendering the text more immediately understandable. Such seems even to be the primary function of this type of exegesis, making the reading of the Septuagint text more accessible for a larger audience.

With this goal in mind, Theodoret proceeds first of all to divide the biblical text as clearly as possible into "chapters,"[53] of which he briefly indicates the general theme. Cautioned and guided accordingly, readers will therefore be in no danger of getting lost in the line-by-line commentary. In some cases this effort is facilitated by the presence of "titles" in the text which indicate the content of the passage,[54] but ordinarily it is the exegete who must take pains to mark out the text, to demonstrate its unity, and, if necessary, to show up its subdivisions. Overall Theodoret performs this task quite ably, proving his ability to master his material. In this division of the text, history was a tremendous aid. The succession-lists of kings and the mention of principal events in their reigns provided useful chronological reference-points. But not every biblical text had a distinctly historical character, in which case especially Theodoret manifests his synthetic spirit, knowing full well how to characterize portions of Scripture: e.g., a hymn of praise to God, a song of lament, a satire against a king, a personification (*prosôpopoeia*), and so on. The repetition of stereotyped formulas or comparable syntactical turns, for purposes of ending a development and introducing a new subject,[55] serves to clarify and in many cases to emphasize the coherence of the scriptural text.[56] Within each large section of scriptural text, but often less emphatically (here a "since," a "then," an "after that," followed by a verb meaning to "announce," or "foretell" are ordinarily sufficient), Theodoret introduces subdivisions. It would hardly be exaggerating to say that we already find in his commentary the titles and subtitles that accompany our present-day translations of the Bible.

Once the the framework of the commentary is laid out, Theodoret is ready to determine precisely how verses of Scripture are to be divided in order to read the text correctly, for the manner in which the words are connected to each other can fundamentally alter the meaning of the text and so, too, the substance of its interpretation. In Isaiah 23:4, for example, Theodoret chooses to read,[57] "Be ashamed, Sidon has spoken to you, O sea," rather than as we would expect, "Be ashamed, O Sidon, the sea has spoken." Such cases are nevertheless rather rare; much more frequently Theodoret is inclined to specify the mood—indicative, interrogative, optative—which suits the verse.[58] This is usually explained by an ambiguous redaction (or what passes for such in the fifth century) of the Septuagint text. In many cases, for example, it is a question of emphasizing the interrogative value of a *mê* that could otherwise indicate a negation.[59] To support this reading, the version of one of the three interpreters is eventually quoted, insofar as it unequivocally renders the text in the interrogative mood. Finally, and again relatively frequently, Theodoret indicates the exact tone of the verse so that the reader will not mistake its meaning. Thus, for example, he will emphasize that the prophet is using "irony," or that we are dealing with a *prosôpopoeia* or a figure of speech.

This division of the text and indications concerning the mood in which the verse should be read constitute, we might say, the first step in "literal" explanation. But Theodoret presses ahead, fully aware that the language of the Septuagint or even the Greek of the apostle Paul poses an obstacle to comprehending the texts.[60] Paraphrase is therefore a practical means to reduce the obscurity of the text or to clarify a difficult construction. To this Theodoret adds certain grammatical remarks intended to explain or justify the gender and number of a certain word, to specify its accent or its syntactical value, to draw attention to the use of a certain pronoun, coordinate, or preposition, and so on. Through this kind of literal interpretation Theodoret is able naturally to explain obscure terms in the scriptural text. Not satisfied merely with clarifying Hebrew words (proper or common names[61]) that the Septuagint has not translated into Greek, he also strives to determine the precise meaning of certain Greek words, as much in the Septuagint text as in Paul.[62] In the same way, he knows how to recognize confidently the numerous hebraisms in his biblical text, the most common of which is "enallage," the use of one verbal tense for another.[63] He translates or briefly comments on these "idioms" by comparing them, when the occasion presents itself, with analogous turns of phrase in Syriac.[64] Besides hebraisms, there are other "idioms" as well to which Theodoret alerts the reader. Most often it is a case of obviating any anthropomorphic ideas of God by indicating that Scripture is rooted in a manner of expression that is thoroughly human.[65] In this kind of explanation of the text, Theodoret also frequently solicits clarifications or confirmation of his interpretation from the other Greek versions of the Bible, notably that of Symmachus.

To assign the interpretation according to the literal sense the function merely of explaining the letter of the text would nonetheless be singularly to limit its scope. In reality, its importance is considerable, be it to affirm the orthodox faith or to extract various prophetic messages from the text. In the one case, the basis of interpretation is essentially grammatical or stylistic, while in the other it is ordinarily historical. We have already mentioned Theodoret's devotion to highlighting certain "idioms" which might project an anthropomorphic conception of the Divinity. But this quite literal, indeed, grammatical criticism of the text is just as much a basis for refuting Sabellianism or a "Jewish" conception of God and for providing biblical grounding for trinitarian theology.[66] In the same way, and more often still, Theodoret refutes Arian teachings by using a verse or a word within a verse, taken in its literal sense, to develop an argument which often has the precision of a syllogism.[67] But he knows just as well how to turn to his own advantage the word order, the use of a singular, or the presence of a particular preposition or conjunction for purposes of vindicating the consubstantiality of the Father and the Son.[68] Lastly, Theodoret often requires literal interpretation to prove the cogency of Antiochene teachings concerning dyophysite christology; to do this, he confirms that the verse in question cannot be understood correctly except by relating the terms to one or the other of Christ's natures (divine or human).[69]

In judging the prophecies, literal interpretation once again plays a fundamental role and its historical character is clearly predicated. For it is a question of discovering at what point the prophecy is fulfilled, and of verifying, with the proof of facts (*ta pragmata*), whether a delayed outcome or "end" (*telos, ekbasis, peras*) is exegetically acceptable and accounts for the whole prophecy. In this way the exegete is led to distinguish prophecies which were already fulfilled in the Old Testament, and those which were fulfilled with the advent of Christ. But breaking with the ancient Antiochenes, Theodoret clearly orients his exegesis to the New Testament and uncovers, on the basis of his literal interpretation, a rather large number of messianic prophecies in the Old.

This type of interpretation thus occupies a preeminent place in Theodoret's exegesis, a fact which seems to be further confirmed, when several senses of the text come into play, by the order of their presentation. Certainly this is connected to Theodoret's urge to explain the text, but just as much to the need to establish its real and historical nature. This consistent recourse to literal explanation should not for that reason be taken to mean a "literalism" in the pejorative sense of the word. Theodoret is not satisfied with paraphrasing the text, even if paraphrasing is necessary to understanding it; he can also use the same "letter" of the text to support a demonstration of its true theological, christological, and messianic dimension. He is so convinced of the depth of Scripture that he does not hesitate, when the literal sense is inconsequential, and especially when it appears incoherent or absurd, to move beyond it. Hence it is figurative interpretation which enables him fully to plumb the text.

Figurative Interpretation

In reality, the frontier between literal and figurative meanings is often dynamic enough for Theodoret to present the two interpretations in succession, but almost always in this case he betrays his preference for the figurative sense, which is richer and more "worthy of God." The formulas employed, however, indicate that he envisions this interpretation not as a necessity but as a possibility[70] that permits access to the truth of the prophecy, albeit now at a second level. Most often, in spite of everything, the choice of a figurative interpretation follows on the categorical rejection of the literal sense, whether the letter contradicts historical fact (a prophecy would never be deceitful!) or seems to be absurd or even shocking.[71] In such cases it is necessary "to pass beyond the veil of the letter in order to understand the text figuratively (*tropikôs*) or spiritually (*pnematikôs*). But does the exegete have the right to pursue such a meaning? Does not his interpretation risk making the text say something completely different from what it says? Theodoret does not think so: first, because figurative language is in his view common in Scripture—"Divine Scripture says a multitude of things figuratively"[72]—and second, because it is sufficiently widespread that one cannot be mistaken about the meaning of words. Thus, in Isaiah 23:13, terms evoking construction (rampart, battlements, towers) appear to fall under the category of this figurative meaning, which Theodoret proves on the basis of 1 Corinthians 3:10:

Clearly the prophetic text ascribes to demons the construction of the wickedness on account of which the city [of Tyre] was desolated. And in fact, when the Apostle declares, "I, like a master builder, laid a foundation," we do not think of stones, but of pious words.[73]

On the other hand, Scripture itself advises this figurative reading in several instances. The prophet, for example, will convey clearly what he comes to announce in a veiled manner.[74] This is an invitation not to comprehend the text at the first level, "as we read it," but "to pass beyond the letter which kills" (cf. 2 Cor. 3:6) in order to understand "in a spiritual manner that which is of the realm of the Spirit."[75] The figurative sense as Theodoret conceives it is therefore not an extraneous meaning lent to the text but is its true sense—which is where it differs from allegory—and actually remains a "literal" sense, if we remember that we are dealing in this case not with the literal sense proper but with the *metaphorical* literal sense. This is why the phrase *ek metaphoras,* Theodoret's cherished expression for this kind of interpretation, is particularly well-chosen. The adverb *tropikôs,* which is even more frequently used, seldom has another meaning; but, like our expression "figurative sense," it is a rather general term for variously designating the "metaphorical" meaning, the moral or "spiritual" sense close to anagogy, and even a properly "allegorical" interpretation.[76]

In essence, however, the figurative interpretation is metaphorical in Theodoret's view. Its content proves this, consisting most often in a series of terminological equivalences that he establishes with the help of stereotyped formulas intended to emphasize the parity between terms. One example from Theodoret's commentary on Isaiah 5:2 sufficiently illustrates this procedure:

> It is the people whom he calls "vineyard"... By "tower," he designates the building which resembles a guardshack in an orchard...and by "cistern" the altar of sacrifice... By "hill" he is, in a figurative way, indicating royalty... Moreover, it is Palestine that he calls "fertile place."[77]

The spiritual or moral interpretation differs little in nature, even if the way of noting the equivalences of terms sometimes has less substantiation.

In order to lend credence to his interpretation, Theodoret strives foremost to adhere faithfully to the same system of equivalences. The figurative value of a word cannot depend on the caprices of the exegete or vary according to the needs of interpretation. That does not mean, nevertheless, that the same word only has one possible metaphorical meaning, since meaning can vary according to context, but that the number of equivalences remains quite limited. For example, the terms for "hills" or "mountains," which customarily evoke idolatry and the cult of the demons, can also designate those who enjoy an uplifted spirit and the knowledge of divine mysteries. The term "darkness" sometimes indicates ignorance, sometimes misfortunes, while "light," by contrast, indicates the knowledge of liberation from evil. In spite of this, we sense Theodoret wanting to preserve the unity of interpretation, its overall flow or *akolouthia*, to the point that if he is led to broach an equivalence which appears surprising on the surface, he takes pains to explain it and justify it. Such is the case in Isaiah 35:2 with the equation of "Lebanon" and "Jerusalem," when so often elsewhere "Lebanon" poses as a metonymy indicating idolatry and pagan nations:

> He says, on the other hand, that the honor of Lebanon and the glory of Carmel are given over to the desert. But as we have often said, he calls Judea "Carmel," because from of old it was full of prophetic fruits. "Lebanon" is the name which divine Scripture often gives to Jerusalem. "The great eagle, with the great wingspan, full of claws, who has the design of marching against Lebanon, took the choice parts of the cedar and the cypress" (Ezek. 17:3, 12, 13). So, then, the interpretation that the prophet gives teaches that Jerusalem is "Lebanon," that Babylon is the "eagle," and that the scion of the kingdom is the "choice parts of the cedar."[78]

The example is interesting because it reveals a second preoccupation of Theodoret, the harmony or *symphônia* of Scripture, which is at once a corollary and guarantee of the *akolouthia* sought after in interpretation. Indeed, for Theodoret it is not enough to declare that the assimilation of "Lebanon"/"Jerusalem" is frequent in Scripture, as he proves by returning to a passage from Ezekiel (17:3-4, 12-13) where the prophet himself provides the key to this figurative use of the term "Lebanon." The role of quotations is therefore quite often to elucidate the "symphony" of figurative interpretations and, beyond that, the harmony of all Scripture. Finally, manifesting the same concern for coherence, Theodoret forbids himself from intermingling the literal and metaphorical explanations of a particular passage of Scripture, all the more so in the case of one particular verse. Here, too, there is a certain form of *akolouthia* to respect. Through the different "rules" that he imposes, Theodoret is able to give a certain rigor to his metaphorical interpretation and to guard in all cases against fantastic or cavalier interpretations.

The role of metaphorical interpretation is, to a great extent, comparable to that of literal explanation of texts, since, in both cases the goal is to make the text clear. While not as crucial in metaphorical interpretation as in literal, the role of history, grammar, and style is still not insignificant. This is especially true of history, which quite often determines whether to opt for a figurative meaning, and which, if such an option is taken, makes it possible to discover a number of messianic prophecies or prophecies anticipating the New Testament.[79] The theme of the transfer of promises from the Jewish people to the Christian people, for example, which hold such a prominent place in Theodoret's exegesis, is nearly always developed on the basis of a metaphorical interpretation of the terms "Lebanon," "desert," and "Carmel."[80] But perhaps even more interesting, given Theodoret's time, is the role played by this interpretation in the ongoing christological controversy. Terms such as "temple," "cloud," "quiver," "clothing," etc., were thus commonly understood as figurative designations of the human nature assumed by Christ at his Incarnation.[81] Thanks again to figurative interpretation, Theodoret can, in Isaiah 53:7-8 for example, aver once more his dyophysite concepts, showing the existence of two distinct natures in the one person of Christ:

> For his humanity was slaughtered and his divinity seemed, as it were, stripped of the fleece that constituted his humanity without his divinity being separated from his humanity, even at the moment of his suffering, and clearly without the divinity itself undergoing the suffering.[82]

Certainly we could not claim that all cases of figurative interpretation are of comparable interest. Like the literal explanation of texts, it aims at providing the reader with a basic grasp of the text; but also like the literal exegesis, and often even more than the literal, the figurative interpretation discloses a "hidden" and richer meaning, precisely that "treasure" which Scripture conceals in order to prompt more fervent research into the text.

Typological Interpretation

A third level, so to speak, of Theodoret's exegesis, typological interpretation, distinguishes itself from the two preceding methods to the extent that its goal is not so much to assure immediate comprehension of the text as to disclose its larger significance, which almost always means establishing its ultimate purpose with respect to the Messiah and the New Testament. Yet typology remains closely related to literal explanation because it is based most often on the historical meaning of the text. Once again here, we witness Theodoret's urge to provide an exacting exegesis.

Confident that all prophecy is true and consequently that its realization is certain, Theodoret's task is to specify the exact "end" (*telos, ekbasis, peras*) of its accomplishment. He discovers that some prophecies seem to be fulfilled twice, so that it is permissible to speak of "double prophecies."[83] This expression is nonetheless ambiguous and improper, for in reality, the first fulfillment recognized by the exegete gives incomplete account of the prophecy, and only generates expectation of a second fulfillment which, in truth, is the only genuine end of the prophecy. These two successive realizations are referred to as "type," or figure, and "antitype," the latter being the truth of which the type is merely an image or reflection. Type is to antitype as less is to more. Whether we say that the second fulfillment transcends the first in grandeur, extent, and precision, or that the first realization gives way to the second as a material fulfillment to a spiritual one, the antitype always prevails over its type. The vocabulary that Theodoret uses conveys this relationship well: whatever is realized "figuratively" (*typikôs; kata typon*) is destined to be fulfilled "properly and truly" (*kyriôs kai alêthôs; kat' alêtheian; alêthôs*); whatever is merely an "image" (*eikôn*) must correspond with the reality of facts (*ta pragmata*); whatever finds only an approximate application is called to exactitude (*akribôs; kat' akribeian*) and to a perfect equivalence (*diaphêrontôs; mallon harmottei*). For the most part, the partial and imperfect fulfillment of the prophecy happens within the Old Testament, perceived as a figure or type of what must be fully accomplished with or after the advent of Christ.[84] Typological interpretation therefore plays an important role in determining prophecies that relate to the Messiah and the New Testament. It even provides a glimpse of certain eschatological prophecies. Of these, the existence of the Church is a first fulfillment, but their definitive realization is to be sought in the future life. Thus we can say that one such eschatological prophecy offers multiple schemes of fulfillment, provided the stipulation that it is the exegete's responsibility to introduce a perspective which Scripture has deliberately neglected. In his *Commentary on Isaiah*, Theodoret's comparison between typology and pictorial art demonstrates this principle quite well:

> (Isa. 60:1) "Shine, Shine Jerusalem, for your light has come, and the glory of the Lord has risen upon you."
> Once when the holy apostles were admiring the tremendous size of

the stones of the Temple, the Lord said, "There will not be left here one stone upon another: all will be destroyed" (Matt. 24:1-2). Since they in turn asked the question, "When will this take place, and what will be the sign of your coming?," the Master simultaneously taught these two points, without making any distinction in what he said, but foretelling jointly both events pertaining to the administration of Judea and those pertaining to the administration of the universe. Nevertheless, shrewd minds can make distinctions and recognize what, on the one hand, applies to the end of the Jewish cult, and what applies, on the other hand, to the universal consummation.

In this way, the prediction here simultaneously includes three subjects. It prophesies, as in a sketch (ôs en skiographia), the reconstruction of Jerusalem, which happened under Cyrus and under Darius. Moreover, like a painting that enhances a rather great number of colors, it also shows the more precise contours (typous) of the truth, the splendor of the holy Church. Nevertheless, it also displays in advance the original itself of the painting (auto to tês eikonos archetypon), namely, the future existence and life in heaven. The divine Paul has in turn taught us this distinction: "The law which in truth had a shadow of the realities to come...and not even the image of these realities..." (Heb. 10:1). On the one hand, he calls this immortal and grief-free life, this existence without old age and free of every care, the "realities to come;" and, on the other hand, (he calls) the organization of the Church which, during the present life, imitates as far as possible the realities to come, the "image of realities;" and (he calls) the Law which instructs in a way that is more veiled than the Church's teaching, a "shadow." And indeed, painters have in view the original that they imitate in order to create their painting: they first do a sketch, then they adorn the sketch with colors. If, however, the Jews are opposed (to this interpretation) and attempt to draw all of prophecy to themselves, it is prophecy itself that will permit me, with God's help, to convince them of their deceit. So then, the terms of this prediction apply equally, in some manner, to ancient Jerusalem, which, against all hope, received splendor in the past; but they apply in particular to the Church of God, which has received the light of divine knowledge and encircles the glory of the Savior.[85]

In such a hermeneutical system, the role of history is fundamental. Even at this third level of interpretation, everything, the determination of type and antitype alike, must pass "the test of facts"—so much so that Theodoret often earnestly refuses to retain a certain event or person in the Old Testament as a "type" because they do not in his view meet the prerequisites for this function. Indeed, he cannot be satisfied with a mere resemblance or an excessively vague relation between type and antitype. The "rules" established for typology by the Antiochenes were quite scrupulous[86] (in comparison, say, with the great Alexandrian exegetes). It behooves us, then, to conclude that prophecy was by no means finally fulfilled in the Old Testament (which is, again, why certain potential "types" prove impossible[87]), and that prophecy must ultimately be directly related to Christ or to the New Testament period. Even if we attribute all of this to anti-Jewish polemic and make of it a particular form of Christian exegesis,[88] it still remains true, methodologically speaking, that *history* always decides whether to resort to, or to deny, a typological interpretation.

Considering as a whole the hermeneutical system advanced by Theodoret, its coherence and rigorous self-discipline are striking. There is no break in passing from one type of interpretation into another, for everything rests definitively on the "literal" sense. Whether it is a question of explaining the letter of the text by rendering it in its proper sense, or of having to resort to figurative interpretation, or of establishing a typological interpretation, the process remains the same: to safeguard the "reality" and historicity of the text by demonstrating its truth with the testimony of facts (*ta pragmata*), and by specifying its significance through determining the end (*telos*) which genuinely fulfills the prophecy. Thus we can see how history is one of the privileged auxiliary disciplines in Theodoret's exegesis.

Again, however, this does not lead to a narrowly literal, or "literalistic," exegesis. Each of these three modes of interpretation—literal, figurative, and typological—truly enables Theodoret to show that realities or messages from the Old Testament are genuinely comprehended and fulfilled with the advent of Christ or the life of the Church. Through three different exegetical approaches, Theodoret succeeds in orienting his interpretation to the New Testament, therein establishing two groups of prophecies: those directly related to the New Testament, owing to literal or metaphorical interpretation, and others indirectly related to it, interpreted through a typological lens. Overall, then, the rigorousness of Theodoret's method does not lead him to as narrow a reading of the sacred texts as we find in the ancient Antiochene exegetes.

The Ultimate Goal of Theodoret's Exegesis

One last question remains, not about Theodoret's exegetical method (we have already acknowledged its interest) but about why, in the fifth century, the bishop of Cyrus undertakes this enormous hermeneutical labor. What motivated him to deliver again, after so many other earlier exegetes, commentaries on the same biblical texts? Initially there are reasons given by Theodoret himself and repeated without change from one commentary to the next. Most often he claims to be yielding to the wishes of friends who have besought him to comment on Scripture, sometimes so urgently that they constrain him to modify his original intentions.[89] Actually these outside requests seem merely to provide an immediate occasion for commentaries that Theodoret had already conceived or projected.[90] But doubtless they served to revive in him an awareness of his moral duty, made all the more pressing by his pastoral charge: "divine law" commanded him to transmit the received teaching of the Church and to make use of his talents.[91] Despite appearances, it would perhaps be an exaggeration to see in these motivations, which the Fathers commonly invoke, merely a rhetorical artifice. Not only did Theodoret, in the course of his commentaries, never forget his readership, or to encourage them to profit from the teachings of the Bible,[92] but, with the unique clarity of his interpretation, his heuristic style and his conciseness, he made a useful work of his finished exegetical project.

Are these acknowledged reasons sufficient? The polemical tone of several prefaces indeed betrays other motivations as well, but actually Theodoret simply desires in this case to justify taking up the work others before him had started, and for this reason vigorously criticizes certain "judaizing" methods of exegesis.[93] Our purpose here is principally to identify the originality of Theodoret's own exegetical method, not to set forth the outline of a polemic at the root of his writings. Still, in reading his commentaries one cannot help but notice a triple polemic at work, against idolaters, Jews, and heretics. Before concluding that his exegesis was a weapon of combat against the Church's enemies, however, we must take note of the fact that this battle was hardly raging in full force in the fifth century, and it was of limited interest to Theodoret, insofar as he had already, well before composing his biblical commentaries, written whole treatises against "Greeks," Jews, and various heretical groups.[94] Indeed, by the fifth century the Church no longer had to defend its right to exist against paganism; yet numerous pagan practices still survived, and many a soul was still seduced by a "Hellenism" which was far from admitting defeat. There persisted, then, a certain risk of contamination for the Christian faith. This is sufficient to explain Theodoret's insistence on defining the divine nature in opposition to that of idols, on obviating every kind of anthropomorphism in Scripture, and on vindicating the Unity-in-Trinity of God on the basis of the biblical text. Against the Jews, aside from the traditional accusations in which he has a limited interest, Theodoret strives to show that the Jews' method of reading Scripture is wrong because most of the prophecies that they consider fulfilled in their own history actually must be related to the New Testament. He furthermore devotes himself to refuting their excessively narrow conception of God, since they fail to recognize the oneness of the three hypostases, again for want of a correct reading of the Bible. And finally, Theodoret's polemic against heretics in essence amounts to a refutation of Arian teachings. Certainly, here and there, the names of Sabellius, Marcion, Macedonius, and Apollinaris[95] come up, and their heresies are condemned, but it is principally the "blasphemies" of Arius and Eunomius that Theodoret denounces. Not only does he affirm, each time the text warrants it, the divinity of Christ and his *homoousia* with the Father, but in his diligence in commenting on verses liable to being used as ammunition by the Arians and undoubtedly exploited by them already, we recognize Theodoret's urge to remove all scriptural foundation for the heresy and to establish, instead, that of the Nicene faith. Such appears to be the overall goal toward which his three-edged polemic converges; indeed, this goal justifies the polemic. For Theodoret, then, the need to maintain an exegetical method directed toward establishing the orthodox faith, notably in the domain of christology, overshadows the working out of a polemic of little immediate relevance and necessarily less intense than in his earlier treatises.

The key issue at stake in the fifth-century Church, the one which divided Antioch and Alexandria, was no longer Arianism, but the christological problem posed by Apollinarianism. As is well known, this heresy, which cut short the human nature of Christ to the extent that he ceased to be a "complete human being," provoked a strong reaction from the Antiochenes. They responded emphatically by affirming two complete natures, divine and human, in Christ. Up to that point they were defending the doctrine of Nicea, but everything would change with the emergence of Nestorius, an Antiochene by training, as bishop of Constantinople (423), who championed dyophysitism with a fervency matched only by the awkwardness of his pronouncements.[96] His resounding denial of the *theotokos* ultimately provoked the wrath of Cyril of Alexandria and divided the Church for a long time. And yet Cyril's formula for defining the union of the two natures in Christ[97] in its turn appeared suspiciously Apollinarian and devoid of all scriptural support to Antiochenes. Passions mounted on both sides, and won the day with the Council of Ephesus (431), before being provisionally appeased by the Act of Union (433), of which Theodoret was the primary redactor. The cogency of Antiochene dyophysitism and the legitimacy of the formulas that expressed it (excluding, of course, those of Nestorius) were acknowledged by Cyril, while the Easterners, for their part, were satisfied with Cyril's explanations, accepting the orthodoxy of his famous christological formula, "one incarnate nature of the divine Logos." Officially, an agreement was reached, but each side remained vigilant, sometimes suspecting the other. It is apparently in this period, after the Act of Union, that Theodore composed his exegetical commentaries.

Through all of this we can see more clearly Theodoret's ultimate purpose. Just as Bible reading permitted him to lay an exegetical foundation for the trinitarian theology and christology defined at Nicea, it also gave him the chance to clarify Antiochene dyophysitism. This is precisely why Theodoret is so assiduous in his commentaries to point out what accords respectively with the human and divine natures of Christ. The distinction of natures is recalled again and again, and appears to be grounded in the very "letter" of the text. In addition, metaphorical interpretation legitimates the use of terms originally held suspect by Cyril, such as "temple," "tabernacle," "cloud," for representing the human nature assumed by Christ. At the same time, however, Theodoret is careful, always basing himself on the text, to affirm the reality of the union of Christ's two natures, even if he refrains from describing its exact mode. There are in Christ "two natures," the Son of God and the Son of man, and while they are truly two distinct natures, they constitute only one person. Moreover, to avoid the ambiguity of a vocabulary which had inspired the errors of Nestorius, Theodoret gives up using concrete formulations—"man" and "God"—respectively to designate each of Christ's natures, even though the Act of Union had sanctioned such terminology. Without polemic or passion, but with a methodical discipline, Theodoret once again becomes, through his exegetical commentaries, the defender of Antiochene christological principles. His conscientious respect for the Act of Union of 433 furthermore enabled him, when the controversy with Eutyches struck,[98] to use the testimony of his scriptural commentaries among other proofs of his orthodoxy.[99]

In the fifth century, as in every period when the Christian faith has required precise doctrinal definition, reference to Holy Scripture seems to have been fundamental. It is in such a context that Theodoret's massive exegetical enterprise found its true justification. It makes little difference, in the end, that he devoted himself to commenting on texts that others before him had already interpreted, or even that he borrowed from them, at the risk of passing as a mere compiler. What mattered to Theodoret was to add his own stone to the building, to produce a useful work that permitted even those who already "profited from knowledge" to discover in his commentaries "more to think about."[100] It was by no means a matter of making the text say what he wanted it to; his rigorous exegetical method precluded that danger. In establishing the correct text, as in the task of interpretation properly speaking, we have the importance that Theodoret attaches to the "letter" of Scripture. It is certainly possible to bemoan the lack of a more properly "spiritual" or mystical dimension in his exegesis, but its rational and virtually "scientific" character gives it a power and authority of its own. One cannot help being struck by the coherence of Theodoret's exegetical method, the manner in which he articulates the three levels or modes of interpretation, and by the security of the process. The style of his commentary further reinforces this impression,[101] revealing as it does a more cerebral than emotional temperament; indeed, its clarity, rigor, and brevity leave little room for passion. Such a style simultaneously serves Theodoret's overall plan, for not only did his commentaries have the advantage of being more accessible and more directly useful in understanding the biblical text, but, in the christological controversy of the fifth century, after all the insults, passion, and injustices, they opened up a new approach. The credit must go to Theodoret, one of the principal authors of the Act of Union, for showing that the solution of doctrinal conflict lay in Scripture, not in the conflict of personalities. One and the same method enabled him to show that the foundation of the Nicene faith, the refutation of Arianism, or the evidence for the two distinct natures, united without confusion or admixture in the one person of Christ, could all be discovered in Scripture. Through his exegesis as much as his polemical writings, therefore, Theodoret undeniably contributed to laying the foundation for the orthodox faith.

NOTES

1. See now J.-N. Guinot's expanded study, *L'exégèse de Théodoret de Cyr*, Théologie historique 100 (Paris, 1995).
2. Theodoret commented on all the Prophets, the Psalms, the Song of Songs; and we must add to his commentaries a series of *Quaestiones* on the Octateuch, Kings, and Chronicles. For the Greek text of his commentaries we will refer to the PG of J. P. Migne and, for his *Commentary on Isaiah*, to my own critical edition in SC 276, 295, and 315 (Paris, 1980, 1982). References to the *In Is.* will be made according to volume number in the

SC edition, section number in the commentary (as opposed to page numbers), and lines.

3. *In Ep. Pauli, praef.* (PG 82: 37A).
4. Such is a leitmotif of virtually all the prefaces to his commentaries, and this urge to be concise is also in evidence many times throughout the course of his interpretation. He refuses, for example, to prolong a polemic or, in hopes of avoiding a useless repetition, refers to his earlier works. Moreover, in contrast with the common practice of exegetes of his time, usually prompted by a curious quotation in the text on which the exegete is commenting, Theodoret abstains from entering into a long digression (*ekphrasis*).
5. This proves that antiquity largely shared Photius's opinion expressed in his *Bibliotheca* (ed. R. Henry, Paris, 1962, cod. 203, t. 3, 102-103).
6. See, e.g., *In Cant.* (PG 81: 48C); *In XII proph.* (PG 81: 1548B). Neither does Theodoret hide his reading of commentaries prior to his own: *In Cant.* (PG 81: 32A-B); *In Psalm.* (PG 80: 860C-D); *In Ep. Pauli* (PG 82: 37A).
7. *In XII proph.* (PG 81: 1548B).
8. Most notably he contests interpretations of Theodore of Mopsuestia and sometimes vigorously denounces this "judaizing" type of exegesis; cf. *In Cant.* (PG 81: 29A); *In Psalm.* (PG 80:860C).
9. Cf. the comments of M. Harl in her Introduction to Origen's *Philocalia* (SC 302: 59ff).
10. *In Cant.* (PG 81: 32C).
11. Ibid. (48A).
12. Ibid. (29C-D); see also *In Psalm.* (PG 80: 864A).
13. *In Dan.* (PG 81: 1264A).
14. *In Ezech.* (PG 81: 1073B).
15. Cf. *In Gen.* (PG 80: 76B).
16. In nearly all the prefaces to his commentaries, Theodoret humbly confesses his inability to penetrate the meaning of Scripture unless the Spirit comes and enlightens his intelligence.
17. Theodoret frequently invokes this principle: cf. *In Ezech.* (PG 81: 809B; 957C; 1052A); *In Dan.* (PG 81: 1256C); *In Is.* (SC 295: 8, 84-90).
18. *In Ezech.* (PG 81: 809B-C).
19. *Quaest. in Reg., praef.* (PG 80: 529A).
20. *In Dan.* (PG 81: 1256C): "If it was possible for everyone to uncover the oracles of the divine prophets, to transcend the surface of the letter, to penetrate its profundity and purchase the pearl of thought that is hidden there..."; cf. *In Cant.* (PG 81: 32D): "...and, because they ignore divine Scripture's means of expression, they have no desire to find their way in and pass beyond the veil of the letter so as to attain the spirit within the text and to behold, as in a mirror, a visage discovered, the glory of the Lord."
21. *In Psalm.* (PG 80: 865A); *In Is.* (SC 315: 16, 248-251); *In Ep. Pauli* (PG 82: 37B).
22. *In Is.* (SC 295: 6, 16-19; SC 315: 16, 248-251); *In Ep. Pauli* (PG 82: 44B).

23. *In Psalm.* (PG 80: 864A). On this point Theodoret goes even further than Theodore of Mopsuestia, despite the latter's great admiration for the Septuagint.

24. *Quaest. in Reg., praef.* (PG 80: 529A); *In Cant.* (PG 81: 120A-B).

25. Today we must resist speaking of a "Lucianic recension"; see D. Barthélemy, *Les Devanciers d'Aquila* (Leiden, 1963), 126-127, reprinted in *Études d'histoire du texte de l'Ancien Testament* (Fribourg-Göttingen, 1978), 70-71; also, in Barthélemy's article "Les problèmes textuels de II Sam. 11:2-1 Rois 2:11 reconsidérés à la lumière de certaines critiques des *Devanciers d'Aquila*" (ibid., 218-254), see the postscript entitled "La recension lucianique" (ibid., 243-354). The text used in the churches of Antioch and Constantinople was not, contrary to the long-held view, the work of Lucian of Antioch. This text, which does not display the same characteristics for all books of the Bible, bears the mark of a number of literary touch-ups, mainly in the form of atticisms, and depends essentially on the Origenian recension in the *Hexapla*. Its interest is, therefore, not, as was once believed, to proffer a new hebraicizing recension of the Septuagint, but rather to conserve numerous elements of the ancient Septuagint. It is better to speak, then, as Barthélemy proposes, of an "Antiochene edition" of the Septuagint which was placed later on under Lucian's patronage.

26. He also occasionally confirms their agreement as compared with other versions of the Bible (e.g., *In Is.*, SC 315: 14, 117-119); in any case, the mention of "the Hexapla" or better yet "the text of the Septuagint given in the Hexapla" clearly indicates that Theodoret refers to a text other than that of his lemma.

27. These asterisks appear only in the *Commentary on Isaiah* and seem to be relatively recent. Cf. J. Ziegler, ed., introduction to *Septuaginta: Vetus Testamentum graecum XIV Isaias*, 2nd ed. (Göttingen, 1967), 90-92.

28. It became virtually commonplace, following Origen, to emphasize the clarity of Symmachus's translation; cf. D. Barthélemy, "Eusèbe, la Septante et 'les autres,'" in *La Bible et les Pères* (Paris, 1971), 51-65; this is also, with some reservations, Theodore of Mopsuestia's opinion, as revealed in *Le commentaire de Théodore de Mopsueste sur les Psaumes I-LXXX*, ed. R. Devreesse (Vatican City, 1939), 364,25-365,14.

29. Occasionally the citation is reduced to a single word, introduced as a clearer synonym or as leading to a fundamentally different interpretation (e.g., in Isa. 7:14, *neanis* instead of *parthenos*).

30. See, e.g., *In Is.* (SC 276: 2, 542-545) or the text of Isa. 5:8. *Mê oikêsête* must not be read in the negative but the interrogative mood, as is proven by Symmachus's translation, where the *mê* is replaced with the interrogative particle *âra*.

31. A good example of this ambiguity is revealed by Theodoret in his commentary on Hosea 4:15 ("Do not go up to the house of On"): the term *ôn* could be taken, as some have mistaken it, to be the participle of the verb *eimi*; but, as "the interpreters'" version proves, this *ôn* must

rather be understood as the name of the idol of Bethel (*In Ose.*, PG 81: 1573D-1576A).

32. Such is the reason to which Theodoret appeals in *In Cant.* (PG 81: 120B).

33. See, e.g., Ps. 111:5 (110:5, LXX), which reads, "He provides food for those who fear him." Theodoret comments that "instead of 'food,'" the interpreters have said 'booty.' Now both interpretations are true, each in its own way. For they hastened after the riches of their enemies as if after a booty entirely prepared for them, and it is on that basis that they acquired abundant food" (*In Psalm.*, PG 80: 1777B-C).

34. Cf. *In Psalm.* (PG 80: 957C-D).

35. The way in which he manages to establish this *symphônia* can at times appear rather simple, even artificial: e.g., in Isa. 33:6 he strains to show that the word *pistis* used by the three interpreters agrees with the *nomos* in the Septuagint so as to designate the New Testament (*In Is.*, SC 295: 10, 53-61).

36. One example will be sufficient, taken from his commentary on Isa. 28:17 ("And I will turn judgment into hope, and my mercy into balances [*stathmous*]"); Theodoret remarks: "Symmachus translated this passage as follows: 'And I will issue judgment by way of a plumb-line, and justice by way of a level.' This amounts to saying: I will bring a righteous condemnation against my opponents. Indeed the level shows whether the surface of the foundation-stones is flat and the plumb-line assures that the construction jambs are vertical. With these words he has distinguished justice from condemnation. On the basis of this interpretation let us likewise understand the Septuagint's own reading, according to which the hope is a righteous judgment and mercy is mixed with judgment" (*In Is.*, SC 295: 8, 149-158). See also ibid. (SC 295: 7, 584-588; 8, 65-69; 9, 52-60; 10, 93-102; 11, 95-99; 13, 408-416).

37. Cf. *In Psalm.* (PG 80: 1009C-1012A-B). Here Theodoret confirms that the Septuagint version is the only one that uses the term "sins" in Ps. 22:2, which makes it difficult to apply the verse to Christ. After quoting the versions of Aquila, Symmachus, and Theodotion, which make such an application easier, he is still anxious to return to the Septuagint text and to prove that he is in no way inhibiting its reading, contrary to what certain others have said.

38. This does happen, however, in *In Jonam* (PG 81: 1733D), for example, where Theodoret thinks that an error committed by the Septuagint has been repeated in subsequent copies of this version, whereas the three interpreters' versions, the Hebrew text, and the Syriac text all give a more acceptable reading.

39. The consensus of the seventy inspired men (who translated the Septuagint) indeed appears to him to give their version an authority that cannot be counterbalanced by the agreement of a mere three individuals (*In Is.*, SC 276: 3, 363-366), and certainly not by any one of the three by himself (*In Psalm.*, PG 80: 864C, referring to Aquila).

40. Cf. *In Is.* (SC 276: 3, 367-373), where he declares that the seventy who translated the Bible before the coming of Christ had no reason to corrupt Scripture, whereas the three interpreters, producing their version after the Incarnation, had reasons for doing so, insofar as they had the prejudice of Jews.

41. Just the same we would add that Theodoret does consult the text transmitted by the *Quinta editio*, albeit on a very rare occasion, since he refers to it only twice in the *In Cant.* (PG 81: 157D; 181C) and once in the *In Psalm.* (PG 80:1469B).

42. E.g., in Isa. 37:38, some copies preserved the Syriac *patechron* instead of the Greek *patarchon* that Theodoret read in his text (*In Is.*, SC 295: 11, 390-394; cf. ibid., SC 276: 3, 714-721). See also *In Psalm.* (PG 80: 1953D), where the addition found in some copies is considered to be valid.

43. Thus in the *In Psalm.*, almost every time Theodoret mentions these copies it is to indicate additions that they make to the Hebrew, to the *Hexapla*, or to the three interpreters, whether a word or a title; but quite often these additions that he singles out equally form part of Theodoret's lemma. Must we conclude from this that these *antigrapha* are closely related to his base text?

44. Even though he does give them a certain amount of credit, as was noted above (cf. n. 42), Theodoret still follows his own text most of the time. Two opposing examples will prove this: in the first case (*In Is.*, SC 315: 14, 115-121), he rejects an addition inserted by certain copies as a corruption; in the second case (ibid., SC 315: 19, 133-136), on the contrary, he preserves a word that only his base text has, despite the combined evidence of certain "copies," the *Hexapla*, the three interpreters, and the original Hebrew.

45. In this connection, therefore, he does not follow Theodore of Mopsuestia, who concludes once for all that the Septuagint version is faithful enough that no recourse to the Hebrew is necessary.

46. It is possible, moreover, that Theodoret refers to the Hebrew only through the bias of the *Hexapla*. His use of Syriac allows us to think that he had a cursory knowledge of Hebrew, by virtue of the kinship of the two languages, but this cannot be categorically affirmed.

47. Indeed, it is precisely the Peshitta that we must recognize as designated by his mention of *ho Syros*—contrary to what the critical school of thought associated with Rahlfs has claimed, which saw in this designation merely a Greek version of the Bible that had been produced by some unknown Syrian. Theodoret appears not to have shared Theodore of Mopsuestia's suspicion of this Syriac version (cf. PG 66: 437C, 452C-D, 468A).

48. His use of the Peshitta also varies considerably between commentaries. He mentions it three times in the *In XII proph.*, twice in the *In Is.*, six times in the *In Psalm.*, sixteen times in the *In Ezech.*, but thirty-four times in the *In Jer.*, where, moreover, it is the only version besides the Septuagint that he consults.

49. Cf. *In Is.* (SC 315: 19, 133-136).
50. Ibid. (SC 276: *Hypothesis,* 25-27).
51. *In Ezech.* (PG 81: 1156B).
52. This suspicion is expressed notably in the preface to *In Psalm.* (PG 80: 860C).
53. We should recall here that the formal division of the Bible into chapters and verses was late in coming (respectively in the thirteenth and sixteenth centuries).
54. E.g., the "titles" of the Psalms or those of the oracles of Isaiah against the nations (Isa. 13-23).
55. Typically Theodoret will comment on these transitions this way: "After having announced such an event, he foretells what follows." Frequently, too, he will remark: "He announces after this (*meta touto*) such and such a thing," or "Henceforth (*enteuthen*) he changes the subject in order to declare..."
56. Every chance that he gets, Theodoret certainly tries to show the coherence of the text by justifying the presence of a certain prophecy that seems to have no connection with what precedes and follows it, or that seems to be a useless repetition (e.g., *In Is.,* SC 276: 2, 3-6; SC 295: 6, 2-11; 11, 6-7). But even more consistently, Theodoret quickly notes the logical links which unite the prophecies to each other, using most often in these cases the same syntactical structure, viz., a causal proposition introduced with *epeidê,* followed by a principal expressing the idea to be announced, the logical or causative link frequently being marked by the adverbs "rightly," "with good reason," "necessarily" (e.g., *In Is.,* SC 276: 3, 78-80, 352-356, 559-562; SC 295: 5, 200-204; 6, 196-199, 490-491).
57. *In Is.* (SC 295: 7, 28-35).
58. The more numerous instances are those in which Theodoret indicates that the verse must be read in the interrogative mood although no word indicates it, the interrogative lying solely in the intonation given to the text; and the same holds true in those instances where the interrogative word is not very clear (e.g., *In Is.,* SC 276: 2, 541-545; SC 295: 13, 51-55; SC 315: 14, 559; 16, 11-13, 427-430; 17, 267-270; *In Ep. Pauli,* PG 82: 85B; 161C; 168C-D; 173A-B; 268A). Elsewhere (*In Psalm.,* PG 80: 1301C), he notes the indicative *ara* must be read instead of the interrogative *âra;* or that the prophet is expressing himself in the tone of a wish and that this optative style is common in Scripture (ibid., 1753D; *In Is.,* SC 295: 7, 588-592).
59. Or in still other cases he will encourage the reading of an accented *tís* so as not to confuse it with the indefinite *tis,* or to opt for the exclamative *hôs* rather than the comparative *hôs.*
60. The obscurity of the Septuagint often stems from its literalism (see above); but Paul's Greek is often just as obscure by virtue of its conciseness (*In Ep. Pauli,* PG 82: 820D), some of its constructions (ibid., 832D), and certain strokes of language proper to Paul (e.g., the value of the conjunction *hina*: ibid., 104A-B; 181C).

61. Undoubtedly Theodoret had to refer for this to the *Interpretation of Hebrew Names* (*Onomastica*) that Origen also used (see, e.g., Origen's *Hom. in Num.* 20.3, SC 29: 200). While he refers to it explicitly only one time in his *In Is.* (SC 295: 9, 270), he uses it much more frequently in his *Quaestiones* on the books of Kings and Chronicles.

62. For example, the terms "anathema" (*In XII proph.*, PG 81:1841A-B, 1956C; *In Is.*, SC 295: 5, 27-32; *In Ep. Pauli*, PG 82: 149A-B); "proselyte" (*In Psalm.*, PG 80: 1632C, 1977A); "anointed" (ibid., 1713B; *In XII proph.*, PG 81: 1832C; *In Is.*, SC 315: 14, 73-75); *idiotês* (*In Ep. Pauli*, PG 82: 341C, 344B); *euperistation* (ibid., 769C); and *agapêtê* (ibid., 874A).

63. Like his great exegetical predecessors from the Antiochene school, Diodore of Tarsus and Theodore of Mopsuestia, Theodoret acknowledges that enallage is a common procedure in Scripture (*In Is.*, SC 295: 4, 102-103; *In Ezech.*, PG 81: 952C-D; *In Nahum*, PG 81: 1800C) or, which for him is the same thing, in the Septuagint (*In Psalm.*, PG 80: 1620B, 1676C-D). In the *In Joelem* (PG 81: 1637C), he gives the following reason for it: "Indicating future events as though they had already happened is characteristic of divine Scripture. It uses this procedure not only by reason of the transposing terms from one language into another, but also for purposes of confirming what is being said. For as the prophet declares, these events will happen in this way since we contemplate them as already accomplished and talk of them as already accomplished."

64. E.g., in Isa. 65:20, he takes the expression "the child a hundred years old" to mean "a hundred years" (*In Is.*, SC 315: 20, 455-457), or *kairos* to mean *symphora* (*In Psalm.*, PG 80: 1528A and *passim*).

65. Consequently, nearly every time Theodoret encounters expressions like "the arm" or "the hand" of God in his text, we see him specifically indicating that it is a matter of a human means of expression, and that "hand" must be understood in these sense of God's "power." We should note that these "idioms" at once lead him toward a metaphorical interpretation.

66. Cf., e.g., *In Is.* (SC 276: 3, 66-72), where in Isa. 6:2-3 the singular "Lord" attests, in Theodoret's view, to the one nature of God, while the triple repetition of "holy" refers to the Trinity.

67. See, e.g, *In Is.* (SC 276: 3, 845-846, 852-855 [Isa. 9:5]; SC 295: 7, 571-576 [Isa. 26:13]; 12, 592-598 [Isa. 42:8]; 13, 167-176 [Isa. 43:11], 313-318 [Isa. 44:6]). Theodoret's affinity for syllogism (cf. his *Demonstration through Syllogisms*, PG 83: 317C-336B) corresponds to a precise polemical intention, the desire to refute Eunomius (who was well-known for his passion for this kind of logic) with Eunomius's own weapons.

68. On the importance of the place of word order, see *In Ep. Pauli* (PG 82: 669A); of the preposition *dia*, ibid. (229A, 232B, 509A, 644B); of the conjunction *kai*, ibid. (641C); of a singular in Isa. 45:21, see *In Is.* (SC 315: 14, 338-350).

69. Notably Theodoret attributes the words "slave" and "servant," and every expression "unworthy of God" and liable to providing ammunition

for the Arians, to Christ's human nature. It is important to relate to his human nature everything that is humble (*ta tapeina*), and to his divine nature everything that transcends his humanity, thus providing the exegetical foundation for a dyophysite christology. See, e.g., Theodoret's commentary on Isa. 7:15 (*In Is.*, SC 276: 3, 393-403), where he alternately relates the text to the human nature and the divine nature of Christ.

70. The usual formula is as follows: "Yet if one so desires also to understand (this word) in a figurative way... one will equally discover in this way the truth of the prophecy, and one would not be deviating from the truth." See, e.g., *In Is.* (SC 276: 2, 166-170; 3, 488-490; SC 315: 14, 13-16; 17, 243-244, 484-490; 19, 121-122, 501-502).

71. Here is an example of the procedure taken from Isa. 30:25 ("And on that day there will be flowing water on every lofty mountain and every high hill"): "As for the expression 'waters rushing on every mountain and every hill,' we find that this has not taken place literally (*kata rhêton*), and yet we know that the promise of God is not deceitful. Let us observe precisely why, even if the Jews do not want to do so, it is necessary (*anagkê*) to understand the prediction figuratively (*tropikôs*) and to find its fulfillment after the incarnation of our Lord Christ. For at that time our thirsty human nature received its 'waters' as it were, in the form of the divine apostles" (*In Is.*, SC 295: 9, 200-206); cf. also ibid. (SC 295: 5, 9-13, 417-419; 6, 157-161; 7, 123-127; 10, 202-209). It was precisely through ignorance of the metaphorical sense that certain persons could be shocked at reading the Song of Songs (*In Cant.*, PG 81: 32D).

72. *In Cant.* (PG 81: 33A).

73. *In Is.* (SC 295: 7, 123-127).

74. Thus, for example, in Isa. 5:7, the prophet himself specifies that he used the term "vine" to designate the house of Israel (*In Is.*, SC 276: 2, 521) and, in Isa. 51:1-2, that he uses "rock" and "hollow in the quarry" to designate Abraham and Sarah respectively (ibid., SC 315: 16, 162-163).

75. *In Cant.* (PG 81: 37A).

76. It is rather difficult to determine, however, exactly what Theodoret means by "allegory." Although he claims several times to be interpreting a passage "according to the laws of allegory" (*In Ezech.*, PG 81: 1040B-1124A), it is hard to find what distinguishes this interpretation from a "metaphorical" one, all the more so because he seems to use *allegorikôs* as a synonym for *tropikôs* (ibid., 1040C).

77. *In Is.* (SC 276: 2, 463-482).

78. Ibid. (SC 295: 10, 398-408). Theodoret once again invokes this passage from Ezekiel in the preface to his *In Cant.* (PG 81: 33A-B) to prove that Scripture commonly uses figurative means of expression. It seems, furthermore, that this was virtually a "textbook example;" thus John Chrysostom, in his *Commentary on Isaiah*, benefiting from using Isa. 5:7 ("For the vineyard of the Lord of Hosts is the house of Israel") to recall that we should resort to "allegory" only at the invitation of Scripture,

also appeals to this passage in Ezek. 17:3 (SC 304: 5, 3, 45-59); cf. also Origen, *Hom. in Ezech.* 11 (GCS 8: 424f).

79. E.g., in Isa. 8:6, the expression "waters of Siloam" (*In Is.*, SC 276: 3, 552-555), the "waters" depicted in Isa. 30:25 (cf. n. 71), etc.

80. Cf. *In Is.* (SC 295: 8, 388-398 [Isa. 29:17]; 9, 450-461 [Isa. 32:15-16]; 10, 193-195 [Isa. 33:20]).

81. Cf. ibid. (SC 276: 3, 805-811 [Isa. 9:4]; SC 295: 4, 361-354 [Isa. 11:1]; 6, 203-206 [Isa. 19:1]; SC 315: 19, 588-589 [Isa. 63:2]).

82. Ibid. (SC 315: 17, 112-115).

83. Cf. *In Ezech.* (PG 81: 1156B, 1164D); *In Soph.* (PG 81: 1857C); *In Is.* (SC 295: 7, 185-186, 759-760; SC 315: 19, 42).

84. Cf. *In Ep. Pauli* (PG 82: 244D) on 1 Cor. 2:13: "We indeed have the testimony of the Old Testament and through it we sanction the New, for the latter is equally inspired. And in fact, when we want to demonstrate the figures (*typous*) of our mysteries, we introduce the lamb, the blood smeared on the doorposts, the crossing of the sea, the water springing forth from the rock, the dispensing of the manna, and a host of similar things, and by the figures (*dia tôn typôn*) we exhibit the truth." Cf. also *In Ezech.* (PG 81: 1232B): "For the Old Testament is the figure of the New;" *In Habac.* (PG 81: 1836C): "The ancient realities are clearly the figures of new realities;" *In Zach.* (PG 81: 1917C): "For the ancient realities were the figure of those things which pertain to us."

85. *In Is.* (SC 315: 19, 2-39).

86. Cf. John Chrysostom (PG 51: 247; PG 53: 328-329). See also Theodoret himself, *In Zech.* (PG 81: 1917C): "He agrees that the image had a likeness (*homoiôtêta*) to the archetype."

87. Theodoret frequently denies the possibility of a typological interpretation: *In Amos* (PG 81: 1705B-C); *In Mich.* (PG 81: 1760D); *In Zach.* (PG 81: 1924A); *In Ezech.* (PG 81: 1197A-B); *In Is.* (SC 295: 4, 478-481; 12, 64-70; 13, 217-221; SC 315: 15, 335-340). In certain cases, nevertheless, Theodoret is less adamant and recognizes the possibility of typological interpretation; but one almost always has the sense in these instances that he is merely making a concession (cf. *In Habac.*, PG 81: 1836C; *In Zach.*, PG 81: 1940C).

88. In fact, even if his prophetic exegesis is targeting Jews, it appears (notably in his exegesis concerning Zerubbabel and the return of the Jews from the Babylonian exile) that Theodoret just as much has in view the work of Theodore of Mopsuestia, whose literal and historical exegesis clearly remains within the parameters of the Old Testament itself. See *In Dan.* (PG 81: 1436B-D), where Theodoret lays the blame on "teachers of piety" and no longer only on the Jews.

89. Thus, in the preface to the *In Psalm.* (PG 80: 860A-B), he declares that he would have preferred to give priority to a commentary on the Psalter, but the solicitations of friends constrained him first to compose his commentaries on the Song of Songs, Daniel, Ezekiel, and the twelve Minor

Prophets. Moreover, Jeremiah's prophecy did not appear to him to require a commentary, but again in this case he gave in to the requests of his friends (PG 81: 496A).

90. At least this is the case with the commentary on the Psalter (cf. the preceding note). In the prologue to the *In Is.* (SC 276: *Prol.*, 35-36), Theodoret states that he has to date provided interpretations of all the prophets except Jeremiah. But this statement perhaps expresses more than a simple register of his works; it could be understood as indicating that he already has the intention of commenting on Jeremiah too in order to complete his series on the prophets.

91. *In Is.* (SC 276: *Prol.*, 9-16); cf. *In Dan.* (PG 81: 1257A-C), where Theodoret states that he had been nourished by the Scriptures since his childhood.

92. It is not unimportant, moreover, that each section of his commentaries finishes with a short moral exhortation and a doxology which thus gives them a homiletic quality.

93. Cf. *In Psalm.* (PG 80: 860C): "I have found...that others reconciled the prophecy with certain historical events, such that their interpretation pleaded in favor of the Jews rather than in favor of the children of faith." The criticism appears to be aimed especially at Theodore of Mopsuestia, whose exegesis tended to discover within Jewish history the fulfillment of the majority of prophecies that Theodoret related to Christ or the New Testament. Elsewhere the criticism of Theodore's literalism, as we have seen already, is particularly lively in Theodoret's preface to the *In Cant.* Other prefaces as well, notably those to the *In XII proph.* (PG 81: 1545B-1548) and the *In Ep. Pauli* (PG 82: 36A), reveal that Theodoret himself was subject to criticisms or else feared them, given the forcefulness with which he justified his exegetical enterprise.

94. The majority of these treatises, the memory of which is preserved thanks to Theodoret's correspondence, are today lost, namely his *Against the Arians and Eunomians, Against the Macedonians* (or, *On the Holy Spirit*), *Against the Marcionites,* and *Against the Apollinarians*—all of which were produced before 431. Fortunately, on the other hand, we still have his treatise against "the Greeks," known today as the *Cure for the Greek Maladies,* in which P. Canivet (editor of this work in SC 57) claims also to see the treatise *Against the Jews* that Theodoret mentions several times in his letters (P. Canivet, *Histoire d'une enterprise apologetique au VIe siècle,* Paris, 1958).

95. Contrary to what we might justly expect, given the importance of the christological debate in his time, Theodoret directly attacks Apollinaris only twice in his biblical commentaries (*In Ezech.,* PG 81: 1248C-1256B; *In Aggaeum,* PG 81: 1872C-1873A), and yet his attacks do not bear on the christology of the heresiarch, but on his erroneous interpretation of a historical event.

96. Nestorius in practice came to the point of no longer distinguishing two natures (*physeis*) in Christ, but two persons (*prosôpa*), God and man. He also said that the union of these two natures was only moral and external (*kat' eudokian, kata thêlêsin, kata gnômên*), that the divine Word

indwelled the man Jesus like a temple (*enoikêsis*), and that we should speak not of adoration with respect to Jesus, but of "co-adoration" (*sumproskunêsis*) of the assumed man by virtue of the presence of God within him. From that also arose Nestorius's position regarding the designation of "mother of God" (*theotokos*) given to the Virgin, who, in his view, was entitled, *stricto sensu*, only to be called "mother of the man" (*anthrôpotokos*).

97. Cyril's formula, "One incarnate nature of the divine Word" (*Mia physis tou Theou Logou sesarkômenê*), like his precise nuances concerning the mode of the union as realized "hypostatically," were misunderstood and legitimately suspected by the Antiochenes. Cyril in fact believed in good faith that he was going on the authority of the Fathers (including Athanasius), without realizing that the Apollinarians had disseminated an entire apocryphal literature under their great names. In any event, Cyril's formula would in its turn be exploited and reworked, from the orthodox sense that Cyril himself had given it, to serve the doctrinal position of the Monophysites.

98. At first confined within his diocese by imperial order, Theodoret was deposed from his see by the "Robber Council" of Ephesus in 449, and then exiled to Apamea.

99. Here we have the testimony once again of his correspondence. Cf. *Letter* 82 to Eusebius of Ancyra (Y. Azéma, ed., *Correspondence de Théodoret de Cyr*, SC 98, Paris, 1964, 202-203), and especially his long *Letter* 113 to Pope Leo (ibid., SC 111, Paris, 1965, 64-65); see also *Letter* 116 to the priest Renatus (SC 11: 71-73) and Letter 146 addressed to the monks of Constantinople when he had already regained his episcopal see in Cyrus.

100. *In Dan.* (PG 81: 1257C-D).

101. Photius, referring to the commentary *In Dan.*, judges Theodoret's style to be particularly well-adapted to the genre of the exegetical commentary (Photius, *Bibliotheca*, ed. R. Henry, cod. 203, t. 3, 102-103).

PART III

The Bible in Early Christian
Doctrinal Controversy

10

The Bible in Use among the Marginally Orthodox in the Second and Third Centuries

ALAIN LE BOULLUEC

In the second century and the first half of the third, interpretation of the Bible was at the very center of conflicts that pitted Christians against other Christians and that resulted in the exclusion of some. The principal champions of heterodox doctrines who, while subsisting at first within the ranks of Christianity, came very quickly to be perceived as heretics, were Marcion and his disciples, and the followers of what has customarily been called the Valentinian school, after its great Gnostic teacher Valentinus. The controversy extended well into the third century, as diverse groups of "heretics" continued to live on the margins of the Church. Works of biblical exegesis on the "orthodox" side continued to show traces of anti-heretical polemic at a time when Marcionites and Gnostics were no longer a real danger. These works demonstrate what a profound commotion these groups had stirred, and indicate that the Christian conception of the Bible and the methods of interpreting it were strongly impacted by this doctrinal strife in the earliest Christian centuries.

Marcion was originally from the city of Sinope in the province of Pontus on the Black Sea. He was raised in a Christian family, with a father who appears to have been a bishop. A shipowner by trade, Marcion traveled first in Asia Minor to Ephesus, where his doctrinal views already shocked local church authorities. He came to Rome probably in 139 and made a gift of 200,000 sesterces to the Church there. Not until 144, having failed in his bid to render the Roman clergy sympathetic with his doctrine, was Marcion excluded from the Church and began to found his own. Thanks to his gifts of organization, the energy of his convictions, and the power of his teaching, the Marcionite church grew very quickly. In 150, Justin Martyr anxiously declared that Marcion "has caused men of every nation to blaspheme" (*1 Apol.* 26). The Marcionite church became for some time the great rival of the "catholic" Church. Its significance, and the danger that it posed, can be measured by the forcefulness and the frequency of anti-Marcionite refutations in early Christian literature. Both Justin and Theophilus of Antioch composed treatises *Against Marcion*. Irenaeus indicates his intention to write one in his larger work *Against Heresies* (1.27.4, SC 264), one of the principal targets of which is Marcion himself. Eusebius of Caesarea, in his *Ecclesiastical History,* refers to a certain Modestus, who "more excellently than the others brought to light for all the world the error of this man" (4.25; SC 31). He also quotes extracts of Rhodo, who criticized the theses of Marcion's disciple Apelles (5.13; SC 41). The longest of Tertullian's works is his *Against Marcion* in five books, which is our principal source for our knowledge of Marcion's Bible. Hippolytus of Rome also composed a treatise *Against Marcion* (Eusebius, *Hist. eccl.* 4.22). Clement of Alexandria often attacks Marcionite doctrine in his *Stromateis,* while Origen abundantly discusses the exegetical principles of Marcion and Apelles. The abundance and diversity of this anti-Marcionite literature betrays the powerful lure of Marcionism and the extent of its growth throughout the Roman world. The pagan polemicist Celsus testifies in the second century to the sharpness of the Marcionite controversy. He in fact uses this dissent among Christians as evidence to build his own argument, and he appears to be well informed of the basic theses of Marcionite doctrine (*ap.* Origen, *Contra Celsum* 3.12; 5.54, 61; cf. 2.27; SC 132, 136, and 147). Finally, Eusebius gives evidence of the existence, from the end of the second century, of some Syriac *Dialogues* directed in part against Marcion by Bardesanes of Edessa.

While the Marcionite church declined rather rapidly in the West in the third century, we have proof that it persisted in the East well into the fifth century from the correspondence of Theodoret of Cyrus (SC 98 and 111) and the apologetic summary written in Armenian by Eznik of Kolb, who includes the Marcionites among the adversaries of the Church.

We must limit ourselves in this essay to Marcion's conception of the Bible, but this is the essence and foundation of his doctrine, the key to his system, and the reason for his success. Marcion's primary intuition is the irreducible novelty of the Gospel, the revelation of Jesus Christ. This entirely new message makes known a God who is patient and merciful, an unprecedented Kingdom, a salvation which promises absolute liberation from the world by granting access to a wholly other reality. Marcion sees this perfect God as utterly different from the God who speaks and acts in the Old Testament, who is a vindictive and jealous deity, severe in his justice and violent in his punishments. The decisive criterion is the statement of Luke 18:19: "None is good but God alone." Correlatively, the law of love in the Gospel is squarely opposed to the ancient Law. Marcion considers himself a disciple of Paul, and his doctrine has sometimes justifiably been deemed an intense Paulinism. He retains Paul's contrast between Grace and Law, while hardening it. Marcion alleges that the Church has compromised the absolute newness of the Gospel by recovering the Jewish Scriptures and acknowledging the authority of traditions which have distorted the message of Christ by connecting it up with Judaism. Marcion aspires to be the reformer who must direct Christians back to their authentic and original revelation. Proceeding so singularly but so effectively in his time, Marcion did not claim to be a prophet nor to withhold a secret tradition of some sort. In order to bolster and develop his teaching, he began with texts received in the Church and submitted them to criticism using Pauline themes as his norms. In this respect he is truly the first biblical scholar in the history of Christianity, albeit a scholar who worked exclusively with scissors and scalpel.

In reality, too many elements in the Pauline epistles contradicted the total opposition of Law and Gospel presumed by Marcion, who was convinced that judaizers had not ceased antagonizing Paul, and that they had posthumously falsified his writings. Marcion had set about purging the text of the epistles of all interpolation, in order to recover the original message of the Apostle, who was chosen by God because of the conspiracy that had deluded even the Twelve after Christ's ascension. Marcion's Pauline corpus includes the nine letters to the churches and Philemon (thus excluding the Pastoral Epistles). Once restored, these serve as his model for reconstituting the true Gospel, beginning with texts received in the Church that in his view have been contaminated by Jewish influences.

Marcion bases Paul's superior authority on Galatians 1:12: "I did not receive it (this Gospel) from human beings, nor was I taught it, but it came by a revelation of Jesus Christ." He draws from this same epistle the idea that other apostles had preached a false, judaizing Gospel.

A number of examples will serve to illustrate Marcion's exegetical method.[1] Marcion suppresses the reference to Abraham in Galatians 3, and generally eliminates all quotations from the Old Testament, expressions introduced by the phrase "it is written." In Galatians 5:14, after the phrase "the law is fulfilled," he adds "in you" in order to make clear that such has not happened "among the Jews." In 1 Corinthians 3:17 he replaces the words "God will destroy him" with "he will be destoyed" because God's perfect goodness is incompatible with that kind of destruction. In Romans 1:18, Marcion deprives "wrath" of its genitive complement "of God" and deletes the entire remainder of the chapter, where human crimes appear as divine punishments. He further omits Romans 3:31-4:25 because he could not countenance the idea of "upholding the law," nor the example of Abraham. In Romans 11:33 he eliminates the phrase "How unsearchable are his judgments" because God did not exercise judgment. In Ephesians 2:14-15, he replaces two words, a pronoun and a preposition, such that the Greek text takes on a wholly different meaning: "He destroyed the wall of separation, hostility in *the* flesh. He abolished the law and its commandments *by means of* ordinances" (instead of "He destroyed in *his* flesh the wall of separation, hostility. He abolished the law of commandments *in* ordinances"). In this way the passage signifies that God annulled the Jewish law by the precepts of Christ, and the role of Christ's flesh is fully eclipsed. In Ephesians 2:20, Marcion throws out any mention of the prophets; they cannot belong to the new household of God. The dropping of a single preposition turns Ephesians 3:9 into textual proof of the ignorance of the Creator-God, who does not know the plans of the true, saving God: Paul thus affirms that he received the grace "of making plain how the mystery which has always been hidden *for* the God who created the universe [instead of "*in* God, Creator of the universe"] is realized." All of Marcion's deletions turn the Pauline epistles into inspired documents that attest the distinction between the good, superior, only true God, and the God of the Law; between the "alien" God and the God who created the world; between the God revealed by Christ and the God of the Jews; between the Christ who came from a transcendent world and the human Messiah promised to Israel; between the Savior who, without really becoming incarnate, came to liberate souls from the servitude of the world so as to receive eternal beatitude, and the carnal restorer of a temporal and limited power.

Among the gospels being read in the Church in his time, Marcion retains that of Luke doubtless because of its pagano-Christian character, its emphasis on grace, and its ascetic tendencies. Yet he leaves out the accounts preceding Jesus's birth, the nativity stories, the baptism of Jesus, his Jewish genealogy, and the temptation. A number of Marcion's principal deletions from Luke's gospel are worthy of mention here. He omits the phrase "The old (wine) is good" in Luke 5:39, because it refers back to the Old Testament. Reference to Jesus's mother and brothers disappears from 8:19 because it leaves the impression that Christ, having earthly parentage, was merely born like a human being. Luke 10:24 is reduced to "For I tell you, the prophets did not see what you see." In the lawyer's question to Jesus in 10:25 ("Teacher, what must I do to receive eternal life?), the epithet "eternal" vanishes, since the promises of the God of the Old Testament, which in Marcion's view are the primary interest of the "lawyer" here, have to do only with this world. The parable of the prodigal son is not included, doubtless because it has the son return to the father's house. Christ's disclosure to the Twelve that his Passion and Resurrection will be a fulfillment of prophecy (18:31-33) is eliminated. In the story of Zacchaeus, Marcion understandably deletes the words "because he too is a son of Abraham" (19:9). From the phrase "This cup is the new covenant..." (22:20) he omits "new" because the good God has not yet made any covenant with humanity. Marcion rejects Luke 24:27 and 24:44-46, which relate messianic prophecies from the Old Testament to Christ. Luke 24:39-50 is eliminated because it cannot accord with Marcion's belief that the body of Christ was only an appearance, not a fleshly reality. He also deletes the end of Luke's gospel, which initiates the mission of the apostles to Jerusalem.

Marcion's corrections to Luke therefore consist above all of omissions, as these examples make clear. But he also resorts to other kinds of alterations. He allows for some additions, although these are comparatively rare. In Luke 23:2, for example, he adds to the accusations against Jesus before Pilate the grievance of destroying the Law and Prophets. He also skillfully uses substitutions of single terms to restore what he believes to have been the original text before judaizers introduced their changes in it. He replaces the "justice" of God with "the call" of God in Jesus's rebuke of the Pharisees in Luke 11:42, and substitutes "Christ" for "king of the Jews" in 23:3. Elsewhere, in Galatians 4:24, he replaces the two "covenants," represented by the slave and the free woman, with the two "proofs."

This biblical criticism was further pursued by Marcion's disciples, who admitted into their New Testament canon verses from the other gospels, sometimes by altering them. Thus the words of Matthew 5:17 are reversed: "I have come not to fulfill the Law, but to destroy it." They also include the Pastorals within the Pauline corpus.

Marcion's great exegetical work is often referred to by his adversaries under the title of the *Antitheses*. It is both an introduction to his

New Testament and an application of his fundamental exegetical principles. It is difficult to determine its precise literary form; the sources which allude to it are not sufficiently clear about it. It is certain in any case that Marcion set out in this work, using examples, an exceedingly stark contrast between the Old Testament and the Gospel, by elucidating the oppositions, word for word, between quotations drawn respectively from each. That does not mean, however, that he utterly denied the validity of the Old Testament, for he still recognized its authority as a book of history; he even credited the Creator-God with a form of justice and considered certain aspects of the Mosaic Law to constitute a moral code.

Apelles, one of Marcion's principal disciples, goes further than Marcion in considering the Old Testament inspired by an evil angel and deceitful through and through. His *Syllogisms* are bent on exposing its contradictions so as to conclude that these Scriptures did not come from the true God and that they are the stuff of fables. Origen and Ambrose both know of this work. Tertullian even wrote a treatise *Against the Apelleacs* which has not survived.[2]

There are a number of texts from Luke's gospel which form the pivot of Marcion's doctrine and argumentation, and which come to figure prominently in the *Antitheses* in establishing the opposition between the message of the Jewish God and the revelation of Jesus Christ. They are Luke 6:43 ("no good tree bears bad fruit, nor again does a bad tree bear good fruit"); 16:13 ("No servant can serve to masters..."); 5:36-38 (the new piece of garment and the old garment; the new wine and old wineskins); 6:20-23 (the Beatitudes); and 18:19 ("No one is good but God alone").

The *Antitheses* place in relief the novelty of the Gospel and the differences between the God of the Jews and the God of Jesus Christ. To the judging God, wrathful and bellicose, is opposed the kindly, calm, and benevolent God. From the Demiurge, the God of creation (according to Genesis) who is master of this world, known to human beings and having a name, the God whom the prophet Ezekiel mentions as "made known to Israel" (Ezek. 20:5), is distinguished the hidden and unknown God, who is invisible, nameless, new, alien, other, as Luke 10:22 indicates ("No one knows who the Son is except the Father, or who the Father is except the Son"). The good God never contradicts himself; in all things he manifests his constancy; he is wisdom (cf. 1 Cor. 1:18-21). But the Creator is unstable: he simultaneously forbids the making of images while ordering the design of the ark of the covenant and the Cherubim; he expects offerings from Abel and Cain, yet reproves sacrifices through the voice of the prophets; he rejects Saul after having chosen him. Christ knows the thoughts of human beings and what is the true knowledge of God. But the Creator is ignorant and weak, asking Adam "Where are you?" (Gen. 3:5), and needing to come down and verify the crimes of Sodom and Gomorrah (Gen. 18:21). He is fully ignorant of the fact that there exists another God above him and proclaims "There is no other God besides me" (Isa. 45:21; 46:9). Like the Law, the Creator is neither good nor evil, but righteous and harsh, to the point of "creating woe" (Isa. 45:7). He is the one who provoked the Flood, destroyed Sodom by fire, stirred up the plagues of Egypt, hardened Pharaoh's heart, and revisited the fathers' sins upon the children (Exod. 20:5). He is the one who prohibited the protoplasts from partaking of the tree of knowledge (Gen. 2:17). Christ, on the contrary, reveals a merciful and saving God. This good God sent out the Twelve on a mission without anything for their journey (Luke 9:3), whereas the God of Moses induced the Jews to plunder the Egyptians (Exod. 3:22; 11:2; 12:35ff).

The precept of Jesus in Luke 6:29 ("To him who strikes you on the cheek, offer the other") stands opposed to the Old Testament law of retaliation (cf. Exod. 21:24; Deut. 19:21). Elisha cursed children in the name of Yahweh and forty-two of them were torn to pieces by bears (2 Kings 2:23-24); Jesus said in response: "Let the little children come unto me" (Luke 18:16). Christ is infinitely superior to the Jewish Messiah, promising not the restoration of an earthly and finite kingdom but the salvation of all humanity. Christ bestows heavenly and eternal beatitude, whereas the Old Testament merely promises the Jews rest in the bosom of Abraham (cf. Luke 16:22-23). The Demiurge cursed him who hung on the tree (Gal. 3:13, quoting Deut. 21:23). The Creator-God persecutes true believers, who are caught between his hands like the heart of the king of which Proverbs 21:1 speaks. Marcion even addresses his disciples as his "companions in misery and victims of the same hatred."

The reading of Paul, or rather the selection of certain statements from the Pauline epistles, also grounds Marcion's doctrine of salvation. "Christ redeemed us from the curse of the Law" (Gal. 3:13). Indeed, according to Marcion, the good God saves creatures who do not belong to him, since they are the property of the Demiurge. These are the invisible realities that the good God brought about; Christ, however, enters a world that is foreign to him. The salvation that he brings is directed toward beings who are entirely estranged from him, and this is precisely for Marcion the sign of God's perfect and fully disinterested goodness. The theme of redemption is thus very important in his work. Accordingly he revamps Paul's statement in Galatians 2:20, "The life I presently live in the flesh I live by faith in the Son of God, who purchased me and gave himself for me." He replaces the phrase "who loved me" with "who purchased me" in order to show that the divine love is expressed more by this act of redemption, which liberates a being who is subject to another rule by an initiative of sheer mercy.

Marcion's attitude toward the Old Testament could be seen as implying a captious, indeed excessive, literalism which ends in forcing the text of Scripture. Origen emphasized that Marcion totally rejected allegory (*Commentary on Matthew* 14.3). But he even refused to allow for any prophetic typology. In doing so he broke with all antecedent Christian tradition and with the Church of his time. His set critical purpose at times meets with the most reasonable judgment, such as when he discerns in 2 Samuel 7:12 (2 Kings 7:12, LXX) an allusion to Solomon and not to Christ. He understands the passage in its context. The same is true when, at Isaiah 16:4, he renders "the outcasts of Moab sojourn among you" in exclusively historical terms, whereas Tertullian sees in this phrase a prophecy of conversion to Christianity (*Against Marcion* 3.21). It is not, however, modern philological concern that inspires Marcion, but obsession with distinguishing the Old Testament from the Gospel. For example, he denies that the Old Testament prophesies a suffering Messiah; he does not apply Psalm 72 (71, LXX) to Christ, but confines it in the strict sense to an announcement of a Jewish Messiah. Yet Marcion is furthermore not entirely consistent with himself in his rejection of prophecy. He retains the parable of the rich man and Lazarus, where Abraham, Moses, and the prophets clearly figure prominently. He includes 1 Corinthians 1:19, which quotes Isaiah 21:14, and 1 Thessalonians 5:20 ("Do not despise gifts of prophecy"). He saves Luke 17:26, which invokes Malachi 3:1, as well as 1 Corinthians 5:7 ("For Christ our paschal lamb has been sacrificed"), where Old Testament reminiscences are certainly not lacking. Such inconsistency is not in Harnack's view insurmountable: Marcion had thought that in certain passages the Creator-God had spoken unwittingly under the inspiration of the unknown God.

We can only imagine that this manner of treating the Scriptures scandalized a majority of Christians. There were many who followed Marcion because they were seduced by the force and simplicity of his doctrine and by the ideological impact of the absolute novelty of the Gospel. Many others were won over by an ascetic teaching consonant with an aversion to the world that was already rather widespread in this period. And many other Marcionites still, having been former pagans, were impassioned by Marcion's anti-Jewish sentiments or rather by his refusal to see Christianity reflected in the religion of the Jewish Bible. But there was another important movement, represented precisely by those who barred Marcion from the Church, which could not allow his kinds of attacks on sacred texts. Up to that time the Church had not ceased laying claim to the heritage of the "Old Testament," which originally constituted, in the highest degree, the Scriptures of Christians. Marcion's enterprise provoked an intolerable disturbance. In their responses to this crisis, orthodox exponents tirelessly taxed their wits to demonstrate the unity of the two Testaments. As a result, typological interpretation of the Hebrew Scriptures was emphasized and developed, refining arguments that had been used up to that point in controversies with Jews, as we see in the works of Justin, Irenaeus, and Tertullian. In addition, allegorical interpretation of the Law and the historical books of the Old Testament took on a new impetus, as can be observed in Origen's exegesis.

Marcion's truncated Bible also had a decisive influence on the the formation of the New Testament canon. Though he did not himself create the need for determining precise norms by which to demarcate a "New Testament" that enjoyed the status and authority of Holy Scripture, his meddling with Scripture and his exclusive choices of appropriate texts accelerated the evolution that led to the New Testament canon that was received in the Church by the end of the second century.[3]

Historians have also inquired as to whether Marcion's Bible had an influence on the transmission and text itself of the Latin New Testament in Christian antiquity. On the one hand, most of the better manuscripts of the Vulgate contain Latin Prologues to the Pauline epistles; setting aside the Pastorals, it is certain that these Prologues were of Marcionite inspiration and that they were translated from the Greek. They celebrate Paul's epistles as the instrument of victory or resistance against false apostles who pretended to restore converts "to the Law and circumcision" or "to the Law and Prophets," apostles inspired by submission to the Jewish law. These Prologues were widely diffused in the West. But they must have circulated as a separate collection, one of the first—and rare—introductions to the writings of Paul. Not until the end of the fourth century do they appear to have been admitted in the Church as actual "arguments" of the epistles, at a time when there remained only a handful of Marcionites in the West.[4]

On the other hand, the Latin translation of Marcion's Bible was made in the very same period as the most ancient Latin versions of the New Testament. Research has been conducted to find whether Marcion's work had any impact on these versions. Three principal conclusions have resulted. First, many of the coincidences derived from the fact that there was a shared Greek text to which Marcion and the Latin Christian translators were referring; it was a matter of the "western" text of the New Testament. Second, a small but very limited number of tendentious Marcionite alterations found their way into the ancient Latin tradition and were attested by some manuscripts (e.g., the omission of the last phrase of Luke 11:42, which acknowledges a certain validity in the legal practices and ethical law of the Old Testament; or the insertion into Luke 23:5 of an addition made by Marcion in 23:2, which has the Jews accusing Jesus of leading astray their sons and wives). Third, no special connection is nevertheless found between Marcion's text and any extant manuscript of the *Vetus Latina*.[5]

In conclusion, we can sum up the principal features of the Marcionite conception of the Bible this way. Marcion's selective reading of the Pauline epistles, guided by the opposition between grace and law, governed his full rejection of the Old Testament, which he interpreted in exclusively literal terms. In addition, Marcion's critical work on the Pauline texts and the Gospel (of Luke) resulted in the creation of a New Testament canon and excluded a large number of the texts already received in the Church as Holy Scripture. Marcion's doctrine in turn wreaked havoc on established traditions of the time and obliged the "orthodox" to refine and deepen their interpretation of the Old Testament so as to define more clearly and vigorously their own canon of the New Testament.

Marcion's doctrine was not exclusively biblical, contrary to the image imposed for so long by the magisterial study of Harnack, who was fascinated by the figure of Marcion as a religious reformer. In certain aspects his doctrine rejoined that of the Gnostics, and philosophical preoccupations were hardly foreign to him, as more recent research has tended to show.[6] Marcion and the Gnostics had in common the distinction between the good God and the just God, between the transcendent God and the Creator, as well as disparagement of the Old Testament and hostility toward the world and matter. The great difference has to do with soteriology: the unknown God came to save particular beings, human beings, who are strangers to him, constituted of body and soul, and creatures of the Demiurge. For the Gnostics, on the contrary, the one high God indemnifies himself by saving human beings, who already belong to him by virtue of their highest participation in the divine, namely the intellect or spirit.

If, moreover, the attitude of Christian Gnostics[7] toward the Bible had ramifications similar to Marcion's for the evolution of "orthodox" scriptural doctrine, their hermeneutical methods and their definition of the Scriptures were radically opposed to his.

Marcion took explicit declarations of Paul as his guiding principles, and he undertook a critical reading of the epistles and of the Gospel (of Luke) which led to the establishment of a New Testament that was extremely restricted in relation to the texts circulating as Scripture in the Church. As well, Marcion adhered closely to the literal sense of the Bible. Gnostics, on the contrary, referred to secret traditions and utilized all the writings received in Christian communities, to which they sometimes added Gospels and Apocalypses that they themselves had produced. They made abundant use, moreover, of allegorical interpretation. Marcion concurs with the Gnostics only on one point: interpreting in the most strictly literal sense all Old Testament passages which can serve to contra–distinguish the God of the Jews, or Creator of the world, and the message of Christ, Son of the perfect God.[8] But all texts, prophetic ones in particular, that are capable of supporting or illustrating the Gnostics'doctrine are assimilated by their exegesis.

The great Christian Gnostic teachers of the first generation already placed their esoteric teaching under the authority of persons who had connections with the Apostles. According to Clement of Alexandria (*Strom.* 7.17.106), Basilides referred to a certain Glaucias, an interpreter of Peter (unknown in the New Testament), while Valentinus referred to a certain Theodas, an acquaintance of Paul. Ptolemy, Valentinus's disciple, speaks in his *Letter to Flora* of "the apostolic tradition that we too have received by succession." And many of the Gnostic treatises discovered at Nag Hammadi pose as revelations that Christ's close confidants, James, Peter, John the Son of Zebedee, Thomas, or even Paul were privileged to receive; or else the revelations are placed under their patronage. For the Gnostics, the truths reserved for the elite, the pneumatics, were taught by Christ to his disciples alone, far from the larger multitude of his followers, between the Resurrection and the Ascension. Those who withheld this gnosis from the larger mass could themselves benefit from visions, as in the case of Marcus, reported by Irenaeus (*Against Heresies* 1.14.1).

It has thus been ascertained that for the Gnostics there was no closed list of inspired writings invested with authority and bearing the truth. The Scriptures were a body of writings that could be enlarged and even embellished by the commentaries themselves; moreover, they were not the only basis of knowledge, since revelation could come through other means within a tradition of gnosis which maintained a living and contemporary relation with its source, the Savior himself.

At the same time, however, the Gospel had a primary role; indeed it was the spiritual interpretation of the Gospel that functioned as the norm, model, and sustenance for all Gnostic tradition. The development of apocryphas within the Gnostic milieu was emphasized only toward the end of the second century. Eusebius of Caesarea (*Hist. eccl.* 4.7.7) knows of a certain heresiologist, Agrippa Castor, whose refutation of Basilides mentions a commentary of twenty-four books that the great Alexandrian Gnostic had written on the Gospel. One of Valentinus's disciples, Heracleon, composed a work on the Gospel of John that Origen discusses and quotes in his own *Commentary on John* in the next century (SC 120, 157, 222). Ptolemy, another Valentinian, gives an exposition of Gnostic theology that begins with an interpretation of the prologue to John's Gospel (*ap.* Irenaeus, *Against Heresies* 1.8.5). The existence of the *Gospel of Thomas*, a collection of sayings of Jesus parallel to the synoptic tradition, reveals the tremendous value that was placed in Gnostic communities on the message of Christ.[9] Indeed, in the history of Christianity the Gnostics were the first commentators on the New Testament writings, showing a decided preference for the Gospel of John and the Pauline epistles, which exercised a very strong influence on their theology.[10] Romans 2:28-29 provided for them an incentive for the symbolic and esoteric reading of Scripture. Pauline exegesis in the second century was at first Gnostic. The Church therefore had in its turn to reconstitute an "orthodox" image of Paul.

Early Christian heresiologists did not accuse the Gnostics of falsifying the texts of the Gospels or of Paul so much as of altering their meaning in order to adapt them to their doctrine. In contrast with Marcion, Valentinian Gnostics preserved the integrity of the New Testament writings; intentional tendentious distortions of the texts were rare among them. Yet there are some noteworthy textual modifications.[11] In Jesus's statement in Matthew 5:18 ("Not an *iota*, not a dot will pass from the Law until all is accomplished"), the words "from the Law" are omitted both because the Law is of an inferior status and because the letter *iota*, signifying in Greek the number 10, represents the Decad of the primary Aeons of the divine Pleroma (*ap.* Irenaeus, *Against Heresies* 1.3.2). In John 12:27, the response "I do not know" is added after the question "What shall I say?" in order to emphasize that the Savior manifested the anguish of the Aeon Sophia, who was fallen from the Pleroma (*ap.* Irenaeus, *Against Heresies* 1.8.2). In Romans 8:20, the phrase "Creation was subjected to the vanity of the world not of its own will" is replaced with "He was subjected to the vanity of the world not of his own will," indicating that the Demiurge, while thinking that he was creating by his own power, actually was an instrument of Sophia (*ap.* Clement of Alexandria, *Extracts from Theodotus* 49.1, SC 23).

Irenaeus, and other patristic authors subsequently, reduced Gnostic exegesis to the fabrication of centos (Irenaeus, *Against Heresies* 1.9.4). "They select ambiguous expressions," says Clement of Alexandria, "in order to adapt them to their own opinions; here and there they pluck bouquets of certain words, with no regard for the meaning that is extracted from them, but abusive of the pure and simple literal sense" (*Strom.* 7.16.96). Two things should be said of Clement's objection here. First of all, it disguises a form of literary composition consistently operative in the authentic Gnostic treatises discovered at Nag Hammadi, which consisted in weaving a web of allusions and independent references, and undertaking a labor of rewriting aimed at protecting Gnostic esotericism and producing a mystical sense of Scripture. On the other hand, this insistence on the letter (or literal sense) of the text is not incompatible with the Gnostics' allegorical reading; on the contrary, it is the attention paid to certain words, words capable of evoking the Gnostic myth, that orients Gnostic interpretation toward the hidden sense.

The legitimacy of allegorical exegesis was confirmed for Gnostics by the very form of Christ's own words: "The Savior taught the Apostles, first in figures and in mysteries, then in parables and enigmas, and finally, in the third place, in a clear and direct fashion, when they were alone" (*Extracts from Theodotus* 66). Certain of Paul's statements were exploited in the same sense, especially those which treated of the "mysteries," precisely as in the formula of 1 Corinthians 2:10: "For the Spirit searches everything, even the depths of God." In the same vein, the distinction between pneumatics, those who were alone capable of arriving at the hidden meaning of Scripture, and others who were mere hearers or readers, is drawn from New Testament passages like Mark 4:10-11, Matthew 13:10-13 and 34-36, Luke 8:9, John 16:25, Romans 2:28-29, and 1 Corinthians 2:13-14. Paul himself spoke two languages at the same time: "He announced the Savior in both his aspects: as created and passible, for the sake of those on the left, since they can understand him on this level and believe in him; then on the spiritual level, as born of the Holy Spirit and the Virgin (cf. Luke 1:35), in the way that the Angels on the right know him" (*Extracts from Theodotus* 23.3).

The parables were the cherished terrain of Gnostic speculations. This kind of expression, perfectly suited to the teaching of the mystery, but insufficient by itself, required a key possessed only by "pneumatics." The drama of the Pleroma, revealed by the Savior, must be known in order for the parables to be opened up and their deeper cryptic meaning to be made manifest. Exegesis thus becomes in itself a means of salvation, because it causes the individual to participate in the quest that leads to restoration in the eternal perfection of the pair *Anthropos-Ecclesia*. Such is the meaning of the precept constantly invoked by Gnostics: "Seek and you will find" (Luke 11:9). Contrary, then, to the image that ecclesiastical adversaries of Gnosticism wanted to impose, it was not really a matter of an undefined inquiry, without end, leading to nothing, but of a comforting reminder for the elect that beyond the common or vulgar explanation of Scripture existed another, superior meaning, the perception of which constituted the assurance of salvation and the sign of belonging to the company of pneumatics. Deciphering the truth mimicked the movement symbolized by the parable of the lost sheep: the Savior is in search of the Church dispersed in the world, to cleanse it of its material passions through the illuminating grace of a formation of gnosis, and to re-establish it in the bosom of the Father within the Pleroma. Whoever attains to complete comprehension discovers himself or herself as part of the divine seed imprisoned in the world, becomes aware of his or her exile and his or her true nature, and finds in his or her liberation by Jesus the certainty of salvation.[12]

Recourse to allegory also authorized the Gnostics to accept a large part of the Old Testament. The beginning of Genesis was one of their principal references for cosmology and anthropology. The *Extracts of Theodotus* provide quite rich material evidence in this regard. The Psalms, wisdom books, and prophets were used in conjunction with the New Testament. The expositions and quotations of the heresiologists, as well as certain of the Nag Hammadi treatises, afford numerous proofs of this pattern. Some Gnostic movements remained quite hostile to the Creator-God and his Law, while others, particularly the Valentinians, were more accommodating and acknowledged a partial and relative value in the "psychic" word of the Old Testament God. According to Irenaeus, whose testimony is reliable,[13] they attributed many of the words of the prophets to the spiritual "seed" produced by Sophia-Achamoth in the presence of the angels of the Savior, who came to heal her of her passions: "But the Mother too spoke much, they claim, about things above, and much of what she said came through the Demiurge and through the souls that he created. It is in this way, finally, that they divide up the prophecies, asserting that one part was uttered by the Mother, another by her seed, and a third by the Demiurge" (*Against Heresies* 1.7.3, SC 264: 107f). This tripartite division, corresponding at once to the three levels of interpretation and to their different respective contents, enabled the Gnostics to preserve the prophetic books. The division is further applied to Jesus himself: "Some of the things Jesus said came from the Savior, others from the Mother, and others still from the Demiurge" (*Against Heresies* 1.7.3). Contrary to Marcion, then, these Gnostics did not need to purge the Gospel: the Christ who refers to the Old Testament is the "psychic" Christ issued from the Demiurge in the capacity of a Son, the very one of whom the Demiurge has spoken through the prophets. "It is he who passed through Mary, just as water passes through a duct, and it is on him, at the time of his baptism, that there descended in the form of a dove (cf. Matt. 3:16; Luke 3:22) the Savior who belonged to the Pleroma and who was formed from all the Aeons combined; in him there existed still the spiritual seed which issued from Achamoth" (*Against Heresies* 1.7.2). In all of this we see how close the relationship was between exegesis and christology among the Gnostics.

Retaining the whole of Scripture and preaching resurrection through Christ, the Valentinians considered themselves Christians and claimed the name. They did not deny ecclesiastical tradition, but refused to admit that the content of that tradition represented the essence of Christianity, the revelation characterizing the Gospel. The Valentinians were convinced that they were withholding a superior knowledge and protesting against the Church's claim that its "psychic" and imperfect faith was the only orthodox one. The *Apocalypse of Peter,* one of the Nag Hammadi writings dating from the first half of the third century, forcefully expresses this grievance of the Gnostics against the clerical Church.[14]

Some representatives of the Valentinian school even adopted what was apparently a quite conciliatory attitude toward the "orthodox" conception of the Scriptures, even to the point of recognizing a certain validity in the Old Testament Law. Such is the case with Ptolemy in his *Letter to Flora* (SC 24). Basing himself on passages from the Gospel (Matt. 19:6-8; 15:4-9), he distinguishes three components within the pentateuchal Law:

the Law of God, the additions of Moses prompted by personal interests, and interpolations made by the Elders of the people. The mention of the last two components stems from ideas developed in Jewish-Christian circles.[15] As for the first component, the Law of God, it too is broken down into three parts: the pure law (the Decalogue), which was fulfilled by Jesus; the part that is mixed with evil and injustice (the law of retribution), which the Savior abolished; and a figurative and symbolic part (cultic and ceremonial prescriptions). In some of its features this conception of the Law is analogous to the depictions of it circulating in the Church in the same period, such as that of Justin. And yet Justin developed his scriptural doctrine not only under the influence of the Church's ongoing controversy with the Jews, but also with a view to countering Marcion and the Gnostics. Ptolemy seems therefore to have taken account of the Church's responses to Gnosticism and to have integrated them into his own system. At bottom, however, he made no serious concession to the commonly accepted theses. The "pure law" itself was not even perfect in his view, since it had to be fulfilled by Christ. This incompleteness of the Law was incompatible with the perfection of the "Father of all." In the ontological perspective of gnosis, a perfect author can only produce perfect works. There is no contradiction between this part of the Law and the new commandments, but there is a difference of origin: the Creator gives the former, the Savior the latter. As for the second part of the Law of God, that which is mingled with injustice, it had as its author the Creator, insofar as he was "intermediary" between the "Adversary" and the supreme God. Finally, the third, ritual part of the law, consisting of "figures and images," derived from the Demiurge insofar as he was the "image" of God. Ptolemy's teaching here was only a preliminary initiation. His complete doctrine of Scripture involved knowledge of esoteric theses, such as were revealed through the tradition of the apostles and the words of the Savior—that is, through secret tradition. This appears, at the end of Ptolemy's treatise, as the way to topple the principal objection against his system—i.e., that it distinguishes two gods—by reconciling monotheism with the Gnostic myth. For the secret tradition, writes Ptolemy, taught "how from a single principle of all things, who is simple, incorruptible, and good, were constituted these other natures, the nature of corruption and that of the intermediary, which are essentially dissimilar, whereas it is in the nature of the good to engender and produce only beings similar to and consubstantial with him" (*Letter to Flora* 7, 8).

We can thus declare that, even in a writer like Ptolemy, who is so close in many respects to "orthodoxy," that the conception of the Bible and its interpretation were inseparable from the gnosis which was deposited in the secret tradition. It is understandable, then, how under these circumstances the Church had been led through anti-Gnostic polemics to define its concept of tradition more precisely, in the same way that its response to Marcion compelled it to establish the New Testament canon. As for the exegetical methods of the Gnostic Christians, they did not lead the Church to a renunciation of allegory and typology, but to a deepening of the notion of the unity of the Scriptures, and to a conception of them as an organic whole, or as a fabric with all its threads connecting with each other. Christian hermeneutics thus progressed in the regard for *context,* which concerned not only the larger harmonies of Scripture but the coherence of each individual pericope.

All the marginal currents of Christianity, even beyond those which, like Marcionism and Gnosticism, failed to become dominant in the context of the second-century Church, made the Bible one of their major references. It would take too long to examine the diverse forms that this recourse to the authority of Scripture took among particular movements, as well as the various exegetical methods that derived from them. The heterodox doctrine of one figure, Hermogenes, is nonetheless worthy of notice by virtue of its uniqueness. Theophilus of Antioch attacked him in a lost treatise, the argument of which can still be reconstructed,[16] and Tertullian follows suit in his own treatise *Against Hermogenes.* Hermogenes represented, in the latter decades of the second century, a philosophical Christianity deeply influenced by the Platonism of his time. He attempted to resolve the problem of the origin of evil by arguing for the existence of an uncreated matter. Without going into the details and the sources of his theory, it is appropriate to note here the exegetical argument that he employs. Hermogenes saw, in the imperfect "was" in the Septuagint version of Genesis 1:2a, proof of the eternity of matter: "The land was without order." Before being molded by God and put in order, as indicated in Genesis 1:1, matter existed in an unformed, indefinite state deprived of any qualities. In all created beings there subsisted a reflection of the original disorderliness of matter. The Church's rejoinders to Hermogenes's theses intensified the affirmation of the doctrine of creation *ex nihilo.*[17] What is interesting to remember here is that Hermogenes's perspective inverted the relation between philosophy and

the Bible that was established in Jewish and Christian apologetics: interpretation of the text no longer served to show that Greek ideas derived
from the Bible, but was instead used to confirm a theory of its secular
origin. The accusation of heresy was thus aimed, at least in Tertullian
and Pseudo-Hippolytus, not only at Hermogenean doctrine itself, which
threatened to introduce a new dualism, but also at an exegesis which
appeared to bend the Scriptures to alien representations of its truth. Moreover, Hermogenes's interpretation of Psalm 19:4 (18:5 [LXX])—"in the
sun he has placed his tent"—indicates the esoteric nature of his Christianity, influenced at this point by the philosophical myths of the time
concerning the returning ascent of souls; for in his view this verse signifies that when he ascended into heaven the Lord left his body in the sun
(Clement of Alexandria, *Eclogae propheticae* 56.2; Pseudo-Hippolytus,
Elenchos 7.17).

One other movement worthy of mention, which was spreading
during the last third of the second century, is Montanism, named for its
founder Montanus.[18] His followers were also called "Cataphrygians,"
referring to the region in Asia Minor in which the Montanist movement
had its birth. The most ancient sources do not make of it a heresy. It was
"the new prophecy," of an ecstatic nature. Its fundamental faith was that
of the Great Church, and it recognized all the Scriptures, but it was a
source of disturbance by virtue of the movement's enthusiastic character,
for which reason ecclesiastical authorities were inclined to reprimand it.
Montanus, as well as two prophetesses, Priscilla and Maximilla, uttered
oracles under the inspiration of the Paraclete promised by Jesus in the
Gospel of John (John 14:26); they also announced to their followers the
advent of the Heavenly Jerusalem proclaimed in the Apocalypse. This
movement interests us for three reasons. First of all, the conflict that it
provoked testified to the controversies surrounding the Revelation of John.
While Irenaeus based his eschatology on it in the last book of his master-
work *Against Heresies,* another churchman, Gaius, living in Rome at the
beginning of the third century, rejected its authenticity, along with that of
John's Gospel, out of anti-Montanist prejudice.[19] In the second place, the
debate involving Montanism led part of the Church to define orthodox
prophetism through the interpretation of scriptural examples, as well as
to reject ecstatic phenomena. And finally, the Montanist presence shows
that certain Christian communities, even up to the end of the second century, in Phrygia and elsewhere, believed that revelation was not closed
and that it could be communicated through means other than the Bible.

One of the authors who refuted Montanism furthermore expresses, at the beginning of his work, his own fear of appearing to violate the rule prohibiting any addition to, or subtraction from, the Gospel (Eusebius, *Hist. eccl.* 5.16.3). Gaius for his part goes further and accuses the Montanists, against all probability, for "their audacity in composing new Scriptures" (*ap.* Eusebius, *Hist. eccl.* 6.20.3).

The biblical scholarship of Tatian, an apologist who was Justin's disciple, would also be worth mention here, since his harmony of the Gospels, the *Diatessaron,* is marked by extreme ascetic tendencies and by encratism. But that would lead us into a whole other domain, the history of Syriac and oriental Christianity.

In the second and third centuries, conflicts over the interpretation of the Bible were mainly disputes of ecclesiastical Christianity with Marcionites and Gnostics. The results of these hermeneutical controversies were momentous for the Church. They constrained the Fathers to revise and to articulate more precisely their conception of the unity of the two Testaments; they accelerated the fixing of the New Testament canon; and they generated the development of exegetical methods which for centuries determined the form of Christian interpretation. Moreover, the "gnostic" reading of the Bible, its theory of levels of meaning, the flowering of a literature quite richly animated by allegorical interpretation and nourished by scriptural reminiscences, and an esoteric "Paulinism" and mysticism were some of the elements which made for the originality of a movement born of the encounter between Gnosticism and Christianity. One ultimately finds in the Gnostic conception of the Bible certain features which prepared the way for Manichaeism, which we now confidently know had close historical connections with Christian Gnosticism. The Manichaean *Kephalaia* and the *Hymns* from the Coptic library discovered at Fayoum in 1930 contain numerous allusions to the Bible; moreover, at the end of the fourth century in the West, Augustine's struggle against African Manichaeism had a tremendous influence precisely on his doctrine of the Scriptures.[20]

NOTES

1. An exhaustive study of the Marcionite New Testament was made by A. von Harnack in his *Marcion: Das Evangelium vom fremden Gott* (Leipzig, 1924); trans. J. Steely and L. Bierma, *Marcion: Gospel of the Alien God* (Durham, N. C., 1989). Harnack's analysis was refined and corrected by E. C. Blackman, *Marcion and His Influence* (London, 1948).

2. See the introduction of J.-P. Mahé to Tertullian's treatise *On the Flesh of Christ* (SC 216: 15-21, 94-110).

3. See H. von Campenhausen, *The Formation of the Christian Bible,* trans. J. Baker (Philadelphia, 1972), 147-209.

4. See Blackman, *Marcion and His Influence,* 52-54.

5. See ibid., 128-168.

6. See U. Bianchi, "Marcion: théologien biblique ou docteur gnostique?" *Vigiliae Christianae* 21 (1967): 141-149; J. G. Gager, "Marcion and Philosophy," *Vigiliae Christianae* 26 (1972): 53-59; B. Aland, "Marcion: Versuch einer neuen Interpretation," *Zeitschrift für Theologie und Kirche* 70 (1973): 420-447; and J.-P. Mahé, in SC 216: 69-80.

7. My intention here is only to speak of Gnostics who referred to themselves as Christians.

8. See the article on "Gnosticisme chrétien" by P. Hadot in the *Encyclopaedia Universalis.*

9. See H.-Ch. Puech, *En quête de la Gnose,* vol. 2 (Paris, 1978).

10. See E. H. Pagels, *The Johannine Gospel in Gnostic Exegesis: Heracleon's Commentary on John* (Nashville and New York, 1973); idem, *The Gnostic Paul: Gnostic Exegesis of the Pauline Letters* (Philadelphia, 1975).

11. See L. C. Barth, *Die Interpretation des Neuen Testament in der Valentinianischen Gnosis,* Texte und Untersuchungen 37.3 (Leipzig, 1911), 30-43.

12. See A. Orbe, *Parábolas Evangélicas en San Ireneo* (Madrid, 1972), vol. 2, 477. Orbe's work contains superior studies of Gnostic exegesis of the parables.

13. See F. M. Sagnard, *La Gnose valentinienne et le témoinage de saint Irénée* (Paris, 1947).

14. See K. Koschorke, *Die Polemik der Gnostiker gegen das kirchliche Christentum* (Leiden, 1978).

15. See G. Quispel in SC 24: 20-23.

16. See F. Bolgiani, in the *Mélanges offerts à G. Lazzati* (Milan, 1979), 77-118.

17. See P. Nautin, in the collection *In Principio* (Paris, 1973), 69-79; also, with some differences of perspective, G. May, *Schöpfung aus dem Nichts: Die Entstehung der Lehre von der creatio ex nihilo* (Berlin, 1978), 142-150.

18. See H. von Campenhausen, *The Formation of the Christian Bible,* 225ff; J. Blanchetière, "Le montanisme originel," *Revue des sciences religieuses* 52 (1978): 118-134; ibid. 53 (1979): 1-22; H. Paulsen, "Die Bedeutung des Montanismus für die Herausbildung des Kanons," *Vigiliae Christianae* 32 (1978): 19-52.

19. Gaius's criticisms are known from the bits and pieces of Hippolytus's reply to him, available to us thanks to other authors.

20. See J. Ries, "La Bible chez saint Augustine et chez les manichéens," *Revue des études augustiniennes* 7 (1961): 231-243; ibid. 9 (1963): 201-215; ibid. 10 (1964): 309-329.

11

The Bible in the Arian Crisis

CHARLES KANNENGIESSER

The doctrinal crisis called Arian because of Arius, a member of the Alexandrian clergy, dominated the political and intellectual life of the churches throughout the fourth and even, at least in the West, into the middle of the fifth century. In the vast literature available on the subject, no one has ever attempted a synthesis of modern scholarship concerned with the use of Scripture during the Arian controversy. The present essay is far too limited to achieve such a result, but we will attempt to outline some basic conclusions.

Arius and the Bible

Any interpretation of the Arian crisis depends essentially on the interpreter's preconceptions of Arius himself. The same would be true if someone explored the links between that crisis in its theological and spiritual dimensions using our biblical hermeneutics of today. Two major questions need in the first place some clarification about Arianism in general: (1) What was properly basic to the Arian reading of Scripture? and (2) What effect did the Arian reading of Scripture have on the use of Scripture among anti-Arian interpreters? These questions, which deal at once with the intrinsic nature of Arian exegesis and with its historic significance in the life of the churches, need at first to be addressed in considering Arius personally. But this is precisely what creates a major problem. For the more studies on Arius multiply, the more the figure of the Alexandrian heresiarch becomes blurred. Some of the results of a century-old specialized research on Arius, and certitudes about him solidified over many centuries, have recently been shaken in the light of new critical data. Should a historian currently claim a definitive statement of any sort concerning Arius, he or she would certainly have to be gifted with a supernatural understanding.

A century or century-and-a-half after the emergence of Arius and Arianism, the oldest chroniclers of Christianity felt confident to declare that Arius had become famous in his lifetime for commentaries on Scripture he delivered in preaching to the Alexandrian parish for which he had become responsible under Bishop Alexander. His congregation was astounded by the originality of his interpretations. Hundreds of consecrated virgins were counted among his most fervent followers. When he found himself compromised in a serious quarrel with his bishop, he was already close to his sixties. Here were two men, both formed within the local tradition of theological learning that had developed during the third century before the "Great Persecution" (which lasted in Alexandria from from 303 to 311), now engaged in a public showdown with irreconcilable propositions about the divinity of the Son of God. Both succeeded in transmitting to future generations a plea in favor of their theories, consisting in circular letters and professions of faith. These dramatic documents strike us today more by what they have in common than by their antagonism. Alexander, like Arius, found it normal to expound, in ordinary preaching, theoretical aspects of the doctrine of the relationship between Father and Son: The local "pope" and his learned subordinate, both heirs of Origen's theological legacy, were taking advantage of his pioneering speculation on the Christian Godhead; both also exploited the themes and the technical vocabulary of Origen's biblical exegesis. At the time of the scandal produced by their theoretical differences within the turbulent ecclesiastical community of Alexandria, they already had a long personal history of which we know almost nothing. If their respective readings of Scripture diverge, modern critics can only measure the gap, without being able to explain its cause.

Before entering into the core of this tragic debate, another preliminary observation is needed. Declared the loser early on, Arius was stripped of any right to defend himself in the local community. The same happened to his earliest Alexandrian followers, who...

> ...were stated apostates: Arius and Achillas, Aeithales and Carponis, another Arius and Sarmatas, all former priests; Euzoios and Lucius, Julius and Menas, Helladios and Gaius, former deacons; and with them Secundus and Theonas, who up to now bore the title of bishops.[1]

Being formally accused of heresy, the censured members of the clerical hierarchy under the jurisdiction of Alexander not only had to give up their titles and positions, but were required to expatriate, with all their writings being destroyed. In the cultural context of the time, such a collective ruling was of no surprise. It reduplicated in the name of the apostolic faith an age-old practice in the political and philosophical-religious institutions of the Empire.

As a result, we are reduced to know Arius only through very poor remains of his writings and through the documents used to condemn him. Even so, Arius's scraps are eloquent enough by the cross-references they make possible. Despite being reduced to speaking only through the fatal gag imposed on him by his worst enemies, Arius retains a unique voice, the voice of intellectual passion, bound to rigorous precision in his technical vocabulary and expressed with only a few words in condensed arguments. Probably among experts controversy will never end, be it over defining the exact content of Arius's statements in their literal nature, or over clarifying their proper meaning. For, as we read these extracts, they are arbitrarily deprived of their context and assembled with the sole purpose of reproaching the condemned priest. If truncated quotations or biased paraphrases could appear fair game in an open discussion, they represented a harmful weaponry against an opponent who could no longer defend himself. In short, in Arius's case we are put in the position not only of being ignorant of his doctrinal antecedents, as is broadly the case as well with Bishop Alexander, but of witnessing a systematic demolition of his doctrinal position beginning with the bishop's censure. To what extent was the latter responsible for such hostility? It is difficult to evaluate, but clerical factions, fighting each other with theological slogans, were perfectly in keeping with the cosmopolitan and intellectual metropolis of ancient Egypt.

It is slogans such as these that we have inherited from Alexander, and later from his young successor Athanasius. The famous statements of Arius quoted by Athanasius as extracts from the *Thalia*, a pamphlet Arius composed partially in poetic style and published soon after his condemnation, have much in common with the Arian propositions already mentioned by Alexander in the circular letter mentioned above. These propositions, which made possible a unanimous vote against Arius at the Alexandrian synod convened around 319, resulted from a deliberately vindictive compilation of choice phrases which would prove disastrous for the credibility of their author. Even today, declaring oneself anti-Arian would appear untimely or anachachronistic at the very least; one can hardly engage in a serious discussion of Arian propositions without admitting that a fair evaluation of them was nullified from the start of the controversy in the early fourth century.

Arius was a man of intellectual concerns, open to the philosophical trends of his time, a Christian whose traditional convictions matured slowly, until they fermented in the form of a set of genuinely original intuitions. Arius's originality is itself paradoxical, just as his style is at once unique and deeply Alexandrian. The principal paradox of Arius consists in the fact that, the more he speaks, the more the teaching of Origen comes into view. Better yet, sentence after sentence, Scripture surfaces constantly, but Arius's own logic prevails.

Arius was fascinated by the radical transcendence of the Father in the Christian Godhead long before Alexander chose him to be the head of the popular parish of Baucalis near the harbor of the metropolis. More precisely, like his contemporary and oldest opponent outside of his local church, Marcellus, bishop of distant Ancyra (today the capital of Turkey), Arius spontaneously applied different rational categories when conceiving the radical priority of the Father and when deciding about the status of the Son in the mystery of the Christian Godhead. Having a spirit and nonconformist mindset not unlike Marcellus's, Arius considered himself essentially a Christian *mono*theist. It was easy for him to contemplate the whole revelation of Christ in the transcendent light of a reinforced *mono*theism, according to which God not only was utterly one, but included in his very unity a proper Son and a personified Wisdom. Critics often overlook the striking similarity between the structure of Arius's metaphysical syntheses and the trinitarian (or rather binitarian) system of Marcellus, who was equally obsessed by the radical unity of God in New Testament terms. In all probability, a comparison between those two theologians, as belonging to the same generation still rooted in the third century, would greatly benefit from a systematic analysis of their use of Scripture. For both were eager to apply Scripture in theorizing about God, while using new ideas but also remaining in continuity with third-century theologies.

Arius conceived the notion of the "*un*begotten" Father in an order of reality totally different from any other, marked precisely by the prefix "un-" (in Greek a privative alpha: *a-gennêtos*). Excluded by this negation was not only generation per se, but any mode of becoming. Otherwise God would sooner or later be reduced to a derivative being, like a Gnostic entity. But Arius's fascination did not stop there; otherwise he might have repeated Plotinus's formal metaphysics and lost touch with

Scripture. For his fundamental intuition had not originated from outside the traditional frame of Christian catechesis. His central thought on the radical oneness of the Father projected for him a new light over the basic notions of biblical revelation. He knew of no other God but the one revealed as Father in the New Testament, with whom he identified his metaphysical construct of Godhead. Thus he found himself confronted with the mystery of the Son, and the mystery of divine Sonship was for him at the core of New Testament revelation. Arian "theo-logy" at bottom took the shape of a "theo-dicy" in the strict sense, namely a theoretical justification of God as such, considered in terms of his essential unity as "Father." By such a christology, centering on the divinity of the Son in his very origin, Arius intended to reject Gnostic myths, anthropomorphic forms of polytheism and the ambiguities of Sabellius, which understated the Father's radical transcendence.

To what kind of "reading" of Scripture was Arius inclined? To a paradoxical one, in line with his whole intellectual journey. He took literally the statements of Scripture which had traditionally been assigned a christological meaning, such as the famous verse from Proverbs 8:22: "The Lord created me the first of his works long ago, before all else was made." At the same time he stressed the metaphorical nature of biblical language. Thus, he explained, the Son is truly "created" according to this verse of Proverbs, but he is no ordinary "creature." In the same way, Arius understood the gospel stories concerning Jesus and the Pauline affirmations about Christ as literally true, but at the same time he admitted that these stories and affirmations showed, on the concrete level of salvation history, the transcendent realities of deity like in a Platonic image-scheme: The Father was truly revealed as "greater" than the Son, and the Son confessed indeed not to know the ultimate secret of the Father; the Son "made himself nothing" (Phil. 2:7), because his peculiar divinity allowed it, having been "created" according to Proverbs 8:22.

The paradox of such a use of Scripture became for Arius a fatal trap and a dead-end, as he persisted in taking Scripture verses as literal prooftexts or as metaphors allegedly supporting his own notion of deity. The living context in which he located his hermeneutics was no more the natural context of the verses quoted, namely Scripture itself; it was his own theoretical universe which the interpreter articulated to himself using the language of Scripture. Arius was not an exegete in the traditional sense, but succeeded in giving a biblical or "exegetical" shape to his own thought in the context of his pastoral ministry. Arius's thought presented certain qualities of rigor and speculative invention badly needed by his ecclesiastical community at the start of the Constantinian era, but the misunderstandings and scandals which it provoked in trying to speak out on the level of popular catechesis made his thought an easy target for more conformist theologians.

Had Arius kept his personal doctrine inside the inner circle of his informed disciples, as in the esoteric practice of philosophers, it would have caused no ecclesiastical firestorm, nor would it have been solemnly condemned at the council of Nicea in 325. In his later years, however, Arius must have planned to popularize his private teaching in order to reach out to more people in his pastoral ministry. It led to a complete disaster for himself and his disciples and even for his adversaries henceforth obsessed with destroying the doctrinal construct which he had so patiently built up.

The most spectacular effect of the exegetical scandals provoked by Arius and his friends was the imposition of an "anti-Arian" interpretation of Scripture, more immediately bound to the trinitarian dogma and to the original sentences of the christological creed. Precisely from the man he was controverting, Arius, the isolated metaphysician who was not even recognized as such overseas among his own disciples, Athanasius of Alexandria would inherit the formidable challenges of being an improvising pastoral theologian and interpreter of Scripture, one who would represent the new form of Christian orthodoxy on an Empire-wide scale.

The Anti-Arian Exegesis of Athanasius

When Athanasius became bishop, doctrinal discipline seemed to have been restored in his local church. Arius was definitely the loser in his eyes, despite the international coalition of bishops who tried to defend him. During the summer of 328, three years after the Council of Nicea, Athanasius was elected to the top position in the hierarchy of the Alexandrian church. In his writings of the next forty-five years he would never say a word about his personal contribution to the Nicene synod, which he had attended as a secretary of Bishop Alexander. His first work, the double treatise *Against the Heathen* and *On the Incarnation of the Word*, shows clearly, around 337, that Athanasius had come from a world of prayer and meditation, hardly interested in the theological quarrels of the past twenty years. By the firm consistency of his biblical doctrine, inherited from Clement and Origen through local tradition, Athanasius reveals himself entirely in this initial catechetical synthesis. The work is quite accessible, but its density is strikingly rich; it previews the author and pastor Athanasius was destined to be throughout the doctrinal and administrative crises of his episcopal ministry during his record 45-year tenure. The first treatise, *Against the Heathen*, still conformed to traditional apologetics, setting forth well-worn biblical arguments against idolators, though it seems to have added to some notebook summaries of earlier years a final presentation, much fresher and more elaborate, of the role of the divine Logos in the economy of salvation. Thereby it leads to the exposition *On the Incarnation of the Word*, which results in a second treatise, independent, but complementary to the first.

In his second treatise the apologist becomes more original and consistent, turning into a theologian with a vision of his own. His strongest conviction is Pauline, embedded in reminiscences of the narrative texture of the gospels. At the core of the treatise, the mystery of the death and resurrection of Jesus is explored in terms of all its logical coherence, such as is able to show up the theological importance of this mystery to a Christian doctrine of salvation. The mystery of divine incarnation illuminates the treatise from beginning to end. In the light of this mystery, Athanasius celebrates the continuous experience of the presence of Christ in the church's liturgy and faith, in the death of the martyrs, and in the mass conversion of pagans. In a treatise aimed entirely at educated sympathizers and newly baptized believers eager to deepen their Christian initiation, the young bishop does not utter a word about Arius and the Arians. Despite the omission of any express mention of Arianism, however, the spiritual foundations of what would become the Alexandrian bishop's anti-Arian exegesis are already laid down here in all clarity: The author speaks of God only by inference from ecclesial experience and reality, as we see in his pastoral actualization of the Gospel and its narratives, in his assiduous pedagogy, and his vision of the divine Logos as revealed in the New Testament.

Soon after that first and still modest literary essay, possibly in order to give it a needed complement, in any case because urged to do so by his closest supporters, the young bishop decided to write a polemical work *Against the Arians*. Once more, his effort resulted in a double treatise (it became three treatises only much later), despite the fact that his first intention was to write only a single one. It was not an easy task, as Athanasius himself confesses in a letter addressed to monks, joined to his first draft:

> For the more I desired to write, and endeavoured to force myself to understand the Divinity of the Word, so much the more did the knowl-

edge thereof withdraw itself from me; and in proportion as I thought that I apprehended it, in so much I perceived myself to fail of doing so... Now when you have read this account, pray for me, and exhort one another so to do. And immediately send it back to me, and suffer no one whatever to take a copy of it, nor transcribe it for yourselves...[2]

Taking these private remarks and recommendations with the needed caution, one may note one distinctive mark of the literary work in question in this letter: The anti-Arian exegesis presented in it claims to reflect Athanasius's "knowledge" of the divine Logos. As in the essay *On the Incarnation of the Word*, and against the rules of the polemical genre, the author of *Against the Arians* would wish first of all to communicate his own "knowledge" of the Logos, his typically Alexandrian *gnôsis* of the Logos contemplated in himself, but as a bishop with episcopal responsibilities, he attempts to appropriate it accordingly: namely in preserving the doctrinal concerns of his teaching centered on the Paschal reality of the incarnate Word and constantly applying these concerns to the needs of the church's actual experience. The polemical element, strictly speaking, would then serve in the anti-Arian double treatise as an introduction to the doctrinal teaching of the author, and Scripture would be omnipresent in that teaching.

That is indeed what happens in his *Contra Arianos* (*CA*). First, the popular slogans attributed to the Arians ("there was a time when the Son was not;" "before the Son, the Father was not;" "Like all beings due to becoming, the Son possesses a free will and is therefore exposed to changes," etc.), are brandished like a scarecrow, and a set of arguments are opposed to them ("the Son is not a creature, being eternal; he is entirely in conformity with the Father, being his Son; he is immutable as such, as he is God," etc.); then the Athanasian catechesis takes over in a long sequence of exegeses on Philippians 2:9-10 (*CA* 1.37-45); Psalm 44:7-8 (*CA* 1.46-52); Hebrews 1:4 (*CA* 1.55-61); Hebrews 3:2 (*CA* 2.6-10); Acts 2:36 (*CA* 2.11-17); Proverbs 8:22 (*CA* 2.24-43 and 44-51); and Colossians 1:15 (*CA* 2.62-72). These exegeses represent as many chapters in a modern division of the work. They would be read by the most important theologians in the East and the West. The death of Arius happened on a Saturday of 336, shortly before Athanasius sent to the monks the first draft of *Contra Arianos*: "Being faster (than my letter), you already heard about it from other people," observes the bishop in his letter joined to the draft.[3] In any case, had he lived longer, "Arius" would have been nothing more than a collection of slogans for Athanasius and his addressees. He was not even supported anymore by the few theologians who claimed to share his ideas or at least what they understood his ideas to be. The anti-Arian exegesis of the Athanasian *Contra Arianos* opposed a phantom Arianism, capable of frightening good Christians but hardly in touch with Arius's own thinking. Arius as a dogmatic ghost, with his imaginary Son of God, deficient like every other creature, totally incapable of securing universal salvation, was indeed a horrible nightmare for faithful monks and informed parishioners. Athanasius earned credit for exorcising the fears caused by such a heresy, real or fictitious, in deploying once more, but with stronger arguments and a much richer use of Scripture than in *On the Incarnation of the Word*, the inveterate optimism of his conviction that the God-made-man was still at work in the present life of the church. Gleaning the central message of the many exegeses accumulated in *Contra Arianos*, one cannot help comparing it with the masterpiece of Irenaeus of Lyons, *Against the Heresies*, from the late second century. In each case, an emergency calling for a polemical response led to a synthesis of doctrine which itself, thanks largely to the author's assiduous exploration of Scripture, transcended polemics, thereby making possible sound and coherent answers to the questions which perturbed Irenaeus's and Athanasius's respective communities.

In response to Arian radicalism, perceived by the clergy and other members of the Alexandrian church as blasphemous of Christ, the doctrinal catechesis of all churches would henceforth focus more explicitly on the full divinity of the Savior, the Son declared to be of the same divine substance (*homoousios*) as the Father. The verses of the prologue to John's Gospel or of the Letter to the Colossians, so much discussed by Athanasius, with the common titles "Lord," "Creator," "Logos," "Son" applied to the Savior, would be consistently repeated and explained by Athanasius in his discourses. Rather than analyzing these repetitions, however, it seems more profitable to elucidate what happened to biblical exegesis during the second half of the fourth century, which saw the emergence of a generation of "Neo-Arians" and "Neo-Nicenes" in the Greek-speaking churches.

The Bible among the "Neo-Arians" and "Neo-Nicenes"

Around 350, Athanasius was still the commanding voice of anti-Arian exegesis. In the spring of 356 he published a remarkable circular letter, addressed to all bishops of Egypt and Libya. Paragraph 12 of that letter includes, in a slightly reduced format, the series of extracts from

Arius's *Thalia* and from a pamphlet of Asterius quoted fifteen years earlier in *Contra Arianos* 1.5-6. Whereas these Arian extracts were carefully framed by a prologue written for anti-Arian purposes at the outset of the *Contra Arianos*, and yet totally ignored in the body of the argument (which makes one think that Athanasius added it after the completion of the whole work), they now appear at the center of the circular letter of 356. Placed at the core of that epistolary treatise counting twenty-three paragraphs, this quotation of Arian extracts determines the letter's whole structure; in particular, it receives a direct and systematic response in paragraphs 13-17. In short, Athanasius speaks here as an experienced polemist, which he had not yet become when he wrote the *Contra Arianos*. Now he concentrates his attack on the Arian *Thalia*. All his proofs against it consist, from paragraph 13 on, in a flourish of biblical references, and they are directed from the start by a definitive judgment on Arianism: "All this opposes Scripture."[4] In their details, the arguments of 356 substantially reprise themes already developed in *Contra Arianos*, themes which are now accentuated and sharpened by the numerous biblical references.

The same technique of anti-Arian exegesis is applied in the "third" treatise *Contra Arianos*, joined by a unanimous tradition to *Contra Arianos* 1-2. In a style and a mindset alien to Athanasius, but thoroughly consonant with his christology, and eager to retain his technical vocabulary, a disciple of the aging bishop composed a series of essays destined to update *Contra Arianos* 1-2; they form the so-called treatise "*Contra Arianos* 3," which lacks a compositional unity, but centers, like the circular letter of 356, on a set of biblical references allegedly used by the Arians (§ 26-58). Two short essays (§ 1-25 and § 59-67) frame the central one, building with them the appearance of a unified "treatise." The list of Arian "errors" is no more presented in *Contra Arianos* 3 using the extracts of the *Thalia* repeatedly quoted by Athanasius between 339 and 356; it is instead presented in the form of a set of verses from the New Testament which insolent and blasphemous Arian adversaries have quoted while having one fundamental question in mind: If Christ "received" from the Father, "was ignorant," "grew up;" if he "experienced fear," "cried" and at last expired after agonizing and after the panic of death "troubled" him, how can he be the true Son of God by nature? In their rather abstract identity, the "heretics" offered here an easy target, the more so as the neo-Nicene author of *Contra Arianos* 3 carefully stylises their objections in perfect symmetry with his own theory of "consubstantiality" as enunciated by the Council of Nicea. Thanks to these opponents, largely a product of his own dialectical imagination, the implacable logician clarifies in this treatise his own trinitarian and christological views, thereby enriching anti-Arian exegesis with totally new doctrinal accents. Christology, in particular, assumes in the so-called *Contra Arianos* 3 the shape of a theory about the "unique divine nature of the incarnate Logos;" the attention of the theologian, instead of embracing the global event of the Incarnation in following the gospel narratives as Athanasius always did, focuses henceforth on the mystery of the union between the divine Logos and human flesh. The basic elements of Apollinaris's christology, long before they became "Apollinarian," and even longer before 380, when they were denounced in Rome by Jerome as a heresy, seem to emerge here by a natural drift from the main course of fourth century anti-Arian exegesis.[5]

During these same years 356-361, punctuated by the circular letter of Athanasius and the "third" *Contra Arianos*, an unexpected revival of "pure" Arianism happened in Alexandria, fostered by a former deacon of Antioch, Aetius, better known under the compromising surname "the Atheist". In 359, Aetius condensed his ultra-rationalistic teaching of a decade in a series of syllogisms, edited without a title, and only known as the *Syntagmation*, or "Summary," at the heart of which was a flat denial of any possible likeness between the Father and the Son. Aetius was promptly silenced in February 360. His principal disciple was Eunomius, then bishop of Cyzicus, in Syria. The central neo-Arian thesis, defended with some intransigence by Aetius and Eunomius, consisted in transforming the attribute "unbegotten," proper to the Father (the same attribute which had fascinated Arius in a more neutral philosophical context), into a proper name for the Christian Godhead, a consummately logical name whereby the "Son" was reduced to a sheer metaphor.

A new generation of pro-Nicene theologians thus came together, with Basil of Caesarea as leader, joined by two of his brothers and some friends, all bishops. In September 359, the young, but learned Basil had escorted his bishop to the Eastern synod of Seleucia, in Isauria (in what is now southern Turkey). By letter from there, he implored urgently the renowned Apollinaris of Laodicea to explain to him the true notion of the Nicene *homoousios*, at that time still the object of many controversies. Basil himself and his close collaborators, the "Cappadocian Fathers" of our patrologies, ended in elaborating a very profound theory of trinitarian faith, without trying to determine too much the original meaning of *homoousios* as used at Nicea in 325. These neo-Nicene theologians found themselves directly confronted with neo-Arians like Eunomius. The two books *Contra Eunomius* by Basil and his younger brother, Gregory of Nyssa, count among the finest theological achievements of their century. A rigorous discussion of the forms and rules of human language in general and of the style of Scripture in particular rested, in their works, on a philosophical theory of the possibility of knowing God. This last stage in the history of anti-Arian exegesis is also the most spectacular in regard to the intellectual creativity that Arianism indirectly prompted among the Greek-speaking churches during the fourth century.

A last mention of Athanasius—whom Basil sincerely admired, whom Gregory of Nyssa imitated in his teaching on the Incarnation, and whom Gregory Nazianzen celebrated in a versified eulogy—concerns his initiative in the *Letters to Serapion*, written between 357 and 360, in which he outlined what was to become the anti-Arian doctrine of the Holy Spirit, canonized by the first Synod of Constantinople in 381. The adversaries censured in the *Letters to Serapion* were not Arians themselves; they were objective allies of the Arians by negating the primary divinity of the Spirit. The form of Athanasius's initiative was predictable: He re-employed, to demonstrate the divinity of the trinitarian *Pneuma*, all the logical arguments and exegetical proofs that he had used for over twenty years to develop his anti-Arian notion of the "Son" of God. He also applied a hermeneutical rule specifying in which cases *pneuma* in Scripture meant the Holy Spirit. That same technique, applied to Scripture and to elements of the Christian liturgy, was to be of great help to Basil in his essay *On the Holy Spirit*.

NOTES

1. *Henos somatos* (Encyclical Letter of Alexander of Alexandria, ca. 319), in H. G. Opitz, ed., *Athanasius Werke* 3, 1: *Urkunden zur Geschichte des arianischen Streites 318-328* (Berlin, 1934).

2. *Ad historiam Arianorum ad monachos epistula* 1, 3 (PG 25: 692-693; trans. A. Robertson, NPNF, 2nd ser., vol. 4, 563).

3. Ibid. 3

4. *Epistula encyclica ad episcopos Aegypti et Libyae* 13 (PG 25: 568A, line 14).

5. For a full discussion of the composition and authorship of "*Contra Arianos* 3," see my *Athanase d'Alexandrie, évêque et écrivain: une lecture des traités "Contre les Ariens,"* Théologie historique 70 (Paris, 1983).

12

The Bible and Spiritual Doctrine: Some Controversies within the Early Eastern Christian Ascetic Tradition

PAUL BLOWERS

Let the one who has visions make use of the words of God.

—EVAGRIUS PONTICUS[1]

Numerous theories have been advanced to explain the explosion of ascetic activity and the formation of monastic movements in the Christian East in the fourth and fifth centuries. With greater or lesser success, historians have variously attributed them to socio-economic changes in the Later Roman Empire, the intrusion of Gnostic influences in Egyptian Christianity, protests against the moral tepidity of the Constantinian Church, and the acute needs of Christian society for holy mediators to provide spiritual access to a gracious but judging God.[2] Yet any descriptive account which would take seriously the internal, and genuinely religious, factors in the growth of the early Christian ascetic tradition must also see at the heart of its development a multi-dimensional engagement with the Word of God in Holy Scripture. Whether it be (as in the exemplary conversion of St. Antony and countless others) a simple and unquestioning obedience to the gospel injunction to relinquish worldly attachments and follow Christ,[3] or (as in Pachomius) a whole scripturally-regulated program to reconstruct the *bios apostolikos*[4] and to imitate the virtuous saints of the biblical narratives, or a reverence for the Bible as a mirror of the deepest structures and struggles of the soul, or even (as in Evagrius) a disciplined quest to advance through the contemplation of Scripture and creation to a higher knowledge of the Trinity, the Bible at once challenged and inspired, perplexed and captivated the pioneers of Christian monasticism.[5]

Indeed, the Bible was the primary touchstone of all enduring Christian models of the ascetic life and of the spiritual doctrine which developed in orthodox Christian monasticism, both in its eremitic and cenobitic expressions. But—as will be the particular focus of this essay—this does not mean that the monastic appeal to, and use of, the Bible were free of significant controversies over the precise rule of Scripture or the interpretation of specific scriptural texts in connection with monastic theology and praxis. Nor does it mean, moreover, that canons of scriptural authority and interpretation in monastic contexts always developed in strict isolation from the theological and hermeneutical claims of the larger Church. What it does mean is that the formative role of the Bible in early Christian monasticism is a complex one, one which we must infer by carefully considering the ways and means of biblical usage in the full gamut of the thought, language, symbolism, spiritual disciplines, and practical experience of early Christian ascetics.

Living "In" the Bible, Living Out the Bible: Controversy over Scripture in the Desert Fathers

The deserts of Egypt, Syria, and Palestine, in which early Christian monasticism first thrived in the fourth and fifth centuries, constituted their own microcosmic culture of biblical interpretation, in which the "stakes" of interpretation were heightened by the profoundly *eschatological* character of the monastic life itself. Most who flocked into desert hermitages, or into the Pachomian monasteries of the Upper Nile, were motivated less by spiritual heroics than by an urgency to find salvation in the "last days." The "Word in the desert," as Douglas Burton-Christie has termed it in his fruitful studies of the early monastic engagement with the Bible, was essentially a word of redemption and transformation.[6] Contrite disciples posed the paradigmatic question to their elders, "Abba, what must I do to be saved?—clearly reminiscent of the rich young man's query to Jesus in Matthew 19:16. And the paradigmatic response was quite often a word of salvation from the abba in the form either of a quotation from Scripture or a prescribed course of action informed by Scripture.[7]

Much has been written of late on the "performative" nature of biblical interpretation, the fact that it is never a matter purely of mechanically extracting an objective content or meaning, but rather of processing and enacting the Word "mimetically" in the continuum of action, experience, and traditioned understanding.[8] Accordingly, sacred texts hold their force (*dynamis*) precisely by constantly being tested and exposed to the hazards of existence in time and space. This description perfectly fits the situation of the desert, for the clear goal of monks whose existence literally turned on a word of Scripture or on a sage's inspired utterance, and who did not have the luxury of a distanced reflection on the Bible's meaning, was to *perform* the Word concretely, to *embody* their spiritual commitments, and indeed their salvation, in demonstrative acts.[9] As Burton-Christie has shown, the "desert hermeneutic" thoroughly fused horizons, collapsing the distance between the sacred text and the purview of the monks, who found themselves on the same existential plane with the biblical saints, fighting the very same moral and spiritual battles.[10] Much of the appropriation of Scripture in the desert naturally focused, therefore, on the great exemplars of wisdom and virtue, the "living icons" of the Bible and among the venerable sages of the desert, whose actions spoke louder than words, and continued to speak by *mimêsis* in the good works of the monks.[11]

It would not be exaggerating to say that the monks of the desert believed themselves to live "in" the Bible as they lived out its commandments and imitated its saintly characters. The fifth-century monastic theologian Nilus of Ancyra, drawing on Origen's axiom that the whole biblical history could be allegorically "transposed" into the life of the individual soul, considered the ascetics of the present day to inhabit, as it were, the same spiritual cosmos as the Bible's saints (and sinners). Basing himself on Paul's statement in 1 Corinthians 3:22 to the effect that the "world is ours," Nilus deduced that the whole past of the biblical history lived on *today* (*sêmeron*) in the ascetic life: "We *are* the world" now (*hêmeis esmen ho kosmos*). There may be no Joseph, no ancient Egypt, no King Hezekieh, no Judas, no Lazarus, no Simon Magus still alive today, but the wise man today *is* a Joseph, the adulterous woman *is* ancient Egypt, the pious ruler *is* a Hezekiah, the betrayer of the word of truth *is* a Judas, the man made alive through repentance *is* a Lazarus, the man baptized with water but without the Spirit *is* a Simon Magus.[12]

Modern skeptics might want to contend that such "performance" of Scripture may or may not constitute interpretation. Not all of the Bible, after all, is reducible to ethical commandments or to principles of spiritual progress, and not all obedience to Scripture is necessarily "informed" obedience. Surveying the *Apophthegmata patrum*, superficial evidence could doubtless be culled to support that skepticism. Knowledge of Scripture in the desert was often strictly mediated by the sages, and where elders did allow the private reading of the Bible over and beyond the readings delivered in the *synaxis* (liturgical office),[13] they frequently discouraged "speculative" questions about its higher theological meanings such as could distract monks from their practical commitments. Traditional wisdom had it that the Bible was the staple of the monk's life, but could also be a dangerous book, conducive to controversy.[14]

Closer scrutiny, however, requires us to take into account the peculiar nature of spiritual pedagogy in the desert. To be sure, we are a far cry here from the controlled *disputatio* of the monastic and cathedral schools of medieval Europe, but the abba's ostensible stifling of inquiry sometimes betrayed a deeper heuristic purpose, and his own silence could be instructive. In one short conference in the *Apophthegmata patrum*, which could just as easily have appeared in a rabbinic tractate, a group of monks approach Abba Zeno with the query, "What does the saying in the book of Job mean: 'Heaven is not pure in his presence' (Job 15:15)?" The old man replies "The brothers have passed over their sins and inquired about heavenly things. This is the interpretation of this saying: 'God alone is pure...[therefore] heaven is not pure.'"[15] The abba throws the apparent "plain sense" of the text in the face of any further speculation; it is enough that the monks be reminded of their own impurity before God. Abba Zeno surely presumes that there is a great mystery in the "heavenly things," but at present it is simply none of the monks' business. Abba Copres is said to have refused inquiries about the mysterious figure of Melchizedek for analogous reasons,[16] while Antony reportedly praised a disciple for gaining insight into the Bible precisely because the disciple earnestly admitted that he did not know what a certain text meant.[17] Abba Pambo, moreover, was acclaimed as advanced in the knowledge of Scripture on the basis of his reluctance (i.e. his trained reticence) to speak forthrightly about its meaning.[18]

Such stories reveal an environment in which putting questions to Holy Scripture was not so much dismissed as utter foolishness as it was forcefully subjugated to the exigencies of strict ascetic discipline and practical concerns. Extended conversation about the Bible or the teachings of the Fathers could lead to distraction or foment pride, such as in the case of a monk who confessed to his abba, "When I read the Scriptures, my mind is wholly concentrated on the words so that I may have something to say if I am asked."[19] In another story, an elder chides a group of monks for conversing too much about the Bible, telling Abba Antony, "No doubt they are good, but they do not have a door to their house and anyone who wishes can enter the stable and loose the ass." The point is not so much that they are being inquisitive about scriptural ideas; it is that they have not yet grown to a spiritual stature to manage such ideas wisely. As the redactor adds here, the old man "means that the brethren said whatever came into their mouths."[20]

The literature ultimately produced by this once predominantly oral culture of desert monasticism, however, betrays the fact that putting questions to the sacred texts did go on consistently. As Burton-Christie remarks, "the desert fathers show themselves again and again willing to enter into a risky conversation with the texts, to suspend their former understanding of the world, and to allow themselves to be 'taken up' into the world of the sacred texts."[21] In effect, their very lives *were* the conversation with Scripture. And at times, as in the case of the monk Theodore, who was spurred on in his monastic vocation precisely by hearing (second hand) Pachomius's awe-inspiring theological exegesis of the Tabernacle and Holy of Holies (Heb. 9:1-5, etc.),[22] it was more than a straightforward *applicatio* or *exemplum* from Scripture that changed lives. Moreover, while "dialectic," strictly speaking, may have been absent in the desert, it was the variegated genre of *quaestio-responsio,* much of it focused on queries about the Bible, that was destined to become the consistent hallmark of early monastic literature, from the pithy "conferences" of the *Apophthegmata patrum* to the stylized monastic dialogues of John Cassian's *Collationes* or of the *Quaestiones et responsiones* of the later sixth-century Palestinians Barsanuphius and John.[23]

"Origenists" and "Anthropomorphites"

One of the most far reaching controversies in early Greek Christian monasticism took the shape, in part at least, of a debate over how to interpret Scripture. The crisis was for a long time pegged purely as a struggle between more intellectual "Origenist" monks, inspired by the great Alexandrian master's speculative theology and allegorical approach to Scripture, and the mass of rustic or illiterate "Anthropomorphite" monks whose less sophisticated piety carried with it a more literal approach to the Bible. Such a depiction, based on a preliminary reading of the remarks of John Cassian and other ancient writers on the dispute, is too simplistic. More recent research has demonstrated that the "Anthro–

pomorphite controversy" (and so too the more embracing "Origenist Controversy") was in fact a quite complex affair in which issues of anti-paganism, ascetic discipline, biblical interpretation, theological anthropology, and the contemplation of the Divine were all interconnected.[24] For our purposes, the controversy provides a fascinating example of how the monastic reading of Scripture was tied to theological and exegetical concerns that went beyond the hermitages and monasteries of the desert.

With most of our evidence for the polarization of Origenists and Anthropomorphites coming from the late fourth and early fifth centuries, and presenting a rather stereotyped picture at that, it is difficult to discern the formation of such factions of monks in Egypt earlier in the fourth century. Two of the most prolific of the Origenist monks, Evagrius Ponticus and Palladius, did not appear in Egypt until the 380s, and the evidence for a substantial influence of Origen's works on Egyptian monks before that time is highly disputable.[25] Antoine Guillamont, among others, has cast doubt on the authenticity of Pachomius's alleged condemnation of Origen and Origenist teaching in the Greek *Life of Pachomius* and in the Pachomian *Chronicles*.[26] Stories in the *Apophthegmata patrum*, moreover give no real hint of any vigorous contention in which literalistic Coptic monks were accusing Origenist "allegorizers;"[27] on the contrary, modest allegory was already very much a part of the sages' moral exposition of Scripture. Conversely, there is no hard evidence from the *Apophthegmata*, the *Letters of Antony*, the Pachomian literature, or even the works of Evagrius for a distinctive "Anthropomorphite" faction emerging in the desert, absorbed with too literal an understanding of Scripture or exercising too graphic an imagination of the Divine.[28]

And yet, by the 370s, we have Epiphanius openly castigating Origenist monks in Egypt;[29] and in 399, we find Theophilus of Alexandria, in a festal letter addressing the subject of the incorporeality of God, formally condemning Anthropomorphism among the Coptic monks—an action which only precipitated a furor of protest from monks who stormed the archepiscopal city and induced the bishop abruptly to about-face and condemn the Origenist monks instead.[30] The suddenly fevered pitch of this controversy, as Elizabeth Clark has shown, owes much to the political interests of Theophilus and his association with the devoutly anti-Origenist circle of men like Epiphanius and Jerome, but also to genuine theological factors.[31] For one thing, Theophilus's initial anti-anthropomorphite posture expressed his urge to extirpate all vestiges of pagan "idolatry" among Coptic monks who might be tempted, out of their indigenous Egyptian context, to taint their Christian prayers and contemplation using *human* mental images of God.[32]

A number of sources indicate that a focal point of controversy was the possibility that human beings, after the fall, retained the *image* (*eikôn*) of God in which humanity was created, implying as a corollary that the incorporeal God could thus be legitimately represented in the crass form of the human body or of corporeal thoughts.[33] John Cassian tells of a certain Serapion of Scete and other Egyptian monks who were ensnared by too literal a reading of Genesis 1:26—who had, in other words, failed to grasp the higher spiritual sense of that text (dear to the Origenists). Wooed by the learned deacon Photinus's arguments against reducing the transcendent God to any corporeal image, Serapion allegedly forsook his anthropomorphic habits, but not without first anguishing that in his future imageless prayers to an imageless God, he would "have no one to hold on to."[34] On the other hand, the intriguing Coptic *Life of Ape Aphou of Pemdje*, which reports the story of an elder Anthropomorphite monk registering his protest against Theophilus's festal letter of 399, and which likewise focuses on the doctrine of the image, presents Aphou as staging his own formidable theological and scriptural defense in favor of the human retention of the image.[35] Georges Florovsky has argued that the point of the positions of Serapion and Aphou in particular, and the so-called "Anthropomorphism" in general, was to bring into play the *incarnational* (and eucharistic) mystery, the fact that human beings are created in the image of the *incarnate Son*, an endowment which they cannot lose even after the fall; furthermore, this reality correlatively sanctioned the discreet use of human or somatic "images" of God in theological discourse or in spiritual disciplines like prayer or mediation on Scripture. The "Anthropomorphite controversy" accordingly took the shape of a battle between competing spiritualities, "evangelical realism" and "Origenistic symbolism."[36]

Alexander Golitzin has lately argued that Ape Aphou was effectively (and more controversially) arguing that human bodies were created in the image of the transcendent "Body" of the Second Person of the Trinity, a position which could have posed a genuine threat to Nicene orthodoxy. But however we interpret the gist of his arguments, Aphou does not appear as a simpleton incapable of articulating a theological case; he seems to represent a "school of thought" in Coptic monasticism that had developed its spiritual doctrine on the basis of a careful, and in its own way sophisticated, reading of Scripture. Indeed, the author of the

Life of Ape Aphou wants to credit him as the one who changed Theophilus's mind about the Anthropomorphites.

So whether one sees the "Anthropomorphites" as a purely polemical creation, the stereotype of a current deeply rooted in the indigenous Coptic theological and spiritual tradition,[37] or as actually representing a mass of unlettered monks whose fetish for corporeal images of God was an affront to Nicene theology, they were a force to be reckoned with by the turn of the fifth century, as their riot in Alexandria in 399 shows. And likewise on the other side, the presence and influence of Evagrius in Egypt in the late fourth century provided the needed impetus to a more consolidated and identifiable monastic Origenism,[38] such as could further bring this conflict of spiritual worldviews to a head. Here was a theological genius who not only articulated an Origenist "system" in which allegorical interpretation was allied with various philosophical presuppositions about creation, the fall, and the apokatastasis, but who further used this system as a theoretical basis for the ascetic disciplines of the monastic life.[39] For Evagrius, the battle over "images" was not simply a theologians' struggle over what language or ideation was suited to a God who defies imagination or even conceptualization; it was a monk's own raw battle with the constant flood of vain thoughts (*logismoi*), fantasies, and memories that were shot through with passion and that were the vehicles of demonic assault.[40] The monk engaged in prayer or meditation on Scripture was an open target for such demonic machinations: doubtless Evagrius would have seen the monk Serapion as consorting with demons by succumbing to the use of mental "images" of the Divine. Memory and imagination, as lower psychic functions habitually allied with the body and continuously suggesting themselves to the mind (*nous*), were inherently frail, scarcely capable of sustained concentration on God, and always in need of purgation if the intellect was to ascend contemplatively to achieve an imageless "pure prayer" or a graced state of knowledge (*gnôsis*) of the Divine essence, the very Trinity.[41] Still, Evagrius's alleged gnosticism and "internalized iconoclasm," as Elizabeth Clark has termed it,[42] was thoroughly trained by ascetic experience. One in fact finds in his teaching much common ground with the wisdom of the Coptic ascetic tradition (e.g., the apotropaic use of Scripture to ward off demons or counteract impassioned thoughts;[43] the value of silence; the need for compunction, etc.). But on the whole, and stereotypes notwithstanding, Evagrius unquestionably championed a different set of spiritual insights from those of the Egyptian monks accused of Anthropomorphism.

The integrity of the Eastern Christian monastic tradition was born precisely of the chemistry of diverse spiritual currents, some of them standing in clear tension with each other. Indeed, the interlocking Anthropomorphite and Origenist controversies were an important testing ground for the tempered approach to the Bible and spiritual doctrine which over time came to characterize this tradition. John Cassian, for all his attachments to the Origenist legacy, already revealed in his *Conferences* a moderating and synthesizing trend. Like Evagrius, he was fully aware of the instability of memory and imagination as instruments in the service of contemplation,[44] and he, too, envisioned the mind as ever needing to be drawn, by grace—especially that grace communicated *now* through the food of Holy Scripture and the invocation of the powerful name of the Lord[45]—beyond sensible proclivities. Given the graphic, evocative, and thought-provoking nature of Scripture itself, a monk could all too easily get caught up in its web of texts and meanings and fail to have it lift him beyond himself.[46] But in his pastoral treatment of the case of the Anthropomorphite Serapion of Scete (Serapion needs further training, not repudiation as a heretic!), in the meticulous relation that he established between ascetic praxis and the contemplative concerns of prayer and the interpretation of Scripture,[47] and in the way he furthermore grounded the *via contemplativa* solidly on the reality of the Incarnation without, however, fixating it wholly on the earthly or historical Jesus,[48] Cassian aspired to a brilliant integration of desert wisdom and the Origenist spiritual vision.

The Bible as a Mirror of the Ascetic Strivings of the Soul: The Messalian Controversy

In the controversy over Messalianism, as in the upheaval over Anthropomorphism, historians have had to pose the question of whether we are we dealing with a spiritual current or "tendency" (in this case of Syrian Christian origin) liable to stereotyping by its opponents, or rather with a heterodox monastic sect having a clearly defined spiritual doctrine. The framing of Messalianism took place through a series of heresiological condemnations and conciliar censures stretching chronologically from the fourth to the eighth centuries, and geographically from the Christian Orient to Asia Minor.[49]

Early on, the Messalians (from the Syriac, "those who pray"; thus the Greek "Euchites") were pegged as a radically dualistic and enthusiast sect of Mesopotamian origin, one which spurned manual labor and focused its attention exclusively on prayer.[50] In the late fourth and early fifth centuries, the sect apparently sprung up in Pamphylia and Lycaonia in Asia Minor, prompting strong reactions from local synods at Side (ca. 390), Constantinople (426), and general condemnations both in the Council of Ephesus (431) and in the *Theodosian Code* (16.5.65). Further surfacings of Messalian radicals are indicated by more local condemnations in Armenia (477), Persia (486), and Syria (532-34). In seventh-century Persia still, Babai the Great was strongly attacking Messalians for their idleness and devotion to prayer unaccompanied by good works. A more definitive, albeit polemical, picture emerges in the lists of alleged Messalian teachings drawn up by Timothy of Constantinople (sixth century) and John Damascene (eighth century). The following were among the targeted tenets: (1) the idea that after the fall of Adam every human being was inhabited by a wicked demon attaching itself metaphysically to the soul; (2) the assertion that baptism (or any other sacrament) was wholly ineffectual in ridding the soul of this demonic scourge; (3) the belief that prayer alone could usher in the Holy Spirit to vanquish the demon within; (4) the conviction that a person could immediately experience a feeling of certitude and assurance of the Spirit's operations within the soul; and (5) the insistence that the spiritual subject, fully cleansed by the Spirit and not before, had already arrived at a state of utter impassibility (*apatheia*), at which point any ascetic exercises were rendered superfluous.[51]

A turning point in the study of the Messalian phenomenon was the discovery that the celebrated *Spiritual Homilies* attributed to Macarius of Egypt were in fact the work of an author (or authors) linked to Messalianism and to the Syrian Christian frontier, and subsequent research has shown that "Pseudo-Macarius" represented a mitigated Messalianism, rehabilitating its constructive elements and language while toning down or rejecting its more radical tendencies.[52] Remarkably, it has also been demonstrated that the Cappadocian Fathers were directly and positively influenced by Pseudo-Macarius's "reform" of ascetic theology.[53] Moreover, later monastic theologians such as Mark the Hermit, Diadochus of Photikê, Dorotheus of Gaza, and even Maximus the Confessor all show up important thematic and terminological influences from this "moderating" Messalianism of Pseudo-Macarius. The later we move, the more diversified the Messalian profile becomes. As Aelred Baker has written, "there were Messalians and Messalians," although it is difficult to determine who were more representative at any given point.[54] Given the standing evidence, however, it remains doubtful whether we can ever totally extract individual Messalian groups from the Messalian controversy,[55] or to put it another way, isolate what Messalian asceticism *was* in Syria and Mesopotamia from what "Messalianism" was *becoming* as it advanced into the dynamic, highly diversified Greek ascetic culture of the fourth and fifth centuries

Columba Stewart's thesis that the Messalian controversy, spreading as it did across the cultural fault-line between Syrian and Greek Christianity, had the *ambiguities of the language of spiritual experience* at its root, is an important one,[56] especially when we also factor in the different translations of the Bible that lay in the background of this controversy, *and* the "ambiguous" nature of the Bible's own language of spiritual or ascetic experience. While it is risky to make sweeping generalizations about the use of Scripture in this controversy—given that we have none of the original Messalian *Ascetikon* intact and are dependent on polemical or mitigating sources—it is nonetheless possible to detect patterns of interpretation with certain particularly vulnerable biblical texts that emerged in the struggle to delineate, repudiate, or rehabilitate "Messalian" doctrines. Pseudo-Macarius, Mark the Hermit, and Diadochus of Photikê clearly direct counter-exegeses against ascetic radicals, be it by attacking unwarranted literalism, modifying extreme interpretations, or simply adducing alternative scriptural prooftexts.

Texts concerning Manual Labor

One such vulnerable text was Jesus's injunction in John 6:27 to work not for perishable food but for that which endures unto eternity. According to Epiphanius (whose own observations must be carefully scrutinized), some Messalians took this text quite literally simply out of naiveté; others because they were inspired by Manichaeism.[57] Elsewhere, in the *Apophthegmata patrum*, we hear of one such "naive" Euchite monk who, defending his abstience from manual labor, cites not only John 6:27 but also Luke 10:38-49, trying to play off Mary against Martha (i.e., Jesus's ostensible preference of Mary's spirituality to Martha's domesticity). But the sage's reply, rather than offering a straightforward counter-interpretation, aims to put these passages into the properly ascetic perspective of the monk's growth toward spiritual perfection, for which labor is foundational. The answer appears precisely when the Euchite monk comes looking for a meal:

> "Why did you not call me?" The old man said to him, "Because you are a spiritual man and do not need that kind of food. We, being carnal,

want to eat and that is why we work. But you have chosen the good portion (Luke 10:42) and read the whole day long and you do not want to eat carnal food. When he heard these words the brother made a prostration saying, "Forgive me, abba." The old man said to him, "Mary needs Martha. It is really thanks to Martha that Mary is praised."[58]

A similar logic obtains in another lesson from the desert, where some Euchite monks appear before a sage quoting Paul's injunction in 1 Thessalonians 5:17 to "pray without ceasing." The wise man proposes an answer which explains how the "literal" observance of the commandment is best realized in the practice of manual labor in common with other monks:

> I will show you how, while doing my manual work, I pray without interruption. I sit down with God, soaking my reeds and plaiting my rope, and I say, "God, have mercy on me, according to your great goodness and according to the multitude of your mercies, save me from my sins"...So when I have spent the whole day working and praying, making thirteen pieces of money more or less, I put two pieces of money outside the door and I pay for my food with the rest of the money. He who takes the two pieces of money prays for me when I am eating and when I am sleeping; so, by the grace of God, I fulfil the precept to pray without ceasing.[59]

Already these anecdotes betray the monks' consciousness of the potential "slide" between baldly literal or figurative interpretations of the New Testament's commands about work. Pseudo-Macarius's own homiletic exposition of the Mary and Martha pericope clearly elicits a moderating trend that negotiates between the two ascetic principles perceived to stand in tension in the text. On the one hand, Mary's earnest devotion to Jesus, her choice of "the good portion which shall not be taken away from her" (Luke 10:41), reveals the superiority of prayer and the ministry of the Word (cf. Acts 6:2-6) to every virtue, and signals the reception of a divine spirit and power in the soul that can only obtain permanently and not be lost.[60] On the other hand, "after a time the things that Martha had done so eagerly as domestic service brought her to that gift of grace [which Mary had]; for she also obtained divine power in her soul."[61] Pseudo-Macarius is happily unconcerned that his exegesis still leaves in tension the two principles of spiritual devotion and manual labor; he is characteristically comfortable with such tensions and paradoxes as intrinsic to the ascetic life. He simply affirms the indispensability of domestic labor alongside the absolute superiority of devotion and prayer. After all, he says in his *Great Letter*, "if it [domestic labor] were nothing, how could the Lord have shared in Martha's service himself, as when he washed the feet of his disciples?"[62]

Texts concerning Sin, Baptismal Grace, and Christian Ethics

The dynamism of exegetical patterns in the Messalian controversy becomes more obvious the deeper we move into its consuming theological and spiritual-doctrinal issues. As "inside" sources, Pseudo-Macarius and Mark the Hermit demonstrate the crucial role of Romans 1-8 (especially chapters 5 and 7) in the debate with Messalian extremists over sin, grace, and ethics. In the Messalian use of Romans, we find that curious mixture of ideas which earned the sect the reputation of being both "Manichaean" and "Judaistic" among its contemporaries, and in some sense both "Augustinian"[63] and "Pelagian"[64] among various of its analysts today. In his treatment of Romans 5-7, Pseudo-Macarius provides a view into the Messalian version of original sin, according to which an inhabiting demon, or else Satan himself, became rooted in human souls through Adam's sin (cf. Rom. 5:19ff; 7:17).[65] Retained is this sense of a demonic inhabitation as the universal legacy of Adam, creating estrangement between demonic and spiritual principles within the human soul, turning it into that "body of sin" (Rom. 6:6) or "body of death" (7:24) that Paul himself experienced.[66] Yet Pseudo-Macarius consciously obviates the possible Manichaean overtones of such an interpretation.[67] In a manner paralleling the classic early rabbinic understanding of human sinfulness, he notes the soul's simultaneous natural inclinations toward good and evil,[68] asserting that it is under no ontological compulsion to the demonic presence, as it still enjoys the image of God and is always free to resist evil and choose the good.[69] By contrast, in one homily he speaks of the Adamic legacy in Romans 5 totally without reference to any indwelling demon, describing it (in a way consonant with Greek patristic views on original sin) as an inheritance of evil passions that have become "virtually natural for us" (*hôsper physin hêmôn*) through habit (*syntheia*) and propensity (*prolêpsis*).[70] Again, Pseudo-Macarius thrives on the fluidity of his interpretations, showing no disposition to systematize a doctrine of "original sin."

Romans 7 and a number of other Pauline passages were vital in the extremists' denial of the efficacy of baptismal grace. In his treatise *On Baptism*, Mark the Hermit, an abbot probably living in fifth-century Egypt,[71] directly counters Messalian critics of baptism[72] and cites their prooftexts in order to refute their calumnies.

> Others [Messalians]...say that old sin is cleared away through ascetic struggles, and they too use the testimony of Scripture, when it says, "Let us *cleanse ourselves* of all defilement of the flesh and spirit" (2 Cor. 7:1), at once finding in themselves the very same efficacy of sin *after baptism*. What shall we say to these arguments? Are we to believe them?[73]

Extremists and moderates alike, including Pseudo-Macarius himself, were taking the apostle Paul as the prototype of the monk who struggles ascetically with post-baptismal sin.[74] The difference lay in their spiritualizing inferences from Paul's own experience, especially as outlined in Romans 7:14-25. Mark again quotes his opponents who ask, "Did not Paul sin after baptism, seeing as he was unwillingly agitated? For he says, 'I see another law warring against the law of my mind' (Rom. 7:23)?"[75] Mark in his turn disclaims that Paul is really speaking of his own post-baptismal experience in Romans 7; he is, rather, conscientiously adopting the perspective of unbelieving Jews who have not, like himself, been freed through the "spiritual law" (Rom. 7:14), and who have not received the grace of the Spirit that is conferred mystically *through baptism*.[76] At one point, Mark exhibits his own flourish of New Testament testimonies to the effect that sin cannot be purged from the soul through ascetic struggles apart from the baptismal grace of the indwelling Christ, cooperating with the human will:

> For he is "working in you, both to will and to work for his good pleasure" (Phil. 2:13). Having set forth this phrase "for his good pleasure," he indicates that good pleasure in the virtues is our responsibility. And the statements, "Apart from me you can do nothing" (John 15:5), and "You did not choose me, but I chose you" (John 15:16) tend toward the same idea. Perhaps we must understand the following in the same way—"All things were made through him, and apart from him was not anything made" (John 1:3)—if indeed "all things" includes that which has to do with us. Also this statement: "No one comes to the Father unless it is through me" (John 14:6).[77]

Equally disconcerting for Mark the Hermit are the extremists' *ethical* inferences from Paul's teaching on the "spiritual law" (Rom. 7:14-25; 8:2), or the "law of freedom" as James 1:25 calls it.[78] Mark curiously accuses the extremists at once of a pneumatic antinomianism that abandons good works in the quest for a liberating inner experience of the Spirit,[79] and of a sort of "works-righteousness" in the conviction that the Spirit's grace could somehow be "merited" through internal ascetic struggles against evil ("corporeal works," as Mark ironically labels them) in advance of having fulfilled the ethical commandments.[80] Pseudo-

Macarius's exegesis of Romans 7:14-8:2 perhaps betrays the Messalian logic more accurately: For him the "spiritual law" idea develops precisely in Paul's attempt to grapple with entrenched post-baptismal sin and carnality; it is the law unfolded dynamically through ascesis and good works, albeit commensurate with the indwelling presence of Christ or his Spirit.[81] For Mark, again, the spiritual law is the grace of Christ received *in baptism*, gradually revealing itself through practical obedience to Christ's commandments.[82] But the attractiveness of Pseudo-Macarius's interpretation is obvious. The animus in these ascetic interpretations of Romans 7 was not precise theological distinctions (e.g., "grace" versus "works") but the quest for that insight which most effectively bespoke the monks' own psychological and existential struggle with sin and experience of ethical incapacitation even after baptism. The more appealing interpretation of the "spiritual law" may well have been that which comprehended the mysterious coexistence of efficacious grace, entrenched sin, and absolute freedom in the soul.

Texts concerning Spiritual Experience and Ultimate Impassibility

Some accusers in the Messalian controversy indicted the extremists for viewing the ascetic life as totally oriented to the ultimate, conscious experience of the Holy Spirit inhabiting the soul and vanquishing the demonic power within. The danger then became the conviction of a state of utter impassibility, a sort of "eternal security" in which ascetic struggles and progress were rendered obsolete. The state supposedly could not be lost because the Holy Spirit was either fully present in the soul, or not present at all.

By all indications, Ephesians 4:13, Paul's projection of Christians attaining "to mature manhood, to the measure of the stature of the fullness of Christ," was a central testimony used by all sides in the Messalian controversy. It was a question of whether this "fullness" is possessed all at once as a final and unmistakable impassibility in the Spirit, or whether it is a matter of progressive degrees of achievement. As a "moderate," Pseudo-Macarius sees Ephesians 4:13 as referring to a progressive growth, "little by little...(and) not, as some say, 'Off with one coat, and on with another (*ekdusai, endusai*).'"[83] Here he is almost certainly quoting a proverb of Messalian extremists who take this text to refer to a sudden arrival at impassibility. Pseudo-Macarius has a rich and extensive use of Ephesians 4:13, which he cites in the context of his discussion of the progressive advance of the spiritual life. Attaining to this perfect maturity, this "measure of the stature of the fullness of Christ," comes about as the grace of Christ, hidden at first within the soul, interacts with the obedient will in overcoming sin, advancing in virtue, and putting off "childish" ways.[84] Mark the Hermit analogously argues that Ephesians 4:13 is about the synergy of *baptismal* grace and human volition.[85]

> Christ, being perfect God, bestows on the baptized the grace of the Spirit. We add nothing to that grace; it is revealed to and manifested in us in proportion to our execution of the commandments, and provides us the added assistance of faith, "until we all attain to perfect manhood, to the measure of the stature of the fullness of Christ" (Eph. 4:13).[86]

That is not the end of it. Pseudo-Macarius believes that this reaching of maturity in Ephesians 4:13 would entail a profound experiential aspect, a "full assurance of the Spirit;" in fact he reclaims a classic Messalian catchphrase in urging his disciples to "pray to partake of the Holy Spirit *in full assurance and experience (en plêrophoriai kai aisthêsei)*."[87] Perhaps this phrase was originally coined with Ephesians 4:13 in mind, but its more immediate scriptural basis was probably Philippians 1:1-9 (Paul's mention of love abounding "in full experience," *en...pasê aisthêsei...*),[88] or perhaps 1 Thessalonians 1:5 ("Our gospel came to you not in word only, but in power and in the Holy Spirit *and with much assurance*").[89] Mark the Hermit employs the phrase in conjunction with Ephesians 3:14-17 ("[being] filled with the *fullness of God*"). The phrase shows up again in Diadochus of Photikê, who connects it with Luke 10:27 (loving God "with all your heart, and with all your soul...and with all your mind").[90] On closer scrutiny, to be sure, the original meaning of this phrase "in full assurance and experience," evincing as it does the Messalian insistence that the full and conscious experience of the Spirit assures the monk of having arrived at a new state of grace and impassibility from which he cannot lapse, has been revamped in those writers of orthodox credential who have appropriated it. As Mark the Hermit asserts, this conscious experience of the Spirit is only the divulgence of that hidden baptismal grace already at work within the Christian.[91] Or as Diadochus concludes, our goal is not visions or ecstasies per se, but the sheer perception of the love of God within the heart.[92]

This same concern, moreover, leads these writers to reiterate, against the Messalian extremists, that the Spirit does not make its appearance in the soul all at once. The image of the Spirit as "fire" was a powerful one in Messalian asceticism,[93] and much seems to have been made of texts like Matthew 3:11 ("He shall baptize you with the Holy Spirit and with fire") or Hebrews 12:29 ("Our God is a consuming fire") in expounding the idea that the Spirit in a dramatic tour de force consumes evil in the soul and confers impassibility.[94] Orthodox critics were pressed in turn to demonstrate that the advent of the Spirit is only *gradual,* and proportionate to the monk's *voluntary* battle against sin and performance of the commandments. Indeed the Spirit does co-exist with sin in the soul and wins the day only commensurately with the monk's own active progress in grace. Pseudo-Macarius, Mark the Hermit, and Diadochus of Photikê all appeal here to Paul's injunction in 1 Thessalonians 5:19, "Do not quench the Spirit," and Ephesians 4:30, "Grieve not the Spirit." As Pseudo-Macarius says of these texts, "it is not that God is mutable and feeble, or that the Holy Spirit is (literally) quenched, rather, human beings themselves do not concur (*symphônousi*) with grace, on account of which they go astray and fall into multiple vices."[95] The Spirit's presence is relative, and even those who have received grace and been perfected, like the apostles, have to put forth moral effort lest they "quench the Spirit."[96] Or as Mark the Hermit states,

> Learn from the Apostle that we are the ones who grieve the Spirit, extinguishing him in ourselves; as he says, "Do not quench the Spirit, do not despise prophecy" (1 Thess. 5:19); and again, "Do not grieve the Holy Spirit, in whom you have been sealed for the day of redemption" (Eph. 4:30). We introduce these testimonies not as if to suggest that every man who has been baptized and obtained grace is henceforth immutable and no longer in need of repentance, but to say that through baptism, according to Christ's gift, the complete grace of God is granted to us for the fulfillment of the commandments. Henceforth each one who receives it mystically, and yet does not fully perform the commandments, is activated by sin in proportion to their failure—the sin not of Adam, but of the one who is negligent.[97]

The same theological principle obtains where Messalian ascetics presumably applied the scriptural image of the "heavenly Jerusalem" (Heb. 12:22; Gal. 4:26), the city of pure peace, to the state of the soul once it has achieved impassibility: It is the ultimate "realized eschatology," as it were, since this sublime state can be experienced "already" in its fullness. Pseudo-Macarius candidly affirms the monk's experience of inner peace and repose at the end of his ascetic struggles as an entry into the "heavenly Jerusalem,"[98] but this in no way warrants a complacency or presumptuousness.[99] The perfect, so long as they remain in the flesh, are still subject to fear, temptation, and sin.[100] Mark the Hermit similarly describes the present reality of finding the "heavenly Jerusalem:" After all, he asserts, Hebrews 12:22 does say that "you *have arrived* [perfect tense] at Mt. Zion, and the city of the living God," which is the benefits of baptismal grace; only those of steadfast faith, those who continue observing the commandments, truly make it there.[101] Besides, there remains still the *future* aspect of the heavenly Jerusalem, attainment to which is not exhausted by any means in the present spiritual life.[102]

Messalian extremists seemed to have been fixed on this idea that impassibility, once realized in the soul in its fullness, and incapable of being lost, abruptly excluded the faintest hint of passion. Does not 1 John 4:18 say clearly that "perfect love casts out fear"? The radicals' use of this text, evincing as it did a false sense of security among the "perfect," prompted a classic exegetical response in the Byzantine monastic heritage, as a whole series of ascetic theologians sought to reconcile the "perfect love" of God with at least some measure of "fear." The pattern in this exegetical tradition—which includes John Cassian, Diadochus of Photikê, Dorotheus of Gaza, and even Maximus the Confessor—is the same: Texts from the Psalms (in particular Psalm 34:9 [33:10, LXX]) are adduced over against 1 John 4:18 to demonstrate that "fear," far from being irreconcilable with the "perfect love" of God, is a godly virtue; moreover, fear and love are thoroughly compatible when situated within the framework of the different levels or grades of perfection among the saints.[103] Beginners start with the mere fear of divine punishment, but by the time they advance to the level of perfect love, they still have that pure "fear" which is a holy reverence for God.

Conclusion

A few general concluding observations are in order concerning the patterns of the monastic encounter with the Bible. First, the monks' interpretation of Scripture was profoundly "performative," provided we understand that term in the broadest sense: That is, much of the appropriation of the Bible in the desert was doubtless focused on explicit and concrete injunctions from Scripture concerning all aspects of the moral and spiritual life; and yet, as we see most conspicuously in the Origenist tradition, Scripture was also understood to be projecting a higher spiritual vocation that urged souls beyond "the letter" and the sensible reality in an inner spiritual journey that was no less "performative" by virtue of the strict course of ascetic disciplines that it inculcated. We learn from the interconnected Anthropomorphite and Origenist controversies, moreover, that an overly exaggerated polarization of "pragmatist" (or "literalistic") and "gnostic" (or "allegorizing") approaches to the Bible in the desert breaks down, insofar as "Anthropomorphites" had genuinely theological concerns, just as Origenists believed that no one could ascend to the heights of contemplation without having matured in the practical performance of the commandments and the cultivation of the virtues. In the Messalian controversy, furthermore, it is especially clear that the "performance" of Scripture in a patently ascetic context carried with it a host of critically important theological ramifications. Interpretation of specific texts with a view to fulfilling the "spiritual law" engaged overarching questions of grace and free will, the infection of sin, the efficacy of the sacraments, the nature of the Holy Spirit's indwelling presence, and so on. In all of these controversies, we have seen that the theological and hermeneutical issues in the background of the monastic "performance" of Scripture often transcended the monastic milieu itself and invited the involvement and critical scrutiny of the larger Church.

We should not fail to highlight in this connection the properly *controversial* dimension of the early monastic appropriation of the Bible. Monastic exegesis developed within a self-consciously *eschatological* context[104] in which the stakes of commitment (to the faith of the Church, and immediately to the vocation of renunciation of the world and separation [*anachorêsis*] from it) naturally also exaggerated the stakes of interpretation of the scriptural revelation. The righteousness of the Kingdom of God within and among the monks (cf. Luke 17:21; Matt. 6:33) would not be birthed without birthpangs. The saving Word had to be received, taken to heart, its convicting and transformative power demonstrated, in these "last days" anticipating judgment and resurrection. Discerning the mysterious Word of God, fathoming its power to cut to the very quick of the spiritual life, be it in the context of dialogue with elder sages or in the ongoing paideusis of monastic discipline itself, could never happen without conflict—sometimes overt, sometimes latent, or even subliminal—over the precise exigencies of that Word. Earlier we noted how stories of monks being hushed or reprimanded for their inquisitiveness merely betrayed their wrestling with the Word and its spiritual doctrine. Silence, and confessions of ignorance, even on the part of sages, veiled the quest of a faith seeking understanding, albeit an understanding achievable only through experience and the painstaking traditioning of ascetic wisdom.[105] One may too casually deduce that the doctrinal parameters of the Anthropomorphite, Origenist, or Messalian controversies, *qua* "controversies," were ultimately defined more by ecclesiastical authorities or observers than by the monastic communities themselves. At the root of these crises, again, were hermeneutical problems inextricable from the concrete ascetic struggles of monks who, in their scriptural mediation, prayer, physical labors, acts of self-renunciation, and strivings toward a higher contemplation of God, recognized full well the elusiveness and eschatological character of the Gospel's truth. The "romance" of their quest, if there ever really was such a thing, was constantly exploded by the apocalyptic power of a Word at once gracious and convicting.

In the end, *discernment,* both as a spiritual gift and as an interpretative "habit," is a crucial concept in comprehending the monastic appropriation of the Bible. John Cassian, who will have the last word here, indicates this in his second *Conference* when he states unequivocally that, after all the searching and striving for the ultimate ascetic virtue that would lead to perfection, the monk had to have discernment in order to avoid the extremes of presumptuousness and carelessness and to see things in a truly divine perspective.[106] Called in Scripture the "lamp" of the body (Matt. 6:22-23), the "sun" that must never set on anger (Eph. 4:26), the "guide" of life (Prov. 11:14), the "wine" of the soul (Ps. 104:15 [103:15, LXX]), "wisdom," "sound judgment," "intelligence" (Prov. 24:3-4), the "solid food" for the mature (Heb. 5:14),[107] this discernment ultimately represented the indwelling of the Word (and Spirit), which *is* salvation. Cassian accordingly quotes Hebrews 4:12: "The Word of God is living and active, more cutting than any two-edged sword, reaching through to mark off the soul from the spirit and the joints from the marrow, and discerning the thoughts and wishes of the heart."[108] The quest for *discernment,* for graced flashes of insight amid ignorance or broken knowledge at best, for the real but bittersweet presence of the Word in the heart, ties together the properly *performative* and *controversial* aspects of the early monastic appropriation of Scripture and elucidates, from within the monks' own experiential horizon, the fierceness of the debates over the Bible and spiritual doctrine outlined in this essay.

NOTES

1. *De proverbiis et eorundem expositionibus* 40, ed. J. Muyldermans, *Evagriana Syriaca,* Bibliothèque du *Muséon* 31 (Louvain, 1952), 138. Translations of primary works in this essay are my own unless otherwise noted. Primary works will normally be cited by volume number in series, pages, and (where necessary) lines.

2. For an excellent concise review of some of these theories of Christian monastic origins, see R. M. Price, Introduction to *Theodoret of Cyrrhus: A History of the Monks of Syria*, Cistercian Studies 88 (Kalamazoo, 1985), xxiii-xxix. In recent years Peter Brown's theory concerning the mediatorial role of holy men and women in late antique society has received especially wide acclaim. See his "The Rise and Function of the Holy Man in Late Antiquity," *Journal of Roman Studies* 61 (1971): 80-101; and more recently his *The Body and Society: Men, Women and Sexual Renunciation in Early Christianity* (New York, 1988).

3. See Athanasius's *Vita Antonii* 2ff (PG 26: 841Bff). Antony's "conversion" of course became a model to scores of later ascetics, including Augustine (*Confessions* 8.12).

4. See the *Instructions of Theodore* 2.1, ed. and trans. A. Veilleux, *The Pachomian Koinonia*, Cistercian Studies 45-47 (Kalamazoo, 1982), vol. 3: 91-92.

5. For a comprehensive review of the Bible's varied role in early Christian monasticism, see J. Biarne, "La Bible dans la vie monastique," in *Le monde latin antique et la Bible*, ed. J. Fontaine and C. Pietri (Paris, 1985), 409-429.

6. See D. Burton-Christie, *The Word in the Desert: Scripture and Quest for Holiness in Early Christian Monasticism* (New York, 1993). See also his shorter study in our present volume, "Oral Culture, Biblical Interpretation, and Spirituality in Early Christian Monasticism," 415-440.

7. Cf. the following examples and variations from the *Apophthegmata patrum, Alphabetical Collection* (hereafter *AP*): Antony 19 (PG 65: 81B); Ares 1 (132C); Hierax 1 (232C-D); Macarius 25 (272D); Nisterius 2 (305D); Pambo 153 (360B); Pambo 162 (361A); Sisoes 38 (404C). Cf. also, from a later generation of monks in sixth-century Palestine, Barsanuphius and John, *Quaestiones et Responsiones*, letter 88 (PO 31.3: 566); ibid., letter 93 (PO 31.3: 572).

8. For an important recent study of "performative" interpretation in the Fathers, see F. M. Young, *Virtuoso Theology: The Bible and Its Interpretation* (Cleveland, 1993).

9. See Burton-Christie, *The Word in the Desert*, 108-111, 150-166.

10. Ibid., 20-23.

11. Early monastic literature is teeming with "exemplarist" interpretation. In the *AP*, see, e.g., John the Persian 4 (PG 65: 237D-240A); Nisterius 2 (305D-308A); in the *Pachomian Koinonia*, see *Pachomian Instructions* 1.1-6, 12, 17-18, 25, in Veilleux, ed., vol. 3: 13-14, 17, 19, 23-24. This epigram of Pachomius (ibid. 1.17) is typical: "If you cannot get along alone, join another who is living according to the Gospel of Christ, and you will make progress with him. Either listen, or submit to one who listens; either be strong and be called Elijah, or obey the strong and be called Elisha. For obeying Elijah, Elisha received a double share of Elijah's spirit (cf. 2 Kings 2:9, 15 [4 Kings 2:9, 15, LXX])." On the *exempla* tradition, cf. also R. L. Wilken, "The Lives of the Saints and the Pursuit of Virtue," in his *Remembering the Christian Past* (Grand Rapids, 1995), 121-144; P. Brown, "The Saint as Exemplar in Late Antiquity," in *Saints and Virtues*, ed. J. S. Hawley (Berkeley, 1987), 3-14; Burton-Christie, *The Word in the Desert*, 167-170.

12. Nilus of Ancyra, *Epistulae* 2.223 (PG 79: 316B-317A). See also my *Exegesis and Spiritual Pedagogy in Maximus the Confessor: An Investigation of the "Quaestiones ad Thalassium"* (Notre Dame, Ind., 1991), 115-116.

13. Possession of a Bible by a monk for private use in his cell was rarely touted (see *AP*: Epiphanius 8-9, PG 65: 165A-B), and discouragement of it can be inferred (cf. *AP*: Gelasius 1, PG 65: 145C-148A; Theodore of Pherme 1, 188A). See also H. Dörries, "Die Bibel in ältesten Mönchtum," *Theologische Literaturzeitung* 72 (1947): 216-217; Burton-Christie, *The Word in the Desert*, 111-117.

14. See in particular *AP*: Amoun of Nitria 2 (PG 65: 128C-D); trans. Benedicta Ward, *The Sayings of the Desert Fathers*, Cistercian Studies 59 (Kalamazoo, 1975), 31-32.

15. *AP*: Zeno 4 (PG 65: 324A); trans. Ward, 56.

16. *AP*: Copres 3 (PG 65: 252D).

17. *AP*: Antony 17 (PG 65: 80D).

18. *AP*: Pambo 9 (PG 65: 369D-372A); also Palladius, *Historia Lausiaca* 10 (Pambo) (PG 65: 1033B).

19. *AP*: Sisoes 17 (PG 65: 397B); trans. Ward, 216.

20. *AP*: Antony 18 (PG 65: 81A), trans. Ward, 5.

21. Burton-Christie, *The Word in the Desert*, 22.

22. *The (Boharic) Life of Pachomius* 29, in Veilleux, ed., *Pachomian Koinonia*, vol. 1: 53-54.

23. See the extended analysis of the *quaestio-responsio* genre in early Christian monastic literature in my *Exegesis and Spiritual Pedagogy in Maximus the Confessor*, 36-73.

24. See G. Florovsky, "The Anthropomorphites in the Desert," and (pt. 2), "Theophilus of Alexandria and Apa Aphou of Pemdje," in his *Aspects of Church History* (Belmont, Mass., 1975), 89-129; and more recently the important study of E. A. Clark, *The Origenist Controversy: The Cultural Construction of an Early Christian Debate* (Princeton, 1992), esp. 43-84; also G. Gould, "The Image of God and the Anthropomorphite Controversy in the Fourth Century," in *Origeniana Quinta*, ed. R. J. Daly (Leuven, 1992), 549-557; A. Golitzin, "The Vision of God and the Form of Glory: Some Thoughts on the Anthropomorphites," paper delivered to the annual meeting of the North American Patristics Society, 30 May-1 June 1996 (publication forthcoming).

25. On this controversial evidence, see G. Gould, "The Influence of Origen on Fourth-Century Monasticism: Some Further Remarks," in *Origeniana Sexta: Origène et la Bible/Origen and the Bible*, ed. G. Dorival and A. le Boulluec (Leuven, 1995), 591-598; cf. S. Rubensen, *The Letters of St. Antony: Origenist Theology, Monastic Tradition, and the Making of a Saint* (Lund, 1990), who makes the case that Antony and other early, intellectually oriented monks served as a conduit of Origen's influence on earliest monasticism in Egypt.

26. Cf. *The (Greek) Life of Pachomius* 31, in Veilleux, *Pachomian Koinonia*, vol. 1: 317-318; *Pachomian Chronicles* 7, in Veilleux, *Pachomian Koinonia*, vol. 2: 28-

29; and A. Guillamont, *Les "Kephalaia Gnostica" d'Évagre le Pontique et l'histoire de l'Origénisme chez les grecs et chez les syriens* (Paris, 1962), 55-56.

27. In the alphabetical *AP,* there is only one brief anecdote in which an elder monk is censured for being enamored with the works of Origen: Lot 1 (PG 65: 253-256). But even here, allegorism is not a specified target.

28. See Gould, "The Image of God and the Anthropomorphite Controversy," 552-553.

29. Epiphanius, *Ancoratus* 82 (GCS 25: 102-103); cf. idem, *Panarion* 64.4.1 (GCS 31 [revised ed.]: 410).

30. Cf. Socrates, *Hist. Eccl.* 6.7 (PG 67: 684B-686C); John Cassian, *Collationes* 10.2 (CSEL 13: 287).

31. Clark, *The Origenist Controversy*, 35-38.

32. This concern is explicitly noted by John Cassian in *Collationes* 10.5 (CSEL 13: 290-291). See also Clark, *The Origenist Controversy,* 57-58.

33. For detailed sketches of the controversy over the image, see Gould, "The Image of God and the Anthropomorphite Controversy," 550-553; Clark, *The Origenist Controversy,* 58ff.

34. John Cassian, *Collationes* 10.3 (CSEL 13: 289,12-14).

35. See the Coptic text of the *Life of Ape Aphou*, ed. with a French trans. by E. Drioton, "La discussion d'un moine anthropomorphite audien avec le Patriarche Théophile d'Alexandrie en l'année 399," *Revue de l'Orient chrétien* 20 (1915-1917): 92-100, 113-128; Florovsky has also translated a large section of the dialogue in "Theophilus of Alexandria and Apa Aphou of Pemdje," 112-117.

36. Florovsky, "The Anthropomorphites in the Desert," 89-96; "Theophilus of Alexandria and Apa Aphou of Pemdje," esp. 112-128.

37. See Gould, "The Image of God and the Anthropomorphite Controversy," 549-550: "the anthropomorphite monk is a fixed point in our scematisations of doctrinal development, standing along with the other representatives of the literalist and biblicist element in early Christianity in opposition to the allegorist, hellenistic, and philosophical." Cf. also Guillamont (*Les "Kephalaia Gnostica,"* 83), who argues that the titles "Origenist" and "Anthropomorphite" alike were originated by adversaries who used them for their own purposes; such labels were inherently deprecatory and an "inévitable exagération."

38. See Clark, *The Origenist Controversy,* 50, 60-84.

39. See, e.g., Evagrius's *Scholia on Proverbs* (ed. P. Géhin, SC 340, Paris, 1987), for a view into how Evagrius utilizes spiritual or allegorical exegesis, informed by his overarching theological principles, as a means to render the Bible a veritable index of the moral and intellectual struggles of the ascetic life. On Evagrius's larger system of thought, see his *Kephalaia Gnostica*, Syriac text ed. with French trans. by A. Guillamont, PO 28.1 (Paris, 1958); also Guillamont, *Les "Kephalaia Gnostica,"* 102-119.

40. Cf., e.g., Evagrius, *Practicus* 34 (ed. A. Guillamont and C. Guillamont, SC 170 [Paris, 1971], 578); 48 (SC 170: 608); 50 (SC 170: 614-616); 54 (SC

170: 624-626); 65 (SC 170: 650); *Capita cognoscitiva* 2, 4, 22 and *passim* (ed. J. Muyldermans, *Evagriana* [Paris, 1931], 38-44).

41. Cf., e.g., Evagrius, *De oratione* 10 (PG 79: 1169B-C); 44-46 (1176C-D); 66 (1181A); 72 (1181D); 114 (1192D); 117 (1193A); 120 (1193B); *Cap. cognos.* 17-18 (ed. Muyldermans); *Keph. Gnost.* 5.84 (PO 28.1: 213).

42. Clark, *The Origenist Controversy*, 75.

43. See in particular Evagrius's *Antirrheticos*, ed. W. Frankenberg, *Evagrius Ponticus* (Berlin, 1912), 472-545. Cf. also J. Kirchmeyer, "Écriture sainte et vie spirituelle" (II. Dans la tradition; 4. Le monachisme; 4. Évagre et l'antirrhétique), *Dictionnaire de spiritualité*, vol. 4.1: 164-166.

44. See, e.g., *Collationes* 14.12-13 (CSEL 13: 413-416).

45. Ibid. 8.3 (CSEL 13: 218-221); 10.10-11 (CSEL 13: 297-306); 14.10-11 (CSEL 13: 410-413); cf. Evagrius, *De oratione* 97 (PG 79: 1188D-1189A); perhaps also *De octo vitiosis cogitationibus* (PG 40: 1275).

46. See John Cassian, *Collationes* 10.13 (CSEL 13: 306-307).

47. See, in particular, ibid. 14.1-4, 8-9, 16 (CSEL 13: 398-401, 404-410, 418-421).

48. Cassian took to heart Paul's statement in 2 Cor. 5:16 ("Even though we once regarded Christ in the flesh, we no longer regard him in this way") as enjoining the believer not to be preoccupied with the earthly Christ, but to ascend in the contemplation of the glorified and divine Christ: cf. *Collationes* 10.6 (CSEL 13: 291-292); idem, *De incarnatione* 3.3 (CSEL 17: 263-264). See also O. Chadwick, *John Cassian*, 2nd ed. (Cambridge, 1968), 107-109.

49. This process has been ably reconstructed in a sequence of studies: cf. H. Dörries, "Urteil und Verurteilung. Kirche und Messalianer: Zum Umgang der alten Kirche mit Häretikern," in his *Wort und Stunde* (Göttingen, 1966), vol. 1: 334-351; J. Gribomont, "Le dossier des origines du messalianisme," in *Epektasis: Mélanges patristiques offerts au Cardinal J. Daniélou* (Paris, 1972), 611-625; A. Baker, "Messalianism: The Monastic Heresy," *Monastic Studies* 10 (1974): 135-141; A. Guillaumont, "Messaliens," *Dictionnaire de spiritualité*, vol. 10: 1074-1083; and most recently C. Stewart, *"Working the Earth of the Heart": The Messalian Controversy in History, Texts, and Language to AD 431* (Oxford, 1991), 1-69, 244-279.

50. See Epiphanius, *Panarion* 80 (GCS 37 [revised ed.]: 485-493).

51. Cf. Timothy's list in PG 86: 45C-52C; John Damascene's in PG 94: 729A-732B. See also the general analyses of these indicted tenets in Guillaumont, "Messaliens," 1079-1082; Stewart, *"Working the Earth of the Heart,"* 52-69.

53. See L. Villecourt, "La date et l'origine des 'homilies spirituelles' attribuées à Macaire," *Comptes rendus de l'Academie des Inscriptiones et Belles-Lettres* (Paris, 1920), 250-258; H. Dörries, *Symeon von Mesopotamien: Die Überlieferung der messalianischen "Makarios"-Schriften* (Leipzig, 1941); idem, *Die Theologie des Makarios/Symeon* (Göttingen, 1978); J. Meyendorff, "Messalianism or Anti-Messalianism? A Fresh Look at the 'Macarian' Problem," in *Kyriakon: Festschrift Johannes Quasten*, ed. P. Granfield and J. Jungmann (Münster, 1970), vol. 2: 385-390.

54. In particular, Gregory of Nyssa's treatise *De instituto christiano* has been found to be largely a reworking of the *Great Letter* of Pseudo-Macarius:

see J. Gribomont, "Le *De instituto christiano* et le Messalianisme de Grégoire de Nysse," *Studia Patristica* 5 (Berlin, 1962), 312-322; R. Staats, *Gregor von Nyssa und die Messalianer* (Berlin, 1968). Basil of Caesarea's *Asceticon* shows up clear parallels with the Pseudo-Macarian corpus as well. In fact, the struggle against more radical Messalianism appears to have been a common interest of Pseudo-Macarius and the monastic reform of Basil. See Dörries, *Symeon von Mesopotamien*, 451-465; J. Gribomont, "Le monachisme au IVe siècle en Asie Mineure: De Gangres au Messalianisme," *Studia patristica* 2 (Berlin, 1957), 400-415.

55. A. Baker, "Messalianism: The Monastic Heresy," 137, 139. Cf. also J. Gribomont, "Le monachisme au sein de l'Église en Syrie et en Cappadoce," *Studia Monastica* 7 (1966): 19. As Stewart himself admits, "clearly one cannot produce a history of the Messalian movement, but only of the Messalian controversy" (*"Working the Earth of the Heart,"* 5).

56. See ibid., 70-233, 237-240.

57. Epiphanius, *Panarion* 80 (GCS 37 [revised ed.]: 489).

58. *AP*: Silvanus 5 (PG 65: 409B-D), trans. Ward, 223. Cf. John Cassian, *Collationes* 1.8 (CSEL 13: 14-16).

59. *AP*: Lucius 1 (PG 65: 253B-C), trans. Ward, 120-121. On the background of this anecdote, see H. Dörries, "Mönchtum und Arbeit," in his *Wort und Stunde*, vol. 1: 280, 287.

60. *Hom. spir.* 12.16 (ed. H. Dörries, E. Klostermann, M. Kroeger, *Die 50 geistlichen Homilien des Makarios*, Patristische Texte und Studien, Bd. 4), 116-117. (Hereafter cited: PTS 4).

61. Ibid. (PTS 4: 117,221-223).

62. Pseudo-Macarius, *Ep. mag.* (ed. W. Jaeger, *Two Rediscovered Works*, 288,7-8).

63. Cf. Andrew Louth, "Messalianism and Pelagianism," *Studia patristica* 17.1 (Oxford and New York, 1982), 127-135, and esp. 130ff. Louth notes the similarity between Messalianism and Augustinianism in their evaluation of the contrariety of sin in the dark side of the soul, leaving them both prone to the charge of "Manichaean" tendencies.

64. Cf. F. Dörr, *Diadochus von Photike und die Messalianer: Ein Kampf zwischen wahrer und falscher Mystik im 5. Jahrhundert* (Freiburg, 1937) 63ff; J. Meyendorff, "Basil, the Church, and Charismatic Leadership," in *The Byzantine Legacy in the Orthodox Church* (Crestwood, N.Y., 1982), 210.

65. Cf. *Hom. spir.* 15.48-49 (PTS 4: 154-155); ibid. 4.8 (PTS 4: 32-33). Cf. also V. Desprez, "Les citations de Romains, 1-8, dans les 'Homilies' macariennes," *Parole de l'Orient* 3 (1972): 96-97.

66. *Hom. spir.* 1.7 (PTS 4: 8-9). Cf. Desprez, "Les citations," 98-99.

67. On the ramifications of the metaphor of "indwelling" sin, in Pseudo-Macarius, see the detailed linguistic analysis of Stewart, *"Working the Earth of the Heart,"* 203-208.

68. *Hom. spir.* 15.25 (PTS 4: 142,347-351).

69. *Hom. spir.* 1.7 (PTS 4: 8-9); ibid. 15.25 (PTS 4: 142). Cf. Desprez, "Les citations," 96, 99.

70. *Hom. spir.* 4.8 (PTS 4: 32,125-33,129).

71. See O. Hesse, ed., *Markus Eremita: Asketische und dogmatische Schriften*, Bibliothek der griechischen Literatur 19 (Stuttgart, 1985), 106-111.

72. Ibid., 66-79.

73. *De baptismo*, Quaestio 1 (PG 65: 985A). Emphasis added in translation.

74. We see the same example of Paul in Pseudo-Macarius, whose "thorn in the flesh" (2 Cor. 12:7) indicates his own liability to sin even *post gratiam* (*Hom spir.* 7.4 [PTS 4: 73-74]).

75. *De baptismo*, Quaestio 4 (PG 65.992D).

76. Ibid., Responsio 4 (PG 65: 993A-B).

77. *De baptismo*, Responsio 5 (PG 65: 1008A).

78. This forms the central theme in Mark's anti-Messalian treatises *On the Spiritual Law* and *On Those Who Think They are Justified by Works*, both of which are translated in *The Philokalia*, vol. 1, ed. and trans. G. E. H. Palmer, P. Sherrard, and K. Ware (Boston, 1979), 109-146.

79. E.g., *De his qui putant se ex operibus justificari* 57 (PG 65: 940A); cf. also *De lege spirituali* 59, 85, 143 (PG 65: 913A, 916B, 924A) where Mark mentions those who are claiming that they are exempted from fulfilling the commandments by the fact that they do not know intellectually what is good; then (*De his qui putant...* 5, 7, 12 [PG 65: 932A, C]) there are also those who have the "theoretical" knowledge of the good but do not act on it (cf. 1 Cor. 8:1). Cf. also Hesse, *Markus Eremita*, 65-66, 112-115.

80. Int. al., *De his qui putant...* 11, 17 (PG 65: 932B, D).

81. For his exegesis of the "spiritual law," see the texts adduced and analyzed by Desprez, "Les citations," 197-202, 218-220. As Desprez concludes: "Macarius...wants to see in the 'law of the Spirit' a dynamic reality emanating from Christ and interior to the human being, a *pneuma*, a breath of life identical either with Christ or with the Spirit, and which is at the same time a norm of action, a *logos* (Neue Homilien 8.1) inscribed in the heart" (219-220).   •

82. Int. al., *De his qui putant...* 56, 85, 137 (PG 65: 937D, 944A, 952A-B).

83. *Hom. spir.* 15.41 (PTS 4: 151,571-152,583). Cf. also Stewart, "*Working the Earth of the Heart,*" 82-83.

84. Cf. *Hom. spir.* 3.5 (PTS 4: 24); 18.11 (PTS 4:182); 32.10 (PTS 4:257); 37.7 (PTS 4: 267-268); also idem, *Logos* 2.6 (*Makarios/Symeon: Reden und Briefe*, ed. H. Berthold, GCS, Berlin, 1973), vol. 1: 18,6-20. Cf. also *Ep. mag.* (ed. Jaeger, *Two Rediscovered Works*, 236,13-237,10), and the modification of Ps-Macarius's use here of Eph. 4:13 by Gregory of Nyssa (*De instituto Christiano*, GNO 8, pt. 1: 44,27-46,7), who enhances even more the progress, rather than the goal, as the essence of Eph. 4:13. On this point, see Staats, *Gregor von Nyssa und die Messalianer*, 30-31.

85. *De bapt.* Responsio 5 (PG 65: 1008C). Cf. ibid. 17 [PG 65: 1028B-C]), where Mark writes: "Christ, being perfect God, bestows on the baptized the grace of the Spirit. We add nothing to that grace; it is revealed to and manifested in us in proportion to our execution of the commandments, and provides us the added assistance of faith, 'until we all attain to perfect manhood, to the measure of the stature of the fullness of Christ' (Eph. 4:13)."

86. Ibid. Responsio 17 (PG 65: 1028B-C).

87. *Hom. spir.* 37.7 (PTS 4: 267).

88. See E. des Places, *Diadoque de Photiké: Oeuvres spirituelles,* SC 5, rev. ed. (Paris, 1966): 38.

89. Cf. Pseudo-Macarius, *Ep. magn.* (ed. Jaeger, *Two Rediscovered Works,* 235,14-21) Gregory of Nyssa, *De instituto christiano* (GNO 8, pt. 1: 44,3-11); cf. Staats, *Gregor von Nyssa und die Messalianer,* 28-29. On the linguistic background of this phraseology in the Messalian controversy, see Stewart, *"Working the Earth of the Heart,"* 110-114.

90. *Cent. gnost.* 40 (SC 5: 108,14-19). Cf. ibid. 44 (SC 5: 110,23-111,2); 68 (SC 5: 129,5-8); 90 (SC 5: 150,19-23); 94 (SC 5: 156,14-16).

91. *Consultatio intellectus* (PG 65: 1108D). See also K. Ware, "The Sacrament of Baptism and the Ascetic Life in the Teaching of Mark the Monk," *Studia patristica* 10 (Berlin, 1970), 447.

92. *Cent. gnost.* 40 (SC 5: 108,5-19).

93. Cf. Dörries, *Die Theologie des Makarios/Symeon,* 19, 154, 180, 205.

94. This image of the Spirit working as "fire" is used with some degree of caution by Pseudo-Macarius: cf. *Hom. spir.* 15.53 (PTS 4: 157); 32.4 (PTS 4: 253-254); 47.1, 10 (PTS 4: 304, 308).

95. *Hom. spir.* 15.36 (PTS 4: 148,510-515); cf. ibid. 27.9; *Logos* 33.1-2 (*Reden und Briefe* 2: 28,28-29,8). See also the same point in Diadochus, *Cent. gnost.* 28 (SC 5: 99).

96. *Hom. spir.* 17.8 (PTS 4: 171).

97. *De bapt.* Responsio 5 (PG 65: 1004B-C).

98. Cf. *Hom. spir.* 4.12 (PTS 4: 36,180ff); 25.7 (PTS 4: 203,103-105); 27.2 (PTS 4: 219,11ff); 43.4 (PTS 4: 287,62-288,67).

99. Cf. M. Canévet, "Pseudo-Macaire (Symeon)," *Dictionnaire de spiritualité,* vol. 10: 38.

100. Pseudo-Macarius, *Hom. spir.* 26.23 (PTS 4: 216) .

101. *De bapt.* Responsio 8 (PG 65: 1009B); cf. ibid. Responsio 4 (993C-D).

102. Ibid. Responsio 5 (1008A-B). See also Hesse, *Markus Eremita,* 151.

103. Cf. John Cassian, *Collationes* 11.11-13 (CSEL 13: 325-330); Diadochus of Photikê, *Cent. gnost.* 16 (SC 5: 92,15-93,16); Dorotheus of Gaza, *Didaskaliai* 4.47-49 (SC 92: 220-224); and Maximus the Confessor, *Quaestiones ad Thalassium* 10 (CCSG 7: 83-87). See also my discussion of this tradition of godly fear in *Exegesis and Spiritual Pedagogy in Maximus the Confessor,* 58-59.

104. See Burton-Christie, *The Word in the Desert,* 181-212.

105. On this traditioning process (the "tradition of the elders") with a view to instilling "discernment," see John Cassian, *Collationes* 2.10-15 (CSEL 13: 48-59).

106. Ibid. 2.2 (CSEL 13: 40-42).

107. Ibid. 2.4 (CSEL 13: 43-44).

108. Ibid. (trans. C. Luibheid, *John Cassian: Conferences,* Classics of Western Spirituality [Mahwah, N.J., 1985], 64).

PART IV

The Bible and the Cultural Setting
of the Mediterranean World

13

Celsus: A Pagan Perspective on Scripture

MARCEL BORRET

Through the history it retraces and the meaning that it gives itself, Scripture is the soil that nourishes the Christian message. Under various historic forms, however, anti-Christian polemic, in its turn, willingly refers back to Scripture in order to attack, at their very roots, the doctrines that it combats, thereby discrediting the sacred texts on which they are based. The Christian reaction is to examine anew the tenor of the disputed passages in the light of the contexts and larger themes of which they were a part; the result, then, is to register, in the balance-sheet of research, a progress in Christian knowledge of the Bible. This is precisely the pattern that we see with the first great polemic written against Christianity, known to us through Origen's *Contra Celsum*. Origen transcribes in fragments the substance of Celsus's *The True Doctrine,* a radical denunciation of the Christian faith and fervent eulogy of pagan piety.[1]

After some brief repartee, Origen sets out, in pages full of apologetic and doctrinal discourse, a full-scale treatise covering the scriptural, theological, and spiritual elements of things. The respective works of Celsus and Origen really represent two kinds of apology: the one marked by invective and praise; the other by response and demonstration. Sixty-nine years separate the two works. Yet the difference between them is blurred by the sheer drama of the dispute. And beyond the passionate excesses on both sides due to offended beliefs, and in spite of ideas and issues of the time that do not immediately interest us but are instructive for the history of ideas, there is good reason to be concerned with this explosive confrontation between two champions from a vast culture; for they present the claims of their respective religious belief-systems for the approval of human beings in all times. Given the brevity of this essay, however, we must forgo direct treatment of Origen and limit ourselves to examining the role of Scripture in Celsus's criticism of Christianity.

This ever vigilant criticism takes diverse forms, beginning with an argument from ancient tradition: its history, philosophy and literature, cultural and social institutions. There is ample material evidence, distributed in fragments transcribed by Origen. Out of a distinctly documentary interest, these extracts were identified, located, and interpreted at the time of the renewal of scholarly studies of Celsus.[2] The result, however, is paradoxical. *The True Doctrine* has been restored as a manifesto of Celsus's philosophy and even his faith, such that the pagan man of letters is better known than the anti-Christian pamphleteer. But what of his work? Has its perspective not been modified by virtue of the presence of Christianity? For, in a word, the preface of Celsus's treatise is about Christians, the conclusion against them; and, in the main body of his argument, direct criticisms of Christianity fill up the first part, and abound in the other two parts, where they include testimonies drawn from ancient religions and cultures. It is against the Christian tradition that Celsus's treatise mobilizes the pagan tradition. Its tone and form are constantly aggressive. If there is a pagan profession of faith here, it is enveloped in anti-Christian polemic.

But it is through Scripture that the events, persons, doctrine, and moral laws of Christianity, all of which pagan critics take to task, are known. The critic sets his sites on these things attested in Scripture in order to diminish their significance, vulgarize them, and discredit them. By providing a complete list of these points of attack he contributes to the study of his own work; for indeed, everything that concerns Scripture concerns us believers. It is to the mission of casting doubt on Scripture, denying its specific doctrinal value, and accusing it of inconsistencies that the pagan haughtily devotes himself, thinking he can wreak havoc on Christian interpretation. Ironically, at any rate, the pagan critic can lead the way toward its refinement and strengthening, a task which Origen himself undertook in his response to Celsus. Besides, observing texts undergoing a pagan's assaults has an enduring interest in and of itself. Most of those texts were destined subsequently to provoke the same incredulity from pagan critics. Celsus, in the thoroughly profane manner in which he explains away the sacred Book, is the first link in a long chain of authors critical of the Bible. The scriptural passages that he attacks fall into three groups, according to their subject matter: (1) the life of Jesus and some observations of Pauline origin; (2) certain Christian doctrines, which are a pale reflection of those of the ancient pagan tradition; and (3) contradictions between the message of Moses and that of Jesus.

The New Testament

The Life of Jesus

The first part of Celsus's lampooning of Christianity is a prosopopoeia where he stages a Jewish interlocutor true to his faith, who first inveighs against Jesus and then debates with his former coreligionists who have become Christians. Only in this part does Celsus continually question the figure of Jesus; there are few allusions to him in the other two parts of Celsus's attack.

Origins. From the outset, Celsus's Jew reproaches Jesus, first impeaching his birth "from a virgin" as one of his fabrications. In a Judean village, a poor country girl, convicted of adultery with a soldier named Panthera, driven away by her husband who was a carpenter by trade, became a disgraceful vagabond and gave birth to Jesus in secret (*Contra Celsum* 1.28). The theme of an ignoble birth here was customary in invectives leveled by Greco-Roman orators. There is an analogous distortion of the flight to Egypt: Poverty-stricken, Jesus hired out his services as a workman and learned the tricks of sorcery on account of which, when he returned home, he was reputed to be God (1.28). Was this an echo of slanderous local traditions, later fixed in certain Jewish sources?[3] Perhaps the mention of "Judea," "Egypt," and the "carpenter" echoes the gospel of Matthew, from which Celsus knows the annunciation to Joseph, mentioned further on in his treatise,[4] and the visit of the Magi, which he is about to examine. But already the author's procedure is evident. He selects a few texts of Scripture and then applies his own caustic reading to them. He strips them of every miraculous or providential feature, but retains certain concrete details that he incorporates into his invectives, interpolating them and highlighting them as needed. Reflecting on the patterns of the literature he is using, Celsus determines that nothing in these records of Jesus's origins lends itself to the fiction of a divine birth, such as certain myths contrive. He makes fun of the mother of Jesus with the idea that God could have fallen in love with her, just as Zeus fell in love, once upon a time, with certain mortals (1.37-70; esp. 1.39).

The Visit of the Magi. Celsus's Jewish interlocutor also attacks the account of the visit of the Magi.[5] "Chaldeans, according to the account of Jesus," Origen transcribes, "were moved to come to his birth to worship him as God although he was still an infant." They reported to the king who had his men massacre "those born just at that time" (cf. Matt. 2:1-2; 2:7, 16) for fear that "after he had lived for the time sufficient for him to grow up, he should become king" (1.58; trans. Chadwick, 53). Immediately the alleged royal candidacy of the infant elicits a caricatural recollection of the adult:

> Why then when you were grown up did you not become king, but, though son of God, go about begging so disgracefully, cowering from fear, and wandering up and down in destitution (1.61; trans. Chadwick, 56).

The flight of the baby is but a prelude to the fugitive existence of the man Jesus.[6] What could be more unconscionable than a claim to royalty? Inserted into the middle of the account, Celsus's exaggerated invective undermines it as nothing more than a legend. While any true Jew would admit in principle a providential passage of the family and even an angelic intervention, the Jewish interlocutor of the pagan Celsus rejects them. Celsus rejects them. Returning to the scriptural text, Celsus sifts it through his critical logic. Would a Son of God be afraid of death? Was it necessary for an angel to come from heaven to set up an escape?

> Could not the great God, who had already sent two angels on your account, guard you, His own son, at that very place? (1.66; trans. Chadwick, 60).

Fear, the need for help, escape—all are incompatible with divine omnipotence. Thus, internal criticism alone of the scriptural story demonstrates its improbability and dispels the wonderful halo with which it is arrayed. Neither historical nor mythical, the story of the visit of the Magi is an abortive fiction.

The Baptism of Jesus. Meanwhile the author, drawing "from the gospel according to Matthew and perhaps also from the other gospels," takes up the baptism of Jesus by John (1.40; trans. Chadwick, 174).[7] To his kinsmen, the Jew would present the fact as one of the proofs of the Jewish origin of Christianity, in truth its apostasy from the mother religion, as Origen's protest testifies: "What sort of objection is it to Christianity that 'John who baptized Jesus was a Jew'?" (2.4; trans. Chadwick, 70). He therefore does not deny the historicity of the ceremony. It is the theophany that he repudiates with disdain:

> When you were bathing near John, you say that you saw what ap-
> peared to be a bird fly toward you out of the air...What trustworthy wit-
> ness saw this apparition, or who heard a voice from heaven adopting
> you as son of God? (1.41; trans. Chadwick, 39).

Celsus's Jew can only see these miraculous features as clumsily inserted
into the story. And who are the witnesses? Only the beneficiary, Jesus,
and the single stooge John ("one of the men who were punished with
you")—that is, two accessories destined for the same penalty of death
(1.41; trans. Chadwick, 39).[8]

Miracles. So how then is Celsus to dismiss the whole series of
miracles in the life of Jesus? Using Matthew's gospel, Celsus's Jew mentions several of them (1.34). He gives no thought to comparing them
with miraculous elements in the Bible, with the sequence of the mighty
acts of the Lord and their revelatory significance. He is not his own race's
witness, but the mouthpiece of Celsus; meanwhile the pagan is musing
on mythical marvels, relishing the beauty of Greek literature, of which he
recalls as many titles as he quotes extracts. To be sure, he is less a believer
in the mythical traditions than an aesthete; nevertheless, real or imaginary, the exploits of the Greek heroes find favor in his eyes; they fit the
persons of the demigods:

> But as for you, what have you done in word or deed that is fine or
> wonderful? You showed nothing to us, although they challenged you in
> the temple to produce some obvious token that you were the son of God[9]
> (1.67; trans. Chadwick, 62).

Excluded from the world of the Greek hero, Jesus nonetheless
impressed his own disciples who related their remembrances of his deeds.
Celsus concedes this.[10] But instead of submitting one of Jesus's acts of
power and goodness to critical examination, he simply likens the whole
of them to the practices of the Egyptian sorcerers, of which he is happy to
provide a list.[11]

The reaction of Celsus's Jew is more brutal toward his fellow Jews
who have allegedly told him,

> ...we regarded him as Son of God for this reason, because he healed
> the lame and the blind... (2.48; trans. Chadwick, 102).

Is not this alleged restoration of health, of life itself, merely a de-
lusion? The Jew avoids the question, and drowns his own interlocutors
in a flood of indignation, reminding them of Jesus's own mention of other

sorcerers and of Satan.[12] Jesus does so, as Celsus reiterates later in his treatise, for fear of possible rivals:

> He declares that even Satan himself will appear in a similar way to that in which he has done and will manifest great and amazing works, usurping the glory of God. We must not be deceived by these, nor desire to turn away to Satan, but must believe in him alone[13] (6.42; trans. Chadwick, 357).

Jesus is thus likened to the sorcerers and is among the worst of them because he adds to their kind of deception a sectarianism with respect to false messiahs, with respect to Satan, and foremost with respect to his own circle of followers.[14] Flippant behavior for a God! In the three cases, the signs are the same: Were they acts of divine power, they would give sanction to all who perform them; since they are nothing but sorcery, they discredit all who do them, including Jesus and his followers. Each time Celsus repeats the argument and dispenses with any critical assessment of the testimonies.

Public life. This recollection of the figure of Jesus tells the whole story: His public life was full of misery, impotence, and malevolence. But it is precisely in his physical constitution and demeanor that we observe characteristics unworthy of God. The body of a God would not be like that of Jesus, nor born like he was (1.69-70); nor would a God eat the meat of sheep, nor drink vinegar or gall[15] (7.13).

> If a divine spirit was in a body, it must certainly have differed from other bodies in size or beauty or strength or voice or striking appearance or powers of persuasion. For it is impossible that a body which had something more divine than the rest should be no different from any other[16] (6.75; trans. Chadwick, 388).

Celsus's Jew had said the same thing:

> The body of a God does not use a voice of that kind, nor that method of persuasion (1.70; trans. Chadwick, 64).

> [Jesus] utters threats and empty abuse whenever he says, Woe unto you, and, I declare unto you.[17] For in these words he openly admits his inability to carry conviction, which no god, nor even a sensible man, would fail to do (2.76; trans. Chadwick, 123).

In short, not a trace of the divine supernatural can be found in Jesus's entire life. So how would there have been any trace of it in his Passion and death?

Passion. The Jewish interlocutor formulates his principal indictment right out of his invective against Jesus: In his suffering, "he was not helped by his Father, nor was he able to help himself" (1.54; trans. Chadwick, 50). Instead, he orchestrated it in discussion with his followers. From his torture to being suspended on a cross, he underwent the phases of the experience; yet in his conduct there was not a trace of heroism, only passivity and total powerlessness, and the attitude of a guilty man, justly punished. The circumstances were like an ultimate challenge, a putting to the test, a sort of ordeal from which he would have to emerge the victor. His inability to meet the challenge gave the lie to any divine quality either antecedently pretended by him or later on attributed to him. By itself the Passion demonstrates his imposture and justifies refusal to believe in him.[18]

How miserable henceforth was the expedient to which the disciples of Jesus resorted in order to obviate an inevitable objection to Jesus's reputation! The Jew indicts them accordingly:

> As the disciples of Jesus were unable to conceal the self-evident fact, they conceived this idea of saying that he foreknew everything (2.15; trans. Chadwick, 81).

For Celsus, this prediction is authentic, at least in the sense that the scriptural authors recorded it just that way in their account. It was not historical, as Jesus never uttered it, but was interpolated in the text. Many factors would prove that the authors were bent on developing the text in such a way as to stave off what was doubtless a frequent allegation against Jesus. For one thing, a prediction like this was inconceivable, counter to the very nature of things and the obvious incompatibility of Jesus's servile condition with the stature of a divine being.[19] In addition, were it really that of a divinity, the prediction would have been effective. Apprised ahead of time, a god, demon, or even a sensible human being would not have fallen headlong into danger (2.17). And if the disciples were informed ahead of time by the very one whom they considered God, "why did they not fear him as God, so that the one did not betray him nor the other deny him?" (2.18, trans. Chadwick, 83; cf. 2.19). Besides, if the prediction were actually God's, it would render the resultant event inevitable. God would then have to assume responsibility for it:

> A god, therefore, led his own disciples and prophets with whom he used to eat and drink[20] so far astray that they became impious and wicked.

But a god above all ought to have done good to all men, in particular to those who have lived with him[21] (2.20; trans. Chadwick, 84).

Finally, if he was God and willed what happened to him, the mistreatments would have been "neither painful nor grievous to him" (2.23; trans. Chadwick, 87).

Why then does he utter loud laments and wailings, and pray that he may avoid the fear of death, saying something like this, 'O Father, if this cup could pass by me'?[22] (2.24; trans. Chadwick, 88).

The Jew can thus conclude: We are dealing with a false prophet, and the authors of the gospels have falsified the truth (2.26-27).

Undoubtedly Christians added the prophecies of the Old Testament to Jesus's own predictive prophecy. But it was all in vain. Celsus's Jew reiterates that the prophecies could be applied to an infinity of other characters "far more plausibly than to Jesus" (2.28; trans. Chadwick, 91; cf. 1.50, 57). Dispensing with rigorous logic[23] for the sake of another effective contrast, he declares:

The prophets say that the one who will come will be a great prince, lord of the whole earth and of all nations and armies (2.29; trans. Chadwick, 91)...

As the sun which illuminates everything else first shows itself, so ought the Son of God to have done (2.30; trans. Chadwick, 92).

Nor can the sophisms of Christians vouch for the promise of such a glory,

when they say that the Son of God is the very Logos himself,...[and yet] do not bring forward as evidence a pure and holy Logos, but a man who was arrested most disgracefully and crucified (2.31; trans. Chadwick, 92-93)...

[or when] the men who compiled the genealogy of Jesus boldly said that Jesus was descended from the first man and from the kings of the Jews[24] (2.32; trans. Chadwick, 93).

Moreover, since the noble pagan is more celebrated than the educated Jew, Celsus's Jewish interlocutor makes the gospel story appear more miserable to the pagan when he asks, "What fine action did Jesus do like a god? Did he despise men's opposition and laugh and mock at the disaster that befell him?" (2.33; trans. Chadwick, 94). Jesus had no assurance before God;[25] and there was no punishment of the one who condemned him,[26] any more than of...

266

those who mocked him and put a purple robe round him and the crown of thorns and the reed in his hand[27] (2.34; trans. Chadwick, 95).

In short, there is nothing of the hero of the classical authors in the victim of this drama: no action, word, or distinctive bodily sign;[28] on the contrary, there is an attitude unworthy even of an ordinary human being. When given the vinegar and gall on the cross,

...he rushed greedily to drink[29] and did not bear his thirst patiently as even an ordinary man often bears it (2.37; trans. Chadwick, 96).

And the ultimate scandal of Jesus's Passion is that one cannot conceive of any final purpose for as many sufferings; yet Christians allege that...

he endured these sufferings for the benefit of mankind, in order that we also may despise punishments (2.38; trans. Chadwick, 97).

An absurd rationalization in the eyes of an indignant author. One could just as easily apply it to all even more miserable executed criminals, to whom one could attribute the same ability to predict future sufferings as Jesus allegedly had (2.44). The Christians' claim that his suffering "was meant to destroy the father of evil" provokes the same response[30] (2.47; trans. Chadwick, 102).

Resurrection. The account of Jesus's Resurrection is treated as an appendix to that of his death, with the same acerbic criticism aimed at unraveling the moral of the story. Once again Celsus's Jew raises the issue of Jesus's power of prediction.

What led you to believe, except that he foretold that after his death he would rise again? (2.54; trans. Chadwick, 108).

Introducing an account of extraordinary adventures with a prediction is the practice of unscrupulous individuals. It is a literary motif at the beginning of narratives which dramatically portray famous persons and make them disappear and then reappear.[31] One must, however, observe the nature of these persons' recorded acts in order to determine the proper account to be given of them:

But we must examine this question whether anyone who really died ever rose again with the same body (2.55; trans. Chadwick, 109).

The answer, here implied as self-evident, is developed at length elsewhere in Celsus's treatise: The resurrection of the flesh is impossible; the very supposition of it is repugnant (5:14). From then on, prediction and the staging of its fulfilment belong to the same phantasmagory: Prophecy has no object; it is fictional narrative, a fable. The only acceptable biographical evidence of the Passion is the diverse vicissitudes of the drama, stripped of every interpolated element. What should strike us, however, is how this story unfolds as a thoroughgoing fairy-tale through a dramatization of death that defies all standards:

> Or do you think that the stories of these others really are the legends which they appear to be, and yet that the ending of your tragedy is to be regarded as noble and convincing—his cry from the cross when he expired, and the earthquake and the darkness?"[32] (2.55; trans. Chadwick, 109).

For Celsus, the Resurrection is part of the same fairy-tale as the Passion, in total defiance of the apostolic testimonies.[33] Celsus can hardly touch on two points from the Resurrection accounts in the gospel without his scorn being aroused:

> While he was alive he did not help himself, but after death he rose again and showed the marks of his punishment and how his hands had been pierced. But who saw this? A hysterical female, as you say, and perhaps some other one of those who were deluded by the same sorcery...[34] (2.55; trans. Chadwick, 109).

Was the Resurrection anything other than the resuscitation of a memory or a figment of the imagination? Was it not merely the vision of an excited woman, or of someone naturally prone to dreaming or else deceived by an imaginary representation ("an experience which has happened to thousands"), or better yet, a phenomenon of hallucination (2.55)? Further along in his treatise, Celsus would dispel the myth of another glorious appearance from the Resurrection stories:

> Furthermore, they say that an angel came to the tomb of this very man (some say one angel, some two), who replied to the women that he was risen (5.52; trans. Chadwick, 305).

The angels' intervention here is no more admissible than the intervention of angels in the stories of Jesus's infancy, the latter of which he had not mentioned until now[35] (5.52).

Thus reduced, the portrayal of the resurrected Jesus is appended to the embellished portrayal of Jesus's death as a kind of *deus ex machina* meant to quell the abuse of a badly composed story by throwing in an episode from a wonderful fairy-tale. Poor pastiche, muses the educated interlocutor of Celsus, pretending to correct it:

> [Jesus] ought, in order to display his divinity, to have disappeared suddenly from the cross...he ought to have appeared to the very men who treated him despitefully and to the man who condemned him and to everyone everywhere...he ought to have called all men clearly to the light and taught them why he came down (2.68, 63, 73; trans. Chadwick, 118, 114, 122).

Christians. Celsus adds little to the criticisms of his Jewish spokesman on this point.[36] Christian propaganda becomes the target of violent satire. An elite had been called to initiations into the ancient mysteries, but only a rabble was summoned to initiation into Christianity.

> Whosoever is a sinner, they say, whosoever is unwise, whosoever is a child, and, in a word, whosoever is a wretch, the kingdom of God will receive him[37]...What others would a robber invite and call? (3.59; trans. Chadwick, 168; cf. 3.44).

Christians deny the divinization of the Greco-Roman heroes, yet affirm that...

> after Jesus died he appeared to his own confraternity...[but they say] he appeared even then only as a phantom (3.22; trans. Chadwick, 140).

Imagining God as a corporeal being in human form, Christians desire a physical resurrection in order to attain it corporeally. Would that they would go to the temples where gods appear in human form!

> One may see them, not merely making a single appearance in a stealthy and secretive manner like the fellow who deceived the Christians, but continually having communion with any who so desire[38] (7.35; trans. Chadwick, 423).

One last time, in connection with oracles, Celsus the pagan honors some ancient heroes who have become the object of a divine myth, and then some sages from history for their superhuman courage as manifested by what they said when they were tortured: "What comparable saying did your God utter while he was being punished?" And he concludes this long discussion by saying that Jesus was even inferior to certain figures from the Bible!

> A far more suitable person for you than Jesus would have been Jonah with his gourd, or Daniel who escaped from wild beasts,[39] or those of whom stories yet more incredible than these are told (7.53; trans. Chadwick, 440).

St. Paul

Celsus uses a Pauline source to ridicule some of the Christian prating. Origen in his turn establishes the authentic quotation from Paul that he is using and interprets it in the light of its context and parallels.

For Celsus, a rebellious spirit has characterized Christianity from its inception and throughout its history (3.5-14). Probing into the Christians' doctrine of God,[40] among other of their beliefs, he discovers a whole proliferation of sects, and the ultimate scandal of it is that the whole lot of them, "who disagree so violently and by their strife refute themselves to their utter disgrace," will wear themselves out repeating the phrase "The world is crucified unto me and I to the world" (Gal. 6:14) (5.64; trans. Chadwick, 314). They justify their ignorance and their contempt of culture when they say, "The wisdom in the world is an evil, and foolishness a good thing" (1.9; trans. Chadwick, 12), or "the wisdom possessed by men is foolishness with God" (6.12; trans. Chadwick, 325). Origen of course corrects this misrepresentation by quoting and explaining Paul's actual words in 1 Corinthians 3:19 (6.12-13).

To the intolerance of Christians, Celsus counters: "If, as they say, they abstain [from partaking of meat sacrificed to idols] to avoid feasting with demons" (8.28; trans. Chadwick, 471), then they will have to give up the things the demons bestow for the sustenance of life, the human and social activities over which the demons preside, and, indeed, the health of the body, parts of which are entrusted to as many demons (8.24-33, 53-58). Origen's response, point by point, has a Pauline inspiration, namely the passage concerning meat sacrificed to idols and the defense against "entering into communion with demons..., participating in the Lord's table and the table of demons" (cf. 1 Cor. 10:20, 21, quoted by Origen in 8.24).

We should add that the term *skubala*, "rubbish," which Paul uses to describe his own Jewish credentials and his own righteousness before God (Phil. 3:8), is known by Celsus, who in turn applies it to Christians.[41]

Scripture and Ancient Tradition

The Gospel as literature is inferior in comparison with the Greco-Roman myths and tales; Christianity and Judaism are inferior as religions in comparison with paganism. Celsus gives the reason for these facts, in the fragments which follow his Preface, by outlining a history in three intervals. In the beginning there was a liberal religion in which faith in the supreme God coexisted with the cult of subordinate and intermediary deities.[42] Moses distorted it into a sectarian monotheism, thus fanaticizing his uncultivated people; and Jesus, who was an adherent to the Jewish faith, in turn came to introduce another change by passing himself off as the Son of God (1.26). Two impostors, a double apostasy. Succession and degradation. The process that revealed the "true doctrine" of God proved its integrity among all remaining peoples of the earth, until the advent of Christianity, which is destitute of all originality and beauty.

In relation to the pagan tradition of doctrine and custom (*logos* and *nomos*), descended from time immemorial and genuinely shared among barbarian and Greek peoples alike, the Christian innovation, being severed from this majestic heritage of thought and practice, offers only pieces, poor plagiarisms, counterfeits. What is more, the doctrines of multisecular culture had received from the Greeks an admirable literary and intellectual legacy.[43] Among Christians, however, form is as impoverished as thought. In Celsus view, there is, on the level both of human beings and cultures, very high nobility on the one hand and common stock on the other. Celsus plays with this contrast, exalting and demeaning as he wills. In accordance with a ritual common in the literary genre of the eulogy, he composes or transcribes an anthology of long quotations from renowned authors whom he honors as sages, scholars, philosophers, poets, holy men, inspired persons, divines. In contrast with this brilliant mosaic, he presents a medley of obscure forms,[44] or at best poor imitations. And like Jesus and his community, they are, together with their devotees, sitting ducks for insult, irony, sarcasm, pressing troubles, and other forms of invective.[45] They are denounced throughout Celsus's treatise for corrupting ideas and vulgarizing form.[46] His criticism pounces on St. Paul, on the Gospel, and especially on the book of Genesis.

St. Paul

Celsus innovatively denounces Paul and one of his maxims popular with Christians, that "Human wisdom is foolishness with God" (1 Cor. 3:19). Christians say this precisely because they "aim to convert only the uneducated and stupid," but in fact "this notion was invented by us...and was taken over from the Greek wise men who said that human wisdom is one thing and divine wisdom another" (6.12; trans. Chadwick, 325, 326). As proof of the plagiarism, he quotes both Heraclitus and Plato.[47]

The Gospel

Jesus' judgment against the rich, when he said "It is easier for a camel to go through the eye of a needle than for a rich man to enter the Kingdom of God", was manifestly borrowed from Plato[48] (6.16; trans. Chadwick, 329).

Passages relating to the Kingdom of God and to the supercelestial God come right out of "inspired utterances" of Plato on the King of the universe and the divine essence[49] (6.17-19).

271

> They have also a precept to this effect—that you must not resist a man who insults you. Even, he says, if someone strikes you on one cheek, yet you should offer the other as well (7.58; trans. Chadwick, 443).

Celsus opposes this short gospel saying with a whole handsome page from Plato, where it is said in substance that one must not commit injustice, nor do any wrong to others, but must refrain from responding to injustice with injustice, or rendering evil for evil[50] (7.58).

In the Christian "doctrine about Satan" Celsus sees the fearful expectation Jesus had of a rival sorcerer or of many such rivals, and the absurd notion that he sustained chastisement from the devil. Even in this distorted form, this doctrine recalls the "divine war" hinted at enigmatically in tales told by ancient Greek authors, though it obviously possesses not even a fraction of the nobility of these venerable myths (6.42).[51]

One of Celsus's more violent criticisms is directed against the notion of God as Spirit, employed with respect to Jesus, "the Son" whom Christians allege is a "spirit derived from God who was born in a human body" (6.71-72; trans. Chadwick, 385-386); but there is no allusion to any Scripture other than John 4:24.[52] Celsus judges that when Christians say "God is spirit,"

> ...there is in this respect no difference between [Christians] and the Stoics among the Greeks, who affirm that God is spirit that has permeated all things and contains all things within itself (6.71; trans. Chadwick, 385).

Genesis

Celsus takes to task those passages from Genesis having to do with divine intervention, the creation of Adam, the history of the patriarchs, allegory, and the origins of the world and humanity.

Divine intervention. Jews and Christians alike claim in their favor a divine intervention in the world,[53] and a divine descent to earth in order to judge its inhabitants (4.2). Celsus thus sees here another travesty of an ancient belief in the cosmic cycle return punctuated by the alternation of deluge and conflagration.[54] In mythology, the myths of Deucalion and Phaethon explained this grand cosmological thesis; in the Bible, the story of a divine punishment through water and fire.

> The Jews say that as life is filled with all manner of evil it is necessary for God to send someone down that the wicked may be punished and everything purified, as it was when the first flood occurred (4.20; trans. Chadwick, 197).

Celsus—"for some unknown reason," says Origen—sees the destruction of the Tower of Babel as serving the same purpose as the Flood in Genesis (4.21; trans. Chadwick, 197). Apparently he did so in order to denounce another plagiarism: "Moses...corrupted the story about the sons of Aloeus when he composed the narrative about the tower" (4.21; trans. Chadwick, 198). Celsus further compares the myth of Phaethon with Moses's story of Sodom and Gomorrah, which were destroyed because of their sin (4.21).[55]

> Christians also add certain doctrines to those maintained by the Jews, and assert that the Son of God has already come on account of the Jews, and that because the Jews punished Jesus and gave him gall to drink[56] they drew down upon themselves the bitter anger of God (4.22, trans. Chadwick, 198).

Yet Christians and Jews alike ridiculously presume that they are the center of the world, the objects of God's preferential treatment.[57] He recalls in particular the Jews' sense of a special election, and ridicules it using a classic antisemitic stereotype from Greek literature.[58]

The origin of the first man. Already among ancient peoples, Celsus asserts, certain men were said to have been born of the soil of the earth.

> Jews, being bowed down in some corner of Palestine, were totally uneducated and had not heard of these things which were sung in poetry long before by Hesiod and thousands of inspired men. They composed a most improbable and crude story...

Looking over the second creation account (Gen. 2:4b-3:24), Celsus discovers merely the makings of a fable:

> ...that a man was formed by the hands of God and given breath, that a woman was formed out of his side, that God gave commands, and that a serpent opposed them and even proved superior to the ordinances of God[59]— a legend which they expound to old women, most impiously making God into a weakling right from the beginning, and incapable of persuading even one man whom He had formed (4.36; trans. Chadwick, 212).

Continuing his reading of the Genesis account, Celsus scarcely finds anything better:

> Then they tell of a flood and a prodigious ark holding everything inside it, and that a dove and a crow were messengers.[60] This is a debased and unscrupulous version of the story of Deucalion; I suppose they did not expect that this would come to light, but simply recounted the myth to small children (4.41; trans. Chadwick, 217).

The history of the patriarchs. Celsus similarly glances over the history of the patriarchs in Genesis, isolating anecdotes that he considers ridiculous, salacious, and unbelievable:

> Utterly absurd also is the begetting of children when the parents were too old (cf. Gen. 21:1-7);...the conspiracies of the brothers (25:29-34; 27:18-29);...the father's grief (37:33-35);...the treacheries of mothers (27:5-17);...[that] God entered into the closest contact with [these men];...[that] God made a present to the sons of asses, sheep, and camels (13:2; 30:43); ...[that] God also gave wells to the thirsty (16:14; 21:19; 26:22);...the marriages [and] the intercourse of [righteous] men with [different] women...brides and maidservants (16:1ff);...[the story of] daughters...more iniquitous than Thyestian sins (19:30-38);...[stories of] hatred (27:41-45);..[of those who] went forth because of the insult to their sister (34:25-31);...brothers trading [and] a brother sold (37:26-28);...a father who was deceived (37:31-35);...[stories of] dreams [and] their explanation (40:1-19; 41:1-36);...[that] the one who was sold was kind to his brothers who sold him...(42-44);...[that Joseph] made himself known (45:1-4);...[that] the man who was sold to be a slave, was set free and with a solemn procession returned to his father's tomb (50:4-14);..[that] by him [Joseph] the distinguished and marvelous race of the Jews, which in Egypt had increased to a multitude, were commanded to live somewhere outside and to tend their flocks in land that was valueless;...[and that there was a] flight [of the Jews from Egypt]... (4.42-47; trans. Chadwick, 218-222).

Doubtless Celsus sees in these passages from Genesis a heap of legends, lampooning and branding them in the way that he designates and characterizes them.

The refusal of allegory. Celsus does not ignore allegorical interpretation; indeed he allows it for the the Greek myths and Egyptian mysteries (cf. 6.42). But in the case here of the Hebrew Scriptures it would be groundless, in spite of the contrary view of "the more reasonable Jews and Christians [who] allegorize these things" (4.48; trans. Chadwick, 223). He knows that such an intellectual elite exists, but he categorically refuses them the alternative of allegory.[61] The divine intervention that they allege is simply impossible; not only in the sense of God intervening in their favor—they are unworthy of it!—but in the sense that it is intrinsically contrary to the immutable perfection of God and to the invariable order of the world.[62] False too is the idea of God creating the material creation, and vain is the hope of a divine judgment. Every anthropomorphic interpretation of these cosmic events is absurd. Moreover, in the order of nature, what appears superficially an evil can be useful for oneself, for others, and for the whole universe (4.70). This is why it is a crude error to ascribe to God "angry utterances" against the impious, and "threats" against sinners. To attribute human passions to God is an impiety (4.71-72). History itself gives the lie to this pretended "wrath" of God.[63]

The origins of the world and of humanity. Celsus returns to the matter of cosmic origins and refutes Judeo-Christian conceptions, but even more vehemently the biblical narrative itself. First, he levels against the account as a whole:

> Therefore both the Jews and these people [Christians] have the same God... Obviously the members of the great Church confess this, and believe that the story of the making of the world (cf. Gen. 1-2) current among Jews is true even in respect of the six days and the seventh in which...God rested (2:2-3);...[of the first man, Christians] say he was the same man as the Jews do, and...trace the genealogical descent from him like them (1:26-27; 11:10-32);...[Christians] tell of the same plots of brothers against one another as the Jews do (4:8; 27:41-45);...[and of] the same departure to Egypt as they do, and the same...flight... (5.59; trans. Chadwick, 310).

Leaving the patriarchs, Celsus further criticizes the Genesis cosmogony as naive and stupid:

> Besides, the cosmogony too is very silly...[and] the record of the origin of man is also very silly...the paradise planted by God (Gen. 2:8), and the life which the man lived in it in the first place, and that which came to pass through force of circumstances when the man was banished on account of his sin and made to live opposite the paradise of luxury (3:24)... (6.49; trans. Chadwick, 365, 366).

> Is it anything more than a bad poem?[64]

Celsus then turns his criticism to the specifics of the first creation story (Gen. 1:1-2:4a):

> ...far more silly is to have allotted certain days to the making of the world before days existed. For when the heaven had not yet been made, or the earth yet fixed, or the sun borne round it, how could days exist? (6.60; trans. Chadwick, 375).

Not only the idea of days before days even existed, but the whole sequence of divine commands and workings on those days, and the fatigue inherent in God's labor (as if God needed a holiday to rest!) are all nothing more than human and materialistic representations unworthy of the first and supreme God (6.60-62). It only follows that Celsus would reject another important statement in the biblical account:

Nor did he make man his image (cf. Gen. 1:26-27); for God is not like that, nor does he resemble any other form at all (6.63; trans. Chadwick, 378; cf. 7.62).

Moses and Jesus

Between the two worlds of the venerable culture of antiquity on the one hand, and the lack of culture among Jews and Christians on the other, Celsus sees only a great abyss. The first world is homogeneous; the second is not. And in the third major part of his polemic, Celsus carries out his labor of dissection no longer between these two worlds, but within the second, or rather within the Scripture that Judaism and Christianity share. As part of his strategy he juxtaposes the Marcionite sect, among others, with the Great Church; in fact, he borrows from the Marcionite position, combats its theology, and takes inspiration from its method all in the course of his argumentation. Celsus mentions the principal thesis of Marcionism: that there is a demiurge, or evil creator of an evil world, and a good God, alien to the world, from whom Jesus comes.[65] He attacks this view as though it were common among all Christians. And yet, like the Marcionites, he designates in the biblical text certain *antitheses*[66] between Moses and Jesus, their laws, and their Gods.

Setting the stage, Celsus mentions certain groups in the foreground. Beside "the members of the great Church," who have the same God as the Jews and the same tradition about the origins of the world (5.59; trans. Chadwick, 310), there are among the sects...

> those who because of the teaching of the name of Jesus have departed from the Creator as an inferior being, and have gone to a God whom they regard as superior, who is Father of him who came... (5.54; trans. Chadwick, 306; cf. also 5.61).

Elsewhere the distinction of groups seems to break down. Having eulogized the Mithraic rite of initiation (6.22), and in order to accentuate "the difference between them" (6.24; trans. Chadwick, 337), Celsus denigrates "a mystery of the Christians" with sarcastic and obscure allusions. The Mithraic rite aims at the application of a "seal" in the presence of seven angels of light and seven archontic angels; accordingly, "the chief of those called archontic angels is said to be an accursed God," that is...

> the God of the Jews...being the God who sends rain and thunder, and who is the Creator of this world and the God of Moses, described in his accounts of the creation of the world (6.27; trans. Chadwick, 342, 343).

276

This being the teaching of Marcion, Celsus sees it as further reinforced in the doctrine of another group (the Ophites, whom he does not mention by name):

> Such a God deserves to be cursed in the opinion of those who hold this view of him, because he cursed the serpent which imparted to the first men knowledge of good and evil[67] (6.28; trans. Chadwick, 343-344).

Would Celsus suddenly ignore how lightly he had taken the Genesis account of the origins of the world? He guards against doing so, having kept his critical distance. What he speaks of is "in the opinion of those who hold this view." The opinion is not his own; he is simply reporting it. As for the Marcionite teaching, he indiscriminately attributes it to Christians by a kind *coup de théâtre* that he loves to employ. Entering the scene, he explodes into a tirade against them and their notion of two Gods:

> What could be sillier or crazier than this blockheaded wisdom? For why did the Jews' lawgiver make a mistake? And if he did, why do you accept his cosmogony or the law of the Jews interpreting it as an allegory, as you say, while you only grudgingly praise the Creator of the world, you most impious fellow, though he promised the Jews everything, declaring that he would increase their race to the ends of the earth[68] and would raise them up from the dead with the same flesh and blood, and inspired the prophets; and yet you pour abuse on him? But when you are put in difficulties by the Jews, you confess that you worship the same God. Yet when your master Jesus and Moses, in whom the Jews believe, lay down contradictory laws, you try to find another God instead of this one who is the Father (6.29; trans. Chadwick, 344-345).

Celsus develops this theme of contrary laws in one of the sections that he dedicates to the superiority of the pagan oracles to the Jewish prophets. He honors the power of the oracles, and then, having unleashed against the vaticinators of Phoenicia and Palestine, resumes his criticism of prophecy, which he had already undertaken in connection with the Passion.[69] And yet his examination of the prophetic message furnishes a new reason for rejecting it. Celsus discovers a contradiction which would seem to originate with God: God gives certain laws to Moses, and through his son predicts contrary laws. Celsus provides a whole list of legislative antitheses:

> If the prophets of the God of the Jews foretold that Jesus would be his son, why did he give them laws by Moses that they were to become rich and powerful and to fill the earth (cf., e.g. Gen. 8:17; 9:1-7; 16:10) and to massacre their enemies, children and all, and slaughter their en-

tire race (Exod. 17:13ff; Num. 21:34ff), which he himself did, so Moses says (Exod. 34:11; Deut. 29:1-2), before the eyes of the Jews? And besides this, if they were not obedient, why does he expressly threaten to do to them what he did to their enemies (Deut. 1:26ff; 7:4)? Yet his son, the man of Nazareth, gives contradictory laws, saying that a man cannot come forward to the Father if he is rich (Matt. 19:24) or loves power (Matt. 20:25-27) or lays claim to any intelligence or reputation (Matt. 11:25), and that he must not pay attention to food or to his storehouse anymore than the ravens, or to clothing any more than the lilies (Matt. 6:25-31), and that to a man who has struck him once he should offer himself to be struck again (Matt. 5:39)? Who is wrong? Moses or Jesus? Or when the Father sent Jesus had he forgotten what commands he gave to Moses? Or did he condemn his own laws and change his mind, and send his messenger for quite the opposite purpose? (7.18; trans. Chadwick, 409).

There is a certain train of thought in the pamphleteer's ideas. He crashes the Law and the Gospel into each other in order to disqualify Scripture, Moses, Jesus, and God all at once.

Conclusion

"Jews demand signs and Greeks seek wisdom" (1 Cor. 1:22). The pagan Celsus demands both, but only such signs and wisdom as his culture reveals to him. From his own cultural landscape he recalls, indeed he admits uncritically, the whole marvelous Greco-Roman tradition of myths and fictions, with their heroes haloed in the glory of superhuman acts. But with the outstanding features in Celsus's caricature of Jesus— his unusual birth; his hard up youth, which forced him into exile for a time; his uprooted life; his suffering as a weakling; his death as a culpable criminal; his message, which amounted to nothing more than a pretension to being God's Son; the fact that his pretension was built on magic tricks learned in Egypt, and undermined by his fear of the rivals he denounced and by his inability to persuade anyone, and betrayed by his empty threats—we are far from the Greco-Roman myths. With such a profile, we are also far removed, however, from the gospel story, from the memories the disciples had of Jesus while they were on the road, and from the "prophet mighty in deed and word before God and all the people" (Luke 24:19). Such vitriol ultimately hinders the process of Celsus's criticism: How can it really penetrate deep faith? Celsus's is an impassioned reclamation of the autonomy of reason, and of the culture that it procures, over against the mystery of the incarnate and redemptive Word, of the living God of Scripture who intervenes in human history. Celsus's rejection of this basis of faith renders the whole of Christianity incomprehensible and ridiculous.

Origen welcomes the divine intervention that Scripture attests. He rereads the biblical texts, brings them together, compares them, and uses them to reinforce each other. The historicity of the life of Jesus is admitted on the basis of faith in witnesses; and his identity as God-Man, in all the circumstances and acts of his birth, life, Passion , and Resurrection, even though that identity was disclosed through diverse "aspects" (*epinoiai*), is discernible according to the spiritual capacity of the believer. Origen alludes to this divine-human life of Jesus as rooted in sacred history. Distinct from pagan predictions, Old Testament prophecies announced Jesus and he in turn fulfilled them. Jesus himself pronounced other prophecies, some of which came to pass and others of which, like those concerning universalism, were on their way to being fulfilled. Distinct from the pagan marvels, miracles of the biblical prophets prefigured those in the Gospel, and Jesus's miracles on human bodies symbolized his spiritual action of healing and life. His power continued always to be exerted, in visible and invisible effects, in churches constituted of converts, most of whom were simple people, nonetheless people liberated from sin and devoted to virtue. In short, Origen linked the life of Christ to the whole of Scripture, which he interpreted by itself, and to the whole life of the Church.

The same goes for Christian doctrines. Celsus dismantles them even more than the scriptural stories, setting against them beautiful extracts from ancient authors aimed at making innovators aware of their dependence on, and imitation of, that venerable tradition, and of their inferiority to it in foundation and in form; this Celsus underscores with abusive interjections. Origen agrees that Scripture is very simple in its style. But he praises it as such for being more accessible and having an entirely different efficacy (6.1-2), and he demonstrates in particular the profundity of its thought. Origen reconciles the Christian theme of the light of grace coming from God with Platonic themes of the interior illumination required for knowing the Sovereign Being. He compares the wisdom of Solomon, the apostle Paul, and other saints with that of Plato and the ancients (6.5, 13-14; 3.45 and 34). He brings to life the richness of the biblical tradition in confronting every subject raised by Celsus. The quite human history of the patriarchs is accepted as actual; yet Origen at the same time speaks of allegory and illustrates the allegorical interpretation of that history (4.43ff). Moreover, the events preceding the patriarchal history really did happen, understanding here particularly the flood and Noah's ark, of which Origen gives an elaborate description (4.41). The second creation account in Genesis is richer in its hidden teaching than any comparable page from Hesiod or Plato. But every resemblance to mythical depictions is purely accidental, and thus to refer to them as sources is wholly arbitrary.[70] By itself, the first creation account is not a narration: Creation was an act of God, but it was not recounted in chronological order, and the anthropomorphisms applied to God within it have only an allegorical meaning.

The same holds true for certain of the Mosaic laws, with respect to crass expressions concerning wealth, power, domination, and massacre. As Origen spends many chapters showing (7.18-25), these cannot be taken literally in many passages of the Old Testament as well as the New. In certain cases—the massacre of enemies, for example—the proper sense of the text amounts to a moment in the divine economy, where the survival of the people whom Providence is leading to the more perfect kingdom of Christians must be assured. But such a disposition to slaughter is no longer valid for those Gentile or Jewish converts, subject to Roman law, who would come to faith in Jesus Christ; indeed it is no longer valid even for Jews who are currently deprived of their city and of the temple where they once celebrated their service to God through cult and sacrifice (7.26). Like the ancient institutions of the Old Testament, the ancient law has no more value than its spiritual meanings, which are made explicit through the inspired letter and providential events. Neither Moses nor Jesus contradict themselves or speak untruths. They express the one will of God. In this way, Origen the apologist presented an able defense of his cause, and could say, with his teacher Paul, "We preach Christ crucified, a stumbling block to Jews and folly to Gentiles, but to those who are called, both Jews and Greeks, Christ the power of God and the wisdom of God (1 Cor. 1:23-24).

NOTES

1. See *Origène: Contre Celse*, critical ed. of the Greek text with French trans. by M. Borret, Sources chrétiennes [SC] 132, 136, 147, 150, 227 (Paris, 1967, 1968, 1969, 1976). For the dates of the *Contra Celsum*, see SC 132: 15-21; and of Celsus's *The True Doctrine*, SC 227: 122-129. On the pagan book itself, see SC 226: 9-121; and on Origen's "demonstration," ibid., 207-246. On the principal features of Celsus's attack on Christianity, see R. L. Wilken, *The Christians as the Romans Saw Them* (New Haven and London, 1984), 94-125. The best English translation of Origen's apology is H. Chadwick, ed. and trans., *Origen: Contra Celsum* (Cambridge,

1965). (Chadwick's translation of the *Contra Celsum* has been used throughout this English edition of Borret's essay—Ed.).

2. Cf. SC 227; for the German publisher of the *Contra Celsum*, see ibid., 36 (n. 2) and 144ff; on the more recent research, see the critical bibliography, ibid., 145-198; on the results that utilize and prolong our attempt at analysis, ibid., 29-121.

3. There is a double reference to Jewish sources in SC 132: 151ff, notes. On the possible Jewish polemical sources used by Celsus, see M. Lods, "Études sur les sources juives de la polémique de Celse contre les chrétiens," *Revue d'histoire et de philosophie religieuses* 21 (1941): 1-33.

4. Cf. Matt. 2:1, 13-14; 13:55; *Contra Celsum* 5.52.

5. He is mistaken about the identity of the visitors and of the reigning prince: not Chaldeans but Magi; not Herod the Tetrarch but his brother, Herod the Great.

6. Indigence and flight are other themes common in rhetorical invective. Used of the pauper Mary, we see it enhanced again here with respect to Jesus—the [ig]noble monarch with his court to match, a handful of individual birds of the same feather! "Jesus collected around him ten or eleven infamous men, the most wicked tax-collectors and sailors, and with these fled hither and thither, collecting a means of livelihood in a disgraceful and importunate way" (1.62; trans. Chadwick, 56). "When he was alive he won over only ten sailors and tax-collectors of the most abominable character, and not even all of these..." (2.46; trans. Chadwick, 101). The accusation of escape is repeated against Jesus and his family (1.66; 5.52), Jesus at his arrest (2.9), and the Jewish people exiting Egypt (4.47).

7. Origen accuses Celsus of disturbing the order of the facts, one example among others of his lack of method.

8. Celsus doubtless depends here on Matt. 3:16-17 and John 1:32. But, Origen replies, the assimilation of Jesus and John does not fit the character of the Jew: "For the Jews do not connect John with Jesus, nor the punishment of John with that of Jesus" (1.48, trans. Chadwick, 46; cf. 1.89-98).

9. Cf. John 10:23-24. The Synoptic Gospels attribute the challenge to the high priest (cf. Matt. 26:63). But here the testimony is truncated. Jesus's response—"The works that I do in my Father's name, they bear witness to me" (John 10:25)—is omitted. Origen, without quoting it, opposes the legendary exploits of the Greek heroes with the idea of God's ever current action: "We affirm that the whole human world has evidence of the work of Jesus since in it dwell the churches of God which consist of people converted through Jesus from countless evils" (1.67; trans. Chadwick, 62).

10. He pretends to concede what the Scriptures had to say about "cures or resurrection or a few loaves feeding many people, from which many fragments were left over (cf. Matt. 13:14-21; 15:32-38)..." (1.68; trans. Chadwick, 62).

11. "[the Egyptian sorcerers] drive daemons out of men and blow away dis-

eases and invoke the souls of heroes, displaying expensive banquets and dining-tables and cakes and dishes which are non-existent, and...make things move as though they were alive although they are not really so, but only appear as such in the imagination" (1.68; trans. Chadwick, 63). Suddenly having done with his mockery, he becomes fearful: "Since these men do these wonders, ought we to think them sons of God? Or ought we to say that they are the practices of wicked men possessed by an evil daemon?" (ibid.). On the context and ramifications of the dispute between Celsus and Origen over the figure and miracles of Jesus, see E. Gallagher, *Divine Man or Magician: Celsus and Origen on Jesus* (Chico, Cal., 1981).

12. "O light and truth, with his own voice he [Jesus] explicitly confesses, as even you have recorded, that there will come among you others also who employ similar miracles, wicked men and sorcerers, and he names one Satan as devising this (cf. Matt. 7:22-23; 24:24-25; Luke 10:18): so that not even he denies that these wonders have nothing divine about them, but are works of wicked men...In fact, even he admitted that these works were not produced by any divine nature, but were the signs of certain cheats and wicked men" (2.49; trans. Chadwick, 104).

13. Cf. Matt. 24:23-27; 2 Thess. 2:2-4, 9. Celsus continues: "This is blatantly the utterance of a man who is a sorcerer, who is out for profit and is taking precautions against possible rivals to his opinions and to his begging" (6.42; trans. Chadwick, 357).

14. Origen had previously quoted Celsus as saying that "because he foreknew that others too would get to know the same formulas and do the same thing, and boast that they did so by God's power, Jesus expelled them from his society" (1.61; trans. Chadwick, 10).

15. An allusion, on the one hand, to the paschal Lamb (cf. Luke 22:15) and, on the other hand to the Passion (cf. Matt. 27:48, 54).

16. The usual antithesis then follows: "Yet Jesus's body was no different from any other, but, as they say, was little and ugly and undistinguished" (6.75; trans. Chadwick, 388-389).

17. Cf. perhaps Jesus's discourse against the scribes and Pharisees in Matt. 23:13-29, and his invective against the cities in Matt. 11:20-24.

18. "How could we regard him as God when in other matters, as people perceived, he did not manifest anything which he professed to do, and when he had convicted him, condemned him and decided that he should be punished, was caught hiding himself and escaping most disgracefully, and indeed was betrayed by those whom he called disciples? And yet,...if he was God he could not run away nor be led away under arrest, and least of all could he, who was regarded as Saviour, and Son of the greatest God, and an angel, be deserted and betrayed by his associates who had privately shared everything with him and had been under him as their teacher" (2.9; trans. Chadwick, 73). Such misfortune would be unimaginable for "a good general who led many thousands," even for "any wicked robber-chieftain, who was captain of very bad men." But Jesus, "who was betrayed by those under his authority, neither ruled like a good

general; nor, when he had deceived his disciples, did he even inspire in the men so deceived that goodwill, if I may call it that, which robbers feel toward their chieftain" (2.12; trans. Chadwick, 77).

19. "It is as if someone, while saying that a certain man is righteous, shows him to be doing wrong, and, while saying that he is holy, shows him to be a murderer, and, while saying that he is immortal, shows him to be dead, and then to all this adds that he had predicted it" (2.16; trans. Chadwick, 81). Concerning the prophets, Celsus further writes: "So we should not consider either whether they did or whether they did not foretell it, but whether the act is worthy of God and is good... How, then, is it anything but blasphemy to assert that the things done to Jesus were done to God?" (7.14; trans. Chadwick, 406).

20. Cf. Acts 10:41; but Peter here speaks of the resurrected Christ.

21. No one conspires against dinner guests, still less if the host is God... "And what is more outrageous still, God himself conspired against those who ate with him, by making them traitors and impious men" (2.20; trans. Chadwick, 84-85).

22. Celsus cuts the verse (Matt. 26:39) in half. Origen accordingly protests and quotes the second half, "Nevertheless, not as I will but as thou wilt," as well as Jesus's further insistence in vs. 42, "If this cannot pass from me unless I drink it, thy will be done" (2.24; trans. Chadwick, 88).

23. He speaks here in 2.29 of *prophets* (pl.) announcing the coming of a figure whose glory is unique. He had spoken of a prophecy (sing.) that would apply to a limitless number of other persons known for extravagant conduct (cf. 1.50, 57; and esp. 7.9). "But my prophet said once in Jerusalem that God's son would come..." (1.49; trans. Chadwick, 46). An irrelevant remark, Origen thus asserts: this unique prophet could only be Moses, but, in Moses's books (the Pentateuch), there is no mention yet of Jerusalem; and the Jews did not expect the Son but rather the Messiah of God (1.49, 57). Recent history had only acknowledged four adventurers, for their fleeting action, as claimants to the title of Jewish Messiah (Theudas, Judas the Galilean, Dositheus the Samaritan, and Simon the Magician) (1.57; 6.11). Nothing, moreover, stood in starker contrast with the agitations of vaticinators than the dignity of the true prophets' lives and the seriousness of their mission (7.1-17). Criticizing Celsus' lack of quotation from Scripture, Origen puts together little by little an important collection of scriptural texts, developing the essence of what would constitute the prophetic argument in traditional Christian apologetics. Cf. SC 227: 214-221.

24. The genealogy of Jesus is traced back to Adam according to Luke 3:23-38, and begins with Abraham according to Matt. 1:1-17.

25. As did Bacchus, whom he quotes from Euripides: "The god himself will set me free whenever I wish it" (2.34; trans. Chadwick, 94).

26. As in the case of the one who condemned Pentheus and consequently suffered "by going mad or being torn to pieces" (2.34; trans. Chadwick, 95). On Bacchus and Pentheus, cf. SC 132: 366ff, n. 2.

27. Cf. Matt. 27:28-29. Celsus will say later in his treatise: "the men who

tortured and punished your God in person suffered nothing for doing it, not even afterwards as long as they lived" (8.41; trans. Chadwick, 481).

28. "What does he say while his body is being crucified? Was his blood like 'Ichor such as flows in the veins of the blessed gods'?" (2.36, trans. Chadwick, 96); cf. Homer, *Iliad* 5.340; and see also SC 132: 371, note.

29. Cf. Matt. 27:48, 34: it is not a matter of greed. Celsus finds the vinegar and gall especially unworthy of God (cf. still 4.22 and 7.13). For Origen, they were prophesied (cf. Ps. 69:21 [68:22, LXX]); they were offered to Jesus, and symbolized the malice and perversity of future enemies of the Gospel and the truth (cf. 2.37 and 7.13). We have here an example of Origen's usual method, that of using biblical history, gospel history, and church history to interpret each other. The method is notably deployed for the interpretation of miracle stories, the area where Origen's exegesis has become the least obsolete.

30. See also below, n. 51.

31. Celsus gives seven such examples of third pattern (2.55), and later on develops an eighth (3.26).

32. Cf. Matt. 27, respectively vss. 46, 50, 51, 54, 45.

33. He says nothing of the preaching, life, and death of the apostles, nor of their theological reflections on the mystery. Although they would in principle render themselves trustworthy (no one lives or dies for the sake of fairy tales that he or she has made up), Celsus quotes none of their written attestations, such as Paul's long list of beneficiaries of appearances of the resurrected Christ (1 Cor. 15:3, 5-8), any more than of the ancient prophets. Origen insists on all these things, as well as filling out Celsus's references to the Gospel (cf. SC 226: 229-131).

34. For the appearance to the disciples and Thomas, see John 20:24-29; to Mary Magdalene, see John 20:11ff. Celsus's Jew concludes: "He appeared secretly to just one woman and to those of his own confraternity" (2.70; trans. Chadwick, 120).

35. Cf. Matt. 28:2; Mark 16:5; Luke 24:4; and John 20:12. Celsus comments: "The Son of God, it seems, was not able to open the tomb, but needed someone else to move the stone. What is more, an angel came to the carpenter to defend Mary when she was pregnant, and another angel that they might rescue the infant and escape" (5.52; trans. Chadwick, 305).

36. Celsus's Jewish interlocutor could fall out with his turncoat kinsmen, Jewish Christians, claiming victory: "these objections come from your own writings, and we need no other witness; for you provide your own refutation" (2.74; trans. Chadwick, 122). To faithful Jews, he could propose the common hope of a bodily resurrection and faith in the Messiah who would be a model and initiator of that resurrection. But like them, he too remains in waiting: "Where is he then, that we may see and believe?" (2.77; trans. Chadwick, 126).

37. Is he thinking of Jesus's call, "Come to me, all who labor and are heavy laden...," and the welcome he reserves for children (cf. Matt. 11:28ff; 18:3-5)?

38. See, in the fragment of Celsus that follows (7.36), one very violent inter-
    pellation among others.
39. Cf. Jonah 4:6; Dan. 6:16-23. See also SC 150: 140ff, n. 1 and 2.
40. By virtue of Jesus's defense that "It is impossible for the same man to
    serve several masters" (Matt. 6:24), which Celsus repeats in 7.68 and 8.2.
41. "An impressive God, indeed, who desires to be the father of sinners
    condemned by another and of poor wretches who, as they say themselves,
    are but dung (*skubala*)..." (6.53, trans. Chadwick, 369; cf. Origen, 2.2).
    Origen is shocked at Celsus's ignorance of the work and genius of the
    apostle Paul (cf. 5.64; 3.20). He himself considers Paul the source and
    model of spiritual interpretation of Scripture, and continuously refers to
    him in order to expound the theological, mystical, and moral dimensions
    of Christian doctrine. See, for example, H. de Lubac, *Histoire et esprit:
    L'intelligence de l'Écriture d'après Origène*, Théologie 16 (Paris, 1950), 69-77.
42. In short, the pagan religion that Celsus would defend against Christian
    intolerance (7.62-8.63). His outline begins thus: "There is an ancient
    doctrine which has existed from the beginning, which has always been
    maintained by the wisest nations and cities and wise men" (1.14; trans.
    Chadwick, 17). These he enumerates in a double list (1.14 and 1.16).
    Moses, having known it through hearsay and understood it indirectly,
    transmitted it such as it was to his followers (1.21), but "the goatherds
    and shepherds who followed Moses as their leader were deluded by
    clumsy deceits into thinking that there was only one God...[and it was]
    without any rational cause [that] these goatherds and shepherds aban-
    doned the worship of many gods" (1.23; trans. Chadwick, 22).
43. "The Greeks are better able to judge the value of what the barbarians
    have discovered, and to establish the doctrines that put them into prac-
    tice by virtue" (1.2; trans. Chadwick, 7). Such was a commonplace un-
    contested at the time (cf. SC 132: 182ff, n. 1).
44. Within this medley, Celsus compares the hieratic arrangement of the cer-
    emonial ladder in Mithraic initiation, with its degrees, gates, precious met-
    als, stars, and divinities, to the jumbled heap of expressions and strange
    rites which were, in his view, used in Christian initiation (6.22; and 6.34-39).
45. The pamphleteer unleashes on the Christians in connection with some
    teachings of Plato. Having quoted some extracts from Plato on the sov-
    ereign Good, he writes: "After Plato has said this, nevertheless he does
    not relate some incredible tale, nor does he check the tongue of the man
    who wants to inquire what in fact it is which he professes, nor does he
    at once order people to 'start by believing that God is like this and He
    has a Son like that, and that the latter came down and walked and talked
    with me'" (6.8; trans. Chadwick, 321). Before speaking of the knowl-
    edge of God, who is not carnal at all but spiritual, he says: "Let them
    listen to me, if so cowardly and carnal a race are able to understand
    anything" (7.36; trans. Chadwick, 423)... "You are completely bound to
    the flesh and see nothing pure" (7.42; trans. Chadwick, 430). After dis-
    tinguishing between the "intelligible" and the "visible," according to

Plato and the ancients, he insists to Christians: "If you are unable to understand [these doctrines], keep quiet and conceal your own lack of education, and do not say that those who see are blind and those who run are lame, when you yourselves are entirely lamed and mutilated in your souls and live for the body which is a dead thing" (7.45; trans. Chadwick, 433).

46. This double-sided reproach introduces a list of eleven comparative themes (see SC 227: 93-95). On the one hand, writes Celsus, "we must speak of all the misunderstandings and corruptions of the truth which they have made through ignorance" (5.65; trans. Chadwick, 315); and elsewhere: "But what I have said on this point may be a sufficient example for all the other doctrines which they corrupt" (7.58; trans. Chadwick, 444). On the other hand, he affirms: "These ideas have been better expressed among the Greeks, who refrained from making exalted claims and from asserting that they had been announced by a god or the son of a god" (6.1; trans. Chadwick, 316); and elsewhere: "This too is old stuff, and was better said before them. But they expressed it in more vulgar terms" (7.58; trans. Chadwick, 443).

47. From Heraclitus: "The character of man has no common sense, but that of God has," and "A man has the reputation of being a fool before a god just as a child before a man" (*Fragm.* B 78-79; Diels-Kranz I: 168-169; *ap.* C. *Cels.* 6.12; trans. Chadwick, 326). And from Plato: "For I, men of Athens, have come to have this name for no other reason than that of wisdom. But what sort of wisdom is this? It is a wisdom that is perhaps attainable by man; for in truth I venture to affirm that I am wise in that respect" (*Apol.* 20D; *ap.* C. *Cels.* 6.12; trans. Chadwick, 326).

48. Cf. Matt. 19:24. Celsus continues: "Jesus corrupts the Platonic saying where Plato says that 'It is impossible for an outstandingly good man to be exceptionally rich' (*Laws* 743A)" (6.16; trans. Chadwick, 329).

49. Celsus quotes from Plato, *Ep.* 2, 312E-313E, and *Phaedrus* 247C.

50. Cf. Luke 6:29; Matt. 5:19; Plato, *Crito* 49B-C.

51. For the scriptural allusions, see above, n. 12. Authors, quotations, and myths occupy two pages in Celsus's discourse here. I note only his concluding point: "The punishment of the Son of God by the devil is to teach us that when we are punished by the same being we should endure it patiently. All this also is ludicrous. In my opinion he ought to have punished the devil; certainly he ought not to have pronounced threats against the men who had been attacked by him" (6.42; trans. Chadwick, 359).

52. In Celsus's view, the notion of God (and his Son) as spirit renders inexplicable Jesus's immortality, resurrection, incarnation, and lack of physical superiority (6.72-73, 75, 77), and it renders incomprehensible the fact that, instead of being sent to people who were the most inspired from the beginning, like the Chaldeans and others, the Son of God was sent "into one corner" of the earth, to the Jews, in view of the fact that "they will presently perish" (6.78-80; trans. Chadwick, 391, 393). Celsus otherwise sees this as evidence once again of the literary inferiority of Christian Scrip-

ture to the pagan classics: "The comic poet wrote that Zeus woke up and sent Hermes to the Athenians and Spartans because he wanted to raise a laugh in the theatre. Yet do you not think it is more ludicrous to make the Son of God to be sent to the Jews?" (6.78; trans. Chadwick, 391).

53. In the whole second part of his discourse (*ap.* Books 3-5 of the *C. Cels.*), Celsus rejects three forms of this divine intervention: the coming of a Savior to humanity, which is ruled out as a falsehood by history itself; the descent of a God or Son of God, which is is ruled out as an absurdity by critical reason; and the sending of an exceptional angel, which is contradicted by the order of providence and found to be an untenable pretension. This criticism of the idea of a divine descent does not distinguish between the eschatological consummation, the historical punishments recorded in Genesis, in which Jews and Christians alike believe, and the Incarnation, which Jews and Christians debate. He simply attacks the very thought of a divine descent.

54. On the flood and conflagration, Celsus asserts, Christians "misunderstood what is said by the Greeks or barbarians about this matter... This idea occurred to them because they misunderstood the doctrine of the Greeks and barbarians, namely, that after cycles of long periods and after returns and conjunctions of stars there are conflagrations and floods, and that after the last flood in the time of Deucalion the cycle demands a conflagration in accordance with the alternating succession of the universe. This was responsible for their mistaken opinion that God will come down and bring fire like a torturer" (4.11; trans. Chadwick, 190). On this cyclic concept and its broad dissemination, see SC 136: 210ff, n. 3; 318ff, n. 2; and 346ff, n. 2. For the accusation of plagiarism, see ibid., 232, n. 3. In response to the accusations of a lack of intelligence and the pillaging of ancient tradition, Origen begins by recalling the antecedence of Moses (see SC 227: Index, s.v. "Moïse, ancienneté," 331). To be sure, Origen adds other reasons in defense. He declares as absurd the thesis of predetermined world cycles, corrected within the tradition of ancient Stoicism, according to which, in every cycle, there is a return of a state of affairs, things, beings, of history of persons and events which are either "identical" or "altogether similar" (4.67-69; 5.20-21). On the possibility of successive worlds, Origen hesitates—he hopes still, indeed he affirms, the victory of love and the triumph of the Logos (Pref. 3; 8.72).

55. For the Flood account, Gen. 10:7ff; the Tower of Babel, Gen. 11:1-9; Sodom, Gen. 19:1-29. On the sons of Aloeus, see SC 136: 232, n. 2.

56. Cf. Matt. 27:34; and above, n. 29. Note here the word-play in Greek: gall–wrath (*cholên–cholon*).

57. "The race of Jews and Christians [is like] a cluster of bats or ants coming out of a nest, or frogs holding council round a marsh, or worms assembling in some filthy corner, disagreeing with one another about which of them are the worse sinners... [They say] 'There is God first, and we are next after Him in rank since He has made us entirely like God, and all things have been put under us...'" (4.23; trans. Chadwick, 199-200).

58. "The Jews were runaway slaves who escaped from Egypt; they never did anything important, nor have they ever been of any significance or prominence whatever" (4.31; trans. Chadwick, 206; see ibid, 207, n. 1, for the antecedents of this stereotype in Greek literature). Celsus adds: "They shamelessly undertook to trace their genealogy back to the first offspring of sorcerers and deceivers, invoking the witness of vague and ambiguous utterances..." (4.33; trans. Chadwick, 209).

59. Cf. Gen. 2:7ff; 3:1ff.

60. Cf. Gen. 6:14ff; 8:6-7, 8-12.

61. According to Celsus, this elite, "because they are ashamed of [these stories], take refuge in allegory...but they are incapable of being explained in this way, and are manifestly very stupid fables" (4.48, 50; trans. Chadwick, 223, 225; cf. also 1.27 earlier). Celsus continues: "At any rate, the allegories which seem to have been written about them are far more shameful and preposterous than the myths, since they connect with some amazing and utterly senseless folly ideas which cannot by any means be made to fit" (4.51; trans. Chadwick, 226). Would this perhaps be a response to interpretations, known at least by hearsay, like that of the story of Hagar and Sarah in Gal. 4:21-31 or in its rather different form in Philo, e.g. *De Congressu* 71ff?

62. A general providence controls the progress of the world, which is virtually automatic. And if there is a purification at the end of the cyclic return of cosmic periods, it is a matter of natural law inscribed in nature itself, not of an episodic action. Celsus expresses this view in many fragments of Book 4, but without reference to Scripture.

63. "Is it not ridiculous that when a man [Titus] was angry with the Jews and destroyed them all from the youth upwards and burnt down their city, in this case they were annihilated; yet when the supreme God, as they say, was angry and wrathful and sent His Son with threats, he suffered such indignities?" (4.73; trans. Chadwick, 242).

64. "Moses wrote these stories because he understood nothing, but did much the same as the poets of the Old Comedy who mockingly wrote, 'Proteus married Bellerophon, and Pegasus came from Arcadia'" (6.49; trans. Chadwick, 366).

65. On Marcion, his theology of Scripture, and his determination of a biblical canon, see A. le Boulluec, "The Bible in Use among the Marginally Orthodox" in this volume, 197-216.

66. *Antitheses*, as is well known, was the title of a lost work of Marcion.

67. Cf. Gen. 2:17; 3:5, 14.

68. Cf., for example, the promises made to Abraham in Gen. 12:2-3; 15:5; 22:17-18, etc., and extended to the people in Deut. 1:10.

69. Cf. above, 265-266 and n. 20.

70. The resemblances of scriptural themes to those of Greco-Roman mythology are still greatly overestimated by modern authors. See H. de Lubac, *Exégèse médiévale*, pt. 1, t. 2 (Paris, 1959), 373-396.

14

The Bible in Greek Inscriptions

DENIS FEISSEL

There has not been an attempt at synthesis in this field since Louis Jalabert's essay on "Citations bibliques dans l'épigraphie grecque"[1] appeared in 1914. We are clearly indebted to this work for the extent of its quotations and its variety of perspectives. And yet this work demands updating, if not replacement. The regional inventory of 247 epigraphic quotations,147 from Syria and Palestine, 66 from Egypt (including 20 ostraka), and a mere 30 from Europe and Asia Minor, needs in particular to be completed. New contributions continue to redress the regional imbalance, even though Syrian inscriptions remain numerically dominant, and the investigation, extending over a larger area, is covering more diverse quotations. Cataloging these citations, although an important undertaking, and for many regions lacking an epigraphic corpus, an inevitably provisional one, is not necessary for the present study. It seems more expedient instead to indicate, by region, the principal collections which contain the sources used in this essay.[2] The geographical background thus defined, we must specify the chronological parameters of the documentation, which, on the whole, dates from after the Peace of the Church (313). The few non-Christian quotations prior to this date will be examined first. All the rest will be classified without reference to their dates or origin, but with regard to the destination of the particular inscription, such as belonging to churches, houses, or tombs. For lack of an exhaustive catalog of inscriptions, this will enable us to draw up an inventory of some particularly frequent quotations and to focus upon certain monuments of exceptional epigraphic importance. Some brief remarks will be devoted, in conclusion, to the choice of quotations and the state of the text.

Non-Christian Inscriptions

The oldest epigraphic quotations of the Bible were most often Jewish or at least show up Jewish influence. On the island of Rheneia near the end of the second century or beginning of the first century B.C.E., two inscriptions[3] call for divine vengeance, each for the murder of a young Jew. The language clearly reflects scriptural expressions, drawn particularly from Numbers 16:22 and Leviticus 23:29. Later on, formulas based on maxims and curses from the Old Testament were aimed at protecting a certain monument or tomb from destruction. The exception was a Hermes erected by Amphicles of Chalcis, a rhetor and student of Herod Atticus, in memory of his son. The text of this monument combines pagan curses with those of Deuteronomy 18:22 and 28. The author, as illustrated by L. Robert,[4] was certainly influenced by Judaism. At Akmonia in Phrygia, two Jewish epitaphs[7] invoke the "curses written in Deuteronomy" as a whole, without quoting a particular passage, while two other inscriptions also from Akmonia call upon "the sickle of the curse"[6] (an allusion to Zechariah 5:2-4, LXX). From Bithynia and Scythia Minor,[7] in the third century, some ostensibly pagan inscriptions also intended to protect sepulchers, proclaim: "Do unto no one what you hate," in which I find an echo of Tobit 4:15. From the fourth century C.E. on, nearly all the biblical quotations are found in Christian inscriptions. The most remarkable exception is an inscription from a Samaritan synagogue at Thessalonica.[8] It reproduces Numbers 6:22-27 from a version of the Pentateuch which differs here from the Septuagint text both in the order of the verses and in certain details in the vocabulary. It seems, according to E. Tov, to be a revision of the Septuagint text following a Hebrew original; at points it differs from the Masoretic text, but independent of the Samaritan targum.

Inscriptions from Churches

Among the quotations engraved on churches the most frequent by far is that of Psalm 118:20 (117:20, LXX): "This is the gate of the Lord: the righteous shall enter through it."[9] The quotation is found principally in Syria (up to six times in various churches in the cite of El Anderîn[10] alone) but also occurs in Palestine,[11] Arabia,[12] Sinai,[13] sporadically in Asia Minor[14] and as far as Corfu.[15] This quotation is most often found on door lintels of churches, sometimes on the west side (*IGLS*, 1683, 1693, 1700) and sometimes on the south side (*IGLS*, 271, 1841). Rarely does this quotation decorate non-sacred buildings; such is the case, however, for three Syrian fortresses (*IGLS*, 1673, 1682, 2524).

With the exception of this highly favored quotation from Psalm 118, few scriptural texts enjoyed a wide diffusion in inscriptions on churches. I will cite two examples, which, in the absence this time of Syrian documentation, will show the need to extend this epigraphical investigation to the rest of the Greek world. The prophecy of Isaiah 11:6-8, "The wolf shall feed with the lamb, and the leopard shall lie down with the kid...."accompanies several mosaics with scenes of paradise. Aside from the eschatological meaning, we can discern here an allusion to the circumstances surrounding the reconciliation of the orthodox and monophysite churches.[16] In the inside of churches the liturgical furnishing also carried quotatons. I have indicated elsewhere the frequency with which Psalm 29:3 (28:3, LXX) "The voice of the Lord is upon the waters"[17] was used particularly on bronze vases (at Corinth and in various museums) or marble vases (primarily in Venetia); sometimes the quotation was associated with Isaiah 12:3.

Without unduly lengthening the list of scriptural quotations with sporadic examples, at least three groupings must be mentioned here which are remarkable for the way each accumulates, in a single church, a series of scriptural texts. They are precious clues to local aspects of biblical culture in Syria, Egypt, and Asia Minor. The church of Nawa[18] in northern Syria juxtaposes verses from the Psalms (Ps. 84:11-12 [83:11-12, LXX]; 100:4-5 [99:4-5, LXX]; 118:19-20 [117:19-20, LXX]) with verses from the Song of Songs (4:1, 3 , 4, 7; 5:2). Such is a "spontaneous exegesis" according to L. Jalabert, which identifies the bride of the Song of Songs with the newly built church. In Egypt, a rock church in the Thebaid is decorated with painted inscriptions.[19] Inscriptions of Psalms 32, 41, 112, 119, and 128 (31, 40, 111, 118, and 127, LXX), all of which commence with the word "blessed," are borrowed from the Old Testament. From the New Testament the inscription painters borrowed the first verses of each of the four gospels (Luke 1:14; John 1:1-5; Matt. 1:1-3; and Mark 1:1-2). Finally three inscriptions found near Afyon, in Phrygia, doubtless belong to the same church; one of them (*MAMA*, VI, 385) is made up of extracts of the Psalms (Ps. 32:1; 34:9; 34:6; 27:1; 97:11 [31:1; 33:10; 33:7; 26:1; 96:11, LXX]). The other two are composed of verses from Isaiah.[20] W. Ramsay has legitimately compared the choice of the passages with long quotations of Isaiah in Eusebius of Caesarea's *Panegyric* on the new church at Tyre (*Hist. eccl.* 10.4.48-52).

House Lintels

Nearly half of epigraphic quotations of the Bible are found on the doors or windows of simple homes. This engraving of lintels is an almost exclusive trait of the villages in ancient Syria. The object of such inscriptions, far from being purely apotropaic (designed to avert an evil),[21] was to praise God and to proclaim the faith of the inhabitants protected therein. The Psalms offered a vast repertory of quotations for this use which the Syrians mined with great variety. Psalm 121: 8 (120:8, LXX: "The Lord will guard your going out and your coming in") is distinguished by its large diffusion, over forty examples[22] of which occur in Syria, with only a few appearing elsewhere. Psalm 46:7 or 11 (45:8 or 12, LXX: "The Lord of hosts is with us; The God of Jacob is our refuge") is found on doorways principally in Apamea.[23] Psalm 91:1 (90:1, LXX: "He who dwells in the shelter of the Most High"), other uses of which will be seen below, was also aimed at protecting houses.[24] Aside from the Psalms, the phrase *Gloria in excelsis* (Luke 2:14) enjoyed a certain amount of local favor.[25] Unlike churches, each house was ordinarily content with one or two brief quotations. Thus it is only by grouping the quotations by location that certain characteristic preferences can be highlighted. If one considers, for example, the great *kômê* (or village) of El Bara in Apamea, out of 29 inscriptions (*IGLS*, 1453-1481) there are 13 lintels containing scriptural quotations. Some quotations occur only once (Ps. 4:8; 23:1 [22:1, LXX]; 33:22 [32:22, LXX]; 46:8 [45:9, LXX]; and Eph. 4:5); however, two examples of Psalm 113:7 (112:7, LXX), three of Psalm 120:8 (119:8, LXX) and four of Luke 2:14 (followed in one case by Ps. 113:7 [112:7, LXX]) are counted.

Funerary Inscriptions

Whereas funerary epigraphy is almost always the most common in all places, biblical quotations are relatively rare within this category, only a few dozen out of thousands of epitaphs.[26] Again the Psalms are predominant here, but we do not find a predilection for any particular passage, only gleanings which vary in tenor and in application. On rare occasions , as we see in the third century, the quotations were concerned with protecting a tomb against violators. I call attention to an inscription from Cyprus[27] which functions in this manner. Found on a tile covering a coffin it quotes Psalm 35:4 (34:4, LXX): "Let them be turned back and confounded who devise evil against me." Three epitaphs from Argos and shortly after, another one from Attica, threaten anyone who would break into the tomb with sharing the fate of those guilty souls who said, "Away with him, crucify him!" (John 19:15).[28]

Certain scriptural formulas served to eulogize the dead. Such was the case for Psalm 45:3 (44:4, LXX) in Palestine (*Revue biblique*, 1898, p. 127); Wisdom of Solomon 4:8-9 in Thrace (Beshevliev, no. 240); and Romans 15:1 (abbreviated): "Bearing with the scruples of the weak, as it is written" (Bandy, no. 56). In Cappadocia, 1 Timothy 5:10 (abbreviated and paraphrased) is applied to a deaconess "who, according to the Apostle, took care of children, practiced hospitality, washed the feet of the saints, and distributed her bread to the afflicted" (*SEG*, 27, 948). Elsewhere contempt for the world borrows as its maxim Ecclesiastes 1:2 , "Vanity of vanities. All is vanity!" (*IGLS*, 1438). Epitaphs likewise quote numerous verses from the Psalms evoking divine mercy and the remission of sins: Psalm 25:5-7 (24:5-7, LXX) (Lefebvre, no. 283); Psalm 32:1 (31:1, LXX) = Romans 4:7, which is characteristic of a series of epitaphs from Cilicia;[29] Psalm 51:1 (50:3, LXX) ((*IGLS*, 1488; Lefebvre, no. 663).

An epitaph in Athens[30] adapts Psalm 118:19 (117:19, LXX) in an original way to make it a prayer for the dead: "May the Lord open the gates of righteousness to him." In a transposition similar to that of the Jerusalem temple to the celestial home, a funerary mosaic in Albania[31] quotes Psalm 84:1-3 (83:1-3, LXX): "How lovely is your dwelling place O Lord of hosts..."

Aside from these isolated examples, two rather complex groups are particularly interesting. In Crimea, on a tomb dating from 491 C.E. found in Kertch,[32] verses from various Psalms (Ps. 27:1 [26:1, LXX]; 102:1ff [101:1ff, LXX]; 121:7-8 [120:7-8, LXX]) are brought together with the complete text of Psalm 91 (90, LXX). We have already seen Psalm 91:1 (90:1, LXX) inscribed upon lintels of homes. This affirmation of faith in God could be adapted equally well to funerary use (also *IGLS*, 1488; Thomsen, no. 168), perhaps with the same prophylactic value as this Psalm certainly enjoyed when engraved upon jewelry.[33] At Hâss in Apamea the inscriptions on the tomb of Diogenes are borrowed again from the Psalms. *IGLS* 1519 freely connects Psalms 65:9 and 60:2 (64:10 and 59:4, LXX), where it is inscribed: "You visited the land and saturated it; heal its breaches, for it has been shaken." In this I see a probable allusion to a real earthquake. *IGLS* 1520 quotes Psalm 118:26-27 (117:26-27, LXX: "Blessed is he who comes in the name of the Lord. The Lord is God, and he has manifested himself to us"). These verses are part of the most ancient liturgies. Psalm 106:4-5 (105:4-5, LXX) is also integrated within the context of a developed liturgical prayer: "...O Christ, visit your servant Antôninos with your salvation..., that he may behold the good of your elect ones" (*IGLS* 1522).

The Choice of Biblical Books and the State of the Biblical Text

From this rapid tour of the landscape of epigraphy containing scriptural quotations, an obvious predilection for the Psalms emerges. The Psalter provided, for the spontaneous gleanings of the faithful, as well as for the liturgy and sometimes through the liturgy, a rich resource of praise and prayer. All totaled, approximately a third of the 151 Psalms are found represented, in quite variable length and frequency, in epigraphic quotations.[34] Those which were most widespread have been indicated throughout this essay: Psalm 29:3 (28:3, LXX) which appears 17 times; Psalm 91:1 (90:1, LXX), 15 times; Psalm 118:20 (117:20, LXX), 31 times; and Psalm 121:8 (120:8, LXX), 43 times. Among the other Old Testament books, quoted in only twenty inscriptions, Isaiah is the best represented. Nine different extracts from this book are quoted (see note 20), and all appear only once except Isaiah 6:3 (the Trisagion: "Holy, holy, holy is the Lord of hosts!") and 11:6 (see note 16). Quotations from the New Testament[35] are nearly three times less frequent than those of the Old Testament and none of them enjoy as privileged a use. We should note, however, the relative frequency of Luke 2:14 (see note 25) and Romans 8:31 ("If God is for us, who is against us?") on Syrian lintels.[36]

The usefulness of these engraved quotations of Scripture for biblical text criticism is limited at once by the small number of verses actually attested and by the relatively late date of their inscription. We must furthermore keep in mind the liberties taken by the redactors in abridging texts, adapting them to their own interests, and arbitrarily linking fragments that have very different origins in the Bible. Bearing this in mind, epigraphy can contribute to determining the state of a biblical text in use at a given period in a given part of the Greek world, and to discerning its connections to various manuscript traditions. In this field, in spite of several detailed studies (cf. Jalabert, col. 1754), the lack of a comprehensive treatment is regrettable. I will limit myself here to pointing out several examples of the kinds of problems which arise.

Old Testament epigraphic quotations independent of the Septuagint are rare and generally produced by non-Christians. We have already noted a quotation of Numbers 6:22-27 from Thessalonica which draws upon a revised version of the Pentateuch. On the other hand, the Jews of Akmonia (see note 6) read Zechariah 5:2-4 in the Septuagint recension. Only rarely did the Septuagint text undergo significant alteration in inscriptions. Such was the case with a mosaic found at Mopsuestia in Cilicia, which represented the story of Samson and quoted Judges 16:1-4. The revising of the story seems to have been taken either from the Jewish Targum tradition or from a Christian emendation similar to the Jewish Targum.³⁷ The same sort of confusion over a Christian or Jewish origin surrounds an inscription from Cyprus presently housed at the Louvre,³⁸ which quotes all of Psalm 15 (14, LXX) and which, according to P. Perdrizet, could come from either a synagogue or a church. The text itself has only minor variations from the Septuagint. Two other inscriptions have preserved a Psalm in its entirety or virtual entirety. The first comes from a lead scroll found in Rhodes whose antiquity has sometimes been exaggerated.³⁹ In this case Psalm 80:2-16 (79:2-16, LXX) is used as an *apotropaion* for the protection of a vineyard. The second is found in the tomb at Kerch (in the Bosphorus), dated from 491, which reproduces all of Psalm 91 (90, LXX) (see notes 32 and 33). The interest in these lengthy quotations, which have been known of for some time, should not distract from more fragmentary, but more abundant, examples which remain for critical investigation.

Two examples drawn from the New Testament will at last illustrate how epigraphy can enrich the text-critical history of a passage of Scripture. As we have already observed, a series of lintels from Syria contain inscriptions of Luke 2:14 (see note 25), not according to the received text ("Peace on earth to men of goodwill") but with the nominative *eudokia* ("peace on earth, goodwill toward men"). These inscriptions share this reading with several manuscripts. It logically follows that a text from the same family circulated in Syria around the fifth century, but this fact, important as it is, is of little help in choosing one or the other of the readings. Our second example is the inscription, identified early on as a version of the *Lord's Prayer* according to Matthew 6:9-13, found on a fragment of a clay tablet discovered at Megara (on the isthmus of Corinth).⁴⁰ An important epigraphic parallel appears on a lintel in Syria (*IGLS*, 2546 with commentary). Of particular note is the variation *aphiomen* (verse 12) common to both inscriptions and to several Matthaean manuscripts. On the other hand, the Megara tablet did not add a doxology at the end of the prayer, whereas the Syrian inscription contained an ending found neither in Matthew nor in the liturgies. It is obvious from these all too lacunary pieces of evidence that epigraphy, so varied in time and space, did not even come close to using a uniform biblical text; yet, perhaps in a more modest way, it can be one helpful source in trying to understand the history of the formation and corruptions of the text of the Bible.

NOTES

1. *Dictionnaire d'archéologie chrétienne et de liturgie*, III, 2 (Paris, 1914), col. 1731-1756 (hereafter abbreviated: Jalabert). For lack of a recent edition of an inscription, I will refer the reader to the regional inventory of 1914, citing simply: Jalabert, nos. 1-247.

2. The principal regional collections (with abbreviations) to be used in this essay include the following:

EUROPE

Bandy: A. C. Bandy, *The Greek Christian Inscriptions of Crete* (Athens, 1970) [nos. 56, 68].

Beshevliev: V. Beshevliev, *Spätgriechische und spätlateinische Inschriften aus Bulgarien* (Berlin, 1964) [nos. 166, 240].

ASIA MINOR

Grégoire: H. Grégoire, *Recueil des inscriptions grecques chrétiennes d'Asie Mineure*, I (Paris, 1922) [nos. 7, 108, 128, 165].

Ramsay: W. M. Ramsay, *The Cities and Bishoprics of Phrygia* (1895-1897) [nos. 674-678].

MAMA: Monumenta Asiae Minoris Antiqua, vol. II (London, 1930), 107; III (1931), [nos. 112, 125, 190, 195, 196, 242*b*, 458]; IV (1933) [no. 33]; VI (1939) [nos. 316, 335, 335*a*, 385]; VII (1956) [no. 567]; VIII (1962) [no. 256].

SYRIA

Wadd.: H. Waddington, *Inscriptions grecques et latines de la Syrie* (Paris, 1870).

IGLS: Inscriptions grecques et latines de la Syrie, vol. II (Paris, 1939) Antioch, [nos. 271, 285, 414, 524, 613, 642, 675]; III (1950-1953) [nos.770, 1984]; IV (1955), includes Apamea with a large number of quotations (scriptural index, 364-367); V (1959), Emessa (index, 335).

Limes: R. Mouterde and A. Poidebard, *Le limes de Chalcis* (Paris, 1945) [nos. 31, 53, 57, 58, 61].

PALESTINE

Thomsen: P. Thomsen, *Die lateinischen und griechischen Inschriften der Stadt Jerusalem* (Leipzig, 1922) [nos.22, 24, 168-170].

EGYPT

Lefebvre: G. Lefebvre, *Recueil des inscriptions grecques chrétiennes d'Egypte* (Cairo, 1907).

Other Abbreviations:

BCH: Bulletin de correspondance hellénique.

Bull. ép.: Bulletin épigraphique de la *Revue des Etudes grecques.*

CIG: *Corpus inscriptionum graecarum* (Berlin, 1828-1977; reprinted New York, 1977).

CRAI: *Comptes rendus de l'Académie des Inscriptions et Belles-Lettres.*

SEG: *Supplementum epigraphicum graecum* (reprint ed., Amsterdam, 1979-).

ZPE: *Zeitschrift für Papyrologie und Epigraphik.*

3. M.-Th. Couilloud, *Les monuments funéraires de Rhénée* (Paris, 1974), no. 485.

4. *Inscriptiones graecae*, VII, 9, 955 and 1179, explained by L. Robert, *CRAI* (1978), pp. 245-252.

5. *MAMA*, VI, 335 and 335a (the latter is dated from 248-249 B.C.E.).

6. *Corpus inscriptionum judaicarum* (Rome and Paris, 1936-1952), II, 769 and *MAMA*, VI, 316. Also see L. Robert, *Hellenica* (Paris, 1960), XI-XII, pp. 399-400. This expression comes from the Septuagint and not the Hebrew version of the Bible.

7. *Bull. ép.*, 1953, 194, and 1971, 434.

8. See my *Recueil des inscriptions chrétiennes de Macédoine, du IIIe au Vie siècle* (Athens and Paris, 1983), no. 291 with the previous bibliography.

9. Variants: "This is the gate that the Lord has blessed" (*IGLS*, 1706) or "that the Lord has made" (*IGLS*, 1841).

10. *IGLS*, 1683, 1688, 1693, 1694, 1700, 1706. Elswhere in Syria: *IGLS*, 271, 1841, 1947, 1966; Wadd. 2413 a. It is not certain that nos.1744, 1844, 1982 come from churches.

11. Jalabert, nos.77-78; Thomsen, nos.24; *SEG*, 8, 235; *Israel Expl. Journal*, 1974, p. 227.

12. *SEG*, 1167 and 1186.

13. *Dumbarton Oaks Papers*, 20 (1966), p. 262, nos.1 and 3.

14. In Cilicia, at the beginning of *CIG*, 8857, which I will reedit; in Lycia, Grégoire, no. 288; in Cataonia (*Bull, corr. Hell.*, 1883, p. 140, no. 25) and in Armenia (ibid., 1909, p. 42, no. 17).

15. *Inscriptiones graecae*, IX, 1, 720.

16. In Palestine, *Revue biblique*, 1938, p. 233. In Cilicia, *MAMA*, II, p. 107 and M. Gough, *Mélanges Mansel* (Ankara, 1974), I, pp. 411-419, from whom this interpretation comes. For the same quotation at Anemurium, cf. J. Russel, *Türk arkeoloji dergisi* 25 (1980): 283, fig. 18.

17. *Aquileia nostra*, 1976, col. 167-172 and ibid., 1980, col. 338.

18. *IGLS*, 1945-1949, with commentary. The church dates from around 598-599 C.E.

19. G. Lefebvre, *Annales du service des antiquités de l'Egypte* (Paris, 1909), pp. 263-269 (Jalabert, no. 180).

20. Ramsay, no. 674 (Isa. 1:16-18) and no. 675 (Isa. 61:1 = Luke 4:18; Isa. 61:10 and 25:63). In another church in Phrygia, we read Isa. 60:1-3 (Ramsay, no. 676).

21. On this point, Jalabert (col. 1749-1753) devoted himself for a long time to refuting the largely obsolete theory of W. K. Prentice.

22. The following catalogue will illustrate the growth in documentation since 1914 (Jalabert, nos. 81-107, 164,233). Northern Syria: *IGLS*, 223, 378, 525,

642 1456, 1466-1468, 1531, 1562, 1567, 1571, 1677, 1680, 1702, 1704, 1719, 1724, 1725, 1750, 1751, 1755, 1812-1815, 1887, 1969, 1993, 2204, 2235, 2516, 2537; *Limes*, nos. 57, 71; *ZPE*, 47 (1982), p. 86, no. 24; Southern Syria: Jalabert, nos. 103 to 105; Jerusalem: Thomsen, nos. 22, 24; Hebron: *Bull. ép.*, 1950, 215; Egypt: Jalabert, no. 164; Crimea: Jalabert, no. 233; Armenia: Le Bas-Waddington, *Add.* 1814 c.

23. *IGLS*, 1428, 1453, 1687, 1723, 1726 (on a tower), 1743 (fortress dated from 566 B.C.E.). Also found on a mosaic in Cyrene (*SEG*, 18, 768), dated from 539, with Ps. 93:5 (92:5, LXX).

24. *IGLS*, 341, 675, 1675, 1747, 1748. Also see Jalabert, no. 45. See note 33 below.

25. *IGLS*, 1407, 1454, 1455, 1464, 1478, 1482.

26. Among the inscriptions of biblical quotations, epitaphs are also relatively rare (30 from 247 according to Jalabert).

27. T. B. Mitford, *Byzantion* 20 (1950): 134-136, no. 9, fig. 9.

28. The examples brought together by D. Feissel, *BCH* 104 (1980): 466.

29. *MAMA*, III, 125, 190, 195, 458. As we mentioned previously the same quotation was found in two churches in Egypt and Phrygia.

30. K. Konstantopoulos, *Harmonia* (Athens, 1900), p. 35, no. 35.

31. S. Anamali, *Iliria* 3 (Tirana, 1975), p. 353, pl. 5.

32. J. Kulakowski, *Römische Quartalschrift* 8 (1894): 49-87 and 309-327 (Jalabert, col. 1744-1745).

33. As with the tomb in Kertch, Psalm 91 (90, LXX) was inscribed in its entirety in a residence of Salamis of Cyprus (see my study in *BCH*, 1984 with parallels). A series of ten bracelet/amulets quoting the beginning of this same Psalm have been brought together by M. Piccirillo, *Studii biblici Fransciscani liber annuus* (Jerusalem, 1979), pp. 244-252.

34. Jalabert, col. 1746, pointed out the quotation of 48 different Psalms . The present total has grown to a mere 56. Newly discovered inscriptions most often reproduce previously known quotations.

35. Without taking into account the ostraka from Egypt of which Jalabert, nos.193-214, quotes twenty.

36. *IGLS*, 1442, 1448 to 1450, 1576, 1577, 1784, 1846.

37. See R. Stichel, *Byzantinishe Zeitschrift* 71 (1978), pp. 50-61: "Die Inschriften des Samson-Mosaiks in Mopsuestia und ihre Beziehung zum biblischen Text."

38. P. Perdrizet, *BCH* 20 (1896): 349-351; definitive text found in T. B. Mitford, *Byzantion* 20 (1950): 168.

39. Grégoire, no. 128. The editor argues against the generally accepted date (third or fourth century) in favor of a later dating (fifth or sixth century). In verse 16 one finds "the son" which conforms to the Hebrew rather than "the son of man."

40. R. Knopf, *Athenische Mitteilungen* 25 (1900): 313-324 (Jalabert, col. 1746). The editor dates the inscription from the fourth century.

15

The First Biblical Scenes
Depicted in Christian Art

PIERRE DU BOURGUET, S.J.

Whatever its matrix, iconography is never spontaneously produced. There is always the passage from story or portrait, as an imagined scene, to the actual plan of representation, be it sketched, colored, or sculpted.

In the case of Christian iconography, the sudden appearance in places of worship of scenes and personages from the New and Old Testaments was not achieved in the obviously most natural manner. Events from the life of Christ and the person of Jesus himself, which were the focal point of apostolic preaching (i.e., the gospels), were, in themselves, of primary importance, foundational to Christian faith. We would expect that they constituted the premier basis of Christian iconography. But this is not so. Instead the two themes are rare, since they were introduced virtually in secret, and the very principle of depicting their essential protagonist, Jesus Christ, was slow in being established. The clearest subjects decorating earliest Christian monuments were borrowed from the Old Testament, and therefore more from Christianity's pre-history than from its own foundation and life; and yet these subjects were explicitly, even dangerously real-to-life.

The paradox here stems from the fact that the Old Testament is rich in colorful and graphic stories, stories in which unforgettable characters emerge. And yet, in strict fidelity to the prohibition on "engraving sacred images," not a single such person appears on Hebrew monuments until the beginnings of the Common Era. Outstanding figures of the Old Testament had to wait for the advent of Christianity before being deemed worthy of depiction in largely painted or sculpted form, mainly for the purpose of illustrating Christianity. It was Christianity that opened wide the doors for iconographic depiction of these celebrated persons. Initially these Old Testament figures flooded Christian art, to the point even of taking over and dominating it for an extended period, without, however, completely excluding New Testament subjects, and indeed gradually conceding to them the preeminent position in Christian iconography. We must assume that the iconography emerging from the Christian age, and from the reality of Christianity itself, necessarily had to pass, like the history of the "people of God," through an initial recollection of the Old Covenant in order to blossom in the New, which was still its true and proper domain. The fact of this Christian artistic exploitation of Old Testament themes is all the more surprising considering that the first converts in each Gentile town visited by the Apostles were Jews, frequently even Pharisees, like the one who had been commissioned to bring the Good News to the Gentiles. No matter how disconcerting, this iconographic practice would endure and spread unabatedly for several centuries, and the decrease in the number of subjects borrowed from the Old Testament did not lead to their complete disappearance.

This briefly surveyed evolution, which led from the dominance of Old Testament artistic subjects to a balance which favored New Testament themes, came about in periodic stages in the early history of Christianity.

We see a gradual progression in early Christian art from the third century to the fourth century. By the fifth century, concern for the doctrinal teaching of the Church gave rise to a new emphasis on the image of Christ as heir, in a new light, to the Old Testament; this image in turn was adorned with a pomp heretofore reserved only for the emperor, even with the emperor's own consent. The sixth century, especially in Byzantine art (which constituted the principal Christian art of the time), saw Christ represented quite intentionally in the Old Testament symbol of the Lamb. In the seventh century, the Byzantine Empire, permeated with "achiropoietic" images ("not made with human hands"), sounded the need to depict the reality of the person (*hypostasis*) of Christ.

This preliminary sketch, which is detailed enough for our purposes, underscores the double antinomy which seems to have impeded the normal development of Christian art, and from which Christian art did not free itself until the end of the seventh century: first, the artistic priority of Old Testament subjects over those of the New; and second, the numerical preponderance of the former over the latter for a rather significant length of time. Over the course of the early Christian period, this contradiction was clearly fundamentally reduced by the reality of the religious fervor of the earliest Christians. Yet it merits a fuller examination in order to view it more in depth.

Logically, the legitimacy of sacred images should have been contested by the first Christian converts, most of whom were Jews from the Diaspora synagogues. But this is not the case. No echo of this kind of exclusion of images resounds in Acts (which is nonetheless attentive to other kinds of bans and the controversies they caused), nor does this exclusion of images show up later on, whereas normally the bond among members of communities alienated from their place of origin consists in fidelity to external forms such as bans. Such a psychological reaction common among expatriated Jews surely demanded exclusion of any penetration of pagan practices. We would think that the influence of Jerusalem, which was preponderant in this period, should have demanded adherence to a ban on images on the part of pagan converts to Christianity, who would naturally defer to their Jewish Christian coreligionists. Such an influence thus ought to have produced the same reservations toward images as those which were directed against Paul's liturgical and sacramental innovations.

In fact, however, the prohibitions against images observed by Jews had already lost their force during the time of Christ. Jewish sarcophagi from the first century C.E. in Jerusalem, the seat of Jewish thought, include figurative reliefs.[1] This is not the thinking of the primitive nomads to whom these prohibitions had originally been addressed in Mosaic law. The profound separation between God and the idols was no longer as essential when the danger hardly remained any more of placing them on the same level or even of according the idols a secondary status. The progress in this refinement of Jewish thought on images is triumphantly displayed in the renowned iconography of the synagogue at Dura-Europos from the first half of the third century C.E.

It seems that Christian converts, even the Jewish converts to Christianity, directly by virtue of their faith in the "novelty" of the Incarnation of the Son of God, as was foundational to their conversion, would have felt obliged, more than anyone else, to embrace and proclaim the consequences of the Incarnation, the most obvious one being the legitimacy of representing an infinite God who had willed to become visible and thus representable. From our perspective, therefore, it is all the more paradoxical that this visible God is practically never represented in the mural paintings and sarcophagi sculptures of the third century, which together provide the clearest examples of early Christian iconography.

Here we must interject a word about a factor from this period which, oddly enough, is usually only accorded relative importance if any, though it is actually fundamentally important. The thought of the time, particularly in religious or official matters, but even in social relations, was expressed deliberately using allegory and symbol. A great person, even of the same social rank, was called upon or mentioned only by a quality of his function or person, either of which was allegorical. Such forms of address as "Your Excellency" or "Your Majesty" are a legacy of this custom even today. Proof of this practice shows up in the fourth century in the letters exchanged between bishops as closely connected as Gregory of Nazianzus and Basil of Caesarea. Elsewhere in the Greco-Roman world, the symbol supported pagan mythology in projecting the human spirit toward the heights of the gods. The religious thought of the earliest Christians proceeded in the same way.[2] This is indeed the normal process of religious thought. It cannot attain, nor consequently formulate, the goal of its prayer or contemplation except by this act of the spirit, which, through relay, through a sensible reality, reaches to the invisible reality of God. Is not the very word "God" (*deus; dieu*) itself, through its root which signifies the light of day (*dies*), a symbol of the ineffable luminous reality of the infinite Being? One confirmation of this disposition to symbolize was the Christian artistic use of subjects as far removed from Judeo-Christian perspectives as the pagan myths: namely, Eros and Psyche, Orpheus, the "rescuer" dolphin, the Seasons, and the Elysian Fields. Their admittance to and choice for the Christian repertoire are explained only by the symbols that they contain, which are, respectively, love, the pursuit of the Good, salvation, eternity, and Paradise.

In this vein, it was even a contradiction in terms during this period directly to depict scenes and persons from the New Testament. On the contrary, it was altogether appropriate to hint at these scenes and persons using the images from the Old Testament that had foretold them: namely, prophecies enriched with all of history as the gratuitous action of divine election, prophecies which flowed into and found their ineffable fulfillment in the person of Christ and in his acts.

Third-Century Christian Art

This profusion of Old Testament subjects left its mark, as we will see, on the earliest Christian iconography, that of the catacombs in Rome.

During the third century, when the Church was forced to lead a semi-clandestine life, the only walls capable of Christian decoration were those confined to subterranean areas which imperial authorities conceded to Christians for burying their martyrs; such were the kinds of "concessions" obtained by secular confraternities (*collegia*) in this period.[3] In addition to murals, there were also decorative reliefs on sarcophagi kept in the catacombs.

The guiding principle for choosing images could not have been completely based, as J. Wilpert believed,[4] on the sequence of episodes constituting the "Prayer for the recommendation of the soul," the most ancient manuscript of which dates from no earlier than the ninth century; nor could it have been based purely on the historical (as opposed to symbolic) sense of facts from salvation history, as P. Styger suggested.[5] On the basis of drilling through the catacomb walls into the actual burial cells, some of which still contained bones and some of which were sealed by a burial stone, both Wilpert and Styger concluded that the catacombs had been used as general cemeteries by the Christians. In fact, the catacombs could never have sufficed for the Christians as a whole, who instead normally shared the use of public necropolises that were open to all, such as the one at Ostia. Moreover, it appears from inscriptions on most of the tombstones from the catacomb cells that the practice of using these cells as sepulchres for the Christian faithful was not instigated until the end of the third century, when the cult of the martyrs was beginning to take shape, a cult destined to flourish in the catacombs after the Peace of the Church. Hence we must envision the third-century iconography from the catacombs less in connection with death than with martyrdom and those who suffered martyrdom.

Two series of subjects are found in multiple examples in the catacombs; those italicized below constitute the largest group of examples.

The first series of subjects treats of everything recalling persecution: Susanna as an object of the lusts of the two elders, *the three Hebrews in the fiery furnace,*[6] *Daniel in the lion's den,*[7] and Job on his rubbish heap.[8]

The second series relates the Covenant and its ultimate consequences in the Hereafter: *the temptation of Adam and Eve,*[9] *Noah and the ark,*[10] *the sacrifice of Abraham, Moses making water gush from the rock in the desert,*[11] the ascension of Elijah, David armed with a sling-shot, Tobias and the fish, and *Jonah and the whale.*[12]

From the New Testament, only the following are retained to any significant degree in this period: *the Good Shepherd,*[13] an image already rooted in the Old Testament, which was extended to depict Christ simultaneously in the manner of the bucolic figure of Orpheus[14]; *the raising of*

Lazarus,[15] which was a theme of hope for the martyrs; and finally, the *adoration of the Magi*,[16] in which already Mary is recalled and depicted in close association with the baby Jesus. This last scene was certainly cherished by pagan converts to Christianity, who could recognize in it the justification of their martyrs through the extension of the New Covenant to them. Added to these are some representations of the eucharistic Banquet,[17] symbolizing the sacrifice of the mass as the eschatological Banquet in the coming Kingdom, of which Jesus's multiplication of the loaves and his miracle at the wedding feast in Cana are similarly symbolic. Finally, there are a number of miracles depicted in relation to the faith for which the martyrs died: the healings of the *paralytic*, the woman with a hemorrhage,[18] the bent woman, the lepers, the man blind from birth, as well as events crowning the earthly mission of Christ, such as his Baptism or his teaching (found in the Hypogeum of the Aurelii).[19] We should also mention here the beautiful portraits of the Apostles, also found in the Hypogeum of the Aurelii.[20]

One striking foreshortening which unites the two Testaments is a scene portraying Balaam showing the star to the Virgin.[21]

Two things are notable for their absence in this art: the Passion and the Resurrection. (The childhood of Jesus could also be added here, for this would not begin to develop in Christian art for another two centuries). But even in this case, the early Christians' urge to use symbols negates the apparent discrepancy. The Good Shepherd, who gives his life for the sheep and who saves the lost sheep so as to extend its life, serves as a dual symbol of the Passion and Resurrection. The sacrifice of Abraham is itself also a symbol of the Passion, and in some sense even of the Resurrection. Moreover, does not Christ himself use the biblical story of Jonah being swallowed and vomited by the whale as a symbol of his own eventual Resurrection (Matt. 12:39-40)? It seems also that the raising of Lazarus depicted in the catacombs must be interpreted as adumbrating Christ's Resurrection, precisely as it is presented in the Gospel of John and recalled by Christians henceforth.

A slightly different perspective inspires the choice of iconography on the baptistry of the "Christian House" excavated at Dura-Europos. There once again the iconography is functional, adapted to the sacrament which is being administered within the walls of the church. On the canopy which overhangs the cistern, above and beside the figures of Adam and Eve, appear the Good Shepherd, the paralytic carrying his pallet, Jesus holding his hand out to Peter (who has fallen into the lake), and the Samaritan woman close to her well.[22] On the wall are various scenes, including one of the three Marys near the sepulchre of Jesus. The saving water on the canopy and the Resurrection on the wall are depicted here less as symbols than as the "substance" of the sacrament.[23] Yet in each case they are represented with scenes from the Old and New Testaments which directly illustrate the intentions of Christ and the Church. Here symbols play a different role from what we saw in the catacombs. In the baptismal setting, they are highlighted by virtue of the deeper efficacy that has been conferred on them, whereas in the catacombs they served to recall the faith for which some had suffered martyrdom. This difference all the more accentuates the value of symbols overall in Christian iconography in this period.

Fourth-Century Christian Art

At the end of the third century and throughout the fourth, Christian symbolism was dulled by a certain realism of the times. Two factors are responsible for this: first, the increased impact of Christianity in the social milieu of the Empire (which furthermore prompted the revival of persecution under Decius, and especially under Diocletian); and second, the subsequent freedom granted to the Church after 313.[24]

In fourth-century paintings from the catacombs, the Old Testament repertoire was kept to the minimum essentials. Adam and Eve, Jonah and the whale, were used concurrently with subjects borrowed from mythology and exploited for their symbolic value: Eros and Psyche, Orpheus, and the Seasons. The New Testament scenes, which included the adoration of the Magi, further presented Jesus, still in the figure of the Good Shepherd, but also using new figures which left behind those of the third century: Jesus teaching his Apostles, presiding over the miraculous catch of fish, crowning a martyr, and above all being enthroned in majesty between Peter and Paul.

On the sarcophagi, which offered the same iconography, the crossing of the Red Sea was added to the Old Testament repertoire, while the Nativity of Jesus and Jesus and Zacchaeus were added to the New Testament group. On the tomb of Junius Bassus, dating from 359 (Vatican Caves), appear Jesus's entry into Jerusalem and the arrest of Jesus, but also Jesus as an ephebe enthroned above the cosmic figure of Coelus.[25] Elsewhere, Peter's denial and Christ joining the hands of a married couple are also depicted.

One of the catacombs discovered in 1955 under the Via Latina in Rome[26] distinguishes itself for the parallel religious origins of its subjects, some clearly pagan and others Christian. This contrast has led to the conclusion that the various members of the family had different religious affiliations. Subjects honored in the preceding century, frequently or not, were now detailed in cycles. An example is the fall of Adam and Eve, to which were added the expulsion from Eden and the reception of Cain and Abel bearing the fruit of their labor. To Noah and the ark were added the flood or Noah succumbing to drunkenness. To the sacrifice of Abraham was added the whole cycle including the vision at Mamre, the escape from Sodom, Isaac's meal and the blessing he gave to Jacob, Jacob's vision at Bethel, and further still the Song of Joseph, the arrival of Jacob's family in Egypt, and the benediction pronounced by Jacob on Ephraim and Manasseh. To the scene of Moses striking the rock in the desert were joined the rescue of the infant Moses from the waters, Moses before the burning bush or else presiding at the crossing of the Red Sea; also added were the pillar of fire and full-length portraits of an Egyptian soldier and an Israelite. To the scene of Balaam pointing out the star is added the interruption of his journey by the angel. The story of the three Hebrews in the fiery furnace again appears, and scenes from the story of Jonah are portrayed in detail rather than in an overlapping group on the same panel. Finally, a long Samson cycle is represented in three scenes.[27] The New Testament is given less representation in the sarcophagi of the catacombs. But to the essential scenes inherited from the third century—the adoration of the Magi, Jesus and the Samaritan woman, the multiplication of the loaves, the raising of Lazarus, and the Good Shepherd—are added the Sermon on the Mount, the soldiers casting lots for the robe of the teaching Jesus, and Jesus seated among the Twelve or between Peter and Paul.[28]

This new aspect of Christ, the Christ who is already enthroned, is found in the mosaics of the *Traditio Legis* and the *Traditio Clavium* in the Mausoleum of Santa Costanza in Rome.[29] A half-length portrait (or bust) of the bearded Christ occupies a panel in the ceiling paintings of the Catacomb of Commodilla.[30] He is also depicted holding a book between two martyrs or as a lamb blessing the loaves.

Whether in the paintings or the sarcophagi of the catacombs, Mary appears in an attitude of prayer, and henceforth in a role more clearly capable of a theological significance. In one stone panel originally from Fayûm in Egypt, Mary is engraved sitting on a cushioned bench holding the Child, in an attitude discreetly connected with that of Christ.

The Apostles, up to this point portrayed individually (e.g., Peter's denial of Christ in the Catacomb of Commodilla), are presented in a group with Christ, as we see, for example, in the Catacomb of the Giordani.[31]

Objects of smaller and more manageable dimensions allow for freer art and even freer inspiration. Such is the case with the ivory artifacts, namely, casket-linings, pyxes, and diptychs. The repertoire, which contained engravings of Susanna and the elders, Daniel with the lions, Jonah and the whale or else the raising of Lazarus, the miracle at Cana, and Christ with his Apostles, was now expanded to include some new subjects. From the Old Testament were added Jacob and Rachel at the well, Moses rescued from the waters or else praying at Horeb, the crossing of the Red Sea, the duel between David and Goliath, and Jeroboam near the altar at Bethel. New Testament additions included Jesus and Zacchaeus, Jesus in Gethsemane, Jesus before Caiaphas, Jesus before Pilate, the holy women at the tomb, the imprisonment of Peter, the episode of Ananias and Sapphira, the hanging of Judas, and Paul teaching or before the Roman proconsul. The small dimensions of these pieces favored the fourth-century penchant toward the concrete and, consequently, the representation of Christ. The gilded silver reliquary discovered in the Church of San Nazaro Maggiore in Milan depicts scenes on its sides and lid from the Old and New Testaments alike: Joseph and his brothers, the judgment of Solomon, the adoration of the Magi, the three Hebrews in the furnace, and the miracle of Cana.[32] On a glass cup originally from the region of Arras and now in the Louvre in Paris, Susanna and the elders, Daniel with the lions, Adam and Eve, and Daniel slaying the dragon are all depicted surrounding the Christian monogram.[33] The wealth of painted glass which seals the slabs covering the burial cells in the corridors of the catacombs offers the same variety.

Thus the proliferation of subjects, the addition of concrete details, and the separation of scenes from a subject or from a cycle all point to a realism which, without violating the symbolism of the thought, gives it more of a concrete or theological consistency.

Representations of Christ enthroned, in portraits with a beard, or even at the center of the college of Apostles, illustrate this synthesis. They therefore merit a closer look. Until recently the tendency has been to see here the application of the emperor's attributes and role to Christ as Ruler of the universe. His position above Coelus on the sarcophagus of Junius Bassus (noted earlier), the portrayal of him with a beard in imitation of the third-century emperors, his posture of enthronement, or the posture of Peter and Paul bowing toward him or assisting him, all would seem to support this "imperial" interpretation. And indeed, many features of imperial iconography are in evidence here. Yet the true significance goes much further, for the very nature of this kind of imperial representation is fundamentally transformed. This transformation is hinted at in a late-fourth-century painting from the Cemetery of SS. Peter and Marcellinus in Rome. Portrayed here as the *imperator,* Christ is victorious. The tools of his victory, however, are not the material ones of the emperor, but spiritual weapons that run counter to prevailing Roman values. They consist of Christ's sacrifice, his humility, his powerlessness, and his human defeat. His "imperial" attributes directly contradict the power wielded by the emperor. This effect is furthermore enhanced in this fresco by the lamb positioned (below Christ) at the center, flanked by the principal Apostles and along the same axis as the bearded Christ who is enthroned between St. Peter and St. Paul.[34] Clearly this is the sacrificial Lamb. In later monuments Christ would continue to appear in these two forms (*imperator* and sacrificial lamb) until asserting himself in sixth- and seventh-century art as the Lamb crowned with a halo, often with a cross or in the symmetry of the cross, sitting on a throne. Once again in this case, we must consider the representation of the enthroned Christ to be a symbol following on earlier precedents. What is more, there is no pursuit of a physical resemblance to Christ, which would be pretty much impossible after three centuries, unless we are to speculate that even in this short duration there was an attempt to establish Christ's actual characteristics.

In this second panel of Christian iconography, Old Testament themes are no longer dominant; the New Testament clears a place for itself. But the panel lives on with a symbolic significance marked by the thought of the time in which it was produced.

Meanwhile we must not fail to mention, from the end of the third century and throughout the fourth, the insertion of concrete scenes depicting professions or persons of the time. We see this, for example, with the coopers shown in the Catacomb of Priscilla in Rome,[35] or the agricultural instruments in the scene found in the hypogeum of Trebius Justus in Rome, where the deceased is portrayed among his parents and servants,[36] or further still the rich gowns of Lady Veneranda in a cubicule in the Cemetery of Domitilla, where the woman is portrayed as being introduced into paradise by St. Petronilla.[37] It is here that subjects or details that were earthly and in some ways profane, but acceptable given the standing or social rank of the individuals concerned, won their way right into Christian representations, according to a conception of art that conformed with the consequences of the Incarnation. It is nonetheless a characteristic which further highlights an orientation toward realism at this stage in early Christian art, and which further nuances the use of symbolism in this period.

Fifth-Century Christian Art

During the fifth century, Christian art, which had derived its basic style from Late Antiquity, began to sketch out, depending on location, the first of what were destined to be its unique constitutive features. At the forefront were those features directly supervised by the Church's hierarchy or the Christian emperor. Among the other features, we see expressions from local elites, such as Coptic Christian art in Egypt, which succeeded pagan Coptic art, contrasting it somewhat and here and there providing its own unique characteristics.

At the end of the fourth century, Theodosius I issued edicts proclaiming Christianity to be the official state religion (380) and banning pagan worship (391). These decrees allowed the Church in the West to proclaim the power that Christ had conferred on it, and allowed the emperor in the East to emphasize, notably in the realm of art, the exercise of his functions as vicar of Christ in the Empire (a role with which Constantine had felt he was invested by virtue of his vision of the battle of the Milvian Bridge).

In a mosaic in the apse of the basilica of Santa Pudenziana in Rome, Christ, depicted beneath the heavenly Jerusalem, is the dominant figure.[38] He sits enthroned between Peter and Paul, who are being crowned, as they sit among the other apostles, by two feminine figures, allegorically representing the Church of the Circumcision and the Church of the Gentiles respectively. The portrayal is not based on any particular New Testament scenes, but is a figurative interpretation of the doctrine preached by Christ and of its consequences. At this point we pass from the level of concrete life and story to the level of figurative theology; the passage is nonetheless in the form of allegories. In this way, the progressive and conscious preeminence of the New Testament is confirmed through a deepening of its fundamental principles. The two allegories of the Church reappear in the same century in Santa Sabina's in Rome. Clearly, then, the Church was posing in its mission, as heir of Christ, to make him triumphant in all the world.

We see this intellectual advance again in the basilica of Santa Maria Maggiore in Rome. It is not as dramatic, insofar as we are still seeing concrete scenes, again in mosaics, in the series of panels along the upper periphery of the walls of the nave and on the triumphal arch.[39] But the didactic intent is clear and conforms well to the educational responsibilities with which the Church saw itself invested. The believer is led through the scenes from the life of Abraham[40] and Jacob on the left side of the nave and those of the life of Moses and Joshua on the right[41]—and thus through the history of the Old Covenant, of which Mary is the flower—to the representation, on the triumphal arch, of the mother of him who is in person the New and eternal Covenant, Jesus Christ. On the arch, then, are scenes from the cycle of Jesus's childhood (the Annunciation, the presentation of the infant at the Temple, the adoration of the Magi, the Holy Family before the Egyptian governor Affrodosius, the massacre of the innocents, the Magi before Herod),[42] ending with depictions of Bethlehem and Jerusalem. While the Holy Child is enthroned as king among the angels and Mary and not far from the Magi, everything is arranged around the dogma of the Mother of God, which had been promulgated the previous year at the Council of Ephesus. In addition, the symbolic throne flanked by St. Peter and St. Paul at the summit of the arch symbolically affirms the role of the Church. The same role is recalled in a scene on the Baptistery of the Sôtêr in Naples, where Christ is depicted as giving the gift of the Law to the Princes of the Apostles; likewise we will see it in the "Mausoleum" of Galla Placidia in Ravenna.

Without boasting its function in theological "guidance," the art of the emperors indeed goes hand in hand with the creative movement at Ravenna.

In the so-called Mausoleum of Galla Placida, everything emanates from the gilded cross on the crossing where the church's nave and transept intersect, a symbol which clearly recalls the particular character of Christ's victory and power.[43] The interpretation of them is particularly pronounced in the lunette on the north side, where the beardless Savior is seated in a supple pose among sheep to whom he stretches his hand in a gesture of tenderness, while holding upright a cruciform shepherd's crook.[44] Truly he appears as the King of the universe through the peace that issues from his cross. Elsewhere, in the lower lunette, St. Lawrence advances toward the rack of his martyrdom,[45] signalling the importance accorded to the cult of the martyrs (beyond that reserved up to this time for the Apostles) even in figurative interpretation. A reminder of the Old Testament, Psalm 42 in particular, is placed on the arms of the transept where, in an ornament of acanthuses, two deer bend toward a small lake surrounded with grass.[46] Whether, however, the cross is thus being subtly evoked or explicitly represented, it is notable that it still does not bear the Crucified; it remains only a symbolic reminder of him.

In the Baptistery of the Orthodox at Ravenna (the theme of which would be resumed in a more mechanical style in the Baptistry of the Arians built in the sixth century), the sacrament of baptism is enhanced by the decoration inside the octagonal building, which presents itself functionally in tiers from the domed ceiling down to the baptismal cistern at ground level.[47] From the cupola, whose *emblêma* portrays the Baptism of Christ,[48] the light of the Holy Spirit, symbolized by the presiding dove, descends onto successive rings which capture the light: the retinue of Apostles holding their martyr's crowns[49]; the liturgical tools of their teaching, particularly the Gospel and the cross; sculpted stuccos in which, under frontons or niches, prophets and apostles are portrayed; and finally the lunettes, where Daniel in the lions' den, Jonah being freed by the whale, and the triumphant Christ are all portrayed.

At Ravenna as well, we should not forget the Christ Militant, with a breastplate under his robe and armed with a cross, depicted in the archiepiscopal palace.[50]

In various other monuments in which the mosaic reigned supreme as an art form, be it in the East, or especially in Rome and much of the West, the Old Testament left the door open for the New. For one thing, scenes drawn from the gospels assumed a more substantial role. Once again at the Baptistery of the Sôtêr at Naples, we find the holy women at the tomb, the Samaritan woman, and the wedding at Cana; but we also see a new scene, the calling of Peter and Andrew by the Sea of Galilee. For another thing, representations of holy martyrs, the "witnesses" of the New Covenant, multiply. We have already mentioned St. Lawrence's presence in a mosaic in the Mausoleum of Galla Placidia in Ravenna. Elsewhere, in St. George's church in Salonica (Thessalonika), seventeen Eastern martyrs, including Cosmas and Damien depicted at prayer,[51] occupy eight architectural compartments; and in the same city, St. Demetrius stands between two founders of the church which bears his name.[52] Furthermore, St. Victor is portrayed in bust framed by a crown of laurels in a mosaic on the cupola of Milan's martyrium chapel of San Vittore[53]; here too in mosaics appear St. Ambrose on one side (albeit not himself a martyr), between the martyrs Gervais and Protais,[54] and on the other side, the bishop Maternus between St. Nabor and St. Felix.

In the freer technique of mausoleum painting, as found in two small chapels at Bagawat (oasis of Kharga) in southwestern Egypt, Old Testament themes persist, mingled with scenes from the New. In the one called the Chapel of the Exodus, some traditional Old Testament scenes show up: Adam and Eve; the sacrifice of Abraham; Noah and the ark; Daniel in the lions' den; the three Hebrews in the furnace[55]; Jonah thrown into the sea, swallowed, thrown up by the whale, and resting in the shade of the vines; the stricken Job; Susanna and the elders; and Moses striking the rock. But there are also some new scenes or ones showing a new technique: Eliezar and Rebekah at the well of Nahor; Jethro; the Israelites being pursued by the Egyptians[56]; the virgins of Jerusalem (from Lamentations) advancing in single file toward a small building; Jeremiah the prophet; and the martyrdom of Isaiah. Others are scenes from the New Testament or based on its theological development: a shepherd among his sheep; St. Thecla at her martyrdom; the vine (which covers the cap of the cupola; groups of three crosses, with the central one an ankh, or ansate cross, appearing at the apex of the arches. In a mausoleum nearby, called the Chapel of Peace, arranged in a style that is decidedly Byzantine, albeit provincially so, appear Daniel in the lions' den; two feminine allegorical figures entitled *Dikaiosunê* (Righteousness) and *Euchê* (Prayer), who are respectively related to facts in the lives of the subjects which follow them, the three Hebrews in the furnace and Susanna; then come Jacob at prayer; Noah's ark[57]; Mary; St. Thecla; St. Paul; Adam and Eve in Eden; the sacrifice of Abraham; and finally the allegorical figure of *Eirênê* (Peace), as related to Daniel and the lions.

Ivory pieces from this period, while not abandoning certain Old Testament subjects such as the sacrifice of Abraham, Moses at the rock, and the three Hebrews in the furnace, draw most of their scenes from the New Covenant. Naturally the adoration of the Magi, the Baptism of Christ, the miracle at Cana (yet with the Twelve included in the depiction), the healings of the paralytic and the woman with a hemorrhage, Peter's denial, the women at the tomb,[58] and the Ascension, all emerge again. But appearing as well on the ivory casket-linings preserved in the British Museum are the Annunciation (near a spring), the Song of Joseph, the Nativity (which includes an ox and a donkey), the preaching of John the Baptist, the arrest of Christ together with Judas's intervention, the way of the cross, the hanging of Judas, and for the first time, it seems, the Crucifixion, along with other scenes from the Passion[59] and Resurrection. Still other scenes in ivory derive from Acts, such as Tabitha with Peter, and Paul reading. A large number of subjects, as even some of the iconographic details in traditional scenes show, are inspired by apocryphal writings; a characteristic example here is the group of St. Paul and St. Thecla depicted on the ivories in the Chapel of Peace at Bagawat in Egypt.

Another piece of Coptic art worth noting is a relief painted on wood, now at the Louvre, which presents a fragmentary Annunciation scene from which the archangel has almost entirely disappeared. The Virgin Mary is depicted as seated at work spinning, conforming to a model which was frequent in Syria in the same period. The style and technical details alike leave no doubt of the Coptic origin of this fragment. In an entirely different and more animated style, a lintel from the Church of Al-Muallaqah in Old Cairo, preserved in the Coptic Museum, portrays Jesus's entry into Jerusalem and the Ascension;[60] a detail in the lintel, inscribed in Greek, connects it to the first half of the fifth century and to the enduring influence of Alexandrian art.

By means of these small-scale arts, concrete details were added to the biblical stories and accentuated them, the stories themselves being more realistic than the official Christian art which portrayed them. The inspiration was such that it did not hesitate on occasion—as we see, for example, in the two adjacent panels of a diptych from the Treasury of the Cathedral in Milan—to enwrap the haloed Lamb with a triumphal crown of laurels, or to adorn the Cross of Calvary (as indicated by its position below the Temple veil) with imitations of precious stones.[61]

On the whole, the fifth century marked a new step toward the penetration of Christian life into the world. While subjects drawn from the New Covenant ultimately outweighed those of the Old, and even while concrete details of profession or dress were introduced, the preponderance of allegorical and symbolic representation was still left intact. The key sign of this was the select place reserved for the Good Shepherd and the mystical Lamb.

Sixth-Century Christian Art

The sixth century saw the first flowering of Byzantine art, properly speaking, which was and would continue to be uniformly constituted of Christian iconography, or iconography profoundly impacted by Christianity.

Just before Byzantine art assumed its unique orientation under the influence of Justinian, it appears that, through a convergence of Eastern and Western features, as much in Rome as in Constantinople, some saints were confirming their presence, others making their entrance for the first time in Christian iconography. As always, the Princes of the Apostles, St. Peter and St. Paul, made their presence felt, as we see in an (Eastern) painting of Peter on wood at St. Catharine's Monastery at Mt. Sinai (generally ascribed to a school of the "Second Rome," Constantinople),[62] or in another (Western) portrayal of him in company with the other apostles in the Baptistery of the Arians in Ravenna.[63] In Rome itself, it is precisely a Byzantine soldier, St. Theodore, who is portrayed in the church consecrated by Pope Felix IV to SS. Cosmas and Damien, who were themselves of Eastern origin. At any rate, the convergences are always limited to Apostles and to certain of the martyrs.

The concern for "visual" instruction inaugurated by Rome's Church of Santa Maria Maggiore was passed on in devotional objects of ordinary personal use, be they plaques or ivory or metal chests. It was natural that such concern inspired the illustration of monuments which were the primary source for knowledge of texts of the Old and New Testaments. The artistic transition occurring in this period turned more toward the expression of life. It reveals itself in Greek manuscripts, where the letters are traced in gold on a purple parchment background. Surviving miniatures, about twenty in each codex, include episodes from Genesis, in the Vienna Genesis codex[64] belonging to the Austrian National Library in Vienna, as well scenes from the gospels, respectively in the Rosanno Gospel codex[65] held in the archiepiscopal Museum of Rossano (Calabria), and in the Sinope Gospel codex[66] held in the Bibliothèque Nationale in Paris. Despite the search for imperial extravagance and some elegance of form in some scenes from the Rossano Gospel and most of the scenes from the Sinope Gospel, the severity with which persons are depicted in the Sinope Gospel, as well as the stockiness of the figures throughout it, otherwise seem to suggest a Syro-Palestinian origin. Such an origin is perhaps confirmed through comparison with the high colorings on a neutral background seen in the Rabbula Gospels,[67] attributed to a Syrian monk from the monastery of Zagba, as well as paintings on wood from a pilgrim's souvenir chest found nearby, belong to the Vatican Museum. The picturesqueness of the gospels was enhanced in this way precisely in the interest of teachings based on the biblical narratives.

With ivory artifacts, the ratio between Old and New Testament subjects, while favoring those of the New, remains fairly balanced. Subjects appearing for the very first time are few in number and duplicated rather rarely. For example, there is a depiction of the story of Joseph in Egypt on the Throne of Maximian in the archiepiscopal palace at Ravenna; the same includes scenes from the cycles of Moses and Jonah, the three Hebrews in the furnace, and Daniel and the lions. Scenes from the life of Christ—the Baptism by John the Baptist, the miracles, notably the multiplication of the loaves,[68] the healings of the woman with a hemorrhage, the paralytic, the man blind from birth,[69] and the Samaritan woman, as well as the raising of Lazarus—are frequent. These scenes are intentionally arranged around the figure of Christ, between two pillars. Scenes from the life of Mary connected with the childhood of Jesus continue to be detailed. Gospel diptychs in ivory consistently depict people around the figure of Christ enthroned between Peter and Paul, and yet, in an adjacent panel, the central motif can in some cases be—as we find in the diptych from the Echmiadzin treasure from Armenia, now in the Bibliothèque Nationale in Paris[70]—the Virgin enthroned between two angels, surrounded by scenes from Christ's childhood with picturesque details borrowed from apocryphal gospels. Mary thus assumes a more prominent place in iconography on pedestals connected most closely with the more "official" art of the Christian Empire, a theological upshot of the Council of Ephesus of 431 and its strong affirmation of the "Mother of God" (*theotokos*). The Princes of the Apostles too, in their function of recalling the Church, do not lack representation in this expensive artistic medium of ivory carving. The cycle of holy martyrs also begins to appear as a subject at this point, such as that of Menas depicted on a pyx found in Rome and held in the British Museum.[71]

In this properly Byzantine period, symbolism maintained its importance. Indeed its value was not diminished by the realism and naturalism which pervaded the artistic rendering of these episodes from the Bible. But no longer was it a matter of such scenes being displayed in sacred places simply as dictated by the peculiar religious function of those sites, as we saw from the third century in the Roman catacombs or the baptistery at Dura-Europos. Now the biblical scenes being portrayed, those based on the New and Old Testaments alike, were assembled around important moments in the life of Christianity, especially liturgical and paraliturgical ceremonies. Tied to such ceremonies by their symbolic significance, the biblical episodes began to pass beyond the level of mere symbolic recall and took on a patently mystical meaning, supported by theology. This is the case, for example, in the souvenir chest mentioned above, and in pilgrim's ampullae found at Monza[72] and Bobbio[73] (Italy), some of which are decorated with scenes from the holy places whose soil or water they contain.

The situation is the same for mosaic monuments. We see it in the magnificent scenes which decorate the front of the chancel in Ravenna's Church of San Vitale: on the north wall, the hospitality of Abraham,[74] and near it the sacrifice of Isaac, and on the south wall the sacrifices of Abel and Melchizedek[75]; these respectively follow, in the presbyterium, Justinian's offering of the paten and Theodora's offering of the chalice, each of them standing at the center of their own corteges, with the whole ensemble oriented, clearly for symbolic purposes, toward the altar in the eucharistic sanctuary.[76]

No less significant, in this perspective, is the presence, also in San Vitale, of the mystical Lamb with halo in the center of the cupola which tops the entire edifice, clearly evoking Christ's triumph by virtue of his sacrifice.[77] The terrible reality of the sacrifice is recalled by the cross which is held up by the Victories at the curvature of each of the four arcades, above the aforementioned biblical scenes. Included in this supporting imagery, we find, at the cornerstones, Isaiah, who sang of the slaughter of the Lamb, and Moses before the burning bush,[78] where the Eternal offered to him his Word. The theme of triumph is further exalted in the apse, where Christ, enthroned upon the world, holds out the victor's crown to St. Vitalis.[79]

The beautiful mosaics of Ravenna's Basilica of Sant' Apollinare Nuovo share precisely the same symbolic and liturgical vision. Here two corteges, one of the martyrs, led by St. Lawrence and St. Martin, the other of virgins, led by the Magi, process respectively toward Christ and toward the Virgin and Child.[80] Even the scenes from the life of Jesus, which (in thirteen panels on each side) decorate the upper walls of the nave between the windows and the ceiling, do not deviate from this intention. These panels were commissioned by the Arian king Theodoric when he had this basilica built in the Savior's honor, in a style clearly bearing the influence of his connections with the Byzantine court. On the left side are the traditionally depicted miracles, to which have been added the parables of the pharisee and the publican and the widow's mite.[81] On the right side, beginning with the Last Supper, are scenes from the Passion (excluding the Crucifixion itself) and Resurrection narratives.[82] This use of iconography extends the liturgical and catechetical function of this art, but by particularly emphasizing the Eucharist and its foreshadowings (the miracle at Cana and the multiplication of the loaves), as well the healing of the paralytic and appearance of Christ to the Apostles—all of which are located close to the altar—the mystical significance of Christ's victorious sacrifice is exalted all the more.

A strong symbolic urge distinguishes the portrayal of the Transfiguration in the apse of Ravenna's Basilica of Sant' Apollinare in Classe.[83] Instead of reproducing the persons and details which make up the story, it recalls them only through the half-figures of Moses and Elijah who, situated in thin clouds above three lambs (Peter, James, and John), flank a large jeweled cross. The cross itself is inscribed on an encircling background of myriad stars (the realm of glory), and has at its center a small medallion with a bust of Christ. Dimensionally speaking, this sublime ensemble pales in comparison with the erect figure of St. Apollinaris which hovers over the apse, precisely in the place where we would expect to find the figure of Christ. But the figure of Christ situated here would constitute a useless repetition in view of the bust already at the center of the cross. Moreover, if the twelve sheep, depicted here in two groups of six, were aligned at the feet of Jesus Christ, the principal figure in the whole scene, instead of at the feet of St. Apollinaris, the scene's true purpose would not be served.

As in Santa Maria Maggiore in Rome in the preceding century, where the Virgin bore the insignias of an "Augusta," Mary is painted with the attributes of a queen in the Church of Santa Maria Antiqua, also in Rome. Such accorded with the invocations of the acathiste hymn composed in her honor in Greek, a hymn which was prized more in the West than in the East in this period, and which was focused more on Mary's spiritual role.

At Parenzo, on the Dalmatian coast, in the Basilica of St. Euphrasius, sixth-century mosaics in the central apse reveal the Virgin-Mother enthroned between two angels and two saints, and those of the Annunciation and Visitation[84] further emphasize the foundations of Mary's role in this respect. The Parenzo mosaics favor all the more, perhaps, those figures who seem to enhance the doctrine of Incarnation: the archangel Michael holding a globe; the prophet Zachariah preaching; John the Baptist with a cross; the beardless Christ, seated on a globe between the twelve Apostles at the summit of the apse, or else blessing SS. Cosmas and Damien, and Ursus and Severus; on the facade, the Transfiguration (which is now missing), and Christ teaching the Apostles; on the sides of the central apse, busts of saints in medallions which progressively lead toward the divine Lamb. We can see this as a response to monophysitism; the didactic intent would surpass, but does not in the meantime weaken, the symbolism.

In St. Catharine's Monastery at Mt. Sinai, a mosaic of the Transfiguration,[85] likewise dating from the sixth century (specifically the time of Justinian's reign), occupies the apse of the community's large church; it is surrounded with medallions containing busts of prophets and of the Apostles who were not present at the Transfiguration. The subject is new, but it is envisioned, through the presence of the person of Moses (with the Transfigured Christ) in the New Covenant, as the proper result of the Old Covenant, which is signified by the figure of Moses on Mt. Sinai, on the left side of the arch, and Moses receiving the Law on the right side. Moreover, we cannot separate from these depictions the two painted portraits of St. Peter and of Mary enthroned between two angels and two saints.

In Coptic art, the remains of wall frescos in the church of the cave monastery of Deir Abu Hennis in the Nile Valley of Middle Egypt align themes relating mainly to the cycle of Jesus's Childhood. At the monastery of Bawît in the western desert a little further south, some devotional chapels are decorated with painted scenes, including the Baptism of Christ, some holy monks, and a bust of Christ in a circle born by angels, above the portraits of holy knights. Here we discover, in a style more characteristic of Alexandria, two directions which seem to share in the evolution of iconographic inspiration in this period of Christian artistic usage: first, a certain realism achieved by breaking down gospel scenes into their proper details, and by introducing contemporary saints into the repertoire; and second, the application of theological thinking to the role of Christ. These two parallel tendencies are reflected in the monastery of Jeremiah in Saqqarah, in paintings of a group of holy monks, including Apa Apollo,[86] founder of the monastery at Bawît, which are now preserved in the Coptic Museum in Cairo. In the same monastery, we also see these two tendencies in sculptured representations under the niche of the enthroned Mary and in paintings of Mary nursing. By the changes in proportion of the subjects, notably Mary, the characteristically Coptic style stands out, a style scarcely represented in Constantinople.

Thus, with pictorial illustrations or decoration intended to be instructive, like those themes passed down in ivory-decorated liturgical objects, the proliferation of detailed scenes from the gospels—which surpassed those of the Old Testament without wholly abolishing them—granted increasing access to the "reality" which, up to this point, had been represented for the most part symbolically. In addition, reflection on the role of Christ, with which the role of his mother was closely associated, tended to exalt him, in an artistic extension (from the symbolic into the mystical) that aspired to enhance the mystical sources of Christian doctrine. These two directions in theological thinking and its artistic translation could not help but reinforce each other.

Christian Art in the Seventh Century and Beyond

Of these two artistic currents, inherited by the seventh-century Church, the first was quite naturally perpetuated in ivory carvings, and more so in painting; the second continued to express itself in official mosaic art. The latter is exemplified in the apse of the Baptistry of the Chapel of San Venanzio in Rome's Church of San Giovanni in Laterano, where, beneath a bust of Christ giving a blessing between two angels, Mary is portrayed kneeling in prayer between two saints, with other attending saints lining the walls.[87] At this point in time, certain saints also began to obtain comparable honors, such as St. Agnes, who is depicted between Popes Symmachus and Honorius in the Church of Santa Agnese fuori le Mura (St. Agnes Outside the Walls) in Rome.

Ivories in fact diminished in use in this period, and disappeared completely by the eighth century; only in the tenth century did their use resume, and in a completely different style. This rupture has been linked to economic difficulties prior to iconoclasm and to the repression of refinements of luxury in Constantinople. But this was not only the doing of the Byzantines, and we should perhaps observe here a change of tendencies, if not of tastes, in this period. The only subjects which appear to have survived from the seventh century are the Nativity and the miracles of Christ.

Henceforth it was frescos that captured the realism, indeed the picturesqueness, of Christian iconography of the day. Yet the only surviving examples of these frescos come from the West, in contrast with the Byzantine artistic surface, which was characteristically more sensitive to light playing on the gentle asperities of the mosaic. If the technique for rendering details and figures is freer in painting than in mosaics, its style still remains noble. It is equally significant that it occurred to fresco painters to borrow from the apocryphal gospels.

319

Toward the middle of the seventh century, at Rome's Church of Santa Maria Antiqua, several frescos reflect the grand classical composition, which still betrayed a Byzantine influence since the inscriptions which accompany them are in Greek. Three subjects are noteworthy: St. Anne carrying Mary in her arms, the Annunciation, and Salomone, mother of the Maccabeans (an Old Testament subject symbolizing the sufferings of the Virgin). In the same hieratic style, a figure of the face of St. Luke is fixed on a wall of the Roman catacomb of Commodilla, dating from the last quarter of the century. Near the turn of the eighth century, an entire cycle of the Childhood of Christ is represented north of Milan at the Church of Santa Maria di Castelseprio. The cycle goes from the Annunciation to the death of Zechariah, while passing through the song of Joseph, the journey to Bethlehem, the announcement to the shepherds, all in a circle around a portrait of the bust of the Savior.[88] The subjects, as much in their choice and arrangement as in their details, are clearly borrowed from the apocryphal *Protevangelium of James*. Without losing any of their classical nobility, a slight animation pervades the characters of the fresco.

It is in Coptic Egypt, nevertheless, albeit at a slightly later date, that we find paintings inspired even more distinctly by theology. In one chapel of the monastery at Bawît, in a mandorla (almond-shaped picture) beneath the enthroned Christ and held up by four symbols of the evangelists, Mary is depicted as an erect orant;[89] in another place she is the Virgin-Mother (again beneath the enthroned Christ), herself enthroned at the center of the group of Apostles who serve as her spectators.[90] Elsewhere in the chapels of Bawît, walls are lined with the paintings of sainted Coptic monks.

Among the smaller-scale arts, Christians subjects, though no longer presented in ivory carvings, found expression in other mediums.

The symbol of the Victory of Christ, which is affirmed in the depiction of the mystical Lamb, had continued in the sixth century. At the end of the sixth century, for example, in the silver cross of Justin II preserved in the Vatican Museum, the Lamb appears, haloed and with his body supporting a cross, in a medallion at the intersection of the cross's branches. The extremities of the shaft of the cross bear the bust of Christ in a medallion, while those of the arms respectively carry busts of the emperor and his wife, likewise in medallions.[91]

Subjects drawn from the gospels are more highly developed and consequently represented in far greater concrete detail, as attested by the "Communion of the Apostles from the hand of Christ" on a silver paten found at Riha, Syria, and now in the Byzantine antiquities collection at Dumbarton Oaks.[92] Meanwhile, Old Testament subjects retain their more modest frequency.

Some of these subjects, especially New Testament ones, are elaborated in such a way as to be immersed in the concrete reality of the moment. We see this in wedding jewelry where Christ is depicted standing slightly behind the married couple and placing his hand on their joined hands. Such is found, for example, on a gold belt buckle now belonging to the Louvre.

In this period, the saints, at the side of Christ and the Virgin, gain greater representation. The Apostles maintain their privileged position, and are most often depicted in bust in medallions. They are portrayed this way, for example, in the large Coptic tapestry of the Virgin and Child enthroned between the archangels Michael and Gabriel, now in the Cleveland Museum of Art.

Portraits on wood followed existing ones from the sixth century, notably from Coptic Egypt, and from the seventh century, from the Sinai. We are talking here mainly of portraits of Mary, and in one instance, Peter. At Rome, Mary was still portrayed with the Holy Child. One portrait, the oldest of her on wood in the West, dates from the beginning of the seventh century and is located at the Pantheon, while another, originally from Rome's Church of Santa Maria Antiqua, is now in the sacristy of the Church of Santa Francesca Romana (previously known as Santa Maria Nuova); both of these examples show up a hieratic style. By contrast, in Egypt, in the style so peculiar to Coptic art, two paintings on wood present venerated holy men. One portrait from Bawît now preserved in the Louvre depicts Abba Menas, superior of a monastery, being protected by Christ, who holds his arm around the abba's shoulders in a gesture inherited from the ancient Pharaohs.[93] Another, from Saqqarah, now in the collection of the Berlin Museum, displays a bust of the bishop Abraham.

One movement of popular origin that revealed itself in the second half of the sixth century, by reinforcing the emphasis on the concrete, paralleled more "official" tendencies toward expression of the concrete evident in objects of liturgical or devotional usage. The movement is effectively manifested in an *achiropoietic* (not made with human hands) "portrait" of Christ discovered in a niche overhanging the gate of the town of Edessa (Syria), a portrait which had allegedly delivered the city from foreign occupation after it had been besieged by the Persians in 544. It presents the face of Christ, which had been miraculously affixed on a veil. Supposedly the apostle Thaddeus had brought it to King Abgar of Osrhoene in response to a letter the king had sent to Christ imploring him to heal him of leprosy. The mention on the veil of the formula *En toutô nika* induced certain Byzantine historians of the late-sixth and early-seventh centuries to interpret the representation here as a new *labarum* (Christian insignia), at this point figurative and, by the same token, functioning as a pledge of victory. Four other such portraits existed at the same time around the Byzantine Empire. Emperors like Heraclius used them at the time for military purposes. This portrait would occupy a privileged place on the emperor's throne, as much in churches as in the imperial palace in Constantinople; indeed, it would enjoy the same honors as the emperor. For everyone it became an effective symbol of the victory over evil. It was the point of departure for the "icon" and for the icon's present value for believers, a value which was extended to the Virgin and the saints. The abuses to which iconography was exposed would lead in the eighth century to the extended iconoclastic controversy in Constantinople and across the Empire. Thanks to the work of St. John Damascene (and after him, St. Theodore the Studite) in articulating a revised theological defense of iconography, the icon would reemerge in the ninth century purified and triumphant throughout the territories and spheres of influence of the Byzantine Empire.

This immersion of the symbol in the features of concrete reality and in the customs of daily life is doubtless partially responsible for the redaction of article 80 in the decrees of the Quinisext Council held in Constantinople in 692. This article explicitly rejected *symbolic* representations of Christ, but it confirmed ipso facto the tremendous value which Christians up to this time had attached to the use of figurative means of expression in depicting persons from the Old Testament and the New. The Lamb is specifically cited in the article as the most esteemed example of a symbol used to represent Christ and to be a depiction of him. The article instead prescribes the enhancement of the Savior's human attributes as the means of expressing his divinity, based on the doctrine of the Incarnation. It furthermore recommends pursuing not the real physical likeness of Christ, but the tracing of those human characteristics which "suit" the divinity of Christ, and thus the decree did not ultimately stifle the spiritual movement at the heart of symbolic thought. It was a turning point, but it still left the way open for symbolic usage. Its importance would not be diminished until the emergence of the secularizing abuses of the Renaissance. In the meantime, while the theme of the mystical Lamb was discouraged, that of the enthroned Christ would endure and be amplified even more. It was destined to symbolize, in its own unique way, the victory over evil won with the weapon of Christ's own *kenôsis*, his total self-giving in humility, the very gift which he brought from his heavenly Father.

NOTES

1. Cf. J. L. Harry, *The Jews of Ancient Rome* (Philadelphia, 1960), fig. 10, fig. 14; also H. Leclercq, *Manuel d'archéologie chrétienne depuis les origines jusqu'a VIIIe siècle* (Paris, 1907), vol. 1, 122-123.

2. Cf. H. Stern, *Le calendrier de 354* (Paris, 1953), *passim*.

3. See P. du Bourguet, *Early Christian Art*, trans. T. Burton (New York and Amsterdam, 1971), 40ff.

4. J. Wilpert, *Le pitture delle catacombe romane* (Rome, 1903), 141. See also du Bourguet, *Early Christian Art*, 56 and n. 34.

5. P. Styger, *Die römischen Katacomben* (Berlin, 1933); and du Bourguet, 56 and n. 36.

6. See plate in du Bourguet, *Early Christian Art*, 25. (Citations of major reference works on early Christian art, which contain illustrations or plates of many of the pieces described in this essay, have been added to this English edition of Bourguet's essay, in the interest of facilitating the reader's access to the primary artistic material itself. —Ed.).

7. For an example, see A. Grabar, *Christian Iconography: A Study of Its Origins* (Princeton, 1968), appendix, fig. 1.

8. See fig. in du Bourguet, *Early Christian Art*, 98.

9. See plate, ibid., 89; also Grabar, *Christian Iconography*, fig. 28.

10. See plate in du Bourguet, *Early Christian Art*, 85.

11. See fig., ibid., 95, and plate, ibid., 97.

12. See fig., ibid., 102; Grabar, *Christian Iconography*, fig. 4; also idem, *Early Christian Art: From the Rise of Christianity to the Death of Theodosius*, trans. S. Gilbert and J. Emmons (New York, 1968), 33 (fig. 31).

13. See plates in du Bourguet, *Early Christian Art*, 9, 21; Grabar, *Christian Iconography*, fig. 2.

14. See fig. in du Bourguet, *Early Christian Art*, 10, and plate, ibid., 53.

15. See Grabar, *Christian Iconography*, fig. 25; also idem, *Early Christian Art*, 25 (fig. 22).

16. See fig. in du Bourguet, *Early Christian Art*, 46.

17. See figs., ibid., 50, 51.

18. See plate, ibid., 81.

19. See Grabar, *Early Christian Art*, 109 (fig. 107).

20. See plate in du Bourguet, *Early Christian Art*, 19; Grabar, *Early Christian Art*, 209 (fig. 230).

21. See plate in du Bourguet, *Early Christian Art*, 11.
22. See Grabar, *Early Christian Art*, 69-71 (figs. 60-63); idem, *Christian Iconography*, fig. 44.
23. See Grabar, *Early Christian Art*, 69 (fig. 59).
24. For a more extensive discussion of this transition, see du Bourguet, *Early Christian Art*, 119ff.
25. See figs., ibid., 166, 167; Grabar, *Christian Iconography*, fig. 29.
26. On the Via Latina discoveries, see Grabar, *Early Christian Art*, 225-233; also L. Kötzsche-Breitenbruch, *Die neue Katakombe an der Via Latina in Rom: Untersuchungen zur Iconographie der altestamentlichen Wandmalereien* (with plates), Jahrbuch für Antike und Christentum, Erganzungband 4 (Münster Westfalen, 1976).
27. A number of the scenes in the Via Latina paintings mentioned above can be seen in Grabar, *Early Christian Art*, 229-235 (figs. 252-254, 257, 259-260); also idem, *Christian Iconography*, figs. 242, 272.
28. See plate in du Bourguet, *Early Christian Art*, 121; also Grabar, *Early Christian Art*, 217 (fig. 238).
29. See plate in du Bourguet, *Early Christian Art*, 129, and fig., ibid., 131.
30. See plate, ibid., 123.
31. See plate, ibid., 121.
32. See plate and figs., ibid., 185-187.
33. See fig., ibid., 206.
34. See fig., ibid., 171.
35. See plate, ibid., 157.
36. See Grabar, *Early Christian Art*, 222 (fig. 244).
37. See plate in du Bourguet, *Early Christian Art*, 153.
38. See Grabar, *Christian Iconography*, figs. 80, 172.
39. See G. Schiller, *Iconography of Christian Art* (New York, 1971), vol. 1, plate 52.
40. See Grabar, *Christian Iconography*, figs. 143, 274.
41. Ibid., figs. 132, 133, 135, 137, 141, 286.
42. See Schiller, *Iconography*, vol. 1, plates 66, 230, 250, 256, 301.
43. See R. Krautheimer, *Early Christian and Byzantine Architecture*, 4th ed. (Harmondsworth, 1986), 183 (fig. 146).
44. See G. Bovini, *Ravenna Mosaics* (New York, 1957), plate 2.
45. Ibid., plate 3.
46. Ibid., plate 4.
47. See Krautheimer, *Early Christian and Byzantine Architecture*, 178 (fig. 142).
48. Grabar, *Christian Iconography*, fig. 291.
49. See fig. in Bovini, *Ravenna Mosaics*, 14; also plates 6-8.
50. Ibid., plate 14.
51. See Grabar, *Christian Iconography*, fig. 192.
52. See fig. in K. Weitzmann, ed., *Age of Spirituality: Late Antique and Early Christian Art, Third to Seventh Century* (New York, 1979), 554 (no. 500).
53. See Grabar, *Christian Iconography*, fig. 180.
54. Ibid., fig. 184.

55. See plate in du Bourguet, *Early Christian Art*, 161.
56. Ibid.
57. See fig., ibid., 163.
58. See fig. in du Bourguet, *Early Christian Art*, 195.
59. See R. Lovelace, *Byzantium* (Cambridge, Mass., 1988), 11 (fig. 8), 15 (fig. 15).
60. See fig. in *The Coptic Encyclopedia*, ed. A. Atiya (New York, 1991), vol. 1, 245.
61. See Schiller, *Iconography*, vol. 1, plates 53, 423.
62. See K. Weitzmann, *The Monastery of Saint Catharine at Mount Sinai: the Icons* (Princeton, 1976), plates VIII-IX.
63. See Schiller, *Iconography*, vol. 1, plate 355.
64. See Grabar, *Christian Iconography*, figs. 219-221.
65. Ibid., figs. 226-227.
66. Ibid., figs. 228-229, 236.
67. Ibid., figs. 230-231.
68. Ibid., figs. 257-258.
69. Ibid., fig. 65.
70. See Schiller, *Iconography*, vol. 1, plate 58; Grabar, *Christian Iconography*, figs. 204-205; cf. the sixth-century diptych from Constantinople (now in Berlin's Staatliche Museum), fig. in Weitzmann (ed.), *Age of Spirituality*, 528-529 (no. 474).
71. See figs. in Weitzmann (ed.), *Age of Spirituality*, 575 (no. 514).
72. See Grabar, *Christian Iconography*, figs. 176, 194, 209, 275, 296, 303, 317, 318, 320.
73. Ibid., figs. 295, 319.
74. Ibid., fig. 273.
75. Ibid., fig. 341; Bovini, *Ravenna Mosaics*, plate 41. See also, more recently, S. Schrenk, *Typos und Antitypos in der frühchristlichen Kunst* (with plates), Jahrbuch für Antike und Christentum, Erganzungband 21 (Münster Westfalen, 1995).
76. See Bovini, *Ravenna Mosaics*, plates 28-37.
77. See Grabar, *Christian Iconography*, fig. 341.
78. See Bovini, *Ravenna Mosaics*, plate 42.
79. See Grabar, *Christian Iconography*, fig. 340.
80. See Bovini, *Ravenna Mosaics*, plates 20-22, 26.
81. See Schiller, *Iconography*, vol. 1, plates 428-437; also Bovini, *Ravenna Mosaics*, plates 23, 24.
82. See Schiller, *Iconography*, vol. 2, plates 67, 141, 158, 159, 185, 196, 197, 208; also Bovini, *Ravenna Mosaics*, plate 27.
83. See Schiller, *Iconography*, vol. 1, plate 405.
84. See Grabar, *Christian Iconography*, fig. 314.
85. See Schiller, *Iconography*, vol. 1, plate 407.
86. See J. Quibell, *Excavations at Saqqara* (Cairo, 1908), plate 44.
87. See Grabar, *Christian Iconography*, figs. 322, 107.

88. Ibid., plate 312.
89. Ibid., plates 325, 326.
90. Ibid., plate 324; cf. plate 323.
91. See D. Talbot Rice, *The Art of Byzantium* (London, 1959), fig. 71.
92. See the *Handbook of The Byzantine Collection* (Dumbarton Oaks) (Washington, 1967), plate 61.
93. See fig. in Weitzmann (ed.), *Age of Spirituality*, 552 (no. 497).

PART V

The Bible and Religious Devotion
in the Early Greek Church

16

Biblical Themes
in Greek Eucharistic Anaphoras

IRÉNÉE-HENRI DALMAIS, O.P.

"The Lord's Supper," the Memorial left by Jesus to his disciples at the Last Supper on "the night he was betrayed," the Christian Eucharist, has always and in all places looked to conform faithfully to the primitive tradition passed on by Paul to the Corinthian church which was considered to exemplify the characteristic traits of this meal. Paul described the tradition in this way: "The Lord Jesus on the night when he was betrayed took bread, and when he had given thanks, he broke it, and said, 'This is my body which is for you. Do this in remembrance of me.' In the same way also the cup, after supper, saying, 'This cup is the new covenant in my blood. Do this, as often as you drink it, in remembrance of me'...." (1 Cor. 11:23-25). It is the prayer of benediction (*berakah*) over the bread and the cup which constitutes the original root of all eucharistic prayers or Christian anaphoras that wish to remain faithful to tradition. Unfortunately we have little information about "table benedictions" used in hellenized Jewish communities. Yet we can assume that essentially they conformed to what we have come to know as rabbinic tradition and what, in the process of development, determined the shape of later rituals that have come down to us.[1] According to rabbinic tradition, which has been well attested since the third century C.E., all "benedictions" must make mention of the divine Name and of the Kingdom.

In recent years, however, more attention has been paid to a nuance of vocabulary that has been neglected far too often. Christians had favored the word *eucharistia* very early on, even as early as the writing of the Pauline epistles. This term occurs very rarely in the Septuagint. It or its various derivatives appear only a dozen times. No Hebrew equivalent can be found except for a rather insignificant passage in Proverbs 11:16. *Eucharistia* and its derivatives appear in texts which were written in Greek or have come down to us only in Greek.[2] By contrast, Aquila uses *eucharistia* nine times to translate the Hebrew *tôdah*, most notably in the Psalms. Attention is thus drawn to a type of sacrifice which, though having only a secondary status in the priestly redactions, seems probably to belong to the most ancient source of the Mosaic cult, notably in the Deuteronomic tradition, and to have been considered by the psalmists as the most perfect form of the sacrificial cult. Elsewhere in Philo, *eucharistia* again appears as the expression par excellence of spiritual worship.[3] Furthermore, it is the word *hôdôt* or *hôdayôt*, stemming from the same root as *tôdah*, that refers in the Qumran community to an important collection of hymns. H. Cazelles concludes his important study devoted to this problem of apparently secondary vocabulary by writing:

> The destruction of the Temple should have finished the role of *tôdah* in the Jewish community. But it had its place in the Christian community where the true Temple was the body of Christ. The Christian community was able to take over these triumphal hymns from 2 Maccabees (2 Mac. 1:11, 2:27, 10:7) and celebrate and confess the victory of God in his Christ....Thus the Christian Eucharist is more a proclamation of the victory of Christ through his passion and resurrection than a gesture of thanksgiving. The words of the consecration evoked this proclamation in a context which was destined to become an anaphora.[4]

This is certainly the tone which characterizes the most ancient "Eucharist" transmitted to us in the Greek language from the *Didache* (chapters 9-10). Whether this is a "eucharistic prayer" or "anaphora" in the technical sense that these expressions have assumed in liturgical traditions is probably impossible to determine. Furthermore, as we have come to recognize, such a distinction would have been meaningless in this ancient context. Yet recent studies have increasingly brought to light that in the four-part structure of Jewish graces or benedictions given at the table, a new perspective is introduced which integrates the rather abundant legacies of biblical tradition.[5] W. Rordorf, who prefers to consider at least the formula in *Didache* 10 as a *praefatio*, points out several aspects of this new perspective at the levels of christology, ecclesiology and eschatology. He writes:

> According to the *Didache*, which reproduces in this connection formulas used in the primitive Church, Jesus had not abolished Jewish

messianic expectations but rather revealed the deeper meaning, and the verb *gnôrizein*, which appears three times in 9.2-3 and 10.2 is thus quite suggestive... The ecclesiology of the eucharistic prayers in the *Didache* is equally quite characteristic. In these prayers, the Church, that is, God's chosen people, is essentially founded on the messianic vocation of Israel. She is the "vine of David" (9.2), the living temple of God (10.2), the place of salvation where "life, knowledge, and immortality" (9.3 and 10.2) are found on the one hand, and "food and spiritual drink" (10.3) on the other... As for the eschatology of the eucharistic prayers in the *Didache*, it too retains the same perspective since it expresses the experience of the anticipated realization of the society of the elect. Yet this realization is incomplete and transitory, and so the community prays intensely for the fulfillment of the divine promises... In these conditions, the Jewish prayers of benediction at the table appear to be profoundly reworked in the *Didache*. Henceforth they would refer to Jesus, the Messiah who fulfilled the promises made to the people of Israel, so that hope no longer turned exclusively towards the future by evoking the past. Now the church was assured of the experience of the divine presence. In all cases, the eucharistic prayers of the *Didache* are still very Jewish in their structure and their conception. This is why in all likelihood they derived from the earliest Christian communities of Palestine and Syria.[6]

This ancient structure and conception, so profoundly rooted in the traditions of Jewish prayer and so pregnant with biblical resonances evoking the whole mystery of salvation, come to expression exclusively in Christian communities under heavy semitic influence. Such is the environment of Mesopotamian Christianity in which the Aramaean (Syriac) language prevailed. Elsewhere eucharistic prayers would be modeled more or less directly on the trinitarian structure of the baptismal confession of faith. They would develop a christology that emphasized as much the doctrine of the Logos as the historic moments of the work of salvation accomplished in Christ, by explicitly setting forth the tradition of the story of the institution within the framework of the Last Supper and the perspective of the Passion.

The essential lines of this schema are already observable in the formulation found in Hippolytus's *Apostolic Tradition*. While the original Greek text has unfortunately not survived, the quite literal Latin translation, and the Ethiopian version which has survived in liturgical usage from at least the fifteenth century, permit us to restore it.[7] As is well known, the Eucharistic Prayer II from the Roman missal of Pope Paul VI (1969) is rather strictly inspired by the *Apostolic Tradition*. Jesus Christ is described as *païs*, the child-servant, conforming to the ancient christology which made use of Deutero-Isaiah. The Ethiopian version interprets this as "son" according to a more highly developed christology. He is declared to be both "Messenger of the [divine] counsel" (an allusion to Isa. 9:5) and the "Inseparable Word through whom you have created all things." Doubtless the sacerdotal character of the offering was underlined by the expression *hierateuein*, which is somewhat watered down in the Latin version with the simple term *ministrare*. If one notes that the invocation (*epiclêsis*) of the Holy Spirit (in so far as this portion can be considered to belong to a primitive redaction) asks that this Spirit come to bring about the "gathering" of those who participate in this sacred act "for the confirmation of their faith in the truth," it appears that in several very sober expressions this schema of eucharistic prayer was recalling the decisive moments in the ministry of salvation as accomplished by Christ. It began with the time he "was sent from heaven into the womb of a virgin" and was "manifested as your Son, born of the Holy Spirit and the Virgin," and moved on to the moment when "Fulfilling your will and preparing for you a holy people, he stretched forth his hands to suffer that he might deliver from suffering those who trust in you... and might abolish death, shatter the bonds of the Devil, tread hell under foot, enlighten the righteous, establish the ordinance, and demonstrate the resurrection." Such was the decisive work of liberation, accomplishing beyond all hope that which, certainly from the time of Deutero-Isaiah, appeared as the epitome of divine self-revelation. It was the manifestation of a God who revealed himself by delivering his people from all slavery and gathering them together in peace. It was with this thread, which merits the title of "apostolic tradition," that the anaphoras subsisting in liturgical usage were variously embroidered.

Although it is doubtful that the eucharistic liturgy as it has been handed down to us in Book 7 of the *Apostolic Constitutions*, which was designed to replace the *Apostolic Tradition,* was ever actually used, it is impossible to pass over it in silence here. This "Clementine liturgy," as it is frequently called, proves exceptionally rich in biblical allusions. In it one can hear the echo of the Jewish Christian communities of northern Syria. W. Bousset drew attention to the links between this text and several typically Jewish Christian "benedictions" inserted from their prayer book into Book VII of the *Apostolic Constitutions* after having been adapted in the *Didache* (*Apost. Const.* 7.33-38). But it is chiefly Fr. Louis Ligier who, in various works has illuminated the links between the long eucharistic prayer of remembrance of divine blessings in the work of creation and the history of Israel, inserted before the angelic Trisagion, and the *Avodah*,

or service of the high priest for *Yom Kippur*.[8] Ligier has personally translated several versions of this particular service. After a detailed recollection of the work of creation, the original beatitude in paradise, the gift of
natural law, the fall and its consequences, and the sermon promising
resurrection to Adam, the service calls to mind the righteous, from Abel
to Moses and Joshua, whose name points to Christ the new guide who
will lead the people of God into the true promised land. Then, in a detailed recounting of the great moments from Christ's life, the story of the
institution of the Last Supper is highlighted at the center of the anaphora,
thus becoming its capstone. During the entire eucharistic anamnesis of
the great figures from the old covenant, the sacerdotal perspective is
strongly highlighted. It is taken up again after the story of the institution in
the prayer asking for recognition of the offering. The similarities to the
formulas of the priestly *Avodah* for *Yom Kippur* and the fact that the formula
of the *Apostolic Constitutions* is found within the framework of an episcopal ordination have led M. Metzger to suggest that our anaphora could
have been used for episcopal ordinations.[9] The anaphora of the *Apostolic
Tradition* already underscores the continuity between the apostolic ministry of Christian bishops and the priestly office of Mosaic tradition. In elucidating at length what was only briefly hinted at before, the redactor of the
Apostolic Constitutions places the accent, perhaps more clearly than ever
before, on the sacrificial character—sacrificial in the sense of the expiation
of sins as expressed in the liturgy of *Yom Kippur*—of the Memorial of the
Covenant that is constitutive for the celebration of the Eucharist. Therein
we are reunited to the perspective from which the priestly redactors had
reordered various traditions to constitute the *Torah*.

This perspective was nevertheless not destined to be as clearly
embraced by the various eucharistic anaphoras which, during this same
early Christian era, found the form they would maintain in liturgical usage. The form under which they have been transmitted to us is certainly
the result of a long period of development, which doubtless came to term
only around the eighth and ninth centuries, the period from which our
most ancient manuscripts derive.[10] All of them bear witness to the complex interplay of influences and exchanges between various local traditions and to a truly ecumenical consensus on the structure of the eucharistic prayer. Also discernible, however, is the decisive role played by
several large cultural, theological, and spiritual centers which laid claim
to apostolic tradition, namely Antioch, Alexandria and Jerusalem. The
pivotal part played by the Cappadocian Fathers in the doctrinal and

ecclesiological struggle that made possible an acceptable solution to the interminable Arian crisis would insure the prestige of the anaphoras transmitted under the patronage of Basil, particularly when one of the Basilian recensions came to be, along with an Antiochene anaphora under the patronage of John Chrysostom, one of the official formulas in the liturgy of the Great Church in Constantinople. The desire to bring to light, in the face of risks of Arian deviation, the contested aspects of the orthodox faith as defined at Nicea and more precisely articulated at Constantinople (381), would result in the reshaping of these ancient anaphoras within a more or less explicit trinitarian structure. As a result, the biblical references would often be less obvious. At least this was the case for the principal anaphoras in use in the Greek-speaking world since, in reaction, the locales that were the most strongly attached to specifically Antiochene traditions and to biblical rigorism would rework two anaphoras translated into Syriac, undoubtedly during the fifth century. According to certain manuscripts these translations were made by the Catholicos Mar Aba around 540 C.E., and they remain in use in the so-called Nestorian churches identified under the patronage of Nestorius and Theodore of Mopsuestia. If the first tradition primarily testifies to the compilation of anaphoras from Basil and Chrysostom, the second tradition is a veritable rhapsody of New Testament and particularly Pauline allusions, in line with the one whom these churches venerated as the "Interpreter" par excellence of Scripture.[11]

The Greek text of the Alexandrian anaphora,[12] said to have come from Mark, comes down to us only through later redactions strongly influenced by the traditions of Cappadocia and Jerusalem. But a Coptic version under the patronage of Cyril of Alexandria and fragments preserved in this same language enable us to speculate about more ancient recensions. The work of creation was only briefly sketched but the role of the Logos was highlighted: "You have created everything through Wisdom, the true Light, your Son, our Savior and Lord Jesus Christ." In order to characterize the 'spiritual sacrifice' which constitutes the eucharistic oblation, Malachi 1:11 is quoted. As in the anaphora attributed to Bishop Serapion,[13] the introduction to the *Sanctus* quotes Ephesians 1:12 word for word and joins with it a biblical cento made up of Daniel 7:10, Ezekiel 1:5-18, Revelation 4:6-8, and Isaiah 6:2-3, describing the celestial liturgy of praise.[14] Throughout the anaphora, the strong emphasis is on divine holiness and the sanctification communicated through the eucharistic celebration.

More numerous and significant are the biblical allusions adorning the anaphora from Jerusalem, whose patronage is credited to James the "brother of the Lord." Noticeably the most distinctive trait here is the reference made in the initial glorification (after the hymn of praise celebrating "the heavens of the heavens and all their powers, the sun and the moon and the whole retinue of stars, the earth, the sea and everything found therein") to "Jerusalem, heavenly city, assembly of the first-born enrolled in heaven." This reference to Hebrews 12:22-23 would be developed in the subsequent Greek text by the recalling of "the spirit of the righteous and the prophets, the souls of martyrs and apostles" before mentioning the diverse ranks of celestial powers which are joined to the earthly church in Isaiah's Trisagion acclamation. This is the case for most of the anaphoras. It should be noted that in the hymn of praise for visible creation in Mark's subsequent anaphora no reference is made to Jerusalem, the celestial city, church of the first-born enrolled in heaven. This pericope from Hebrew 12, so dear to the Jerusalem community, remains somewhat enigmatic and commentators do not agree on its exact interpretation. The *Mystagogical Catecheses* (5.6) attributed to Cyril of Jerusalem appear ignorant of this addition; hence it stops with the mention "Of heaven, of earth and the sea, of the sun and moon, the stars, of all creation, rational and irrational, visible and invisible" as well as various orders of angels. The Alexandrian anaphora in its various recensions and the "Prayer of Bishop Serapion" agree in introducing the Memorial of the eucharistic institution by basing it on the glory which fills heaven and earth. The epiclesis of each petitions God to deign to fulfill the sacrifice offered through his benediction with a visitation (*epiphoitêsis*) of the Holy Spirit.

The Jerusalem anaphora, along with the rest of the Eastern and Western eucharistic prayers, initiates (beginning with the acclamation of divine holiness about to be proclaimed) a rehearsal of the salvific interventions which culminate in the offering of the body and blood of Christ. The divine holiness emphasized here manifests itself not only in works of terrific power but more so in the compassionate goodness which the Creator unceasingly demonstrates. In the definitive Greek recension, mercy is explicitly mentioned, particularly regarding humanity who was fashioned from earth and who, as the latest version explains, was made "in your image and likeness." Through the formulations recovered in the recent *Fourth Eucharistic Prayer*,[15] the grand stages of this long and complex pedagogy are traced, from the prophetic interventions to the Son's advent in the world: "...our Lord Jesus Christ, in order to renew his image. Descending from the heavens, he assumed the flesh through Mary, holy Virgin and Mother of God; he dwelled among men and arranged for the salvation of our race." After this detailed recital of the Institution, the formula for the offering evokes the formidable character of this non-bloody sacrifice, and requests that we not be judged according to our errors and offenses but "according to your mercy and philanthropy (see Bar. 2:27) which blot out the sins of those who entreat you." The highly developed epiclesis details the manifestations of the Spirit, Lord and Giver of life, consubstantial and coeternal with the Father and the Son: "He has spoken in the Law and Prophets; in the new Covenant he descended in the form of a dove on our Savior Jesus Christ in the Jordan River, (then) he descended on the holy apostles in the form of tongues of fire in the upper room of holy and glorious Zion on the day of Holy Pentecost."

Certainly it is the theme of merciful and divine philanthropy, along with the emphasis on the privileged position of "holy Zion," that characterize this eucharistic prayer from Jerusalem. The place held by the notion of philanthropy in Cyrillian catechesis has already been pointed out.[16] Another characteristic trait is the importance accorded the manifestations of the Spirit in salvation history. The formulas are so close to those inserted into the Confession of Faith of Constantinople that a relation of dependence is highly probable, though it is impossible to determine how that dependence worked. On the other hand, the development of the theophanies of the Spirit, which are frequently found in Syrian anaphoras of a later date, could very well have been originally set in relief within the matrix of the Christian communities of Jerusalem.

All these references to salvation history are almost entirely absent in the Antiochene anaphora of the apostles which, with certain developments and modifications, would become (especially once it began to be ascribed to the patronage of John Chrysostom in the eleventh century) the most common formula in use in the Church of Constantinople and all churches that followed the rites of the Great Church of Hagia Sophia. Consequently, biblical allusions appear at first glance to be less numerous. In fact the initial doxology, certainly in the definitive Greek text of the Divine Liturgy, abundantly develops a contemplation of the ineffable mystery of God with a series of apophatic qualifiers reminiscent of Wisdom of Solomon 7. The invocation of the work of creation and salvation is expressed in one sentence of extraordinary density: "It is you who has brought us from non-being into existence and, after we were fallen, you raised us up and did not cease working all things until you had restored us to heaven and had bestowed on us the gift of your coming Kingdom." Likewise the glorification of divine holiness, introduced by the angelic Trisagion, using Johannine expressions, recognizes its paradigmatic manifestation in this love with which God so loved the world that He gave up his only Son for it (John 3:16), "that all who believe in him would not perish but aquire everlasting life; who, having come and fulfilled the whole Economy for our sake, on the night that he was betrayed, or rather when he gave himself up for the life of the world," consecrated and broke bread, and circulated the cup as a Memorial of the gift of his body and his blood. It should be pointed out that in contrast to what one finds in most of the ancient eucharistic prayers, the Greek text of this anaphora does not recall Christ's own commandment to his disciples during the Last Supper to celebrate as a memorial what he was doing in the Supper. It is all the more surprising that the text instead refers simply to this "saving commandment" when it is found in explicit terms in the Syriac version, which translates the most ancient formula. Likewise the text of the Byzantine liturgy ignores the solemn diaconal admonition, which, among the Syrians, introduces the epiclesis: "How terrible is this hour, how fearful it is, my beloved, this moment when the Holy Spirit leaves the heavenly heights and descends like a dove on this oblation and consecrates it. Stand up and pray in silence and in fear." These expressions of holy fear and reverence certainly fall within the Antiochene tradition; indeed, this same notion of godly fear is developed in John Chrysostom's own *Homilies on Divine Incomprehensibility*. One might speculate that such reverential expressions disappeared after the introduction of the anaphora into the common liturgy of the Great Church in Constantinople, just when the apophatic character of the initial doxology was developing.

Of all the anaphoras in Greek, those of Cappadocian origin are doubtless the most replete with biblical resonances. This is especially so for the most important anaphora, the only one which survived in use in the Byzantine liturgical tradition. It even seems that this was, for several centuries, the habitual form of the eucharistic prayer in the Great Church of Hagia Sophia before it was reserved exclusively for Lenten Sundays and for the vigils for the Nativity, Theophanies, and Easter. Transmitted under the name of Basil, an association confirmed by internal analysis, the anaphora has come down to us in two recensions. The shorter, translated into Coptic or Arabic, became the common anaphora for the Coptic

Church after having been in use for a long time in the Egyptian Melkite Church. The more developed recension was adopted by the Byzantine tradition. Numerous hints lead one to believe that one or the other of these redactions bears the personal mark of Basil.

With its balance and firmness of trinitarian structure, its doctrinal density and richness in biblical allusions, this Cappadocian anaphora, particularly in its Byzantine recension, can be considered the jewel in the crown of eucharistic prayers from the Christian East. Certainly some authors prefer James's anaphora. It is more sober and undoubtedly closer to the primitive formulas, before the Arian controversy and the refinements of theological expression which resulted from it left their mark on this solemn confession of faith. The initial doxology here in the Cappadocian version is exceptionally elaborate, in order to explain with multiple qualifiers the right balance of the confession of trinitarian faith. "Who can exalt your power, make known your praises, Lord, or proclaim at all times your marvelous deeds?" In order to answer this question in reverence of the incomprehensible mystery of the divine essence, the Byzantine version, like the anaphora of John Chrysostom, recovers several expressions from Chrysostom's *On the Incomprehensibility of God*, Homily 3.[17] The elaborations of the manifestation of the Word and the Spirit echo what was said in Basil's treatise *On the Holy Spirit* concerning the principle of the trinitarian economy. The Word appears here preeminently as the revealer of the Father above all else. It is also by the Word that the Holy Spirit is revealed: "Spirit of Truth, Gift of adoption, Pledge of the future inheritance, Firstfruits of eternal goods, lifegiving Virtue, Source of sanctification; every intelleigent and spiritual creature, strengthened by you, serves you and addresses you with the eternal hymn of glory."

Having acclaimed with the celestial powers the infinite and ineffable holiness of the Triune God, the anaphora develops at length his manifestation not so much in the works of creation as in in his merciful interventions which mark salvation history. For,

> It is with all justice and by an equitable sentence that all things happen to us. Having created man from the mud of the earth but honored him with your likeness, O God, you placed him in a paradise of delights, promising him immortality and enjoyment of your eternal benefits if he observed your commandments. But, having disobeyed you, you the true God who created him, being seduced by the craftiness of the serpent, he was subjected to death of his own fault. In a just sentence, O God, you cast him from paradise in this world, returning him to this land from which he had been drawn, but sustaining him through your

Christ with the salvation of regeneration.

After recounting the numerous interventions of the prophets, the gift of the Law and the mission entrusted to the angels on behalf of humanity, the anaphora recalls the sending of the Son in the fullness of time, which is evoked using expressions from the prologue of Hebrews and from the *kenôsis* hymn in Philippians 2:6-11: "He who, being the radiance of your glory and the form of your substance, bearing all things by his powerful word, did not consider grasping equality with you, you God and Father, but being God himself from all eternity, he appeared on the earth, sharing in the life of human beings."

In contrast with the anaphora of James, where the accent is placed on merciful divine philanthropy, the Basilian anaphora emphasizes the paradoxical manner in which justice, violated by human sin, is reestablished. It presents the salvific work of Christ along the lines of the Pauline epistles, above all Romans:

> And as through man sin made its entry into the world, and through sin death, it pleased your only Son, him who is in your own bosom, God and Father, him who was born of a woman, the holy Mother of God and ever virgin Mary, to set himself under the Law and to condemn sin in the flesh, in order that those who died in Adam would be made alive by him, your Christ. Having lived in the world and given us the commandments of salvation, and having wrested us from the seduction of idols, he led us to know you, you God and Father; he thereby took us unto himself as his chosen people, a royal priesthood, a holy nation. After purifying us through water and santifying us by the Holy Spirit, he ransomed us from the death to which we were held captive, sold as we were under the reign of sin.

This salvific work culminates in the liberating mystery of Christ's death and the Resurrection, which is emphasized as well in Basil's treatise *On the Holy Spirit* (chaps. 14 and 30).

The anaphora of Basil especially highlights the renewal of creation, of which the Resurrection is the constitutive first-fruits:

> Having descended through the cross into hell, in order to accomplish all things on his own, he delivered us from the pains of death. Resurrected on the third day, and having opened up to all flesh the way of resurrection from the dead—because it was impossible for the author of life to be subject to corruption—he became the first-fruits of those who are asleep, the first-born from among the dead in order to have primacy in all things.

As L. Bouyer has remarked of Basil's anaphora,

> There is scarcely another example, in a developed liturgical text, of as perfect a fusion between the theological developments of the end of the fourth century and a vision of the Eucharist that is faithful to the substance and the original unity of its content. As such, far from being a mere mosaic of biblical texts artificially pieced together, this composition, with its command and organization of the texts it brings together, is but an express representation of the most primitive stratum of the Eucharist. Its speculation hardly breaks free from the first movement of the divine word, remaining so profoundly and completely rooted in that movement that it naturally assumes the most diverse expressions. Yet it draws them togther, not factitiously, but in an order that renders simple and clear their underlying connections.[18]

It is an exceptional success made possible by a perfect assimilation of the most fundamental lines of biblical tradition. In this way, Basil's anaphora illustrates how the eucharistic celebration is the Memorial of the mystery of salvation in the fullness of its unveiling.

NOTES

1. See I. Elbogen, *Der jüdische Gottesdienst in seiner geschichtlichen Entwicklung* (Frankfurt, 1931), 4-5; cited by K. Hruby in *Eucharisties d'Orient et d'Occident* (Paris, 1970), I: 24-25. See also the more recent raising of the question in Th.-J. Talley, "De la 'berakah' à l'Eucharistie, une question à réexaminer," *La Maison-Dieu* 125 (1976): 11-39; and the very important study of E. Mazza, *The Origins of the Eucharistic Prayer*, trans. R. E. Lane (Collegeville, Minn., 1995), 12-35.

2. H. Cazelles, "L'Anaphore et l'Ancien Testament," *Eucharisties d'Orient et d'Occident*, I: 11-22.

3. J. Laporte, *La doctrine eucharistique chez Philon d'Alexandrie*, Théologie historique 16 (Paris, 1972).

4. H. Cazelles, op. cit., 20-21.

5. W. Rordorf, "Les prières eucharistiques de la *Didache*," in *Eucharisties*, I: 76-82.

6. W. Rordorf, "Intro." to the *Didaché* (SC 248: 43-47). More recently, see the analysis of the background and theology of the eucharistic prayers of the *Didache* in E. Mazza, *The Origins of the Eucharistic Prayer*, 12-41.

7. See G. Dix, ed., *The Treatise on the Apostolic Tradition of St. Hippolytus of Rome*, vol. 1 (London and New York, 1937). On the background of the anaphora of the *Apostolic Tradition*, see Mazza, *The Origins of the Eucharistic Prayer*, 98-176.

8. L. Ligier, *Péché d'Adam, péché du monde*, Théologie 48 (Paris, 1961), vol. 2, 403-406. See also Mazza, *The Origins of the Eucharistic Prayer*, 42-65.

9. *L'Eucharistie des premiers chrétiens*, Le point théologique 17 (Paris, 1976), 208.

10. For a review of the early history of the Byzantine anaphoras, see H.-J. Schulz, *The Byzantine Liturgy* (New York, 1986), 4-20.

11. B. Botte, in *Eucharisties...*, II, 11-18.

12. See Mazza, *The Origins of the Eucharistic Prayer*, 177-218.

13. See ibid., 219-239.

14. R. G. Coquin, in *Eucharisties...*, II, 65.

15. On this newer anaphora, see A. F. Detscher, "The Eucharistic Prayers of the Roman Catholic Church," in *New Eucharistic Prayers: An Ecumenical Study of Their Development and Structure*, ed. F. C. Senn (New York, 1987), 37-42.

16. A. Paulin, *Saint Cyrille de Jérusalem catéchète*, Lex Orandi 29 (Paris, 1959), 75-76.

17. See the text in J. Daniélou, ed., *Jean Chrysostome: Sur l'incompréhensibilité de Dieu*, SC 28bis (Paris, 1970), 190, l. 53.

18. L. Bouyer, *Eucharistie* (Paris, 1966), 290.

17

The Influence of the Bible
in Early Christian Martyrology[1]

VICTOR SAXER

My habit in dealing with hagiographic literature is to stick closely to the document in its most ancient form. In the case of different ancient versions, I customarily concentrate on alterations in the text which might still date from the fourth century. In dealing with the biblical connections of this literature, moreover, my controlling interest, more than the evolution of the scriptural argument in texts, is the use of that argument in its most ancient forms.

Typically, hagiographic works report the thought and words of the martyr and those of his or her biographer. But it is interesting as well to observe the outlines by which and in which scriptural terminology is expressed and reworked in this literature. We will examine that process here in terms of six martyrological themes: (1) martyrdom as witness; (2) martyrdom as confession of faith; (3) martyrdom as combat; (4) martyrdom as liturgy; (5) martyrdom as charism; and (6) martyrdom as parousia. For each of these themes, I will focus on showing at once how it comes to expression in the *Acts of the Christian Martyrs* and how it is connected with the Bible in these works.

Martyrdom as Witness

Etymologically speaking, martyrdom *is* a witness. In Christian language, the testimony is one of blood, and the title of "martyr" is reserved only for those believers who, during the persecutions, were handed over to a Roman tribunal, confessed their faith before it, were condemned to death by it, and were actually executed for their faith.

The vocabulary of martyrdom was the object of lively controversies over how that language passed from the juridical sense of testimony before qualified court authorities to the martyrological sense of death for the faith. Delehaye, in his study of the emergent cult of the saints, has already dealt with these controversies, so we need not return to them here.[2] Ruysschaert has more recently taken up this problem with respect to the *Letter* on the Martyrs of Lyons, but the debate which has followed clearly shows that the era of great controversies over the language of martyrdom has already come to end.[3] The best exposition of these questions for the period of biblical and patristic origins is still found in Kittel's *Theological Dictionary of the New Testament*.[4]

I have no intention here of reopening these debates nor raising again all the issues at stake in them. My purpose is limited exclusively to those martyrological *Acts* which can pass as authentic, with a view to recovering their conception of martyrdom and their connections with the Bible.

The Personal Sentiments of the Martyrs

Not all of the *Acts of the Christian Martyrs* recount what the martyrs themselves thought of their own experience, which makes all the more precious the task of gathering the rare personal testimonies that they have left. We will mention them here in their chronological order.

In the *Martyrdom of Polycarp,* the bishop in his prayer blesses the Lord for allowing him to be included among the martyrs. He expresses it this way: "I bless you because you have thought me worthy of this day and this hour, to have a share among the number of the martyrs in the cup of your Christ" (*M. Polyc.* 14.2).[5] The "day and hour" are, in the Synoptic Gospels, those of the return of Christ, when he will come like a thief (Matt. 24:36; 25:13; Luke 12:46), while in John's Gospel the "hour" is that of the passion of Christ (John 7:30; 8:20; 12:23, 27; 13:1; 17:1) and likewise that of his disciples (John 16:2). Here the "hour" is that of Polycarp's passion, by virtue of the fact that God has numbered him among the martyrs. Clearly the intention is to affirm that the martyrs participate in the death of Christ.

We know in particular the statements of the martyrs of Lyons about how they should be judged. They refused to be called martyrs orally or in writing, in spite of the burns, wounds, and bites which their bodies could show as evidence. They insisted only on being called "simple, humble confessors," reserving the title of martyr only for those who had died for their testimony: Christ, "the true and faithful witness," and Stephen, "the perfect martyr."[6] Indeed, in their view, as they themselves explicitly declared, "They were indeed martyrs whom Christ has deigned to take up in their hour of confession, putting his seal on their witness by death."[7] These "martyrs" of Lyons thereby distinguished two categories of witnesses to whom we now customarily give the title of martyrs: incomplete martyrs, those engaged in testifying to their faith, whom they called "confessors," and complete martyrs, those alone whom they deemed truly worthy of the title of *martyrs*.

When, in the *Martyrdom of Perpetua and Felicitas*, the imprisoned African catechumen Saturus described in his turn the "martyrs" that he had seen in a vision (the vision mentions a certain Quintus, and some other anonymous martyrs),[8] he placed them already in paradise.

One last personal reference to the martyrs in this literature comes from Phileas, an imprisoned bishop from the Thebaid in Egypt who claimed "that the apostles and the martyrs were his kin."[9] We can already detect echoes of the Gospel in Phileas's words (cf. Matt. 12:46-50; Mark 3:31-35; Luke 8:19-21). But more important here is the fact itself that he placed the martyrs on the same footing with the apostles.

It is rather difficult to trace an evolution in the thinking of the martyrs themselves about how they were to be considered and what they were to be called. In fact only the statements of the martyrs of Lyons are sufficiently explicit on this point. It is clear, nonetheless, that a difference existed between them and the Africans: While the former refrained from admitting a full evolution in the "martyr" terminology (i.e., from "witness" in the juridical sense to "witness" by virtue of dying for the faith), the latter simply presupposed the change. Probably this evolution took place not during the transition from a Greek to a Latin martyrological vocabulary, but already in the Greek usage itself. This would suggest that it was a divergence in usage rather than a real discrepancy of perspective between the martyrs in Africa and the narrator of the story of the martyrs in Lyons.

The Biblical Substratum

By calling Christ "the true and faithful witness," the martyrs of Lyons were referring to Revelation, where the Greek term *martys* is used twice to describe Christ (Rev. 1:5; 3:14) but is used of other persons as well (Rev. 2:13; 11:3; 17:6). Antipas in particular (2:13) was not a *martys* because he had been put to death, but was rather put to death because he was a *martys*, which is why, like Christ, he was called both "witness" and "faithful." What, then, was their shared witness? Jesus's witness consisted at once of the message about God that he communicated to humanity and the testimony that God rendered to him concerning the fulfillment of his earthly mission. For Jesus's own mission was to "bear witness to the truth" (John 18:37), which is precisely what he did before Pontius Pilate (1 Tim. 6:13). His testimony precipitated his death, thus making him the consummate prototype of the Christian "martyr." Analogously, the witnesses of Christ were those who continued his work by spreading his message even to the point of death (Acts 22:20; Rev. 2:13; 17:6). What is more, it was because of their faithfulness to this mission that the dragon persecuted them (Rev. 12:17) and that they were put to death in their turn (Rev. 6:9; 20:4). "What we find in the Johannine writings, especially Revelation, but also in some verses in Acts, forms a preliminary step toward the martyrological concept of the witness (*martys* = martyr) which emerged at once in the Early Church."[10] The martyrs of Lyons made a decisive impact on the evolution of martyrological terminology by retaining the honor of "martyr" and reserving it exclusively for those who had died for the faith.

Martyrdom as Confession of Faith

If, etymologically, martyrdom was a witness or testimony, and if, in spite of its conceptual evolution, the title of martyr always kept this original connotation, then in what precisely did the martyr's testimony consist?

We must glean the object of this testimony from extant hagiographic documents. They reveal two aspects of the testimony, one positive and related to the content of the Christian faith, the other negative and opposing that faith to the contemporary Greco-Roman cults. Both the affirmation of the faith and the critique of the cults were built on assorted arguments and biblical references.

The Content of the Faith

The martyr's confession of faith could be reduced to a simple declaration of the truth of Christianity. In the spirit of the martyr, it was enough simply to justify his or her refusal to sacrifice to the gods: I am a Christian, I cannot sacrifice.[11] Here there is no trace of biblical references. In general, however, the confession of faith was more nuanced. It included, first of all, adherence to monotheism, for this was a touchstone of Christianity and Judaism alike. The worship of the one God excluded devotion to any other gods. Pionius and Phileas both enunciate this principle explicitly, the one referring to Exodus 20:3 and the other to Exodus 22:20,[12] thereby appealing to the charter of biblical monotheism which constituted the Covenant Code. Normally this monotheism included two component principles: the oneness of God and his activity in creation. This is certainly how numerous early Christian martyrs defined it.[13] The formula with many of them is the same: "The one God who made heaven and earth, the sea, and all that is in them."[14] Even this formula originated from the Covenant Code itself (Exod. 20:11), but it was also repeated time and time again in the Bible.[15] Indeed, it is characteristic of biblical monotheism. Likewise it was destined to become part of the Christian Creed from the very beginning, and has been reaffirmed again and again by theologians and in symbols (formal confessions) of the faith.[16] Finally, it was destined to be found on the lips of the Christian, in his or her turn, when confronted with the choice between the Christian God and false gods.

Yet the formula was sometimes subject to modifications. Speratus, the premier leader of the Scillitan martyrs, proclaimed his faith in the invisible God; Justin expressed it in philosophical terms; Phileas developed it in terms of the apophatic theology in vogue among the Christian apologists and the Alexandrians.[17] But the variations themselves had a biblical foundation.[18] At any rate, the various formulations of this monotheistic faith testified to the different cultural backgrounds of their authors and to fundamental differences in content.

The specificity of Christian monotheism, however, lay in the belief in the divinity of Jesus Christ. Ancient hagiographic documents refer to Christ as "child of God" (pais Theou);[19] Polycarp invokes Christ as the "beloved and blessed child" of God.[20] This title recalled Isaiah's "Servant of Yahweh," with whom Christ identified himself.[21] It conforms as well to the most ancient christology.[22] The word is simultaneously synonymous with "son," indeed with the "only Son of God" as some of the passion accounts of the martyrs reveal,[23] echoing the New Testament.[24] These stories ascribe other titles as well to Christ: Savior,[25] Lord,[26] Word of God,[27] God.[28] All this titling was of New Testament origin when applied to Christ.[29]

Christ's mission to humanity is generally treated from three perspectives in the passion accounts of the martyrs. The martyrs indeed recognized Christ as the one who had made God known to them, who had come to earth and suffered death on the cross to save them, and who

346

would return one day to judge them according to their works.[30] These themes were at the heart of the Christian revelation in the New Testament and sometimes reinterpreted ideas from the Old.[31] They receive a more precise treatment in two hagiographic works. Justin actually used the argument from prophecy as proof of Jesus's divinity and mission, while basing himself on the early preaching of the apostles.[32] Phileas for his part took up the prophetic argument again with respect to the "crucified God," but he also coupled it with a florilegium of New Testament references concerning the miracles of Christ.[33] After all it was Christ himself who, appearing to the disciples from Emmaus, had initiated such an exegesis:

> "O foolish men, and slow of heart to believe all that the prophets have spoken! Was it not necessary that the Christ should suffer these things and enter into his glory?" And beginning with Moses and all the prophets, he interpreted to them in all the scriptures the things concerning himself (Luke 24:25-27, RSV).

All of the martyrs at last saw in Christ the very one who was with them in martyrdom,[34] and believed that in death they were entrusting their souls to him[35] and that they would receive from him eternal recompense.[36] All of them were therefore imbued more or less with this mysticism of the imitation of Christ and of union with him through martyrdom—a mysticism championed by Ignatius of Antioch, and which had Paul himself as its primary source.[37]

Hence, from the passion accounts of the martyrs arose a consensus of faith on two key articles, biblical monotheism and belief in the divinity of Jesus Christ. It was by confessing these ideas that the martyrs put their lives on the line. But their confession also revealed that the Bible, especially the New Testament, nourished their faith.

As for knowing whether the martyrs referred directly to the Bible or rather quoted it via a symbol of the faith, the hagiographic literature does not allow us to answer this question uniformly. Yet it is worth remembering that, among the Scillitan martyrs, Speratus carried with him the Epistles of Paul,[38] while Euplus of Catania bore copies of the four gospels while being cross-examined by an imperial governor.[39] For others, however, the question can remain open. Then again, the question could be pointless to the extent that testimonies of martyrs and primitive symbols of faith, being so replete still with biblical content and so far from theological formulations, became a kind of vernacular of the confession of Christian faith.

Criticism of the Greco-Roman Cults

The martyrs were confronted with a paganism whose gods they completely repudiated and whose cults they sometimes criticized openly. On the other hand, they also engaged in a rather exceptional criticism of Judaism. This double-sided polemic deserves more of a brief characterization in order to know to what extent it was dictated by the Bible.

The martyrs' repudiation of paganism was general and absolute. There could be no compromise. From the perspective of the Roman state, Christianity had no right to exist;[40] on the other side, Christian "atheists" denied the pagan gods really existed and deemed their cults merely vain idolatry. There was total opposition and lack of understanding. As two of the martyrs uttered in their wrath against pagan deities, "May the gods be destroyed who have not made heaven and earth!"[41] Borrowed from Jeremiah 10:11, this imprecation originated from a deutero-canonical chapter and constituted as well an Aramaic gloss on the verse which followed it. It expressed a fundamental and devout anti-paganism. Carpus leveled basically the same criticism of the worship of idols before the proconsul of Asia: "They look like men, but they are unfeeling. Deprive them of your veneration, and, since they are unfeeling, they will be defiled by dogs and crows."[42]

Apollonius took a different tack from this popular criticism of the gods, presenting a systematic indictment of idolatry in the presence of cultivated Roman gentlemen after he was brought before the *praefectus Urbi* in Rome. He reprehended the statues of gods which were accorded divine honors, but he went further and took to task the entire pagan pantheon together with the mythology that explained it:

> ...I am a pious man, Perennis, and I may not worship artificial idols. Hence I do not bow before false gods made of stone or wood, who can neither see nor hear: for these are but the work of craftsmen, workers in gold and bronze; they are the carvings of men and have no life of their own...
>
> Men who humble themselves to worship things preserved by human skill commit sin: such are but the cold carving of stone, dry wood, hard metal, or dead bones. What nonsense and deception![43]

Having offered concrete examples of the religious practices of the Egyptians, Athenians, and others, he returned to his critique of idolatry. These statues, he claimed, were deceitful:

> Their entire form is indeed a lie: for though they have ears, they hear not, they have eyes but cannot see, they have hands but cannot

348

move them, they have feet but cannot walk. Their appearance cannot change their nature.[44]

For more compelling reasons Apollonius found it necessary to upbraid those who worship products of nature, like the people of Pelusium who worship onion and garlic as gods, even though they are things that pass through the stomach and eventually end up in the sewer.[45] Finally, we find in Apollonius an echo of the Euhemerist critique when he says,

> ...Men sin against heaven when they worship creatures endowed with reason, that is, human beings who function as gods. They give the name of gods to men of former times, as their myths prove. Dionysus they claim was torn to pieces; Heracles was brought alive to the flames; Zeus was buried in Crete. Of a piece with this is the discussion of the gods' offspring in the myths, whose names are well known. Especially because of their impiety I must reject them.[46]

This criticism of idolatry was biblical through and through. Vituperating against "dead gods," Carpus was expounding on a prophetic and sapiential theme (cf. Ep. Jer. 17-27 [15-26, LXX]; Wisd. 14:8-15). The beasts who came frequenting the statues are also mentioned here in Scripture, though it is not said that they left their excrements there. In the *Martyrdom of Apollonius*, this biblical arsenal of arguments against idolatry is exploited methodically, with several expressions from the Bible being transmitted as is. Such is the case with the author's mention of digested food passing through the stomach and being evacuated into a sewer (Matt. 15:17; Mark 7:19). But it is especially obvious in the themes of "immobile gods," "idols made with human hands." The first expression, already present in the *Acts of Carpus and Companions*, is amplified in the *Martyrdom of Apollonius* according to a well known polemic from the Bible (Ps. 115:4-8; =113:12-16, LXX; and 135:15-18; =134:15-18, LXX) which was a virtual stereotype of Old Testament teaching against idolatry.[47] The second expression ("idols made with human hands") was linked to the first and attested by the same biblical passages.[48] In the Septuagint we find precisely the same formula as in our *Acts* of the martyrs: *eidôlon cheiropoiêton* (Wisd. 15:8). The prophetic tradition and the book of Wisdom recalled or described both the primary material of the idols and the artisan who fashioned them. But at this point we are not yet to the polemic against the Egyptian gods, particularly in their animal form (Wisd. 15:14-19), nor to the theory of Euhemerus of Messina (Wisd. 14:14-20), neither of which would have appeared yet when the last book of the Old Testament was produced.

It seems clear, however, that this critique of paganism, especially in the developed form given it in the *Martyrdom of Apollonius*, shows up erratically within the ancient passion accounts of the martyrs. As for the critique of Judaism, I would note from the outset its rarity in these stories; in fact I have found it only in two works. One is the anti-Jewish slant of Phileas's remark when he says, "The Scriptures on which the Jews rely foretold his coming down and his death."[49] The Latin recension of this same text sharpens the point even more: "For the sacred Scriptures (which the Jews think they adhere to, but do not) had predicted all this."[50] It was on this same issue of scriptural interpretation that disputes between Jews and Christians had emerged in the apostolic age (Acts 7:2-53; 13:16-41; 26:22-23), but these were only apologists claiming to deprive the Jews of the Old Testament.

The *Martyrdom of Pionius* is our other case in point. Two strong indictments are leveled here against Judaism.[51] The first is addressed almost entirely and directly toward Jews present in the agora of Smyrna during the persecution of Christians. The martyr reproaches them for their past and present infidelity to the Law to which they laid claim. The discourse here is in the same vein as Christ's invectives against the Pharisees,[52] for Pionius's accusation ends, just like Christ's seven curses against the Pharisees, with the threat of condemnation (cf. Matt. 23:33-36). It is Pionius's second discourse, however, that ostensibly explains the virulence of the preceding polemic. In prison, the martyr had in fact received a visit from apostates who came to request his help. He warned them against the attempts at seduction on the part of the Jews, who would be altogether happy to make proselytes of those apostates excluded for the time being from the Church. To prevent this from happening, Pionius, after having decried the ravages of the persecution, exhorted his visitors not to submit to the Jews and not to forfeit their faith to the calumnies that the Jews propagated against Christ and his religion. As proof of the falsehood of their attacks he expounded at length on the biblical episode of the witch of Endor (1 Sam. 28:8ff [1 Kings 28:8ff, LXX]).

It should come as no surprise that these discourses against the Jews were full of biblical quotations.[53] The only surprise would be to find as much biblical erudition in a person in a similarly desperate situation.

These different aspects of the martyrs' confession of faith raise certain questions when we consider the knowledge of the Bible that they imply. The martyrs' confession touched on two articles of the faith, monotheism and the divinity of Jesus Christ, but the level of stability in the formulation of each of these articles was different. Things were pretty much fixed as far as the principle of monotheism was concerned, the only variants being redactional ones. The other article was much more dynamic in its articulation and is actually absent from some of the passion stories. Indeed, it is not mentioned, for example, in the *Acts of the Scillitan Martyrs*, which may be due to the fact that the question of Christ's divinity simply had not been posed to the martyrs in this case. It could also be explained by the fact that, confronted with pagan polytheism, Christians doubtless had a tendency to emphasize their own monotheism foremost. Be that as it may, the simplicity of certain of the declarations is striking.[54] Even when the second article is mentioned, its formulation is rudimentary and limited mainly to the filiation and the Lordship of Jesus.

Ultimately this difference in the stability of the two articles must be explained on historical grounds. The fixity of the first article was already verifiable in the Old Testament. It had the benefit of antiquity and of a canonical authority when the Christian Credo was formulated, and it simply entered that Credo without any further ado. The second article was by definition linked to Christian history. Its existence appeared only over the course of time, to judges who inquired about the faith of the Christians who were presented to their tribunals. The Christians' responses revealed a christology still in the process of realizing its proper dimensions. They often gave it, furthermore, a popular form, for indeed, among the martyrs, not all were bishops or theologians. On a theme still on its way to fixed formulation, the martyrs each gave account of their faith in Christ to the extent of their abilities. And so by the testimony of these passion stories, the common belief in the divinity of Christ came to expression in diverse ways according to the times, locations, and cultural contexts of the witnesses themselves.

Compared, then, with the confession of faith that was shared in common by all the martyrs, the polemic against contemporary religions was quite irregular, and poses a double problem for our research: first, to know whether, and to what extent, the anti-pagan and anti-Jewish polemic belonged from the very outset to the stories that contained it; and then, having determined the extent to which that polemic was original (if it was), to know the scriptural orchestration proper to this polemic in primitive hagiographic redactions. It seems to me, however, that such questions have little chance of being answered using the sources we have.

Martyrdom as Combat against the Devil

The interrogation of a martyr by a Roman magistrate sometimes assumes the look of an oratorical contest. Such a procedure would be especially characteristic of those passion stories that have been editorially modified. But martyrdom itself was considered a combat from the very beginning. This theme is fundamental in the *Letter of the Churches of Lyons and Vienne,* and we must compare other hagiographic documents with evidence from this work in order to know how this image was rooted in the Bible.

Images of Combat

Applied to martyrdom, the vocabulary of combat did not express simply the idea of an athletic competition in which the better competitor won, but a bloody struggle whose victims were the true victors. Its stakes exceeded those of a human kind, since there stood in the background the great struggle going on against the Adversary.

Rarely did this vocabulary designate circus combats in their original form. Yet the *Letter of the Churches of Lyons and Vienne* speaks of singular combats of gladiators (*monomachos*), and the *Martyrdom of Perpetua and Felicitas* of the gladiatorial "games" (*munus*). The first expression indicates one-on-one combat, the second the whole group of circus games in their variety. The martyrs of Lyons considered the tortures inflicted on them to be like a combat;[55] Perpetua similarly considered her exposure to beasts in the arena as such a combat.[56] In the *Martyrdom of Polycarp,* it is a contest with beasts (*thêriomachia*); the young Germanicus, it says, actually "fought manfully with the beasts."[57] Ignatius had already proposed to do the same in the event that the beasts would show some unwillingness to attack.[58] Hence the combat could become very real. In general, however, the martyr triumphed through patience. As it was said of Polycarp, "By his perseverance he overcame the unjust governor and so won the crown of immortality,"[59] so becoming a model "for the training and preparation" of those who would eventually do the same.[60]

The best illustration of this image of martyrdom as combat comes in the final vision of Perpetua. Here she is depicted in a struggle with an Egyptian, who actually symbolizes the Devil, just as her battle symbolizes martyrdom.[61] In the *Epistle of Barnabas,* it is the Black One (*ho melas*) which carries the same meaning.[62] Already Paul himself had referred to the demons as "princes of darkness" (Eph. 6:12). As Perpetua and her adversary thus prepared to do battle, her assistants rubbed oil on her, while the Egyptian rolled in the dust, each contestant wanting to make the other's victory more difficult to attain. A man appearing to be an athletic trainer emerged to act as an umpire for the contest. Both as his badge and as the instrument of his duty, he carried a baton (*virga*). He also carried a green branch with golden apples on it, being both the victory prize and the symbol of life.[63] The extraordinary stature of the umpire which the vision describes clearly designated him as a heavenly being. The best parallel to this passion story on this point is found in the *Shepherd of Hermas,* where there similarly appears "a man of great stature, such that he was taller than the tower."[64] But this man was further designated as the Son of God himself.[65] The struggle between Perpetua and the Egyptian took the form of a pancratium rather than a boxing match. It is easy to understand why. The pancratium required much more agility than strength, and better suited a young 22-year-old woman who could hope to tire her adversary by her mobility. Similar engagements were depicted in painted form on Greek vases from Antiquity. Always in these depictions, there are three persons: two combatants and a trainer, the latter with a baton. Moves are portrayed in this art of which our text here also speaks: seizing an opponent by the leg or foot, or by the head in a choke-hold.[66] When Perpetua gets the better of the Egyptian, she steps on his head, presupposing that the adversary had been put to the ground. David made the same move on Goliath (1 Sam. 17:51 [1 Kings 17:51, LXX]). It signified victory.[67] The reactions of the spectators in Perpetua's combat were also traditional,[68] as were the bestowing of the prize to the victor and the exit through the Gate of Life.[69] The kiss of peace, on the other hand, and the expression which the trainer uttered to the victorious Perpetua—*Pax tecum,* "Peace be with you"—belonged to the Christian liturgy and underscored the religious meaning of the combat.

The Theme of Combat in the Bible

We already know that around the beginning of the Common Era, the vocabulary and theme of combat (*agôn*), borrowed from Greek philosophy, were introduced into Jewish religious literature, and made their way from there into the New Testament.[70] While in Luke 13:24 we find the verb *agônizesthai* applied to the Christian life, it was most notably Paul who developed the combat theme in Christian terms, first in the general sense[71] and then applying it more specifically to the preaching of the Gospel,[72] which ultimately devolved upon the martyr[73] and entitled him or her to the martyr's crown.[74] But Paul did not really approach the hidden sense of this combat, which would be disclosed elsewhere in Scripture as a struggle waged with the Devil himself.[75]

Martyrdom as Liturgy

Martyrdom has been compared with baptism as well as with the Eucharist. In this sense, martyrdom is seen as a liturgy which the "victims" of this baptism and Eucharist celebrated in honor of their God. The question is whether this kind of interpretation of martyrdom has a foundation in the extant hagiographic texts.

Only the *Martyrdom of Perpetua and Felicitas* specifically compares martyrdom with baptism (the "second baptism"); the analogy appears twice in this work.[76] The easiest allusion to understand describes the deacon Saturus at the moment he was attacked by a leopard in the arena:

> And immediately as the contest was coming to a close a leopard was let loose, and after one bite Saturus was so drenched with blood that as he came away the mob roared in witness to his second baptism. "Well washed! Well washed! For well washed indeed was one who had been bathed in this manner."[77]

We have here an example of interpretation on two levels, reflecting two different mindsets. The crowd of spectators had shouted to the victim the greeting that was addressed to those who were leaving the baths, a custom of which we have various archaeological attestations from Africa and elsewhere. An analogous greeting was addressed to the bather who was entering the water. These two salutations are sometimes found together in African inscriptions.[78] The acclamation here in the story of Saturus from the *Martyrdom of Perpetua and Felicitas* thus corresponds to a contemporary African custom that is amply documented.

For his part, the compiler of the *Martyrdom of Perpetua and Felicitas* lent it a Christian interpretation by seeing in it the "witness to the second baptism," that is, martyrdom—or better yet, by interpreting martyrdom as a second baptism. Even this interpretation is amply attested in early Christian literature from North Africa.[79] It is rooted, furthermore, in the New Testament. Indeed, the prospect of the Passion is for Christ a source of anguish, and the passion itself, a baptism which would plunge him into an abyss of sufferings (cf. Luke 12:50). F. J. Dögler inquires as to whether indeed, through certain Old Testament conceptions,[80] it was not necessary still to link this theology of martyrdom to Greek and Hellenistic ideas on the function of blood as a means of regeneration and salvation.[81]

The other allusion comes in the story of Felicitas at the moment when she was led into the amphitheater, "glad that she had safely given birth so that now she could fight the beasts, going from one blood bath to another, from the midwife to the gladiator, ready to wash after childbirth in a second baptism."[82] Here the interpretation is simple, and uniquely the doing of the compiler. It is obvious how the comparison was occasioned: Felicitas went from the blood of childbirth to the blood of her martyrdom. The compiler merely completed the analogy: The bath of martyrdom was comparable to the washing of a woman after labor.

The relations between martyrdom and eucharistic rites were amply examined by two early Christian authors, Ignatius of Antioch and Cyprian of Carthage, who furthermore had occasion to put their doctrine into practice.[83] But these connections were never seriously envisioned within the *Acts of the Christian Martyrs* themselves. Unfortunately they are sometimes simply read back into the *Acts* from the work of Ignatius and Cyprian without taking pains to verify whether such a transfer of evidence was legitimate.[84]

Martyrdom as Mystical Experience

Confronted with death, the martyrs had different reactions. Some kept silent awaiting the mortal blow;[85] others prayed in silence;[86] still others prayed aloud.[87] This tranquil assurance, common among the martyrs, in certain cases took the form of religious enthusiasm: Perpetua went to her martyrdom singing;[88] Agathonicê offered herself for martyrdom spontaneously, after having heard Carpus tell of the glory of the Lord that he had envisioned.[89] This assurance and enthusiasm can be explained in terms of the martyrs' very sense of no longer being the masters of their own lives and actions, but of having become the instruments of God, who was acting and suffering through them. In truth this action was conceived as exercised not by God directly, but through the mediation of Christ or the Holy Spirit. I want here briefly to describe two facets of this mysticism of martyrdom while showing to what extent they reflect biblical thought.

The Martyr and Christ

Christological mysticism had its most decisive impact on the *Acts of the Christian Martyrs*. The reason for this perhaps lies in the model which martyrs and hagiographers discovered in the epistles of Ignatius of Antioch. For Ignatius, as Th. Camelot has written, "death is not only testimony rendered to the truth, nor the supreme gesture of love, it is the reproduction of the death of Christ."[90] "Death allows one to discover Christ, not only through an empirical reproduction of his sufferings but by communion with his life...since it is by death that Christ is 'true life,' and the Christian by dying does not seek anything other than "birth into life.'"[91]

The influence of this mysticism on Polycarp seems to be indisputable. He is described as a "witness in accordance with the Gospel."[92] In order to bring to light this conformity with the Gospel, the hagiographer drew out and perhaps accentuated Polycarp's resemblance to Christ, and the similarity of his martyrdom to Christ's Passion, "Like Jesus...Polycarp did not offer himself for death and wait to be handed over (*Martyrdom of Polycarp* 1.2; 5.1); he went to hide on an estate near the city just as Jesus went to Gethsemane (5.1); he was betrayed by people of his own house, just as Jesus was by Judas (6.1), and the police captain who arrested him was named Herod, just as Jesus was arrrested by a Herod; it happened on a Friday around the dinner hour (7.1), and once again like Jesus, Polycarp prayed for a long time before being handed over to his enemies (7.3)."[93] It was thereupon understandable that in imitating Christ's model to the point of death, Polycarp could have the assurance of "the resurrection unto eternal life (cf. John 5:29) of both the soul and the body in the immortality of the Holy Spirit."[94]

The Ignatian influence doubtless made itself felt as well in the *Letter of the Churches of Lyons and Vienne*. The martyrs "refuse the glorious title of martyrs, which is only fitting for Christ, the only faithful and true witness; they merely want themselves to be 'emulators and imitators of Christ' (Eusebius, *Hist. Eccl.* 5.2.2-3); and when Blandina is bound to a stake to be devoured by ferocious animals unleashed against her, the martyrs believe with their bodily eyes that they are seeing in their sister the one who was crucified for them (*Martyrdom of Perpetua and Felicitas* 1.41)."[95]

The narrator from Lyons did not limit to Blandina his intention to identify the martyrs with the Christ of the Passion. Sanctus bore on his body the stigmata of the Suffering Servant of Isaiah.[96] Pothinus was abused by the mob "as though he were Christ himself."[97] The narrator could say as well that Christ himself suffered in Sanctus and triumphed in Pothinus.[98] What is more, if Blandina herself appeared to her companions in suffering as the image of the Crucified, it was because, "tiny, weak, and insignificant as she was...she had put on Christ (cf. Rom. 13:14; Gal. 3:27), that mighty and invincible athlete."[99] Imitators of Christ, the martyrs of Christ followed in his footsteps: "they sped on to Christ."[100] Blandina not only pursued Christ, she found him and had conversation (*homilia*) with him.[101] Vettius Epagathus, who was "a true disciple of Christ," continued in the hereafter "following the Lamb wherever he goes (Rev. 14:4)."[102]

These christological features, which recur rather frequently in primitive Asiatic hagiography, show up more discreetly in other *Acts of the Christian Martyrs*. In the *Acts of Carpus, Papylus, and Agathonicê*, the deacon Papylus (Pamfilus in Latin) bore his suffering "like a brave athlete," explaining to the proconsul the reason for his endurance:

> "I feel no pain because I have someone to comfort me (cf. Phil. 4:13); one whom you do not see suffers within me."[103]

In this way, not only was the martyr's union with Christ affirmed, but even the presence of Christ within the martyr. The Greek version of the same work highlights another aspect of this christological mysticism. Here Carpus at his death blesses Christ for having found him "worthy of this share in you,"[104] by which he means dying like Christ as a witness to God in order to share with him the glory of God.[105]

The *Martyrdom of Perpetua and Felicitas* as well contains some comparable interpretations. The compiler begins the work with the desire that it will inspire Christians such that they "may have fellowship with the holy martyrs an-d, through them, with the Lord Christ Jesus (cf. 1 John 1:1, 3)."[106] It is interesting to focus again on this original desire, for if martyrdom enables the one who suffers to enter into communion with Christ, the Church's commemoration places its members in communion with the martyrs. We are therefore seeing here the outline of a graduated mediation between the faithful and God through the communion of saints. Accordingly, martyrdom takes on an ecclesial as well as personal dimension. As for the theme of Christ suffering in his martyrs, it is taken up again by Felicitas herself just as she falls prey to the pains of childbirth prior to her martyrdom. At that moment it is she who suffers; later, at her martyrdom, Christ will suffer in her:

> "What I am suffering now," she replied, "I suffer by myself. But then another will be inside me who will suffer for me, just as I shall be suffering for him."[107]

To take part in the Passion of Christ meant not only to die with him but, again like him, to endure the torments which precede death.

357

Indeed, this is precisely what the redactor calls participating in the Passion of Christ:

> ...The crowds became enraged and demanded that [the martyrs] be scourged before a line of gladiators. And they rejoiced at this that they had obtained a share in the Lord's sufferings.[108]

The share that the martyrs obtained was to be scourged like Christ before death. As was the case for Christ, so too their own passion was therefore the whole array of sufferings which led them from the Roman tribunal to their death.

We need not dwell at length on the origins of this christological mysticism; it was rooted in the writings of the New Testament itself. Whereas the Passion of Christ was conceived from the beginning in terms of the sufferings of the Servant described in Isaiah,[109] the martyr in his or her turn was seen as bearing the cross of Christ (Matt. 16:24; Mark 8:34; Luke 9:23). Likewise the apostle Paul could recommend to the faithful to imitate the humility of the Lord who died on the cross (Phil. 2:8), and demand that they "put on" Christ (Rom. 13:14; Gal. 3:27); but Paul spoke of himself as crucified with Christ so that Christ was living in him (Gal. 2:19-20). Because this christological mysticism is already well known, I have presented just some brief examples here, which are enough to reveal its influence in the *Acts of the Christian Martyrs*.

The Martyr, the Spirit, and Montanus

Whether or not it is true to say that Ignatius was a mystic, a spiritual theologian living by the movement of the Spirit and endowed with a prophetic charism,[110] there was at least one time in which he claimed to be speaking under the direct inspiration of the Spirit.[111] Here he resembled Stephen, who was likewise "full of the Holy Spirit" (Acts 7:55), the Spirit "with which he spoke" (Acts 6:10). In the *Acts of the Christian Martyrs*, on the other hand, this privilege was never claimed by the martyrs themselves, but was always attributed to them by their hagiographers.

Such is the case with Polycarp. Indeed, three days prior to his arrest he had a vision in which his pillow caught on fire while he was praying, a forecast of his death. "He turned and said to his companions, 'I am to be burnt alive.'"[112] When sentence was actually passed that he be burnt alive, the narrator comments: "For the vision he had seen regarding his pillow had to be fulfilled, when he saw it burning while he was at prayer and turned and said to his faithful companions: 'I am to be burnt alive.'"[113] This is why the same hagiographer characterized Polycarp as "a teacher in the apostolic and prophetic tradition."[114] He was *apostolikos* in the sense that he was one of the last witnesses of the apostolic age. As for enjoying a "prophetic" charism, this was often the case with the martyrs, as we shall see.

In the *Letter of the Churches of Lyon and Vienne*, the Spirit's operation is even more conspicuous. We see this, first of all, in the case of Vettius Epagathus, who was "fervent in the Spirit" (cf. Acts 18:25).[115] Under this influence of the Spirit were included his tremendous love for God and neighbor, and his gift of being "untiring in his service of his neighbor, possessing great devotion to God..."[116] It was in this mind that he subsequently undertook the defense of his unjustly accused friends and personally went before the Roman tribunal itself. Such is why he deserved to be called "the Christians' advocate (*paraklêtos*)," since "he possessed the Advocate within him, the Spirit that filled Zachary, which he demonstrated by the fullness of his love, consenting as he did to lay down his life in defense of his fellow Christians."[117]

We should emphasize the play on diverse senses of the term *paraclêtos* in this passage. It is used in the first place in the juridical sense of defense or advocacy before a court. But it is also used in its properly theological sense such as we find in the New Testament. 1 John refers to Christ as an advocate for sinners before God (1 John 2:1). In the Gospel of John, the term designates a different defender or paraclete sent by God to replace Christ. The mission of this new Paraclete is complex: He perpetually helps the faithful in fulfilling the commandments of Christ (John 14:16); he recalls those commandments and renders Jesus's teaching comprehensible (John 14:26); he bears witness to Jesus, so that the faithful too can bear witness to him (John 15:26-27); and finally, the Paraclete's testimony, in convicting the world of sin and projecting justice and judgment, manifests the very rationale, cogency, and meaning of the action and redemptive suffering of Christ (John 16:7-11). John explicitly identifies this Paraclete with the Holy Spirit.[118] Such, then, is precisely the Spirit, or Paraclete, who filled Vettius Epagathus, and it is the very same charism which turned him into a defender of his fellow Christians. His conduct likewise rendered him worthy to become a witness like the Paraclete in John's Gospel; indeed, "when he admitted he was [a Christian] in the clearest tones, he was accepted into the ranks of the martyrs."[119]

It has been argued that this "fervency in the Spirit" marked out Vettius Epagathus as a sympathizer, if not a devotee, of Montanism.[120]

The same could be said, then, of Alexander, whom the *Letter* praises for "his love of God and his outspokenness in preaching the word," proof that he too had a share in "the charism of the apostles."[121] The same has been said again of Alcibiades, whose abstinences have been interpreted as Montanist. Even the martyrs have been stereotyped this way in view of their treatment of the *lapsi*.[122] For they ostensibly "had a mother's compassion"toward them.[123] They "made a defense of their faith to all, but accused no one; they loosed all, but bound none."[124] And they believed that the God "who does not desire the death of a sinner but shows him the favour of repentance, makes it sweet for them."[125] Pierre de Labriolle has effectively countered these stereotypes by asserting that neither the "fervency of the Spirit" nor the prophetic charism was a Montanist monopoly; that the asceticism practiced by Alcibiades was no longer the privilege purely of the Phrygian sect; and that rigorism toward apostates was an issue in the Novatianist crisis, not the Montanist controversy.[126]

Martyrdom as Parousia

The rarity of the word "paradise" in the New Testament is striking (Luke 23:43; 2 Cor. 12:4; Rev. 2:7).[127] The same is true in the hagiographic literature. On the one hand, of all the images of the hereafter, that of paradise is the most rare, while that of the feast and that of the crown are frequent; on the other hand, the consistent preoccupation is less with the hereafter itself than with the Christ who opens access to it. This is why martyrdom was not primarily a door into earliest Christian eschatology; essentially it represented a parousia of Christ coming to meet his witnesses.

At the heart of this conception was the conviction that the righteous would receive their due recompense in the hereafter. Justin conveys this conviction in his responses to the Roman prefect Rusticus:

> The prefect turned to Justin: "You are said to be learned and you think you know the true doctrine. Now listen: if you are scourged and beheaded, do you suppose that you will ascend to heaven?"
>
> "I have confidence," said Justin, "that if I endure all this I shall possess his mansions. Indeed, I know that for all those who live a just life there awaits the divine gift even to the consummation of the whole world."
>
> The prefect Rusticus said: "You think, then, that you will ascend to heaven to receive certain worthy rewards?"
>
> "I do not think," said Justin, "but I have accurate knowledge and am fully assured (*peplêrophorêmai*) of it."[128]

360

It is noteworthy that Justin shares this conviction with other martyrs and that he uses analogous expressions for being "convinced," in particular the verb *plêrophorein*.[129] I want to focus here, however, on those images which translated this "conviction" and on how they might illuminate the martyrs' eschatological notions. Their conceptions of the hereafter were arranged around four fundamental ideas: triumph, paradise, the eschatological meal, and eschatological marriage. The images of the bosom of Abraham and of the eternal tabernacle are not found in their eschatological repertoire. But we must also note at once that, except in the *Letter of the Churches of Lyons and Vienne* and (to a lesser extent) in the *Martyrdom of Perpetua and Felicitas*, which are exceptionally rich in this kind of imagery, such imagery is scant elsewhere in the *Acts of the Christian Martyrs*.

Triumph

The idea of triumph came to expression in two images in the hagiographic literature: the procession, and, more frequently, the victor's crown.

The image of the triumphal procession appears first of all in the *Letter of the Churches of Lyons and Vienne*, in the story of the venerable Pothinus, who was associated with the triumphant Christ as he was dragged through a public humiliation with a train of angry accusers.[130] Clearly the notion of the Christian's identification with the victory of Christ had roots in the New Testament (cf. 2 Cor. 2:14; Col. 2:15).

The compiler of the *Martyrdom of Perpetua and Felicitas* seems to have had the same image in mind. In fact he associates the *dies victoriae* with the procession of martyrs advancing from prison toward the amphitheater.[131] Accordingly, the organizers of the games had wanted to create a pagan procession, by dressing the men up as priests of Saturn, and the women as priestesses of Ceres. The Christians rejected the sham parade in the name of their religious liberty, for which they paid with their lives. This is why, it seems to me, the compiler, by identifying the martyrs' "procession" with their "victory," more or less conscientiously transformed their parade into a "triumphal procession." Yet the image here is more suggestive than explicit.

The image of the victor's crown appears twice in the *Martyrdom of Polycarp*,[132] three times in the *Letter of the Churches of Lyons and Vienne*,[133] once in the *Acts of the Scillitan Martyrs*,[134] once in the *Martyrdom of Pionius*,[135] and twice in the Greek version of the *Acts of Euplus*.[136] The biblical inspiration of much of this imagery is obvious.[137] In some of these passages it is called a "crown of immortality"[138] or a "crown of incorruptibility"[139] (cf. 1 Cor. 9:25; James 1:12; Rev. 2:10; 4 Macc. 17:15), in one place an "unfading crown" (cf. 1 Peter 5:4),[140] and in one other a "crown of ortho-dox belief."[141] The first two of these descriptions reappear in the Fathers.[142]

The crown, which was drawn into the imagery of triumph through the idea of combat in early Christian martyrology, also had equivalent im-ages. The most frequent was the "prize" (*bravium; brabeion*). The equiva-lence of the two words is strongly underscored in the *Martyrdom of Polycarp*, where they are placed in parallel.[143] The *Martyrdom of Apollonius*, by con-trast, highlights the connection of the term with the victory that was the prize of combat with the Devil: "Today was the day established on which he was to obtain his prize of victory (*to brabeion tês nikês*) over the Evil One."[144]

A similar symbol appears in the *Martyrdom of Perpetua and Felicitas*. The umpire of her combat with the Egyptian carried in one hand the ba-ton of an athletic trainer, in the other "a green branch on which there were golden apples."[145] The meaning of the branch was obvious: if Perpetua won, she would receive it. She actually accepted it after her victory, and concluded her story by saying: "I realized that it was not with wild animals that I would fight but with the Devil, but I knew that I would win the victory."[146] This image too had clear biblical roots and was carried on in patristic literature.[147]

While the crown was from the beginning the badge of the mar-tyrs' victory, the idea of royalty and of reigning seems to have been con-nected with it very early on. The words *basileia* and *basileuein* began to appear in martyrological doxologies, designating the eternal reign of Christ.[148] Indeed, such designations honoring Christ were already present in Revelation (Rev. 11:15, 17; 19:6). The *Acts of the Scillitan Martyrs*, how-ever, ends with a doxology in which martyrdom is not only identified with the crown but associated with the reign of the Trinity.[149] A similar trinitarian doxology appears in both alternative endings to the *Martyr-dom of Polycarp*.[150] This kind of phraseology and conceptualization as well appears in Revelation (Rev. 20:4; 22:5).

Occasionally martyrdom is associated with the theme of perfume. The martyrs of Lyons are said to have spread the "sweet odor of Christ" when they submitted themselves for torture, "so that some thought they had anointed themselves with a perfume of this world."[151] In the *Martyr-dom of Polycarp*, it is the burning body of the martyr that emitted this de-lightful fragrance, "as though it were smoking incense or some other costly perfume."[152] In the *Martyrdom of Perpetua and Felicitas,* perfume is the sustenance of the blessed in the hereafter.[153] The image of perfume was related, in the first place, to the Old Testament idea that the sacrifice pleasing to God was a sacrifice of good fragrance. This is precisely the meaning behind the sweet fragrance given off by the burning body of Polycarp: His holocaust was fully acceptable to God, as indicated in the symbol of the spreading fragrance. This fundamental sense was carried on in the New Testament in the image of the "aroma of Christ" (2 Cor. 2:15) which henceforth characterized those whose life, before they died, was a pleasant fragrance to God. This new sense of the expression found its way into the *Letter of the Churches of Lyons and Vienne,* and was clearly behind the subsequently commonplace image of the fragrance spread by the bodies of the saints. But the aroma served not only to distinguish the good from the wicked; ultimately it was also, according to 2 Corinthians 2:14-16, a principle of life or death. This is the other sense of the image in the *Martyrdom of Perpetua and Felicitas,* where the fragrance becomes the very food of immortality for the martyrs in paradise.

Paradise

As in the New Testament, the image of paradise is rare in the hagiographic literature. It appears only in the *Martyrdom of Perpetua and Felicitas,* but there are several occurrences of it.

In her first vision, after having climbed the last steps of the great bronze ladder into heaven, Perpetua sees opened before her an immense garden, and in it a tall, grey-haired shepherd who was milking sheep.[154] The vision of Saturus displays a comparable image. After their death, the martyrs are transported "toward the east" by four angels.[155] The subsequent scene is worth including in its entirety:

> And when we were free of the world, we saw an intense light... While we were being carried by these four angels, a great open space appeared, which seemed to be a garden, with rose bushes and all manner of flowers. The trees were as tall as cypresses, and their leaves were constantly falling. In the garden there were four other angels more splendid than the others...
>
> Then we came to a place whose walls seemed to be constructed of light. And in front of the gate stood four angels, who entered in and put on white robes. We also entered and we heard the sound of voices in unison chanting endlessly: "Holy, holy, holy! (Rev. 4:8)." In the same place we seemed to see an aged man with white hair and a youthful face, though we did not see his feet. On his right and left were four

elders, and behind them stood other aged men. Surprised, we entered and stood before a throne: four angels lifted us up and we kissed the aged man and he touched our faces with his hand. And the elders said to us: "Let us rise." And we rose and gave the kiss of peace. Then the elders said to us: "Go and play."[156]

A number of biblical elements are observable in this vision of paradise. Paradise is "toward the east" as in Genesis 2:8. It is in an elevated place, toward which Perpetua climbs a ladder, while Saturus and his companions are transported there by angels. The ladder appears to recall the ladder in Jacob's vision in Genesis 28:12. The *Martyrdom of Perpetua and Felicitas* twice compares paradise to a garden,[157] quite obviously evoking Genesis 2:8ff once again. In the purview of the text, the original paradise must be reopened at the end of time. The rose-bushes which Saturus sees, and the trees as tall as cypresses, could be reminiscent of Sirach, where Wisdom and her pious children are said to grow tall like the roses of Jericho, planted at the bank of a stream of water (Sir. 24:14; 39:13; cf. 50:8).

Whereas in Perpetua's vision the garden has no compartments, and has the old shepherd (symbolizing the Lord) tending sheep there, Saturus's vision, by contrast, distinguishes the garden from the Lord's abode. The depiction here of the Lord's abode is rather reminiscent of the New Jerusalem in Revelation, whose walls are made of precious stones and whose light is the Lord himself (Rev. 21:11; 22:5).

Needless to say, the Lord is depicted in both visions as an aged man, seated; the depiction is even more nuanced in Saturus's vision. Indeed, according to Saturus the old man has white hair and a youthful face, and is seated on an elevated throne. Clearly he sits in the pose of Yahweh in the sublime visions of Isaiah (Isa. 6:1) and Daniel (Dan. 7:9). Furthermore, both the visions of Perpetua and Saturus have paradise as the scene of a liturgy. For Perpetua it was an earthly and quasi-eucharistic event, in which she was given milk by the old man in her cupped hands.[158] For Saturus it was a heavenly liturgy, in which the martyrs were conducted by angels before the Lord and heard the chanting of the Trisagion.[159] It appears much like the ritual of Isaiah 6:3 as reworked in Revelation 6:11 and 4:8.

In addition to the biblical influence on these visions, there is an observable influence from the visionary and apocalyptic literature which flourished around the turn of the Common Era. J. A. Robinson pointed out two works which had a determinative influence on the *Martyrdom of*

Perpetua and Felicitas: the *Shepherd of Hermas* and the so-called *Apocalypse of Peter*. His argument on the impact of *Shepherd of Hermas* is quite convincing, but more evidence is needed as far as the second source is concerned. This is not the place to deal with it. It is enough simply to indicate some of the peculiarly apocalyptic elements in the text. Angelic transporters of the martyrs, successive heavens, giant trees in paradise, brilliant light, white vestments, and so on, appear in biblical writings, but are especially characteristic of visionary literature.[160]

Marriage and Feasting

The last theme to be examined within the parousia ideal is that of martyrdom as a marriage between the Christian and God. This theme includes certain secondary components insofar as the Church was understood both as the Bride of Christ and the Mother of the faithful. The Church was not, however, an abstraction; it was concretely realized in all its members, and particularly in the martyrs. Indeed, the martyrs went to their death as if they were going to a wedding; they suffered the pains of childbirth by bringing stray Christians back to the faith. They themselves therefore deserved the title of the Bride of Christ. Such ideas were developed in the *Letter of the Churches of Lyons and Vienne*,[161] and can be understood as a legacy of the Bible.

The most frequent theme is that of the Mother, which the *Letter* develops particularly with regard to those who have strayed from the faith. Among the arrested Christians, it says, most were ready to receive martyrdom, but some were incapable. About ten persons denied their faith, and are referred to by the redactor as "stillborn."[162] The *Letter* later reports, however, that these renegades returned to their senses thanks to the intercession of the martyrs, a restoration which was conceived as new birth.

> The dead were restored to life through the living; the martyrs brought favour to those who bore no witness, and the virgin Mother experienced much joy in recovering alive those whom she had cast forth stillborn. For through the martyrs those who had denied their faith for the most part went through the same process and were conceived and quickened again in the womb and learned to confess Christ. Alive now and strengthened they came before the tribunal that they might again be questioned by the governor; for God, who does not desire the death of a sinner (Ezek. 12:23; 33:11) but shows him the favour of repentance, made it sweet for them.[163]

The same image reappears at the end of the *Letter* with reference to the "motherly compassion" (*mêtrika splanchna*) which the martyrs showed toward penitents.[164] It also comes up briefly in the *Letter's* description of a certain Phrygian named Alexander, who stood firm in his confession and helped to restore apostates:

> He had been standing in front of the tribunal, and by his attitude he had been urging the Christians to make their confession; and hence to those who were standing in the area of the tribunal it was clear that he was as one who was giving birth.[165]

In short, by speaking of the "virgin Mother" from whom apostates were "stillborn," the *Letter* was by no means thinking of the Virgin Mary, but of the Church, which, as the mother of the children of God, remains a virgin by the power of the Holy Spirit.[166] This conception of the Mother-Church, moreover, had not yet taken on the abstract and hierarchical character that it did later on; the martyrs *are* the Church.[167]

This concrete conception of the maternal nature of the Church is eminently biblical. Indeed, maternal imagery occupies an important place in the Bible,[168] from which it was assumed directly into the *Letter of the Churches of Lyons and Vienne* and appeared for the first time in patristic literature.[169]

The figure of the Mother presupposed that of the Bride. The latter appears in passing in the *Martyrdom of Perpetua and Felicitas*.[170] The expression *matrona Christi* in fact carried with it all the connotations of the ancient matron, but was understood definitively in the ideological context of the female martyr as bride and mother. In the *Letter of the Churches of Lyons and Vienne,* the theme appears three times, always with regard to the fidelity of the Christian to his or her commitments. For the martyrs, their prisoners' chains were thus like a bridal ornament, comparable to that described in Psalm 45:14 (44:15, LXX) and again in Revelation 21:2.[171] Whereas the martyrs were attired in the proper garb required by the Gospel for those invited to the wedding (Matt. 22:11-13), the "sons of perdition did not possess the "wedding garment."[172] Blandina in her turn hastened to follow her companions in martyrdom, "rejoicing and glorying in her death as though she had been invited to a bridal banquet instead of being the victim of beasts."[173]

In this last passage, the nuptial theme and the theme of eschatological feasting are explicitly integrated. The *Acts of Carpus, Papylus, and Agathonicê* make the same connection. Agathonicê, who was present at the torture of Carpus, had heard him proclaiming the glory of God that he envisioned at his death. She thus felt herself called in her turn to receive martyrdom, and cried out, "Here is a meal that has been prepared for me. I must partake and eat of this glorious repast."[174] The hagiographic text here was citing none other than the parable of the wedding banquet in Matthew 22:4, where the king says, "I have prepared my meal" (*to ariston mou hêtoimaka*).

We can therefore see how the *Acts of the Christian Martyrs* conflated two themes already confluent in in the Old Testament itself: the messianic banquet, to which Yahweh calls all peoples (Isa. 25:6-10), and the marriage based on love, which he has established with his Covenant people (Hos. 2:19; Isa. 54:4-10; 62:4-5; Ezek. 16). The two themes were joined again in the New Testament in the theme of the nuptial banquet at the end of time.[175] But we simultaneously see another important image factoring in with the theme of martyrdom as marriage, and that, as was noted above, is martyrdom as second baptism. In patristic commentaries, the baptismal liturgy already had strong nuptial overtones.[176] It therefore should come as no surprise to find them in the context of this nuptial theology of martyrdom.

Summation

When one peruses the *Acts of the Christian Martyrs,* at least those select works which we can consider authentic documents of the early Christian martyrological tradition, one cannot help but be impressed by the substantial influence of the Bible. We could try to quantify that influence by counting up the number of biblical quotations which were made or could have been made in the ancient hagiographic writings. But the influence of the Bible is conspicuous above all in the sheer frequency of biblical allusions and in the profound debt owed by every page of these *Acts* to the thought and word of Holy Scripture.[177]

NOTES

1. See also the companion essays by S. Deléani-Nigoul, "Les exempla bibliques du martyre," and "L'utilisation des modèles bibliques du martyre par les écrivains du IIIe siècle," in *Le monde latin antique et la Bible*, Bible de tous les temps 2 (Paris, 1984), 243-260, 315-338.
2. H. Delehaye, *Sanctus: Essai sur le culte des saints dans l'Antiquité* (Brussels, 1927), 74-121.
3. J. Ruysschaert, "Les 'martyrs' et les 'confesseurs' de la Lettre des Eglises de Lyon et Vienne," *Les Martyrs de Lyon (177): Lyon, 20-23 septembre, 1977* (Paris, 1978), 155-164; discussion of this communication, 164-166.

4. See G. Kittel, ed., *Theological Dictionary of the New Testament* [hereafter *TDNT*], Eng. ed. and trans. G. W. Bromiley (Grand Rapids, 1964-1976), vol. 4, s.v. *martys* (et al.), 474-514.

5. Greek text with Eng. trans. in Herbert Musurillo, ed., *The Acts of the Christian Martyrs*, Oxford Early Christian Texts (Oxford, 1972), 12-13.

6. *Letter of the Churches of Lyons and Vienne* 2.2, 5 (ed. Musurillo, 82-83).

7. Ibid. 2.3 (ed Musurillo, 82-83).

8. *Martyrdom of Perpetua and Felicitas* 11.8; 13.8 (ed. Musurillo, 120-121, 122-123).

9. *Acts of Phileas* (Latin recension) 6.4 (ed. Musurillo, 350-351).

10. *TDNT*, vol. 4, s.v. *martys* (et al.), 502.

11. *Martyrdom of Polycarp* 10.1; 12.1 (ed. Musurillo, 10-11); *Letter of the Churches of Lyons and Vienne* 1.19, 20, 50 (ed. Musurillo, 66-67, 68-69, 78-79); *Acts of Justin and Companions* 3.4; 4.1-6, 9 (ed Musurillo, 50-51); *Acts of the Scillitan Martyrs* 10, 13 (ed. Musurillo, 88-89); *Martyrdom of Pionius* 18.1-3, 9 (ed. Musurillo, 160-161, 162-163); *Acts of Phileas* (Latin recension) 1.1; 2.2 (ed. Musurillo, 344-345).

12. Cf. *Martyrdom of Pionius* 3.3 (ed. Musurillo, 138-139); *Acts of Phileas* (Latin recension) 1.1 (ed. Musurillo, 344-345).

13. *Martyrdom of Apollonius* 2 (ed. Musurillo, 90-91); *Martyrdom of Pionius* 8.3; 9.6; 16.3; 19.8 (ed. Musurillo, 146-147, 148-149, 156-157, 160-161); *Acts of Cyprian* 1.2 (ed. Musurillo, 168-169); *Martyrdom of Agapê, Irenê, Chionê, and Companions* 5.2 (ed. Musurillo, 288-289); *Acts of Phileas* (Latin recension) 3.4 (ed. Musurillo, 348-349).

14. *Martyrdom of Apollonius* 2 (ed. Musurillo, 90-91); *Acts of Cyprian* 1.2 (ed. Musurillo, 168-169); *Acts of Phileas* (Latin recension) 3.4 (ed. Musurillo, 348-349).

15. Cf. Neh. 9:6; Ps. 146:6 (145:6, LXX); Acts 4:24; 14:15; 17:24; Rev. 10:6; 14:7.

16. See A. Hahn, ed., *Bibliothek der Symbolen und Glaubensregeln der alten Kirche* (Bresslau, 1897), 6 (Irenaeus, *Adversus haereses* 1.9.4), 21 (Aphrahat), 28 (Credo), etc.

17. *Acts of the Scillitan Martyrs* 6 (ed. Musurillo, 86-87); *Acts of Justin and Companions* (Recension B) 2.5 (ed. Musurillo, 48-49); *Acts of Phileas* (Greek recension), col. 10 (ed. Musurillo, 27-28).

18. Cf. *Acts of the Scillitan Martyrs* 6 (ed. Musurillo, 86-87); John 1:18.

19. See *Acts of Justin and Companions* (Recension B) 2.5 (ed. Musurillo, 48-49).

20. *Martyrdom of Polycarp* 14.1, 3 (ed. Musurillo, 12-13, 14-15).

21. Isa. 42:1-4; 49:1-6; 50:4-9; 52:13-53:12; Matt. 12:15-21.

22. *TDNT*, vol. 5, s.v. *pais*, 652-717, and esp. 700-717 (on the *pais theou* terminology).

23. *Acts of Justin and Companions* (Recension B) 2.6-7 (ed. Musurillo, 48-49); *Martyrdom of Agapê, Irenê, Chionê, and Companions* 4.2 (ed. Musurillo, 286-287).

24. *TDNT*, vol. 8, s.v. *huios*, 366-397; vol. 4, s.v. *monogenês*, 737-741.

25. *Acts of Justin and Companions* (Recension B) 6.1 (ed. Musurillo, 52-53); *Martyrdom of Apollonius* 36 (ed. Musurillo, 100-101); *Martyrdom of Pionius*

16.4 (ed. Mursurillo, 158-159); *Acts of Phileas* (Latin recension) 6.1 (ed. Musurillo, 350-351).

26. *Acts of Justin and Companions* (Recension B) 5.6 (ed. Musurillo, 52-53); *Acts of Carpus, Papylus, and Agathonicê* 7, 39, 41, 42 46 (ed. Musurillo, 22-23, 26-27, 28-29); *Martyrdom of Agapê, Irenê, Chionê, and Companions* 4.2 (ed. Musurillo, 286-287); *Acts of Phileas* (Greek recension), col. 5 (ed. Musurillo, 334-335).

27. *Martyrdom of Apollonius* 5, 26, 35 (ed. Musurillo, 90-91, 96-97, 98-99); *Martyrdom of Pionius* 4.24; 8.3; 9.6 (ed. Musurillo, 142-143, 146-147, 148-149).

28. *Acts of Phileas* (Greek recension), cols. 5-6 (ed. Musurillo, 334-335); *Acts of Euplus* (Greek recension) 2.4 (ed. Musurillo, 312-313).

29. *TDNT*, vol. 7, s.v. *sôter*, 1015-1021; vol. 3, s.v. *kyrios*, 1086-1095; vol. 4, s.v. *logos*, 124-136; vol. 3, s.v. *theos*, 104-106.

30. *Martyrdom of Polycarp* 14.1 (ed. Musurillo, 12-13); *Martyrdom of Apollonius* 36 (ed. Musurillo, 100-101); *Martyrdom of Pionius* 4.24; 8.3; 9.6 (ed. Musurillo, 142-143, 146-147, 148-149); *Acts of Justin and Companions* (Recension B) 5.1-5 (ed. Musurillo, 50-51, 52-53). Other passion narratives of the martyrs speak only of the judgment of God: *Acts of Carpus, Papylus, and Agathonicê* 40 (ed. Musurillo, 26-27) = ibid. 4.4-5 (Latin recension) (ed. Musurillo, 32-33); *Martyrdom of Apollonius* 25, 37, 42 (ed. Musurillo, 96-97, 100-101, 102-103).

31. *TDNT*, vol. 9, s.v. *phaneroô* (etc.), 4-7; vol. 3, s.v. *krinô* (etc.), 936-942. For Christ's action as Savior (*sôter*), see above, n. 29.

32. *Acts of Justin and Companions* (Recension B) 2.5 (ed. Musurillo, 48-49).

33. *Acts of Phileas* (Greek recension), cols. 6-7 (ed. Musurillo, 334-335, 336-337).

34. *Letter of the Churches of Lyon and Vienne* 1.29-30, 42 (ed. Musurillo,70-71, 74-75); cf. *Martyrdom of Perpetua and Felicitas* 15.3 (ed. Musurillo, 122-123); cf. ibid. 18.2 (ed. Musurillo, 126-127), where Perpetua is called a "wife of Christ" (*matrona Christi*).

35. Acts 7:59; *Martyrdom of Polycarp* 14.2 (ed. Musurillo, 12-13); *Martyrdom of Pionius* 21.9 (ed. Musurillo, 164-165).

36. *Martyrdom of Polycarp* 14.2 (ed. Musurillo, 12-13); *Acts of Carpus, Papylus, and Agathonicê* (Greek recension) 40-41 (ed. Musurillo, 26-27); ibid. (Latin recension) 4.4-6 (ed. Musurillo, 32-33, 34-35); *Acts of Justin and Companions* (Recension B) 5.2 (ed. Musurillo, 52-53); *Martyrdom of Apollonius* 46 (ed. Musurillo, 102-103).

37. See Th. Camelot, ed., *Ignace d'Antioche, Polycarpe de Smyrne: Lettres*, SC 10: 33-36, 116, n. 1.

38. *Acts of the Scillitan Martyrs* 12 (ed. Musurillo, 88-89).

39. *Acts of Euplus* (Greek recension) 1.1-4 (ed. Musurillo, 310-311).

40. *Martyrdom of Apollonius* 23 (ed. Musurillo, 96-97).

41. *Acts of Carpus, Papylus, and Agathonicê* 10 (ed. Musurillo 22-23); *Acts of Euplus* (Latin recension) 2.5 (ed. Musurillo, 316-317).

42. *Acts of Carpus, Papylus, and Agathonicê* 2.2 (ed. Musurillo, 30-31).

43. *Martyrdom of Apollonius* 14, 16 (ed. Musurillo, 94-95).

44. Ibid. 19 (ed. Musurillo, 94-95).
45. Ibid. 20 (ed. Musurillo, 96-97).
46. Ibid. 22 (ed. Musurillo, 96-97).
47. Cf. Isa. 40:18-20; 41:6-7; 42:8, 17; 44:9-20; 45:16, 20; 46:6-7; Jer. 2:5-13; 10:1-16; Hos. 2:7-15; Ep. of Jer. (in its entirety); Wisdom 13:10-15, 19.
48. See the preceding note.
49. *Acts of Phileas*, col. 7 (ed. Musurillo, 336-337).
50. Ibid. (Latin recension) 4.5 (ed. Musurillo, 348-349).
51. *Martyrdom of Pionius* 4.5-24; 13.1-14.16 (ed. Musurillo, 138-139, 140-141, 142-143, 152-153, 154-155, 156-157).
52. Matt. 15:1-9; Mark 7:1-12; Matt. 16:5-12; Mark 8:16-21; Luke 12:1; Matt. 23 (in its entirety).
53. Rhetoric alone will not suffice to explain this abundance. We must still take into account the virulent anti-Jewish polemic which these discourses develop.
54. See V. Saxer, *Saints anciens d'Afrique du Norde* (Vatican City, 1979), 21.
55. *Letter of the Churches of Lyons and Vienne* 1.38, 40, 42 (ed. Musurillo, 74-75, 78-79).
56. *Martyrdom of Perpetua and Felicitas* 10.1-14 (ed. Musurillo, 116-117, 118-119).
57. *Martyrdom of Polycarp* 3.1 (ed. Musurillo, 4-5).
58. Ignatius, *Ep. to the Romans* 5.2 (*The Apostolic Fathers*, vol. 1, ed. with Eng. trans. by Kirsopp Lake, Loeb Classical Library [Cambridge, Mass., reprinted 1975], 232-233).
59. *Martyrdom of Polycarp* 19.2 (ed. Musurillo, 16-17).
60. Ibid. 18.3 (ed. Musurillo, 16-17).
61. *Martyrdom of Perpetua and Felicitas* 10.1-15 (ed. Musurillo,116-117, 118-119); cf. also ibid. 18.1-9 (ed. Musurillo, 124-125, 126-127).
62. *Ep. to Barnabas* 4.9; 20.1 (*Apostolic Fathers*, vol. 1, Loeb ed., 352-353, 406-407).
63. See F. J. Dögler, *Die Sonne der Gerechtigkeit und der Schwarze*, Liturgiegeschichtliche Forsuchungen 2 (Münster-W., 1919), 52.
64. *Shepherd of Hermas*, Simil. 9.6.1 (*Apostolic Fathers*, vol. 2, Loeb ed., 230-231, 232-233).
65. Ibid. 9.12.8 (*Apostolic Fathers*, vol. 2, Loeb ed., 250-251, 252-253). Cf. also *Martyrdom of Marian and James* 7.3, 6 (ed. Musurillo, 202-203, 204-205).
66. See C. Daremberg and E. Saglio, eds., *Dictionnaire des antiquités grecques et romaines d'après les textes et les monuments*, vol. 3.2, 1340-1347; figs. 4619-4620; vol. 4.1, 754-760, fig. 5861.
67. Cf. 1 Sam. 17:51 (=1 Kings 17:51, LXX); Joshua 10:24; Ps. 110:1 (=109:1, LXX).
68. Cf. Ps.-Tertullian, *De ieiunio* 13.
69. The *Portia Sanavivaria* (*Martyrdom of Perpetua and Felicitas* 10.13; 20.7, ed. Musurillo, 118-119, 128-129), as opposed to the *Portia Libitinensis* through which the dead and dying passed.
70. *TDNT*, vol. 1, s.v. *agôn*, 135-140.
71. 1 Cor. 9:24-27; 2 Tim. 2:5.

72. 1 Thess. 2:2; Col. 1:19; 1 Tim. 6:12; 2 Tim. 4:7.

73. 2 Tim. 4:6-8; Phil. 2:16-17; 1 Tim. 6:12; Heb. 10:32-34; 11:33-40; 12:1-2.

74. 2 Tim. 4:8; James 1:12; Rev. 2:10; 9:11; 6:2.

75. Rev. 2:10; Heb. 2:14.

76. *Martyrdom of Perpetua and Felicitas* 18.3; 21.2 (ed. Musurillo, 126-127, 128-129). See also F. J. Dögler, "Gladiatorenblut und Martyrerblut: Eine Szene der Passio Perpetuae in kultur- und religionsgeschichtlicher Beleuchtung," *Vorträge der Bibliothek Warburg*, vol. 3 (Leipzig, 1926), 196-214; idem, "Tertullian über die Bluttaufe: Tertullian, *De baptismo* 16," *Antike und Christentum*, vol. 2 (Münster-W., 1930), 117-141.

77. *Martyrdom of Perpetua and Felicitas* 21.2 (ed. Musurillo, 128-129, 130-131).

78. Dögler, "Gladiatorenblut und Martyrerblut," 199-201; also *Dictionnaire d'archéologie chrétien et de liturgie*, vol. 3, 430-431.

79. See Tertullian, *De baptismo* 16; *De pudicitia* 22.9; *Scorpiace* 6; Cyprian, *Epp.* 57.4; 73.22; *Ad Fortunatum*, praef. 4; Anon. (Ps.-Cyprian), *De rebaptismate* 14; Anon. (Ps.-Cyprian), *De singularitate clericorum* 34.

80. Cf. Lev. 14:4ff; Exod. 24:8.

81. Dögler, "Tertullian über die Bluttaufe," 140.

82. *Martyrdom of Perpetua and Felicitas* 18.3 (ed. Musurillo, 126-127).

83. On Ignatius, see K. Bommes, *Weizen Gottes: Untersuchungen zur Theologie des Martyriums bei Ignatius von Antiochen*, Theophaneia 27 (Cologne and Bonn, 1971), 153-159; and on Cyprian, M. Pellegrino, "Eucaristia e martirio in S. Cipriano," in *Convivium dominicum: Studi sull' Eucaristia nei Padri della Chiesa antica* (Catania, 1959), 135-150. On other aspects, especially the cult of the martyrs, cf. V. Saxer, *Morts, martyrs, reliques en Afrique chrétienne aux premiers siècles* (Paris, 1980), 57ff, 104ff, 170ff.

84. V. Saxer, *Vie liturgique et quotidienne*, 174: "l'eucharistie, préparation au martyre."

85. *Martyrdom of Perpetua and Felicitas* 21.4 (ed. Musurillo, 130-131).

86. *Acts of Carpus, Papylus, and Agathonicê* (Greek recension) 37 (ed. Musurillo, 26-27).

87. Ibid. 41, 46-47 (ed. Musurillo, 26-27, 28-29); ibid. (Latin recension) 5.2 (ed. Musurillo, 34-35).

88. *Martyrdom of Perpetua and Felicitas* 18.7 (ed. Musurillo, 126-127).

89. *Acts of Carpus, Papylus, and Agathonicê* (Greek recension) 42 (ed. Musurillo, 26-27, 28-29).

90. Th. Camelot, *Ignace d'Antioche*, 38.

91. Ibid., 39-40.

92. *Martyrdom of Polycarp* 1.1; 19.1 (ed. Musurillo, 2-3, 16-17).

93. Camelot, *Ignace d'Antioche*, 231.

94. *Martyrdom of Polycarp* 14.2 (ed. Musurillo, 12-13).

95. Camelot, *Ignace d'Antioch*, 38. Cf. *Letter of the Churches of Lyons and Vienne* 2.2-5 (ed. Musurillo, 82-83).

96. *Letter of the Churches of Lyons and Vienne* 1.23 (ed. Musurillo, 68-69).

97. Ibid. 1.30 (ed. Musurillo, 70-71).

98. Ibid. 1.23, 30 (ed. Musurillo, 68-69, 70-71).

99. Ibid. 1.42 (ed. Musurillo, 74-75).
100. Ibid. 1.6 (ed. Musurillo, 62-63).
101. Ibid. 1.56 (ed. Musurillo, 80-81).
102. Ibid. 1.10 (ed. Musurillo, 64-65).
103. *Acts of Carpus, Papylus, and Agathonicê* (Latin recension) 3.5-7 (ed. Musurillo, 32-33).
104. Ibid. (Greek recension) 41 (ed. Musurillo, 26-27).
105. Ibid. 39 (ed. Musurillo, 26-27).
106. *Martyrdom of Perpetua and Felicitas* 1.6 (ed. Musurillo, 106-107).
107. Ibid. 15.6 (ed. Musurillo, 122-123, 124-125).
108. Ibid. 18.9 (ed. Musurillo, 126-127).
109. 1 Peter 1:11 = Isa. 52:13-53:12; 1 Peter 2:22-24 = Isa. 53:5-6, 9.
110. Camelot, *Ignace d'Antioch*, 44, n. 3.
111. Ignatius, *Ep. to the Philadelphians* 7.1-2 (*Apostolic Fathers*, vol. 1, Loeb. ed., 244-145, 246-247).
112. *Martyrdom of Polycarp* 5.2 (ed. Musurillo, 6-7).
113. Ibid. 12.3 (ed. Musurillo, 12-13).
114. Ibid. 16.2 (ed. Musurillo, 14-15).
115. *Letter of the Churches of Lyons and Vienne* 1.9 (ed. Musurillo, 64-65, translation modified).
116. Ibid. (ed. Musurillo, 64-65).
117. Ibid. 1.10 (ed. Musurillo, 64-65).
118. *TDNT*, vol. 5, s.v. *paraklêtos*, 800-814.
119. *Letter of the Churches of Lyons and Vienne* 1.10 (ed. Musurillo, 64-65).
120. P. de Labriolle, *La crise montaniste* (Paris, 1913), 225-227.
121. *Letter of the Churches of Lyons and Vienne* 1.49 (ed. Musurillo, 76-77). The "apostolic charism" here is transposed into a "prophetic charism" in the edition of G. Bardy, SC 41: 19, n. 64.
122. de Labriolle, *La crise montaniste*, 225-230.
123. *Letter of the Churches of Lyons and Vienne* 2.6 (ed. Musurillo, 84-85, translation modified).
124. Ibid. 2.5 (ed. Musurillo, 82-83).
125. Ibid. 1.46 (ed. Musurillo, 76-77).
126. de Labriolle, *La crise montaniste*, 225-230.
127. *Dictionnaire biblique, Suppl.*, vol. 6, 1213.
128. *Acts of Justin and Companions* (Recension B) 5.1-3 (ed. Musurillo, 50-51, 52-53). Cf. also *Martyrdom of Apollonius* 42 (ed. Musurillo, 100-101, 102-103); *Acts of Phileas* (Greek recension), cols. 3-4 (ed. Musurillo, 332-333).
129. Cf. *1 Clement* 42.3 (*Apostolic Fathers*, vol. 1, Loeb ed., 80-81); Ignatius, *Ep. to the Magnesians* 8.2 (*Apostolic Fathers*, vol. 1, Loeb ed., 204-205). Cf. also *Clementine Homilies* 1.17 (the conviction that the soul is immortal); *Acts of Pilate* (Recension B) 15.5 (the conviction that Christ was resurrected). It is thus remarkable that this conviction was based, among other truths of the faith, on the resurrection of Christ as a guarantee of the Christian's own resurrection. We therefore recover here

the reasoning, if not the terminology, of the apostle Paul (1 Cor. 15:12-19, 29-34). Cf. *TDNT*, s.v. *plêrophoreô*, 309-310.

130. *Letter of the Churches of Lyons and Vienne* 1.29-30 (ed. Musurillo, 69-70, 71-72).

131. *Martyrdom of Perpetua and Felicitas* 18.1-5 (ed. Musurillo, 124-125, 126-127).

132. *Martyrdom of Polycarp* 17.1; 19.2 (ed. Musurillo, 14-15, 16-17).

133. *Letter of the Churches of Lyons and Vienne* Prol. 4; 1.36, 42 (ed. Musurillo, 72-73, 74-75). Actually the first citation (prol. 4) must be attributed to Eusebius, and only the two others (1.36, 42) to the redactor of the *Martyrdom of Polycarp*. But there can be no doubt that Eusebius was echoing here the ideas of the work itself.

134. *Acts of the Scillitan Martyrs* 17 (ed. Musurillo, 88n, indicating the MS variant to line 32, for which Codex Vindobonensis latinus 377 and Codex Ebroicensis 37 include the phrase: *omnes simul martyrio coronati sunt*).

135. *Martyrdom of Pionius* 22.2 (ed. Musurillo, 164-165).

136. *Acts of Euplus* (Greek recension) 2.2, 4 (ed. Musurillo, 312-313).

137. See *TDNT*, vol. 7, s.v. *stephanos*, 615-636, esp. 629-633.

138. *Martyrdom of Polycarp* 17.1; 19.2 (ed. Musurillo, 14-15, 16-17); *Letter of the Churches of Lyons and Vienne* 1.42 (ed. Musurillo, 74-75).

139. *Letter of the Churches of Lyons and Vienne* 1.36 (ed. Musurillo, 72).

140. *Acts of Euplus* (Greek recension) 2.4 (ed. Musurillo, 312-313).

141. Ibid. 2.2 (ed. Musurillo, 312-313).

142. I will limit myself to authors only of the first two centuries: Ignatius, *Ep. to the Magnesians* 13.1 (*Apostolic Fathers*, vol. 1, Loeb ed., 208-209); *2 Clement* 7.3 (ibid., 138-139); *Shepherd of Hermas, Simil.* 8.2.1 (ibid., vol. 2, Loeb ed., 192-193).

143. *Martyrdom of Polycarp* 17.1 (ed. Musurillo, 14-15).

144. *Martyrdom of Apollonius* 47 (ed. Musurillo, 102-103, translation modified).

145. *Martyrdom of Perpetua and Felicitas* 10.8 (ed. Musurillo, 118-119).

146. Ibid. 10.14 (ed. Musurillo, 118-119).

147. See 1 Cor. 9:24; Phil. 3:14. And cf. Tatian, *Oratio ad Graecos* 33; Clement of Alexandria, *Quis dives salvetur* 1; Eusebius of Caesarea, *Vita Constantinii* 1.9; John of Thessalonica, *Orationis in dormitionem B. M. V.* 1.3.

148. *Martyrdom of Polycarp* 20.2 (ed. Musurillo, 16-17, 18-19); *Acts of Carpus, Papylus, and Agathonicê* (Latin recension) 3.5-7 (ed. Musurillo, 36-37); *Martyrdom of Apollonius* 47 (ed. Musurillo, 104-105); *Martyrdom of Pionius* 23 (ed. Musurillo, 166-167); *Acts of Cyprian* 6 (ed. Musurillo 5.7, 174-175n, indicating the older MS reading from the ed. in CSEL 3.3, which appends the words: "The most blessed martyr Cyprian suffered in the fourteenth day of September, under the emperors Valerian and Galerius, in the reign (*regnante*) of our Lord Jesus Christ..."); *Martyrdom of Agapê, Irenê, Chionê, and Companions* 7.2 (ed. Musurillo, 292-293).

149. *Acts of the Scillitan Martyrs* 17 (ed. Musurillo, 88-89n, indicating the MS variant to line 32, for which Codex Vindobonensis latinus 377 and Codex Ebroicensis 37 include the phrase: *et ita omnes simul martyrio coronati sunt et regnant cum Patre et Spiritu sancto per omnia saecula saeculorum.*

150. *Martyrdom of Polycarp* 22.3 (18-19, 20-21).
151. *Letter of the Churches of Lyons and Vienne* 1.35 (ed. Musurillo, 72-73).
152. *Martyrdom of Polycarp* 15.2 (ed. Musurillo, 14-15).
153. *Martyrdom of Perpetua and Felicitas* 13.8 (ed. Musurillo, 122-123).
154. Ibid. 4.8 (ed. Musurillo, 110-111).
155. Ibid. 11.1 (ed. Musurillo, 118-119).
156. Ibid. 11.4-6; 12.1-6 (ed. Musurillo, 118-119, 120-121).
157. Ibid. 4.8; 11.5-6 (ed. Musurillo, 110-111, 120-121).
158. Ibid. 4.9 (ed. Musurillo, 110-111, 112-113).
159. Ibid. 12.1-5 (ed. Musurillo, 120-121).
160. J. A. Robinson, *The Passion of Perpetua*, Texts and Studies, vol. 2.1 (Cambridge, 1891), 26-43.
161. This theme in fact appears nowhere else in the extant *Acts of the Christian Martyrs*, save for a brief allusion in the *Martyrdom of Perpetua and Felicitas* 18.1.
162. *Letter of the Churches of Lyons and Vienne* 1.11 (ed. Musurillo, 64-65).
163. Ibid. 1.45-46 (ed. Musurillo, 76-77).
164. Ibid. 2.6 (ed. Musurillo, 84-85, translation modified).
165. Ibid. 1.49 (ed. Musurillo, 76-77, 78-79).
166. See J. Daniélou, *The Bible and the Liturgy* (Notre Dame, Ind., 1956), 47-49.
167. This concrete conception of the Mother-Church has been highlighted by K. Delahaye, *Ecclesia mater chez les Pères des trois premiers siècles* (Paris, 1964).
168. Mother images, notably from the Maccabees (2 Macc. 7:20ff; 4 Macc. 16:12) directly inspired the redactor of the *Letter of the Churches of Lyons and Vienne* (1.55, ed. Musurillo, 78-79). See elsewhere in Scripture the maternal personifications in Isa. 49:15; 50:1; 66:13; Hos. 4:5. For the theme of spiritual paternity/maternity, see 1 Cor. 4:15; Philem. 10; 1 Thess. 2:7-8, 11; Gal. 4:19. For maternity as an apocalyptic symbol, see Rev. 12:1-6; 21:2, 9-10; 22:17, 20.
169. See J. C. Plumpe, *Mater Ecclesiae: An Inquiry into the Concept of the Church as Mother in Early Christianity* (Washington, D.C., 1943); and *TDNT*, vol. 4, s.v. *mêtêr*, 642-644.
170. *Martyrdom of Perpetua and Felicitas* 18.2 (ed. Musurillo, 126-127).
171. *Letter of the Churches of Lyons and Vienne* 1.35 (ed. Musurillo, 72-73).
172. Ibid. 1.48 (ed. Musurillo, 76-77).
173. Ibid. 1.55 (ed. Musurillo, 78-79).
174. *Acts of Carpus, Papylus, and Agathonicê* (Greek recension) 42 (ed. Musurillo, 26-27, 28-29).
175. *TDNT*, vol. 1, s.v. *gameô*, 653-657; vol. 1, s.v. *deipnon*, 34-35.
176. See Daniélou, *The Bible and the Liturgy*, 191-207.
177. The reader will find a more complete exposition of the influence of the Bible in early Christian martyrology in V. Saxer, *Bible et hagiographie: Textes et thèmes bibliques dans les Actes des martyrs authentiques des premiers siècles* (Berne, 1985).

18

The Bible as a Guide for Early Christian Pilgrims to the Holy Land

PIERRE MARAVAL

The history of Christian pilgrimages to the holy places of the Bible began in earnest only with the Peace of the Church in the early fourth century (312 C.E.). Before that time, there are only rare examples of Christian pilgrims journeying to Palestine with the desire to see and to honor the theater in which the events of the Old and New Testaments took place. Certainly political circumstances were hardly conducive to such travel: The third century was a period of tremendous instability; it was also a period in which Christians were frequently the object of imperial persecution. This in itself is enough to explain the rarity of Christians going on pilgrimages, but another factor was doubtless more determinative, namely, the primitive Christian communities' manifest suspicion of attempts to sacralize times and places. Such was a legacy of Judaism, indeed of paganism as well. Reference to the Gospel was made in support of this attitude: The true worshipers of God did not worship on this or that mountain, but in spirit and in truth (cf. John 4:21-24). Earliest Christians, moreover, had little interest in the location of events from the New Testament, or in visiting them for themselves. The Gospels contain little in the way of precise topographical information (with the exception, perhaps, of John); and not much more is found in writers of the first three centuries. Even a scholar as attentive to the biblical text as Origen, who journeyed to Palestine "in search of traces of Jesus, his disciples, and his prophets," provides only meager information on the subject.

The situation would change altogether in the fourth century, when interest in biblical topography would go hand in hand with the influx of pilgrims into the Holy Land;[1] henceforth the Bible would become the guide for the pilgrims' travels. In the first part of this essay we will show how the Bible served in this capacity for pilgrims of the time, using the testimony of certain fourth-century pilgrims for whom this function of the Bible was especially striking. In the second section, we will have occasion to determine the precise contents of the pilgrim's Bible on the basis of the inventory of holy sites that they established for themselves over the three centuries from the Peace of the Church to the capture of Jerusalem by the Arabs in 638.

The Bible as a Guide to Sacred Topography

The Bible was the pilgrim's greatest inspiration, determining the pilgrim's interests, deciding the sites which the pilgrim would visit and venerate during his or her journey. The ancient pilgrim was no mere tourist predisposed to see and admire everything, but instead had the singular goal of visiting the holy places, upon which his or her attention was virtually exclusively focused. The so-called Bordeaux pilgrim was the first to have left us a report of his journey, leaving Bordeaux in 333 and traveling to Jerusalem, then returning from Jerusalem to Milan.[2] He simply noted without commentary the list of provinces through which he traveled before his arrival in Palestine. But upon arriving in the "land of the Bible," his rather lean report is suddenly enlarged, as he recounts all the memories of biblical history that his encounter with the holy places evoked. Serepta (Zarephath) is the town where the prophet Elijah came to live with a widow (1 Kings 17:8ff; =3 Kings 17:8ff, LXX). Carmel is the mountain where he performed his miraculous sacrifice (1 Kings 18; =3 Kings 18, LXX). Caesarea, the metropolis on the coast of the province of Palestine where modern archaeologists have unearthed some remarkable monuments, holds interest for the Bordeaux pilgrim only because he found there the bath (*balneum*—doubtless a baptistery) of the centurion Cornelius (Acts 10). At Garazim he takes up the Samaritan tradition that this was the site of Abraham's sacrifice of Isaac. At Jacob's well he shows his profound knowledge of the Bible, for he is the only one of the ancient pilgrims for whom the well recalls the violence against Jacob's daughter Dinah (Gen. 34). Naturally Jerusalem is the object of his most passionate interest, by virtue of all its monuments (pools, catacombs, towers, aqueducts, synagogues, tombs, etc.) and all its holy places that can be related to events or persons from the Old and New Testaments.

Fifty years later, the pilgrim Egeria would have the same attitude. According to Valerius of Bierzo,[3] she prepared for her trip by completely checking, Bible in hand, all the sites she planned to visit; when she actually came to those places, she specified several times that what she visited, under the guidance of local monks or clerics, were the very sites "that I asked about according to the Scriptures."[4] Her requests were perhaps difficult to fulfill sometimes, when the guides' knowledge—or imagination—failed. Fortunately for her, Egeria met up with guides who were particularly well-versed in the Scriptures; she even specifically mentions that this was the case for three of her guides: the bishop of Arabia in Egypt, the priest of Salem in the Jordan River Valley, and the bishop of Haran in Mesopotamia. This last bishop must have explained to her why one would want to venerate, a mile from Haran, the tombs of Nahor and Bethuel (respectively the brother and nephew of Abraham), since Scripture does not explicitly state that they followed their kinsman when he left the Ur of the Chaldeans (cf. Gen. 11:26-12:5; 24:24). He likewise must have given her the location of the wells from which Jacob had watered Rachel's herds, the location where Terah (Abraham's father) had lived, and "much else besides."[5] This kind of holy curiosity was shared by Paula when she traveled though Palestine in 385, led by a guide who must not have been short on explanations, seeing as it was none other than St. Jerome himself. In the letter recounting this pilgrimage, Jerome specifically writes, "I shall only name such places as are mentioned in the sacred books,"[6] and what follows is a veritable tapestry of biblical quotations and allusions connected with each of the sites visited.

This interest solely in biblical sites most often determined the pilgrim's itinerary itself. Even if the pilgrim, for obvious reasons of convenience, traveled along the major arteries of the time, he or she did not hesitate to divert from them onto difficult backroads that had exclusively biblical significance. So it was with the trip to Mt. Sinai from Clysma (Suez): While partially following a caravan route, it still included the crossing of desert regions and rugged climbs, but almost every step of the way was marked by the memory of the exodus of the Hebrews. The ascent to Mt. Sinai in particular, as well as the visit to the valley below where the Hebrews waited for Moses, enabled the pilgrim who circled the area with Bible in hand (or at least vivid in memory) truly to walk in the footsteps of Moses and the Hebrew people, since all the events recounted in numerous chapters from Exodus were carefully located. Egeria was one of the first Christian pilgrims to have taken this route, which would remain a popular one throughout this period. She was always prepared to use the Bible quite literally as her guide. Hence, when she returned to Clysma after visiting Sinai, she determined to proceed on her journey by a less frequented and less stable route (soldiers had to escort her from fort to fort!), her singular goal being "to see all the places where the children of Israel had been on their way from Rameses to the Red Sea."[7] On another occasion, while traveling to Mt. Nebo—which was already a destination that held only biblical significance—it was enough that a priest among Egeria's escorts indicated to her that by deviating from their route she could see where Moses miraculously extracted water from a rock for the thirsty Israelites (Exod. 17:6; Num. 20:8); she immediately took his advice.[8] In this way, veritable pilgrims' circuits began to be formed beginning in this period. The Sinai route was visibly well organized by the sixth century. Caravans leaving Jerusalem could get there in eighteen days, and along the way several hostels were destined to spring up to provide lodging for the pilgrims. Other pilgrim circuits fell in place all along the principal access roads which radiated around the Holy City of Jerusalem. One work from the first half of the sixth century, the *De situ terrae sanctae* of Theodosius, which was really a guide for Christian pilgrims, describes these routes in sequence, all of them marked by a recollection of biblical events. For example, he writes of the journey south from Jerusalem: "From Jerusalem to the place where Philip baptized the eunuch is sixteen miles. From there it is two miles to the Terebinth which is called the Oak of Mamre. From the Terebinth to the double cave where the patriarchs rest is another four miles. From the double cave to Hebron is two miles: Saint David lived there for seven years when he was fleeing from Saul." Hence the pilgrim traveling the roads of Palestine was constantly breathless recalling biblical events.

These memories very quickly became rather precise. A town or a mountain was too vague to satisfy the religious devotion of pilgrims anxious to see the *ipsissima loca*, the very places where the events they were commemorating took place; if possible they wanted also to lay hold of an authentic relic from such sites. The Bordeaux pilgrim already knew of several such specific holy places. Near Jacob's well he saw plane-trees which he believed had been planted by the patriarch himself. At Bethel he found the almond tree at the foot of which Jacob had had his vision of the ladder and his combat with an angel (Gen. 28:10-17; 32:22-30). In Jerusalem he saw the very vault where Solomon had written his book of

Wisdom, traces of blood of the martyred prophet Zechariah (2 Chron 24:20-22; Matt. 23:35), the marks of the hobnails of his executioners, the rock where Judas Iscariot betrayed his Master (Matt. 26:47-56 and par.), the palm tree from which the children of Jerusalem fetched branches to welcome Christ at his entry into the city (Matt. 28:8 and par.). At Terebinthus (Mamre), the Bordeaux pilgrim discovered the well which Abraham dug, where he also spoke with the angels (Gen. 18:1ff).[9] And the list goes on.

Egeria too gives a number of similarly precise examples. Among the many things that she mentions in her detailed account of her trip to Sinai, she saw the grotto where Moses was positioned on the holy mountain (Exod. 33:22), sprouts from the original Burning Bush (Exod. 3:1ff), the rock on which Moses shattered the tablets of the Law (Exod. 32:19), the large stone where the image of the golden calf had stood (Exod. 32:4).[10] Clysma, which Egeria visited along the coast of the Red Sea, was a place where, as some later sources tell us, one could still see on the banks the tracks of the chariots of Pharaoh's army. Antoninus of Piacenza in the late-sixth century claimed to have seen these tracks as forever petrified;[11] the phenomenon is also mentioned as late as the twelfth century by Peter the Deacon in his *Book on the Holy Places*.[12] On the shore of the Dead Sea, many pilgrims would search for the salt statue of Lot's fated wife. Egeria would be shown the site where it once stood, all the while being assured that the statue itself had disappeared by her time.[13] Other later pilgrims would still frequent the spot anyway. Noticeably, many of the details which distinguished these sites supplemented the biblical narratives when they did not contradict them. This was just as true for many of the New Testament sites, beginning with the "grotto" of Jesus's nativity in Bethlehem. This tendency, moreover, would not diminish with time, and even became more pronounced during these early centuries of Christian pilgrimage to the biblical holy places, marked by the transition from "topographical" relics—grottos, rocks, archaeological remains or geological phenomena—to relics of the biblical events themselves, or better yet of persons who had actually lived those events.

This is precisely how relics from the life of Christ began to flourish. The first known one was the manger, which Origen claimed to have seen in the first half of the third century; then came the column of the flagellation of Jesus, known to the pilgrim of Bordeaux; shortly thereafter followed the most celebrated of all the relics, the actual cross of Christ, discovered sometime around 340. Little by little other relics of the Passion showed up: the reed and the sponge, the spear used to pierce Christ's side, the onyx chalice from the Last Supper, and the crown of thorns, all of which were venerated in Jerusalem in the sixth century in various sanctuaries. Beginning in the fifth century, relics from Christ's childhood and those of the Virgin also gained importance and served to embellish recognized holy sites not only in Jerusalem but in Bethlehem, Nazareth, and even Egypt. A fair number of these relics were connected not with the Bible itself but with apocryphal texts or extra-canonical legends. Thus one could see at Nazareth the bench on which the boy Jesus sat (and which no Jew could lift!), or in the Anastasis Church the rock on which Mary rested during her journey to Bethlehem (the rock having been transported there from Kathisma, the "Old Seat," half-way between Jerusalem and Bethlehem, where, according to one source, Mary had originally rested[14]). All of this attests to the burgeoning popularity of relics in Christian piety of this period, the effects of which were also seen in the various forms of the cult of the martyrs. At least in Palestine, interest in this type of relics does not seem to have overshadowed the original link between a particular site and a biblical event, since such relics were generally venerated at the site itself. But when fragments of these relics began to overrun all regions of the Empire, this link with the Bible would tend to disappear or to assume merely secondary significance. The relics would become talismans, "amulets" (*phylactêria*) like all the rest, perhaps having greater efficacy only because of where they originated. Henceforth the desire to procure such relics became for some the primary motivation for making pilgrimages to the Holy Land.

Certainly there were, nonetheless, Christian pilgrims who avoided this rather narrow perspective. For them, the visit to biblical sites provided the opportunity to recover a privileged link with the biblical text, to offer up meditations or prayers which were directly based on the Scriptures. The most interesting example to recall here is that of Paula, or more precisely Jerome's description of her pilgrimage, which in recounting the visited sites constantly indicates how their significance echoed deep in the pilgrim's soul, as Paula relived the events on account of which they had become holy places. "Before the Cross," Jerome says of her visit to Golgotha, "she threw herself down in adoration as though she beheld the Lord hanging upon it."[15] Concerning her journey to Bethlehem,

> she protested in my hearing that she could behold with the eyes of faith the infant Lord wrapped in swaddling clothes and crying in the manger, the wise men worshipping Him, the star shining overhead, the virgin mother, the attentive foster-father, the shepherds coming by night to see

"the word that was come to pass" and thus even to consecrate those opening phrases of the evangelist John "In the beginning was the word" and "the word was made flesh." (Luke 2:7-15; Matt. 2:1-12; John 1:1, 14). She declared that she could see the slaughtered innocents, the raging Herod, Joseph and Mary fleeing into Egypt... (Matt. 2:13-18).[16]

This same desire to re-actualize biblical events motivated Egeria, as each time she stopped at an important place in her pilgrimage, she would have the pertinent biblical passage read, as well as an appropriate Psalm. Jerome, however, also echoes a deeper kind of reflection in those instances where the visiting of holy sites elicited an exegesis of the texts that those sites had called to mind for the pilgrim. The visit to Mt. Zion recalled a verse from the Psalms in which the gates of Zion appeared as beloved by the Lord (Ps. 87:2 [86:2, LXX]). Reflection was elevated from the ruins of the ancient gates to the "gates" against which hell does not prevail, the gates of the Church (Matt. 16:18).[17] Near the tower of Ader, close to Bethlehem, in the vicinity of which Jacob already had watered his herds, the shepherds heard the angels announce the birth of Christ; the allusion to sheep in turn leads Jerome, in his narration, to elaborate on the symbolism of the lamb, simultaneously the mystical Lamb and its prefiguration in the Jewish Passover. "While they were keeping their sheep they found the Lamb of God; whose fleece bright and clean was made wet with the dew of heaven when it was dry upon all the earth beside (Judges 6:37), and whose blood when sprinkled on the doorposts drove off the destroyer of Egypt (Exod. 12:21-23) and took away the sins of the world."[18]

Even places neglected by pilgrims warranted a spiritual reflection: "she did not care to go on to Kirjath-sepher, that is 'the village of letters'; because despising the letter she found the spirit that giveth life" (cf. 2 Cor. 3:6).[19] Such commentary points to the abiding significance of the exegesis of Jerome, and likewise that of many other patristic exegetes before and after him. This appears to be especially the case for reflection on the holy places of the Old Testament, which did not stop with the physical sites themselves, but sought after their typological meaning. In the twelve stones on the field of Gilgal, near Jericho, the ones which Joshua had pulled from the Jordan River to erect a memorial for the safe passage of the twelve tribes of Israel (cf. Josh. 4:1-5:1), Jerome claims that Paula saw "symbols of those twelve foundations on which are written the names of the twelve apostles."[20] Elisha's fountain, whose water had long ago been made wholesome by the prophet (cf. 2 Kings 2:21-22; = 4 Kings 2:21-22, LXX), recalled "the fountain of the Law most bitter and barren which the true Elisha healed by his wisdom, changing it into a well sweet and fertilising."[21] To be sure, these reflections of Jerome can appear to be *a posteriori* reflections, just as his *Epistle* 108 itself looks like a literary work developed after the fact rather than a simple account of Paula's pilgrimage. It is obvious that Jerome was able to integrate exegeses of biblical texts which the original visit to the holy places had perhaps not actually recalled. Yet his reflections offer a good example, even if it is only an ideal example, of the manner in which Christians, shaped by the culture of the Bible, could experience their pilgrimages to the holy places.

Toward a Biblical Inventory of the Holy Places

The Bible inspired early Christian pilgrims. But which Bible? Or rather, which passages from the Bible? Pilgrims had to choose which episodes from the biblical narratives would be their primary inspiration, a choice often contingent on the geographical limitations of the pilgrims' itineraries, but it was still in many cases an intentional choice. Without giving a complete list of all the sites visited by Christian pilgrims from the fourth century to the sixth, it is interesting to point out, according to the order of the biblical books themselves, those sites most beloved by visitors. Listing them will furthermore disclose some of the criteria that guided the choice of all those, especially during the fourth century, who attempted to provide an inventory of the holy places.

The events narrated in Genesis provided numerous locations of interest to pilgrims. Obviously the first eleven chapters were scarcely as rich in geographical information. Yet one could still locate Adam's tomb (and occasionally his "birthplace") on Golgotha itself. There was no biblical evidence to support this, but the symbolic meaning of this identification spoke for itself. The most significant episodes from the life of Abraham, on the other hand, had unmistakable local references. Abraham's encounter with Melchizedek, on which occasion the latter offered a sacrifice (Gen. 14:17-18), was concurrently identified with two locations, but the one placing the event at Jerusalem—and more precisely at Golgotha—prevailed, mainly because of an existing christological interpretation of the figure of Melchizedek, as well as a eucharistic interpretation of his sacrifice. The visitation of Abraham by a messenger (or more than one) near the oak of Mamre (Gen. 18:1-8), in which patristic exegetes delighted in finding a theophany of the Trinity, turned this site (where, moreover, the oak became a terebinth) into a highly venerated site, one of the first adjacent to which a basilica was constructed. The ruins of Sodom and neighboring towns, together with the statue of salt that had once been Lot's wife (Gen. 19:24-26), likewise attracted the curiosity of pilgrims. For the sacrifice of Isaac (Gen. 22:1-2), Christians did not accept the traditional Jewish location (believed to be echoed in 2 Chron. 3:1), according to which it took place on the mountain where the Temple in Jerusalem was eventually built. Once more Christians located the story at Golgotha. After all, was not the sacrifice of Isaac a prefiguration of Christ's sacrifice? The Jacob cycle provided occasion for some less strained identifications of sites. We will note only the place of his vision of the ladder, Bethel (Gen. 28:12-19), and especially, near Shechem, the well on his land (cf. Gen. 29:2), made famous in conjunction with Jesus's conversation with the Samaritan woman (John 4:5-6). In Egypt, certain sites were connected with the story of Joseph, but Egypt was more an object of curiosity than of places of pilgrimage in the strict sense. Here we will only mention the Christian interpretation of the pyramids, which were considered to be the graineries where Joseph had stored wheat in preparation for the seven years of famine (Gen. 41:48-49).

We are told that the exodus of the Hebrew people from Egypt and all the events that went with it, as recounted in Exodus and Numbers, prompted a careful locating of the sites, and from the beginning there were numerous Christian pilgrims trying to trace its progressive stages. Egeria, at the end of the fourth century, was the first to describe these stages to us in detail, although it is necessary here to supplement her text with the help of Peter the Deacon's *Book on the Holy Places*. Her universal curiosity enabled her to provide us with knowledge of more locations than any subsequent pilgrim, locations which most often included precise topographical details. Without trying to list them all, we will point out that the crossing of the Red Sea (Exod. 14:1-31), the descent of the manna (Exod. 16:1-36), the rock which gushed water (Exod. 17:1-7), the battle with Amalek (Exod. 17:8-16), the lawgiving at Sinai (Exod. 19-20), all of which were on Egeria's itinerary, figured among the cherished narratives used in baptismal catechesis. The site of the burning bush at the foot of Mt. Horeb, theater of one of the most important theophanies in the Old Testament (Exod. 3:1ff), was also a particular object of veneration.

Several of the sites mentioned in Joshua held the attention of Christian pilgrims, in particular all the ones which were connected with the crossing of the Jordan and the entrance into Palestine. These included the ford where the Hebrews crossed (Josh. 3:14-17), the twelve stones erected as a monument at Gilgal (Josh. 4:20), and indeed the "Hill of the

Foreskins" (Gibeath-haaraloth), where Joshua circumcised the Hebrews (Josh. 5:3). At Jericho, the ruins that could be seen there were naturally considered to be those toppled by Joshua (Josh 6:1-21). One especially fascinating site, noted by nearly all visitors, was the house of Rahab, the harlot who hid Joshua's spies and whose goods and relatives were spared (Josh. 2 and 6:22-25)—the same person whom patristic exegesis loved to present as a prefiguration of the Church.

Sites furnished by other books of the Old Testament were not held in as high an esteem. Nonetheless, we will mention two groups which enjoyed sustained interest. The first derived from the connected cycles of Elijah and Elisha. The domain of these two prophets' activity included several holy places, as much in the north of Palestine (in the vicinity of Mt. Carmel or of Samaria and Jezreel) as further to the south in Judea. Among them were the vicinity of the ford of the Jordan River where the passage of the Hebrews had already been located, the grotto from Elijah's journey to Mt. Horeb, in the massive rock of Sinai, and the site of the theophany (1 Kings 19:8-19 [=3 Kings 19:8-19, LXX]). The second group included numerous tombs of Old Testament figures venerated by Christians beginning in the fourth century: tombs of patriarchs, judges, kings, prophets, and even Jewish martyrs like the Maccabean brothers and their mother (2 Macc. 7).

It should come as no surprise that pilgrims were even more interested in all the places in Palestine where they saw, as Gregory of Nyssa puts it, "memorials of our Lord's life in the flesh."[22] The curiosity of pilgrims spawned a multitude of New Testament holy places, for which it was often necessary, as we have already seen, to supplement the somewhat imprecise topographical data of the gospels. This is how the cave in Bethlehem came to be identified very early on (from the second century) as the place of Jesus's birth, when the birth narratives in Matthew and Luke did not specify the location. Likewise, a grotto of the Annunciation appeared at Nazareth, and grottoes have been preserved on the Mount of Beatitudes and the Mount of Olives as well, even though none of them has any textual foundation. The vast majority of episodes from the gospels were gradually located at precise points. We will pass over the sites from Egypt and Nazareth connected with the infancy of Jesus, which were for the most part based on apocryphal texts. In Galilee, numerous locations around the Lake of Tiberias (Sea of Galilee) effectively recalled the beginnings of the apostolic life of Christ: the mountain and grotto of the Beatitudes (Matt. 5:1), Peter's house in Capernaum (Matt. 8:14), the synagogue in this same city where a paralytic was healed (Matt. 9:1), the meadow of the multiplication of the loaves (which was located several kilometers west of Capernaum, despite the rather confused evidence of the Gospels, which seem to place it on the eastern shore of the lake). At Cana could be found the location of the wedding (John 2:1), and Tabor would come to be identified as the Mount of the Transfiguration, though the Gospels merely refer to a high mountain (Matt. 17:1).

In Samaria, we will only draw attention to one site, already noted above: Jacob's well near Shechem. In Judea, beyond Jerusalem, the city of Jericho and, close by, the ford of the Jordan, both attracted Christian pilgrims. Jericho contained a certain New Testament "curiosity" as well, the sycamore tree into which Zacchaeus had climbed to see Jesus passing by (Luke 19:4). The Jordan River naturally had a strong attraction since it was the site of Jesus's baptism (Matt. 3:13-17 and par.); many catechumens loved to be baptized there. Obviously it was Jerusalem, however, that offered the visitor the greatest number of holy places, most of which were related to the final period of Jesus's ministry. At Bethany one could find the tomb of Lazarus (John 11:17), on the Mount of Olives the cave where Jesus delivered his eschatological discourse (Mark 13:3-37 and par.), which some sources claimed was also where he had given his speeches after the Last Supper. The Messianic entry into Jerusalem (Matt. 21:1-9 and par.) was recalled by a palm tree from the Kidron Valley, allegedly the one which had provided palms for those who went out to meet Jesus. Sites connected with the Passion, which had early on been inventoried and provided with churches, were the most venerated: the place of the Last Supper (which had remained uncertain for a long time before finally being located on Mt. Zion) (Mark 14:15 and par.), the site of Jesus's prayer in Gethsemane (Mark 14:35ff and par.), the rock (unmentioned in the Bible) near which Judas had betrayed his Master (cf. Mark 14:43ff and par.), the house of Caiaphas on Mt. Zion (where originally one could find the column of the flagellation) (John 18:28), Pilate's Praetorium in the Tyropoeon Valley (John 18:28), and finally Golgotha itself. (It should be noted in passing that early Christian pilgrims did not follow the modern stations of the Cross on the Via Dolorosa).

All of these sites, down through the centuries, were embellished with relics of the Passion, the foremost and most precious of which was the Cross of Christ. The tomb of Christ, quite close to Golgotha (John 19:42) was the crown jewel, and most venerated, of the holy sites. Its rediscovery in 325, if in fact it was not already behind the emergence of

Christian pilgrimage, was a major impetus to travelers. The "upper room" on Mt. Zion where the disciples reassembled after the Passion was also an important holy place, the location of two appearances of Christ and of the outpouring of the Holy Spirit on Pentecost morning. The summit of the Mount of Olives was the place of the Ascension, and beginning in the fifth century the pilgrim could find there the last prints of Christ's feet. Also noteworthy here are some sites from the Acts of the Apostles which earned the interest of pilgrims. We already mentioned the site of Pentecost; one could also find the spring in which Philip had baptized the Ethiopian eunuch from Queen Candace (Acts 8:36-38) and the bath of the centurion Cornelius at Caesarea (Acts 10:48).

From this rapid tour of the landscape of early Christian pilgrimage to the Holy Land, a number of important facts emerge. One striking fact from the outset is the pilgrims' primary interest in sites which recalled significant events in salvation history. Certainly all of the Bible was "sacred history" to them; yet certain moments in that history were especially conducive to catechesis and preaching in this era, in which those moments were interpreted either as progressive stages in salvation history or as prefigurations of the salvific achievements of Christ or the redemptive benefits of the sacraments of the Church. Great figures of the Old Testament like Adam, Abraham, Isaac, and Moses announced in advance the salvation wrought by Christ, and the key passages about them in the Bible such as were cherished, for example, in the Jerusalem liturgy for Lent, were further illustrated, so to speak, on holy ground. Even more important in this perspective was to establish locations, as well as possible, for all the episodes in the life of Christ, especially those of his passion and resurrection. Particularly evocative in their ability to echo baptismal catechesis were sites where baptisms had taken place, first and foremost that of Christ's own baptism. All of this explains the great care taken in locating these important biblical sites and the success those sites enjoyed with Christian pilgrims.

One other comment will focus us on those who discovered these sites. Numerous holy places evoked the memory of Moses, Elijah, and Elisha. Other factors notwithstanding, there is clear influence here of monks who, as we already know, did much to help identify the holy places. These three Old Testament saints, in their diverse roles, were important in the monastic spirituality of this period, with numerous episodes from their biographies serving as models for the monastic way of life. In areas of heavy concentrations of monks, particularly in the vicinity of Sinai and in the area around Jericho, there were numerous holy places connected with the lives of Moses, Elijah, and Elisha; undoubtedly this was no accident.

We need still to emphasize two other criteria in the pilgrims' choice of holy places to venerate. One was the urge for relics, which induced pilgrims very early on to venerate the tombs of biblical saints, before it became an obsessive search for any and all remains, of greater or lesser authenticity, of the biblical events and their characters. Second was the simple curiosity of the pilgrims, which led them to keep searching, with more tenacity than critical judgment, for the souvenirs which fired their imaginations.

In conclusion, one concrete question confronts us. Did these Christian pilgrims, inspired by the Bible in their search for the slightest remains of biblical events and personalities, really travel around with Bibles in hand? We must remember that the book, or codex, in Antiquity was a rare and expensive commodity possessed only by a privileged few. Certainly there are actual examples of pilgrims who traveled around with one of the biblical books in hand, usually one of the gospels. A case in point is Peter the Iberian in the fifth century, who traveled with a copy of the Gospel of John, in the binding of which was encased a relic of the true cross. But this was an exception to the rule. The Bible of the majority of early Christian visitors to the holy places was foremost the Bible enshrined in the heart. That Bible was sufficient to start them on their journey and to comfort them in their travels.

NOTES

1. On the emergence of early Christian pilgrimage to the Holy Land, there are abundant secondary studies, but see in particular E. D. Hunt, *Holy Land Pilgrimage in the Later Roman Empire AD 312-460* (Oxford, 1982); P. Maraval, *Lieux saints et pèlerinages d'Orient: Histoire et géographie. Des origines à la conquête arabe* (Paris, 1985); and R. L. Wilken, *The Land Called Holy: Palestine in Christian History and Thought* (New Haven, 1992), esp. 108-125.

2. For the critical text of the *Bordeaux Itinerary,* see P. Geyer and O. Cuntz, eds., *Itinerarium Burdigalense,* CCSL 175: 1-26; trans. J. Wilkinson in *Egeria's Travels to the Holy Land,* revised ed. (Warminster, 1981), 153-163. On the importance of the Bible to the Bordeaux pilgrim, see also Hunt, *Holy Land Pilgrimage,* 83-85.

3. See Valerius's *Letter in Praise of the Life of the Most Blessed Egeria,* trans. J. Wilkinson, *Egeria's Travels to the Holy Land,* 174-175.

4. The remains of Egeria's travel diary are translated by J. Wilkinson, *Egeria's Travels to the Holy Land*, 89-147. On the importance of the Bible in her pilgrimage, see also Hunt, *Holy Land Pilgrimage*, 86-88.
5. *Egeria's Travels*, 119-120.
6. Jerome, *Epistle* 108.8, trans. W. H. Fremantle, G. Lewis, and W. Martley, NPNF, 2nd ser., vol. 6 (reprint ed., Grand Rapids, 1979), 198.
7. *Egeria's Travels*, 100-101.
8. Ibid., 106.
9. *Itinerarium Burdigalense*, trans. J. Wilkinson in *Egeria's Travels*, 155, 156, 157, 159, 162-163.
10. *Egeria's Travels*, 94, 96, 97.
11. Antoninus, *Itinerarium* 41 (CCSL 175: 150-151).
12. See Peter the Deacon, *Liber de locis sanctis* (CCSL 175: 91-103); trans. J. Wilkinson in *Egeria's Travels*, 179-210, and esp. 205-206 for Peter's mention of the chariot tracks at Clysma.
13. *Egeria's Travels*, 107-108.
14. See *Protoevangelium of James* 17.2; also Wilkinson, *Egeria's Travels*, 274, n.64.
15. Jerome, *Epistle* 108.9, trans. W. H. Fremantle et al., 198-199.
16. Ibid. 10, trans. Fremantle et al., 199.
17. Ibid. 9.
18. Ibid. 10, trans. Fremantle et al., 200.
19. Ibid. 11, trans. Fremantle et al., 200.
20. Ibid. 12, trans. Fremantle et al., 201.
21. Ibid.
22. Gregory of Nyssa, *On Pilgrimages*, trans. W. Moore and H. A. Wilson, NPNF, 2nd ser., vol. 5 (reprint ed., Grand Rapids, 1979), 382.

19

The Reading of the Bible in the Ancient Liturgy of Jerusalem

CHARLES RENOUX, O.S.B.

"Let only those Scriptures which we read in the Church with complete confidence be the object of your earnest study."[1] It was with this urgent admonition to his catechumens, around the year 348, that Cyril of Jerusalem introduced the list of sacred writings regarded as canonical in the Holy City: twenty-two for the Old Testament (Tobit, Judith, Wisdom of Solomon, Sirach, and Maccabees were not on the list), and twenty-seven for the New (Revelation was not included). "And whatever books are not read in the churches," Cyril adds, "are no longer to be read in private."[2]

A compilation of liturgical readings of the Bible therefore appears to have been in place in Jerusalem in the fourth century. The Bishop himself alludes to it elsewhere, in *Catechesis* 14 on the Resurrection and Ascension of Christ, when he writes, "The course of the teaching on the faith leads me to speak also of the Ascension, but the grace of God arranged things such that, to the extent our weakness allowed, you already heard it yesterday, on the Lord's Day. By the economy of God's grace, the course of readings (*anagnôsmatôn*) delivered in church included the account of our Savior's ascent into heaven."[3] What Sunday was this?[4] How was the system of Scripture lessons organized at this time, such that during the Lenten season, the season in which Cyril was instructing catechumens in preparation for Baptism on Easter, there was one Sunday when the Ascension pericope was read?[5] We simply do not know of any such schedule of biblical readings from the Lord's Day liturgy; no trace of such a lectionary has survived.[6]

At the end of the fourth century, the *Itinerarium Egeriae* (*Egeria's Travels*),[7] the journal of the pilgrim Egeria detailing what she had seen and heard in the holy places and churches of Jerusalem during the years 381-384,[8] gives us several glimpses of the use of a lectionary in the Holy City. For example, at vigils on Sunday, the Gospel account of the resurrection of the Lord was always to be read.[9] On the Saturday before Palm Sunday, prior to the office commemorating the raising of Lazarus, Egeria explicitly mentions the reading of two pericopes: "a reading from the Gospel about Lazarus' sister meeting the Lord;"[10] then, after the ceremony, the presbyter "mounts a platform, and reads the Gospel passage which begins, 'When Jesus came to Bethany six days before the Passover'..."[11] During the offices of Holy Week and Easter, Egeria refers to the reading of numerous Gospel texts recounting the events of the last days of Christ's life, his Passion, and his Resurrection.[12] On the fiftieth day after Easter, she reports that the liturgical reading included the passage from Acts about the descent of the Holy Spirit and the texts from Acts and the Gospel recounting the ascension of Christ.[13]

In each case noted above, the *Itinerarium* does not designate with exactness the biblical texts being read in Jerusalem. But it seems indeed that we are already seeing here, at the end of the fourth century, an organized lectionary of which the pilgrim Egeria has only mentioned a few readings. In the next century, these same pericopes appear perfectly fitted into the structure of a course of scriptural readings that could not have sprung up overnight. Liturgical documents from Jerusalem are therefore of great interest insofar as they are the first evidence of an organization of the reading of biblical texts in the liturgy.

There is considerable uncertainty over the use of lectionaries elsewhere in the Christian world in the fourth and fifth centuries. Echoes of a liturgical reading of the Bible nonetheless come down to us in decisions issued by early councils and bishops. These customarily prescribe that only canonical books be read in church and warn against the use of particular and dubious writings.[14] The *Doctrine of Addai* informs us as well that in Edessa, around 400, the Law, Prophets, Gospel, Pauline letters, and Acts were all read publicly.[15] But there is no evidence of how the faithful listened to these various books, whether the books were read serially or by selections. We must wait until the end of the sixth century, and once again precisely from Edessa,[16] to find the first liturgical lectionary in use beyond the domain of Jerusalem.

The *"Armenian Lectionary of Jerusalem"*

The *Catecheses* of Cyril of Jerusalem, the *Itinerarium Egeriae*,[17] and the *Homilies* of Hesychius of Jerusalem[18] all attest that the liturgy was celebrated in Greek in the Holy City at the end of the fourth century and beginning of the fifth. While patristic works testifying to this period are certainly not lacking, not a single liturgical text in Greek survives. Only with the tenth-century *Typicon of the Anastasis*[19] do we have the first description in Greek of the liturgical rites of Holy Week. Some texts preserved in Georgian nevertheless provide us an access to the rites and the lectionary in use in Jerusalem from the end of the fifth century to the end of the eighth.[20] The breadth of the period that these texts cover and the final state in which we have them, however, make it difficult to use them. The situation is different with the document customarily called *The Armenian Lectionary of Jerusalem*, which bears witness to the state of liturgical rites and liturgical reading of the Bible in the Holy City during the years 417-439. Why do we find this text in an Armenian recension? The distant church of the Caucasus, which developed its own alphabet in the early years of the fifth century after having been without one,[21] undertook in the same period to establish its own religious literature. The Bible was undoubtedly translated first, but along with it "many writings of the Fathers of the church which were composed with the help of divine grace."[22] It is in this context of the creation of an indigenous literature, under the pontificate of the Catholicos Sahak (d. 438), that we must situate the formation of a properly Armenian liturgy[23] and the translation from Greek to Armenian[24] of the *Lectionary* of the Holy City which formed the basis of the Armenian liturgical year.[25]

General Appearance

Three Armenian manuscripts that have since been edited[26] allow us to see how the *Lectionary* of Jerusalem appeared during the years 418-439. While the name *Lectionary* has prevailed as the title of this document (it contained all biblical texts read in the course of the liturgical offices from 5 January to 29 December), the work nonetheless contained just as much that this title would not tell us. Each day that a liturgical office was celebrated in the Holy City, a rubric actually indicated the nature of the feast or the anticipated ceremony, the place and hour of its celebration, and finally the psalm which was to introduce it. Then there appear, transcribed in full, the biblical readings, interspersed with a psalm or a psalm-alleluia and sometimes even followed by another psalm.[27]

More than simply a book of the Epistles or the Gospels, the *Armenian Lectionary of Jerusalem* therefore appears to be a kind of Byzantine liturgical book called a *typicon*.

Origin and Destination

The provenance of this text, the Holy City, as explicitly designated in the preface of one of the three manuscripts, *Paris BN Armenian 44*,[28] leads us to believe that it was the translation of a Greek text. We know for a fact that Greek was the liturgical language of Jerusalem during the fourth and fifth centuries. Cyril of Jerusalem's *Catecheses*, the *Itinerarium Egeriae*,[29] and the *Homilies* of Hesychius of Jerusalem all clearly attest this. In the *Lectionary of Jerusalem* itself, moreover, such a Greek substratum occasionally surfaces. Not only Greek words underlying Armenian words (*kanon = kanôn; marturn = martyrion*), but numerous psalms, chosen by virtue of verbal allusions or because they adapted the Greek text of the Scriptures to the feast or to the place where it was being celebrated,[30] also betray the language of the compilers of this book and its original destination. Topographical allusions to the churches of Jerusalem, which are the continual links between this text and the descriptions given by the pilgrim Egeria, consistently bring the reader within the precincts of the Holy City.

Translated from the Greek, the three known Armenian manuscripts which constitute what we call the *Lectionary of Jerusalem* do not, however, derive from the same original. Numerous differences in rubrics and in text on the same ceremonies can truly be explained only on the basis of recourse to different Greek originals.[31] These three extant manuscripts testify to successive stages in the Jerusalem liturgy; we will have occasion to see how interesting their particularities are for the significance of the *Lectionary*.

The Liturgical Year and Its Delimitations

The *Lectionary of Jerusalem* opens, on the evening of 5 January, with a brief office for the "Shepherds' Field," followed by the Epiphany vigil, a celebration lasting eight days.[32] During this eight-day period, however, there appears on 11 January the first of the commemorations of martyrs and saints which would extend up until 29 March.[33] The texts for the Lenten liturgy, Holy Week, and Easter Week constitute the third and longest part of the *Lectionary*.[34] The last part, that of the feasts of saints, interrupted by the celebration of Ascension and Pentecost, covers the period from 1 May to 29 December.[35]

Within these four blocs—Epiphany, the first sanctoral (cycle of saints), Lent/Easter, and the cycle of saints—Sunday liturgies are noticeably absent, except those of Pentecost. Egeria's account attests the existence of a Lord's Day liturgy,[36] but at the beginning of the fifth century it still preserved the characteristics it had in the fourth century. For those Sundays which lacked any connection with a particular event in the Savior's life there was no prescription for special biblical readings and, consequently, those Sundays had no place in the guidebook to the development of the liturgy. The choice of pericopes to be read on those Sundays was the prerogative of the celebrant, who, as the *Itinerarium Egeriae* shows, took into account the properly Paschal character of Sunday[37] and the progressive course of liturgical time. There, in all probability, lies the answer to the questions posed by the text of Cyril of Jerusalem noted in the beginning of this essay.[38] The liturgical reading of the Bible as such was therefore restricted only to a certain number of liturgical assemblies. As we will see, it was still uniquely during the period of Lent and Easter that pericopes were actually arranged into an organized whole.

Formation and Date

As for the dating of the Greek original of the *Lectionary* which was translated and preserved in Armenian, the commemoration of John of Jerusalem, the most recent bishop of the Holy City, figures into the calendar of the three lectionary manuscripts,[39] which would undoubtedly require us to place the redaction of these documents after 417, the year that Cyril of Jerusalem's successor died. Yet they clearly have an earlier origin. Indeed, the rites fixed by these texts are already those of the end of the fourth century, as we can establish on the basis of a comparison with the *Itinerarium Egeriae*. The liturgy which Egeria attended during the years 381-384[40] conforms to a Greek *typicon* of the same character as that found in the three Armenian manuscripts.[41] Moreover, we already have indications from Cyril of Jerusalem, in the middle of the fourth century, of the development of the Lenten catechesis.[42] The Jerusalem ordo preserved in Armenian therefore has a history dating well before 417, the year of John of Jerusalem's death.

A tradition often repeated in Armenian Christianity had James, the first bishop of Jerusalem, as the author of the lectionary followed in the Armenian Church.[43] Purely a legend, this tradition referred the whole institution of feasts and liturgical times, which we know came along much later, to the apostolic age.[44] We must place the actual redaction of the Greek liturgical books, on which the Armenian translations were based, between 417, the year of John of Jerusalem's death, and 439, the date of the dedication of the Martyrium of St. Stephen.

The "Martyrium of St. Stephen," where one of the celebrations in the *Lectionary of Jerusalem* is located,[45] is doubtless the martyrium built by the Empress Eudocia on the north side of the city and dedicated in 439. More precisely it was the original diaconicon of the church of Mt. Zion, which became the first martyrium of St. Stephen after his relics were relocated there in 415. The Christian community of Jerusalem often gathered at Mt. Zion to hold Lenten stations and certain other celebrations. "Frequently," writes Hesychius of Jerusalem in his panegyric on St. Stephen, "we go up[46] to his wine-press skipping with joy and we sing the nuptial hymn with a vintage song: 'Lord, you have crowned us with your favor as with a shield' (Ps. 5:12 [5:13, LXX])."[47] It is thus before 439, the year that the martyrium on the north side of the city was entered into service, that we must place the redaction of the Greek liturgical ordo underlying the Armenian texts.

The translation of the Greek texts into Armenian cannot be dated precisely. While obviously we must place it after the development of the Armenian alphabet which made possible the appropriation of Greek and Syriac writings into Armenian religious literature, it also appears likely that the translation was finished before the death of Bishop Sahak (d. 438), the first organizer of the Armenian rite.[48] The first steps in the development of the Armenian rite were directed by the liturgical usages of the Jerusalem Church. Indeed, the oldest known lectionary and homiletical witnesses of the time reflect the structures of a *Lectionary of Jerusalem* anterior to 439.

The Schedule of Liturgical Readings of the Bible

Through a document preserved in Armenian, therefore, we have opened to us a very ancient testimony to the lay-out of biblical readings in the liturgy of Jerusalem. While the organization of the readings is hardly thoroughly developed at this point, the *Lectionary* still has its rules.

Offices and Readings

The five different types of offices listed below, less than there were in the *Itinerarium Egeriae*,[49] provide the lay-out of the *Lectionary of Jerusa-*

lem, and all of them, at the beginning of the fifth century, integrate the liturgical reading of Scripture.

The Eucharistic Liturgy. This liturgy was celebrated for all of the Lord's feasts, for the days dependent on those feasts (Epiphany Week, Easter Week), and for the commemorations of the saints.[50] Two or three pericopes could be read on these occasions, and the first was sometimes taken from the Old Testament.

The Lenten Synaxis. This celebration was held twice a week, Wednesday and Friday, at the tenth hour (4:00 P.M.). Two readings are specified in the *Lectionary* for Wednesday, and three for Friday, all drawn from the Old Testament.[51]

Commemorative Stations. These were brief gatherings for the purpose of recalling events from the Gospels at the holy places themselves, with the help of corresponding biblical passages. They took place only during the great celebrations of the liturgical year: Epiphany, Holy Week, Easter, the Sunday after Easter, and Pentecost. Ordinarily these stations included a reading from the Gospels.[52]

Vigils. The scriptural texts for three nocturnal vigils have been preserved in the *Lectionary of Jerusalem*: Epiphany, the night between Maundy Thursday and Good Friday, and the Paschal Vigil. The first and last of these include a set of twelve readings which are pretty nearly identical; the other, a psalmic vigil, ends with a Gospel reading.[53]

Catechetical Assemblies. Instruction given to catechumens during Lent, and to the newly baptized during Easter Week, was introduced by a reading from Scripture.[54]

A special type of office should be added to these liturgical stations, which always followed the same ceremonial procedure. The assembly for the morning of Good Friday, a long office of the adoration of the Cross, consisted of eight parts, each of which included a Psalm and two readings (Old and New Testament); of these parts, the last four included a Gospel reading.[55]

As for the biblical books used in these liturgical offices, the scriptural index of the *Lectionary of Jerusalem* covers barely more than half of the books of our Bible. Only forty-one books were used in the liturgy of the Holy City: Genesis, Exodus, Deuteronomy, Joshua, 1, 2, and 4 Kings, 2 Maccabees, Job, Psalms, Proverbs, Isaiah, Jeremiah, Ezekiel, Daniel, Joel, Amos, Jonah, Micah, Zechariah, Matthew, Mark, Luke, John, Acts, Romans, 1 Corinthians, Galatians, Ephesians, Philippians, Colossians, 1

Thessalonians, 1 and 2 Timothy, Titus, Hebrews,[56] James, 1 and 2 Peter, and 1 John. Thus the *Lectionary* adds to Cyril of Jerusalem's list of books read in church[57] a borrowing from 2 Maccabees for 1 August, the feast day of Eleazar, Samouni, and the Seven Brothers.[58] We should note as well the absence of any reading from Revelation, even though Cyril[59] and Hesychius[60] alike quote this book in their preaching. Lastly we should draw attention to the order of the books of the Bible as used in Jerusalem in the fifth century. The arrangement of passages for Easter Week—Acts of the Apostles, followed by the Epistle of James—follows Cyril of Jerusalem's enumeration and the succession confirmed in, among other sources, the *Peshitta* and the *Armenian Vulgate* (Venice, ed. Zohrapean, 1805).

The number of pericopes borrowed from each of the books listed above by no means approaches a mathematical equality. The books of Joshua, 2 Maccabees, Amos, and Jonah are each opened for reading only on one occasion, while the Psalter appears most often, but always as a song book, which thus removes it from our study here.[61] The most important bloc in the *Lectionary* consists of the pericopes drawn from the Prophets, the Pauline Epistles, and the Gospels. A preeminent place is given to the Gospel of Matthew, since it supplies more than a third of the Gospel texts, and since, especially during Holy Week, the reading of the other Gospels revolves around Matthew.[62] Altogether, 315 pericopes make up the *Lectionary of Jerusalem*, but, considering the frequent repetition of a number of texts, this number falls to 260: 98 from the various Old Testament books, 90 from the Gospels, and 72 from Acts and the Epistles. Tremendous variety prevails in the number of verses read on a given occasion; indeed, it defies all systematization.[63]

Methods of Reading

The respective importance of the biblical books used in the liturgy of Jerusalem, and doubtless also the significance which was attached to them in the Church, appear in the method of reading which they entailed. It goes without saying that the Gospel readings had to be set apart in their own privileged category; they were continuously read in the Eucharistic synaxis.

1. Continuous or Semi-Continuous Reading

Numerous periods within the liturgical year in Jerusalem were marked by the continuous reading of a biblical book. As we will see, this is the case for the festivals and weeks which formed the skeleton of the liturgical year.

1.1 The Feasts of Epiphany. The Gospel readings for Epiphany were taken from Matthew and Luke; almost the whole of the first two chapters of both books were read.[64] Clearly no other texts could be utilized to recall the mystery of the Nativity of the Lord, which was still, along with the events preparatory to it (viz., the Annunciation and Visitation), the only theme commemorated on these days in Jerusalem.[65]

1.2 Lent. During the six weeks of Lent, the reading of the five books listed below regularly recurred at the Quadragesimal[66] synaxis for Wednesdays and Fridays:

Wednesday readings:

i)   Exodus 1:1-5:3 (the story of Israel in Egypt, the birth and call of Moses).

ii)   All of Joel, read as the second reading during the first five weeks, followed on the sixth week by a reading from Zechariah (Zech. 9:9-16a).

Friday readings:

i)   Deuteronomy 6:4b-11:25 (Moses's discourse on faithfulness to the Law, omitting the passage in 8:2-10, which was not read elsewhere).

ii)   Job 6:2-21:34, read as the second reading, and omitting the speeches of Job's friends.

iii) Isaiah 40:1-47:4, the Book of the Consolation of Israel, read as the third reading, with several passages excised.

1.3 Holy Week. For the first days of Holy Week, including Maundy Thursday, the *Lectionary* docketed an exceptional selection of lengthy pericopes drawn in sequence from Genesis and aimed at recalling the great early stages of salvation history: Genesis 6:9-9:17 (the story of Noah, the Flood, and the Noachic covenant); Genesis 18:1-19:30 (Abraham's intercession on behalf of Sodom and Gomorrah); and Genesis 22:1-18 (the sacrifice of Abraham).[67]

Starting on Holy Tuesday, a progressive reading of the Gospel accounts of the Passion ran continuously, mainly in the course of a liturgy of the stations. Priority was given to the Gospel of Matthew, the reading of which began with Jesus's eschatological discourse in Matthew 24:1ff[68] and would continue for the rest of Holy Week. Matthew 28 would be read in its entirety on Easter Sunday.[69]

Mark held second place in the Gospel readings. The reading of Mark, starting with chapter 14,[70] took place on the evening of Maundy Thursday during the Eucharistic liturgy in the church on Mt. Zion, which was beginning to be regarded at that time as the "upper room" (Mark 14:15) where Christ instituted the Eucharist.[71] The last pericope from Mark, read on Easter morning, opened with the story of Christ's burial (Mark 15:42-16:8),[72] a carry-over of a celebration of Easter that was not yet aimed at honoring the Resurrection alone. We should note as well that the *Lectionary of Jerusalem* did not include the reading of the end of Mark (Mark 16:9-20).

The progressive reading of the Passion account in John's Gospel, the third Gospel to be read sequentially during Holy Week, began on the night of Maundy Thursday, at the end of the office of the vigil held in the church on the Mount of Olives. The long farewell discourse of Jesus after the washing of the disciples' feet (John 13:16-18:1) was reread by the Christian community of Jerusalem at the very place where they believed Christ had originally delivered it.[73] The Johannine Passion narrative was read in its entirety over the days of Holy Week. The reading of John's Gospel would then be concluded on the Saturday after Easter,[74] except the story of Christ's appearance to Thomas, which was reserved for the Sunday after Easter.[75]

Coming last,[76] the reading of the Passion narrative in the Gospel of Luke no longer took place on the actual site when the story of the Last Supper (Luke 22:1-65) was delivered in the small church on the summit of the Mount of Olives, the Imbomon.[77] The reading of Luke's Gospel was completed on the Wednesday after Easter (Luke 24:36-40),[78] the last verses of the chapter being reserved for the feast of the Ascension.[79]

Such a distribution of the Gospel narratives of the Passion and Resurrection, arranged on the basis of the preponderance of Matthew, consistently vouches for an origin in Jerusalem. The pericopes were in fact inserted in a stational liturgy which corresponded to the one operative at the end of the fourth century according to the *Itinerarium Egeriae*. From holy place to holy place, from reading to reading, the faithful of Jerusalem relived the last moments of Christ's life and ministry. "Historicizing" liturgical forms, some have said. But were not the full mystery of the Savior and the eternity of the "Eighth Day" always present, as it were, in the spatio-temporal sign of a liturgical act?

1.4 Easter Week. The final example of continuous liturgical Bible reading is the reading of the Acts of the Apostles and the Epistle of James during Easter Week.

The first reading from Acts began on Easter Sunday itself with Acts 1:1-14, the story of the Ascension and of Christ's prayer for his apostles in the upper room. It may seem odd that this text, taken from the readings for the Monday after Easter (Acts 2:22-41), was read on the very Day of the Resurrection, but historians believe that this is a carry-over from the celebration of Easter Sunday before the Feast of the Ascension appeared in the fourth century. The events of the fifty days after Easter were thus originally commemorated on the "first day" of Easter.[80]

The reading of Acts would continue beginning on the Monday after Easter (Acts 2:22-41) and would finish on the Sunday after Easter with Acts 5:34-6:7. In addition to Peter's sermon on Pentecost, this reading included the story of the earliest conversions to Christianity, the first miracles, and the first persecutions in the apostolic age, which the editors of the *Lectionary of Jerusalem* associated, just like the Ascension, with the Easter feast, the celebration of the Christian mystery in its totality. We probably see vestiges here of an ancient conception of the Paschal celebration.[81] The pericope for the Tuesday after Easter (Act 2:42-3:21) furthermore continued the reading of Acts from the vigil the night before,[82] even though the assembly was held at the Martyrium of St. Stephen, where the account of the martyrdom of Stephen was customarily heard.[83]

From the Wednesday after Easter to the Sunday after Easter, the *Armenian Lectionary of Jerusalem* prescribed a reading from James after the pericope from Acts. Which James? James, the first bishop of Jerusalem, had enjoyed a privileged position in this most solemn of liturgical times, and it was on the Wednesday after Easter, the day of the station at the church on Mt. Zion, regarded as the church where James had preached,[84] that the reading from his epistle began.[85] We must remember that even though James was commemorated on 25 December according to the *Lectionary of Jerusalem,*[86] his martyrdom had taken place around Easter in the year 62 according to the *Memoirs* of Hegessipus, as quoted by Eusebius of Caesarea.[87]

2. Select Readings

Besides the continuous readings prescribed by the *Lectionary* for certain weeks and days, a second type of pericopes was designated as "select readings." The celebration of a given feast naturally led to the reclaiming of biblical texts which had a direct link with the feast or which could be associated with it. This mode of liturgical reading of the Bible prevailed exclusively[88] on Palm Sunday, Pentecost Sunday, the Feast of the Ascension, the feast days of the saints, the vigils of Epiphany and Easter, and in the office of the adoration of the Cross on Good Friday. Pericopes were randomly taken from Scripture, as many from the Old as from the New Testament, in accordance with the sole criterion of adaptability, such as was so often invoked in the *Itinerarium Egeriae*.[89] But a rigorous rule obtained in the arrangement of the lectures: Pericopes from the Old Testament were never to be read by themselves before the reading of the Gospel; the latter was therefore to be preceded by a reading drawn from Acts or the Epistles.[90] One approached Christ *through the Church*.

The celebrations of Epiphany, Holy Week, Easter, Ascension, and Pentecost, all integrated, along with the continuous or semi-continuous readings, pericopes which were quite naturally suited to the occasion. The opening of Romans, the opening of Hebrews, Titus 2:11-15 (which was reused several times), and Galatians 4:1-7[91] offered biblical texts perfectly suited to the celebration of the Nativity. Chapters 14 and 16 of John's Gospel could not have been better used than on the occasion of the numerous stations on the day of Pentecost.[92] The feast of a mystery of the Lord was always supplied with a reading from the New Testament which related to the event being celebrated. In their own unique way, passages from Scripture thus turned into "memoirs."

The same concern for adaptability guided the choice of readings for the feast days of the saints of the Old and New Testaments. The calling of a saint, the saint's holiness, achievements, an event in his or her life, and the saint's martyrdom provided an occasion for finding resonances in Scripture.[93] On the feast day of St. Antony, for example, the Gospel lesson was Matthew 10:37-42, the very appeal of Jesus (to the rich young man) which, according to Athanasius's *Vita Antonii* 2,[94] was decisive in Antony's own withdrawal from all worldly things. For the commemoration of the Emperor Theodosius, benefactor of the Christian community of Jerusalem, the reading was Luke 7:1-10, Jesus's healing of the slave of the Roman centurion who had built a synagogue at Capernaum, a text which evoked the imperial sovereign's generosity toward Jerusalem. In response, 1 Timothy 2:1-7 was read, recalling the church's obligation to pray for those in positions of authority.[95] Naturally, the feast day of a particular figure from the Old or New Testament (prophets, apostles) led to the reading of the biblical text in which that figure appeared.[96] If the saint had actually authored an inspired writing, the readings would obviously be drawn from that work.[97]

The location where the congregation met to hear a reading also served as a criterion for the selection of lessons. The devotion of the Jerusalem church to its preeminent deacon, St. Stephen, therefore prompted it to read the story of the death of the great proto-martyr (Acts 6:8-8:2), since the assembly convened at the Martyrium of St. Stephen.[98] During the same Epiphany Week, a liturgical station at the tomb of Lazarus, another holy site cherished by the Jerusalem church, attracted the reading of a Pauline text on the resurrection of the dead (1 Thess. 4:13-18) and John's account of the raising of Lazarus (John 11:1ff).[99]

Finally we must mention one remarkable pericope, even though it appears only once in the *Lectionary*. On the Wednesday of the sixth week of Lent, once the reading from the prophecy of Joel is finished, the *Lectionary* turns to Zechariah 9:9-16, the only lesson from this prophet: "Rejoice greatly, O daughter of Zion! Shout aloud, O daughter of Jerusalem! Lo, your King comes to you..."[100] The "local color" of the *Lectionary* could not be more powerfully elicited.

With these few examples it is already possible to perceive one of the orientations of the *Lectionary*, which we will analyze in more detail in our concluding section. The urge for appropriation and adaptation, which guided the selection of scriptural texts over and beyond the great liturgical seasons, was driven by a constant preoccupation: namely, to cross over time and recover the event and the person, insofar as the celebration of the Christian mystery was grounded in history.

Orientations of the Lectionary

Our presentation of the *Lectionary* up to this point has allowed us quickly to penetrate the motifs which prompted the choice of biblical texts destined to be read in the liturgical celebrations of the Christian community of Jerusalem. Is it possible, to some extent, to systematize the arrangement of these choices in searching for what they signify?

Biblical Readings and "Historicization"

When we examine the pericopes in the *Lectionary of Jerusalem* one by one, their *incipit* and their *desinit*, their insertion in the schedule of readings, their relation to the feast being celebrated, and finally the site of their delivery, the historical coloring of the choice of many of them is overwhelming. We can see how this tendency, which progressively guided the authors of the *Lectionary* as they put it together, continuously reinforced itself.

Let us look at a few examples. The most obvious manifestation of this desire to recall history is during the "commemorative stations,"[101] or on-site liturgies, of which we have numerous examples.

On the eve of Epiphany, 5 January, for the assembly which took place at 4:00 P.M. at the Poimnion, the "Place of the Shepherds" (where the shepherds heard the angelic message), the very same angelic proclamation is made to the Christian faithful through the reading of Luke 2:8-20.[102] Once more recalling the event at the time and place where it had occurred, the reading of the last discourses of Jesus (John 13:16-18:1) were read on the night of Maundy Thursday in the church on the Mount of Olives, where it was thought at that time that Jesus had delivered them.[103] On the night of Easter and on the Sunday after Easter, the accounts of the resurrected Christ's appearances to his apostles constituted the central element in the celebration.[104] It was also possible here, as was done on other occasions,[105] to choose texts from the Old Testament which prefigured these events; the apostolic writings which commented on them could likewise be read. It was the Gospel, and the Gospel alone—relating the very things which the Lord had done in those days and in those places—that was proclaimed to the people. Again we must reiterate this constant urge to recall the events of the Gospel in the presence of the community of Christian faithful.

A preoccupation with the historical also emerges in the choice of readings for numerous feast days of saints. Whenever possible, the saint is introduced into the celebration with the reading of his own writings (Jeremiah, Zechariah, Isaiah, Paul and Peter, James and John),[106] or else, rather surprisingly, with the writings of one who has the same name,[107] or in still other instances, with those writings which mentioned the saint (the holy Innocents, Elisha, the Maccabees, Thomas, etc.).[108]

For saints and figures who could not be honored by these methods for choosing texts, adapted readings were used to revive the memory of them in the mind of the congregation. Cyril and John of Jerusalem were both good pastors: The two readings honoring them recalled their zeal in carrying out their mission (2 Tim. 4:1-8) and their love for their flock (John 10:11-16).[109] Moreover, we have already noted above[110] how, through the figure of the Roman centurion, benefactor of the religious community at Capernaum (Luke 7:1-10), the Jerusalem church was able to honor the benefits that had been granted to it by the Emperors

Constantine and Theodosius, who were respectively commemorated on 22 May and 19 January.[111]

The desire to recall historical realities as fundamental to a liturgical celebration, to recapture the very person of the saint, bishop, or emperor being commemorated, was therefore strikingly obvious in the choice of biblical readings. This orientation to history, as we will see, became more and more entrenched in the tradition of the *Lectionary*. We will in fact refer to it as a process of *historicization*.

The observable differences in Bible readings throughout the liturgical year among the three Armenian manuscripts, our witnesses to the *Lectionary of Jerusalem* used in the fifth century, are not without significance. Materially they consist of a shortening of the length of pericopes either at the beginning or the end. Noticeable especially in one of the manuscripts, *Paris BN 44*, these changes tell us much about the situation which existed in the most ancient Eastern lectionaries from the end of the fifth century and beginning of the sixth.[112]

It was primarily during Holy Week and Easter Week that the new physical appearance of the *Lectionary of Jerusalem* became conspicuous. The intentions of those reforming the course of readings was also quite obvious in the organization and arrangement of the pericopes for this fifteen-day period. Clearly they desired to conform the reading of the Gospels more and more closely to the actual chronology and geography of the final events of Christ's life. Hoping to fulfill this goal, the editors made three types of modification in the *Lectionary*.

First, they put together a continuous reading of the Passion narrative without using any doublets. Consequently the Passion story was not resumed from the beginning with the reading of each Gospel. Instead, the story had one starting point, based on the Gospel of Matthew, and, without going back to the beginning, developed progressively, in accordance with the chronology of the final days of the life of Christ. Numerous omissions were therefore made, particularly in the pericopes of Mark, John, and Luke. The different witnesses woven together in the *Lectionary* helped to unfold a single narrative, the goal of which was to achieve a perfect chronological succession in the events of the Passion.[113] The most important instances of this arrangement of texts were found in the period from Maundy Thursday to Easter Sunday, but we also find instances of it, to a lesser extent, in the time from Palm Sunday to Holy Wednesday, as well as in the readings for the first days of Easter Week.[114]

The second manifestation of this historicizing tendency in the

Lectionary appears in the redactors' concern to accommodate a given pericope to the site where the congregation was gathered. Only by shortening the readings could this result be achieved. All pericopes influenced by this procedure were read during Holy Week.[115]

The third and final kind of historicizing change made in the *Lectionary of Jerusalem* assumed the other two and divulged their true intention: The biblical text had to be adapted to the mystery being celebrated. Such was the case with the Gospel readings for Palm Sunday and for the Easter feast, which will serve as our examples here.

At the end of the fourth century and beginning of the fifth, the Gospel for the Palm Sunday mass consisted of the story of several episodes in the life of Christ: the healing of the two blind men at Jericho (Matt. 20:29-34), Jesus's final entry into Jerusalem (Matt. 21:1-11), the expulsion of the vendors from the Temple (Matt. 21:12-13), the acclamation of the children and Jesus's departure for Bethany (Matt. 21:14-17). By the fifth century, however, as homilies preached during this period attest, the sole object of the feast was henceforth the celebration of Christ's entry into Jerusalem.[116] Clearly an *historical* conception of the liturgical year had imposed itself increasingly at the expense of the previous content of readings, which were more *mystical* in orientation.[117] The lectionaries were modeled on this historical vision and consequently their pericopes were modified. Two of the three manuscripts of the *Lectionary of Jerusalem* prescribed nothing more than the reading of Matthew 21:1-11,[118] and in the *Georgian Lectionaries,* our witness to the liturgy of Jerusalem at the end of the fifth century, the length of the Palm Sunday pericopes was shortened.[119]

The case of the Gospel readings for Easter is even more notorious. By abridging the pericopes from John, Mark, and Luke for the Sunday and Monday after Easter, pericopes which contained the account of Christ's burial and of the discovery of the empty tomb, the Easter feast evolved from a celebration of the fuller mystery of salvation—Christ dead and raised—into a celebration exclusively of the Resurrection.[120] Concern for the chronological truth unfortunately gave way henceforth to a fragmented celebration of the various events in Christ's life.

Readings and Mystery

To end our study with this analysis of a "historicizing" of the Biblical readings, deliberate or simply factual, would nevertheless leave an inaccurate impression of the *Lectionary of Jerusalem* during these years of the fifth century when the liturgy of the Holy City was developing. It was not an exhibition or piece of theater that the editors of the *Lectionary*, with their assiduous attention to historical, chronological, and topographical details, were seeking to deliver to the faithful.

Reading and Christian Life. As in all other Christian churches, the community in Jerusalem celebrated the resurrected and living Christ. Readings from the Bible, often linked to the Eucharistic celebration of Christ the Victor, were not intended only to recall events in the economy of salvation but to give substance to Christian faith and life. The publication of the corpus of homilies of Hesychius of Jerusalem, who preached during the first half of the fifth century, reveals quite well this connection between liturgical reading and living faith. It echoes in the words he utters before the reading of Luke 1:26-38 (the archangel Gabriel's news to the Virgin Mary), read on the fourth day of Epiphany:[121] "Let us too be instructed by the words of the archangel Gabriel about the birth of the Master, let us walk in his footsteps; without searching any further, we too, like him, consider divine the power which presides over this childbirth."[122]

The *Lectionary* itself furthermore contains a beautiful example of this transcendence of history. In the meditative office for Good Friday, each reading from the Prophets, announcing the Passion and sufferings of Christ, was followed by a pericope from the apostle Paul: the prophetic word, fulfilled henceforth in Christ, burst forth in the vision of Christ living and glorified at the right hand of the Father.[123] Hence the authors of the *Lectionary of Jerusalem* desired to set forth more here than a mere historical reconstruction.

Liturgical Readings and the Economy of Redemption. The reading of the Bible in the liturgy is intended to serve in displaying the economy of redemption. Christians can celebrate the various moments in that economy—Nativity, Easter, Ascension, Pentecost—as they do during the liturgical year, but they cannot separate those moments. The *Lectionary of Jerusalem*, like all lectionaries, expressed in numerous instances this global vision which transcends time and history.

The readings for the two great vigils of Epiphany and Easter presented a complete fresco of the economy of salvation. The Epiphany vigil[124] began with the creation of the world and progressed to the birth of Jesus by way of Israel's liberation from Egyptian bondage and the prophecies of a Messiah-Savior. With the Easter vigil, the fresco was further expanded; once again it began with the creation of the world and the liberation from Egyptian bondage, but it also integrated prophetic visions relating to the birth of the Church and the resurrection of humanity, and then climaxed with the glorious light of the resurrected Christ.[125]

In addition to these annual displays of the global economy, the mystery of redemption echoed throughout the readings delivered each Wednesday and Friday during Lent. These dramatic readings portrayed Christ as the Liberator marching with his people (readings from Exodus) and giving his people the law of a New Covenant (Deuteronomy). Through penitence (Joel) and suffering (Job), Christ's people would indeed attain to the heavenly Jerusalem (Zechariah).

The Mystery on a Daily Basis. The daily liturgy of the *Lectionary of Jerusalem*, in which the biblical readings often revealed the authors' "historical" intentions, also conveyed a spiritual pedagogy oriented toward the disclosure of the mystery of salvation. Here we will mention four expressions of this celebration of the mystery in the daily liturgy, and illustrate them with a few examples.

First, the readings drawn from the Old Testament and those which followed them from the New, within one and the same section, were chosen in such a way as to reveal a link between the texts. We have already noted this in the readings for Good Friday; this same pattern was constantly repeated. For the feast of the Ark of the Covenant on 2 July, for example, two readings from the books of Kings recalled the Ark's temporary residence at Kiriath-jearim before its transfer to Jerusalem; these were followed in turn by Hebrews 9:1-10, which disclosed the true sense of the cult surrounding the Ark, namely, that the blood of Christ had taken over the benefits of that cult once and for all, such that the Holy of Holies was now open to all humanity. The Gospel pericope for that day therefore appropriately declared, "I have come not to abolish the Law, but to fulfill it" (Matt. 5:17-20).[126] Thus there was always a quite intentional unity established between the readings. Scripture had to be elucidated by Scripture.

Second, we often see in the *Lectionary* how a succession of readings from the Old Testament gradually disclosed a premeditated teaching, such as in a puzzle, where each piece, one after the other, gradually contributes to constructing the whole picture. For Holy Monday, the first reading, Genesis 1:1-3:24, proclaimed the reality of the fall of humanity. Yet God did not fully abandon the human race, for as the second reading (Prov. 1:2-9) made clear, humanity had received the wise counsel of its Father: "Here, my son, the discipline of your father...It is like a crown of grace for your head." This God-given instruction or discipline induces humanity once more to take heart, as elicited by the remarkable words of the next reading, Isaiah 40:1-8: "Comfort, comfort my people...Speak to the heart of Jerusalem...that her sin is forgiven."[127]

Third, it was sometimes the case in the *Lectionary* that the instruction or interpretation meant to be drawn from of a particular event in the Gospels was delivered *before* the reading of the pericope that related it. Thus during the mass of the Epiphany vigil on the night of 5-6 January, it was not a prophecy of the birth of Christ that was read first, but the text of Titus 2:11-15 on the manifestation of God's grace for the purpose of reclaiming fallen humanity; only after this passage did the audience hear the actual story of the Nativity from Matthew 2:1-12.[128] On Maundy Thursday, during the first Eucharist, the account of the Last Supper in Matthew 26:17-30 was preceded by the reading of the same event according to 1 Corinthians 11:23-32, where Paul, rather than simply telling the story, delivers the true meaning of the Lord's Supper and recalls the requirements for its proper observance.[129]

One final expression of this celebration of the mystery of salvation in the context of the daily liturgy was the fact that the readings were complementary, a feature noticeable particularly on the feast days of saints. The spiritual struggles of the righteous, as narrated in the reading of Hebrews 11:32-40 during the feast day of St. Antony, had Jesus himself as their reason and goal. This was made clear in the complementary Gospel pericope for the same day: "Whoever does not take up his cross and follow me is not worthy of me" (Matt. 10:38).[130]

Summation

The *Lectionary of Jerusalem*, preserved in Armenian, is the most ancient version known to date of the liturgical book that we call a *lectionary*, and contains the ordo which regulated the development of the liturgy of the Holy City and its course of biblical readings during the fifth century. Without question, this great work was profoundly marked by the place where it was born. Yet its origin in Jerusalem did not limit its splendid influence on numerous Churches of the Christian East beyond the Holy Land, which were creating and developing their own particular rites in the same period. To this day, the Armenian liturgy, the ancient Georgian rite, and the Byzantine liturgy contain numerous biblical pericopes that were originally chosen at Jerusalem. In spite of its local roots, the Jerusalem lectionary in fact offered a presentation of the Christian mystery that all the Churches could adopt in their celebrations. This dependence, in the area of biblical readings, is only one of the manifestations of the Holy

City's influence in the fifth century. Research undertaken on the history of the liturgical year and its various feasts, and on the origins of sacramental rites and even of certain architectural forms, has proven the magnetism of the Mother-Church in attracting the scores of pilgrims who visited Jerusalem in this era.

Notes

1. *Catechesis* 4.35 (PG 33: 497C).
2. Ibid. 4.36 (PG 33: 501A).
3. Ibid. 14.24 (PG 33: 856C).
4. For R. Cabrol, in his *Les Églises de Jérusalem: La discipline et la liturgie au IVe siècle* (Paris, 1895), 158, it would have been the second Sunday before Easter. H. Leclerc concurs with Cabrol in his essay in the *Dictionnaire d'archéologie chrétienne et de liturgie*, s.v. "Catechèse," col. 2563. For G. Kretschmar, in his article on "Die frühe Geschichte der Jerusalemer Liturgie," *Jahrbuch für Liturgik und Hymnologie* 2 (1956): 23, it would have instead been Palm Sunday. It appears difficult to determine conclusively which Sunday it was, given our uncertainty over the year or years in which the corpus of Cyril's homilies was preached.
5. Several lines after the passage that we just quoted from *Catechesis* 14, Cyril shows the differences between the Ascension of Christ and the lifting up of Elijah, which had come up for discussion on the Sunday that the Ascension pericope had been read in church: "Remember what was said yesterday concerning Elijah..." (PG 33: 857C). Does this mean that the story of Elijah's translation into heaven (2 Kings 2:1-22) was read at the same time as the pericope of Christ's Ascension? It does not seem so, since Cyril alludes throughout this paragraph to the "annunciations" of the Ascension in the Old Testament. In his fifth homily on the Ascension of Christ, John Chrysostom likewise contrasts the Ascension of Christ and the lifting up of Elijah (PG 40: 450).
6. The first known lectionaries of which we will speak actually include pericopes for Sunday readings during Lent only for Palm Sunday. But the question then arises as to whether the reading of Eph. 1:3-10, at the time of this celebration, authorizes us to confirm that Cyril preached about the Ascension on this particular Sunday, based on this particular text.
7. *Itinerarium Egeriae, cura et studio*, ed. A. Franceschini and R. Weber, CCSL 175: 27-103 (Turnhout, 1965); Egérie, *Journal de voyage*, ed. P. Maraval, SC 298 (Paris, 1982); Eng. trans. J. Wilkinson, *Egeria's Travels to the Holy Land* (Warminster, 1981), 91-232.
8. P. Devos, "La date du voyage d'Egérie," *Analecta Bollandiana* 85 (1967): 165-194.
9. *Itin. Eger.* 24.10 (ed. Franceschini-Weber, 69).
10. Ibid. 29.4 (trans. Wilkinson, 131). She is probably referring here to John 11:20ff.

11. Ibid. 29.5 (trans. Wilkinson, 132). She is referring to John 12:1.

12. *Itin. Eger.* 31-40 (ed. Franceschini-Weber, 77-84).

13. Ibid. 43. (ed. Franceschini-Weber, 84-86).

14. On these questions, see J. Ruwet, "Lecture liturgique et livres saints du Nouveau Testament," *Biblica* 21 (1940): 378-405.

15. See G. Philipps, ed., *The Doctrine of Addai, the Apostle* (London, 1876), 44, 46.

16. F. C. Burkitt, "The Early Syriac Lectionary System," *Proceedings of the British Academy* 10 (1921-1923): 301-338.

17. *Itin. Eger.* 47.3 (ed. Franceschini-Weber, 89).

18. M. Aubineau, ed., *Les homélies festales d'Hésychius de Jérusalem,* Subsidia hagiographica 59, 2 vols. (Brussels, 1978-1980).

19. See A. Papadopoulos-Kerameus, ed., *Analecta Hierosolymitikes Stachylogias,* vol. 2 (St. Petersburg, 1894), 1-254 (in Greek).

20. See M. Tarchnischvili, ed., *Le Grand Lectionnaire de l'Église de Jérusalem (Ve-VIIIe siècle),* Corpus Scriptorum Christianorum Orientalium [CSCO] 188-189, 204-205 (Louvain, 1959-1960).

21. R. Grousset, *Histoire de l'Arménie des origines à 1071* (Paris, 1946), 171.

22. Koriwn, *Patmut'iwn Varuc' s. Mastoc'i,* Texte und Unterstuchungen der altarmenische Literatur, Bd. 1, Heft 1, ed. N. Akinian, 2nd ed. (Vienna, 1952), 41.

23. Lazare de Pharbe, *Histoire d'Arménie des origines à 1071* (Paris, 1946), 267-268. See also the article on "Isaac le Grand (saint)," *Dictionnaire de spiritualité,* vol. 7: 2007-2010.

24. See below, 392, 393, 394.

25. The Armenian rite is fundamentally dependent, in the formation of its liturgical year and in several parts of the celebration of the divine office, on structures of the Jerusalem liturgy prior to 439. See my article "Liturgie arménienne et Liturgie hiérosolymitaine," in *Liturgie de l'Église particulière et liturgie de l'Église universelle,* Bibliotheca Ephemerides Liturgicae, Subsidia 7 (Rome, 1976), 275-288.

26. A. Renoux, ed., *Le Codex arménien Jérusalem, 121,* vol. 1: *Introduction aux origines de la liturgie hiérosolymitaine,* PO 35.1 (Turnhout, 1969); vol. 2: *Édition comparée du texte et de deux autres manuscrits,* PO 36.2 (Turnhout, 1971). Henceforth this work is abbreviated *Cod. arm.*

27. A helpful chart of readings in the *Armenian Lectionary of Jerusalem* is provided by J. Wilkinson, *Egeria's Travels to the Holy Land,* 262-275.

28. "Memorial of the synaxes which were held in Jerusalem in the holy places of Christ..." (cf. *Cod. arm.,* vol. 2, 211).

29. *Itin. Eger.* 47.3 (ed. Franceschini-Weber, 89).

30. *Cod. arm.,* vol. 1, 21-22; vol. 2, 162.

31. Ibid., vol. 1, 34-168.

32. Ibid., vol. 2, no. I-IX, pp. 210-225.

33. Ibid., vol. 2, no. X-XVI, pp. 224-232.

34. Ibid., vol. 2, no. XVII-LII, pp. 232-330.

35. Ibid., vol. 2, no. LIII-LXXIV, pp. 331-373.

36. *Itin. Eger.* 24.8 (ed. Franceschini-Weber, 69).

37. The Gospel account of the resurrection was always read at vigils: see ibid. 24.10; 27.2; 43 and 44.2 (ed. Franceschini-Weber, 69, 73, 84, 86).
38. See above, 389.
39. *Cod. arm.*, vol. 2, no. 16, pp. 94-95.
40. See above, n. 8.
41. It is not unlikely, moreover, that the pilgrim Egeria had before her a document of the same kind in composing her own account. How could the admonitions in *Itin. Eger.* 30.2, 36.5, and 46.6 (ed. Franceschini-Weber, 77-80, 88) and the numerous allusions to the readings themselves, have been quoted from memory?
42. The eighteen lectures previewed in the titles of the catecheses *ad illuminandos* of Cyril (PG 33: 369ff) are those of the section dedicated to "instructional readings" in the lectionaries (*Cod. arm.*, vol. 2, no. XVII, pp. 232-237).
43. See N. Adontz, "Les fêtes et les saints de l'Église arménienne," *Revue de l'Orient chrétien* (3rd ser.) 6 (1927-1928): 74-104, 225-278.
44. See E. Bihain, "Une vie arménienne de saint Cyrille de Jérusalem," *Le Muséon* 76 (1963): 319-348.
45. *Cod. Jer.*, vol. 2, no. 3, p. 217; no. 47, p. 315.
46. According to ancient authors who describe their journey to Jerusalem, one goes up to Zion (cf. *Cod. arm.*, vol. 1, 201). This follows also the biblical usage of "going up" (*anabainein*) to Jerusalem: see, e.g., Mark 10:32, 33; Luke 19:28; Acts 21:12; 24:11; Gal. 1:18; 2:1.
47. *Hom.* 9.3, *In Stephanum* (ed. M. Aubineau, 329). Interestingly, in his introduction to this homily, Aubineau demonstrates convincingly that Hesychius as well, in the terms that he uses, is referring to the diaconicon of Mt. Zion as the Martyrium of St. Stephen.
48. Cf. "Isaac le Grand (saint)," 2007-2010.
49. The *Lectionary of Jerusalem* says nothing of liturgical offices wherein biblical readings did not enter into play.
50. Obviously the Eucharist was celebrated more often, such as on Sundays and on Saturdays during Lent. As for the readings at these celebrations, there was still a tremendous latitude allowed for personal initiative in choosing the scriptural texts.
51. *Cod. arm.*, vol. 2, no. 18-32, pp. 239-255.
52. Cf. ibid., vol. 2, no. 40-42, pp. 273-281.
53. Ibid., vol. 2., no. 1, pp. 211-215; no. 39 *ter,* pp. 271-273; no. 45 *bis,* pp. 297-307.
54. Ibid., vol. 2, no. 17, pp. 233-237.
55. Ibid., vol. 2, no. 43, pp. 281-293.
56. As in Cyril and Hesychius of Jerusalem, the Epistle to the Hebrews is considered Pauline.
57. PG 33: 500.
58. *Cod. arm.*, vol. 2, no. 63, pp. 353-355.
59. See above, n. 2.
60. See Hesychius, *Hom.* 9.26, *In Stephanum* (ed. Aubineau, 348-349).

61. Psalms were sung as introductions to the offices, before and after readings of Scripture, and before the Gospel. Moreover, the same Psalm could be used at all these different points in a liturgy.

62. *Cod. arm.*, vol. 1, 162-163; vol. 2, 175.

63. In one of the three manuscripts of the *Lectionary* (*Paris BN 44*, from the 9th and 10th centuries), the reading of chapters 38 and 39 of Job, which were used as pericopes for the Paschal Vigil and as a reading for catechumens (*Cod. arm.*, vol. 2, 235, 303), discloses a tremendous fidelity to the text of the *Armenian Vulgate*. As in the *Armenian Vulgate* (ed. Zohrapean), the recension of chapters 38 and 39 of Job derives from Origen.

64. *Cod. arm.*, vol. 2, no. 1-9, pp. 211-225.

65. Cf. A. Renoux, "L'Epiphanie à Jérusalem au IVe et au Ve siècle," *Revue des études arméniennes* (new series) 2 (1965): 343-359.

66. See above, 395.

67. *Cod. arm.*, vol. 2, no. 35, p. 261; no. 36, p. 263; no. 37, p. 263; no. 38, p. 267.

68. Ibid., vol. 2, no. 36, p. 263.

69. Ibid., vol. 2, no. 44 *ter*, p. 309.

70. Ibid., vol. 2, no. 39 *bis*, p. 269.

71. Several attestations in Hesychius of Jerusalem (cf. *Hom. fest.* 10.1, ed. Aubineau, 367-368; *Hom.* 5, *In Job*, ed. Renoux, PO 42.1 [Turnhout, 1983], 148-153) confirm the appearance of this belief in the first half of the fifth century.

72. *Cod. arm.*, vol. 2, no. 45, p. 313. The reading of the resurrection narratives in John and Luke also began the same way, with the burial story: see no. 44 *ter*, p. 311; no. 46, p. 315.

73. Ibid., vol. 2, no. 39, p. 273.

74. Ibid., vol. 2, no. 51, p. 323.

75. Ibid., vol. 2, no. 52 *bis*, p. 325.

76. Were this last place accorded to the Gospel of Luke, and the fact that the first reading given at the Imbomon (see the note following) was out of place, perhaps indicative of a preference in the Jerusalem church for Matthew, Mark, and John?

77. *Cod. arm.*, vol. 2, no. 52 *bis*, p. 325. The verses in Luke 22:43-44 on Jesus's sweating of blood were omitted in this reading (see S. Lyonnet, *Les origines de la version arménienne et le Diatessaron* [Rome, 1950], 12-13, 273), which leads us to believe that the original biblical text of the *Lectionary of Jerusalem* had been substituted by Armenian copyists with a text conforming to the version used in Armenian Christian communities during the eighth century. Yet one finds no allusion to Luke 22:43-44 in Cyril or Hesychius of Jerusalem. Did the pericope in the *Georgian Lectionary* (ed. Tarchnischvili, no. 647, p. 93), Luke 22:39-46, contain these two verses?

78. *Cod. arm.*, vol. 2, no. 48, p. 317.

79. Ibid., vol. 2, no. 52, p. 339.

80. V. Larranaga, *L'Ascension de Notre-Seigneur Jésus-Christ dans le Nouveau Testament* (Rome, 1938), 492-531; J. Boeckh, "Die Entwicklung der

altkirchlichen Pentekoste," *Jahrbuch für Liturgik und Hymnologie* 5 (1960): 1-45.

81. See R. Cabié, *La Pentecoste: L'évolution de la cinquantaine pascale au cours des cinq premiers siècles* (Paris, 1964), 46-57.

82. *Cod. arm.*, vol. 2, 315.

83. Ibid., vol. 2, no. 3, p. 217.

84. His episcopal throne was ostensibly preserved here (see Eusebius of Caesarea, *H. E.* 7.19, ed. G. Bardy [SC 41: 193]).

85. When, a number of years later, the station took place at the church on Mt. Zion not on Wednesday but on Tuesday, according to the *Georgian Lectionary* (which testifies to liturgical customs in Jerusalem beginning in the middle of the fifth century), the reading of the Epistle of James still began on Wednesday (ed. Tarchnischvili, CSCO 189, no. 758, p. 118). James and Mt. Zion were linked: see Hesychius of Jerusalem's eulogy to Mt. Zion in *Hom. fest.* 10 *in SS Jacobum et David* (ed. Aubineau, 367-368).

86. *Cod. arm.*, vol. 2, no. 71, pp. 367-369.

87. *H. E.* 2.23.18 (SC 31: 87-88).

88. Indeed, we have observed above that during Epiphany Week, Holy Week, Easter Week, and in certain other cases as well, the rule for daily celebrations sometimes included, with the select readings, a pericope which was a continuation of the one for the preceding day.

89. Cf. *Itin. Eger.* 25.10 (ed. Franceschini-Weber, 72).

90. *Cod. arm.*, vol. 2, nos. 53, 59, 60, 61, pp. 331-333, 345-351.

91. Ibid., vol. 2, no. 2-6 and 8, pp. 215-233.

92. Ibid., vol. 2, no. 58, pp. 339-345.

93. Ibid., vol. 2, nos. 10, 11, 12, 15, pp. 225-229, 231-233.

94. PG 26: 841C; *Cod. arm.*, vol. 2, no. 11, p. 227.

95. *Cod. arm.*, vol. 2, no. 12, pp. 227-229.

96. Ibid., vol. 2, nos. 59, 60, 62, pp. 345, 353, etc.

97. Ibid., vol. 2, nos. 53, 59, pp. 331, 345, etc.

98. Ibid., vol. 2, no. 3, p. 217.

99. Ibid., vol. 2, no. 7, p. 221. The readings for the fifth day of Epiphany (Heb. 12:18-27: "For you have not come to what may be touched..."; Luke 1:39-56: "In those days Mary arose and went with haste into the hill country..."), which could appear to conform to the same motifs, since the station became the church on the Mount of Olives, were actually chosen to commemorate, on that day, Mary's visit to her cousin Elizabeth, a memorial connected with all the mysteries of the Lord recalled by the Eleona. See C. Renoux, "L'Eléona dans la liturgie de Jérusalem," in *Les Amis de l'Eléona* (1981), 4-8.

100. *Cod. arm.*, vol. 2, no. 31, p. 253.

101. See above, 395

102. *Cod. arm.*, vol. 2, no. 1, p. 211.

103. Ibid., vol. 2, no. 39 *ter*, p. 273.

104. Ibid., vol. 2, no. 45 *bis* and 52 *bis*, pp. 313, 325.
105. On Good Friday, for example, during the office of the adoration of the Cross, when the Old and New Testaments were alternately read (ibid., vol. 2, no. 43, pp. 281-293).
106. Ibid., vol. 2, nos. 53, 59, 62, 73, 74, pp. 331, 345, 351, 371-373.
107. For the feast of the prophet Zechariah on 10 June (ibid., vol. 2, no. 59, pp. 345-347), the apostle Philip on 15 November (ibid., no. 69, pp. 363-365), and the apostle James the brother of John (ibid., vol. 2, no. 74, p. 373), the authors of the *Lectionary* took the opportunity from the name of the commemorated saint to choose a pericope from the New Testament (either from an epistle or gospel) which alluded to a person of the same name. This use of Scripture did not imply an error on the identity of the saint whose feast day was being honored, but simply manifested the desire to see his name proclaimed on the day of his feast.
108. Ibid., vol. 2, nos. 55, 60, 63, 65, pp. 335-337, 347, 353, 357-359.
109. Ibid., vol. 2, nos. 15 and 16, pp. 231-233.
110. See above, 400.
111. *Cod. arm.,* vol. 2,, nos. 12 and 56, pp. 227, 237.
112. The *Lectionnaire syriaque, add. BM 14528* (see n. 16); the *Codex syr. Philipps 1388* (ed. Allgeier, in *Oriens Christianus* 6 [1916]: 147-152); the *Fragments géorgiens de Gratz* (ed. Tarchnischvili, CSCO 188, pp. xi-xii).
113. *Cod. arm.* vol. 1, 129-159.
114. Ibid., vol. 1, 110-127, 156-159.
115. Ibid., vol. 1, 110-113, 118-122, 136-141.
116. Cf. J. Noret, "Une homélie inédite sur les Rameaux par Théognios, prêtre de Jérusalem (vers 460?)," *Analecta Bollandiana* 89 (1971): 113-142. See also the *Hom. in Ramos Palmarum,* wrongly attributed to Hesychius of Jerusalem (ed. M. Aubineau, Les Homélies festales, 715-777).
117. By omitting from the pericope of Palm Sunday the episodes of the healing of the two blind men and the expulsion of the vendors from the Temple, in the interest of focusing on the story of Jesus's entry into Jerusalem, the mystical content of the feast was decimated; for the healing of humanity and the holiness of the worship owed to God the Father, such as Jesus's entry into this world signified, were no longer recalled.
118. *Cod. arm.,* vol. 1, 110-112; vol. 2, pp. 256-259.
119. M. Tarchnischvili, *Le Grand Lectionnaire de l'Église de Jérusalem,* vol. 189, no. 582, p. 83. The pericope of Matt. 21:1-17 (no. 594, p. 85), still preserved the episode of the expulsion of the vendors from the Temple.
120. *Cod. arm.,* vol. 1, 156-160; vol. 2, 309-315.
121. Ibid., vol. 2, no. 5, p. 219.
122. *Hom. 6.3, de S. Maria Deipara* (ed. Aubineau, 197).
123. *Cod. arm.,* vol. 2, no. 43, pp. 281-289.
124. Ibid., vol. 2, no. 1, pp. 211-215.
125. Ibid., vol. 2, no. 44 *bis,* pp. 295-309.
126. Ibid., vol. 2, no. 61, pp. 349-351.

127. Ibid., vol. 2, no. 35, pp. 259-261. One can find other examples of this same sort in the study of B. Fischer, "Le Lectionnaire arménien le plus ancien," in *Concilium* 102, 39-45.

128. *Cod. arm.*, vol. 2, no. 1 *bis*, p. 215.

129. Ibid., vol. 2, no. 39, p. 267.

130. Ibid., vol. 2, no. 11, p. 227.

20

Oral Culture, Biblical Interpretation, and Spirituality in Early Christian Monasticism

DOUGLAS BURTON-CHRISTIE

"Try to imagine a culture where no one has ever 'looked up' anything."[1] Such an imaginative leap is necessary if one is to understand the attitudes toward language and biblical interpretation found within the oral culture of early Egyptian monasticism. Words, whether words from Scripture, or from the elders, were central to the spirituality of early monasticism. Yet, while some of the monks were capable of "looking up" words in a book, many others were not. The encounter with words for the monks came not primarily through their eyes, but through their ears. Words for them did not lay inert on a page, but moved on the tongue, sounded in the ear. Theirs was largely an oral culture, one with its own distinctive approach to language and particular interpretive rules. The oral character of early monastic culture dramatically influenced the way the monks absorbed and interpreted Scripture. It is a central part of the desert hermeneutic—that creative confluence of ascetic discipline, biblical interpretation and spiritual vision that flowered in fourth-century Egypt.

A careful consideration of the oral character of early monastic culture can help us to clarify the distinctive accomplishments of the desert hermeneutic and situate it in a meaningful way within the history of biblical interpretation. It is striking that most standard histories of biblical interpretation hardly treat the early ascetic movement at all.[2] There are understandable reasons for this neglect: It does not fit easily into the classical "schools" of interpretation usually associated with Alexandria and Antioch, nor does it have any towering individual interpreters of the stature of Origen of Alexandria or Theodore of Mopsuestia; finally, the desert approach to interpretation is eclectic and synthetic, drawing freely on a number of earlier types of interpretation, without offering anything strikingly new in the way of exegetical method. Still, it does have its own characteristic *style* of interpretation, one which owes much to the oral culture from which it arises and the ascetic project that informs it. Yet, perhaps it is in part this very style, rooted in the back-and-forth movement of conversation, shaped by the ascetic culture within which it arose, acutely attentive to the dynamic power of language, insistent on the need for practically embodied interpretation, yet apparently lacking any theoretical substructure, that has helped relegate the desert hermeneutic to such obscurity.

Consider the historian Hans Lietzmann's contemptuous dismissal of the early monastic practice of memorization of texts: "It should of course be understood that this learning by heart was nothing more than a superficial accomplishment, ascetic in character, a kind of weaving and mental matting....The mechanical memorization did not penetrate the heart; it gave indeed only the faintest biblical tinge to the world of ideas in which the monks lived."[3] It is revealing that the very characteristics that Lietzmann derides, "weaving and mental matting," describe precisely the process by which words and stories are taken up and incorporated into the memory of persons living in an oral culture. Walter Ong has called this process "rhapsodizing," the intricate and complex process of weaving together in the memory layer upon layer of stories and sayings, so that one can later bring them to oral expression.[4] This is but one example of the influence of oral culture upon the interpretive approach found in the desert. However, if we are to overcome the tendency to distort and marginalize this interpretive approach, we will need to begin by learning how to situate such practices within a meaningful cultural context.[5] Paying attention to the oral dimensions of the desert hermeneutic is, in my view, one of the best places to begin.

In what follows, I will focus on three main aspects of this theme, with particular attention to evidence from *The Sayings of the Desert Fathers*.[6] First, I will examine the tensions within early monasticism concerning attitudes towards literacy and learning, tensions that suggest the significant differences that existed between oral and literate cultures. Second, I will describe some of the distinctive hermeneutical approaches arising out of the oral culture of the desert monks, especially the primacy of the oral encounter with the word, the way meaning was "negotiated" within the elder-disciple relationship, the monks' "asceticism of language" and their

416

practical, embodied approach to interpretation. Finally, I will describe the consummate expression of the desert hermeneutic—the transformed life. Throughout, I will argue that only by taking account of the oral character of early monastic culture can we come to understand and appreciate the characteristic approach of early ascetic biblical interpretation.

Oral and Literate Culture in the Desert

There were distinct tensions within early monastic culture between those who were literate and those who were not. Though certain of the monks were apparently literate and valued the "culture of the book," the great majority of those living in the desert were part of a culture which can best be described by the term "residual orality."[7] That is, although they had some experience with written texts and with literacy, their attitudes toward language remained colored by long-standing habits of an oral culture. Although the lines between these two cultures were not always distinct, real tensions nevertheless existed between them, concerning the relative value attributed to books, "literate culture," and learning. The presence of these tensions serves as an important reminder of the tenacity and power of oral culture within early monasticism.

Before proceeding to examine the evidence from the *Sayings*, a brief word needs to be said concerning the evidence of literacy and learning in late antique Egypt arising from recent scholarship. The work of Samuel Rubenson on the *Letters of Antony* has raised questions about an earlier, widely held view that Egyptian monasticism arose from the ranks of rustic, unlearned peasants. Rubenson has argued, on the basis of a fresh examination of the *Letters of Antony*, other monastic sources, and supporting papyrological evidence, that Antony, his immediate followers, and a good number of their fellow monks enjoyed higher levels of literacy and learning and were much more theologically and philosophically sophisticated than has previously been imagined.[8] Rubenson has no doubt provided a much needed corrective to what has been a far too simplistic understanding of early monastic culture. However, his own position needs qualification and nuancing. Recent studies by William Harris, Harry Gamble and Roger Bagnall are instructive in this regard. Using a broad definition of literacy as the ability to read or write at any level, Harris, in his book *Ancient Literacy*, reaches a largely negative conclusion for Western Antiquity generally on the question of literacy. The extent of literacy was, he argues, about 10 percent and never exceeded 15 to 20 percent of the population as a whole.[9] Harry Gamble, in his recent

Books and Readers in the Early Church: A History of Early Christian Texts, argues that there is little evidence to suggest "that the extent of literacy of any kind among Christians was greater than in society at large. If anything, it was more limited."[10] Roger Bagnall, whose book *Egypt in Late Antiquity* generally confirms Rubenson's assessment of a relatively higher level of literacy among the monks than was previously imagined, nonetheless admits that this does not mean that literacy levels in the desert were particularly high. Even given the significant amount of papyrological evidence regarding reading and writing in monastic circles—copied manuscripts, correspondence, accounting, informal inscriptions—Bagnall concludes: "it is not clear that these activities required more than the normal minority of literate personnel found in any Egyptian village."[11] It is more likely the case, he argues, that there were a few monks in any given monastic settlement who, by virtue of their background and education, could read and write. The implication is that most of the others could not do so. While the presence of a literate minority within early Egyptian monasticism cannot be disputed, neither can we say that early monasticism was any more literate than the towns and villages from which it drew its recruits. The evidence from the papyrological sources thus corresponds broadly with the picture that emerges from the early monastic sources to suggest that we have within early monasticism a "mixed culture," with elements of both oral and literate cultures influencing its growth and development.[12]

The presence of literate culture in the desert can be seen from the mention of books, writing, copying and reading in the *Sayings*. We hear, for example, that Abba Gelasius possessed a beautiful and extremely valuable copy of the Bible in parchment, said to contain the whole of the Old and New Testaments.[13] Theodore of Pherme is said to have possessed "three good books" from which he and his brothers derived much profit.[14] Abba Ammoes tells of some monks who possessed "books of parchment" in their cells.[15] The occasional mention of writing and copying provides further evidence of the presence of literate culture in the desert. We hear of a scribe at Scetis who worked in his cell copying books for the brothers. He is portrayed as being very skilled and well known for his ability as a scribe, implying that the demand for written copies of the Sacred Texts was not unusual.[16] Here, we likely have an example of what Eric Havelock has called "craft literacy"—literary skills restricted to specialized craftspersons—something which often develops in oral cultures shortly after the introduction of writing or where reading and writing is relatively rare.[17] There is evidence that at least some monks read texts in their cells. The practice of reading was important enough to Sisoes that, when asked by someone for "a word," he simply referred to his own practice of reading Scripture: "What shall I say to you? I read the New Testament, and I turn to the Old."[18] We hear that Abba John Colobos regularly gave himself over to "prayers, readings, and meditations of the Holy Scriptures."[19] Reading Scripture was believed to provide important nourishment for the soul[20]—one brother asserted that happiness comes to the soul "by means of assiduous reading of the Scriptures."[21]

There is also evidence that the written text of Scripture was sometimes revered by the monks as a sacred object of intrinsic religious value apart from any consideration of its meaning. Studies of oral cultures have shown this to be a common attitude among peoples for whom writing has only begun to make inroads. Jack Goody has noted instances of illiterates who profit from rubbing books on their foreheads, or from whirling prayer-wheels bearing texts they cannot read.[22] The Bible clearly had a similar talismanic effect on the imagination of some of the early desert dwellers beyond any consideration of the meaning of its words.[23] A saying of Abba Epiphanius captures this sense, highlighting a common belief that merely *seeing* sacred books could help bring one to salvation: "The acquisition of Christian books" he says, "is necessary for those who can use them. For the mere *sight* of these books renders us less inclined to sin and incites us to believe more firmly in righteousness."[24]

Clearly, the written word was revered and employed within early desert monasticism. Evidence of monks possessing copies of Scripture, of scribal activity, and of the practice of reading all testify to the significance of Scripture as *text* for the early monks. Yet, despite the importance accorded to the written word by some in the desert, one also finds much evidence of a trenchant critique of book culture. Many of the monks—like others in oral cultures where literacy begins to usurp oral discourse—harbored a deep suspicion toward books and writing.[25] This resistance reflects not only a certain natural conservatism, but an acute sense of the potential loss in a transition from orality to literacy: "The fixing of the holy word in writing always carries with it potential threats to the original spontaneity and living quality of the scriptural text, for it places it ever in danger of becoming only a 'dead letter' rather than the 'living word.'"[26]

The elders could be blunt in their response to those who seemed to place too much faith in their technical knowledge or mastery of the written word, while ignoring the imperatives contained in Scripture.

When a brother boasted to one of the elders at Scetis that he had copied with his own hand the whole of the Old and New Testaments, the old man simply responded, "You have filled the cupboards with paper."[27] Should one even possess a copy of the Scriptures? With an irony characteristic of the desert, some monks argued that to possess a copy of the Scriptures was itself in direct contradiction to the words of Scripture which, after all, required one to renounce everything for the sake of the kingdom. Thus we hear of a brother who "owned only a book of the Gospels," but being inspired by the Gospel call, sold it and gave away the money for the support of the poor saying, "I have sold the very word which speaks to me saying: 'Sell your possessions and give to the poor' (Luke 12:33)."[28] Nor was this merely ascetic "grandstanding." Possessing books was seen as problematic not only because it could distract one from adhering to the gospel call to renunciation, but also because it conflicted with the demands of charity and justice. To Abba Serapion, the accumulation of books was tantamount to robbing the poor. When approached by a brother asking him for a 'word,' Serapion responded: "What shall I say to you? You have taken the living of the widows and orphans and put it on shelves.' For he saw them full of books."[29] Serapion, who used and valued books himself, was not arguing that the possession of books is an evil in itself. Rather he was criticizing the tendency to collect and accumulate books for their own sake, a tendency that could lead one to become insensitive to the dynamic power of the language within.

Books were always in danger of becoming useless objects. Once they became such, the monks could easily grow dull to the imperatives of Scripture and become oblivious to the needs of the vulnerable ones in their midst. This tendency to objectify and thereby reify the written Word would haunt later generations of monks. They looked back with longing to an earlier time in the desert, when the word was alive: "The prophets wrote books," one of them recalled, "then came our Fathers who put them into practice. Those who came after them learnt them by heart. Then came the present generation, who have written them out and put them into their window seats without using them."[30] Such a comment clearly reflects at least in part a tendency among later generations of monks to create an idealized picture of early monasticism. But it also reveals an ongoing tension within monastic culture concerning the best means of apprehending and interpreting Scripture. For many, the further one moved from the dynamic power of oral discourse, the greater the chances that Scripture would be reduced to a dead letter.

Beyond these tensions over the role of books and reading, one also finds differences among the monks regarding the meaning and purpose of learning. In part this had to do with the question of whether classical education had any function within the ascetic world of the desert. John Cassian, who as H. I. Marrou has noted, was "less concerned with learning than with forgetting the poetry and secular knowledge [he] had picked up in the schools before [his] conversion," raises questions on precisely this point.[31] For Cassian, the problem with the old learning was psychological; it prevented the mind from absorbing the new ethos of the Scriptures: "A special hindrance to salvation is added by that knowledge of literature which I seem already to have in some slight measure attained, in which the efforts of my tutor, or my attention to continual reading have so weakened me that now my mind is filled with those trifling fables, and the stories of battles with which from its earliest infancy it was stored by its childish lessons."[32] The rhetorical flourish of this passage signals the complexity of this question among those who had ostensibly renounced their classical training and suggests an irony that pervaded the desert on this question. Many monks, Cassian and Evagrius among them, employed sophisticated philosophical categories to express their spirituality, even while denying their usefulness or appropriateness in the life of the monk.

Still, there appears to have been genuine tension over this issue in the desert. In the *Sayings*, it is expressed as a clash of cultures. A story told about Abba Arsenius, another person of great learning and high social status who came to live in the desert, reflects the shock of realization that apparently greeted some of these learned persons when they came into contact with the wisdom of the unlearned Egyptians.

> One day Abba Arsenius consulted an old Egyptian monk about his own thoughts. Someone noticed this and said to him, "Abba Arsenius, how is it that you with such a good Latin and Greek education ask this peasant about your thoughts?" He replied, "I have indeed been taught Latin and Greek, but I do not know even the alphabet of this peasant."[33]

There was a clear sense among the educated ones who came to the desert that learning would have to start over in this place. In the desert, a clear distinction was made between the kind of knowledge that could be acquired through 'worldly education' and what could be gained through the hard work of the simple desert monks:

> [Evagrius] said to blessed Arsenius, 'How is it that we, with all our education and wisdom have nothing, while these uncultured Egyptians have acquired the virtues by their own hard work.[34]

421

The change in sensibilities among the learned took place not only by observing the simple monks, but sometimes through confrontations between the learned and the unlearned regarding the assumptions the well-educated monks brought with them to the desert. Sometimes such confrontations reflected tensions between Greek-speaking and Egyptian-speaking monks. In one instance, we see Abba Evagrius, one of the most learned of those to come to the desert, presenting a teaching to some of the monks. Although we are not told the precise reason for the conflict, one of the monks gently but firmly rebukes Evagrius:

> "Abba, we know that if you were living in your own country, you would probably be a bishop and a great leader; but at present you sit here as a stranger." He was filled with compunction, but was not at all upset and bending his head he replied, "I have spoken once and will not answer, twice but I will proceed no further."[35]

Such stories reflect the authority enjoyed by the simple Egyptian monks, and the adjustments which the most learned had to make in their apprenticeship in the desert. Evagrius for one showed himself eager to learn. However, he could not, in spite of himself, hide his astonishment at the new teaching he received. Upon hearing one of the elders speak, he was: "pierced to his depths by the word and made a prostration, saying, 'I have read many books before, but never have I received such teaching.'"[36]

The ambiguity and tension regarding the place and function of books, reading, writing and education among the early desert monks suggest, I would argue, the significant differences between oral and literate cultures within early monasticism. Although the written word was highly esteemed by some, others saw that writing could lead to a reification of the Word—something which could eclipse its power and leave the monk with no real sense of its meaning. In their critique of the written word, especially the tendency to objectify the word, the desert monks sought to preserve something of the integrity and power of the living, spoken word. So too the tensions over how or whether to incorporate the assumptions of classical Greek paideia into the new paideia of the desert reveal a clash of cultures. For at least some of the monks, life in the desert demanded the adoption of an alternative approach to wisdom—the hard work of the monk in the cell. The presence in the desert literature of these tensions illuminates the struggle in the desert between two cultures, literate and oral, to define the pedagogical and hermeneutical approaches most appropriate to early monastic life.

Oral Dimensions of Interpretation

How did oral culture shape the desert monks' characteristic approach to biblical interpretation? First, there is the pervasively oral character of the monastic encounter with the word, including the word proclaimed at the *synaxis*, the word uttered in the master-disciple relationship, and the word recited in meditation. Second, there is the way meaning was "negotiated" in the back-and-forth conversation between the elder and disciple. Third, there is what I would call an asceticism of language, the intense scrutiny given by the monks to words of all kinds, especially spoken words, and their effects on the spiritual well-being of the individual and the community. The monks' careful discernment of language, both creative and destructive, created the climate in which authentic biblical interpretation could be carried out. Finally, there is the insistence on praxis, the sense that words of authority—whether those of Scripture or those of the elder—need to be fulfilled, brought to realization in the life of the monk for the interpretive process to be fulfilled. Taken altogether, they suggest the significant influence of oral culture on biblical interpretation in the desert.

Words were *heard* in the desert much more often than they were read. Such hearing of Scripture shaped the life of the desert monks as they gathered to hear the word proclaimed at the weekly *synaxis*, as they listened to the words spoken directly to them by an elder, or as they recited or meditated upon a word in their cells. In each of these instances, it was a word spoken and heard that formed the center of the encounter. The lines between these different kinds of encounter were not always clear. Indeed, one of the characteristic features of the desert hermeneutic is seen in the authority attributed by the monks to both words of Scripture and words of the elders. The word of Scripture proclaimed at the *synaxis* and the word of the elder uttered in response to a question each participated in and expressed a dynamic, revelatory power. As Henry Chadwick has noted, "It was axiomatic that the words of one who lived so close to God would be inspired."[37] The words of the holy ones were seen as participating in and continuing the discourse of the authoritative words of Scripture.

A saying of Abba Antony expresses well these two dimensions of the desert hermeneutic, its predominantly oral character and its sense that authoritative words arise from Scripture and the elders. Some brothers came to Antony and said to him: "Speak a word; how are we to be saved?" The old man said to them, "You have heard the Scriptures. That should teach you how." But they said, "We want to hear from *you too*, father."[38] Two points about this saying are worth noting. First, Antony makes no assumption that his listeners will have studied or even read Scripture. He implies that the authority of the Scriptures could be felt and their message received through *hearing* them proclaimed. This accords well with the evidence seen throughout the *Sayings* and in other desert literature concerning the monks' regular participation in the *synaxis* where Scripture was proclaimed.[39] It was here, in oral form, that Scripture was most often encountered. Antony's response seems to take this for granted. Second, from the brothers' request also to hear from Antony himself (and not only from Scripture) one sees evidence of the kind of authority that the words of the elders enjoyed—an authority comparable to that of Scripture. Although the brothers accepted the words of Scripture as authoritative, they also wanted to hear the words of experience from the mouth of their beloved teacher. What precisely did they hope to hear? An explanation of a particular biblical text (perhaps the one Antony had already referred to: "You have heard the Scriptures.")? An original teaching from the elder? This is not clear. For our purposes here, what is important to note is the dynamic that is at work in this saying: authoritative words come from two sources—Scripture and the elders.

But it is not simply that the monks wanted to hear from the elders *in addition to* Scriptures. Often, they were asking implicitly to hear the words of Scripture from the mouth of the elder or even to hear Scripture interpreted by the elder. This is because in the desert, as in oral cultures everywhere, the monks learned primarily through apprenticeship, or, as Walter Ong says, "by discipleship, which is a kind of apprenticeship, by listening, by repeating what they heard, by mastering proverbs and ways of combining and recombining them."[40] It is not surprising, therefore, that we hear elsewhere in the sayings that the words of the elders are given comparable authority to the words of Scripture. Abba Poemen alludes to this when he talks about the dual sources of the desert teaching on tears and compunction. Weeping, he says, is "the way the Scriptures and our Fathers give us."[41] An anonymous saying suggests that God asks two kinds of obedience of the monks, that they "obey the holy Scriptures, and obey their...spiritual fathers."[42] In some cases, the words of the elder appear to have had an authority which surpassed that of Scripture. One saying tells of Poemen citing a passage from Proverbs, prefacing his citation with the authoritative phrase, "it is written." In this particular instance, however, Poemen felt the need to go beyond what was stated in the biblical text, in order to warn the brothers about the dangers of self-delusion. In doing so, he expressed the authority of his own words in a startling way, introducing his comments on the text with the very same expression Jesus used in the Sermon on the Mount (Matt. 5:22) to announce his new authority: "but *I* say to you...."[43] Poemen's use of this phrase reflects not a cavalier attitude toward Scripture, but rather the "freedom of speech" which characterized the elders of the desert and the authority their words enjoyed.

We see a symbolic expression of the importance attached to such authoritative, charismatic teaching in the desert in a story concerning what is required to be accorded the title Abba. when some of the brothers questioned Poemen about why Agathon, who was very young, should be called Abba, Poemen replied, "because his mouth makes him worthy to be called Abba."[44] In spite of his young age, Agathon's mouth—his words and teaching—were pure and authoritative and gave him the right to be called 'Abba.'

The dual authority enjoyed by words of Scripture and words of the elders helps to explain the significance of the elder-disciple relationship for the work of interpretation. Although it was undoubtedly common for individual monks to hear, interpret and absorb words of Scripture proclaimed at the *synaxis*, the characteristic feature of the desert hermeneutic is the existential "negotiation" of the word in the back-and-forth conversation of the elder and disciple. This is consistent with the process through which words are passed on in oral cultures everywhere. As Walter Ong notes, "Words [in oral discourse] acquire their meanings only from their always insistent habitat, which is not, as in a dictionary, simply other words, but includes also gestures, vocal inflections, facial expression, and the entire human, existential setting in which the real, spoken word always occurs."[45] The concrete setting for such oral discourse, Ong suggests, is always "dense, never fully verbalizable, involving all sorts of elusive but real imponderables."[46]

The questions posed in the desert—including the ubiquitous and seemingly opaque "Abba, give me a word,"—were characterized by just such "elusive but real imponderables." The expression, "give me a word," which opens so many of the conversations in the desert, is both pointed and radically open-ended. Imbedded in this phrase were very particular anxieties such as the health and well-being of one's family, the security of one's home, the threat of debts. However, this question could also express an urgent but unspecified yearning for meaning, a plea for solid ground in the midst of a disintegrating world. One such question can be heard in the voice of a person who pleaded with Abba Theodore: "speak to me, I am perishing."[47] The words uttered in response to these questions likewise were immediate, direct, and open-ended. Their immediacy came from the attempt to give a concrete and direct response to the questioner. In this sense they were "more or less continuous with the rest of life, not so much part of a separate world as [words often] appear to be in text."[48] However, they were also open-ended in the sense that they invited the listener to enter into a heretofore unexplored and fathomless world of meaning.

It is in this setting, then, that we can see how meaning was "negotiated" in the elder-disciple relationship. Since the world of oral discourse is generally one of conversation, in which one utterance gives rise to another, that to still another, and so on, meaning can be said to be negotiated in this process. Such negotiation often begins even before any word is uttered. What one chooses to say in a conversation often depends upon one's conjectures (before one begins to speak) about the other person's state of mind and about the possible range of responses. The actual response on the part of the other to what one says may or may not fit the earlier conjecture. The response makes it possible to discern for oneself and to make clear in a counter-response what the fuller meaning of the words was or can be.[49] Two stories illustrate this process of negotiation at work in the desert.

One concerns a brother who spent three days begging Abba Theodore for a word. Theodore refused to speak to the brother and he eventually departed sadly. A visiting brother who witnessed this exchange asked Theodore for an explanation. Why had he refused to speak to the brother? Theodore said that the tone of the brother's questions revealed him to be "a trafficker [in words] who seeks to glorify himself through the words of others."[50] Here is a case where the word of an elder was withheld precisely because the one seeking the word approached with less than pure intentions. How did Theodore know this? It is possible that the brother had a reputation. However, it is equally likely that something in the brother's facial expression or in the tone of his words revealed to Theodore the carelessness with which the brother was putting his question. In such a climate, no word would be spoken.

Usually, the elders *did* respond to questions, although they gauged or negotiated their words carefully depending on the circumstances. In one such instance, Abba Ares gave some particularly difficult commands to a certain brother who asked for a word; the brother received the commands and attempted to fulfill them as well as he could. However, to most of the others who came seeking a word, Ares assigned much less strenuous tasks. When asked about this inconsistency, Ares responded, "How I send them away depends upon what the brothers came to seek. Now it is for the sake of God that this one comes to hear a word, for he is a hard worker and what I tell him, he carries out eagerly. It is because of this that I speak the Word of God to him."[51] Here, the Word of God exists, not as scratchings on a piece of parchment or papyrus, to be studied and puzzled over in solitude, but as a living response to a question. The utterance of the word, the reception of it, and the possibility of life which the Word offers, all depend on the dynamics of a conversation, and the chance to test the ground into which the seed will fall. The Word does not proceed automatically from the mouth of the elder. It must be drawn out by genuine questions from an honest heart.

Language was a living, dynamic process for the desert monks. This helps to explain why they gave so much attention to what one is to *do* with words—those of Scripture, those of the elders, and, just as importantly, destructive or malicious words cast about carelessly. This was an asceticism of language, a long, painstaking process of discernment—in which words were carefully scrutinized for what they could do to the monk (both positively and negatively), and in which the monk was in turn probed by the words and revealed to himself.

The large number of dicta in the *Sayings* concerning the anatomical parts of the body used to utter words, namely the tongue and the mouth—is revealing. Abba Joseph asked Abba Nisterus, "What should I do about my tongue, for I cannot master it?"[52] One brother was nearly driven to despair by his inability to control his tongue. He asked Abba Moses, "What am I to do? My tongue afflicts me, and every time I go among people, I cannot control it, but condemn them." Matoes tells the brother that this inability to control one's speech is indeed "a sickness" for which the only cure is solitude.[53] Nor were struggles with speech simply a matter of lack of resolve; Abba Agathon reminds his listeners that their inability to control their speech is driven by profound forces: "No passion is worse than an uncontrolled tongue," he says. "It is the mother of all passions."[54] This helps to explain the concern in the desert over "strange conversation," "alien words," "worldly talk" and "loose talk." Relatively harmless in themselves, these habits nevertheless provided easy access to more destructive patterns of speech—recrimination

427

and slander. How deeply could such words wound? A brother came to see Abba Achilles and found him spitting blood from his mouth—he had carried within himself a particularly vicious word of a brother.[55] But it was not only because of the immense harm that words could do to others that the monks sought to refrain from slander. It was also because of what it could do to *the one who uttered the words*. As Abba Or put it: "Slander is death to the soul."[56]

Because of this, the monks spared no effort in their attempt to clarify the relationship between the heart and the mouth, between words and life. A brother asked Abba Sisoes how to "guard the heart." The elder responded with a question of his own: "How can we keep watch over our hearts when our mouth is open?"[57] Abba Poemen encouraged his disciples to consider the reciprocal influence of the heart and the mouth: "Teach your mouth to say that which you have in your heart" and "teach your heart to guard what your tongue teaches."[58] Poemen recognized how easily self-deception could creep in: "A person may seem to be silent," he said, "but if his heart is condemning others he is babbling ceaselessly. But there may be another who talks from morning till night and yet he is truly silent; that is, he says nothing that is not profitable."[59] Isidore of Pelusia provides what amounts to a commentary on Poemen's statement, revealing the kind of integrity valued most by the monks: "To live without speaking is better than to speak without living. For the former is useful even by his silence, but the latter does no good even when he speaks."[60] The *Sayings* testify that this was not just a distant and elusive dream: Certain elders did manage to cultivate an integral relationship between their words and their lives; they were known for precisely this quality. It was said of Abba Or that "he never lied, nor swore, nor hurt anyone, nor spoke without necessity."[61]

This attention to language—to the psychological roots of bitter, destructive words and to the possibility of an integral connection between language and a pure heart—provides the context for understanding the desert hermeneutic. Having initiated the first and most difficult part of the hermeneutical process—a rigorous self-scrutiny—the monk could begin to explore the meaning of the words of the elders and of Scripture. Even here, though, the monks' primary outlook was practical: understanding would emerge from praxis.

What should I *do*? How should a person *behave*? How should we *conduct* ourselves? What good work should I *do* that I might *live* in it?[62] These were the most common questions put to the elders. And this practical ethos also defined the monks' attitudes toward words—Scripture and the words of the elder. Abba Gerontius exhorts his listeners to *"do what is written and guard [your] own heart with all possible care."*[63] Abba Agathon notes: "Unless a person *keeps* the commandments of God, he cannot make progress, even in a single virtue."[64] Abba Antony told his disciples, "whatever you *do* you should always have before you the testimony of Scripture."[65] And when Abba Benjamin was dying, he quoted a text from Scripture to his disciples: "Be joyful at all times, pray without ceasing, and give thanks for all things (1 Thess. 5:16-17)," he told them; *"Do* these things and you can be saved."[66] Nor was this practical response limited to the words of Scripture. Abba Pistus told a story about the obedience of Abba Athres and Abba Or, commenting: "What I have seen, I have done everything in my power to *keep."*[67] Whether a penetrating word of Scripture or a memorable gesture of an elder, one could carry it within oneself and ruminate on it.

What did it mean to translate this practical ethos into the work of interpretation? We see much discussion in the *Sayings* about how to *attain* a saying, how to appropriate it. Poemen declares that if a person has *attained* the word of the Apostle, "to the pure, everything is pure" (Titus 1:15), he sees himself as less than all creatures. Hearing this, one of the brothers raised an objection, posing what might be considered a limit case: "How can I deem myself less than a *murderer*?" Poemen's response is extreme, and telling: "When a person has really *attained* this saying, if he sees [someone] committing a murder, he says, *'he* has only committed this one sin but *I* commit sins every day.'"[68] For Poemen, attaining a saying from Scripture or realizing its truth in oneself implies a deep moral and spiritual transformation. To *attain* a saying, as opposed to merely *understanding* its meaning abstractly, one must somehow *become* that of which the text speaks. In this case, to become pure (of heart) means to realize humility, compassion, to recognize one's common plight with every other human being—even a murderer.

The elders did not underestimate the difficulty of such practical appropriation of the sacred texts. Because of this, the work of interpretation was inextricably bound up with the work of discernment. One elder counseled his listeners: "Every time a thought of superiority or vanity moves you, examine your conscience to see if you have *kept all the commandments,* if you love your enemies, and are grieved by their sins, if you consider yourself as an unprofitable servant and the greatest sinner of all."[69] Attention to practice (especially attention to one's feeble attempts) could keep one from being deceived, from treating words carelessly. We hear of one brother who "began to speak with [Abba Theodore] and inquire about things he had not yet put into practice." Theodore told the brother: "You have not yet found a ship nor put your cargo aboard it and before you have sailed, you have already arrived at the city. *Do the work first*, then you will come to that of which you now speak."[70]

Arriving at the port with the cargo. This is an apt image of what the desert fathers hoped to achieve through their hermeneutic. Abba Poemen provides an example of just how deeply a word must permeate the life of the monk in order for it to be fulfilled. A brother questioned Poemen, asking, "What does 'See that none of you repays evil for evil' (1 Thess. 5:15) mean?" The elder responded: Passions work in four stages—first in the heart; secondly, in the face; thirdly, in words; and fourthly, it is essential not to render evil for evil in deeds. If you can purify your heart, passion will not come into your expression; but if it comes into your face, take care not to speak; but if you do speak, cut the conversation short in case you render evil for evil.[71] Poemen's account of what it means to *interpret* this text from 1 Thessalonians reveals a penetrating psychological insight regarding the different levels at which a text must be fulfilled in the life of the monk. To put this text into practice, one must become "pure of heart;" only then would anger and resentment cease from welling up and casting a shadow across the face; and only then would the monk be able to pull out the roots of bitter words and malicious deeds.

Realizing the Word: A Life Transformed

This demanding approach to interpretation helps to account for the defining feature of the desert hermeneutic and of desert spirituality—a life transformed. The *Sayings* reveal an intriguing hermeneutical trajectory: Words of power burst forth into the world of the monk—whether sacred texts proclaimed at the *synaxis*, the charismatic word of the elder or, just as important, careless, murderous words uttered in anger. Careful scrutiny (discernment) was given to these words: Of what did they speak? What possibilities did they offer? What challenges? What dangers? In this demanding process of discernment, the monks worked assiduously to root out the passions within them that prompted malicious words and to take into themselves those words of power that held out particular promise. They sought to enter the worlds of meaning revealed by these words, to remake themselves in light of them. The *Sayings* witness to a variety of expressions of this transformation in the life of the monk: A telling word, gesture, or facial expression revealed one to have realized the sacred texts within oneself. To have done so was to have in a sense become a new sacred text.

This intense focus on the person is an expression of the relentlessly practical character of the desert hermeneutic. We see here an ascetic culture rooted in an approach to interpretation which George Steiner has called "execution." "An interpreter," he says, "is, in essence, an executant, one who 'acts out' the material before him so as to give it intelligible life. Interpretation is to the largest possible degree, lived."[72] In portrait after portrait in the *Sayings*, we are vividly reminded that the sacred texts *could and did* penetrate one's life. Three biblical themes occupied the monks more than any other: freedom from care, humility, and love. By embodying these texts in their lives, the desert fathers brought them palpably to life for others.

The practice of renunciation and detachment among the monks was inextricably linked to their longing for freedom from care. The struggle to realize these led monks to give prominence to certain biblical texts, like Matthew 19:21 ("If you would be perfect, go, sell what you possess and give it to the poor, and you will have treasure in heaven");[73] Matthew 7:13-14 ("the narrow gate" or "narrow way");[74] and a cluster of texts referring to freedom from care: Matthew 6:34 ("Do not worry about tomorrow");[75] Matthew 6:33 ("Seek first God's kingdom");[76] and Psalm 55:22 [54:23, LXX] ("Cast your cares upon the Lord").[77] Ruminating on these texts would lead, the monk hoped, to a realization of their meaning in one's life. We see this reflected in numerous stories attesting to the monks' realization of detachment and freedom from care. We hear of one brother who "owned only a book of the Gospels." Inspired by the gospel call to renunciation, he sold it and gave away the money for the support of the poor saying, "I have sold the very word which speaks to me, saying: 'Sell your possessions and give it to the poor' (Matt. 19:21)."[78] A similar freedom from the need to own things is seen in numerous stories in the *Sayings* that tell of the monks' response to being robbed. Abba Macarius was returning to his cell one day after having been away and he encountered a man who was plundering his goods. Without hesitation, "he came up to the thief as if he were a stranger and he helped him to load the animal. He saw him off in complete tranquility, saying: 'We have brought nothing into this world, and we cannot take anything out of the world' (1 Tim. 6:7), 'The Lord gave and the Lord has taken away; blessed be the name of the Lord' (Job 1:21)."[79] Abba Euprepius extends this grasp of detachment even further, running after thieves who had robbed his cell to make sure they had taken everything they wanted.[80]

The desert fathers' understanding and practice of humility was informed not only by certain biblical texts, but also by the example of the humble one, Christ. Thus the monks appealed to the scriptural injunction to "act in secret" (Matt. 6:45) when fasting.[81] Similarly, they were encouraged to avoid a false sense of pride in their accomplishments (1 Cor. 10:12), and to maintain a constant awareness of their sins (Ps. 25:18 [24:18, LXX]). There was a cluster of biblical texts that the monks found useful in cultivating a radical kind of humility. They were to "endure affliction" (Matt. 5:11) for the sake of the Gospel, consider themselves to be the "offscouring of all" (1 Cor. 4:13), not to shy away from being despised by others (Luke 18:32), and learn to "bear dishonor" (2 Cor. 6:8). In this school of humility, it was Christ who was the master and the monks looked to his example, especially as it is articulated in the great hymn of *kenôsis* in Philippians 2:6-11.[82] The realization of humility in one's life usually emerged over a long, exacting process of testing. However, the meaning of humility, in one's life and in a broader sense, came to light in a flash. A story tells of an old man who had practiced great fasting and asceticism for over seventy years. One day he asked God the meaning of a "word of Scripture," but the meaning was not revealed to him. Then the old man said to himself, "I have given myself so much affliction without obtaining anything, so I will go to see my brother and ask him." But as he was closing the door behind him to go see his brother, an angel of the Lord was sent to him who said, "These seventy years you have fasted have not brought you near to God, but when you humiliated yourself by going to see your brother, I was sent to tell you the meaning of the word."[83] Humility embodied in a life also conveyed power, especially over the malevolent force of the demons. In one instance, a demon approached Macarius with a knife and tried to cut his foot. However, "because of [Macarius'] humility, he could not do so. He said to Macarius, 'All that you have, we have also; you are distinguished only by humility; by that you get the better of us.'"[84] It is intriguing to note that the realization of humility, which only came through entering into the deepest obscurity, finally issued forth in a power that the monk's contemporaries found astonishing: Of Abba John Colobos, it was asked: "Who is this John, who by his humility has all Scetis hanging from his little finger?"[85]

Above all, the desert hermeneutic was manifested through compassion, something so central to the lives of the monks that they referred to it simply as "the commandment."[86] The monks were asked to consider in the most practical terms what it would mean to realize the commandment to love within the ordinary circumstances of their lives. Two of the most pervasive themes in the *Sayings* which express the monks' idea of love were refraining from anger and not judging others. The text from Ephesians, "Let not the sun go down on your anger" (Eph. 4:26), was one of the primary biblical inspirations behind the monks' efforts to root out anger—what Evagrius called "the fiercest passion."[87] Other texts also figured to keep the monks' mind focused on this task. Abba Agathon, alluding to the chapter on love in Paul's letter to the Corinthians, expresses in stark terms the need to drive anger out: "A man who is angry, even if he were to raise the dead, is not acceptable to God (cf. 1 Cor. 13:1-3)."[88] Abba Poemen told his hearers, "if your brother hurts you by his arrogance and you are angry with him because of it, that is getting angry without cause (cf. Matt. 5:22)." But to drive the point home even more forcefully, he used a striking and unusual juxtaposition of biblical texts: "If [your brother] plucks out your right eye and cuts off your right hand (cf. Matt. 5:29-30), and you get angry with him because of it, that is getting angry without cause."[89] The monks expressed a similar uncompromising attitude toward the temptation to judge others. Their experience taught them that giving into the habit of judging others, no matter how justified it might seem, always eroded the capacity to love. To ascetic extremists, who wished to judge a weak brother, Poemen called to mind the text from Matthew, "First take the log out of your own eye, then you will see clearly to take the speck out of your brother's eye (Matt. 7:5)."[90] The monks were reminded that they should refrain from scorning or judging others because they themselves would stand before the judgment seat of God (Rom. 14:10).[91] Judging others was seen as a far more serious offense than fornication (James 2:11), a reminder that the severest ascetic struggles were not "of the flesh," but those requiring a purging of the seemingly bottomless reservoirs of hidden contempt for others.[92]

The monks were concerned, finally, that love should manifest itself in the ordinary circumstances of their lives. Non-retaliation, toward those who slandered or injured one in some way, was for Abba Poemen part of what it meant for the monks to realize the words of the Gospel, "Greater love has no man than this, that a man lay down his life for his friends (John 15:13.)"[93] There was a particular emphasis on the need for tenderness toward those who were weakest, most in need of help. Poemen reminded his listeners of the concrete meaning of Jesus' words, "'Those who are well have no need of a physician, but those who are sick' (Matt. 9:12). If you do a little good to the good brother, do twice as much for the other. For he is sick."[94] We see this sensibility realized in a story about Abba Moses, who was asked to participate in the communal judgment of one of the brothers who had fallen into sin. Reluctantly, he agreed to follow the brothers to the place of the trial, but insisted on bringing along a large jug, which leaked from his shoulder as he walked along. Pressed by his companions for an explanation of his behavior, he told them, "My sins run out behind me, and I do not see them, and today I am coming to judge another." Seeing this, the brothers gave up their vendetta against the one who had sinned.[95] Another story provides a hint of how deeply some of the monks were transformed by love: Abba Ammonas was said to "have advanced to the point where his goodness was so great, he no longer took any notice of evil."[96] If anyone came asking him to judge another, he would "feign madness" to avoid doing so.[97] And we see love eloquently expressed in the simple tenderness of Poemen toward a brother who could not maintain the ascetic rigors of the monastic regime. Some of the brothers, who were insistent on preserving what they believed to be the necessary strictness in the monastic observances, asked Poemen: "When we see brothers who are dozing at the *synaxis*, shall we rouse them so that they will be watchful?" He responded: "For my part, when I see a brother who is dozing, I put his head on my knees and let him rest."[98]

Here, and in numerous other places in the *Sayings*, we catch glimpses of what the monks themselves believed to be signs of holiness: the realization and concrete expression of the biblical values of freedom from care, humility and love. Equally telling, as expressions of the desert hermeneutic, are sayings depicting the visages of some of the greatest of the elders as reflecting the light of their biblical forbears. Abba Pambo was said to be "like Moses, who received the image of the glory of Adam when his face shone."[99] Abba Arsenius' appearance was angelic, like that of Jacob.[100] Abba Nisterus was said to reflect the glory of Moses, and indirectly, Christ. He was likened to "the serpent of brass which Moses made for the healing of the people (Num. 21:8-9): he possessed all virtue, without speaking he healed everyone."[101] In focusing on these gestures, the monks reflect very much the same sensibility one finds throughout the ancient biographies of holy men and women, whose aim, Patricia Cox Miller suggests, "was to evoke, and thus to reveal the interior geography of the hero's life...; when they sought to 'capture the gesture,' they were negotiating the intersection of the human and the divine."[102] At the same time such images reveal the profoundly biblical character of early monastic culture. As Peter Brown has suggested: "To be a 'man of God' was to revive, on the banks of the Nile, all other 'men of God' in all other ages....Little wonder that strong millennial hopes flickered around the persons of the holy men and around the walled monasteries of the Nile."[103]

Conclusion

The embodied hermeneutic of the early desert monks deserves our close and careful consideration as a significant moment within the history of biblical interpretation. The influence of oral culture on the interpretive patterns of the monks is striking. The tension between oral and literate cultures present in the literature reveals the deep and significant differences among the monks regarding how and where one was to interpret the word. The pervasively oral/aural character of the monks' world blurred the lines of distinction between the words of Scripture and words of the elder, suggesting the potentially revelatory capacity of all language. The negotiated character of meaning indicates the significance of conversation for interpreting texts. The intense scrutiny given by the monks to the power of language and the acute attention paid to how to fulfill the word of God (whether from Scripture or from the elder) makes plain the inherently dynamic character of the desert hermeneutic. Finally, the insistence that the work of interpretation must bear fruit in a transformed life reminds us of the intimate relationship between hermeneutics and spirituality for those who sought holiness in the desert.

NOTES

1. W. Ong, *Orality and Literacy: The Technologizing of the Word* (London and New York, 1982), 31. On oral culture, see also W. Kelber, *The Oral and Written Gospel* (Philadelphia, 1983); E. A. Havelock, *Preface to Plato* (Cambridge, Mass., 1963); idem, *The Muse Learns to Write: Reflections on Orality and Literacy from Antiquity to the Present* (New Haven, 1986); W. A. Graham, *Beyond the Written Word: Oral Aspects of Scripture in the History of Religion* (Cambridge, 1987); L. H. Silberman, ed., *Orality, Aurality and Biblical Narrative,* = *Semeia* 39 (1987).

2. R. M. Grant, with D. Tracy, *A Short History of the Interpretation of the Bible,* 2nd ed., revised and enlarged (Philadelphia, 1984), 3-83; J. Kugel and R. A. Greer, *Early Biblical Interpretation* (Philadelphia, 1986); K. Froelich, *Biblical Interpretation in the Early Church* (Philadelphia, 1984); S. M. Schneiders, "Scripture and Spirituality," in *Christian Spirituality: Origins to the Twelfth Century,* World Spirituality series, vol. 16 (New York, 1987); R. P. C.

Hanson, "Biblical Exegesis in the Early Church," in *The Cambridge History of the Bible*, vol. 1 (Cambridge, 1970), 412-453; J. Fontaine and C. Pietri, eds., *Le monde latin antique et la Bible* (Paris, 1985); M. Simonetti, *Biblical Interpretation in the Early Church: An Introduction to Patristic Exegesis* (Edinburgh, 1994); M. S. Burrows and P. Rorem, eds., *Biblical Hermeneutics in Historical Perspective* (Grand Rapids, 1991).

3. H. Lietzmann, *The Era of the Church Fathers*, trans. B. L. Woolf (London, 1951), 153.

4. Ong, *Orality and Literacy*, 59-60.

5. Part of this will involve recognizing what W. Graham has called "the relentless dominance of textuality in the scholarly mind." See Graham, *Beyond the Written Word*, 47. See also ibid., 9: "For us the written word has become the basic form of language...so tied are we to the written or printed page that we have lost any awareness of the essential orality of language."

6. I am fully aware that *The Sayings of the Desert Fathers* provides only one lens through which to examine the issue of early monastic approaches to Scripture. A fuller treatment of this question would of necessity include an examination of the full range of texts (and distinct hermeneutical outlooks and strategies) produced by the early monastic movement. To speak, as I do in this essay, of the "desert hermeneutic" is in no way to imply that the approach articulated in the *Sayings* is the central or dominant interpretive approach among early Christian monks. Still, it can lay claim, on historical and literary grounds, to being one of the most significant strands of interpretation within early monasticism. The *Sayings* tradition is particularly important for the purposes of this essay because of the influence of oral culture on its development and form. On this particular question, and for a fuller elaboration of the themes presented below, see my *The Word in the Desert: Scripture and the Quest for Holiness in Early Christian Monasticism* (New York, 1993).

References that follow are, for the most part, taken from the Alphabetico-Anonymous *Collection*. For the Alphabetical collection, see J. P. Migne, PG 65: 72-440, supplemented by J.-C. Guy in *Recherches sur la tradition grecque des Apophthegmata Patrum. Subsidia Hagiographica* 36 (Brussels, 1962, reprinted with additional comments, 1984) (hereafter *Recherches*). Eng. trans. B. Ward, *The Sayings of the Desert Fathers* (London, 1975). For the Anonymous collection, see F. Nau, ed., "Histoire des solitaires égyptiens (MS Coislin 126, fol.158f.). Nos. 133-369," *Revue d' Orient Chrétien* 13 (1908): 47-57, 266-83; 14 (1909): 357-79; 17 (1912): 204-11, 294-301; 18 (1913): 137-40 [hereafter *ROC*]. Eng. trans. B. Ward, *The Wisdom of the Desert Fathers: Apophthegmata Patrum from the Anonymous Series* (Oxford, 1975).

Other collections of the sayings to which this essay refers: L. Regnault, *Les sentences des pères du désert: collection alphabetique* (Sablé-sur-Sarth, 1981) [hereafter *SPAlph*]; idem, *Les sentences des pères du désert: Nouveau recueil*, 2nd ed. (Sablé-sur-Sarth, 1977) [hereafter *SPN*]; idem, *Les sentences des pères du désert: Série des anonymes* (Sablé-sur-Sarth/Bégrolles-en-Mauges, 1985) [hereafter *SPAn*]; L. Regnault, *Les sentences des pères du désert: Troisième recueil et tables* (Sablé-sur-Sarth, 1976) [hereafter *SPTr*].

7. W. Ong, "Text as Interpretation: Mark and After," *Semeia* 39 (1987): 14.

8. S. Rubenson, *The Letters of St. Antony: Origenist Theology, Monastic Tradition and the Making of a Saint* 24 (Lund, 1990; reprinted, with new translation of the *Letters*, Philadelphia, 1995). See also: E. Wipszycka, "Le degré d'alphabètisation en Égypt byzantine," *Revue des Études Augustiniennes* 30 (1984): 279-96.

9. W. V. Harris, *Ancient Literacy* (Cambridge, Mass., 1989), 323-37.

10. H. Y. Gamble, *Books and Readers in the Early Church: A History of Early Christian Texts* (New Haven and London, 1995), 5.

11. R. Bagnall, *Egypt in Late Antiquity* (Princeton, 1993), 249-50.

12. The fluidity of the relationship between oral and literate cultures is worth emphasizing. Gamble, *Books and Readers in the Early Church*, 29ff, argues for a less radical cultural division between orality and literacy than does, say, the work of W. Ong and E. Havelock. See also R. Finnegan, "What is Orality—if Anything?," *Byzantine and Modern Greek Studies* 14 (1990): 130-149, for a clear argument for maintaining this sense of fluidity.

13. Gelasius 1 (PG 65: 145CD).

14. Theodore of Pherme 1 (PG 65: 188A).

15. Ammoes 5 (PG 65: 128AB). There is also evidence that some of the desert fathers made use of small, personal copies of the Bible (or parts of the Bible). Serapion is said to have possessed a "Psalter" and a copy of Paul's epistles, these probably being the kind of small, portable codices which were beginning to become more widespread during this time. Cf. Serapion 1 (PG 65: 413D-416C).

16. Abraham 3 (PG 65: 132BC); see also Nau 385 (*ROC* 18: 143), the story in which a brother claims to have copied with his own hand the whole of the Old and New Testaments.

17. Havelock, *Preface to Plato*, 39; Ong, *Orality and Literacy*, 94.

18. Sisoes 35 (PG 65: 404B).

19. CSP I.2 (*SPTr*, 129).

20. J 676.9 (*SPAn*, 289).

21. Pa 40.1 (*SPN*, 2120).

22. J. Goody, ed., *Literacy in Traditional Societies* (Cambridge, 1968), 15-16; cf. Ong, *Orality and Literacy*, 93.

23. This attitude reflects a sensibility not uncommon in the ancient world, namely that the Sacred Book has a power akin to a magical or even talismanic object; see Graham, *Beyond the Written Word*, 45-55; Ong, *Orality and Literacy*, 93.

24. Epiphanius 8 (PG 65: 165A). Epiphanius' sayings are difficult to interpret. He himself could certainly read. However, it may be that he is

thinking of others, less well-educated than himself, to whom these words would apply.

25. B. Gerhardsson, *Memory and Manuscript: Oral Tradition and Written Transmission in Rabbinic Judaism and Early Christianity* (Lund and Copenhagen, 1961), 157; cf. Kelber, *Oral and Written Gospel*, p. 10. The transition from orality to literacy, as Gerhardsson showed long ago, was liable to feed doubts as to whether the new medium was able to "reproduce the full life, power and meaning of the spoken word."

26. Graham, *Beyond the Written Word*, 59-60.

27. Nau 385 (*ROC* 18: 143).

28. Nau 392 (*ROC* 18: 144). Cf. also Theodore of Pherme 1 (PG 65: 188A). Theodore of Pherme, who as we have seen possessed some "excellent books," was troubled enough about them to approach Abba Macarius for advice. He told Macarius that although he and his brothers derived much profit from the books, he was uncertain whether he should keep them or sell them and give the money to the poor. Macarius answered him with startling directness: "Your actions are good" he said, "but it is best of all to possess nothing." Theodore, without any hesitation, sold the books and gave the money away to the poor.

29. Serapion 2 (PG 65: 416C).

30. Nau 228 (*ROC* 14: 361).

31. H. I. Marrou, *A History of Education in Antiquity*, trans. G. Lamb (Madison, Wis., 1982), 330.

32. Cassian, *Conferences* 14.12; trans. E. Gibson, NPNF, 2nd ser., vol. 11 (Grand Rapids, 1973), 441. Cassian's attitude is a good example of a polemic which masks another reality. In spite of his pessimism regarding classical literature, his writings as a whole present a carefully wrought synthesis of classical and Christian thought.

33. Arsenius 6 (PG 65: 89A), translation mine (hereafter indicated with [m]).

34. Arsenius 5 (PG 65: 88D-89A), [m]. Such stories seem to convey, as F. Marcos suggests "a nostalgia" among the monks for a primitive Christian praxis uncontaminated by the culture of the world. F. Marcos, "La Biblia y los origenes del Monaquismo," *Miscelánea Comillas* 41 (1983): 387.

35. Evagrius 7 (PG 65: 178A).

36. Euprepius 7 (PG 65: 172D), [m]. The saying is contained under the name of Euprepius in the *Alphabetico-Anonymous* collection, but there is strong evidence from other manuscripts that the saying comes from Evagrius. See Regnault's remarks in *SPAlph*, 91.

37. H. Chadwick, *The Early Church* (Harmondsworth, Eng., 1967), 178.

38. Antony 19 (PG 65: 81B).

39. For discussion of the *synaxis*, see Burton-Christie, *The Word in the Desert*, 117-122.

40. Ong, *Orality and Literacy*, 9.

41. Poemen 119 (PG 65: 353A).

42. Nau 388 (*ROC* 18: 143); see also N 592/37 (*SPAn*, 223-224): we hear also

that the words of the fathers and of Scripture are both sources of "the word of God."

43. Poemen 114 (PG 65: 352D).
44. Poemen 61 (PG 65: 336D), [m]. Abba Poemen himself was said to have "the gift of speaking," although interestingly, one of the characteristic aspects of this gift in his case was its relationship with silence; see Poemen 108 (PG 65: 348D).
45. Ong, *Orality and Literacy*, 47.
46. Ong, "Text as Interpretation," 13.
47. Theodore of Pherme 20 (PG 65: 192B).
48. Ong, "Text as Interpretation," 14.
49. Ibid., 8.
50. Theodore of Pherme 3 (PG 65: 188C), [m].
51. Ares 1 (PG 65: 132CD-133A).
52. Nisterus 3 (PG 65: 308A-B).
53. Matoes 13 (PG 65: 293C).
54. Agathon 1 (PG 65: 108D-109B).
55. Achilles 4 (PG 65: 125A).
56. Or 15 (PG 65: 440D).
57. Tithoes 3 (PG 65: 428B).
58. Poemen 63 (PG 65: 337A); Poemen 188 (S1, Guy, *Recherches*, 29).
59. Poemen 27 (PG 65: 329A).
60. Isidore of Pelusia 1 (PG 65: 221D).
61. Or 2 (PG 65: 437B).
62. Theodore of Pherme 20 (PG 65: 192B); Poemen 53 (PG 65: 333D); Romanus 1 (PG 65: 392B); Nisterus 5 (PG 65: 305D).
63. Gerontius 1 (PG 65: 153A-B).
64. Agathon 3 (PG 65: 109B).
65. Antony 3 (PG 65: 76C).
66. Benjamin 4 (PG 65: 145A).
67. Pistus 1 (PG 65: 372C-373B).
68. Poemen 97 (PG 65: 345B).
69. Nau 299 (*ROC* 17: 204).
70. Theodore of Pherme 9 (PG 65: 189B).
71. Poemen 34 (PG 65: 332A-B).
72. G. Steiner, *Real Presences* (Chicago, 1989), 7.
73. Poemen 33 (PG 65: 329D-332A).
74. Theodora 2 (PG 65: 201B); Poemen 112 (PG 65: 349C-352A).
75. Poemen 126 (PG 65: 353C).
76. John the Eunuch 1 (PG 65: 223A).
77. Nau 174 (*ROC* 13: 57).
78. Nau 392 (*ROC* 18: 144).
79. Macarius the Great 18 (PG 65: 269B-C).
80. Euprepius 2 (PG 65: 172B).
81. Zeno 8 (PG 65: 177C-D).

82. Arsenius 33 (PG 65: 100CD-101A); Hyperchius 8 (PG 65: 432A).
83. Nau 314 (*ROC* 17: 207), [m].
84. Macarius the Great 35 (PG 65: 277CD).
85. John Colobos 36 (PG 65: 216C).
86. John Colobos 19 (PG 65: 212BC); Theodore of Pherme 11 (PG 65: 189C-D); Cassian 1 (PG 65: 244AB); John Colobos 39 (PG 65: 217A).
87. Syncletica 3 (PG 65: 425C); Epiphanius 4 (PG 65: 164C); Agathon 4 (PG 65: 109B).
88. Agathon 19 (PG 65: 113C).
89. Poemen 118 (PG 65: 352C-D).
90. Poemen 117 (PG 65: 352C).
91. Theodore of Pherme 13 (PG 65: 189D).
92. Theodote 2 (Guy, *Recherches*, S1: 22).
93. Poemen 116 (PG 65: 352B).
94. Poemen 70 (PG 65: 337D-340A).
95. Moses 2 (PG 65: 288B).
96. Ammonas 8 (PG 65: 121BC).
97. Ammonas 9 (PG 65: 121D-124A).
98. Poemen 92 (PG 65: 344C).
99. Pambo 12 (PG 65: 372A).
100. Arsenius 42 (PG 65: 106A).
101. Nisterus the Cenobite (PG 65: 308D-309A).
102. P. Cox, *Biography in Late Antiquity: A Quest for the Holy Man* (Berkeley, 1983), xi.
103. P. Brown, "The Saint as Exemplar in Late Antiquity," in J. S. Hawley, ed. *Saints and Virtues* (Berkeley, 1987), 11.

List of Contributors

PAUL M. BLOWERS is a Professor of Church History in Emmanuel School of Religion, Johnson City, Tennessee.

MARCEL BORRET, S.J., the late patristics scholar from Lyons, France, was the editor of the critical text of Origen's *Contra Celsum* in the series *Sources Chrétiennes*.

ALAIN LE BOULLUEC serves on the faculty of L'École Practique des Hautes Études in Paris.

PIERRE DU BOURGUET, S.J., the late specialist in early Christian art, was honorary Conservateur en Chef of the Musée du Louvre in Paris.

DOUGLAS BURTON-CHRISTIE is Assistant Professor of Christian Spirituality in the Department of Theological Studies at Loyola Marymount University, Los Angeles, California.

IRÉNÉE-HENRI DALMAIS, O.P., a specialist in liturgics and patristics, has been a Professor of History in L'Institut Catholique de Paris.

DENIS FEISSEL has been a member of the Centre National de la Recherche Scientifique in Paris.

JACQUES GUILLET, S.J., has been a member of the Centre Sévres in Paris.

JEAN-NOËL GUINOT is a Director of Research in the Centre National de la Recherche Scientifique in Paris, and Director of the series *Sources Chrétiennes*.

RONALD HEINE is Director of the Institut zur Erforschung des Urchristentums in Tübingen, Germany.

MAURICE JOURJON is Doyen Honoraire of the Catholic Faculty of Theology of the University of Lyons, France.

CHARLES KANNENGIESSER is Huisking Professor Emeritus of Theology in the University of Notre Dame, Notre Dame, Indiana, and is Invited Professor in the Department of Theological Studies in Concordia University, Montreal.

PAUL LAMARCHE, S.J., has been a member of the Centre Sevre in Paris.

PIERRE MARAVAL is a member of the Protestant Faculty of Theology in the University of Strasbourg.

FREDERICK NORRIS is Dean E. Walker Professor of Church History and Professor of Christian Doctrine in Emmanuel School of Religion, Johnson City, Tennessee.

ERIC OSBORN is Professor Emeritus of New Testament and Early Christianity in the Queen's College, University of Melbourne, Australia, and more recently a Visiting Professor in La Trobe University, Bundoora, Victoria.

CHARLES RENOUX, O.S.B., a specialist in oriental Christianity, has been a member of the Centre National de Recherche Scientifique.

WILLY RORDORF is Emeritus Professor in the Protestant Faculty of the University of Neuchâtel, Switzerland.

VICTOR SAXER is retired Director of the Pontifical Institute of Christian Archaeology in Rome.

MARCEL SIMON, the late specialist in Jewish and Christian antiquity, was Professor of the History of Religion at the University of Strasbourg and a Fellow of L' Institut de France.

Index

Index of Biblical References